MUSIC HISTORY DURING THE RENAISSANCE PERIOD, 1520–1550

**Recent Titles in
the Music Reference Collection**

An Index to African-American Spirituals for the Solo Voice
Kathleen A. Abromeit, compiler

Sinatra: An Annotated Bibliography, 1939–1998
Leonard Mustazza

Opera Singers in Recital, Concert, and Feature Film
Sharon G. Almquist, compiler

Appraisals of Original Wind Music: A Survey and Guide
David Lindsey Clark

Popular Singers of the Twentieth Century: A Bibliography of Biographical Materials
Robert H. Cowden

The Printed Elvis: The Complete Guide to Books about the King
Steven Opdyke

One Handed: A Guide to Piano Music for One Hand
Donald L. Patterson, compiler

Brainard's Biographies of American Musicians
E. Douglas Bomberger, editor

The Mozart-Da Ponte Operas: An Annotated Bibliography
Mary Du Mont

A Dictionary-Catalog of Modern British Composers
Alan Poulton

Songs of the Vietnam Conflict
James Perone

A Guide to Piano Music by Women Composers:
Volume I: Composers Born Before 1900
Pamela Youngdahl Dees

ENTERED MAR 9 2005

MUSIC HISTORY DURING THE RENAISSANCE PERIOD, 1520–1550

A Documented Chronology

Blanche Gangwere

Music Reference Collection, Number 85

Westport, Connecticut
London

Library of Congress Cataloging-in-Publication Data

Gangwere, Blanche.
  Music history during the Renaissance period, 1520–1550 : a documented chronology / Blanche Gangwere.
    p.   cm. — (Music reference collection, ISSN 0736-7740 ; no. 85)
  Includes bibliographical references and index.
  ISBN 0-313-29248-5 (alk. paper)
  1. Music—16th century—History and criticism. 2. Renaissance—Chronology. I. Title. II. Series.
  ML172.G27   2004
  780'.9' 031—dc22   2004045245
British Library Cataloguing in Publication Data is available.

Copyright © 2004 by Blanche Gangwere

All rights reserved. No portion of this book may be
reproduced, by any process or technique, without the
express written consent of the publisher.

Library of Congress Catalog Card Number: 2004045245
ISBN: 0-313-29248-5
ISSN: 0736-7740

First published in 2004

Praeger Publishers, 88 Post Road West, Westport, CT 06881
An imprint of Greenwood Publishing Group, Inc.
www.praeger.com

Printed in the United States of America

The paper used in this book complies with the
Permanent Paper Standard issued by the National
Information Standards Organization (Z39.48–1984).

10 9 8 7 6 5 4 3 2 1

Contents

Preface ix

Part I: Reference Material

  Annotated Bibliography 1

Part II: Historical Outline and Study Guide

  Theorists and Theoretical Sources 123
    Pietro Aaron (Aron) 123
    Lodovico Fogliano 126
    Giovanni del Lago (Zanetto) 127
    Martin Agricola 129
    Heinrich Glarean 130
    Giovanni Maria Lanfranco 133
    Sebald Heyden 134
    Auctor Lampadius 134
    Nicolaus Listenius 135

  Musica theorica: **Science of Music** 137
    Introduction 137
    Changes in Modal Theory 138
    Tonality 140
    The Current Conception of the Gamut 142
    Consonances and Dissonances 147
    Interval Ratios: Intonation 148
    Interval Ratios: Temperament 150

  Musica practica: **Performance Didactics** 154
    Introduction 154
    Chromaticism: *Musica ficta* 154
    Chromaticism: "Chain Reactions" 168
    Pitch 169

Text Underlay	170
Ornamentation	173

Musica poetica: **Composition**
Writings by Theorists on *Musica poetica*	177
The Evolution of *Musica poetica*	178

Notation
Part Arrangement	184
Score Arrangement	184
Tablatures	187
Clefs Used in Sixteenth Century Polyphony	193
Accidental Signatures (Key Signatures)	195
Conflicting Signatures ('Partial Signatures')	196
Note nere	197

Sacred Latin Music for the Catholic Church on the Continent
Introduction	199
Polyphony for the Ordinary and Proper of the Mass	200
Music for the Passion	219
Polyphony for the Office	221
The Motet	233
Performance Practices of Sacred Latin Music	253

Sacred Music for the Reformed Church on the Continent
Introduction	256
Lutheran Church Music at Wittenberg	256
Published Sources of Vernacular Music for the Lutheran Church	272
Published Sources of Latin Music for the Lutheran Church	280
The Performance of Lutheran Church Music	282
Lutheran Church Music at Leipzig	283
Published Sources of Lutheran Music at Leipzig	284
Lutheran Church Music at Augsburg	285
Published Sources of Lutheran Music at Augsburg	285
Calvinist Music in Southern Switzerland	285
The Published Psalters in Southern Switzerland	288
Protestant Music in Northern Switzerland	291
Published Sources of Protestant Music in Northern Switzerland	291
The Bohemian-Moravian Brethren (*Unitas fratrum*)	292
Dutch Psalm Books	293

Sacred Latin and Vernacular Music in England
The Pre-Reformation Period in England from ca. 1521 to ca. 1547	295
The Pre-Reformation Rite	297
The Establishment of Distinctive Music for the Pre-Reformation Liturgy	300
The Reformation Period in England from ca. 1547 to ca. 1550	302
The Development of the Music for the Early Anglican Rite	304
The Sacred Latin Music for the Reformed English Church	307

The Sacred Vernacular Music for the Reformed English Church	357
Performance Practices	364

Secular Vocal Music — 367
- The French *Chanson* — 367
- The Italian *Canzone* — 393
- The Italian Madrigal — 395
- The Italian *Villotta* — 422
- The Italian *Villanella* of ca. 1530-1550 — 424
- The Neapolitan *Mascherata* — 436
- English Secular Music — 438
- Solo Song — 442
- Art Song — 446
- The Ceremonial Motet — 451

Instrumental Music — 455
- Keyboard Music: Musical Forms — 455
- Keyboard Music: Liturgical Organ Music — 462
- Music for the Lute — 493
- Music for the Viol — 498
- Music for the Vihuela — 499
- Music for Ensemble — 501

Index of Persons — 507

Index of Works — 511

Subject Index — 527

Preface

This annotated chronology of western music from ca. 1520 to ca. 1550 is the third of a series of outlines covering the history of music in western civilization. The task of documenting the history and historiography of western music in outline form was undertaken because of the realization that, although there are many excellent books on music history, no single source systematically presents concise information on theory, notation, style, performance practices, composition, and music, by incorporating findings from primary sources and the results of subsequent scholarly research. Researchers seeking accurate information at present must consult a wide array of specialized books and periodicals, not all of which may be familiar or readily available. In addition, considerable background knowledge may be needed to assess these materials.

Therefore, in developing the outline for this book, an attempt was made to consult all types of sources, to cover as many facets of importance as possible, and to present the facts in an organized manner. Each topic is presented separately and written chronologically. Thus a vast amount of data is digested for ready access, and further information may be obtained from the sources noted.

As a convenience to researchers, it was decided to document each line of the outline. Abbreviations are used to refer to the sources that are cited in the bibliography. If the larger part of a section is from one source, the abbreviations are placed after the appropriate heading, with only those few lines that are from other sources having separate abbreviations. The bibliography lists these abbreviations alphabetically without regard to whether the sources are books, periodical articles, or music. The nature of the material is made clear in the citation.

All references to pitch are relative as they refer to the pitches of the gamut and those of the extended interlocking hexachords. All square brackets found in the text indicate additions to the material found in the source quoted.

The period covered in this book is the second part of what is commonly known as the Renaissance. The Italian word *rinascita* was used by Matteo Palmieri in the fifteenth century and established by Vasari in 1550. The term Renaissance, denoting a period in European history, was first used in 1855. There has been much controversy as to the meaning of the term and the dates of the historical period it covers. There has been no attempt in this book to define the word or to give the period a definite time frame.

Part I

Reference Material

Bibliography

AarC   Aaron, Pietro. *Compendiolo di molti dubbi, segreti et sentenze intorno al canto fermo, et figurato*...Milan: G. A. Castellione, ca. 1545. Bibliotheca musicae Bononiensis. Sec. 2: *Teoria*, no. 11. Bologna: Arnaldo Forni, 1970.
        This treatise is curiously elementary. It consists of two books. In number one there is a discussion of plainchant and in number two there is a discussion of counterpoint. This is a facsimile edition.

AarCD   _____. *Compendiolo de molti dubbi, segreti et sentenze intorno al canto fermo, et figurato*...Milan, ca. 1545. Monuments of music and music literature in facsimile. Ser. 2: Music literature, no. 66. New York: Broude Brothers.
        This is a facsimile edition. *See* AarC.

AarLM   _____. *Lucidario in musica di alcune oppenioni antiche, et moderne con le loro oppositione, et resolutione*. Venice: Girolamo Scotto, 1545. Bibliotheca musicae Bononiensis. Sec. 2: *Teoria*, no. 12. Bologna: Arnaldo Forni, 1969.
        A facsimile edition. The original is a book containing a treatise on sixteenth century music theory and is found in Biblioteca del conservatorio, Bologna (I Bc). For a full description of this treatise *see* Catalogo della biblioteca del Liceo musicale di bologna, p. 186.

AarLMU   _____. *Lucidario in musica*. 1545 ed. Monuments of music and music literature in facsimile. Ser. 2: Music literature, no. 68. New York: Broude Brothers, 1978.
        A facsimile edition. The original is a book containing a treatise on sixteenth century music theory and is found in Biblioteca del conservatorio, Bologna (I Bc). For a full description of this treatise *see* Catalogo della biblioteca del Liceo musicale di bologna, p. 186.

AarLT   _____. *Libri tres de institutione harmonica*. Bologna 1516. Bibliotheca musicae Bononiensis. Sec. 2: *Teoria*, no. 8. Bologna: Arnaldo Forni, n.d.
        A facsimile edition. The original is a book containing sixteenth century music theory. It is divided into three books with material on plainsong, solmization, counterpoint, Greek genera, and mensural notation.

AarLTI   _____. *Libri tres de institutione harmonica editi a Petro Aaron Florentino interprete Io. Antonio Flam. Forocornelite*. Bologna: Hector, 1516. Monuments of music and music literature in facsimile. Ser. 2: Music literature, no. 67. New York: Broude Brothers, 1976.
        A facsimile edition. The original is a book containing sixteenth century

music theory. It is divided into three books with material on plainsong, solmization, counterpoint, Greek genera, and mensural notation.

AarT Aaron, Pietro. *Toscanello in music*. Translated by Peter Bergquist. 3 vols. Colorado College Music Press Translations, no. 4. Colorado Springs: Colorado College Music Press, 1970.

This translation is based on the last revision of the treatise by Aaron found in the three printings of 1529, 1539, and 1562. The supplement added to the last three printings is the major difference between the original and revised editions.

AarTD _____. *Thoscanello della musica*. Venice: 1523; Repr. Venice: 1529. Monuments of music and music literature in facsimile. Ser. 2: Music literature, no. 69. New York: Broude Brothers, 1969.

This is a facsimile of the 1529 edition which is a reprint of the 1523 edition. It is a general manual with discussions of mensural notation, intervals, genera, counterpoint, chordal formation, etc. There are six leaves of text bound along with this edition.

AarTM _____. *Thoscanello de la musica*. Venice: Bernardino, 1523. Facsimile ed. Ann Arbor, Mich.: University Microfilms, 1965.

This is a facsimile of the 1523 edition. It is a general manual with discussions of mensural notation, intervals, genera, counterpoint, chordal formation, etc.

AarTO _____. *Toscanello in musica*. Venice, 1539. Edited by Georg Frey. Documenta musicologica. Ser. 1: Druckschriften-Faksimiles, no. 29. Kassell: Bärenreiter, 1970.

This is a facsimile of the 1539 edition. There is a Printer's mark on the title page; initials; and a title within woodcut border of flowers and dolphins. There is also a full page illustration of Aaron in his lecture room. The text is a general manual with discussions of mensural notation, intervals, genera, counterpoint, chordal formation, etc.

AarTOS _____. *Toscanello in musica* (1523). 2nd ed., Venice: Bernardino and Matheo de Vitali, 1529. Bibliotheca musicae Bononiensis. Sec. 2: *Teoria*, no. 10. Bologna: Arnaldo Forni, 1969.

This is a facsimile of the 1529 reprint edition of the 1523 treatise. It is a general manual with discussions of mensural notation, intervals, genera, counterpoint, chordal formation, etc.

AarTR _____. *Trattato della natura et cognitione di tutti gli tuoni di canto figurato*. Venice: Bernardino de Vitali, 1525. Bibliotheca musicae Bononiensis. Sec. 2: *Teoria*, no. 9. Bologna: Arnaldo Forni, 1970.

This is a facsimile of the original 1525 edition. Aaron attempts the most systematic exposition of the entire conceivable gamut.

AarTRD _____. *Trattato della natura et cognitione di tutti gli tuoni di canto figurato non da altrui piu scritti, composti per Messer Pier Aaron Musico Fiorentino canonico in Rimini...* Venice: Bernardo di Vitali, 1525; reprint ed. with addenda, 1531. Facsimile ed. Ann Arbor, Mich.: University Microfilms, 1965.

This is a facsimile of the reprint edition of 1531 with an addenda. Aaron attempts the most systematic exposition of the entire conceivable gamut.

AdaF I Adams, Courtney, S., ed. *French Chansons for Three Voices (ca. 1550). Part I*. Recent Researches in the Music of the Renaissance, no. 36. Madison:

A-R Editions, Inc., [c. 1982].
This source contains thirty *chansons* written for three parts. They are transcriptions of *chansons* printed by Gardane in 1541. There are *chansons* by Sermisy (11), Gombert (1), Willaert (1), Guillaume Le Heurteur (3), and others. There are texts, translations, and a critical *apparatus*. There is a discussion of the music of volumes I and II found in the Preface of the first volume.

AdaF II   Adams, Courtney, S., ed. *French Chansons for Three Voices (ca. 1550) Part II: Three-Part Chansons Printed by Gardane (1543[21]) and the Tiers livre de chansons Printed by LeRoy and Ballard (1553[22])*. Recent Researches in the Music of the Renaissance, no. 37. Madison: A-R Editions, Inc., [c. 1982].
This source contains transcriptions, critical commentary, texts and translations of thirteen *chansons* printed by Gardane and twenty-six *chansons* printed by LeRoy and Ballard. The composers of the first part are Sermisy, Certon, and others. The composers of the second part are Gombert, Willaert, Sermisy, Arcadelt, maybe Richafort, and others. There is a list of sources for concordant readings.

AgrA   Agricola, Martin. *Ach Gott von Himmel*. Antiqua Chorbuch, no. I:1. Edited by Helmuth Mönkemeyer. Mainz: B. Schott's Söhne, 1951.
This is a transcription of a German Protestant song found in *Ein Sangbüchlein aller Sontags Evangelien* by Agricola. It was published in 1541.

AgrD   _____. *Deutsche Musica und Gesangbüchlin der Sontags Evangelien...* Nurnberg: Johann Vom Berg und Ulrich Neuber, 1560. Preface by Wolffgangus Figulus, 1525-1591.Wolfenbüttel: Herzog August Bibliothek, 1988. Microfiche.
This source contains canticles and German hymns. Woodcuts precede each canticle. It is indexed in RISM B VI I, p. 69.

AgrE   _____. *Ein kurtz deudsche musica*. Wittenberg: G. Rhaw, 1528. [München]: Bayerische Staatsbibliothek, [1981?]. Microfilm.
This is a facsimile of a music theory treatise. It is indexed in RISM B VI I, p. 70.

AgrM   _____. *Musica figuralis deudsch*. Wittenberg: Georg Rhau, 1532; Facsimile ed., German books before 1601: Roll 13, Item 9. Hildesheim: Georg Rhau, 1969. Microfilm.
This is a facsimile edition. It is written in two parts. In it, Agricola discusses current musical theory and notation. He uses many musical examples, of which many were composed by him. The examples are confined to vocal polyphony.

AgrMD   _____. *Musica figuralis deudsch*. Wittenberg: Georg Rhau, 1534. Micropaque.
This is a facsimile edition. *See* AgrM.

AgrMF   _____. *Musica figuralis deudsch*. Wittenberg: 1532. Original at the Library of Congress. Microfilm.
This is a facsimile edition. *See* AgrM.

AgrMFD   _____. *Musica figuralis deudsch, 1532*. 2 vols. Translated by Gordon J. Kinney. Lexington: M. I. King Library. University of Kentucky, 1977. Microfilm.
This is a translation of a facsimile of the 1532 Wittenberg edition It contains sixteenth century musical theory and musical notation. Agricola uses

many musical examples, of which many were composed by him. The examples are confined to vocal polyphony.

AgrMI Agricola, Martin. *Musica instrumentalis deudsch*. Wittenberg: Gedruckt durch Georg Rhaw, 1532. [Rochester, N. Y.]: . University of Rochester, 1954. Micropaque.

This was filmed from the original manuscript at Sibley Music Library. The treatise contains material on music notation and musical instruments.

AgrMID _____. *Musica instrumentalis deudsch*. Wittenberg: G. Rhaw, 1529. [München]: Bayerische Staatsbibliothek, [1980?]. Microfilm.

This is a facsimile of the 1529 edition. It contains material on music notation and musical instruments. It is indexed in RISM B VI, p. 70.

AgrMU _____. "Musica instrumentalis deudsch." Publikationen älterer praktischer und theoretischer Musikwerke, no. 20. Edited by Robert Eitner. Leipzig: Breitkopf und Härtel, 1896. Ann Arbor, Mich.: Xerox University Microfilm, 1976. Photocopy.

This is a facsimile of the 1528 and 1545 editions of the *Musica instrumentalis deudsch*. There is material on music notation and musical instruments.

AgrMUS _____. *The "Musica instrumentalis deudsch" of Martin Agricola; a treatise on musical instruments, 1529 and 1545*. Translated by William E. Mattrick. Cambridge musical texts and monographs. Cambridge: Cambridge University Press, 1994

This is a translation of the 1529 and 1545 editions. Bibliographical references and an index are included.

AgrR _____. *Rudimenta musices*. A facsimile of the 1539 Wittenberg Edition. Monuments of music and music literature in facsimile. Ser. 2: Music literature, no. 34. New York: Broude Brothers, 1966.

This is a facsimile edition. It is an abridged Latin version of *Ein kurtz deudsche Musica* which was published at Wittenberg in 1539. In this treatise, Agricola discusses the combination of modes and hexachords.

AgrRM _____. *The Rudiments of Music (Rudimenta musices, 1539)*. Translated by Brian Trowell. Classic texts in music education, no. 21. Aberystwyth, Wales: Broethium Press, 1991.

This source contains the Latin version of Rudimenta musices of 1539 along with an English translation.

AgrT _____. *A translation of three treatises by Martin Agricola: Musica choralis deudsch, Musica figuralis deudsch, and Von den Proportionibus*. Translated by Derq Howlett. Ph.D. Thesis, Ohio State University, 1979. Ann Arbor, Mich.: University Microfilms International, 1985.

This source contains English translations of the three music theory treatises.

AgrV _____. *Von den Proporcionibus*. Wittenberg: G. Rhau, 1532. [München]: Bayerische Staatsbibliothek, [1982?]. Microfilm.

This is a supplement to the treatise, *Musica figuralis deudsch*. It is indexed in RISM B VI I, p. 71.

AlbZ Albrecht, H., ed. *Zwölf französische Lieder aus Jacques Moderns "La Parangon des Chansons" [1538]*. Das Chorwerk, no. 61. Edited by Friedrich Blume. Germany: Möseler Verlag Wolfenbüttel, [c. 1957].

This source is divided into two books. Each contains a *Vorwort* in which the music and the composers are discussed. Both contain transcriptions of four-part *chansons* with the original text and a German translation. There are *chansons* by Sermisy, Layolle, Arcadelt, Manchicourt, Coste, etc.

AllM Allaire, Gaston. *The Masses of Claudin de Sermisy*. Ph.D. diss., Boston University, 1960. Ann Arbor, Mich.: University Microfilms, 1960.
This contains musical transcriptions of the Masses of Claudin de Sermisy in modern score, the sources of his parody Masses, and an Anthology of French vocal music of the Renaissance.

AllT _____. *The theory of hexachords, solmization, and the modal system: a practical application*. Musicological studies and documents, no. 24. N. p.: American Institute of Musicology, 1972.
This is an attempt to reconstruct the theory of hexachords and the technique of solmization based on the analysis of music contained in writings of Medieval and Renaissance theorists.

AmaI Amati-Camperi, Alexandra Daniela. "An Italian genre in the hands of a Frenchman: Philippe Verdelot as madrigalist, with special emphasis on the six-voice pieces." Ph.D. Thesis, Harvard University, 1994. Ann Arbor, Mich.: University Microfilms International, 1996. Photocopy.
This contains transcriptions of Verdelot's six-voice madrigals with bibliographical references.

AmbG V Ambros, August Wilhelm. *Geschichte der Musik*. 5 vols. Vol.5: *Auserwählte Tonwerke der berühmtesten Meister des 15. und 16. Jahrhunderts*. Edited by Otto Kade. Republication of 1882 ed. Hildesheim: Georg Olms Verlagsbuchhandlung, 1968.
The *Geschichte der Musik* by Ambrose was never completed. After the author's death, volume four was edited from the manuscript by G. Nottebohm and C. F. Becker. A continuation, by W. Langhans, appeared in 1882-87 under the title, *Die Geschichte der Music des 17., 18., und 19. Jahrhunderts*. Volume one was edited by B. von Sokolovsky; volume two by H. Reimann; volume three and five by O. Kade; and volume four by H. Leichtentritt. This volume contains transcribed musical examples from the works of famous Masters of the 15th and 16th centuries. The settings are in modern notation and are the works of the best known composers cited in volume three.

AmeD Ameln, Konrad, ed. *Das Achtliederbuch: Nürnberg 1523/24, in originalgetreuem Nachdruck*. Kassel: Basel: Bärenreiter-Verlag, 1957.
This has been reproduced from the Gottingen University Library copy of the second issue of the original edition of 1524. The first twenty-three pages contain the *Achtliederbuch* and the final six pages contain a commentary about them by Konrad Ameln. There are German Lutheran hymns by Martin Luther and P. Sperati.

AmeE _____, ed. *Das Erfurter Enchiridion*. Documenta musicologica. Reihe I: Druckschriften-Faksimiles, no. 36. Kassel: Bärenreiter, 1983.
This source contains facsimile reprints of the 1524 and 1525 editions. They were published in Erfurt as *Eyn enchiridion oder Handbuchlein*. There is an introduction in German and English. There are hymns and psalms with the melodies.

AmeG _____, ed. *Gesangbuch der Bohmischen Bruder: 1531*. Compiled by Michael Weisse. Kassel: Bärenreiter, 1957.

6 Bibliography

AmeK
: This is a facsimile of *Ein New Gesang buchlen, MDXXXI*. It contains German hymns with music. There is a preface by Michael Weisse.
Ameln, Konrad, ed. *Das Klug'sche Gesangbuch*, 1533. Documenta musicologica. Reihe I: Druckschriften-Faksimiles, no. 35. Kassel: Bärenreiter, 1983.
The title of the original is *Geistliche Lieder auffs new gebessert zu Wittemberg*. The original lacks leaves 177, 178, and all leaves after 180. It contains principally unaccompanied melodies of German hymns. The words are principally German with some in Latin.

AmeR
: _____. *The Roots of German Hymnody of the Reformation Era*. Church Music Pamphlet Series: Hymnology, no. 1. St. Louis: Concordia Publishing House, [c. 1964].
This is a publication of a lecture presented on September 11, 1961, at the Congress of the Hymn Society of America, New York.

AnaB
: "Anabaptists." *Britannica 2002 Deluxe Edition*. Copyright © 1994-2002 Britannica.com Inc. April 8, 2002.
This is a short history of the Anabaptist movement in Switzerland.

AngB
: "Anglican Communion." *Britannica 2002 Deluxe Edition*. Copyright © 1994-2002 Britannica.com Inc. April 9, 2002.
This contains a discussion of the history of the Anglican Church in England.

AngS
: Anglés, Higini. "Spain and Portugal." In *The New Oxford History of Music. Vol. 4: The Age of Humanism: 1540-1630*, edited by Gerald Abraham, pp. 372-413. London: The Oxford University Press, [c. 1968]; reprint ed., 1974.
There is a discussion of the characteristics of Spanish church music, Charles V and his court chapel, Philip II's attitude to music, the principal cathedral schools, Spanish composers, and music in Portugal.

AntB
: *Anthologies of Black-note Madrigals*. 5 vols. Edited by Don Harrán. Corpus mensurabilis musicae, no. 73. Neuhausen-Stuttgart: American Institute of Musicology: Hänsler-Verlag, 1978.
The madrigals in these volumes were edited from madrigal book collections published in Venice by A. Gardane and G. Scotto from 1540 to 1557. The madrigals have the Italian words which are also printed as texts with English translations on preliminary pages of each volume. Bibliographical references are included.

AntCP
: *Anthologie de la chanson Parisienne au XVIe Siècle*. Réunie pr François Lesure avec la collaboration de N. Bridgman, I. Cazeaux, M. Levin, K. J. Levy, et D. P. Walker. Monaco: Éditions de L'oiseau-Lyre [c. 1953].
This contains forty-eight *chansons* by Certon, Clereau, Jacotin, Janequin, Rore, Sermisy, and others. They are transcriptions with incipits containing original clefs and original notation. There are notes about each composer along with sources and concordances for each *chanson*.

AntF
: Antico, Andrea. *Frottole intabulate da sonare organi*. Edited by Peter Sterzinger. Diletto musicale, no. 891. Wien: Doblinger, 1987.
This contains arrangements of *frottole* for organ. It is edited from the only completely preserved original in the Dobrovsky Library in Prague. There are Prefaces in German and English. Bibliographical references are included.

AntFI
: _____. *Frottole intabulate da sonar organi*. Bibliotheca musica Bononiensis.

	Sec, 4: *Musica practica*, no. 42. Bologna: Forni., 1984.
	This contains facsimiles of keyboard arrangements of nineteen *frottole* by Bartolomeo Tromboncino and four by Marchetto Cara. There are introductory notes in Italian by Giuseppe Radole.
AntM	Antico, Andrea. *Motetti novi e chanzoni franciose a quatro sopra doi.* Venetia: 1520. Geneve: Minkoff, 1982.
	This is a reprint of the original publication. There are motets and thirty polyphonic *chansons,* including five double canons. The early *chansons* of Willaert are included.
AntP	_____, Comp. *Il primo libro de le canzoni franzese.* Venetium: Octavianum Scotum, 1535. Munich: Bayerische Staatsbibliothek. Microfilm.
	This is a facsimile of the original *altus* and *bassus* parts only. Copies of the other part-books appear to be unknown. The title is taken from the last page of the tenor part. There are *chansons* by Willaert, Sermisy, and L'Heritier. There is also one *chanson* by Richafort. It is indexed in RISM B/1, 1535-38 and Chapman thesis (Ph.D) Harvard University, 1964, no. 71, p. 434.
ApeH	Apel, Willi. *The History of Keyboard Music to 1700.* Translated and revised by Hans Tischler. Bloomington: Indiana University Press, [c. 1972].
	This is a comprehensive presentation of keyboard music. It covers organ music and music for stringed keyboard instruments from Antiquity up to the time of Johann Sebastian Bach.
ApeHD	_____. *Harvard Dictionary of Music.* 2nd ed., revised and enlarged. Cambridge: The Belknap Press of Harvard University Press, [c. 1969].
	The aim of this source is to serve as a convenient reference work for laymen, students, performers, composers, scholars, and teachers. Research published in books and periodicals has been taken into consideration. New articles have been contributed and old ones revised. Errors found in the first publication have been eliminated.
ApeN	_____. *The Notation of Polyphonic Music, 900-1600.* 5th ed., revised with commentary. Cambridge: The Mediaeval Academy of America, [c. 1961].
	This is a survey of the notation of European polyphonic music from its beginning to the seventeenth century, plus the notation of polyphonic music of all other nations outside the European development so far as it is preserved in writing.
ApeSI	_____. "Solo Instrumental Music." In *New Oxford History of Music.* Vol. 4: *The Age of Humanism: 1540-1630,* edited by Gerald Abraham, pp. 602-708. London: Oxford University Press, [c. 1968]; reprint ed. 1974.
	This contains a discussion of the music for organ, lute, and other instruments in Italy, Germany, France, and England.
AquA	Aquilecchia, Giovanni. "Ariosto, Ludovico." *Britannica 2002 Deluxe Edition.* Copyright © 1994-2002 Britannica.com Inc. April 16, 2002.
	This is a short summary of Ariosto's life and writings.
AraH	Araiz Martínez, Andres. *Historia de la música religiosa en España.* Coleccion Labor, biblioteca de iniciación V, música, no. 408-409. Barcelona: Editorial Labor, s.a., 1942.
	This is a collection of sacred polyphonic compositions by Spanish composers for four and five unaccompanied voices.
ArcD	Arcadelt, Jacob. *Del primo libro de madragali.* Venetijs: Scotum, 1543.

8   Bibliography

Jena: Universitatsbibliothek der Friedrich-Schiller-Universitat, n.d. Microfilm.

This is a facsimile of two partbooks, the *altus* and tenor, from the original in the Universitatsbibliothek der Friedrich-Schiller-Universitat in Jena (D Ju). It is part of a different issue of the 1541 edition. It is identical to the 1541 edition except for the title page. It contains madrigals by Arcadelt, Jachet Berchem, Corteccia, C. Festa, and F. Layolle. It is indexed in RISM A/I, A 1318 and the Bernstein catalog, no. 17a.

ArcE   Arcadelt, Jacob. *Eight madrigals: for four voices or instruments*. Edited by Thomas Bernard. Italian Madrigal, no. 1. London: London Pro Musica Edition, 1978.

This contains transcriptions of eight madrigals by Arcadelt. The Italian words are translated into English and printed as text on pp. 1-2. The instruments are unspecified.

ArcI   _____. *Il terzo libro de i madrigali novissimi a quattro voci*. Venetiis: Scotum, 1539.. [Munich: Bayerische Staatsbibliothek, n.d.]. Microfilm.

This is a facsimile of four partbooks containing madrigals by Arcadelt and Costanzo Festa. The original is in the Bayerische Staatsbibliothek in Munich. (D Mbs). It is indexed in RISM A/I, A 1374; RISM B/I, 1539-23, and the Bernstein catalog, no. 2.

ArcIP   _____. *Il primo libro de i madrigali i a quatro voci*. Venetijs: Scotum. 1543. Jena: Universitatsbibliothek der Friedrich-Schiller-Universitat, n.d. Microfilm.

This is a facsimile of one partbook, the *cantus*, from the original in the Universitatsbibliothek der Friedrich-Schiller-Universitat in Jena (D Ju). It is part of a different issue of the 1541 edition. It is identical to the 1541 edition except for the title page. It contains madrigals by Arcadelt, Jachet Berchem, Corteccia, C. Festa, and F. Layolle. It is indexed in RISM A/I, A 1317-18; RISM B/I, 1543-19a, and the Bernstein catalog, no. 17a.

ArcIV   _____. *Il Vero secondo libro di madrigali*. Venice: A. Gardane, 1539. Munich: Bayerische Staatsbibliothek, 1986. Microfilm.

This contains twenty-three madrigals for four voices by Arcadelt. The original manuscript is in the Bayerische Staatsbibliothek in Munich. It is indexed in RISM A/1; A 1369 and Lewis catalog, vol. 1, no. 5.

ArcM   _____. *Motecta*. Edited by Albert Seay. Opera omnia / Works, no. 10. Corpus mensurabilis musicae, no. 31. [S.I.]: American Institute of Musicology, 1970.

This source contains transcriptions of motets with Latin words. There is a commentary in English by Albert Seay.

ArcO   _____. *Opera omnia*. Edited by Albert Seay. Corpus mensurabilis musicae, no. 31. [S.I.]: American Institute of Musicology, 1965.

This source contains transcriptions of the Masses, Madrigals, and motets of Arcadelt.

ArcP   _____. *Il primo-quarto libro di madrigali d'Archadelt a qvartro con nvova gionta impressi a qvattro voci*. Venice: Antonio Gardane, 1539. Microcopy of the original.

This contains madrigals for four parts by Arcadelt. It is indexed in RISM 153923; 153924. It is filmed with the 1545 edition of *Qvarto libro di madrigali a qvatro voci d'Archadelt*. The latter source is indexed in RISM

	154518.
AreP	"Aretino, Pietro." *Britannica 2001 Deluxe Edition CD-ROM*. Copyright © 1994-2000 Britannica.com Inc. October 5, 2001.
	This is a short summary of the works by Ariteno.
AriO	Ariosto, Lodovico. *Orlando Furioso*. English translation by Guido Waldman. Oxford world's classics. Oxford; New York: Oxford University Press, 1974; 1998.
	This is a English translation of *Orlando Furioso*. The subject is Roland (Legendary character)--Romances. There is an index.
AstA	Aston, Hugh. *Ave Maria dive matris Anne*. Edited by Nick Sandon. Peterhouse compositions, no. 14. Newton Abbot, Devon England: Antico Edition, [c. 1995].
	This is a transcription of the votive antiphon for five voices. It is edited from partbooks in the Peterhouse collection of manuscripts in the Cambridge University Library (*Mss. 471-474*, no. 14). It is missing the tenor part which is recomposed by the editor. There are historical notes and critical commentary in English. The Latin words are printed as text with an English translation.
AtlAR	Atlas, Allan W. *Anthology of Renaissance Music: Music in Western Europe, 1400-1600*. The Norton Introduction to Music History. New York: W. W. Norton and Co., [c. 1998].
	This volume serves as a companion to *Renaissance Music* by Allan Atlas which appears in the Norton Introduction to Music History series and contains discussions of all 102 pieces included in this volume. The vocal pieces have English, French, German, Italian, Latin, Portuguese, or Spanish words. English translations of the texts are given on pages 487-496.
AtlR	_____. *Renaissance Music: Music in Western Europe, 1400-1600*. The Norton Introduction to Music History. New York-London: W. W. Norton and Company, 1998.
	This book is written for undergraduate music majors, graduate students, and lovers of early music. The main stress is on the music, leaving individual composers to play second fiddle. There is a companion volume, *Anthology of Renaissance Music*. There are ten *intermedi* scattered through the book. Each spans a few years of historical and cultural background. There is an *Epilogue* in which the term "Renaissance" is discussed at length. Bibliographical references are included.
AttC	Attaingnant, Pierre. *Chansons nouvelles en musique à quatre parties: nagueres imprimées*. Paris: Attaingnant, 1528. Versailles: Bibliothèque Municipale, n.d. Microfilm.
	This contains four-part polyphonic *chansons* by Sermisy, Vermont, Jacotin, and Janequin. But, there are only two partbooks, the *altus* and tenor. The original is in Versailles: Bibliothèque Municipale *(F V), Fonds Goujet, 8⁰ G.32*. The manuscript is indexed in RISM B/1, 1528-3 and Heartz catalog, no. 2.
AttCL	_____. *Chansons au luth et airs de cour français du XVIe siècle*. Société française de musicologie, 1 ser., no. 4-5 [i.e. 3-4]. Paris: E. Droz, 1934.
	This is a transcription of *Très brève et familière introduction...* There is an introduction by Lionel de La Laurenice and commentary and study of the sources by G. Thibault. It is transcribed by Adrienne Mairy. It contains the

songs with lute accompaniment.

AttD   Attaingnant, Pierre. *Dixseptiesme livre contenant xix chansons legères très musicales nouvelles à quatre parties.* Paris: Pierre Attaingnant, 1545. Transcribed by Albert Seay. Transcriptions, no. 2. Colorado Springs: Colorado College Music Press, [c. 1979].

This source contains transcriptions of *chansons* by Janequin (6), Gervaise (1), Guion (1), Sanserre (3), Delafont (2), Meigret (1), Romain (1), Vassal (1), DeMarle (1), and Ebran (1). There is an introduction containing a discussion of the *chansons*.

AttDB   _____. *Dixhuit basses dances, 1529.* Die Tabulatur, Heft 4-5. 2 vols. Hofheim am Taunus; F. Hofmeister, 1966.

This contains a lute tablature with modern transcriptions for lute or keyboard instrument. Volume one is titled *Die Basses dances*; Volume two is titled *Balle, haulberroys, branles, pavanes, sauterelles, gaillardes*.

AttDC   _____. *Dixneuf chansons musicales réduictes en la tabulature des orgues espinettes, manicordions et telz semblables instrumentz musicaulx.* Paris: Attaingnant, 1531. [Munich: Bayerische Staatsbibliothek], n.d. Microfilm.

This contains reductions for keyboard of *chansons* by Sermisy and anonymous writers. The original source is in the Bayerische Staatsbibliothek in Munich. It is indexed in RISM B/I, 1531-6 and Heartz catalog, no. 22.

AttDL   _____. *Dixseptiesme livre contenant xix chansons légères tres musicales nouvelles à quatre parties, en deux volumes.* Paris: Attaingnant, 1545. [Munich: Bayerische Staatsbibliothek], n.d. Microfilm.

This contains the *superius* and tenor parts of some four-part *chansons* by Jannequin, Delafont, Meigret, Senserre, Vassal, Guion, Romaine, Ebran, Gervaise and Demarle. These *chansons* are of the *chanson grivoise* style. The original is in Munich: Bayerische Staatsbibliothek, *(D Mbs), Mus. Pr. 4° 103.* It is indexed in RISM B/1; 1545-10 and Heartz catalog, no. 126.

AttDLD   _____. *Deux livres d'orgue parus en 1531 chez Pierre Attaingnant.* Trans. and comp. by Y. Rokseth. Publications de la Société francaise de musicologie, 1. sér. t. 1. Paris: Heugel, 1967.

This is a transcription of arrangements for the organ of two Masses: *Kyrie fons* and *Cunctipotens*, a Magnificat on the eighth tone with *Te Deum laudamus*, and two preludes. These were published by Attaingnant in 1531 in two separate books. There is an introduction by Y. Rokseth.

AttH   _____ et Jullet. *Huitiesme livre contenant xix chansons nouvelles quatre parties de la facture et composition de maîstre Clément Jennequin...* Paris: Attaingnant et Jullet, 1540. [Wolfenbüttel: Herzog-August Bibliothek], n.d. Microfilm.

There are two volumes containing nineteen four-part *chansons* by Clément Janequin. The original is in Wolfenbüttel: Herzog-August Bibliothek *(D W), 2.8.8. Mus.* It is indexed in RISM A/1; J 0445 and Heartz catalog, no. 90.

AttL   _____. *Liber decimus: passiones dominice in ramis palmarum, veneris sancte...* Paris: Attaingnant, 1535. [Wein: Österreichische National Bibliothek, n.d.] Microfilm.

This is a facsimile of the *superius*, tenor, *bassus*, and contratenor partbooks from the original in Österreichische National Bibliothek in Wien. These partbooks contain Passion music composed by Fevin, Claudin, L'enfant,

Muolu, Verdelot, G. Louvet, Divitis, and Jacquet. They are indexed in RISM B/I, 1535-02 and Heartz catalog, no. 61.

AttM   Attaingnant, Pierre. *Missarum musicalium quatuor vocum cum suis motetis, liber tertius.* Parhisiis: Attaingnant et Jullet, 1540. Microfiche. [Jena: Universitatsbibliothek der Friedrich-Schiller-Universität, n.d.].
This is a facsimile of four partbooks, *superius,* tenor, contratenor, and *bassus,* from the original in Universitatsbibliothek der Friedrich-Schiller-Universitat, Jena (D Ju). It contains Masses and motets by Pierre Certon and Claudin de Sermisy.

AttO   _____. *Operum musicalium liber primus, XVII modulorum indes.* Parisiis: Attaingnant, 1545. [Florence: Biblioteca del Conservatorio, n.d.]. Microfilm.
This is a facsimile of the original publication found in Florence: Biblioteca del Conservatori, *(I Fc), Basevi 2496 (1).* It contains four partbooks with motets by Guillaume Le Heurteur. It is indexed in Heartz catalog, no. 122.

AttP   _____. *Primus liber viginti missarum musicalium tres missas continens...* Paris: P. Attaingnant, 1532. [Boston: Boston Athenaeum Library, n.d.]. Microfilm.
This contains three Masses for four voices: one by P. de Manchicourt, one by Mattheus Gascongne, and one by C. de Sermisy. The original is in the Boston Athenaeum Library *(Us Ba).* It is indexed in RISM B/I, 1532-01 and Heartz catalog, no. 33.

AttPI   _____. *Britannica 2001 Deluxe CD-ROM.* [c. 1994-2000]
This is a short discussion of Attaingnant's music printing.

AttQ   _____. *Quarante et deux chansons musicales à troys parties.* Paris, Attaingnant, 1529. Paris: Bibliothèque Nationale, n.d. Microfilm.
This is a facsimile of the original publication. It contains polyphonic *chansons* for three parts attributed to Moulu, Agricola, Fevin, and Clemens. The original is in the Bibliothèque Nationale in Paris.

AttQG   _____. *Quatorze gaillardes, neuf pavennes, sept branles et deux basses danses, le tout réduict de musique en la tabulature du ieu d'orgues, espinettes manicordions & telz semblables instrumentz musicaulx.* Paris: Attaingnant, 1531. [Munich: Bayerische Staatsbibliotek, 1952.] Microfilm.
This is a facsimile. It contains dance music arranged for keyboard instruments. It is indexed in Heartz catalog, no. 28.

AttQL   _____. *Quatorzième livre de motets composes.* Edited by A. Tillman Merritt. Monaco: Éditions de l'Oiseau Lyre, 1964.
This book of motets is a sequel to *Treize livres de motets parus chez Pierre Attaingnant en 1534 et 1535.* It was republished by A. Smijers with facsimiles of the original title page. This was originally titled *Liber decimus quartus.* It contains motets by Pierre de Manchicourt.

AttQLT   _____. *Quartus liber tres missas continet...* Paris: P. Attaingnant, 1532. Microfilm. [Boston: Boston Athenaeum Library, n.d.].
This is a facsimile of masses for four voices. The original is in the Boston Athenaeum Library *(Us Ba).* It is indexed in RISM B/I, 1532-04 and Heartz catalog, no. 36.

AttQU   _____. *Quintus liber tres missas continet...* Paris: P. Attaingnant, 1532. [Boston: Boston Athenaeum Library, n.d.]. Microfilm.
This is a facsimile of three masses for four voices: one by Lupus, one by

Divitis, and one by Prioris. The original is in the Boston Athenaeum Library *(Us Ba)*. It is indexed in RISM B/I, 1532-05 and Heartz catalog, no. 37.

AttS   Attaingnant, Pierre. *Second livre contenant xxxi chansons musicales.* Paris: Pierre Attaingnant, 1536. Transcribed by Albert Seay. Transcriptions, no. 3. Colorado Springs: Colorado College Music Press, [c. 1979]; reprint ed., 1980.

There is an introduction with a discussion of the *chansons* and a short bibliography. There are transcriptions of *chansons* by Claudin (13), Janequin (1), Lupi (3), Guyon (1), Hesdin (1), Jacotin (3), Roquelay (1), Gombert (1), Certon (2), Ysoré (1), Dulot (1), Duboys (1), Le Peletier (1), and Heurteur (1).

AttSC   _____. *Second livre contenant xxix chansons...* Paris: P. Attaingnant, 1549. [Florence: Biblioteca del Conservatorio], n.d. Microfilm.

This contains four-part *chansons* by Certon, Boyvin, Claudin, Sandrin, De villiers, Belin, Constantius Festa, Harchadelt, Maillard, D'auxerre, Gardane, and De la font. There are only two partbooks, the *superius* and tenor. The original is in Florence: Biblioteca del Conservatorio *(I Fc)*, *Basevi 2492 (4)*. It is indexed in RISM B/1; 1549-18 and Heartz catalog, no. 159.

AttSL   _____. *Secundus liber tres missas continet...* Paris: P. Attaingnant, 1532. [Boston: Boston Athenaeum Library, n.d.]. Microfilm.

This contains three Masses for four voices by P. de Manchicourt (1), Claudin (1), and Mouton (1). The original is in the Boston Athenaeum Library *(Us Ba)*. It is indexed in RISM B/I, 1532-02 and Heartz catalog, no. 34.

AttSLC   _____. *Second livre contenant XXXI. chansons musicales...* Paris: Attaingnant, 1535. [Paris: Bibliothèque Mazarine], n.d. Microfilm.

This contains *chansons* by Jacotin, Gombert, Dulot, Certon and Claudin. The original is in Paris: Bibliothèque Mazarine *(F Pm)*, *Rés 30345 A (5)*. It is indexed in RISM B/1; 1536-3 and Heartz catalog, no. 71.

AttSLD   _____. *Sextus liber duas missas habet...* Paris: P. Attaingnant, 1532. [Boston: Boston Athenaeum Library, n.d.]. Microfilm.

This contains two Masses for four voices by Richafort and Gombert. The original is in the Boston Athenaeum Library *(Us Ba)*. It is indexed in RISM B/I, 1532-06 and Heartz catalog, no. 38.

AttSLT   _____. *Septimus liber tres missas habet...* Paris: P. Attaingnant, 1532. [Boston: Boston Athenaeum Library, n.d.]. Microfilm.

This contains three Masses for four voices by Le Heurteur, Claudin, and Gombert. The original is in the Boston Athenaeum Library *(Us Ba)*. It is indexed in RISM B/I, 1532-07 and Heartz catalog, no. 39.

AttT   _____. *Trente et une chansons musicales.* Les Maîtres Musiciens de la Renaissance Française, no. 5. Edited by Henry Expert. Paris: Alphonse Leduc, 1897.

This source contains transcriptions of *chansons* by Sermisy, Gascongne, Janequin, Jacotin, Courtoys, and etc. There are French texts only.

AttTC   _____. *Trente chansons musicales à quatre parties nouvellement et tres correctement imprimés.* Paris: Attaingnant, n.d. Paris: Bibliothèque Nationale, n.d. Microfilm.

This is a microfilm of the original in the Bibliothèque Nationale in Paris. The *chansons* are mostly anonymous with the exception of one by Clau-

	din.
AttTCM	Attaingnant, Pierre. *Trente chansons musicales*. Paris: Attaingnant, 1534. [Munich: Bayerische Staatsbibliothek], n.d. Microfilm. This contains four-part *chansons* by M. Sohier, G. Ysoré, P. Certon, Alaire, Lupus [or Cadéac]. Claudin, and [Morel]. The original is in Munich: Bayerische Staatsbibliothek, *(D Mbs), Mus. Pr. 40/8*. It is indexed in RISM B/1, 1534-13 and Heartz catalog, no. 44.
AttTH	_____. *Trente et huyt chansons musicales à quatre parties nouvellement imprimées*. Paris: Attaingnant, 1529. Eichstätt: Staatliche Bibliothek, (9). Microfilm. The original is in Eichstätt: Staatliche Bibliothek, (9). It contains the contratenor only of four-part *chansons*. Some *chansons* are by Sermisy and Gombert. It is indexed in Heartz catalog, p. 227ff.
AttTL	_____. *Treize livres de motets parus chez Pierre Attaingnant en 1534 et 1535*. 14 vols. Edited by A. Smijers. Vols. 12-14 edited by A. Tillman Merritt. Paris: Éditions de l'Oiseau-lyre: Louise B. M. Dyer, 1934. These contain transcriptions of motets published by Attaingnant with facsimiles of original title pages.
AttTLC	_____ et Jullet. *Tiers livre contenant xxix chansons nouvelles à quatre parties...* Paris: Attaingnant & Jullet, 1540. [Munich: Bayerische Staatsbibliothek], n.d. Microfilm. This contains two partbooks with the contratenor and *bassus* of four-part *chansons* by Certon, Claudin, Mittantier, Sandrin, Godard, Villiers, Le Moisne, Bourguignon, De Porta, Fresneau, Jacotin, Cadeac, Courtoys, and Maillard. The original is in Munich: Bayerische Staatsbibliothek *(D Mbs) Mus. Pr. 4° 103*. It is indexed in RISM B/1; 1540-10 and Heartz catalog, no. 95.
AttTLCN	_____ et Jullet. *Tresiesme livre contenant xix chansons nouvelles à quatre parties, en deux volumes*. Paris: Attaingnant et Jullet, 1543. [München: Bayerische Staatsbibliothek, n.d.]. Microfilm. This contains four-part *chansons* by Certon, Guyon, Janequin, Manchicourt, Godard, Hebran, Josselme, Peletier, Clemens, and Vassal. There are two partbooks containing the *superius*/tenor and contratenor/*bassus*. The contratenor/*bassus* partbook is dated 1545. The original is in München: Bayerische Staatsbibliothek, *(D Mbs)*. It is indexed in RISM B/1; 1543-09 and Heartz catalog, no. 111.
AttTLT	_____. *Tertius liber tres missas continet...* Paris: P. Attaingnant, 1532. Microfilm. [Boston: Boston Athenaeum Library, n.d.]. This source contains masses for four voices by Claudin, Mouton, and Lupus. The original is in the Boston Athenaeum Library *(Us Ba)*. It is indexed in RISM B/I, 1532-03 and Heartz catalog, no. 35.
AttTM	_____. *Treze motetz musicaulx avec ung prélude, le tout réduict en la tabulatur des orgues espinettes et manicordions et telz semblable instrumentz*. Paris: Attaingnant, 1531. [Munich: Bayerische Staatsbibliothek, n.d.]. Microfilm. This is a facsimile of motets (preludes) arranged for keyboard instruments. According to the Heartz catalog, the Bayerische Staatsbibliothek copy has been missing since 1963. It is indexed in RISM B/I, 1531-5 and Heartz catalog, no. 27.

AttTMP	Attaingnant, Pierre. *Treize motets et un prélude orgue*. Transcribed and edited with an Introduction by Yvonne Rokseth. Publications de la Société francaise de musicologie, Ser. 1; no. 5. Paris: E. Droz, 1930. This contains transcriptions of arrangements of music for organ along with the music of the original compositions. The compositions are for three and four voices with Latin and Italian words. This is indexed in Edition of Attaingnant print, Heartz catalog, no. 27 and RISM 1531/5.
AttTP	_____. *Tablature pour le jeu d'orgues espinettes et manicordions sur le plain chant de Cunctipotens et Kyrie fons...* Paris: Attaingnant, 1531. [Munich: Bayerische Staatsbibliothek], n.d. Microfilm. This is a facsimile of a choirbook containing Masses for keyboard instruments. The original manuscript is in the Bayerische Staatsbibliothek in Munich. It is indexed in the Heartz catalog, no. 25 and Brown, H. M. : *Instrumental Music Printed before 1600*.
AttTQ	_____. *Trente et quatre chansons musicales à quatre parties*. Paris: Attaingnant, 1528. Munich: Bayerische Staatsbibliothek, n.d. Microfilm. This contains four-part *chansons* by Claudin or Jacotin, Richafort, Jennequin, [Passereau], Josquin de pres, and Consilium. The original is in Munich: Bayerische Staatsbibliothek *(D Mbs), Mus. Pr. 31/12*. It is indexed in RISM B/1, [c.1528]-6 and Heartz catalog, no. 29.
AttTS	_____. *Trente et sept chansons musicales à quatre parties nouvellement et correctement imprimées*. Paris: Attaingnant, 1529. Paris: Bibliothèque Nationale, n.d. Microfilm. This contains four-part polyphonic *chansons* by Claudin, Vermont, Jacotin, and Jannequin. The original is in Paris: Biblioteque Nationale *(F Pn) Rés. Vm^7 178*. It is indexed in RISM B/1, [c. 1528]-8 and Heartz catalog, no. 9.
AttTSC	_____. *Trente et sept chansons musicale*. Edited by Henry Expert. Les Maîtres musiciens de la Renaissance française: bibliographie thématique, no. 8. Paris: A. Leduc, 1900. This is a thematic catalogue with an index and the author's *Trente et une chansons musicales*.
AttTSCM	_____. *Trente et six chansons musicales à quatre parties*. Paris: Attaingnant, 1530. Eichstätt: Staatliche Bibliothek, n.d. Microfilm. This contains four-part *chansons* by Jennequin, Jacotin, J. de Bechefort, J. de Bonchefort, Claudin, [Hesdin], [Ronsée]. Gobert Cochet, and [Dulot]. The original is in Eichstätt: Staatliche Bibliothek (D E), no. 12 (Ct, defective). There is only the contratenor. It is indexed in RISM B/1, 1530-4 and Heartz catalog, no. 19.
AttTSE	_____. *Trente et sept chansons musicales*. Les Maîtres musiciens de la Renaissance française: bibliogrphie thématique, 8. Edited by Henry Expert. Paris: A. Leduc, 1900. This is volume eight of a projected set of fifteen volumes. Only volumes three and eight were published. There is an index with Attaingnant's *Trente et sept chansons musicales* of 1529. It contains nineteen *chansons* by Janequin and one by Sermisy.
AttTSEP	_____. *Trente et sept chansons musicales à quatre parties*. Paris: Attaingnant, 1431. Munich: Bayerische Staatsbibliothek. Photographic Reproduction, n.d..

This contains four-part *chansons*. Nineteen *chansons* are by Janequin and one is by Sermisy. It is a new and corrected reprint.

AttTT   Attaingnant, Pierre. *Trente troysiesme livre (1549).* Transcribed by Albert Seay. Transcriptions, no. 7. Colorado Springs: Colorado College Music Press, 1982.

There are transcriptions of twenty *chansons* in this source. Eight of the *chansons* are by Du Tertre, five are by Janequin, four are by Symon, two are by Gervaise, and one is by Ebran. There is an introduction by Albert Seay.

AttTTC   _____. *Trente et trois chansons nouvelles en musique à quatre parties.* Paris: Attaingnant, 1531. Eichstätt: Staatliche Bibliothek. Microfilm.

This contains the countertenor partbook only. There are *chansons* by Claudin, Le bouteiller, Jacotin, Le peletier, Consilium, and [Roquelay]. The original is in Eichstätt: Staatliche Bibliothek. It is indexed in Heartz catalog, p. 243.

AttTTL   _____. *Trente troysiesme livre contenant xx chansons nouvelles à quatre en deux volumes.* Paris: Attaingnant, 1549. [Munich: Bayerische Staatsbibliothek], n.d. Microfilm.

This contains the *superius* and tenor parts of four-part *chansons* by Jennequin, Symon, Ebran, Du tertre and Gervaise. The original is in Munich: Bayerische Staatsbibliothek, *(D Mbs) Mus. Tr. 4° 103.* It is indexed in RISM B/1; 1549-23 and Heartz catalog, no. 157.

AttTU   _____. *Trente et une chansons musicales à quatre parties.* Paris: Attaingnant, 1534. [Munich: Bayerische Staatsbibliothek], n.d. Microfilm.

This contains four-part *chansons* by Claudin, Jennequin, Courtois, M. Lasson, Gombert, Heurteur, Roger Patie, Lupi, Alaire, Hesdin, Ronsée, and Mahiet. The original is in Munich: Bayerische Staatsbibliothek *(D Mbs), Mus. Pr. 31/6.* It is indexed in RISM B/1; 1534-12 and Heartz catalog, no. 54.

AttTUL   _____. *Trente & ungyeseme livre contenant xxx chansons nouvelles à quatre en deux volumes.* Paris: Attaingnant, 1549. [München: Bayerische Staatsbibliothek, n.d.] Microfilm.

This contains the *superius* and tenor of *chansons* by Clément Janequin. The original manuscript is in München: Bayerische Staatsbibliothek. It is indexed in RISM A/1; J0448 and Heartz catalog, no. 155.

AttV   _____.*Vingt Deuxiesme Livre (1547).* Transcribed by Albert Seay. Colorado College Music Press, Transcriptions, no. 4. Colorado Springs: Colorado College Music Press, [c. 1980].

This source contains transcriptions of twenty *chansons* that represent a cross-section of works from the mature period of the Parisian *chanson*. There are *chansons* from fifteen different composers with two different types, the *grivioise* and the sentimental. There are *chansons* by Janequin (2), Delafont (3), Du Tertre (2), Sandrin (4), Gardane (4), and one *chanson* each by the following: Plisson, De Villa, Puy, Le Gendre, Certon, Passereau, Boyvin, Ebran, Sohyer, and Vassal. There are three examples of *chansons* in pairs. Original spellings of the French texts are retained. There is a bibliography.

AttVC   _____. *Vingt et cinque chansons musicales réduictes en la tabulature des orgues espinettes, manicordions et telz semblables instrumentz musicaulx.*

Paris: Attaingnant, 1530. [Munich: Bayerische Staatsbibliothek], [1985]. Microfilm.

This is a facsimile of twenty-five *chansons* reduced into tablature for keyboard instruments. It is indexed in RISM B/I/l, 1531p7s and Brown, H. M., *Instrumental music printed before 1600*, 1531b2s.

AttVD   Attaingnant, Pierre. *Vingt deuxiesme livre contenant xxvi chansons nouvelles à quatre parties en deux volumes*. Paris: Attaingnant, 1547. [Munich: Bayerische Staatsbibliothek]. Microfilm.

This contains the *superius* and tenor parts of four-part *chansons* by Sohyer, Gardane, Le Gendre, Jannequin, Sandrin, Ebran, Plisson, Delafont, Puy, De Villa, Certon, Boyvin, Vassal, Passereau, and Du Terre. The original is in Munich: Bayerische Staatsbibliothek *(D Mbs), Mus. Pr. 4° 103*. It is indexed in RISM B/1; 1547-9 and Heartz catalog, no. 145.

AttVH   _____. *Vingt et huit chansons nouvelles en musique à quatre parties*. Paris: Attaingnant, 1530. Munich: Bayerische Staatsbibliothek, n.d. Microfilm.

This contains four-part *chansons* by F. Dulot, Passereau, Gombert, [Renes], Consilium, [Claudin], Lupi, [Isoré], and Barbette. The original is in Munich: Bayerische Staatsbibliothek *(D Mbs) Mus. Pr. 40/6*. It is indexed in RISM B/1, 1531-1 and Heartz catalog, no. 31.

AttVN   _____. *Vingt et neuf chansons musicales à quatre parties*. Paris: Attaingnant, 1530. [Eichstätt: Staatliche Bibliothek], n.d. Microfilm.

The original manuscript is in Eichstätt: Staatliche Bibliothek *(D E), no. 11 (Ct)*. There is only one part book for contratenor of four-part *chansons* by Beaumont, Claudin, Consilium, [Morton], G. Le Heurteur, Lupi, Jennequin, Jacobin, N. Renes, Passereau, and [Mahiet]. It is indexed in Heartz catalog, no. H. 18 and RISM B/1. 1530-3.

AttVQ   _____. *Vingt et quatre chansons musicales à quatre parties*. Paris: Attaingnant, 1533. [München: Bayerische Staatsbibliothek, n.d.]. Microfilm.

This contains four partbooks of *chansons* by Janequin. The original is in München: Bayerische Staatsbibliothek, *(D Mbs)*. It is indexed in RISM A/1; JJ443a and Heartz catalog, no. 40.

AttVS   _____. *Vingt et sept chansons musicales à quatre parties desquelles les plus convenables à la fleuste d'allement...*Paris: Attaingnant, 1533. Microfilm.

There are twenty-seven four-part *chansons* in this source, of which fourteen are indicated as being applicable for the recorder. They are by Gombert (8), Heurteur (6), Manchicourt (1), Passereau (5), and Sermisy (7).

AttVSC   _____. *Vingt et six chansons musicales réduictes en la tabulature des orgues espinettes, manicordions et telz semblables instrumentz musicaulx*. Paris: Attaingnant, 1530. [Munich: Bayerische Staatsbibliothek], [1985]. Microfilm.

This is a facsimile of twenty-six *chansons* reduced into tablature for keyboard instruments. It is indexed in RISM B/I/l 1531p8s and Brown, H. M., *Instrumental music printed before 1600*, 1531b3s.

AttVSCM   _____. *Vingt et six chansons musicales à quatre parties*. Paris: Attaingnant, 1535. [München: Bayerische Staatsbibliothek, n.d.]. Microfilm.

This contains four-part *chansons* by Janequin, Claudin, Passereau, Gombert, Certon, Lupi, Allaire, Cirot, and Heurteur. It is indexed in RISM B/1, 1535-06 and Heartz catalog, no. 62.

AulP   *Aulcuns pseaulmes et cantiques mys en chant*. A Strasburg, 1539. Répression phototypographique précédée d'un avant-propos par D. Delétra. Geneve: A. Jullien, 1919.

This is a reproduction from the original compiled by Jean Calvin found in the Staatsbibliothek in Munich. Twelve of the Psalms are adapted from Marot's paraphrases. The melodies are unaccompanied with French words.

BaiR Bainton, Roland H. *The Reformation of the Sixteenth Century.* Boston: Beacon Press, [c. 1952].

This book covers the religious revival from Luther to Calvin. It discusses the effects of the Reformation on politics, economics, and domestic relations.

BakB *Baker's Biographical Dictionary of Musicians.* 5th ed. completely revised with a 1971 supplement. Slonimsky, Nicolas, ed. New York: G. Schirmer, [c.1971].

This dictionary contains long accepted biographical facts with a bibliography for each entry. Popular music and its purveyors are covered in the supplement.

BarID Barberiis, Melchiore de. *Intabulatura di lauto: Libro sesto di diversi motetti a quatro voce, intabulati & accomodati per sonare sopra il lautto.* Venetiis: [s.n.], 1546. Wolfenbüttel: Herzog-August-Bibliothek, 1986. Microfilm.

This is a facsimile of the sixth book of intabulations for the lute. There are intabulations of twelve motets.

BarIL _____. *Intabolatura di lauto: libro nono intitulato Bembo di fantasie, balli, passi e mezzo, e padoane, gagliarde.* Venetiis: Apud H. Scotum, 1549. Kassel: Deutsches Musikgeschichtliches Archiv, 1986. Microfilm.

This is a facsimile of the ninth book of intabulations for the lute by Barberiis. It contains intabulations of dance music.

BarOI _____. *Opera intitolata contina intabolatura di lauto di fantasie, motetti, canzoni, discordate a varii modi, fantasie per sonar uno solo con uno lauto, & sarsi tenore & soprano...* Venezia: Hieronymum Scotum, 1549. Wolfenbüttel: Herzog August Bibliothek, 1986? Microfilm.

This contains selections from the tenth book of a set of lute tablatures by Barberiis. It includes two lute duets and four short pieces for lute.

BarT Barbour, J. Murray. *Tuning and Temperament: a Historical Survey.* East Lansing: Michigan state College Press, 1953.

A discussion of the theories of tuning and temperament beginning with Greek tunings and ending with the present (1953).

BauH Baumgartner, Frederic J. *Henry II, King of France 1547-1559.* Durham: Duke University Press, 1988.

A political biography of Henry II. It is based on manuscript collections and contemporary materials.

BelD Bellermann, Heinrich. *Der contrapunct, oder Anleitung zur stimmführung in der musikalischen composition.* Berlin: J. Springer, 1862.

This is a book on counterpoint. It contains music illustrations.

BelS Bellingham, B. and E. Evans, eds. *Sixteenth Century Bicinia.* Recent Researches in the Music of the Renaissance, no. 16-17. New Haven: A R Editions Inc., [c. 1974].

This is a complete edition of Munich, Bayerische Staatsbibliothek, *Mus. MS. 260.* There are 106 compositions of which one hundred are duos and four are German Chorale settings in four or more parts. One composition is missing and one is only partly there. Of these 106 compositions there are twenty-six French *chansons* for two voices. There is a Preface, a list of editorial procedures, Concordances, and notes.

BemP   Bembo, Pietro. *Prose della volgar lingua*. Introduction and note by Carlo Dionisorri-Casalone. Torino: Unione tipografico-editrice torinese, 1931. Collezione di classici italiani... Ser. 2, vol. 6. Washington, D.C.: Library of Congress, 19-.

Bembo codifies Italian orthography and grammar essential for the establishment of a standard language. He recommended fourteenth century Tuscan as the model for Italian literary language.

BemPI   _____. Britannica 2001 Deluxe Edition CD-ROM. Britannica.com, Inc. July 22, 2001.

This is a short biography of Pietro Bembo.

BenF   Bent, Margaret. "Musica recta and Musica ficta." *Musica Disciplina* 26 (1972): 73-100.

Margaret Bent attempts to develop a working hypothesis for applying accidentals in performance. Her material is based on theoretical evidence relevant to the early fifteenth century.

BenFD   Benham, H. "The formal Design and Construction of Taverner's Works." *Musica Disciplina* 26 (1972): 189-

The principal formal methods and objectives used by Taverner in his Masses and antiphons are investigated. This includes textural schemes, arrangement of *cantus firmus* statements, and the establishment of a wide range of correspondences in length between various sections and types of texture.

BenL   _____. *Latin Church Music in England c. 1460-1575*. London: Barrie and Jenkins Ltd., [c. 1977].

This source is a study of a body of elaborate large-scale music for the Latin rite of Sarum. There are musical examples at the original pitch, and a table of works for each composer with a list of sources.

BerC   Bernstein, Jane A., ed. *French Chansons of the Sixteenth Century*. University Park: The Pennsylvania State University Press, [c. 1985].

This is an anthology similar to the ones printed in the sixteenth century in that it presents a compendium of *chansons* from all the main musical centers of Europe. Each *chanson* contains the musical setting, a full poetic text with English translation, an historical description, and a brief critical commentary. Original sources, modern editions, emendations, and texted sources are given. This is a concise history of the sixteenth-century *chanson*.

BerCA   _____. *Music Printing in Renaissance Venice: the Scotto Press, 1539-1572*. New York; Oxford: Oxford University Press, 1998.

This book is divided into four parts: Part I: Historical Study; Part II: Catalogue of Music Editions; Part III: Appendices; Part IV: Indices.

BerCL   _____, ed. *Chansons issued by Le Roy and Ballard*. The Sixteenth-century *chanson*, no. 21. New York: Garland Publishing, 1991.

There is a General Introduction, a section on Editorial Methods, and an Introduction for this volume. There are transcriptions of *chansons* for three to six voices with French words. This volume contains *chansons* by François Regnard, Jean Richafort, Rogier Pathie, Luigi Rouince, and Jean Rousée.

BerCO Bernstein, Jane A, ed. *Collected Works / Philip van Wilder*. Masters and monuments of the Renaissance, no. 4. New York: Broude Trust, 1991.
This is divided into two parts. Part 1: Sacred works and Part 2: Secular works, Instrumental works, and Appendices. There are principally motets and *chansons* for four to twelve voices with French and Latin words. English translations are printed with the texts in commentary.

BerCP _____, ed. *Chansons issued by Le Roy and Ballard*. The Sixteenth-century chanson, no. 9. New York: Garland Publishers, 1994.
There is a General Introduction, a section on Editorial Methods, and an Introduction for this volume. There are transcriptions of *chansons* by Beaulieu, Appenzeller, Bercoy, Besancourt, Boyvin, Briault, Cadeac, Chevalier, Ciron, Consilium, Cornet, Crécquillon, La Rue, De la Font, Desbordes, Du Buisson, Du Tertre, and Ebran.

BerCR Berg, Johann. *Lamentationes Hieremiae Prophetae... Noribergae: Montanum & Neuberum, 1549*. [Munchen: Bayerische Staatsbibliothek, n.d.]. Microfilm.
This source contains works for four voices on the *Lamentations of Jeremiah* by Crécquillon, A. Fevin, J. Gardano, P. de la Rue, C. de Sermisy, and others. The original is in Bayerische Staatsbibliothek in Munich.

BerCT Bernoulli, Eduard. *Chansons und Tänze*. 4 vols. Facsimile edition. The original was published by Pierre Attaingnant. The original is in the Library of Congress, Washington D.C.: 1 microfilm reel, n.d. Facsimile edition: München: C. Kuhn, 1914.
This source contains *chansons musicales* arranged for keyboard instruments.

BerD Bergsagel, J. D. "The Date and Provenance of the Forrest-Heyther Collection of Tudor Masses." *Music and Letters* XLIV (1963): 240-256.
This is a review of the manuscript as a whole. Bergsagel makes a few conclusions.

BerE I _____, trans. and ed. *Early Tudor Masses I*. Early English Church Music, no. 1. London: Stainer and Bell, Ltd., 1963-.
This source contains Masses for four to six voices. There is a critical commentary at the end of the volume. There are bibliographical references.

BerE II _____, trans. and ed. *Early Tudor Masses II*. Early English Church Music, no. 16. London: Stainer and Bell, Ltd., 1963-
This source contains Masses for four to six voices. There is a critical commentary at the end of the volume. There are bibliographical references.

BerI _____. "An Introduction to Ludford." *Musica Disciplina* XIV (1960): 105-130.
This is a discussion of the main details of a sketchy outline of the life and music of Nicholas Ludford developed by W. H. Grattan Flood ca. 1918 and an extensive work thirty years later by Dr. Hugh Baillie.

BerL _____. "On the Performance of Ludford's Alternatum Masses." *Musica disciplina* 16 (1962): 36-55.
Bergsagel discusses the problem presented by the composer's use of squares as soloist's material and the *alternatum* style of the music. The question raised is, should the squares be sung or played by the organ either monophonically as they stand or as *canti firmi* for improvisation?

BerLA Berquist, Peter. "Del Lago." In *The New Grove Dictionary of Music and*

	Musicians, p. 345. 20 vols. Edited by Stanley Sadie. 6th ed. London: Macmillan Publishers Limited, [c. 1980].
	This is a short biography of Del Lago.
BerLAN	Berquist, Peter. "Lanfranco, Giovanni Maria." In *The New Grove Dictionary of Music and Musicians*, p. 441. 20 vols. Edited by Stanley Sadie. 6th ed. London: Macmillan Publishers Limited, [c. 1980].
	This is a short biography of Lanfranco.
BerLP	_____. "The Theoretical Writings of Pietro Aaron." Ph.D. diss., Columbia University, 1964.
	This study presents an analysis and discussion of Aaron's five published treatises: *Libri, Toscanello, Trattato, Lucidario, and Compendiolo*. Also, it includes a substantial portion of his surviving correspondence.
BerM	Berger, Karol. *Musica ficta: Theories of Accidental Inflections in Vocal Polyphony from Marchetto da Padova to Gioseffo Zarlino*. Cambridge: Cambridge University Press, 1987.
	A clarification of the meaning and use of the conventions governing the practice of implied accidentals in vocal polyphony from the early fourteenth century to the mid-sixteenth century.
BerMF	Bernstein, Lawrence F. *"La Couronne et fleur des chansons a troys:* A Mirror of the French Chanson in Italy in the Years between Ottaviano Petrucci and Antonio Gardano." *Journal of the American Musicological Society* 26 (1973): 1-69.
	This is an attempt to resolve the contradictions that have complicated the issue of the provenance of this 1536 publication.
BerMM I	_____, ed. *La Couronne et fleur des chansons à troys*. Transcriptions. Masters and Monuments of the Renaissance, no. 3. 2 vols. New York: Broude Trust, 1984.
	There are forty-one pieces, twenty of which are by Willaert and four by Richafort. There is a General Preface and Supervising Editor's Preface, another Preface with a discussion of *La Couronne et fleur des chansons à troys*, and a discussion of editorial principles.
BerMM II	_____. *La Couronne et fleur des chansons à troys. Commentary*. Masters and Monuments of the Renaissance, no. 3. 2 vols. New York: Broude Trust, 1984.
	This second volume is an historical commentary of the *chansons*. There is an introduction, a bibliographical commentary and critical report, a list of printed sources of vocal music, and a bibliography of general sources.
BerN	_____. "Guillaume Le Heurteur." In *New Grove Dictionary of Music and Musicians*, p. 622. Edited by Stanley Sadie. London: Macmillan Publishers, Ltd., 1980.
	This is a short biography of Le Heurteur and his music.
BerP	_____. "The 'Parisian *Chanson*': Problems of Style and Terminology." *Journal of the American Musicological Society* 31 (1978): 193-240.
	The main purpose of this article is to reveal the extraordinary diversity and mutability of the sixteenth century *chanson* cultivated throughout France and disseminated by Pierre Attaingnant.
BerS	Bermudo, Fray Juan. *Declaraciòn de instrumentos musicales, 1555*. Edited by Marcario Santiago Kastner. Documenta musicologica, Reihe I, no. 11. Kassel: Bärenreiter, 1951-.

	This is an enlarged edition of the 1549 publication. In this treatise, Bermudo discusses and recommends a system of notation for organ music
BerT	Bermudo, Juan. *Tientos and Hymns (1555): for 4 instruments*. Edited by Bernard Thomas. Early music library, no. 362. London: London Pro Musica Edition, 200.
	This source contains transcriptions of three hymns and two *Tientos* for four voices by Bermudo. The music is from Bermudo's *Declaración de instrumentos musicales*. There are editorial notes by Bernard Thomas.
BèzP	Bèze, Théodore de. *Psaumes mis en vers français (1551-1562): accompagnés de la version en prose de Louis Budé*. Edited by Pierre Pidoux. Travaux d'humanisme et Renaissance, no. 199. Genève: Librairie Droz, 1984.
	This source contains Psalms written in French verse by Théodore Bèze. They are taken from the prose version of Louis Budé. There are bibliographical references.
BiaI	Bianchini, Domenico. *Intabolatura de lauto...ditto rossetto di recercari motetti madrigali canzoni francese napolitane et balli*. Venetia: Antonio Gardane, 1546. London: British Museum, n.d. Microfilm.
	This is a facsimile of intabulations for the lute. It contains works by Willaert, Arcadelt, Certon, Gombert, Sermisy and others. It is indexed in RISM A/1, B 2596; RISM B/1, 1546-24, and Brown, no. 1546/5, p. 78. The original publication is in the British Museum in London (GB Lbm).
BibA	*Biblioteca apostolica vaticana: Manuscript, Capella Sistina 155*. 1538. [Citta del Vaticano]: Biblioteca apostolica vaticana, 1983. Microfilm.
	This is a facsimile of a choir book that was copied in Rome for use by the Capella Sistina. The music is for four to six voices with Latin words. It contains *Missa De beata Virgine* by Arcadelt, *Missa Domini est terra* by Sermisy, *Missa chiare dolci fresche aque* by Jacquet of Mantua, and *Missa Ave Regina caelorum* by Arcadelt.
BibAV	_____. *Manuscript, Lat. 5318*. [Citta del vaticana]: Biblioteca apostolica vaticana, 1980. Microfilm.
	This manuscript contains letters on music theory by Giovanni del Lago, Giovanni Spataro, Pietro Aaron, and others.
BibE	*Biblioteca estense (Modena, Italy): Manuscript, Mus. L. 451 (Alpha, n, 1, 1): Messe a 5 e 6 voci per autori diversi*. N.p.: n.p., ? 1700 1799. [S.l.: s.n., 1977?]. Microfilm.
	The title is supplied by the U. C. Music Library. It is a manuscript and is indexed in Bollettino dell 'Associazione dei Musicologi Italiani Catalogo dele opere musicali, serie VIII. It contains three Masses by Della Viola, one by Luzzaschi, and one by Willaert.
BicH	Bicknell, Stephen. *The History of the English Organ*. Cambridge, England; Cambridge University Press, 1996
	This is an attempt to write the first history of the English organ that treads a critical path between traditionally accepted accounts and the modern understanding of documents and surviving instruments. It covers a period from ca. 900 to 1980 and beyond. There are many plates and a glossary of terms related to the organ.
BlaC	Blackburn, Bonnie J., Edward E. Lowinsky, and Clement A. Miller. *A Correspondence of Renaissance Musicians*. Oxford: Clarendon Press; New York: Oxford University Press, 1991.

This correspondence consists of 110 letters written between 1517 and 1543 by fifteen sixteenth-century performing musicians living in Italy. It is known as the *Spataro Correspondence*, so called after its main author.

BlaOC   Blackburn, Bonnie J. "On Compositional Process in the Fifteenth Century." *Journal of the American Musicological Society* 40 (1987): 210-284.

This is an attempt to confirm that simultaneous conception of composition arose early in the fifteenth century and existed side by side with successive composition through the fifteenth and sixteenth centuries.

BleT   Blezzard, Judith, ed. *The Tudor church music of the Lumley books.* Recent researches in the music of the Renaissance, no. 65. Madison [Wis.]: A-R Editions, [c. 1985].

This music is edited from the partbooks in *Royal appendix 74-76* in the British Library, London. The *bassus* is missing but it has been reconstructed by the editor. The music is principally for four voices. It consists of prose and metrical psalms, canticles, two anthems, a Litany, a doxology, and a 1552 Kyrie.

BluE   Blum, Michael. *Enchiridion geistlicher Gesenge und Psalmen fur die Leien...* (1530). Edited by Hans Hofmann. [Leipzig: Quelle & Meyer, 1914].

This is a facsimile reprint of German hymns to which are appended critical notes.

BluPR   Blume, Friedrich. *Part I: The Period of the Reformation.* Revised by Ludwig Finscher. Translated by F. Ellsworth Peterson. In *Protestant Church Music: a History*, by Friedrich Blume, pp. 1-124. New York: W. W. Norton and Co., [c.1974].

This section covers the assimilation and development of substances of all spheres of pre-Reformation music culture, i.e., German folk song and dance, the German art song, and the sacred and secular art of the Netherlanders, along with the Latin-Catholic sphere. The period covered is the sixteenth century.

BohP   Bohemian Brethern. *Piesne Chwal Bozskych...* Edited by Zdenek Tobolka. Monumenta Bohemiae typographica, no. 3. Prague: s.n., 1927.

This is a facsimile reprint of the original hymn book of 1541 compiled by Jan Roh. There is a title also in English, *Pavel Severynz Kapi Hory and his printed text Songs of divine praise dated 1541.*

BooF   Boorman, Stanley. "False Relations and the Cadence." In *Essays on Italian Music in the Cinquecento,* pp. 221-265. Edited by Richard Charteris. Sydney: Frederick May Foundation for Italian Studies, 1990.

This is an attempt to show that certain composers of the early sixteenth century expected theoretically forbidden false relations to occur in performance. Also, that they apparently liked the sonority of false relations and composed accordingly.

BorF   Borren, Carles van den. "The French *Chanson.*" In *The New Oxford History of Music.* Vol. 4: *The Age of Humanism: 1540-1630*, edited by Gerald Abraham, pp. 1-31. London: Oxford University Press, [c. 1968]; reprint ed., 1974.

This is a a discussion of the origin, characteristics, sources, and composers of the *chanson.*

BouL   Bourgeoise, Louis. *Le premier livre des pseaulmes de David contenant xxiiii pseaulmes...* Lyon: Godefroy & Marcelin Beringen, 1547. [Orléans: Bibliotheque municipale, n.d.]. Microfilm.

This is a facsimile of a partbook containing French sacred part songs. The texts are Psalms. The original is in the Bibliotheque municipale in Orléans. It is indexed in RISM A/I, B 3814.

BouLP Bourgeoise, Louis. *Pseaulmes, de David, roy et prophete...* Lyon: Godefroy & Marcelin Beringen, 1547. [Orléans: Bibliotheque municipale, n.d.]. Microfilm.

This is a facsimile of a partbook containing French sacred part songs. The texts are Psalms. The original is in the Bibliotheque municipale in Orléans. It is indexed in RISM A/I, B 3815.

BouV _____. *Vingt-quatre psaumes a 4 voix*. Edited by Paul-Andre Gaillard. Schweizerische Musikdenkmäler, Bd. 3. Bale: Edition Baerenreiter, 1960.

This is a transcription of the Psalms for four voices. There is a preface and a critical commentary in French.

BoyC Boyce, William. *Cathedral music: being a collection in score of the most valuable and useful compositions for that service, by the several English masters of the last two hundred years*. 3 vols. 2nd edition. London: Printed for John Ashley, 1788.

This contains anthems that were selected and carefully revised by Dr. William Boyce. The anthems have English words.

BoyCA _____. *Cathedral music: being a collection in score of the most valuable and useful compositions for that service, by the several English masters of the last two hundred years*. 3 volumes. 2nd edition. Nendein, Liechtenstein, Kraus Reprint ed., 1975.

This is a facsimile of the 1788 edition published by John Ashley. It contains anthems that were selected and carefully revised by Dr. William Boyce. The anthems have English words.

BowC Bowers, Roger. "To chorus from quartet: the performing resource for English church polyphony, c. 1390-1559." In *English Choral Practice, 1400-1650,* pp. 1-47. Edited by John Morehen. Cambridge Studies in Performance Practice. Cambridge: Cambridge University Press, 1995.

This is a discussion of the change that took place in liturgical choirs from previously small ensembles of all adult male soloists to a chorus of boys and men.

BraD Brandolini, Raffaele Lippo. *On music and poetry = De musica et poetica: 1513*. Translated by Ann E. Moyer. Medieval and Renaissance texts and studies, no. 232. Tempe, Ariz.: Arizona Center for Medieval and Renaissance Studies, 2001.

This is a translation of *De musica et poetica* by Brandolini. It was translated with the assistance of Marc Laureys. There is an introduction and notes by Ann E. Moyer.

BraE Bray, Roger. "Editing and Performing *Musica speculativa.*" In *English Choral Practice, 1400-1650,* pp. 48-73. Edited by John Morehen. Cambridge Studies in Performance Practice. Cambridge: Cambridge University Press, 1995.

This article discusses the problems facing an editor attempting to make performable an obscurely notated original illustrating *musica speculativa*. The question of how far should an editor go in trying to establish what form a lost prototype of a surviving arrangement might take is discussed.

BraM   Bray, Roger. "Music and Musicians in Tudor England: Sources, Composition Theory and Performance." In *Music in Britain: the Sixteenth Century*, pp. 1-45. Edited by Roger Bray. The Blackwell History of Music in Britain, no. 2. Oxford: Blackwell Publishers Ltd., [c. 1995].

Roger Bray has attempted to bring together the strands which tie together the activity of the entire sixteenth century, to show how the treatises from the end of the century related to comments found early in the century, how musical sources from the end of the century include music from the early part of the century, how the Anglican service and Catholic service are related, and how the attitudes of the performers at the end of the century are related to those of the beginning.

BraMB   _____, ed. *Music in Britain: the Sixteenth Century*. The Blackwell History of Music, no. 2. Cambridge, Maine: Blackwell Publishers, Ltd., [c.1995].

The period covered is ca. 1450 to 1668. But, the periods other than the sixteenth century are covered only lightly where necessary to establish or maintain the context of the sixteenth-century musicians. This is a group of essays covering music and musicians in Tudor England, sacred music to Latin texts, sacred music to English texts, secular vocal music, keyboard music, and ensemble and lute music.

BraMQ   _____. "Music and the quadrivian in early Tudor England." Music and Letters 76 (1995): 1-18.

This article discusses the combining of *musica speculativa* and *musica practica* by Oxford and Cambridge in the sixteenth century. Students were required to compose a composition proving their competence in academia. Such compositions were not required to be performable.

BraP   _____. "The Part-Books Oxford, Christ Church, MSS 979-983: An Index and Commentary." Musica disciplina 26 (1972): 179-197.

The index and commentary cover music from the final years of Henry VIII's reign to music composed after Elizabeth's accession or during the Marian *interregnum*. The Part-Books are thought to have been copied by John Baldwin between 1580 and 1603.

BraS   _____. "Sacred Music to Latin Texts." In *Music in Britain: the Sixteenth Century*, pp. 46-93. Edited by Roger Bray. The Blackwell History of Music in Britain, no. 2. Oxford: Blackwell Publishers Ltd., [c. 1995].

Bray shows a continuous line of development from Leonel Power to the early Tudor period. He then presents the music, sources, and composers of the early Tudor period, the reformation period, and the post-reformation period..

BraT   Brauner, Mitchell P. "Traditions in the Repertory of the Papal Choir in the Fifteenth and Sixteenth Centuries." . In *Papal Music and Musicians in Late Medieval and Renaissance Rome*, pp. 167-177. Edited by Richard Sherr. Oxford: Clarendon Press; Library of Congress, Washington, 1998.

The author discusses categories of works and the types of pieces, to which were attached ceremony, lore, and symbolism, that created tradition.

BriC I   British Museum. Department of Manuscripts. "Catalogue of manuscript music in the British Museum." Vol. I: "Sacred vocal music." Edited by Augustus Hughes-Hughes. London: Printed by order of the Trustees, 1991. [Des Moines, Iowa]: LBS Archival Products, 1991. 26. Photocopy.

This is volume I of three. It is classified, with author, subject and title

	indexes.
BriL	Bridgman, Nanie. "Latin Church Music on the Continent-1: (a) The Franco-Flemings in the North." In *The New Oxford History of Music*. Vol. 4: *The Age of Humanism: 1540-1630,* edited by Gerald Abraham, pp. 218-237. London: Oxford University Press, [c. 1968]; reprint ed., 1974.

This is a discussion of Josquin's successors, Nicolas Gombert, Thomas Crécquillon, Clemens non Papa, Jean Richafort, and Pierre de Manchicourt.

BriM British Library: *MS. Add. 29996. Music for Organ or Virginal.* London: British Museum Photographic Service, [196-]. Microfilm.

This source contains compositions in multiple forms for keyboard by John Redford, Thomas Preston, and Thomas Tompkins. The compositions are composed on chant melodies. The manuscript is fully described in the Catalogue of manuscript music in the British Museum, A. Hughes-Hughes.

BroAL Brown, Alan. "England". In *Keyboard Music before 1700*. Edited by Alexander Silbiger. New York: Schirmer Books, [c. 1995].

There is a discussion of keyboard music from the late fourteenth century through the seventeenth century in England. This includes a discussion of manuscripts, composers, and performance practices. There is a Guide to Literature and Editions, Notes, and a Selected bibliography.

BroC Brown, Howard Mayer, ed. *Chansons for Recorders: for recorder quartet.* American Recorder Society Editions, no. 52. New York: Galaxy Music Corporation, n.d.

This contains four *chansons* taken from two volumes of music published by Attaingnant in Paris in 1533. All of these *chansons* were specifically marked as being particularly suitable for recorders. The French texts are included in the upper voice. Translations of the first line of poetry are given.

BroCR _____. "The *Chanson rustique*: Popular Elements in the 15th- and 16th-Century *Chanson*." *Journal of the American Musicological Society* 12 (1959): 16-26.

This is a discussion of monophonic *chanson* melodies of the fifteenth and early sixteenth centuries. A definition is given for the *chanson rustique* that distinguishes it from the *chanson musicale*.

BroE _____. *Embellishing Sixteenth-Century Music.* Early Music Series, no. 1. London: Music Department Oxford University Press, [c. 1976].

This is a discussion of graces and *passaggi* as presented by theorists during the sixteenth century. There are tables of ornaments and examples of their use in different types of compositions for vocal and instrumental, solo and ensemble performance.

BroES _____. "Embellishment in Early Sixteenth Century Italian Intabulations." In *Proceedings of the Royal Musical Association*, no. 100, pp. 49-85. Edited by Edward Olleson. N.p.: The Royal Musical Association and the Authors, 1974.

This essay concentrates on embellishments in Italy as that was the country most Europeans looked to for guidance. Also, all the treatises on embellishment and the largest body of intabulations come from Italy. There is a list of sources containing the intabulations for lute and many examples of the embellishments used.

BroG   Brown, Howard Mayer. "The Genesis of a Style: the Parisian *Chanson*." In *Chanson and Madrigal, 1480-1530. Studies in Comparison and Contrast.* Edited by James Haar, pp. 1-50. Cambridge, Mass.: Harvard University Press, 1964.
    A description of the musical events that led to the appearance of the *chansons* published by Attaingnant in his two-volume set of *Chansons nouvelles* in an effort to relate them to their own tradition. At the end of the article there is a discussion between three panelists and Mr. Brown.

BroMF   _____. *Music in the French Secular Theater, 1400-1550.* Cambridge, Mass.: Harvard University Press, 1963.
    A discussion of the popular music of the period and a description of the normal musical practices of the theater.

BroS   Brobeck, John T. "Style and Authenticity in the Motets of Claudin de Sermisy." *Journal of Musicology* 16:1 (1998): 26-90.
    This is a comprehensive and style-critical examination of motets securely attributed to Sermisy. The conclusion is that Sermisy used highly consonant, *chanson*-like rhythmic motives and he lacked contrapuntal elaboration and motivic development in his motets. Also, it is concluded that his music is unusual in the extent to which it mirrors the textual syntax and the systematic way in which it pursues this goal.

BruA   Brumel, Antoine. *Antonii Brumel Opera omnia.* Corpus mensurabilis musicae, no. 5. Edited by Barton Hudson. [S.l.]: American Institute of Musicology, 1969.
    This source contains Masses, Mass sections, motets, Magnificat, and *Opera profana*. The title on the series title page is *Collected works*.

BruS   Bruinsma, Henry A. "The Souterliedekens and its relation to psalmody in the Netherlands." Ph.D. diss., University of Michigan, 1948. Ann Arbor: University Microfilms International, 1980, (Doctoral dissertation series; publication no. 1160). Photocopy of typescript.
    This dissertation includes paraphrases of the Psalms set to folk tunes. The texts have been attributed to W. van Zuylen van Nyevelt. There are also transcriptions of the unaccompanied melodies, leaves 129-568. The dissertation is abstracted in Microfilm abstracts, vol. 9 (1949) no. 1, p. 148-149.

BucF   Buchner, Johann. *Fundamentum, sive ratio vera...* [n. p.: 1520.] Zurich: Staatsbibliothek, *MS. 284.* Microfilm.
    This is a facsimile of Buchner's *Fundamentum*. It contains organ music and a Latin treatise on playing the organ.

BucT I   Buck, Percy C. and Edmund H. Fellows, A. Ramsbotham, R. R. Terry, and Sylvia Townsend Warner, eds. *Tudor Church Music.* Vol. I: *John Taverner, c. 1495-1545: Part I.* New York: Broude Brothers, 1923-1948.
    These volumes are a presentation, in score, of all that is known to remain of English composers for the Church in the sixteenth and early seventeenth centuries. Complete works are reproduced as well as the extant incomplete works of the greater composers and the fragments of the lesser men which appear most significant. Volume I contains transcriptions of eight Masses by John Taverner, an historical survey of Tudor church music, and an appendix containing documents relating to the Taverners.

BucT III   _____. *Tudor Church Music.* Vol. III: *John Taverner, c. 1495-1545: Part II.* New York: Broude Brothers, 1923-1948.

	Volume III contains transcriptions of Taverner's liturgical music and two Masses.
BucT VI	Buck, Percy C. and Edmund H. Fellows, A. Ramsbotham, R. R. Terry, and Sylvia Townsend Warner, eds. *Tudor Church Music*. Vol. VI: *Thomas Tallis, (1505-1585)*. New York: Broude Brothers, 1923-1948.
	Volume VI contains transcriptions of Tallis's liturgical music and two Masses.
BucT X	_____. *Tudor Church Music*. Vol. X: *Hugh Aston, 1485(?)-(?); John Marbeck, 1510(?)-85(?); Osbert Parsley, 1511-85*. New York: Broude Brothers, 1923-1948.
	Volume 10 contains transcriptions of the music by the three composers, a short biography of each, a list of manuscripts where the music may be found, and the words of the motets.
BunP	Bunjes, Paul, ed. *Postremum vespertini officii opus...* Musikdruche aus den Jahren 1538-1545 in praktischer Neuausgabe, no. 5. Kassel: Bärenreiter, 1970.
	This contains the *discantus, altus*, tenor, and *bassus* of Magnificats for four voices. There is a Preface and notes in English. Portions are translated into German by Peter Schmidt. The music is transcribed into score from photocopies of the four partbooks at the Universitetsbiblioteket, Uppsala, Sweden.
BurG	Burney, Charles. *A general history of music from the earliest ages to the present period: to which is prefixed a dissertation on the music of the ancients*. 4 vols. London: Printed for the author, 1776-1789. London: Royal College of Music, 1982. Microfilm.
	This is a facsimile of the original books in the library of John Stafford Smith with some autograph notes by him. The books are in English and contain music history and criticism.
BusC	Bush, Helen. "The Recognition of Chordal Formation by Early Music Theorists." *Musical Quarterly* 32:2 (1946): 227-243.
	This is a discussion of chordal formation and the possible arrangement of voices discussed by theorists from Johannes de Muris of the early fourteenth century to Thomas Morely of the late sixteenth century.
BusO	Buszin, Walter E., ed. *101 Chorales Harmonized by Johann Sebastian Bach*. Minneapolis: Schmitt, Hall and McCreary Co., [c. 1952].
	These chorales have been presented according to the church year. The contents includes the name of the author or source of text and translator and the composer or source of the melody. There is a short biography of Bach.
ButG	Butt, John. "Germany and the Netherlands." In *Keyboard Music before 1700*. Edited by Alexander Silbiger. New York: Schirmer Books, [c. 1995].
	There is material on Conrad Paumann and the Buxheim Organ Book, the early sixteenth century, the later sixteenth-century tablatures, Jan Pieterszoon Sweelinck and his German pupils, Samuel Scheidt, Heinrich Scheidemann, and the mid-seventeenth century.
CalC	Calvin, Jean. *Christianae religionis institutio*. Basileae: 1536.
	This is a facsimile reprint of the Latin text of the 1536 Basel edition. It sets out Calvin's views of God, man, and the church.
CalI	_____. *Institutes of the Christian religion*. Bibliotheca Calviniana. Edited by

Ford Lewis Battles. Grand Rapids, Mich.: H.H. Meeter Center for Calvin Studies, Eerdmans, 1995.

This is an English translation of *Institutio Christianne religionis* by John Calvin. It is edited from the 1536 Latin ed. It sets out Calvin's views of God, man, and the church.

CalL   Calvin, Jean. *La forme des prières et chants ecclésiastiques (1542)*. A review by Pierre Pidoux. Kassel: Bärenreiter, 1959.

This is a facsimile of the copy in the Bibliothek in Stuttgart that was probably printed by Jean Gérard at Geneva. It contains a sixteenth-century liturgy of l'Église de Gèneve, thirty-five Psalms, the Song of Simeon, the Prayer of our Lord Jesus Christ, and the Ten Commandments.

CalLM   _____. *La Manyère de faire prières aux églises françoyses*... Centre International de Publications Oecuméniques des Liturgies. Genève: J. Knoblsch, 1965. Paris: CIPOL-Alminter, 1973. Microfiche.

This is an English translation and transcription of *La Manyère de faire prières aux églises françoyses* which contains the Liturgy and ritual, and psalms and melodies of the French Reformed Church. The original is in the Musée Historique de la Réformation in Geneva. The catalog no. is Rés. MHR A 27.1 (42). It is cited in *Initiation à la Liturgie de l'Église Réformée de France* by J. D. Benoit, published in Paris in 1956, p. 117.

CalMO   Caldwell, John, ed. and trans. *Early Tudor Organ Music I: Music for the Office*. Early English Church Music, no. 6. London: Stainer and Bell, 1966.

This contains transcriptions of antiphons, hymns, the Te Deum, and a Magnificat. There is an Introduction, Editorial Commentary, List of Sources, Critical Commentary, and two Appendices. The first appendix contains the plainsong for each organ composition.

CalO   _____. *The Oxford History of English Music*. Volume 1: *From the Beginnings to c. 1715*. Oxford: Clarendon Press, 1991.

This is the first volume of two written as a replacement for Ernest Walker's *History of Music in England*. The definition of English music is wide and flexible as Welsh and Irish matters are touched upon now and again. The second volume begins with the arrival of Handel in London in the second decade of the eighteenth century.

CanZ   "Canzona" *Britannica 2001 Deluxe Edition CD-ROM*. [c. 1994-2000]. Britannica.com Inc. May 19, 2001.

This is a short definition of the term.

CanO   Cannon, John and Ralph Griffiths. *The Oxford Illustrated History of the British Monarchy*. Oxford: Oxford University Press, [c. 1988]; Reprint ed., 1989.

This is a story of the monarchy as a political and social force from Anglo-Saxon times to the present.

CanT   *Cantiones septem, sex et quinque vocum. Longe gravissimae, juxta ac amoenissimae, in Germania maxime hactenus typis non excusae*. [Augsburg]: M. Kriesstein, 1545. Munich: Bayerische Staatsbibliothek, n.d. Microfilm.

This is a facsimile containing five partbooks for *discantus, altus*, tenor, *bassus*, and *quinta vox*. The partbooks contain sacred part songs for five, six, and seven voices. For the contents see RISM, B/I, p. 149. This is a microfilm of the original in the Bayerische Staatsbibliothek in Munich.

CarA   Cardamone, Donna G., ed. *Adrian Willaert and His Circle: Canzone Villa-*

nesche Alla Napolitana and Villotte. Recent Researches in the Music of the Renaissance, no. 30. Madison: A-R Editions, Inc., [c. 1978].

There is a Preface and Key to Abbreviations along with Critical Notes, Texts, and Translations. There are transcriptions of twenty songs for four voices, four songs for three voices, five lute intabulations, and three intabulations for voice and Vihuela.

CarCV I Cardamone, Donna G.. *The canzone villanesca alla napolitana and Related Forms, 1537-1570.* Vol. 1. Ann Arbor: UMI Research Press, [c. 1981].

This is an investigation of the origins and development of the *villanesca* as a poetic-musical form. It focuses on the corpus of printed music sources issued with only slight variants in terminology between 1537 and 1570.

An attempt is made to clarify the derivation of the *canzone villanesca* from earlier popular manifestations in the southern *strambotto* repertory. Some consideration is given to companion forms which originated in Naples and are often included in *villanesca* prints, *i.e.* the Neapolitan *mascherata* and the *moresca*.

CarCV II _____. *The canzone villanesca alla napolitana and Related Forms, 1537-1570.* Vol. 2 Ann Arbor: UMI Research Press, [c. 1981].

Volume two contains catalogues of Neapolitan dialect songs, three series of *Villanesca* Prints, some *Canzoni Napolitane* from music prints of the period found in books of popular poetry, a list of models and arrangements of four-voice compositions, and some transcriptions.

CarF Cara, Marchetto. *Canzoni, frottole, & capitoli da diversi excellentissimi musici composti novamente stampati & corretti; libro primo de la croce.* Roma: Giunta; printed by G.G. Pasoti & V. Dorico, 1526. [Wien: Österreichische Nationalbibliothek, n.d.]. Microfilm.

This contains *frottole* for four voices by M. Cara, S. Festa, F. P. (fra Pietro da Hostia?), and Ruffin d'Assisi. The original is in Österreichische Nationalbibliothek at Wien (A Wn). It is indexed in RISM B/1, 1526-06.

CarMM Carpenter, Nan Cooke. *Music in the Medieval and Renaissance Universities.* Norman: University of Oklahoma Press, [c. 1958].

This is an investigation of the study and cultivation of music as a university discipline. This is done by presenting the history of music as a subject of higher learning from the founding of the universities until the end of the Renaissance (ca. 1600).

CarMN Carapetyan, Armen. "The *Musica nova* of Adriano Willaert." *Journal of Renaissance and Baroque Music,* 3 (1946): 200-221.

This article was written to introduce the collection of motets and madrigals by Willaert. There is a discussion of the date of publication versus the date the music may have been written. There also is a discussion of the style of the music.

CarR _____. *Rabelais and Music.* University of North Carolina studies in Comparative Literature, no. 8. Chapel Hill: The University of North Carolina, [c. 1954].

This is an investigation of the use of musical terms and ideas in the novel, *Gargantua et Pantagruel,* by Rabelais. His attitude concerning music is strictly that of an intellectual and connoisseur and not that of a practicing musician. He uses musical terms for the expression of his wit and satire. The musical references present a cross section of musical practices and

	ideas of the sixteenth century.
CarSV	Carter, Tim. "Secular Vocal Music." In *Music in Britain: the Sixteenth Century*, pp. 147-209. Edited by Roger Bray. The Blackwell History of Music in Britain, no. 2. Oxford: Blackwell Publishers Ltd., [c. 1995].

The first part of the chapter covers the early Tudor manuscripts, music in courtly entertainment, the influence of continental repertories on the secular music of England, the music of Philip van Wilder, and *chansons* and part-songs during the first half of the century. The next part of the chapter covers the secular music of the last half of the century. |
| CasI | Castellino, Aluvise. *Il primo libro delle villote...da lui composti li versi et il canto*. Venetiis: Gardano, 1541. Wien: Österreichische Nationalbibliothek, n.d. Microfilm.

This contains *villote* for four voices by Aluvise Castellino. The original manuscript is in Österreichische Nationalbibliothek in Wien. It is indexed in RISM A/1; C 1458. |
| CavD | Cavazzoni, Girolamo. *Dal I e II libro di Intavolature per organo*. 5 parts in 1 vol. Edited and transcribed by Giacomo Benvenuti. Classici della musica italiana, no. 6. Milano: Istituto editorale italiano, 1919.

This is a transcription of books one and two of *Intavolature for the organ* by Girolamo Cavazzni. There are five parts in one volume. Parts one and two contain the Masses, part three the hymns, part four the Magnificats, and part 5 the *ricercari* and *canzoni*. |
| CavI | _____. *Intavolatura libro primo: cioè, recercari, canzoni, himni, magnificati*. Venetiis: [s.n.], 1542. Bologna: Civico Museo Bibliografico Musicale, 1986. Microfilm.

This is a facsimile of book one which contains instrumental music for an unspecified keyboard instrument. |
| CavIC | _____. *Intavolatura cioè recercari, canzoni, himni, magnificati*. 2 vols. Venezia: B. Vitali, 1543. N.p.: Negative film reproduction, n.d.

This is a facsimile of both volumes of the *Intavolatura cioè*. The original is in Bologna, Conservatorio di Musica "G.B. Martini" (S 411). |
| CavO | _____. *Orgelwerke*. 2 vols. Edited by Oscar Mischiati. Mainz: B. Schott's Söhne; New York: Schott Music Corp, 1959.

The first volume is a transcription of *Intavolatura cioè Recercari, Canzoni, Hinni, Magnificati...* and the second volume is a transcription of *Intabolatura d'organo cioè Misse Himni Magnificati...libro secondo*. There is a Forward in German and a Preface in Italian, both by Oscar Mischiati, and a Critical Report in both German and Italian. |
| CavR | Cavazzoni, Marco Antonio. *Recerchari, motetti, canzoni: Libro primo*. [Venetiis: Bernardinu, Vercelensem. 1523. [London: British Museum, n.d.]. Microfilm.

This is a facsimile of keyboard music. There are eight compositions for organ by Cavazzoni. The original manuscript is in the British Museum in London. It is indexed in RISM A/I, C 1574 and Brown, no. 1523/1, p. 25. |
| CavRE | _____. *Recerchari, motetti, canzoni...* Monuments of music and music literature in facsimile, 1st ser., *Music*, no 12. New York: Broude Brothers, 1974.

This is a reprint of the Venice edition of 1523. It contains eight compositions for the organ by Cavazzoni. It is one of the most significant sources of organ music of the sixteenth century. |

CazF   Cazeaux, Isabelle. *French Music in the Fifteenth and Sixteenth Centuries.* Oxford: Basil Blackwell, 1975.

This book presents a study of how music penetrated the life of the French people in the fifteenth and sixteenth centuries. It is intended to be a companion volume to such works as those by Reese: *Music in the Renaissance,* Lang: *Music in Western Civilization,* and the *New Oxford History of Music.*

CerC   Certon, Pierre. *Cinquante Pseaulmes de David, mis en musique a quatre parties imprimez en quatre volumes.* Paris: Le Roy & Ballard, 1555. [Paris: Bibliotheque nationale, n.d.]. Microfilm.

This is a facsimile of the tenors of fifty Psalms for four voices printed in four volumes. The original is in the Bibliotheque nationale in Paris. It is indexed in RISM A/I, C 1712 and F. Lesure et G. Thibault catalog, no. 17, p. 64.

CerC I   _____. *Chansons polyphoniques publiées par Pierre Attaingnant, livre I (1533-1539).* Edited by André Verchaly and Henry Expert. Maîtres anciens de la musique française, no. 2. Paris: Hugel, 1966.

This source contains *chansons* for four voices with French words. It has Notes, Sources and an Introduction in French.

CerC II   _____. *Chansons polyphoniques publiées par Pierre Attaingnant, livre II (1540-1545).* Edited by André Verchaly and Henry Expert. Maîtres anciens de la musique française, no. 3. Paris: Hugel, 1966.

This source contains *chansons* for four voices with French words. It has Notes, Sources, and an Introduction in French.

CerC III   _____. *Chansons polyphoniques publiées par Pierre Attaingnant, livre III (1540-1550).* Edited by André Verchaly and Henry Expert. Maîtres anciens de la musique française, no. 4. Paris: Hugel, 1966.

This source contains *chansons* for four voices with French words. It has Notes, Sources, and an Introduction in French.

CerCC   _____. *Complete chansons published by Le Roy and Ballard.* Edited by Jane A. Bernstein. Sixteenth-Century *Chanson,* no. 6. New York: Garland Publishers, 1990.

There is an introduction containing a short biography of Certon and a discussion of his music. All of Certon's *chansons* published by Le Roy and Ballard are in this volume. Sources are given along with a checklist of Certon's *chansons,* with the number of voices, the poet, and the modern edition. There is a table of original clefs and notes.

CerCZ   _____. (ca. 1510-1572). *Zehn Chansons, zu 4 Stimmen.* Edited by Albert Seay. Das Chorwerk, no. 82. Edited by Friedrich Blume. Wolfenbüttel: Möseler pref., 1961.

These are transcriptions of ten four-part *chansons* with French words and German translations.

CerLP   _____. *Premier livre de psalmes mis en musique...* Transcribed by Guillaume Morlaye. Paris: Fezandat, 1554. [Munich: Beyerischen Staatsbibliothek, [n.d.]. Microfilm.

This is a facsimile of Psalms by Certon transcribed into chants accompanied by the lute. The *superius* is in mensural notation and the accompaniment is in French lute tablature. The original is in the Bayerischen Staatsbibliothek in Munich. It is indexed in RISM A/I, M 3690 and Brown, no.

1554/5, p. 160.

CerM   Certon, Pierre. *Messes à quatre voix: Sus le pont d'Avignon, Adiuva me, Regnum mundi*. Monuments de la musique française au temps de la Renaissance, no. 2. New York: Broude Bros., ? 1940 1949.

This is a facsimile of the three Masses. They are indexed in RISM A/I, C 1715 and in F. Lesure et G. Thibault catalog, no. 42, p. 76.

CerMP   _____. *Missa pro defunctis cum quatour vocibus, nunc primum in lucem aedita. Lutetiae*: Le Roy & Ballard, 1558. . [Uppsala: Universitetsbiblioteket, n.d.]. Microfilm.

This is a facsimile of the *Missa pro defunctis*. The original is in Universitetsbiblioteket, Uppsala (S. Uu). It is indexed in RISM A/I, C 1713 and in F. Lesure et Thisbault catalog, no. 41, p. 76.

CerMR   _____. *Messe "Regnum Mundi."* Repertoire populaire de la musique Renaissance. Paris: M. Senart, 193-.

This is a transcription of the Mass, *Regnum Mundi* for four voices.

CerMT   _____. *Missae tres, nunc primum in lucem aedite, cum quatuor vocibus, ad imitationem modulorum: Sus le pont d'Avignon, Adiuva me, Regnum mundi.* Lutetuiae: Le Roy & Ballard, 1558. . [Uppsala: Universitetsbiblioteket, n.d.]. Microfilm.

This is a facsimile of the three Masses. The original is in the Universitetsbiblioteket, Uppsala (S. Uu). This is indexed in RISM A/I, C 1715. It is also cataloged in F. Lesure et G. Thibault catalog, no. 42, p. 76.

ChaB   "Chanson." *Britannica 2001 Deluxe Edition CD-ROM*. Britannica.com Inc. [c. 1994-2000].

This is a short outline of the *chanson* from the twelfth century to 1600

ChaH   Charles, Sydney Robinson. *A Handbook of Music and Music Literature in Sets and Series*. New York: The Free Press, [c. 1972].

This source is meant to be a supplement to existing works. It is not meant to be comprehensive. It attempts to clarify the contents and organization of each set from the point of view of the user. It has alphabetical indices and explanatory paragraphs. There are four divisions: monuments, complete works, monographs, and periodicals.

ChaP   Chapman, Catherine Weeks. "Printed Collections of Polyphonic Music Owned by Ferdinand Columbus." *Journal of the American Musicological Society* 21 (1968): 34-84.

The purpose of this article is to furnish revisions and additions to standard bibliographies in order to supply information about lost books that may serve to identify partbooks and fragments yet to be brought to light.

ChuB   Church of England. *The Booke of common praier noted, 1550*. London: Imprinted by Richard Grafton printer to the Kinges Maiestie, 1550.

This is a musical score containing Anglican chants. It is signed on p. 135 at the end of the text by Jon Merbecke. It is written in plainsong notation. The title is in black and red within architectural borders.

ChuC   _____. *Cranmer's first litany, 1544 and, Merbecke's Book of common prayer noted, 1550*. London; New York: Society for Promoting Christian Knowledge; Macmillan, 1939. Doetinchem, Holland: Microlibrary, Slangenburg Abbey, 1980. Microfiches.

This contains facsimiles of the two works in their entirety along with three other facsimiles. The original titles are: (1) *An exhortation unto prayer,*

	thoughte mete by the Kinges Majesties, and his clergy, to be read to the people in every church afore processyons. Also a letanie with suffrages to be said or song in tyme of the said processyons. London: T. Berthelet, 1544. Also, (2) *The Booke of common praier noted*. London: Grafton, 1550. There is a list of the extant copies of the *Booke of common praier noted* on pp. 27-28, and a list of works by John Merbecke, pp. 39-40.
ChuF	Church of England. *The first and second Prayer Books of Edward VI*. Everyman's Library. Theology and philosophy, no. 448. London: J. M. Dent; E. P. Dutton, 1938; 1910.
	These were first published in 1549 and 1552. There is an introduction by E. C. S. Gibson. They contain the texts of the Liturgy of the Church of England. A bibliography is included.
CimC	Cimello, Giovanni Thomaso. *Canzone villanesche al modo napolitano a tre voci...libro primo*. Venetiis: Gardane, 1545. München: Bayerische Staatsbibliothek (D Mbs). Microform.
	This is a copy of the original manuscript. There are three partbooks containing the *cantus*, tenor, and *bassus* of twenty Italian Villanelle. This is indexed in RISM A/1; C 2487 and the Lewis catalog, vol. 1, no. 64.
CimCH	_____. *The collected secular works*. Edited by Donna G. Cardamone and James Haar. Recent researches in the music of the Renaissance, no. 126. Madison, Wis.: A-R Editions, 2001.
	This contains transcriptions of *Canzone villanesche al modo napolitano: (1545)* and *Libro primo de canti a quatro voci (1548)*. There are *villanelle*, madrigals, polyphonic *chansons*, sacred songs, *villanelle (musique)*, and *madrigaux italiens* for three to four voices. There are Italian and French words as well as printed texts with English translations in Critical report.
CleM	Clemens non Papa, Jacobus. *Missa cum quatuor vocibus ad imitationem Cantilenae Miséricorde*. Lovanii: Pitri Phalesii, n.d. Wien: Oesterr, National Bibliothek, [19--]. Microfilm.
	This is a facsimile of *Missa Misérichorde* for four voices.
CleO	_____. *Opera omnia*. 21 vols. Edidit K. Ph. Bernet Kempers. Corpus mensurabilis musicae, no. 4 Rome: American Institute of Musicology, 1951-1976.
	The title on the series is *Collected Works*. The supplements are to volume eleven. Volumes I, V, VI, VII, and VIII contain Masses; volume II contains *Souterliedekens*; volumes II, XV, XVI, XVIII contain motets; volume IV contains magnificats; volumes IX, XIV, IXX, XX, and XXI contain *Cantiones sacrae*; volumes XII, XIII, and XVII contain *Cantiones ecclesiasticae*; and volumes X and XI contain *chansons*. The *chansons* are printed in the same chronological order as those listed in the catalogue found in *Musica disciplina*, 15 (1961): 187- 200. Incipits of the original clefs and notation, as well as the French texts, are given.
CleS	_____. *Souterliedekens*. Collectio operum musicorum batavorum saeculi XVI, no. 11. Berolini: Trautwein, 1857.
	This source contains selections from the *Souterliedekens* composed by Clemens non Papa and published by Susato in 1556.
CleS, I,II,III	_____. *Souterliedekens, I, II, III*. [Antwerp]: Tielman Susato, 1556. Books printed in the Low Countries before 1601; roll 188, items 5, 6, and 7. Cambridge, Mass.: General Microfilm Co., [19--].
	This contains the three-voice *Souterliedekens* composed by Clemens using

the melodies and texts of the 1540 *Souterliedekens*.

CoaP Coates, Henry and Gerald Abraham. "Latin Church Music on the Continent-2. The Perfection of the *A cappella* style." In *The New Oxford History of Music*. Vol. 4: *The Age of Humanism: 1540-1630*, edited by Gerald Abraham, pp. 312-369. London: The Oxford University Press, [c. 1968]; reprint ed., 1974.

This chapter contains a discussion of three composers and their music: Palestrina, Lassus, and de Monte.

ColS [*Collection of 16th century music theory treatises*]. 1496 to 1556. Washington, D.C.: Library of Congress, 196-. Microfilm.

This contains facsimiles of seven treatises: Martin Agricola (1), Aaron (3), Hermanni Finckii (1), Franchini Gafori (1), and Sebaldi Heyden (1).

ComB Commer, Franz, ed. *Collectio operum musicorum batavorum saeculi XVI*. 12 vols. Berolini: Trautwein, 1884. [S. l: s. n., 1954?]. Microfilm.

This is a facsimile of works by Clemens non Papa, Josquin Depres, and others. There is a complete index in volume twelve. This is also indexed in Paul Hirsch.. *Katalog der Musikbibliothek Paul Hirsch*, Bd. 4 Berlin: Breslauer, 1937.

ConS *Contrapunctus seu figurata musica super plano cantu missarum solennium totius anni*. Lugduni: Guaynard, 1528; Firenze: Biblioteca Nazionale Centrale, n.d. Microfilm.

This is a facsimile of the original found in the Biblioteca Nazional Centrale in Florence. It contains Masses, Propers, and motets. There are thirteen Mass Propers as well as three motets by Francesco de Layolle. Most of the music is anonymous, but the Masses may be by Layolle also. The choirbooks are bound with *Omnes in Domino* by Landini. It is indexed in RISM B/I 1528-1.

CopC Copernicus, Nicolaus. *Copernicus: on the revolutins of the heavenly spheres*. Edited and translated by Alistair Matheson Duncan. Norwalk, Conn.: The Easton Printing..., 1993.

This has been translated from the Latin, *De revolutionibus orbius coelestium*, that was first published in Nuremberg in 1543. It is a discussion of the Solar system.

CorC Corteccia, Francesco. *Collected Sacred Works*. Music of the Florentine Renaissance, no. 11. Edited by Frank A. D'Accone. Corpus mensurabilis musicae, no. 32. Hänssler-Verlag: American Institute of Musicology, 1996.

This contains transcriptions of *Music for the Tridum Sacrum*. The transcriptions are of motets (Latin hymns) for three to five voices with Latin words. They are for the Tenebrae service. There is an Introduction and there are Notes.

CorCQ _____. *Canticorum liber primus cum quinque vocibus (quae passim motecta apellantur)*. Venetijs: Gardani, 1571. [Firenze: Biblioteca Nazionale Centrale, n.d.]. Microfilm.

This is a facsimile of five partbooks for *cantus, altus,* tenor, *quintus,* and *bassus*. The original partbooks are in the Biblioteca Nazionle Centrale, Firenze (I Fn). It is indexed in RISM A/I, C 4156.

CorCS _____. *Canticorum liber primus cum sex vocibus (quae passim motecta dicuntur)*. Venetijs: Gardani, 1571. [Firenze: Biblioteca Nazionale Centrale, n.d.]. Microfilm.

This is a facsimile of six partbooks for *cantus, altus,* tenor, *quintus, bassus,* and *sextus*. The original is in the Biblioteca Nazionle Centrale, Firenze (I Fn). It is indexed in RISM A/I, C 4155.

CorD   Corteccia, Francesco. *Due motetti a 5 voci miste*. Edited by Piero Gargiulo. Roma:Fondazione Guido d'Arezzo: Pro Musica Studium, 1985.

This source contains two five-voice Psalms: *Ecce nunc benedicite* and *Gaudete in domino semper*. It is edited from the 1571 edition, *Canticorum liber primus*. The Preface and critical notes are in Italian. There are Latin words printed as texts. Bibliographical references are included.

CorE   _____. *Eleven works to Latin Texts*. Edited by Ann McKinley. Recent Researches in the Music of the Renaissance, no. 6. Madison {Wis.}: A-R Editions, 1969.

This source contains unaccompanied sacred part-songs and Latin hymns. There is one secular motet.

CorF   _____. *The First Book of Madrigals for Four Voices*. Francesco Corteccia; Collected Selected Works, no. 1. Music of the Florentine Renaissance, no. 8. Edited by Frank A. D'Accone. Corpus mensurabilis musicae, no. 32. Neuhausen-Stuttgart: American Institute of Musicology, 1981.

This contains thirty-five madrigals by Corteccia. There are Italian words printed as texts.

CorFB   _____. *The first book of madrigals for five and six voices*. Music of the Florentine Renaissance, no. 10. Edited by Frank A. D'Accone. Corpus mensurabilis musicae, no. 32. Neuhausen-Stuttgart: American Institute of Musicology; Hänssler-Verlag, 1981.

This contains Italian madrigals by Corteccia. The words are printed as texts, p. xv-xvi.

CorH   _____. *Himnario secondo l'uso della chiesa romana et fiorentina*. Microfilm. Firenze: Biblioteca medicea laurenziana, [1985].

This is a facsimile of the Firenze: Biblioteca medicea laurenziana, *Ms. Palat. 7*. It contains one choirbook of thirty-two Latin Vesper hymns.

CorHS   _____. *Hinnario secondo l'uso de la chiesa romana et fiorentina*. Edited by Glen Haydon. Musica liturgica, vol. 1, fasc. 4; vol. 2, fasc. 2. Cincinnati: World Library of Sacred Music, 1958.

This contains transcriptions of thirty-two Latin hymns arranged in the order of the church year. They are for three to six voices.

CorL   _____. *Libro primo de madriali [sic] a quattro voci*. Venetiis: Scotum, 1544. Wolfenbüttel: Herzog-August-Bibliothek, 1986. Microfilm.

This contains facsimiles of thirty-five madrigals by Corteccia. This edition is dedicated to Cosimo I, duke of Florence. There is a lengthy dedication explaining Corteccia's reasons for publishing his works.

CorLPM   _____. *Libro primo de madrigali [sic] a cinque & a sei voci*. Venetia: A. Gardane, 1547. München: Bayerische Staatsbibliothek, 1986. Microfilm.

This contains madrigals for five and six voices by Corteccia.

CorLS   _____. *Libro secondo di madrigali a quattro voci...* Venetia: Gardane, 1547. [Wein: Österrechische Nationalbibliothek, n.d.]. Microfilm.

This contains madrigals for four voices by Francesco Corteccia. The partbooks are in Wein: Österrechische Nationalbibliothek, (*A Wn*). They are indexed in RISM A/1; C 4159 and Lewis catalog, vol. 1, no. 105.

CorM   _____. *Motet in 8 voices and madrigal in 9 voices from Musiche fatte nella*

36 Bibliography

nozze (1539). Edited by Martin Grayson, George Bate, and Rosemary Bate. [England?]: Alfredston Music, 1994.

These selections are music for a Medici wedding. They are edited from the original version published in 1539 and a concordance published in 1547. Historical information, performance notes, and a translation of the texts in English are included.

CorMT Corteccia, Francesco. *Music for the Tridum Sacrum*. Collected sacred works 3 [*i.e.* 4]. Music of the Florentine Renaissance, no. 11. Edited by Frank A. D'Accone. Corpus mensurabilis musicae, no. 32. Neuhausen/Stuttgart: American Institute of Musicology, 1985.

This contains transcriptions of Holy Week music for three to five voices. Included are *Responsoria omnia, Residuum cantici Zachariae prophetae*, and *Psalmi Davidis quinquagesimi*.

CorS _____. *The second book of madrigals for four voices*. Music of the Florentine Renaissance, no. 9. Edited by Frank A. D'Accone. Corpus mensurabilis musicae, no. 32. Neuhausen-Stuttgart: American Institute of Musicology; Hänssler-Verlag, 1981.

This is transcriptions of madrigals by Corteccia collected by Frank D'Accone. The Italian words are printed as texts on p. xiii-xvi.

CouT "Council of Trent." *Britannica 2001 Deluxe Edition CD-ROM*. [c. 1994-2000]. Britannic.com Inc. May 9, 2001.

This article is a discussion of the Council of Trent from 1537 to 1545 under the direction of Pope Paul II

CovG Coverdale, Miles. *Goostly psalmes and spirituall songes for the coforte and consolacyon of soch as loue to rioyce in God and his worde*. [s.l.: s.n., n.d. Oxford, England: Bodleian Library, [1963]. Microfilm.

This is a facsimile of a book of tunes for English hymns. It was originally published in 1539 or 1540.

CreL Crécquillon, Thomas. *Le tiers livre de chansons à quatre parties*. Anvers: Susato, 1544. Wien: Österreichische Nationalbibliothek, n.d. Microfilm.

A Microfilm of the third book of *chansons* published by Susato. It contains polyphonic *chansons* for four voices written by Thomas Crécquillon.

CreO _____. *Thomasii Crequillonis opera omnia*. Works. Edited by Barton Hudson, Mary Tiffany Ferer, and Laura Youens. Corpus Mensurabilis musicae, no. 63. Neuhausen-Stuttgart: American Institute of Musicology, 1974.

This contains transcriptions: Vol. 1: *Missae quatuor vocum*, Vol. 2: *Missae quatuor vocum*, Vol. 3: *Missae quinque vocum*, Vol. 4: *Missae sex vocum*, Vol. 5-<9>: *Motetta quinque, tres, sex, et octo vocum*, Vol. 11<12>: *Motetta quatuor vocum*, and Vol. 14: *Cantiones quatuor vocum*.

CroH Crocker, Richard L. *A History of Musical Style*. New York: McGraw-Hill Book Company, [c. 1966].

This book is designed as a text for college music majors. It covers western musical style from the earliest written records to the present.

CumH G. J. Cuming. *A History of Anglican Liturgy*. London: Macmillan, [c.1969]

The object of this source is to arouse interest in the history of the *Prayer Book*, and also to provide a basis for further study. There is an historical narrative containing a discussion of each successive edition of the *Prayer Book*. Pertinent documents are placed at the end of the main body of the work.

CusV	Cusick, Suzanne G. *Valerio Dorico: music printer in sixteenth-century Rome*. Studies in musicology, no. 43. Ann Arbor, Mich.: UMI Research Press, 1981. This is a revision of the author's thesis written at the University of North Carolina in 1975. There is a discussion of music printing in Rome, an index and bibliography.
D'AcC	Frank A. D'Accone. "Corteccia, (Pier) Francesco". L. Macy, ed.: grovemusic.com (2001). <http://www.grovemusic.com> (Accsessed 30 August 2001). This contains a short biography of Corteccia and a discussion of his works. There is also a list of his works and a bibliography.
D'AcL	_____. "Layolle, Francesco de [Francesco dell'Aiolle, dell' Aiolli, dell'Ajolle, dell'Aiuola]", L. Macy, ed.: grovemusic.com (2001), <http://www.grovemusic.com> (Accessed 16 May 2001). This is a short biography of his life and works. There is also a short bibliography.
D'AcP	_____: "Pisano [Pagoli], Bernardo", L. Macy, ed.: grovemusic.com (2001), <http://www.grovemusic.com> (accessed 20 July 2001). This is a short discussion of Pisano's life and musical style. There also is a list of his sacred and secular music and a bibliography.
DahS	Dahlhaus, Carl. *Studies on the Origin of Harmonic Tonality*. Translated by Robert O. Gjerdingen. Princeton: Princeton University Press, [c. 1990]. The original edition of this work let each source speak in its own tongue. The reader was left to translate the various passages as he saw fit. This translation in English includes the original language after each quotation. Dahlhaus traces the evolution toward harmonic tonality through the changes in the function and disposition of cadences. He also describes an intermediate stage that led to the transition to harmonic tonality. Complete groups of works are analyzed in the fourth chapter.
DanC	Daniel, Ralph T. "*Contrafacta* and Polyglot Texts in the Early English Anthem." In *Essays in Musicology: a Birthday Offering for Willi Apel*. Edited by Hans Tischler. Bloomington, Indiana: School of Music, Indiana University, [c. 1968]. This is a survey of surviving English anthems found in sources dating from the first century of the existence of the Anglican Church. This was done in order to identify the anthems which were adapted from motets, secular pieces, or instrumental works. Only about thirty instances of *contrafactum* were found from the first century of the evolution of the English anthem.
DanD	Danckerts, Ghiselin. *Differentia musicale sententiata...* 1551. Roma: Dr. M. Vivarelli and V. Gulla, [19--]. Microfilm. This is a facsimile of the manuscript in the Biblioteca Vallicelliana in Rome. It contains forty-three manuscript pages of music and theory.
DarI	Dart, Thurston. *The Interpretation of Music*. N.p.: Hutchinson and Co., 1954; reprint ed., New York: Harper and Row, 1963. This is a survey of some of the problems involved in the present-day performance of music written between 1350 and 1850.
DavH	Davison, Archibald and Willi Apel, eds. *Historical Anthology of Music*. Vol. 1: *Oriental, Medieval and Renaissance Music*. Cambridge, Mass.: Harvard University Press, 1946 and 1949.

This source contains a representative collection of music from the periods mentioned. A considerable amount of the music had never been transcribed into modern notation prior to the time of publication. Foreign texts have been translated and there is reference to phonograph records for a number of the selections. There is also a commentary with notes on the sources.

DayC   Day, John. *Certaine notes set forth in foure and three parts to be song at the morning Communion and evening praier...* London: J. Day, 1560. London: British Museum, [1960]. Microfilm.

This source contains parts for *medius* and *bassus* of anthems and sacred part-songs. There are works by T. Causton, R. Hasilton, Heath, R. Johnson, Knight, Oakland, J. Sheppard, T. Tallis, Whitbroke, and Anonymous.

DélA   Delétra, D. *Aulcuns pseaulmes et cantiques mys en chant.* A Strasbourg, 1539. A facsimile edition. Genève: A. Jullien, 1919.

This is a reproduction of the original compiled by Calvin that is found in the Staatsbibliothek, Munich. It contains twelve psalms adapted from Marot's paraphrases. There are supplementary comments by D. Delétra.

DenD   Dentice, Luigi. *Duo dialoghi della musica.* Roma: V. Lucrino, 1553. Italian Books before 1601; roll 603, item 15. Watertown, Mass.: General Microfilm Co., [19--]. Microfilm.

DenM   Dent, Edward J. "Music and Drama." In *The New Oxford History of Music.* Vol. 4: *The Age of Humanism: 1540-1630,* edited by Gerald Abraham, pp. 784-820. London: Oxford University Press, [c. 1968]; reprint ed., 1974.

This contains a discussion of Renaissance Drama, The *Intermedii,* Venetian Festive Music, The *Camerata* in an *Intermedio,* Festive Music in Germany, Jesuit and Protestant School Dramas, Schütz's Daphne, *Seelwig,* English Comedians in Germany, Religious and Secular Drama in Spain, The *Mascarade* in France, Influence of Baïf's Academy, 'Le Balet Comique de la Royne', Later Ballets de Cour, Continental Influences in England, The Masque, and Music in the English Theatre.

DenS   _____. "The Sixteenth-Century Madrigal." In *The New Oxford History of Music.* Vol. 4: *The Age of Humanism: 1540-1630,* edited by Gerald Abraham, pp. 33-94. London: Oxford University Press, [c. 1968]; reprint ed., 1974.

This is a discussion of the musical style, the literary language, the poems, and the composers of the madrigal and related forms in Italy and England.

DieN   Dietrich, Sixtus. *Novum ac insigne opus musicum 36 antiphonarum, 1541.* Edited by Walter E. Buszin. Georg Rhau, Musikdrucke aus den Jahren 1538 bis 1545 in praktischer Neuausgabe, Bd. 7. Kassel; St. Louis: Bärenreiter, 1955-; Concordia Pub. House, 1964.

This is a transcription of antiphons by Sixtus Dietrich, principally for *discantus, altus,* tenor, and *bassus.* There are Prefaces in English and German and Critical Notes on Pages 85-92.

DieNO   _____. *Novum ac insigne opus musicum triginta sex antiphonarum.* Vitebergae: G. Rhaw, 1541. Kassel: Deutsches Musikgeschichtliches Archiv, 1977? Microfilm.

This is a facsimile of four partbooks for *discantus, altus,* tenor, and *bassus* containing thirty-six antiphons by Sixtus Dietrich.

DieNOV   _____. *Ausgewahlte Werke Erster Teil, Hymnen (1545)... I. Abteilung,* edited by Hermann Zenck. Leipzig: C. F. Peters, 1942. Das Erbe deutscher

Musik. Erste Reihe, Reichsdenkmale, Bd. 23. Ausgewahlte Werke einzelner Meister, 3 . Bd. [Washington, D.C.]: Library of Congress Photoduplication Service [1970]. Microfilm.

This is a transcription of Latin hymns for three to five voices by Sixtus Dietrich. The hymns are principally for *discantus, altus,* tenor, and *bassus.* There are Latin words and critical matter in German. The alternate title is *Novum opus musicum tres tomos scarorum hymnorum continens.*

DobL Dobbins, Frank. "Lyons: Commercial and Cultural Metropolis." In *The Renaissance: from the 1470s to the end of the 16th century,* pp. 197-215. Edited by Iain Fenlon. Man and Music Series. Englewood Cliffs, N.J.: Prentice Hall, [c. 1989].

A discussion of the music found in the literature of Lyons such as the court music, ceremonial entries and church music. There is also a discussion of music copying and printing from the 1470s to the end of the sixteenth century.

DobM _____. *Music in Renaissance Lyons.* Oxford Monographs on Music. Oxford: Clarendon Press; New York: Oxford University Press, 1992.

The focus of this book is on the sacred music composed in Lyons for both the Catholic and Reformed churches. The instrumental music which appeared there also is covered along with the town's professional musicians, particularly the instrumentalists. There are appendices listing musicians, singers, instrumentalists, instrument makers, the music printed in Lyons, and the resident and visiting patrons of music.

DobO _____, ed. *The Oxford Book of French Chansons: Chansons Françaises; Französischen Chansons.* Oxford and New York: Music Department, Oxford University Press, [c. 1987].

This source contains transcriptions of eighty-four *chansons* reflecting the significant contributions of major and minor composers. Also, an attempt is made to represent fairly the favored poets. There is an index by composer, introductions in English, French, and German, notes listing each source used followed by concordant sources, and translations.

DoeE Doe, Paul, transc. and ed. *Early Tudor Magnificats, I.* Early English Church Music, no. 4. London: Stainer and Bell, 1962.

This source contains transcriptions of two anonymous Magnificats, and one Magnificat each by Robert Fayrfax, William Cornysh, Edmund Turges, Henry Prentyce, and Nicholas Ludford. They are for five and six voices.

DoeT _____. *Tallis.* Oxford Studies of Composers, no. 4. London: Oxford University Press, 1968.

This source covers Tallis's career which took place during the middle fifty years of the sixteenth century. It discusses the old tradition in music, the ritual music of the mid-century, the Elizabethan motets, English Church music, and instrumental music.

DomS "Dominant strands of Renaissance philosophy." *Britannica 2001 Deluxe Edition CD-ROM.* [c. 1994-2000]. Britannica.com Inc. May 6, 2001.

This article contains a short summary of the history of Philosophy with the emphasis on Renaissance Philosophy.

DorF Dorico, V. *Fior di motetti e canzoni novi composti da diversi excellentissimi musici.* International Inventory of musical Sources (Organization); Österreichische Nationalbibliothek. Roma: Giunta: Printed by G.G. Pasoti & V.

Dorico, 1526. Wien: Österreichische Nationalbibliothek, n.d. Microform. This contains Italian part-songs by Jean Lhéritier, Claudin de Sermisy, Philippe Verdelot, Laurus Patavus, J. Lebrung, and Francesco Seraphin. Parts of the imprint are illegible. The original is in Österreichische National-bibliothek at Wien (A Wn).

DorM Dorico, V. *Madrigali novi de diversi excellentissimi musici: libro primo de la Serena*. Roma: M. Valerio, 1533. Munich: Bayerische Staatsbibliothek, 1980. Microfilm.
This contains the *superius* and *altus* parts of twenty Italian and French pieces by Carlo, C. Festa, C. Janequin, M. Jhan, Jacapo de Tho(s-cana?), and P. Verdelot. Two of these pieces are French *chansons*. The madrigals were originally written for four voices. Eight of these madrigals are by Verdelot.

DraB "Drama." *Britannica 2001 Deluxe Edition CD-ROM*. Copyright © 1994-2000 Britannica.com Inc. October 5, 2001.
This is a short discussion of Drama in Italy from the first tragedy of Italian vernacular literature to a comedy written in 1582.

DuCP Du Chemin, Nicolas. *Premier livre de chansons à quatre: 1550*. Tours: Centre de musique ancienne, [c. 1994]. Microfilm.
This is a facsimile reproduction of polyphonic *chansons*. There are four *chansons* by Certon and two by Janequin as well as others. Critical commentaries in English and French are included.

DuCS _____. *Second livre de chansons à quatre: 1549*. Verger de musique, no. 1. Tours: Centre de musique ancienne, [c. 1993]. Microfilm.
This is a facsimile reproduction of the original in British Museum, London: *(GB Lbm), MK. S.i.4.* There are polyphonic *chansons* by Du Tertre, Brigard, Janequin, Sevault, Pagnier, Le Brum, Goudimel, Du Bar (Clemens), Regnes, C. Martin, Du Four (Certon), Le Gay Hyer, Le Gendre, Crecquillon, Clemens, Maillart, and Hugou.

DurS V Durant, Will. *The Story of Civilization*. Vol. 5: *The Renaissance: a History of Civilization in Italy from 1304-1576 A.D.* New York: Simon and Schuster, 1953.
A philosophical history that covers the economic basis and background of Italian cities. It is a story of great men; royalty, poets, painters, sculptors, philosophers, scientists, historians, engravers, and architects.

DurS VI _____. *The Story of Civilization*. Vol. 6: *The Reformation: a History of European Civilization from Wyclif to Calvin: 1300-1564*. New York: Simon and Schuster, 1957.
this is a discussion of a social and religious revolution told through the lives of the men who lived it.

EbyE Eby, Frederick. *Early Protestant Educators: The Educational Writings of Martin Luther, John Calvin, and Other Leaders of Protestant Thought.* New York: 1931; Reprint ed., New York: AMS, 1971.
There are brief sketches of the lives and works of the various authors along with translations of some of their works.

EgeA Egenolff, Christian. *Achtzehn weltliche Lieder aus den Drucken Christian Egenolffs, zu 3 bis 5 Stimmen*. Edited by Hans-Christian Müller. Das Chorwerk, no. 111. Wolfenbüttel: Möseler Verlag, 1970.
This is a transcription of German songs for three to five voices taken from

collections published by Egenolff at Frankfurt in 1535, 1536, and 1544.

EgeG　Egenolff, Christian. *Gassenhawer und Reutterliedlin.* Frankfurt am Meyn: Egenolff, 1535. München: Bayerische Staatsbibliothek, n.d. Microfilm.

This is a facsimile of three partbooks containing German songs by Adam von Fulda, J. Brack, S. Dietrich, H. Fritz, J. Fuchswild, W. Grefinger, M. Greiter, H. Heugel, P. Hofhaimer, H. Isaac, Josquin, J. Schechinger, J. Schönfelder, L. Senfl, T. Sporer, S. Virdung, M. Wolff, P. Wüst, and others. The original is in München: Bayerische Staatsbibliothek (D Mbs). It is indexed in RISM B/1; [c.1535]-13.

ÉglF　Église française de Strasbourg. "La manyere de faire prierès aux Égliese francoyses...ensemble pseaulmes & canticques..." Strasbourg: J. Knobloch, 1542. [South Hamilton, Mass.: Goddard Library, Gordon-Conwell Theological Seminary, 1981]. Photocopy.

This is a photocopy of a photocopy of a microfiche owned by University Libraries, University of Notre Dame, published in 1973. It contains the sixteenth-century liturgy of the French Church of Strasbourg. The imprint on page 159 states that it was published in Rome by Théodore Bruss on February 15 by command of the Pope. This imprint was a ruse. Actually Pierre Brully initiated the printing for publication in Strasbourg by J. Knobloch. This was done without papal approval. It is also known as *The French evangelical Psalter.* The original is in the Musée Historique de la Réformation in Geneva.

EinI　Einstein, Alfred. *The Italian Madrigal.* Translated by Alexander Haggerty Krappe; Roger Sessions; and Oliver W. Strunk. 3 vols. Princeton: Princeton University Press, 1949.

This contains the history of the Italian madrigal and its composers. **Volume three contains the texts and scores of ninety-seven madrigals.**

EitBQ　Eitner, Robert. *Biographisch-bibliographisches Quellen- -lexikon der Musiker und Musikgelehrten der christlichen Zeitrechnung bis zur mitte des neunzehnten jahrhunderts.* Leipzig: Breitkopf & Härtel. 1900. Lakewood, Colorado.: Dakota Graphics, 19--. Microfilm.

There are additions to volumes 1 to 10: vol. 10, p. 370-479. Supplements to Eitner's *Quellen-lexicon* appeared as *Bellagen* to *Monatscheft fur Musikgeschichte*, 1904, no. 1, 11-12 and 1905, no. 1-5. There is a criticism of *Quellen-lexicon* by Michel Brenet (Marie Bobillier) in *La Revue musicale* (1905): 480-489. It contains numerous corrections. *Quellen-lexicon* was supplemented by *Miscellanea musicae bio-bibliographica*, edited by H. Springer, M. Schneider, and W. Wolffhelm.

EitC　_____, ed. *Chansons zu vier Stimmen aus der I. Hälfte des 16. Jahrhunderts von französischen und niederländischen Meistern.* Publikationen älterer praktischer und theoretischer Musikwerke, no. 23. Berlin: 1 873-1905.

This contains sixty four-part *chansons* with French words selected from works originally compiled and published by Pierre Attaingnant. It contains works by thirty-five composers, some of whom are Jacob Arcadelt, Pierre Certon, Clemens non Papa, Guillaume Heurteur, Jacotin, Clément Janequin, Pierre de la Rue, and Claude de Sermisy. It is a reprint of the 1899 edition published by Breitkopf & Härtel of Leipzig.

EitD　_____, ed. *Das deutsche Lied des XV. und XVI. Jahrhunderts in Wort, Melodie und mehrstimmigem Tonsatz.* 2 vols. Monatshefte für Musik-geschichte.

42 Bibliography

Beilage. Berlin: L. Liepmannssohn, 1876 1880.
   The first volume contains quodlibets, instrumental pieces, dance pieces, and drinking songs. The second volume contains manuscripts of compositions from the fifteenth century. The poetry is early modern, 1500 to 1700. The introductions are signed by Robert Eitner.

EitE II   Eitner, Robert, Ludwig Erk, and Otto Kade, eds. *Ein Hundert Fünfzehn weltliche u. einige geistliche Lieder...gesammelt und im Jahre 1544 zu Nürnberg...herausgegeben von Johann Ott.* Publikationen älterer praktischer und theoretischen Musikwerke, no. 2. Leipzig: Breitkopf & Härtel, 1899.
   This contains transcriptions of four-voice songs by Isaac, Senfl, Richafort, Crécquillon, Gombert, Lupus, Verdelot *et al.* There are biographical references and indexes.

ElcK   Elcombe, Keith. "Keyboard Music." In *Music in Britain: the Sixteenth Century,* pp.210-262. Edited by Roger Bray. The Blackwell History of Music in Britain, no. 2. Oxford: Blackwell Publishers Ltd., [c. 1995].
   This chapter is divided into liturgical organ music and secular keyboard music. There are subdivisions on liturgical organ music before 1559, organ music after 1559, and secular keyboard music up to 1570. There is also a discussion on musical instruments.

EllO   Ellis, Alexander. "On the History of Musical Pitch." In *Studies in the History of Musical Pitch: Monographs by Alexander Ellis and Arthur Mendel.* Amsterdam: Frits Knuf, 1968.
   This is a correction and supplement to Ellis' paper on "The Measurement and Settlement of Musical Pitch" of 1877. It is presented in English and German.

EllT 12   Ellinwood, L., ed. *Thomas Tallis: English Sacred Music: I Anthems.* Early English Church Music, no 12. London: Stainer and Bell, [c. 1971].
   This contains transcriptions of anthems for mixed voices with organ accompaniment. There is an Introduction, an Editorial Commentary, Notes on Performance, a List of Sources, a Critical Commentary, and a Chronology.

EllT 13   _____, ed. *Thomas Tallis: English Sacred Music: II Service Music.* Early English Church Music, no 13. London: Stainer and Bell, [c. 1971].
   This contains transcriptions of service music for mixed voices with organ accompaniment. There is an Introduction, Editorial Commentary, Notes on Performance, a list of sources, and a Critical Commentary.

ElúA   Elústiza, Juan B. de ed. *Antologia musical, siglo de oro de la musica litúrgica de España.* Barcelona: R. Casulleras, 1933. New York, N. Y.: New York Public Library, 19--. Microfilm.
   This source contains a collection of sacred motets by Spanish composers taken from two manuscripts: one preserved in the church of Santiago at Valladolid and the other an anonymous, early sixteenth century manuscript in the Biblioteca Colombina, Seville.

EslL   Eslava, Hilarión. *Lira sacro-hispana...* 10 vols. Madrid: M. Salazar, 1869. Los Angeles, Cal., University of California, Los Angeles, 19--. Microfilm.
   This source contains the ten volumes in five. The music is unaccompanied or with various accompaniments for three to twelve voices. All compositions are sacred and by Spanish composers. The contents are listed in *Grove's dictionary of music and musicians,* 5th edition, vol. 2, p. 970.

FelC Feller, Karl Gustav. *The History of Catholic Church Music.* Translated by Francis A. Brunner. Baltimore: Helicon Press, 1961.

The purpose of this book is to trace the varied and various relationships of music to the liturgy in the twenty centuries of Catholic Church history. It is concerned with the contribution of the composers to the musical currents and their links with the century in which they worked. It attempts to follow the characteristic movements of each epoch, along with the continued fortunes of traditional forms.

FelE Fellowes, Edmund H. *English Cathedral Music.* New edition revised by J. A. Westrup. Methuen and Co., Ltd., 1941; 5th ed. revised by J. A. Westrup, 1969.

This is an account of the music written for English Cathedrals and collegiate churches and chapels in which professional choirs were established by ancient endowments for the performance of the daily choral services. Two types of composition are covered, the 'service' and the anthem.

FelT _____. *Tudor Church Music: Appendix with Supplementary Notes.* New York: Broude Brothers, n.d.

This source contains descriptions of ten manuscripts not known to the editors at the time the original ten volumes were published. There is also an index of their contents. There are new transcriptions of some of the music previously published in *Tudor Church Music* along with text that was formerly lacking.

FenI Fenlon, Iain and James Haar. *The Italian Madrigal in the Early Sixteenth Century: Sources and Interpretation.* Cambridge, New York: Cambridge University Press, 1988.

This book emphasizes the Florentine origins of the madrigal, and to a much lesser extent the Roman origins. It begins with a study of the manuscripts containing madrigals known to have been written before 1540. Then the study is broadened to include all the manuscript sources of the madrigal before ca. 1550. There is a substantial revision of the currently held theories about the rise of the madrigal. The assumption that the madrigal was influenced by the *frottola* is questioned. There are lists of manuscript sources and printed sources with inventories, concordances and remarks.

FenMS Fenlon, Iain. "Music and Society". In *The Renaissance: from the 1470s to the end of the 16th century,* pp. 1-62. Edited by Iain Fenlon. Man and Music Series. Englewood Cliffs, New Jersey: Prentice Hall, [c. 1989].

This is an exploration of some broad themes such as humanism, religious change, the impact of printing, and the growth in influence of the bourgeoisie, sometimes by reference to some of the essays which follow, and sometimes by introducing different illustrative material. It covers the period from the 1470s to the end of the sixteenth century.

FenR _____, ed. *The Renaissance: from the 1470s to the end of the 16th century.* Man and Music Series. Englewood Cliffs, N.J.: Prentice Hall, [c. 1989].

This book is a part of a chronological series of eight books conceived in conjunction with television programs of the same name. The object of the book is to show in what context and the result of what forces, such as social, cultural, and intellectual, musical forms came into being and took particular shape. The discussion covers what happened, why it happened,

44 Bibliography

        and why it happened when and where it did. There is a chronology at the end of the book covering Music and Musicians; Politics, War and Rulers; Literature, Philosophy, and Religion; Science, Technology and Discovery; Fine and Decorative Arts; and Architecture during the period from 1471 to 1615.

FenV   Fenlon, Iain. "Venice: Theatre of the World." In *The Renaissance: from the 1470s to the end of the 16th century*, pp. 102-132. Edited by Iain Fenlon. Man and Music Series. Englewood Cliffs, N.J.: Prentice Hall, [c. 1989].

        This is a discussion of the evolving official policy of Venice which thought of the state and the music and ceremonial of the Venetian church as intimately related. This intimate relationship was seen as a vital component of the elaboration, through artistic means, of the "myth of Venice." This myth upheld the reputation and unique qualities of Venice and deployed them as a powerful weapon of propaganda The period covered is mostly that which follows the establishment of St. Mark's in the decades after the appointment of Willaert as *maestro di cappella*.

FerC   Fernandez Alvarez, Manuel. *Charles V: Elected emperor and hereditary ruler*. Translated from the Spanish by J. A. Lalaguna. London: Thames and Hudson, [c. 1975].

        This book covers the life of Charles V (1500-1558). At the end of the book there is a summary of his life, a genealogical table, and maps of the period.

FerK   Ferguson, Howard. *Keyboard Interpretation: from the 14th to the 19th century*. New York and London: Oxford University Press, 1975.

        This contains information concerning keyboard instruments, their music, and its interpretation. But, musical problems involved exclusively for the organ are not discussed.

FesC   Festa, Costanzo. [*Collection containing 8 Magnificats, 30 hymns, 2 motets, 4 Benedicamus dominos*] *(1539)*. Vatican City: Biblioteca apostolica vaticana, [1972]. Microfilm

        This is a facsimile of the Biblioteca apostolica vaticana, Ms. *Cappella sistina 18*. It is indexed in Census-catalogue of manuscript sources of polyphonic music 1400-1550. IV. 32 (VatS 18).

FesM   _____. *Magnificat, tutti gli otto toni, a quattro voce*. Venetiis: Scotum, 1554. Roma: Biblioteca Apostolica Vaticano, n.d. Microfilm.

        This is a facsimile of Festa's complete set of eight Magnificats for four voices. No known publication before this one presented Festa's complete set. The original manuscript is in Biblioteca Apostolica Vaticana in Rome (I Rvat). It is indexed in RISM A/I, F 0642 and the Bernstein catalog, no. 122.

FesML   _____. *Madrigale de M. Constantio Festa. Libro primo*. [Venice?]: n.p., 1538. [Oxford: Bodleian Library, n.d.]. Microfilm.

        This source contains madrigals by Festa. There are twenty-two madrigals originally written for four voices, two madrigals originally written for five voices, and one madrigal originally written for six voices. There are only two part-books known to be extant. There are single copies of the *cantus* and *altus* part-books. The place of publication and printer are unknown. But it is thought that it may have been published in Rome by the composer himself. It is indexed in RISM A/1; FF [0]642a. There is a discussion of it in "Libro primo of Constanzo Festa" found in *Acta musicologica*, L11 (1980): p. 147-155. The contents are listed in Nuovo Vogel, no. 970.

FesO   Festa, Costanzo. *Opera omnia*. Edited by Alexander Main. Corpus mensurabilis Musicae, no. 25. 8 vols. Vol. 1: *Missae, Fragmenta Missarum*; Vol. 2: *Magnificat*; Vol. 3: *Motetti I*; Vol. 4: *Motetti II*; Vol. 5: *Motetti III*; Vol. 6: *Lamentations et litaniae*; Vol. 7: *Madrigali*; Vol. 8: *Madrigali*. N.p.: American Institute of Musicology, 1962-.

The title on the series title page is *Collected works*. Volumns III to V are edited by Albert Seay. They include critical notes in English by Albert Seay.

FesS   _____. *Sacrae cantiones, 3, 4, 5, 6 vocibus*. Edited by Eduardo Dagnino. Monumenta polyphoniae Italicae, no. 2. Romae: Pontif. Institutum Musicae Sacrae, 1936.

This source contains motets for 3, 4, 5, and 6 voices with Latin words. The text of the Preface is in Italian and Latin in parallel columns. There is an errata slip.

FesSM   _____. *16 Magnificats (15-)*. . Vatican City: Biblioteca apostolica vaticana [191], n.d. Microfilm.

This is a facsimile of sixteen Magnificats from Biblioteca apostolica vaticana, *MS. Cappella Giulia XII 5*. It contains Magnificats by Festa (8) and Carpentras (8). It is indexed in *Census-catalogue of manuscript sources of polyphonic music 1400-1550*, IV, 17 (VatG XII.5).

FesSV   _____. *Sacred vocal music. Selections. Hymni per totum annum: 3, 4, 5, 6 vocibus*. Edited by Glen Haydon. Monumenta polyphoniae Italicae, no. 3. Romae: Pontificum Institutum Musicae Sacrae, 1958.

This source contains transcriptions of the polyphonic settings of hymns for the liturgical year. They are written for one to six voices. According to the Preface, "The present edition makes the complete hymns of Costanzo Festa available in print for the first time." There is a Preface and some Editorial Notes in English.

FesV   _____. *Il vero libro de madrigali a tre voci...* Venetiis: Antonium Gardane, 1543. [Krakow: Biblioteka Jagiellonska, 1986]. Microfilm.

This contains sacred part-songs and Italian madrigals for three voices. The original manuscript is in the Biblioteka Jagiellonska in Krakow (*Mus. ant. pract. F270*). It is indexed in Eitner's Quellen-Lexicon III, p.433.

FioM   *Fior de motetti e canzoni novi composti da diversi excellentissimi musici*. Roma: Giunta?, 1526. Wien: Österreichisch Nationalbibliothek, n.d. Microfilm.

This source contains three partbooks, the *superius*, tenor, and *altus*. The *bassus* is missing. There are works by C. de Sermisy, Laurus Patavus, J. Lebrung, J. Lheritier, Francesco Seraphin, P. Verdelot, and anonymous. The original is in Österreichisch Nationalbibliothek, Wien (A Wn). It is indexed in RISM B/I, [c. 1526]-05, p. 102. It contains the Latin and Italian words.

FloD   *Florilège du concert vocal de la Renaissance*. Publié par Henry Expert. Paris: Cité des livres, 1928. Reprint ed., New York: Broude Bros., 1964?

This source contains transcriptions of *chansons*, airs, *psaumes*, and duos by Janequin, Orlando de Lassus, Guillaume Costeley, Pierre Bonnet, Claude le Jeune, Jacques Mauduit, Claudin de Sermisy, Peletier, Guillaume le Heurteur, and Antoine Gardane. There is a separate introduction in French for each section. The music of each composer is presented in a separate section with concordances given for each composition.

FogM Fogliani, Lodovico. *Musica theorica...docte simul ac dilucide pertractata: in qua quamplures de harmonicis intervallis: non prius tentatae: continentur speculationes.* Venice: de Sabio, 1529. Bibliotheca musicae Bononiensis. Sec. 2: *Teoria*, no. 13. Bologna: Arnaldo Forni, 1970.

This is a facsimile edition. The treatise is divided into three sections. Number one: musical proportions; number two: the application of those proportions in forming consonances; number three: the division of the monochord.

FogMT _____. *Musica theorica.* Venice, 1529. Monuments of music and music literature in facsimile. Ser. 2: Music literature, no. 93. New York: Broude Brothers, n. d.

This is a facsimile edition. *See* FogM.

FonC Fontana, Vincenzo. *Canzone villanesche...a tre voci alla napolitana: libro primo.* Venice: Gardane, A. Kassel: Deutsches Musikgeschichtliches Archiv, 1986. Microfilm.

This contains twenty-three *canzone villanesche* written for three parts.

FonN _____. *Nine villanelle: for three voices or instruments.* Thesaurus musicus, no. 33. London: London Pro Musica Edition.

This contains nine *canzone villanesche* for three voices. There are Italian words printed as text for the second and succeeding verses. There are English translations of the texts on the inside of the back cover. There are historical and editorial notes by Bernard Thomas.

ForC Forney, Kristine K., ed.. *Chansons published by Tielman Susato.* The Sixteenth-century *chanson*, no. 29-30. New York: Garland, 1994.

There are three introductions, one general and one to each volume, and a discussion of editorial methods. Volume 29 has transcriptions of *chansons*. Benedictus Appenzeller has (4), Antoine Barbe (1), Eustache Barbion (2), Josquin Baston (4), Cornelius Canis (10), Johannes Castileti (Guyot) (5), Jean Courtois (3), and Thomas Crécquillon (12). Volume 30 has transcriptions *chansons*. Jean Descaudain (Rémy) has (1), Hanache (1), Damien Havericq (1), Jean de Hollande (2), Christian Hollander (1), Jean Larchier (2), Jean Le Cocq (3), Jean Le Roy(1), Pierre Lescornet (1), Pierre de Manchicourt (6), Clément Morel (1), Nicolas Payen (1), Loyset Piéton (1), Pierre Rocourt (1), Tielman Susato (11), and four anonymous. The introduction to the first volume discusses the Susato Publishing Firm and the *chanson* publications. There is a chronology of the composers and a table of the geographic distribution of the composers. There is a discussion of the *chansons* and a list of Susato *chanson* publications.

ForE Forster, Georg. *Ein ausszug guter alter und newer teutscher Liedlein...* Nürnberg: Petreius, 1539. München: Bayerische Staatsbibliothek, n.d. Microfilm.

This is a facsimile of Georg Forster's first collection of part-songs for four voices. It contains works by Erasmus Lapicida, Laur. Lemlin, Mahu, Forster, Ludovicus Senfl, J. L. Blanckmüller and others. The original partbooks are in Bayerische Staatsbibliothek, München (D Mbs). It is indexed in RISM B/1,; 1539-27 and Teramoto/Brinzing catalog, no. 10.

Bibliography 47

ForF — Forster, Georg, comp. *Frische teutsche Lieden (1539-1556); I. Teil: Ein ausszug guter alter und neuer teutscher Liedlein (1539)*. Edited by Kurt Gudewill; *Textravision* by Wilhelm Heiske. Das Erbe deutscher Musik, no. 20. Wolfenbüttel: Möseler, 1964.
This is a transcription of Georg Forster's first collection of part-songs for four voices, The words are German.

ForFT — ____, comp. *Frische teutsche Lieden (1539-1556); 2. Teil (1540)*. Edited by Gudewill and Hinrich Siuts. Das Erbe deutscher Musik, no. 60. Wolfenbüttel: Möseler Verlag, 1969.
This contains a transcription of Georg Forster's second collection of part-songs for four voices. There are German words, a critical commentary on pp. [121]-133 and an alphabetical list of *Liedenfänge* on p. 134.

ForS — Fortune, Nigel. "Solo Song and Cantata." In *The New Oxford History of Music*. Vol. 4: *The Age of Humanism: 1540-1630*, edited by Gerald Abraham, pp. 125-215. London: Oxford University Press, [c. 1968]; reprint ed., 1974.
This is a discussion of the style of the music, and the sources, composers, and poets of Italy, Germany, England, and France.

FraI — Francesco, da Milano. *Intaolatura de viola o vero lauto I-II*. 2 vols. in 1. Genève: Minkoff Reprint, 1988.
This is a facsimile reprint of the 1536 edition published by J. Sultzbach in Naples. It is an Italian lute tablature. There is a Preface by d'Arthur Ness and it is indexed in Index de Claude Chauvel.

FraID — ____. *Intabolatura de lauto*. Venetia: A Gardane, 1547. Washington: Library of Congress, n.d. Microfilm.
This contains intabulations of madrigals and *canzone francese*. The original publication is in the Library of Congress in Washington D.C. It is indexed in RISM B/1; 1547-21 and Brown, no. 1547/2, p. 95.

FraO — ____. *Opere complete per liuto*. Transcribed by Ruggero Chiesa. 2 vols. Milano: Edizioni Suvini Zerboni, 1971.
This music is transcribed into modern notation. Volume one contains original compositions. Volume two includes scores of the original compositions by Milano and others. There is a preface in Italian, English, and German. Also included is a list of the composer's works, concordances, and critical remarks.

FreC — "The French chanson and English madrigal." *Britannica 2001 Deluxe Edition CD-ROM*. Britannica.com Inc. [c. 1994-2000]
This is a short discussion of the sixteenth century *chanson*, the sixteenth and seventeenth century madrigal and the glee of the eighteenth and nineteenth century.

FreP — Freedman, Richard. "Paris and the French Court under François I." In *The Renaissance: from the 1470s to the end of the 16th century*, pp. 174-196. Edited by Iain Fenlon. Man and Music Series. Englewood Cliffs, N.J.: Prentice Hall, [c. 1989].
Freedman points out the fact that, in spite of the pressures exerted on musicians at the royal court, the musical products of that age transcended those circumstances in subtle ways that we have only begun to understand.

FroE — Frost, Maurice. *English & Scottish psalm and hymn tunes: c. 1543-1677*. London; New York: SPCK; Oxford University Press, 1953.

This source contains "Old version' Psalters, a description of their contents", on pp. [1]-52 and " Tunes [partly in score] associated with Old version' 1556-1677" on pp. [53]-531.

FroG   Frotscher, Gotthold. *Geschichte des Orgelspiels und der Orgelkomposition.* 2 vols. Edition Merseburger, 1124. Berlin: Merseburger, [c. 1959].

Volume I contains a history of German, Dutch, Italian, French, Spanish, and English organs, organ music and organists from the Middle Ages up through Johann Gottfried Walther (1684-1748). There are music illustrations and bibliographical footnotes. The language is German.

FroO   Froidebise, Pierre, trans. *Œuvres d'orgue de Juan Bermudo (1555).* Orgue et liturgie, no. 47. Paris: Éditions musicales de la Schola cantorum et de la Procure générale de musique, 1960.

These organ pieces are transcriptions of selections from the *Declaración de instrumentos musicales* of Juan Bermudo. There are five hymns, seven free compositions, and one Tiento. There is a Preface in French.

FroS   Fromson, Michele. "Secular vocal works", Macy, ed." grovemusic.com (2001), <http://www.grovemusic. com> (Accessed 30 August 2001).

This is a short discussion of Willaert's *chansons*, madrigals, and *canzoni*.

GafPR   Gafurius, Franchinus. *The Practica musicae of Franchinus Gafurius.* Translated by Irwin Young. Madison: University of Wisconsin Press, 1969.

This edition of the *Practica* is based on the original edition published in 1496. The original edition was a collection of treatises which eventually became a single unit. These treatises contain discussions of church music, the gamut, solmization, mensural notation, counterpoint, *musica ficta*, proportions, and modes.

GaiT   Gains, Charles Thomas. "Tricinia, 1542." S. M. D. Thesis. Union Theological Seminary, n.d. Ann Arbor, Mich.: University Microfilms, 1972. Photocopy.

This is a photocopy of two volumes. Volume I: "Commentary" and Volume II: "The edition." Volume II contains sacred and secular part songs with Dutch, French, German, or Latin words.

GanMR   Gangwere, Blanche M. *Music History during the Renaissance Period, 1425-1520: a documented chronology.* Music Reference Collection, No. 28. New York: Greenwood Press, [c. 1991].

Contains material in outline form on the background, philosophy, theory, notation, musical style, manuscript sources, theoretical sources, classes of music, composers and instruments of the period. There are definitions and translations of foreign words and titles along with an extensive bibliography.

GanO   Ganassi, Sylvestro. *Opera Intitulata Fontegara, Venice 1535: A treatise on the art of playing the recorder and of free ornamentation.* Edited by Hildemarie Peter. English translation by Dorothy Swainson. Berlin=Lichterfelde: Robert Lienau, [c. 1956] and [c. 1959].

This treatise combines two historical aspects of practical musicianship in the sixteenth century, namely, the art of playing the recorder and the art of playing divisions on a given basic theme. This work is intended for practical, not theoretical, use. There are 175 examples of divisions for a cadence on a basic form of six notes, a composite chart of Ganassi's recorder fingerings, and a bibliography.

GanR	Ganassi, Silvestro. *Regola Rubertina*. 2 vols. Bibliothea musica Bononiensis, Sezione II, n. 18a-b. Bologna: Forni, 1970. This is a facsimile of *Regola Rubertina* and *Lettione seconda*. Both volumes include instruction and study of the viol. There are musical examples and exercises.
GanRR	_____. *Regola Rubertina: first and second part: a manual of playing the viola da gamba and of playing the lute, Venice 1542 and 1543*. Edited by Hildemarie Peter. Translated by Daphne and Stephen Silvester. Berlin-Lichterfelde: R. Lienau, 1972. This is a translation from the German edition. It contains instruction on playing the viol and lute. There are musical studies and exercises.
GarC	Gardane, Antonio, 1509-1569. *Canzoni francese (1539). Il primo libro de canzoni francese a due voci*. Transcribed by Albert Seay. Transcriptions, no. 1. Colorado Springs: Colorado College Music Press, 1979. The purpose of this publication is not a scholarly one. The purpose is to make available a complete volume of simple *chansons* at a reasonable price. Nevertheless, musicologically sound standards are not discarded. There is a short introduction containing sources and background. The *chansons* are for amateur and professional alike. There are *chansons* by Heurteur, Claudin, Peletier, and Gardane.
GarCF	Gardane, Antonio. *Conzoni francese a due voci buone da cantare et sonare*. Venetia: A. Gardane, 1539. Wien:Österreichische Nationalbibliothek, 1986. Microfilm. This contains twenty-eight *chansons* for two parts, *cantus* and tenor or *bassus*.
GarCL	_____. *Canticorum liber primus cum quinque vocibus (quae passim motecta apellantur)*. Venetijs: Gardani, 1571. [Firenze: Biblioteca Nazionale Centrale, n.d.]. Microfilm. This contains motets for five voices, *cantus, altus,* tenor, *quintus,* and *bassus*. The original is in the Biblioteca nazionale Centrale in Florence. It is indexed in RISM A/I, C 4156.
GarCLP	_____. *Canticorum liber primus cum sex vocibus (quae passim motecta dicuntur)*. Venetijs: Gardani, 1571. [Firenze: Biblioteca Nazional Centrale, n.d.]. Microfilm. This contains motets for six voices, *cantus, altus,* tenor, *bassus,* and *sextus*. The original is in the Biblioteca nazionale Centrale in Florence. It is indexed in RISM A/I, C 4155.
GarDI	_____. *Di Baldissera Donato il primo libro di canzon villanesche alla napolitana a quattro voci...Aggiontovi anchora alcune villote di Perissone...* Venice: A. Gardane, 1550. [Lincoln microfilm gift]. Torino Italy: Biblioteca nazionale, [1978]. Microfilm. This contains music by Perissone Cambio, B. Donato, Tiberio Fabrianese, and "Anonymous". It is indexed in RISM B/1 1550-19 edition and H. B. Lincoln, *The Italian madrigal and related repertories*.
GarF	_____. *Flox florum, primus liber cum quator vocibus, motetti del fiore a 4*. Venetijs: Gardane, 1545. [Munich: Bayerische Staatsbibliothek, n.d.]. Microfilm. This is a facsimile of the original in Bayerische Staatsbibliothek, Munich (D Mbs). *4p0s pr 42/1*. It contains motets by Lerither, Lupus, Archadelt, Loy-

set, Pieton, Hilayre Penet, N. Paignier, Lasson, Gose, Io. Courtois, N. Gombert, Verdelot, Io. Lupi, Dambert, F. de Lys, Manchicourt, Richafort, and Adrianus Willaert. It is indexed in RISM B/I, 1545-4.

GarI   Gardane, Antonio. *Il terzo libro di motetti a cinque voci*. Venetia: Gardane, 1549. Microfilm. Koln: Universitats und Stadbibliothek, n1974.

This is a facsimile of five partbooks, *cantus, altus,* tenor, *bassus,* and *quintus.* The original is in the Universitats- und Stadbibliothek, Koln. It contains motets by Rore (6), Jacquet (3), Josquin Baston (1), Claudin (1), Morales (1) (attributed to Clemens non Papa in all other sources), Carchillion (1) (*i.e.* Crécquillon), and Francisco della Viola (1). It is indexed in RISM B/I, 1549-8 and Lewis catalog, v. 1, no. 134.

GarIP   _____. *Il primo libro de madrigali cromatici a cinque voci: libro primo.* Venetiis: A. Gardane, 1544. Boblogna: Civico Museo Bibliographico Musicale 1986. Microfilm.

This is a facsimile of thirty-seven madrigals for five voices by Cipriano de Rore. There are five partbooks, the *cantus, altus,* tenor, *bassus,* and *quintus.*

GarM   _____. *Motectorum nunc orimum maxima diligentia in lucem exeuntium, liber primus quinque vocum.* Venetijs: Gardane, 1544. [Washington (D.C.): Library of Congress, n.d.]. Microfilm.

This is a facsimile of five partbooks for *cantus, altus,* tenor, *quintus,* and *bassus.* They contain motets by C. Canis, P. Certon, A. Gardane, C. de Rore, Willaert, and others. They are indexed in Lewis catalog, v. 1, no. 56 and RISM B/I, 1544-06.

GarMD   _____. *Motetti del frutto a quatro primus liber cum quatuor vocibus.* Venice: A. Gardane, 1539. Kasseel: Deutsches Musikgeschichtliches archiv, 1986. Microfilm.

This is a facsimile of four partbooks containing music by Berchem, Gombert, Lheritier, Gero, Ponte, Alardy, Lupi, Verdelot, Lasson, Arcadelt, Billon, Gardane, Gosse, Garnier, and Phinot. It is indexed in RISM B/I, 1539-13.

GarMF   _____. *Motetti del frutto: Primus liber cum quinque vocibus.* Vinetia: A. Gardane, 1538. [Munich, Germany]: Bayerisch Staatsbibliothek, [1987?]. Microfilm.

This is a facsimile of seventeen five-voice Latin motets by D. Finot, Antonio Gardane, N. Gombert, Jachet and Lupi. This is the earliest work known to have been printed by Gardane. The original manuscript is in Bayerische Staatsbibliothek, $kManuscript: *Mus. Mss. 56/7* in Munich. It is indexed in RISM, 1538-4.

GarMP   _____. *Motetti del frutto: Primus liber cum quinque vocibus.* Vinetia: A. Gardane, 1538. Washington, D. C.: United States Library of Congress, 19--. Microfilm.

This is a facsimile of seventeen five-voice Latin motets by D. Finot, Antonio Gardane, N. Gombert, Jachet and Lupi. This is the earliest work known to have been printed by Gardane. It is found in the Bayerische Staatsbibliothek, $kManuscript: *Mus. Mss. 56/7.* It is indexed in RISM 1538-4.

GarMQ   _____. *Motect a quatuor vocum nunc primum diligentissime recognita ac suo candori...Liber primus.* Venetijs: Gardane, 1545. [London: British Li-

brary, n.d.] Microfilm.
This source contains motets for four voices. The original is in the British Library in London. The title page varies. The title is taken from the *cantus* partbook.

GarMQV Gardane, Antonio. *Musica quatuor vocum...* Venezia: A. Gardane, 1549. Vienna: Österreichische Nationalbibliothek, [19--]. Microfilm.
This contains sacred motets. There are twenty-two motets by Willaert.

GarMT _____. *Motetta trium vocum: Ab pluribus authoribus composita, quorum nomina sunt Iachetus Gallicus, [et al.].* Venetiis: Gardane, 1543. [London: British Museum, n.d.]. Microfilm.
This is a microfilm of three partbooks containing motets for three voices by Iachet, Morales, Constantius Festa, and Adrianus. The original is in the British Museum in London (GB Lbm), K.3.d.7. It is indexed in RISM B/1, 1543-6.

GarMTV _____. *Motetta trium vocum.* Venetijs: Gardane, 1551. [Munich: Bayerische Staatsbibliothek, n.d.] Microfilm.
This contains motets for three voices by Iachet, Morales, Constantius Festa, and Adrianus. The original is in Bayerische Staatsbibliothek in Munich *(D Mbs), 4p0s mus. pr 117-8.* It is indexed in RISM B/I, 1551-3 and Lewis thesis (Ph.D.) Brandeis University, 1979, v. 2, no. 161.

GarP _____. *Primus liber cum sex vocibus, Mottetti del frutto a sei voci.* Venetia: A. Gardane, 1539. N.p.: n.d. Microfilm.
This is a facsimile of six partbooks for *cantus, altus,* tenor, *bassus,* and *quintus pars* and extra *pars.* It is indexed in RISM B/I, p. 123.

GarPL _____. *Primo libro di motetti...* Venetia: Antonio Gardane, 1540. Vienna: Österreichische Nationalbibliothek, 1977. Microfilm.
This source contains motets for five voices. The original is in Österreichische Nationalbibliothek in Vienna.

GarPM _____. *Primo libro di madrigali d'Archadelt a tre voci con la gionta di dodese canzoni franzese et sei motteti novissimi.* Venezia: A. Gardane, 1543. Lincoln microfilm gift. Vienna: Oesterrische Nationalbibliothek, [198-?]. Microfilm.
There are three partbooks containing madrigals and motets by Arcadelt, Certon, Cosson, Courtois, F. Du Boys, C. Festa, G. Isoré, Jacotin, Lhéritier, Lupus, M. Hermann, P. Moulu, C. Sermisy, M. H. Werrecore and "Anonymous". Music incipits of the madrigals are found in *The Italian madrigal and related repertories* by H. B. Lincoln. There are incipits and complete contents of the motets in Lincoln's *The Latin Motet,* p. 742. It is indexed in RISM B/1; 1543/21.

GarQ _____. *Quatuor vocum mottecta a nuperrime suonitori restituta et quam emendatissime typis iterum excusa.* Venetijs: apud Antonium Gardane, 1545. Cologne: Universitats -und Stadtbibliothek, 1974. Microfilm.
These are motets for four voices, but the *cantus* and *altus* parts are missing. The original is in Universitats -und Stadtbibliothek in Cologne.

GarQL _____. *Il quinto libro di madrigali di Archadelt a quatro voci Novamente stampato et posto in luce.* Venetijs: Gardane, 1544. Modena, Italy: Fotografo C. Orlandini, 1970. Microfilm.
This is a facsimile of four partbooks containing madrigals by Arcadelt, Hubert Naich, Leonardus Barre, La Martoretta, Verdelot, M. Ihan, Pier-

esson, and anonymous. The original is in Accademia Filarmonica, Verona (*I VEaf*), *N. 150,III*. It is indexed in RISM A/1; A 1382; RISM b/1; 1544-16 and Lewis catalog, vol. 1, no. 50.

GarT Gardane, Antonio. *Tutti li madrigali del primo et del secondo libro a quattro voci*. Venetia: Gardano, 1556. Munich: Bayerische Staatsbibliothek, 1998. Photoreproduction.

This is a facsimile of madrigals by Festa, Constanzo (3) Jacquet of Mantua (1), Willaert (3), Barre, Leonardo (1), Festa, Sabastiano (1), and Verdelot (40). It is indexed in RISM B/I, 1556-27.

GásL Gásser, Luis. *Luis Milán on Sixteenth-Century Performance Practice*. Bloomington: University of Indiana Press, [c. 1996].

This is an investigation of Luis Milán and his ideas of musical structure and organization as well as his social, political, religious, and personal circumstances. This can be used as an instructional text on early sixteenth-century performance practices, theoretical conventions and historical context.

GayL Gay, Claude, Dom. *Les Maîtres de l'orgue du siècle d'or espagnol*. 2 vols. Collected and restored by Dom Claude Gay. Liguge: Editions Europart-Music, 1999.

These volumes contain music by Juan Bermudo, Cabezón, Francisco Fernandez Palero, Francisco de Peraza, Thomas de Santa Maria, Francisco Soto de Langa, and Pedro Alberto Vila. The music has been collected and restored from the manuscripts and books in the bibliothèques de l'Esucurial in Madrid, B.N. and Coimbra.

GeeO Geer, Harold E. *Organ Registration in Theory and Practice*. Glen Rock, New Jersey: J. Fischer and Brothers, [c. 1957].

There is a discussion of scientific and technical information concerning acoustics and the organ sound, the application of the technical information, the application of the theory of tone combination to musical interpretation, and the media of performance.

GérP Gérold, Théodore. "Protestant Music on the Continent." In *The New Oxford History Of Music*. Vol 4: *The Age of Humanism: 1540-1630,* pp. 419-465. Edited by Gerald Abraham. London: Oxford University Press, [c.1968].

This is a discussion of the music of the countries which adopted the ideas of Luther and those which followed the precepts of Calvin.

GinI Gintzler, Simon. *Intabolatura de lauto: de recercari motetti madrigali et canzon francese...* Venetia: Gardane, 1547. London: British Museum, n.d. Microfilm.

This contains original music for lute by Gintzler and intabulations of music by Josquin, Verdelot, Jachet (Berchem), Senfl, Moton, Willaert, Archadelt, Lupus, and Sandrin. It is indexed in RISM A/1, G 2092; RISM B/1, 1547-22, and Brown, no. 1547/3, p. 96. The original publication is in the British Museum in London (GB Lbm).

GinR _____. *6 Ricercari für Renaissance laute*. Edited by Stefan Lundgren. München: Lundgren Musik-Edition, 1982. Reproduced by holograph.

This is a reproduction of six *ricercari*. There is a Preface in German and one in English.

GlaD Glarean [Glareanus], Heinrich. *Dodecachordon*. 2 vols. Translated by Clement A. Miller. Musicological Studies and Documents, no. 6. [Rome]: American Institute of Musicology, 1965.

Volume I of this work contains a translation of Book I and II of the original text. Volume II contains a translation of Book III.

GlaDD   Glarean [Glareanus], Heinrich. *Dodecachordon (1547)*. Publikationen älterer praktischer und theoretischer Musikwerke, no. 16. German translation by Peter Bohn. Berlin: 1873-1905.

This is a facsimile edition. Maria Rika Maniates, in the book, *Mannerism in Italian Music and Culture, 1530-1630*, states that the *Dodecachordon* represents the first critical essay on music. Also that it is an attempt to subject music to historical and stylistic analysis along the same lines as writings on literature and the visual arts. There are new ideas about the modal system, a wealth of biographical information on composers of the period, and an anthology of more than 120 compositions by such composers as Josquin, Obrecht, Isaac, and even Ockeghem

GlaDO   _____. *Dodecachordon*. Basel, 1547. Monuments of music and music literature in facsimile. Ser. 2: Music literature, no. 65. New York: Broude Brothers, 1967.

A facsimile edition. *See* GlaDD.

GlaI   _____. "Isagoge in musicen (Basel, 1516)." Edited and translated by Frances Berry Turrell. *Journal of Music Theory* 3 (1959): 97-139.

The purpose of this article is to call the attention of the reader to the work and to indicate certain salient points.

GlaIM   _____. *Isagoge in musicen*. Basileae: J. Froben, 1516. Watertown, Mass.: General Microfilm Co., [19--]. Microfilm.

The title within the woodcut border is by Hans Holbein, the younger. There is a Preface dated Basileae, 1516. The work is appended with continuous signatures: Due elegiarum libri Henrici Glareani Helvetii ad Videricum. Zinglium Doggium, Basileae, 1516. It contains a discussion of church modes, Greek modes, scale construction, intervals and consonances, the Pythagorean scale and Guidonian syllables.

GomM   Gombert, Nicolas. *Musica quatuor vocum vulga motecta liber primus*. Venice: Scotto, 1539. [New York, N.Y.: Public Library, n.d.] Microfilm.

This is a facsimile of four sacred motet partbooks. The original is in the Public Library in New York. It is indexed in RISM A/1, G 2977 and Bernstein catalog, no. 3.

GomMC   _____. *Missa cum quatuor vocibus, ad imitationem cantionis Ie suis déshéritée*. Paris: du Chemin, 1557. [Paris: Bibliotheque nationale, n.d.]. Microfilm.

This is a facsimile of *Ie suis déshéritée*. The original is in the bibliotheque nationale in Paris. It is indexed in RISM A/I, G 2976 and F. Lesure et G. Thibault, no. 63, p. 322.

GomMO   _____. *Motectorum, quinque vocum, maximo studio in lucem editorum, liber secundus*. Venetiis: Scotum, 1541. [Wien: Österreichische Nationalbibliothek, n.d.]. Microfilm.

This is a facsimile of five partbooks containing motets by Gombert. The original manuscript is in the Österreichische Nationalbibliothek in Wien. It is indexed in RISM A/I, G 2984 and the Bernstein catalog, no. 20.

GomMQ   _____. *Musica quatuor vocum (vulgo motecta nuncupatur)...liber primus*. Venetijs: Scotum, 1541. [München: Universitatsbibliothek, n.d.]. Microfilm.

This is a facsimile of four partbooks containing works by Gombert, Morales, Hieronymus Sotto, Ivo, Iachet, and Scobedo. The original manuscript is in the Universitatsbibliothek in Müchen (D Mu). It is indexed in RISM B/I, 1541-04; RISM A/I, G 2978, and the Bernstein catalog, no. 18

GomMQV   Gombert, Nicolas. *Motetta cum quinque vocibus liber... secundus.* Venezia: H. Scotum, 1550. Munich: Bayerische Staatsbibliothek, 1975. Microfilm.

This is a facsimile of five partbooks containing motets for *cantus, altus, tenor, bassus,* and *quintus.* The original manuscript is in the Bayerische Staatsbibliothek in Munich. It is indexed in RISM A/I, G 2985.

GomMU   _____. *Musica...(vulgo motecta quinque vocum nuncupata).* Venice: Antonio Gardane, 1539. Munich: Bayerische Staatsbibliothek, 1977. Microfilm.

This is a facsimile of five sacred motet partbooks. The original is in the Bayerische staatsbibliothek in Munich. It is indexed in RISM A/1, G 2981 and Bernstein catalog, no. 4.

GomO   _____. Opera omnia. 11 vols. Edited by Joseph Schmidt-Georg. Corpus mensurabilis musicae, no. 6. N.p.: American Institute of Musicology, 1975.

This source contains transcriptions with the words printed as text. The volumes are as follows: Vol. 1: *Missae IV vocum*; Vol. 2: *Missae V vocum*; Vol. 3: *Missae VI vocum*; Vol. 4: *Magnificats*; Vol. 5: *Cantiones Sacrae*; Vol. 6: *Cantiones sacrae*; Vol. 7: *Motecta*, 5 vols.; Vol. 8: *Motecta,* 5 vols.; Vol. 9: *Motecta,* 6 vols.; Vol. 10: *Motetta* 4, 5, 12 v., 2 vols.; Vol. 11: *Cantiones saeculares,* 2 vols.

GomS   _____. *Sex misse dulcissime modulationis aures omnium mulcentes vocibus quinque.* Venice: Gardane, 1547. [Wolfenbüttel: Herzog-August Bibliothek, n.d.]. Microfilm.

This is a facsimile of six Masses: one by Jacquet of Mantua, three by Nicolas Gombert, and two by Jachet de Berchem. The original manuscript is in the Herzog-August Bibliothek in Wolfenbüttel. It is indexed in RISM A/I, G 2975; RISM B/I, 1547-3; and Lewis catalog, vol. 1, no. 109.

GreCM   Greer, Thomas H., gen. ed. *Classics of Western Thought.* Vol. 2: *Middle Ages, Renaissance, and Reformation.* Edited by Karl F. Thompson. New York: Harcourt, Brace and World, Inc., [c. 1964].

A chronological collection of primary documents. Each document is introduced by a brief account of the author's life, his role in the shaping of the Western tradition, and the significance of the particular work.

GriT   Griesheimer, James C. *The antiphon, responsory, and psalm motets of Ludwig Senfl.* Ann Arbor, MI: University of Microfilms International, [c. 1991]. Microfilm.

This is a thesis written for a Ph.D. at Indiana University in Bloomington in 1990. It is in three volumes. Volume 1 contains a Biographical sketch, Textual aspects of the motets, Technical aspects of music, and Motet chronology and stylistic considerations; volume 2 has Appendices; volume 3 has Transcriptions and critical report.

GudG   Gudewill, Kurt. "German Secular Song." In *The New Oxford History Of Music.* Vol. 4: *The Age of Humanism: 1540-1630,* edited by Gerald Abraham, pp. 96-123. London: Oxford University Press, [c. 1968]; reprint ed., 1974.

This is a discussion of the songs and the composers, Lassus, Jacob Regnart, Le Maistre, Christian Hollander, Hans Leo Hassler, Heinrich Schütz,

Johann Hermann Schein and others.

GuiR Guilliaud, Maximilian. *Rudiments de musique practique reduits en deux briefs traictez...* Paris: N. du Chemin, 1554. [Paris: Bibliotheque nationale, 1980]. Microfilm.

This is a facsimile of a treatise on music theory. It is indexed in RISM B VI I, p. 387.

HaaC Haar, James, ed. *Chanson and Madrigal, 1480-1530: studies in Comparison and Contrast.* Harvard University, Isham Library Papers, no. 2. Cambridge, Mass.: Harvard University Press, 1964.

This is a discussion of the comparison and contrast of the *chanson* and madrigalian types to their predecessors as discussed by Howard M. Brown, Walter H. Rubsamen, and Daniel Heartz. Each article is followed by a panel discussion. At the end of the book there are musical examples.

HaaF _____. "False relations and Chromaticism in Sixteenth-Century Music." In *The Science and Art of Renaissance Music,* p. 93-121. Edited by Paul Corneilson. Princeton, New Jersey: Princeton University Press, 1998.

The author discusses aspects of sixteenth-century chromaticism apparent on the surface of the music. There is no attempt to generalize on the larger tonal significance of the phenomena. His thesis is that chromaticism in this music is the result of a genuine liking for the cross-relation, not only among avowed chromaticists but also in the work of composers who wrote basically diatonic music.

HaaFC _____. "Festa, Costanzo", L. Macy, ed.: grovemusic.com (2001). <http://www.grovemusic.com> (Accessed 8 August 2001)

This contains information about the life and works of Festa.

HaaN _____. "The Note Nere Madrigal." In *The Science and Art of Renaissance Music,* p. 201- 221. Edited by Paul Corneilson. Princeton, New Jersey: Princeton University Press, 1998.

The subject of this study is where to draw the fine line between notational fad and stylistic advance, and how best to characterize music written in this "chromatic" notation.

HaaO _____: "Italy, Sixteenth Century", L. Macy, ed: grovemusic.com (2001), <http://www.grovemusic.com> (accessed 19 July 2001).

This is a general discussion of the composers, poets, and cultural relations that played a part in the development of a transitional madrigal style from 1520 to 1570.

HamCC Hamm, Charles, gen. ed. *Census-Catalogue of Manuscript Sources of Polyphonic Music 1400-1550.* 5 vols. Renaissance Manuscript Studies, no. 1. Neuhausen-Stuttgart: American Institute of Musicology, 1979.

This is a Census-Catalogue of Renaissance music manuscripts. It is a detailed bibliographical book. There are no tablatures or printed music. It does not contain manuscripts catalogued in RISM B IV/3-4.

HanJ Hand, Colin. *John Taverner, his Life and Music.* London: Eulenburg Books, [c. 1978].

Hand discusses Taverner's life, his music, and his musical style. In his section on Taverner's life, he questions the accuracy of certain statements usually written about Taverner's life and then discusses the facts that can be documented. An Appendix lists manuscript sources.

HarEL Harper, John. "Ensemble and Lute Music." In *Music in Britain: the Sixteenth*

Century, pp. 263-322. Edited by Roger Bray. The Blackwell History of Music in Britain, no. 2. Oxford: Blackwell Publishers Ltd., [c. 1995].

This is a discussion of the ensembles and players, the sources, foreign music in England, and the style, chronology and genre of the music.

HarEP   Harrison, Frank Ll. "English Polyphony (c. 1470-1540." In *New Oxford History of Music.* Vol. 3: *Ars Nova and the Renaissance: 1300-1540*, edited by Dom Anselm Hughes and Gerald Abraham, pp. 303-348. London: Oxford University Press, [c. 1960]; reprint ed., 1974.

This chapter discusses elements in English music, choral foundations, liturgical forms, style, composers, music, and sources of the period.

HarM   _____. *Music in medieval Britain.* Studies in the history of music. New York, Praeger [1959, c1958]

The period covered by this source is from the establishment of Norman constitutions and liturgies following the Norman conquest to the liturgical and institutional changes brought about by the Reformation. The institutions and their choirs, the liturgy and its plainsong, and the polyphony of the liturgy is covered.

HarME   _____. "Church Music in England." In *The New Oxford History of Music.* Vol. 4: *The Age of Humanism: 1540-1630*, edited by Gerald Abraham, pp. 465-520. London: Oxford University Press, [c. 1968]; reprint ed. 1974.

This is a discussion of the reform of the church and liturgy, the musical innovations, the use of instruments, and the composers and their music.

HarmO   Harmen, Alec, ed. *The Oxford book of Italian madrigals.* London: Oxford University Press, 1983.

This contains Italian madrigals for three to seven voices with Italian words. There is an English translation, of the words, p. 315-322.

HarN   Harrán, Don, ed. *The Anthologies of Black-note Madrigals.* 5 volumes. Corpus mensurabilis musicae, no. 73. Rome: Neuhausen-Stuttgart: American Institute of Musicology, 1978.

This contains four partbooks for *cantus, altus*, tenor, and *bassus*. The words are in Italian but also are printed as text with English translation. There is a critical commentary in English.

HarO   _____. "Orpheus as Poet, Musician, and Educator." In *Essays on Italian Music in the Cinquecento*, pp. 265-277. Edited by Richard Charteris. N.p.: Frederick May Foundation for Italian Studies, [c. 1990].

This essay discusses the various stages in the diffusion of the myth of Orpheus from writings of the ancients through those of the Church Fathers, to those of the Renaissance Neoplatonists, and beyond to conceptions of poetry and music in the Romantic era.

HarTH   _____. "The Theorist Giovanni del Lago: a New View of the Man and His Writings." *Musica Disciplina* 27 (1973): 107-151.

Harrán discusses the contents of the letter to Fra Seraphim and compares it with its version in the *Breve introduttione di musica misurata*. He reconstructs del Lago's theory of counterpoint by supplementing his precepts in the letter with those in the treatise.

HarW   _____. *Word-Tone Relations in Musical Thought: from Antiquity to the Seventeenth Century.* Musicological studies and documents, no. 40. Neuhausen Stuttgart: American Institute of Musicology, Hänsler-Verlag, 1986.

A survey of writings from the ancients to the early seventeenth century on

	the question of word-tone relations.
HayI	Hayes, Gerald. "Instruments and Instrumental Notation." In *The New Oxford History of Music*. Vol. 4: *The Age of Humanism: 1540-1630*, pp. 709-784. Edited by Gerald Abraham. London: Oxford University Press, [c. 1968].
	A discussion of instruments and instrumental notation as discussed by a great number of instrumental texts that began to appear after the beginning of the sixteenth century.
HayM	_____. "Musical Instruments." In *The New Oxford History of Music*. Vol. 3: *Ars nova and the Renaissance: 1300-1540*. Edited by Dom Anselm Hughes and Gerald Abraham, pp. 466-500. Oxford: Oxford University Press, [c.1960]; reprint ed., 1974.
	In this chapter there is a discussion of a large body of medieval and renaissance music in which it is clear that instruments were employed. Also, there is a discussion of the literary and artistic evidence of the same periods that reveals a great wealth of varied instruments in everyday use.
HeaCH	Heartz, Daniel. "The *Chanson* in the Humanist Era." In *Current Thought in Musicology*, pp. 193-231. Edited by John W. Grubbs. with the Assistance of Rebecca A. Baltzer, Gilbert L. Blount, and Leeman Perkins. Austin: University of Texas Press, [c. 1976].
	This is a survey of a genre and a period through the examination of a few works by leading poets and composers. Some facsimiles from original sources are included. The discussion is limited to that which was connected with Paris.
HeaK	_____, ed. *Keyboard dances from the earlier sixteenth century*. Corpus of early keyboard music, no. 8. [N.p.]: American Institute of Musicology, 1965.
	This contains transcriptions of two collections of dances that were originally published by Pierre Attaingnant in 1531 and Antonio Gardane in 1551.
HeaL	_____. "Les Goûts Réunis or the Worlds of the Madrigal and the *Chanson* Confronted." In *Chanson and Madrigal, 1480-1530: Studies in Comparison and Contrast*. Edited by James Haar, pp. 88-138. Cambridge, Mass.: Harvard University Press, 1964.
	A discussion of the exchanges of personnel and music between France and Italy.
HeaP	_____. *Pierre Attaingnant: Royal Printer of Music; a historical study and bibliographical catalogue*. Berkeley, University of California Press, 1969.
	The invention and application of printing and the repertory of Attaingnant, the first French music publisher, furnish the subject matter of this source. The historical study is divided into five sections: section one contains a broad picture of the Parisian scene, sections two and three contain a chronological panorama of the reign of Francis I from the beginning to midpoint, the fourth section discusses the publishing trade, and the fifth section states conclusions. The catalogue contains 174 items. It includes the title page and contents of each item with the text incipit and the name of the composer. There is also a list of modern editions.
HeaPC	_____, ed. *Preludes, chansons and dances for lute*. Publications de la Société de musique d'autrefois; Textes musicaux, t. 2. Neuilly-sur-Seine: Société de musique d'autrefois, 1964.
	This contains a facsimile of Oronce Finé's *Epithoma musice instrumenta-*

58   Bibliography

                     lis..., and modern transcriptions of *Tres breve et familiere introduction...* (1529) and of *Dixhuit basses danses* (1529). There are bibliographical references. It is indexed in RISM I, 1530.

HelL   Hellinck, Lupus. *Liber secundus missarum quatuor vocum.* Antverpie: Susato, 1545. Kassel: Murhard'sche Bibliothek der Stadt Kassel und Landesbibliothek, n.d. Microfilm.

                     This is a facsimile of four partbooks containing Masses by T. Crécquillon, L. Hellinck, and A. Barbe. The original manuscript is in Murhard'sche Bibliothek der Stadt Kassel und Landesbibliothek in Kassel. It is indexed in RISM B/I, 1545-01 and Meissner, vol. 2, p. 35.

HelS   Helm, Everett. "Secular Music in Italy (c. 1400-1530)." In *New Oxford History of Music.* Vol. 3: *Ars nova and the Renaissance: 1300-1540*, edited by Dom Anselm Hughes and Gerald Abraham, pp. 381-405. London: Oxford University Press, [c. 1960]; reprint ed., 1974.

                     This chapter discusses popular music and courtly improvisation, carnival songs, *laudi*, the *frottola*, and *frottola* forms.

HelSC   _____. "The Sixteenth Century French *Chanson*." *Proceedings of the Music Teachers National Association* 36 (1942; for 1941): 236-243.

                     Helm presents a broad outline of the subject and suggests ways in which musicological research can be of real benefit to practical music and musicians by making available an intelligible music which has hitherto been neglected. The article covers a period of 1529 to ca. 1550.

HerT   Hertzmann, Erich. "Trends in the Development of the Chanson in the Early Sixteenth Century." *Papers of the American Musicological Society* (1940): 5-10

                     Hertzmann traces the *chanson* from the publication of the *Odhecaton* through the publication of *chansons* by Attaingnant and concludes that the *chanson* with the aid of printed publications contributed towards the process of the secularization of music.

HerV   _____, ed. *Volkstmliche italienische Lieder: zu 3-4 Stimmen.* Das Chorwerk, no. 8. Wolfenbüttel: Mösler Verlag, 1959.

                     This contains transcriptions of *Canzone villanesche alla napolitana* by Willaert, Castellino, Nola, Cimello, Perissone, Lasso, and Corneti. There are Italian and German words.

HeyD   Heyden, Sebald. *De arte canendi.* 1540. Translation and transcription by Clement A. Miller. Musicological studies and documents, no. 26. N.p.: American Institute of Musicology, 1972.

                     This translation is based on the 1540 edition of *De arte canendi* published by Petreius in Nürnberg. There is an Introduction, a list of composers and compositions used as examples, a listing of the chapter headings, and a bibliography. There is a discussion of the elements of music and *tactus*-mensuration theories. There is a commentary in which a number of the polyphonic examples are discussed, as well as some aspects of Heyden's *tactus*-mensuration theories. The latter discussion was included in order to clarify the meaning of the theories.

HeyDA   _____. *De arte canendi.* Monuments of music and music literature in facsimile. Ser. 2.: Music literature, 139. Nürnberg: Petreius, 1540; New York: Broude Brothers, 1969.

                     This contains a discussion of the elements of music and Heyden's theory of *tactus*. There are polyphonic music examples by Alexander Agricola, Antoine Brumel, Ghiselin, Heinrich Isaac, Josquin des Prez, Jacob Obrecht, Johannes Ockeghem, Marbriano, Piltz Nicolaus (?), Pierre de la Rue, Ludwig Senfl, and Gaspar van Weerbecke.

HeyDAC   Heyden, Sebald. *De arte canendi*. Nürnberg: Petreius, 1540. German Books before 1601, roll 605, Item 14. Watertown, Mass.: General Microfilm Co., 19--.

There is a discussion of the elements of music and Heyden's theory of *tactus*. The examples are polyphonic music by Alexander Agricola, Antoine Brumel, Ghiselin, Heinrich Isaac, Josquin des Prez, Jacob Obrecht, Johannes Ockeghem, Marbriano, Piltz Nicolaus (?), Pierre de la Rue, Ludwig Senfl, and Gaspar van Weerbecke.

HeyMU   _____. *Musicae, id est, artis canendi libro duo*. Nürnberg: Petrius, 1537. London: British Library, n.d. Microfilm.

This is a microfilm of the original publication found in the London British Library. The 1537 edition is an enlargement of the *Musicae...* of 1532 and the source for the enlargement of *De arte canendi* of 1540. It contains Heyden's theories and musical examples which include canons, fugues, part-songs, and sacred music. The compositions are by Josquin des Prez, P. Moulu, M. de Orto, Jacob Obrecht, J. Ockeghem, L. Senfl, and others.

HolM   Hollaway, William Wood. *Martin Agricola's Musica instrumentalis deudsch: a translation*. PhD. diss. North Texas State University, 1972. Ann Arbor, Mich.: University Microfilms, 1972.

This is a translation of Agricola's book written in German in 1528. It contains a discussion of musical instruments and practices of his time. Also, there is a section devoted to a comparison of the material in this book with other books and treatises on the same and related subjects written at approximately the same time or written in the next hundred years.

HugH   Hughes, David G. *A History of European Music: the Art Music Tradition of Western Culture*. New York: McGraw-Hill Book Co., [c. 1974].

This is a discussion of "serious" music; presented as a history of musical styles. It begins with Gregorian Chant and ends with late nineteenth century music.

HumB   "Humanism." *Britannica 2002 Deluxe Edition*. Copyright © 1994-2002 Britannica.com Inc. April 10, 2002.

This contains a discussion of the history of humanism, the definition of humanism, and its beliefs.

HunC   Hunt, J. Eric. *Cranmer's First Litany, 1544 and Merbecke's Book of Common Prayer Noted, 1550*. New York: The Macmillan Co., 1939.

This is a facsimile of both works. There are also extracts from all Merbecke's literary works and a biographical note.

HüsA   Hüschen, Heinrich. "Agricola, Martin." In *The New Grove Dictionary of Music and Musicians*, p. 166. 20 vols. Edited by Stanley Sadie. 6th ed. London: Macmillan Publishers Limited, [c. 1980].

This is a short biography of Martin Agricola.

HusB   "Hussite." *Britannica 2001 Deluxe Edition CD-ROM*. [c. 1994-2000] Britannica.com Inc. May 10, 2001.

This traces the history of the Hussites from 1414 through the fifteenth century to the Unity of Brethren and to the Moravian Church of 1722.

60 Bibliography

JacH Jacquet of Mantua. *Himni vesperorum totius anni secundum Romanam curiam diligentissime recogniti...cum quatuor et quinque vocibus.* Venice: Scotto, 1566. Milan: Biblioteca del Conservatorio "Giuseppe Verdi", 1975. Microfilm.
This contains Vesper hymns in four partbooks for *cantus, altus,* tenor, and *bassus.* The original publication is in the Biblioteca del Conservatorio "Giuseppe Verdi" in Milan. It is indexed in RISM A/I, J22, and Bernstein catalog, no. 269.

JacHV _____. *Himni vesperorum totius anni...* Corpus mensurabilis musicae, no. 54; Opera omnia, no. 2. [S. l.]: American Institute of Musicology, 1972.
This contains translations of Latin Vesper hymns and transcriptions for five voices. There is an Introduction in English and Latin by Philip T. Jackson. It is indexed in Bernstein catalog, no. 269.

JacO _____. *Opera omnia.* Edited by Philip T. Jackson and George Nugent. Corpus mensurabilis musicae, 54. [S.l]: American Institute of Musicology, 1971.
This source contains six volumes. Vol. I: *Missa in dei triibulationis, Missa Chiare dolci e fresche acque, Missa Peccata mea,* and *Missa Anchor che col partire.* Vol. II: *Hymni vesperorum totius anni: 1566.* Vol. III: *Messe del fiore a cinque voci, Libro primo (1561).* Vol. IV: *Primo libro dei motetti a quattro voci (1539).* Vol. V: *Primo libro motetti a cinque voci (1539).* Vol. VI: *Missa Hercules dux Ferrariae, Missa Ferdinandus dux Calabriae, Missa Ave [fuit] prima salus, Missa In illo tempore,* and *Missa De mon triste deplaisir.*

JacPL _____. *Primo libro dei motetti a quattro voci (1539).* Corpus mensurabilis musicae, no. 54. Opera omnia, no. 4. [S.l.]: American Institute of Musicology, 1982.
This source contains motets for four voices with Latin words. There is an English introduction by George Nugent.

JacPLM _____. *Primo libro dei motetti a cinque voci (1539).* Corpus mensurabilis musicae, no. 54. Opera omnia, no. 5. [S.l.]: American Institute of Musicology, 1986.
This source contains motets for five voices with Latin words. There is an English introduction by George Nugent

JanB Janequin, Clément. *Missa La bataille.* Edited by Frank Dobbins. Fazer editions of early music. Espoo, Finland: Fazer Music, 1995.
This Mass is for mixed voices and is a parody on Janequin's popular *chanson.* There is a preface and critical notes in English. Bibliographical references are included.

JanBA _____. *Messe, La bataille.* Anthologie chorale, supplement aux Maîtres Musiciens de la Renaissance Française. Paris: Salabert, 1947.
This contains transcriptions of Masses. There is a preface signed by Henri Expert.

JanC _____. *Chansons polyphoniques.* Édition complète avec une Introduction par A. Tillman Merritt et François Lesure. 6 vols. Monaco: Éditions de L'oiseau Lyre, 1965-1971.
These volumes contain transcriptions of the *chansons* of Janequin published in the chronological order of their publication. Original clefs are indicated at the beginning of each piece. There is an introduction at the beginning of the first volume in which the *chansons* are discussed. The *chan-*

	sons are divided into three phases: the Bordelaise period (1505-1531), the Angevine period (1531-1549), and the Parrisienne period (1549-1558). This is a complete edition.
JanCA	Janequin, Clément. *Chansons (Attaingnant 1529(?)).* Les Maîtres Musiciens de la Renaissance Française, no. 7. Paris: Maurice Senart, 1898; reprint ed., New York: Broude Brothers, n.d.
	This source contains transcriptions of five program *chansons*: *Le Chant des Oiseaux* (The Song of Birds), *La Guerre* (The War), *La Chasse* (The Hunt), *L'ALouette* (The Lark), and *Las, povre coeur* (Alas! poor heart). There are historical notes and criticisms.
JanCS	_____. *Congregati sunt.* Monaco: Éditions de l'Oiseau Lyre, 1949.
	This is a transcription of a sacred motet for four voices by Clément Janequin.
JanCZ	_____. *Zehn Chansons.* Edited by Albert Seay. Das Chorwerk, no. 73. Edited by Friedrich Blume. Germany: Möseler Verlag Wolfenbüttel, n. d.
	There are transcriptions of ten four-part *chansons* with the original text and a German translation.
JanH	Janson, H. W. and Joseph Kerman. *A History of Art and Music.* Englewood Cliffs, N. J.: Prentice-Hall, Inc., n.d.
	This is a brief history of art and music from prehistoric man through the twentieth century. It is designed as an introduction to these fields in the framework of a general humanities course. Each discipline has been treated separately but with a common pattern.
JeaS	Jeans, James, Sir. *Science and Music.* Cambridge: Cambridge University Press, 1937; reprint ed., New York: Dover Publications, Inc. 1968.
	This source describes the main outlines of such parts of science, both old and new, as are particularly related to the questions and problems of music. Jeans conveys precise information in a simple non-technical way. The book is for the amateur, as well as the serious student, of music.
JepI	Jeppesen, Knud, ed. *Die italienische Orgelmusik am Anfang des Cinquecento.* Vol. II: *Altitalienische Orgelmusik.* Kopenhagen: W. Hansen Musikforlag. Edition: 2. *Neubearbeitete und wesentlich erw.* Augs., 1960.
	This source contains transcriptions of Marco Antonio Cavazzoni's *Recerchari Motetti Canzoni, Libro Primo (1523)* and transcriptions of *Ricercari* by Jacopo Fogliano da Modena, Marcantonio [Cavazzoni] in Bologna, Jaches [Brumel], and Julio da Modena. There is also a Mass, *Messa de la dominicia* by Jaches [Brumel].
JosE	Josephson, Nors S., ed. *Earley sixteenth-century sacred music from the Papal Chapel.* Corpus mensurabilis musicae, no. 95. Neuhausen-Stuttgart: American Institute of Musicology, 1982.
	This source contains mainly Masses, motets, and Passion music for two to eight voices. Some monophonic chant is included. It contains works by Josquinus Dor, Andreas Michot, Vincentius Misonne, Johannes Beauserron, Charles d'Argentil, and others. It is edited principally from manuscript sources in the Cappella Sistina, Cappella Giulia, Biblioteca apostolica vaticana. Critical notes and bibliographical references are included.
JosJ	Josephson, David S. *John Taverner: Tudor Composer.* Studies in Musicology, No. 5. Ann Arbor: University Microfilms International, [c. 1975]; reprint ed., 1979

62   Bibliography

    This is a revision of the author's dissertation on John Taverner. Musical chapters have been expanded and biographical chapters have been compressed. Considerations of form, style, liturgy, ritual, or performance practices are not treated at length.

JosW Josquin, des Prez. *Werken.* Edited by A. Smijers. Leipzig: C.F.W. Siegel, 1921-1969.

    There are fifty-five parts in eleven volumes. Parts two to twenty-one have the imprint Amsterdam: G. Alsbach; parts thirteen to twenty-one have the imprint Leipzig: F. Kistner. They were issued in consecutively numbered parts but were intended to be bound according to type of composition. The volumes contain French part-songs, sacred part-songs, and Masses.

JudI Judd, Robert. "Italy." In *Keyboard Music before 1700*. Edited by Alexander Silbiger, p. 235-312. New York: Schirmer Books, [c. 1995].

    There is a discussion of Political Considerations, Problems of Documentation, Instruments, The Liturgy, The Music, and a Guide to Literature and Editions.

KauF Kaufmann, Henry W. "Fogliani (Fogliano), Lodovico." In *The New Grove Dictionary of Music and Musicians,* p. 687. 20 vols. Edited by Stanley Sadie. 6th ed. London: Macmillan Publishers Limited, [c. 1980].

    This is a short biography of Lodovico Fogliano.

KemBJ Kempers, K. Ph. Bernet. "Bibliography of the Sacred Works of Jacobus Clemens non Papa." *Musica Disciplina* 18 (1964): 85-150.

    This contains a *Documenta vitae,* a list of additional literature, and a bibliography of the sacred works. The bibliography lists the title, year, number of voices, later editions, editor of publications, list of libraries and manuscripts, and index of pieces in the *Opera omnia* edited by Kempers.

KemJ _____. "Jacobus Clemens non Papa: *Chansons* in their Chronological Order." *Musica Disciplina* 15 (1961): 187-200.

    This source lists a chronological order of the first edition of Clemens non Papa's *chansons*. It also gives reference to later editions, to tablatures, manuscripts, and scores with annotations. Indications as to where the original sources are to be found, along with original editors and reprinters are listed.

KenD Kennedy, Michael. *The Oxford Dictionary of Music.* Oxford: Oxford University Press, 1985.

    This dictionary contains entries on musical subjects such as composers, performers, orchestras, titles and descriptions of individual works; operas, and ballets; musical forms and terms; instruments, institutions, and writers on music

KleD Kleber, Leonhard. *Die Orgeltabulatur des Leonhard Kleber*. Edited by Karin Berg-Kotterba with a Concordance by Martin Staehelin. 2 vols. Das Erbe deutscher Musik, Bd. 91-92. Frankfurt: H. Litolff's Verlag, 1987.

    This contains compositions to be played on the manuals of the organ as well as arrangements which use the pedals. There are religious and secular song settings, arrangements of motets, settings of dance tunes, and free compositions. This source is edited from the *Ms.* in the Staatsbibliothek Preussischer Kulturitz Berlin (West), Musikabteilung, Signatur *Mus. Ms. 40 026*. There is a critical commentary, concordances, and an index in vol. 2.

KleE	Klerk, Dirk de. "Equal Temperament." *Acta Musicologica* 51 (1979): 140-150.
This is a discussion of intonation and temperament and an attempt to find new feasible tuning systems by means of a computer.
KluG	Klug, Joseph. *Geistliche Lieder zu Wittemberg/ Anno 1543*. Wittenberg: Joseph Klug, 1544.
This source is found in the Richard C. Kessler Reformation Collection in the Pitts Theology Library. It contains Lutheran hymns. It is indexed in VD 16; G 850.; Benzing, Lutherbibliographie; 3559.; Wackernagel; 463.; and RISM, 1544-05.
KraO	Krautwurst, Franz, ed. *Officia de nativitate: Wittenberg 1545*. Musikdrucke aus den Jahren 1538 bis 1545 in praktischer Neuausgabe, no. 12. Kassel: Bärenreiter, 1999.
This source contains Christmas and Epiphany music for the Propers and the Ordinary. The music is written for four parts; *discantus, altus*, tenor, and *bassus*. There is a Preface in German and English. Bibliographical references and indexes are included.
KriE	Kristeller, Paul Oskar. *Eight philosophers of the Italian Renaissance*. Stanford: Stanford University Press, 1964.
This work is based on the Arensberg Lectures given at Stanford University in 1961. The lectures gave a brief survey of Italian thought during the Renaissance period. There is a ninth lecture that has been added as an appendix which concerns only humanism.
KriR II	_____. *Renaissance thought II: papers on humanism and the arts*. New York: Harper and Row, 1965.
A collection of previously published long, documented papers dealing with aspects of Renaissance humanism, the theory of the arts, and a few short specimens of studies dedicated to Renaissance Platonism and Renaissance Aristotelianism.
KugC	Kugelmann, Hans. *Concentus novi...* Augsburg: Kriesstein, 1540. [Wien: Österreichische Nationalbibliothek, n.d.]. Microfilm.
This is a facsimile of four partbooks containing sacred German and Latin hymns by G. Blankenmuller, H. Heugel, H. Kugelmann, V. Schnellinger, T. Stoltzer, and others. The original is in Österreichische Nationalbibliothek in Wien. It is indexed in RISM B/I, [1540]-08.
KugCO	_____. *Concentus novi*, 1540. Das Erbe deutscher Musik. Sonderreihe: Bd. 2. Edited by Hans Engel. Kassel: Bärenreiter-Verlag, 1955.
This source contains thirty-nine German and Latin hymns for three to eight voices. There is a critical report, pp. 105-106.
LagB	Lago, Giovanni del. *Breve introduttione di musica misurata*. Venice: Ottaviano Scotto, 1540. Bibliotheca musicae Bononiensis. Sec. 2: no. 17. Bologna: Arnaldo Forni, 1969.
This is a facsimile edition. The object of the treatise is to instruct the reader on how to compose music that is sensitive to the text on several levels, such as the general mood, units of thought or sentences, punctuation, accentuation of words, and length of syllables.
LamC	Lampadius, Auctor. *Compendium musices*. Bernae: M. Apiarius, 1541. New York: New York Public Library, 1951. Microfilm.
The first edition was printed in Bern in 1537. There is a Preface by Eber-

hard von Rumlang, and a dedication, dated 1537. The original publication is in the New York Public Library.

LanE Langer, William L., comp. and ed. *An Encyclopedia of World History*. 5th ed. Boston: Houghton Mifflin Co., [c. 1972].

This source contains a chronology of events from the prehistoric period to 1970. It includes summaries of cultural activities, science, and social movements.

LanSC Lanfranco, Giovanni Maria. *Scientille di musica...che mostrano a leggere il canto fermo, et figurato, gli accidenti delle note misurate, le proportioni, i tuoni, il contrapunto, et la divisione del monochordo, con la accordatura de varii instrumenti*...Brescia: Britannico, 1533. Bibliotheca musicae Bononiensis. Sec. 2: *Teoria*, no. 15. Bologna: Arnaldo Forni, 1970.

This is a facsimile edition. The purpose of the treatise is the training of choir boys. Part one discusses notes; part two, rhythms and mensural signs; part three, the eight modes; and part four, basic counterpoint, and names of instruments and their tuning. Toward the end of the treatise, Lanfranco describes and discusses string instruments.

LanSM _____. *Scintille di musica*...Brescia, 1533. The original is in the Sibley Music Library, Eastman School of Music. Microfilm.

This is a facsimile edition. See LanSC.

LayC Layolle, Francesco de. *Collected motets for 2, 3, 4, 5, and 6 voices*. Music of the Florentine Renaissance, no. 5. Edited by Frank A. D'Accone. Corpus mensurabilis musicae, no 32. [Dallas?]: American Institute of Musicology, 1973.

This source contains transcriptions of motets by Francesco de Layolle. Latin words are printed as text on pp. xvi-xxii.

LayCC _____. *Cinquanta canzoni a quatro voci*. Lione: Moderne, 1540 1549. Wolfenbüttel: Herzog-August-Bibliothek, 1986. Microfilm.

This contains fifty madrigals for four voices by Layolle.

LayCS _____. *Collected secular works for 2, 3, 4 and 5 voices*. Music of the Florentine Renaissance, no. 3; Corpus mensurabilis musicae, no. 32. Edited by Frank A. D'Accone. Rome: American Institute of Musicology, 1969.

This contains Layolle's *Venticinque canzoni a cinque voci* and other works from various collections. There is an introduction, printed texts, a list of sources, and notes on individual works.

LayCSW _____. *Collected secular works for four voices*. Music of the Florentine Renaissance, no. 4; Corpus mensurabilis musicae, no. 32. Edited by Frank A. D'Accone. [s.l.]: American Institute of Musicology, 1969.

This contains Italian part-songs for four voices. There are forty-nine madrigals by Layolle and an anonymous madrigal "Per la morte di M. Francesco de Layolle". There are instrumental settings by Io. Maria da Crema, Antonio Rotta, and Simon Gintzler, as well as an embellished version of *Lasciar il velo* by Gio. Camillo Maffei. The Italian words are printed as text on preliminary pages. There is a list of sources and notes on individual works.

LayM _____. *Masses and penitential Psalms*. Music of the Florentine Renaissance, no. 6; Corpus mensurabils musicae, no. 32. Edited by Frank A. D'Accone. [Dallas?]: American Institute of Musicology, 1973.

This source contains transcriptions of the Masses and Psalms, a list of sources, and notes.

LayV	Layolle, Francesco de. *Venticinque canzoni a cinque voci*. Lione: Moderno, 1540. Wolfenbüttel: Herzog-August-Bibliothek, 1986. Microfilm. This contains the *superius, altus,* tenor, and *bassus* parts only of twenty-five madrigals by Layolle. It is indexed in RISM, L 1178 and Pogue, S. F., no. 24.
LeaB	Leaver, Robin A, ed. *The booke of common praier noted, 1550*. Courtenay facsimile, no. 3. Oxford, England: Sutton Courteney Press, 1980. This source includes a two color facsimile reprint of the 1550 edition, and original signatures preserved without modern pagination.
LeaJ	_____, ed. *The Work of John Marbeck*. Introduced and edited by R. A. Leaver. The Courtenay Library of Reformation Classics, no. 9. Oxford: The Sutton Courtenay Press, n.d. This source is an evaluation of Marbeck's significance within the disciplines of music and theology. There are extracts from his printed works, contemporary documents relating to him, details of his life and work, and an investigation of the subsequent understanding of them.
LeaL	_____. "The Lutheran Reformation." In *The Renaissance: from the 1470s to the end of the 16th century*, pp. 263-285. Edited by Iain Fenlon. Man and Music Series. Englewood Cliffs, N.J.: Prentice Hall, [c. 1989]. This is a discussion of the patterns of choral and vocal music combined with liturgical monody and congregational hymnody that produced the liturgical music for the Lutheran liturgy. These patterns became the common practice and were firmly established by the end of the sixteenth century. There is also a discussion of the differences between the Lutheran liturgy and the Roman Mass.
LeeG	Lee, Barbara. "Giovanni Maria Lanfranco's Scintille di musica and Its Relation to Sixteenth Century Music Theory." Unpublished Ph.D. diss. Cornell University, 1961. This contains an English translation of Lanfranco's treatise. The purpose of the treatise is deduced and its relation to its background and to its contemporaries are discussed.
LeHM	Le Huray, Peter. *Music and the Reformation in England, 1549-1660*. New York: Oxford University Press, 1967. This book covers the events of the period that influence the music, the organization and practices of the Chapel Royal, performance problems, and composers. There are three appendices covering a list of printed books containing devotional music, organ music in modern editions, and a list of modern editions.
LeHT	_____, ed. *The Treasury of English Church Music*. Volume 2: *1545-1650*. London: Blandford Press Limited, [c. 1965]. This source contains transcriptions of sacred music representing the 'golden age' from the Reformation until the death of Charles I. There is an Introduction, a List of Sources, Editorial Method, Textual Commentary, Modern Editions, Bibliography, and Discography.
LenS	Lenaerts, R. B. "The 16th-Century Parody Mass in the Netherlands." *Musical Quarterly* 36:3 (July, 1950): 410. This source is a study in the comparison of certain parodies of different periods found in the polyphony of the Netherlands. It shows the diversity of the technique.

LeRoP Le Roy, Adrian. Psaumes: *Tiers livre de tablature de luth, 1552; Instruction, 1574.* Edited and transcribed by Richard de Morcourt. Le Roy, Adrian,; ca. 1520-1598; Lute music. Paris: Éditions du Centre national de la recherche scientifique, 1962.

This contains music for voice and lute presented in tablature and modern notation. The music also is performable as lute solos. There are twenty-one Psalms of the *Tiers livre de tablature de luth, 1552* and eight Psalms taken from *A briefe and plaine instruction, 1574*

LesB Lesure, François and Thibault, G. *Bibliographie des éditions musicales publées par Nicolas du Chemin (1549-1576).* Paris: Société de Musique d'Autrefois, 1953.

This is a catalog of the music editions published by Nicolas du Chemin. There is a discussion of French music printing. This is in French. There is an abstract in the *Annales musicologiques*, volume I. It is autographed by Lesure and Thibault.

LesF Lesure, François. "Latin Church Music on the Continent-1. (b) France in the Sixteenth Century (1520-1610)." In *The New Oxford History of Music.* Vol. 4: *The Age of Humanism: 1540-1630*, edited by Gerald Abraham, pp. 237-253. London: Oxford University Press, [c. 1968]; reprint ed., 1974.

This is a discussion of the composers, music, and style of the period.

LesM _____. *Musicians and Poets of the French Renaissance.* Translated from the French by Elio Giantureo and Hans Rosenwald. New York: Merlin Press, [c. 1955].

This contains a discussion of the fusion of music and poetry in the sixteenth century.

LeuL Leupold, Ulrich S., ed. *Luther's Works: Liturgy and Hymns*, no. 53. Helmut T. Lehmann, gen. ed. Philadelphia: Fortress Press, [c. 1965].

This volume is number fifty-three of fifty-five volumes planned of an American edition of Luther's works. It contains translations of "The Basic Liturgical Writings", "The Occasional Services", "The Hymns", and "Prefaces to Hymnals and Other Musical Collections". The first thirty of these volumes contain Luther's expositions of various books of the Bible. The remaining volumes contain what is usually called his "Reformation writings" along with other occasional pieces. The final volume will be an index and glossary. Not all of Luther's writings will be translated in their entirety..

LewA Lewis, Mary S. *Antonio Gardano, Venetian Music Printer 1538-1569: a Descriptive Bibliography and Historical Study.* Vol. I: *1538-1549*. Garland Reference Library of the Humanities, no. 718. New York and London: Garland Publishing, Inc. 1988.

The object of this source, according to the author, is to depict a musical culture of northern Italy and especially the Veneto in the middle years of the sixteenth century through the activities of the Venetian music printer, Antonio Gardano. In order to do this, the author has chosen a diversity of approaches-bibliographical, historical, socio-cultural, and musical. There are four volumes. This volume contains the Descriptive Bibliography, with detailed information on each edition published by Gardano. There are notes on the individual copies, and lists of concordances for all the pieces. There is an overview of the historical and social context within which early music printing developed with a brief biography of Gardano.

LewG   Lewis, Mary S, ed. *The Gardane motet anthologies...* Sixteenth-century motet, no. 13. New York: Garland Publishers, 1993.
>This contains motets for four, five, and six voices. There are Latin words. The motets are edited from anthologies originally collected and published by Antonio Gardane. There is an introduction as well as bibliographical references.

LhéO   Lhéritier, Jean. *Opera omnia.* Edited by Leeman L. Perkins. Corpus mensurabilis musicae, no. 48. [S.l.]: American Institute of Musicology, 1969.
>This source contains mostly motets for four to nine voices. There are Latin or French words.

LinE   Lindley, Mark. "Early 16th Century Keyboard Temperaments." *Musica disciplina* 28 (1974): 129-153.
>This article is a presentation of an interpretation of the kind of temperament Arnolt Schlick, Pietro Aaron, and Giovanni Maria Lanfranco had in mind. The author thinks J. Murray Barbour misconstrued the kind of temperament these theorists had in mind.

LinL   _____. *Lutes, viols and temperaments.* Cambridge: Cambridge University Press, 1984.
>This is a discussion of the tuning of the lute and viol and the spacing of the frets. The discussion is based on the writings of some thirty players and theorists who wrote about the problem between the 1520s and the 1740s.

LisM   Listenius, Nicolaus. *Music = Musica.* Translations, Colorado College Music Press, no. 6. Translated by Albert Seay. Colorado Springs: Colorado College Music Press, 1975.
>This is a translation of a revision of the author's *Rudimenta musicae.* There is a bibliography.

LisMN   _____. *Musica Nicolai Listenii: ab authore denuo recognita multisque novis regulis et exemplis adaucta.* Veröffentlichungen der Musik-Bibliothek Paul Hirsch, no. 8. Edited by Georg Schunemann. Berlin: M. Breslauer, 1927.
>This is a German translation. The first edition of 1533 and several of the subsequent editions were published under the title, *Rudimenta musicae.*

LisR   _____. *Rudimenta musicae in gratiam studiosae juventutis diligenter comportata.* Vitebergae: apid Georgium Rhau, 1533. Zug, Switzerland: Inter Documentation, [1976]. Microfiche.
>This is a reproduction of the original publication. In the treatise, Listenius divides the study of music into three branches: *theorica* (science), *practica* (performance didactics), and *poetica* (composition). The *Rudimenta musicae* was later published under the title, *Musica Nicolai Listenii.*

LloL   Lloyd, L. S. "The Lesson of Mean-Tone Tuning." *Music Review* 5:4 (1944): 14-227.
>This is an attempt to prove that mean-tone tuning was a practical approximation to the scale system distilled from the great masters of the sixteenth and seventeenth centuries and that it tells us about the essential problems of all tunings of keyboard instruments.

LocDM   Lockwood, Lewis, ed. *Drei Motetten über den Text "Quem dicunt homines".* Das Chorwerk, no. 94. Wolfenbüttel: Mösler Verlag, n.d.
>The three motets are by Richafort, J. Pionnier, and Gombert. They are written for four and six voices. Each motet is written for the text, *Quem dicunt homines.* Both Latin and German texts are included. There is a *Vor-*

	wort and the *Quellen und Anmerkungen zur Musik*.
LocSP	Lockwood, Lewis. "A Sample Problem of Musica Ficta: Willaert's Pater Noster." In *Studies in Music History: Essays for Oliver Strunk*, pp. 161-182. Edited by H. S. Powers. Princeton: Princeton University Press, 1968.
	A reflection on the nature of the problem of unspecified accidentals and on the character of some provisional conclusions that might be reached for a particular composition.
LonM	Long, Kenneth R. *The Music of the English Church*. London: Hodder and Stoughton, [c. 1971].
	This is a discussion of the growth and development of the art of liturgical music and of the circumstances under which it was written and performed. There is an effort to show English church music as being a part of a far wider pattern of western European musical culture. Also, the author has sought to project the music against its religious, political, economic, and social background. There is a thumbnail sketch of organ building.
LowAW	Lowinsky, Edward E. "Adrian Willaert's *Chromatic 'Duo'* Reexamined." In *Music in the Culture of the Renaissance and Other Essays*, vol. 2, pp. 681-699. Ediited and with an Introduction by Bonnie J. Blackburn with Forewords by Howard Mayer Brown and Ellen T. Harris = *Tijdschrift voor Muziekwetenschap* 18 (1956-59): 1-36. Chicago: The University of Chicago Press, [c. 1989].
	This is an attempt to answer many unanswered questions concerning Willaert's *Chromatic "Duo"*.
LowC	Lowinsky, Edward E. "Conflicting Views on Conflicting Signatures." In *Music in the Culture of the Renaissance and Other Essays*, vol. 2, pp. 665-681. Edited and with an Introduction by Bonnie J. Blackburn. With Forewards by Howard Mayer Brown and Ellen T. Harris. Chicago: University of Chicago Press, [c. 1989] = *Journal of the American Musicological Society* 7 (1954): 181-204.
	The conflicting view is that of Richard H. Hoppin in his article "Partial Signatures and *Musica ficta* in some Early 15th Century Sources." Lowinsky questions his presentation, method, logic, and terminology.
LowCR	_____. "Cipriano de Rore's Venus Motet: Its Poetic and Pictorial Sources. " In *Music in the Culture of the Renaissance and Other Essays*, vol. 2, pp. 575-595. Edited by Bonnie J. Blackburn. With Forewards by Howard Mayer Brown and Ellen T. Harris. Chicago: University of Chicago Press, [c. 1989]. = *Journal of the American Musicological Society* 7 (1954): 181-204.
	This essay is a discussion of the text of Rore's motet along with a discussion of the paintings in Ferrara that may have been the inspiration for the NeoLatin poem.
LowE	_____. "English Organ Music of the Renaissance." In *Music in the Culture of the Renaissance and Other Essays*, vol. 2, pp. 841- 867. Edited by Bonnie J. Blackburn. With Forewards by Howard Mayer Brown and Ellen T. Harris. Chicago: University of Chicago Press, [c. 1989].
	The repertory begins with early Tudor composers such as Allwood, Taverner, Farrant, and Shelby and continues with later ones, such as Munday, Heath, Tye, and Whyte. There are eighteen compositions by Tallis, eight by Sheppard, and thirty-five by Redford. This is the main source of Redford's compositions. .

LowF	Lowinsky, Edward E. "The Function of Conflicting Signatures in Early Polyphonic Music." *Musical Quarterly* 31 (1945): 227-260 = *Music in the Culture of the Renaissance and Other Essays*, vol. 2, pp. 647-665. Edited and with an Introduction by Bonnie J. Blackburn. With Forewords by Howard Mayer Brown and Ellen T. Harris. Chicago: University of Chicago Press, [c. 1989].
	A discussion of several theories concerning conflicting signatures offered by different musicologists. This discussion is followed by Lowinsky's theory on the subject.
LowH	_____. "Humanism in the Music of the Renaissance." In *Medieval and Renaissance Studies*, edited by Frank Tirro, pp. 87-220. Durham, North Carolina: 1982 = *Music in the Culture of the Renaissance and Other Essays*, vol. 2, pp. 154-221. Edited and with an Introduction by Bonnie J. Blackburn. With Forewords by Howard Mayer Brown and Ellen T. Harris. Chicago: University of Chicago Press, [c. 1989].
	Lowinsky presents a different view from the usual one that has considered the humanist movement as hardly touching music and, at any rate, not seriously affecting its evolution.
LowMA	_____. "The Musical Avant-Garde of the Renaissance; or, the Peril and Profit of Foresight." In *Music in the Culture of the Renaissance and Other Essays*, vol. 2, pp. 730-754. Edited and with an Introduction by Bonnie J. Blackburn with Forewords by Howard Mayer Brown and Ellen T. Harris. Chicago: The University of Chicago Press, [c. 1989].
	This is a sketch of the evolution of avant-gardism in the music of the Renaissance through the music of Josquin, Willaert, Greiter, Clemens non Papa, Nicola Vicentino, Cipriano de Rore, Orlando di Lasso and others. Lowinsky shows how avant-garde music acquired its impetus and inspiration from classical antiquity and gradually became synonymous with music set to texts written in the native tongue of the composer and audience.
LowMG	_____. "Matthaeus Greiter's *Fortuna*: An Experiment in Chromaticism and in Musical Iconography." In *Music in the Culture of the Renaissance and Other Essays*, vol. 1, pp. 240-262. Edited by Bonnie J. Blackburn. With Forewords by Howard Mayer Brown and Ellen T. Harris. Chicago: The University of Chicago Press, [c. 1989].
	This source contains a discussion of a canon, *Omnia facit Fortuna in omnibus*, by Matthaeus Greiter. It is a chromatic piece involving D♭, G♭, C♭, F♭, and B♭♭. Lowinsky states that Greiter has joined Listenius as a German theorist who has enlarged the concept of *musica ficta* into that of a logical modulation in the circle of fifths.
LowMR	_____. "Music of the Renaissance as Viewed by Renaissance Musicians." In *Music in the Culture of the Renaissance and Other Essays*, pp. 87-106. Edited by Bonnie J. Blackburn. With Forewords by Howard Mayer Brown and Ellen T. Harris. Chicago: the University of Chicago Press, [c. 1989].
	This is a paper read at the Fourth Annual Conference on the Humanities sponsored by the Graduate School of Ohio State University on the 27th to the 28th of October in 1961. It is a discussion on the conception that the man of the Renaissance had of himself and his civilization, and, in particular, the views of the musicians writing in the fifteenth and sixteenth centuries.

LowN — Lowinsky, Edward E. "A Newly Discovered Sixteenth-Century Motet Manuscript at the Biblioteca Vallicelliana in Rome." *Journal of the American Musicological Society* 3 (1950): 173-224 = *Music in the Culture of the Renaissance and Other Essays,* vol. 2, pp. 433-483. Edited by Bonnie J. Blackburn. With Forewords by Howard Mayer Brown and Ellen T. Harris. Chicago: The University of Chicago Press, [c. 1989].

This is a description of the manuscript, its history and contents. There are six volumes containing a repertory of ninety motets for five and six voices. There are twenty-one by Verdelot, fifteen by Willaert, seven by Jaquet (Jachet of Mantua), six by Archadelt, six by Lirythier (Lherithier), six by Josquin, five by Constanzo Festa, three by Lupus, three by Consilium, two by Andrea de Silva, and one each by Corteccia, Lafage, Richafort, and Gombert. Appendix I contains the texts of the historical motets; Appendix II is a Catalog; and Appendix III is a Thematic Catalog of Unica.

LowON — _____. "On the Use of Scores by Sixteenth-Century Musicians." In *Music in the Culture of the Renaissance and Other Essays,* pp. 797-803. Edited and with an Introduction by Bonnie Blackburn. With Forwards by Howard Mayer Brown and Ellen T. Harris. Chicago: The University of Chicago Press, [c. 1989] = *Journal of the American Musicological Society* 1 (1948): 17-23.

This paper deals with the earliest theoretical reference to the practice of writing in score. It also covers the emergence of the score in the sixteenth century and the function of the score in the musical composition of that time.

LowR — _____. "Renaissance Writings on Music Theory." In *Music in the Culture of the Renaissance and Other Essays*, vol.2, pp. 797-803. Edited and with an Introduction by Bonnie J. Blackburn. With Forewords by Howard Mayer Brown and Ellen T. Harris. Chicago: The University of Chicago Press, [c. 1989].

Lowinsky states that he wishes to deal with writings on music by Renaissance theorists in order to confront the need for an international discussion of standards, procedures, and methods of editorial problems.

LowS — _____. *Secret Chromatic Art in the Netherlands*. Translated from the German by Carl Buchman. Columbia University Studies in Musicology, 6. New York: Russell and Russell, [c. 1946]; reprint 1967.

This is an attempt to answer the two questions, "What is the technique and the meaning of secret chromatic art?" and "What are the reasons for the secrecy employed?"

LowSC — _____. "Secret Chromatic Art Reexamined." In *Music in the Culture of the Renaissance and Other Essays*, vol. 2, pp. 754-779. Edited and with an Introduction by Bonnie J. Blackburn. With Forewords by Howard Mayer Brown and Ellen T. Harris. Chicago: The University of Chicago Press, [c. 1989].

This is a reexamination of the theory of the secret chromatic art and its criticism in the light of the new evidence accumulated.

LowT — _____. *Tonality and atonality in sixteenth-century music*. With a forward by Igor Stravinsky. Berkeley: University of California Press, 1961.

Lowinsky attempts to define tonality and atonality from the standpoint of the theorist who thinks in terms of fixed conceptual entities and the historian who regards them as living things with embryonic beginnings. He examines these two strands in the texture of musical thought and practice of the sixteenth century. He uses the repertories which do not fit the traditional system of the eight modes.

LucH III Lucki, Emil. *History of the Renaissance, 1350-1550.* Vol. 3: *Education, Learning, and Thought.* Salt Lake City, Utah: University of Utah Press, 1963-1965.

This is an attempt to investigate the claim that after many centuries of darkness, culture was finally reborn. Also to investigate what Renaissance culture was like, to what extent it was new, and to what extent it developed out of Medieval culture.

LucH IV _____. *History of the Renaissance, 1350-1550.* Vol. 4: *Literature and Art.* Salt Lake City, Utah: University of Utah Press, 1963-1965.

This book is divided into two parts with each part beginning with an examination of the nature of the works prevailing on the eve of the Renaissance. This is followed by a survey of the developments in each field.

LucH V _____. *History of the Renaissance, 1350-1550.* Vol. 5: *Politics and political theory.* Salt Lake City, Utah: University of Utah Press, 1963-1965.

This is an attempt to give a wider coverage to the politics and political theory of the period than has hitherto been given, and to place a different emphasis on the subject.

LudC I Ludford, Nicholas. *Collected Works.* Vol. 1: *Seven Lady-Masses.* Edited by John D. Bergsagel. Corpus mensurabilis musicae no. 27. Rome: American Institute of Musicology, 1963.

This source contains transcriptions of the seven Lady-Masses.

LudC II _____. *Collected Works.* Vol. 2: *Festal Masses and Magnificat.* Edited by John D. Bergsagel. Corpus mensurabilis musicae no. 27. Neuhausen-Stuttgart: American Institute of Musicology: Hanssler-Verlag, 1967.

This source contains transcriptions of Ludford's Festal Masses and the six-voice Magnificat, *Benedicta*.

LudD _____. *Domine Jesu Christe, Ave cujus conceptio.* Edited by Nick Sandon. Devon, England: Antico Edition, 1993.

This is a transcription of the treble, mean, contratenor, tenor and bass of the antiphons. The tenor part was completed by the editor. The transcription is based on the partbooks, Peterhouse *MSS 471-474*. There are Latin words with English translations printed as texts.

LudMA _____. *[7 Masses]. 1525. Manuscript.* Original in the British Library. British Library: Manuscript, *Royal appendix 45-48*. London: British Library, [1955]. Microfilm.

This is a facsimile of the original manuscript found in the British Library.

LudMM _____. *Masses for each day of the week.* Music manuscripts, no. 98. Ann Arbor, Mich.: University Microfilms, [1976]. Microfilm.

This is a facsimile of the original manuscript.

LudMS _____. *[Masses for each day of the week].* 1530. London: British Museum Photographic Service, [1986?]. Microfilm.

This is a facsimile of the original manuscript.

LuiA Luisi, Francesco, ed. *Apografo miscellaneo marciano: frottole, canzoni e madrigali con alcuni alla pavana in villanesco...* Edizioni Fondazione Levi; Serie 1: Musica rinascimentale; A: Edizione integrale del corpus delle frot-

tole; 1: Fonti manoscritto. Venezia: Fondazione Levi, 1979.
This contains Italian part-songs, *frottole*, and madrigals for four voices with Italian words. The words are also printed as texts. This is edited from a manuscript in the Biblioteca nazionale marciana. There is a bibliography.

LuoR Luoma, Robert G. "Relationship between Music and Poetry." *Musica disciplina* 31 (1977): 135-154.
This study was prompted by Berhard Meier's brief description of Cipriano de Rore's madrigal, "Quando signor lasciaste". The editor of Rore's, *Collected Works* points out the composers remarkable coordination of mode with meaning. Luoma investigates the effects of the words on the texture, melody, and mode of Rore's work.

LutD Luther, Martin. *Deudsche Messe und Ordnung Gottis Diensts*. Wittemberg: [Michael Lotther], 1526. German books before 1601; roll 8, item 1.1. Cambridge, Mass.: General Microfilm Co., [19--]. Microfilm.
This is a facsimile of Luther's German Mass. It contains the text of the Lutheran liturgy and music. This material is also found in the first edition of *Luther's Werke, Kritische Gesammtausg.* (Weimer, 1883-) vol. 19 (189) p. 60.

LutDM _____. *D. Martin Luther's Werke: Kritische Gesamtausgabe*. Weimer: H. Bohlau: H. Bohlaus Nachfolger, 1883.
The imprint varies. The later volumes were published by H. Bohlaus Nachfolger. The subseries *Tischreden; Die deutsche Bibel; and Briefwechsel* are numbered separately and catalogued separately. The *Revisionsnachtrage* are also catalogued separately. Bibliographical references are included.

LutF _____. *Formula missae et communionis pro ecclesia Vuittembergensi*. [Strasbourg: Wolfgang Kopfel, 1523. Flugschriften des frühen 16. Jahrhunderts; Fiche 1787, Nr. 4591. Zug, Switzerland: Inter Documentation Co., 1987. Microfiche.
This is a facsimile of Luther's Latin Mass. It is indexed in VD 16 L 4727; Benzing (Luther) 1699; and Benzing (Strasbourg) 1160.

LutG _____. *Geystliche Lieder: mit einer newen vorrhede*, 1545. Documenta musicologica. Reihe I: Druckschriften-Faksimiles, no. 38. Leipzig: V. Babst, Bärenreiter-Verlag, 1966. Reprint ed., 1988.
This contains German hymns and Psalms by Luther and others with the melodies. There is a Preface by Martin Luther and an Introduction by Konrad Ameln with bibliographical references. The words are principally in German with some in Latin.

LutH _____. *The Hymns of Martin Luther*. Edited by Leonard Woolsey Bacon and Nathan H. Allen. New York: Charles Scribner's Sons, 1883.
This book contains the original German hymns with English translations. Also, it contains the tunes that were set to the hymns of Luther during his lifetime. The four-part arrangements of the tunes are those of the older masters such as H. Shein, M. Praetorius, and J. S. Bach.

LutT _____. *Three Treatises*. Philadelphia, Pa.: The Muhlenberg Press, [c. 1943]; reprint ed., 1947.
This book contains translations of the three treatises, *An Open Letter to the Christian Nobility of the German Nation..., A Prelude on the Babylonian Captivity of the Church,* and *A treatise on Christian Liberty*. The translations are by C. M. Jacobs, A. T. W. Steinhaeuser, and W. A. Lambert, re-

spectively. These were reprinted from the Philadelphia (Holman) edition of the *Works of Martin Luther* with minor revisions. All three treatises were written in 1520. There are introductions to the treatises by Jacobs, Steinhaeuser, and Lambert.

MadT　*Madrigali a tre et arie napolitane*. [n.p., 1537.] [Wolfenbüttel: Herzog-August-Bibliothek, n.d.]. Microfilm.
This source contains madrigals by Jacob Arcadelt and Costanzo Festa as well as ten *canzone villanesca*. There are only two partbooks, the *cantus* and tenor. The original is at Wolfenbütel in the Herzog-August-Bibliothek. It is indexed in RISM B/1, [1537]-08.

MajT　"Major theatrical styles, and forms." *Britannica 2001 Deluxe edition CD-ROM*. Copyright 1994-2000 Britannica.com Inc. October 3, 2001.
This is a discussion of the early sixteenth-century theater and Ariosto and Ruzante.

MalTP　Maldeghem, R. J. van, ed. and transc. *Trésor musical. collection authentique de musique sacrée & profane des anciens maîtres belges*. Ser. II: Musique Profane, 29 vols. Bruxelles: C. Marquardt, 1865-1893. Washington: Library of Congress. Microfilm.
This contains transcriptions of secular music for three to ten voices. It has the Latin of French words. There are parts for practical performance included in volume twenty-nine of each series. For an annotated index see "Maldeghem and his buried treasure: a bibliographical study" by Gustave Reese, in *Music Library Association Notes*, December 1928, 2nd series, vol. 6, no. 1, p. 75-117.

MalTR　_____, ed. and transc. *Trésor musical. collection authentique de musique sacrée & profane des anciens maîtres belges*. Ser. I: Musique religieuse, 29 vols. Bruxelles: C. Marquardt, 1865-1893. Washington: Library of Congress. Microfilm.
This contains transcriptions of sacred music for three to ten voices. It has the Latin of French words. There are parts for practical performance included in volume twenty-nine of each series. For an annotated index see "Maldeghem and his buried treasure: a bibliographical study" by Gustave Reese, in *Music Library Association Notes*, December 1928, 2nd series, vol. 6, no. 1, p. 75-117.

ManI　Maniates, Maria Rika. *Mannerism in Italian Music and Culture, 1530-1630*. Chapel Hill: University of North Carolina Press, [c. 1979].
This is an attempt to prove the viability of Mannerism as an historic-stylistic concept that arises out of musical patterns evident in the practice of and thought about music between the years of 1530 to 1630.

ManM　Manchicourt, Pierre de. *Opera omnia*. Corpus mensurabilis musicae, no. 55. [S.I.]: American Institute of Musicology, 1971.
This contains transcriptions of motets and Masses. There are six volumes: Vol. 1. Attaingnant motets, Vols. 2-5. The Masses, Vol. 6. Motets from various sources. Volumes 2-6 are edited by Lavern J. Wagner. An introduction in English includes bibliographical references.

ManMP　_____. *Motets by Pierre Manchicourt edited and transcribed by J. D. Wicks*. Cambridge, MA: Harvard College Library, [1959]. Microfilm.
This contains transcriptions of motet selections by Manchicourt. The original manuscript is in the possession of John Doane Wicks.

74   Bibliography

ManMV   Manchicourt, Pierre de. *Motets from various sources.* Edited by Lavern J. Wagner. *Opera omnia:* Pierre de Manchicourt, no. 6. Corpus mensurablilis musicae, no. 55.
[S.l.]: Neuhauser-Stuttgart: American Institute of Musicology, 1984.
This contains transcriptions of motets with Latin words. There is a preface in English by Lavern J. Wagner.

ManL   _____. *Liber decimus quartus: XIX. musicas cantiones continet.* Paris: Attaingnant, 1539. [Wien: Österreichische Nationalbibliothek, n.d.] Microfilm.
This source contains nineteen four-part motets by Manchicourt. It is a facsimile of the original in Österrichische Nationalbibliothek, Wien (A Wn). It is indexed in RISM A/I, M 0269 and Heartz catalog, no. 85.

ManLD   _____. *Liber decimus quartus: XIX. musicas cantiones continet.* Paris: Attaingnant, 1539. [Paris: Bibliotheque Nationale, 1976.] Microfilm.
There are nineteen motets written for four parts. The original is in Ancienne Bibliothèque du Chapitre, Noyon.

ManN   _____. *Le neufiesme livre des chansons à quatre parties, auquel sont contenues vingt et neuf chansons nouvelles, convenables tant à la voix comme aux instrumentz...* Anvers: Susato, 1545. Wien: Österreichische Nationalbibliothek, n.d. Microfilm.
A microfilm of the ninth book of *chansons* published by Susato. It contains twenty-nine *chansons* composed by Pierre de Manchicourt.

ManT   _____. *Twenty-nine Chansons.* Edited by Margery Anthea Baird. Recent Researches in the Music of the Renaissance, no. 11. Madison: A R Editions, Inc., [c. 1972].
There is a Preface containing notes about Manchicourt and a discussion of the music. There are French texts, Notes on Performance and Pronunciation, and a Critical Commentary. The source of the *chansons* is *Neufiesme livre des chansons a quatre parties* published by Tylman Susato at Antwerp in 1545. These are transcriptions.

MarC   Marot, Clément. *Cinquante pseaumes de David: mis en françoys selon la vérité hébraïque.* Edited by Gérard Defaux. Textes de la Renaissance, no. 1. Paris: H. Champion, 1995.
This is an edited edition of the text of the original publication in 1543 at Geneva by Jean Gérard. It contains an introduction, variable readings on the text and notes by Gérard Defaux.

MarFV I   Marshall, Lowen H. "The Motets-A Critical Study". In *The Four-voice Motets of Thomas Crequillon. ?Collected Works.* Institute of Mediaeval Music, no. 21. Brooklyn, N. Y., Institute of Mediaeval Music *1970-
This book contains literature about Crécquillon, a discussion of the manuscripts containing his music, a discussion of the problems of attribution, the texts of the motets in Latin and English, and aspects of his musical style.

MarFV II   _____ "The Motets of the *Opus sacraum cantionum*". In *Four-voice Motets of Thomas Crequillon. ?Collected Works.* Institute of Mediaeval Music, no. 21. Brooklyn, N. Y., Institute of Mediaeval Music *1970-
This volume contains transcriptions of seventeen compositions and eleven *Secunda partes.*

MarFV III   _____. "The Motets from the Miscellaneous Printed Editions". In *Four-voice Motets of Thomas Crequillon. ?Collected Works.* Institute of Mediaeval

	Music, no. 21. Brooklyn, N. Y., Institute of Mediaeval Music *1970-
	This volume contains transcriptions of nineteen compositions and nine *secunda partes.*
MarFV IV	Marshall, Lowen H. The Motets found only in Manuscript. In *Four-voice Motets of Thomas Crequillon. ?Collected Works.* Institute of Mediaeval Music, no. 21. Brooklyn, N. Y., Institute of Mediaeval Music *1970-
	This volume contains transcriptions of ten compositions and seven *secunda partes.*
MarMI	Marcuse, Sibyl. *Musical Instruments*: A Comprehensive Dictionary. New York: W. W. Norton and Co., Inc., [c. 1975].
	This is an encyclopedic guide to musical instruments the world over. It tells when, how, and by whom the instruments have been used. It covers a period from pre-history to the electronic instruments of today.
MasA	Mason, Wilton. "The Architecture of St. Mark's Cathedral and the Venetian Polychoral Style: a Clarification." In *Studies in Musicology: Essays in the History, Style, and Bibliography of Music in Memory of Glen Haydon*, p. 163-179. Ed. by James W. Pruett. Chapel Hill: University of North Carolina Press, [c. 1969].
	Wilton Mason cites studies that support the fact that the relationship between the architecture of St. Mark's Cathedral and the music composed there has been called into question as early as 1929. He attempts to clarify the confusion over the contribution the architectural characteristics of St. Mark's made to the formation of the *cori spezzati* technique.
MasB	*Masses.* Brussels/Mechlin: s.n., ?1530 1531. [Netherlands: Diazo duplikaat, 1997.]
	This source contains eight masses and 1 motet. There are works by Pierre de la Rue (1), P. de la Rue or Josquin (1), P. Moulu (2), J. Richafort (1), and three anonymous works. It was copied by Netherlands court scribe Petrus Alamire. It is listed in Census-Catalogue of manuscript sources of polyphonic music, 1400-1550.
MatG	Mattfeld, Victor H. *Georg Rhaw's Publications for Vespers.* Musicological studies, no. 11. Brooklyn: Institute of Mediaeval Music, Ltd., [c. 1966].
	This is a discussion of the musical liturgical situation in the Protestant church in the early Reformation period, from 1517 to ca. 1550.
MatH	_____. "Haiden" (1) "Sebald Heyden". In The New Grove Dictionary of Music and Musicians. Edited by Stanley Sadie. 20 vols. 6th ed. London: Macmillan Publishers, Ltd., [c. 1980].
	This is a short biography of Sebald Heyden.
McGM	McGee, Timothy J. *Medieval and Renaissance Music: a Performers Guide.* Toronto: University of Toronto Press, [c. 1985].
	This book was written for those who wish to perform early music written before 1600. Chant is not included. The object is to present information that will assist the performer to present historically accurate performances of the early repertory.
McKF	McKinley, Ann Watson. "Francesco Corteccia's Music to Latin Texts." Master's thesis, University of Michigan, 1962. 2 vols. Ann Arbor, Mich.: University Microfilms, 1974. Xerographic copy of typescript.
	Volume two consists of "a representative collection of compositions... four hymns, six responses, a setting of the Canticle of Zachary, and seven mo-

	tets." A bibliography is included.
MeiD	Meissner, Ute. *Der Antwerpener Notendrucker Tylman Susato...* Berliner Studien zur Musikwissenschaft, Bd. 11. Berlin: Merseburger, 1967. This was issued as a thesis. Music is included. There are two volumes. Vol. 1: Bibliographische Studie und Anhang and Literaturverzeichnis. Vol. 2: Bibliographie. The thesis includes French part-songs--Bibliography, Flemish part-songs--Bibliography, and Sacred part-songs--Bibliography.
MenP-I	Mendel, Arthur. "Pitch in the 16th and Early 17th Centuries." In *Studies in the History of Musical Pitch: Monographs by Alexander J. Ellis and Arthur Mendel*, pp. 88-105. Amsterdam: Frits Knuf, 1968 Part I is basically a discussion of *Spiegel der Orgelmacher und Organisten* by Schlick.
MenP-II	_____. "Pitch in the 16th and Early 17th Centuries." In *Studies in the History of Musical Pitch: Monographs by Alexander J. Ellis and Arthur Mendel*, pp. 106-128. Amsterdam: Frits Knuf, 1968. Part II discusses pitch as stated by Praetorius. There is a table on the compass of organ keyboards before 1620. Also a table of pitches described by Schlick and Praetorius.
MenP-III	_____. "Pitch in the 16th and Early 17th Centuries." In *Studies in the History of Musical Pitch: Monographs by Alexander J. Ellis and Arthur Mendel*, pp. 124-150. Amsterdam: Frits Knuf, 1968. Part III discusses the clefs used during this period and their meaning. There are bibliographical references.
MenP-IV	_____. "Pitch in the 16th and Early 17th Centuries." In *Studies in the History of Musical Pitch: Monographs by Alexander J. Ellis and Arthur Mendel*, pp. 151-169. Amsterdam: Frits Knuf, 1968. This part of Mendel's treatises discusses Rocco Rodio's *Regole di musica* published in Naples in 1609. Also, conclusions are given as to the results of Mendel's investigation of pitch from about 1500 to 1859.
MenPW	_____. "Pitch in Western Music Since 1500: a Re-examination." *Acta musicologica* 50 (1978):1-93. Mendel writes about relativity of pitch-standards, evidence concerning absolute pitches before 1834, tuning forks, and absolute standards proposed in terms of frequencies. The article covers a period from the 16th century to the late 19th century.
MerD	Merian, Wilhelm. *Der Tanz in den deutschen tabulaturbüchern, mit thematischen Verzeichnissen...* Hildesheim, Olms; Wiesbaden: Breitkopf & Härtel, 1968. [Reprografischer Nachdruck der Ausgabe Leipzig 1927]. This contains thematic catalogs of the keyboard tablatures of J. Kotter and several other late sixteenth- and seventeenth century composers. There are also transcriptions of many complete pieces and some history and criticism up to 1800. There are bibliographical references and indexes. This book is written in English.
MerTL	Merritt, A. Tillman, ed. *Treize livres de motets parus chez Pierre Attaingnant en 1534 et 1535: Neuvìe livre.* Les Remparts, Manaco: Éditions de L'oiseu Lyre, [c. 1962]. This contains transcriptions of motets. There are motets by Gascongne-*Laetatus sum*; Lupus-*In convertenus*; Mouton-*Confitemini Domino*; and Lupus-*In te Domine, Vermont Primus, and In Domino confido* and others.

MeyC	Meyer, Ernest H. "Concerted Instrumental Music". In *The New Oxford History of Music. Vol. 4: The Age of Humanism: 1540-1630*, pp. 550-598. Edited by Gerald Abraham. London: Oxford University Press, [c. 1968]; reprint ed., 1974. This is a discussion of music for voices or instruments, purely instrumental music, dance forms, and free instrumental forms found in Italy, France, Spain, Germany, Poland, Bohemia, and England during the sixteenth and early seventeenth centuries.
MilC	*Milan, Biblioteca del Conservatorio di Musica Giuseppe Verdi, The Tarasconi Codex*. Renaissance Music in Facsimile, no. 11. New York: Garland Publishing, Inc., 1986. This codex contains 229 compositions. 214 of these compositions are Italian madrigals, 12 are French *chansons*, and three are fragments of a larger composition or they are counterpoint exercises. It contains the music of thirty-six composers of whom most were active in the second half of the sixteenth century.
MilD	Miller, Clement A. "The *Dodecachordon*: Its origins and influence on Renaissance musical thought." *Musica disciplina* 15 (1961): 156-166. This article points out the origins of the material in the *Dodecachordon* and produces evidence that the *Dodecachordon* had a profound and far-reaching effect on the musical thought of the time.
MilL	Milán, Luis. *Libro de música de vihuela de mano intitulado El maestro*. Valencia: 1535. Chicago (US Cn): Newberry Library. Reproduction: Microfilm. This source contains *vihuela* music, songs with *vihuela*, and lute music. There are fantasias, *pavanes, villancicos*, sonnets, and romances for *vihuela* in tablature notation. The words of the songs are in Spanish, Portuguese or Italian. The original manuscript is found in the Newberry Library in Chicago.
MilLM	_____. *Libro de música de vihuela de mano: intitulado El maestro*. Transcribed and edited by Leo Schrade. Publikationen älterer Musik: 2. Jahrg. Leipzig: Breitkopf & Härtel, 1979. This contains music composed by Luis Milán in its original notation as well as a transcription of it into modern notation. There are fantasias, *pavanes, villancicos*, sonnets, and romances for *vihuela*. The words of the songs are in Spanish, Portuguese or Italian. There is a composer's preface in Spanish and an editor's preface in German.
MilT	Miller, Leta E., ed. *Thirty-six Chansons by French Provincial Composers (1529-1550)*. Recent Researches in the Music of the Renaissance, no. 38. Madison: A R Editions, Inc., [c. 1981]. These are transcriptions. The Preface includes a discussion of the composers and the style of the music. There are critical notes, a chronological index of *chansons*, and the French texts with translations.
ModC	Moderne, Jacques. *Le Parangon des chansons. Cinquiesme livre: 1539?* Originally published by Jacques Moderne. Transcribed by Albert Seay. Transcriptions, no. 5. Colorado Springs: Colorado College Music Press, 1980. This is the fifth book of the *Parangon* series. It is edited from the copy published by Moderne in the British Museum, London. In general, the contents resemble those of a typical Attaingnant collection. At the end of the

volume there is an Italian work. There is an introduction, and a bibliography. Many of the composers are from Lyons. There are *chansons* by Layolle, Clereau, Jannequin, Sandrin, Heurteur, Certon, and others.

ModCM   Moderne, Jacques. *Christophori Morales Hyspalensis missarum Liber primus.* [Lyons: Jacques Moderne, 1546. Coimbra: Biblioteca Universidad, 1975. Microfilm.

This source contains eight Masses for four to six voices. The original manuscript is in the Biblioteca Universidad in Coimbra.

ModCMH   _____. *Christophori Morales Hyspalensis missarum Liber secundus.* Lyons: Jacques Moderne, 1551. [Rochester N. Y.: Sibley Music Library, 1992.]. Microfilm.

This source contains eight Masses for four to five voices

ModD   _____. *Le difficile des chansons: Second livre contenant xxvi chansons nouvelles à quatre parties en quatre livres...* Lyon: Moderne, 1544. [Augsburg: Staats- und Stadtbibliothek, n.d.]. Microfilm.

This contains the tenor, *superius,* and *altus* of *chansons* by Flecha, Dambert, Maillard, H. Fresneau, Loys-Henry, Janequin, P. de la Farge, Leo. la Saigne, Du Metz, Bonvoisin, and Gentian. The original of the tenor and *superius* is in Staats- und Stadtbibliothek in Augsburg and the original of the *altus* is in Bibliothèque Nationale in Paris. It is indexed in RISM B/1, 1544-09 and Pogue, S.F., no. 40.

ModDD   _____. *Le difficile des chansons: Premier livre contenant xxii chansons nouvelles à quatre parties en quatre livres.* Lyon: Moderne, 1540. [Paris: Bibliothèque Nationale, n.d.]. Microfilm.

This contains the *altus* only of *chansons* by Janequin. The original is in Bibliothèque Nationale in Paris. It is indexed in Pogue, S.F., no. 27.

ModF   _____. *Four-voice motets from the Motteti del fiore series.* Edited by Richard Sherr. The Moderne motet anthologies; Sixteenth-century motet, no. 9-10. New York: Garland, 1998-1999.

These two volumes contain transcriptions of the four-voice motets found in the four books of the four-voice series. They are edited from anthologies collected and originally published by Jacques Moderne. There is a Preface and critical notes in English. Bibliographical references are included.

ModFI   _____. *Five-and more-voice motets from the Motteti del fiore series.* Edited by Richard Sherr. The Moderne motet anthologies; Sixteenth-century motet, no. 11-12. New York: Garland, 1999-2000.

These two volumes contain transcriptions of the five- and six-voice motets found in the four books of the five- and six-voice series. They are edited from anthologies collected and originally published by Jacques Moderne. This also contains *Harmonidos Ariston, Tricolon, Ogdoameron* published by Moderne at Lyon in 1547. There is a Preface and critical notes in English. Bibliographical references are included.

ModL   _____. *Liber decem missarum a praeclaris musicis contextus...* Lugduni: Modernus, 1532. Bologna: Bblioteca Musicale, n.d. Microfilm.

This is a choirbook containing Masses and motets by P. Moulu, F. de Layolle, Richafort, Ia. Mouton, Guillaume Preuost, Gardanne, Lupus, Ianecquin, Io. Sarton. Two of these [ten] Masses and the three motets are by Francesco de Layolle. The original is in the Bologna: Biblioteca Musicale, *(I Bc), R. 139.* It is indexed in Pogue, S. F., no. 3.

Bibliography 79

ModLD   Moderne, Jacques. *Liber decem missarum a praeclaris et maximi nominis musicis contextus... Lugduni: Modernus*, 1540. Vienna: Nationalbibliothek, n.d. Microfilm.
This choirbook contains Masses and motets by P. Moulu, F. de Layolle, Richafort, Ia. Mouton, Guillaume Preuost, Gardanne, Lupus, Ianecquin, and Io. Sarton (erroneously identified as Io. Certon.) Two of these [ten] Masses and the three motets are by Francesco de Layolle. The Masses and motets are the same as the 1532 edition except two more Masses are appended, one by P. de Villiers and one by Francesco de Layolle. The original is in the Vienna: Nationalbibliothek, (A Wn).It is indexed in Pogue, S. F., No. 22.

ModM   _____. *Mariae cantica vulgo magnificat dicta; psalmata octo tetraphona.* Lugduni: Modernum, 1550. [London: British Museum, n.d.]. Microfilm.
This is a facsimile of Magnificats for four voices by Morales, Jacquet, and Richafort. The original manuscript is in the British Museum in London (GB Lbm.) *K.9.a.10*. This is indexed in RISM B/I, 1550-4; RISM, A/I, M 3595; and Pogue, S. F., no. 54.

ModP   _____. *Primus liber cum quatuor vocibus: motetti del fiore*. Lugduni: Modernum, 1532. [Vienna: Österreiche Nationalbibliothek, n.d.]. Microfilm.
This source contains thirty-three motets by Courtois (2); Gombert (3); Layolle (3); L'Héritier (2); Lupus (4); Piéton (2); Richafort (4); along with De Silva, Sermisy, Verdelot, Willaert, and others.

ModP I   _____. *Le Parangon des chansons: premier livre: Lyons, 1538; and Le Parangon des chansons: second livre contenant xxxi chansons...: Lyons, 1540*. Edited by Jane A. Bernstein. Sixteenth-Century *chanson*, no. 24. New York: Garland, 1992.
This volume contains book one and book two of *Les Parangon*. The first book contains transcriptions of twenty-seven pieces. Two pieces by Layolle are Italian madrigals. The second book has transcriptions of thirty-one *chansons*. The composers are Sandrin, Layolle, Gombert, Claudin, Certon, Passereau, Richafort, Jannequin, and others. There is a general introduction, Editorial methods, and an introduction to this volume containing information about Moderne and the series. There is a list of sources, a table of original clefs, and notes.

ModP II   _____. *Le Parangon des chansons: tiers livre contenant xxvi chansons...: Lyons, 1538; and Le Parangon des chansons: quart livre con tenant xxii chansons à deux et à troys parties: Lyons, 1539*. Edited by Jane A. Bernstein. Sixteenth-century *chanson*, no. 25. New York: Garland, 1993.
This volume contains book three and book four of *Les Parangon*. The composers in these volumes are Claudin, Certon, Jannequin, Layolle, Passereau, Gardane, Heurteur, and others. There are transcriptions of twenty-six *chansons* in the third volume and thirty-two in the fourth. Book III has *chansons* for four voices and contains La Fricasée by Henry Fresneau. This is a quadlibet containing fragments from one-hundred different *chansons*. Book IV contains *chansons* for two and three voices. There is a general introduction, Editorial methods, and an introduction to this volume containing information about Moderne and the series. There is a list of sources, a table of original clefs, and notes.

ModP III   _____. *Le Parangon des chansons: cinquiesme livre contenant xxviii chan-*

sons...: *Lyons, 1539; and Le Parangon des chansons: sixiesme livre contenant xxv chansons nouvelles..: Lyons, 1540.* Edited by Jane A. Bernstein. The Sixteenth-century *chanson*, no. 26. New York: Garland, 1993.

This volume contains book five and book six of *Le Parangon*. There are twenty-eight *chansons* in the fifth volume and twenty-five *chansons* in the sixth. The composers are Layolle, Cléreau, Jennequin, Sandrin, Heurteur, and Certon. Book VI has an extended *chanson spirituelle*. There is a general introduction, Editorial methods, and an introduction to this volume containing information about Moderne and the series. There is a list of sources, a table of original clefs, and notes.

ModP IV Moderne, Jacques. *Le Parangon des chansons: septiesme livre contenant xxvii chansons...: Lyons, 1540; and Le Parangon des chansons: huytiesme livre contenant xxx chansons...: Lyons, 1541.* Edited by Jane A. Bernstein. The Sixteenth-century *chanson*, no. 27. New York: Garland, 1993.

This volume contains book seven and book eight of *Les Parangon*. There are twenty-seven *chansons* in the seventh volume and thirty *chansons* in the eighth. All have French texts except the two Latin graces found in the eighth volume. There is a general introduction, Editorial methods, and an introduction to this volume containing information about Moderne and the series. There is a list of sources, a table of original clefs, and notes.

ModP V _____. *Le Parangon des chansons: neufuiesme livre contenant xxxi chansons...: Lyons, 1541; and Le Parangon des chansons: dixiesme livre contenant xxx chanson...:Lyons, 1543.* Edited by Jane A. Bernstein. The Sixteenth-century *chanson*, no. 28. New York: Garland, 1993.

This volume contains book nine and book ten of *Les Parangon*. There are thirty-one *chansons* in the ninth volume and thirty *chansons* in the tenth. All of the compositions in both volumes have French texts except one in volume ten. It contains an interpolated version of a Latin fragment from the Lamentations of Jeremiah. There is a general introduction, Editorial methods, and an introduction to this volume containing information about Moderne and the series. There is a list of sources, a table of original clefs, and notes.

ModPC _____. *Le parangon des chansons & délectables chansons que oncques ne furent imprimées au singulier prouffit & délectation des musiciens.* Lyon: J. Moderne, 1538-1548. München: Bayerische Staatsbibliothek, 1955. Microfilm.

This source contains facsimiles of the ten books of *chansons* published by Moderne under the title, *Le parangon des chansons*. The original is in Munich: Bayerische Staatsbibliothek. The ten books have been reproduced from copies at the University of Chicago. The title is taken from the first book.

ModQ _____. *Le Parangon des chansons: quart livre (1538).* Originally compiled by Jacques Moderne. Transcribed by Albert Seay. Transcriptions, no. 6. Colorado Springs: Colorado College Music Press, 1981.

This source contains thirty-two *chansons* for two and three voices. There is an introduction and a bibliography.

ModQL _____. *Quartus liber cum quatuor vocibus: motetti del fiore.* [Luguduni: Modernum, 1539. Munich: [Bayerische Staatsbibliothek, n.d.]. Microfilm.

This contains four voice motets by P. Colin, P. de la Farge, Robert Naich,

Lupus, G. Coste, Claudin, Morales, and others. It is indexed in RISM B/I, 1539-11 and Pogue, S. F., no. 18.

ModQLM　Moderne, Jacques. *Quartus liber mottetorum ad quinque et sex voces*. Lugduni: Modernum, 1539. [Munich: Bayerische Staatsbibliothek, n.d.]. Microfilm.

This is a facsimile of four partbooks containing motets for five and six voices. There is a preponderance of antiphons and a number of psalms and responsories. The composers are F.de Layolle, P. Manchicourt, Io. du Billon, Jaquet, N. Gombert, M. Ihean, Ia. Buus, N. Fouchier, Gardane, Gosse, Lheritier, Archadelt, Io. du Moulin, and Lupi. The original is in the Bayerische Staatsbibliothek in Munich. It is indexed in RISM B/I, 1539-5 and Pogue, S. F., no. 19.

ModQM　_____. Quintus liber mottetorum ad quinque et sex et septum vocum. Lugduni: Modernum, 1542. [Munich: Bayerische Staatsbibliothek, n.d.]. Microfilm.

This source contains mainly liturgical pieces. The older generation is represented by one motet attributed to Gombert, one to Benedictus, and three to Jaquet. The latter three had already appeared in Moderne's fourth book with an attribution to Gombert. The original is in the Bayerische Staatsbibliothek in Munich. It is indexed in Pogue, S. F., no. 35.

ModS　_____. *Secundus liber cum quatuor vocibus: motetti del fiore*. Lugduni: Modernum, 1532. [Munich: Bayerische Staatsbibliothek, n.d.]. Microfilm.

This source is a facsimile of the partbooks containing motets by N. Gombert, Archadelt, P. de Manchicourt, Gosse, Loyset Pieton, Lupus, Verdelot, F. de Layolle, Io. Lupi, Dambert, Benedictus, P.de Villiers, I. du Molin, N. Poignier, and Adrianus Villart. There are psalms, antiphons, responsories, and three motets related to the burial service. It contains the first published works by Arcadelt and Manchicourt.

ModSL　_____. *Secundus liber cum quinque vocibus*. Lugduni: Modernum, 1532. [Munich: Bayerische Staatsbibliothek, n.d.]. Microfilm.

This source contains motets for five voices. Some of the composers are Richafort (4); Willaert, L'Héritier, and Gombert, (3) each; Courtois, Jacquet, and Verdelot (2) each; Lupus, La Fage, and Moulu (1) each. Also Andreas de Silva is represented. The original manuscript is in the Bayerische Bibliothek in Munich. It is indexed in RISM B/I, 1532-9 and Pogue, S. F., no. 6.

ModT　_____. *Tertius liber cum quatuor vocibus; motetti del fiore*. [Lugduni: Modernum, 1939. [Munich: Bayerische Staatsbibliothek, n.d.]. Microfilm.

This source contains motets by F. de Layolle, A. Villart, Archadelt, Jaquet, Lupus, A. Mornable, Lheritier, N. fouchier, Benedictus, Hotinet Bara, P. Manchicourt, Pieton, Hugier, Io. du Billon, Carette, Gardane, P. de Villiers, F. de Lys, C. Dalbi, Consilium, H. Fresneau, and N. Gombert. It is indexed in RISM B/I, 1539-10 and Pogue, S. F., no. 17.

ModTL　_____. *Tertius liber mottetorum as quinque et sex voces*. Lugduni: Moderni, 1538. [Vienna: Österreichische Nationalbibliothek, n.d.]. Microfilm.

This source contains four partbooks containing motets for five and six voices. There is music by Courtois, Lupi, Gombert, Willaert, Arcadelt, Verdelot, Guillaume le Heurteur, Costanzo Festa, Jacquet, L. Paminger, Mathias, F. de Layolle, and Benedictus. It is indexed in RISM B/I, 1538-2 and Pogue, S. F., no. 15.

ModTS "Modern Skepticism." *Britannica 2001 Deluxe Edition CD-ROM.* [c. 1994-2000]. Britannica.com Inc. May 7, 2001.
This is a discussion of Modern Skepticism that emerged in the sixteenth century.

MonO Monte, Phillipe de. *Opera /.* Edited by C. van den Borren, J. van Nuffel, and Georges van Doorslaer. Series Vetera, no. 1. [Brugis: Desclée, De Brouwer, 1927.
This source contains Masses, madrigals, and motets. The volumes are edited variously by Charles van den Boren, Jules van Nuffel, and Georges van Doorslaer. Each volume has a separate Title page in Latin. The text is chiefly Latin with some Italian and French. The Prefaces are in Dutch, French, English, and German. There are notes in Dutch and French. Volumes six to nine are autograph presentation copies from Jules van Nuffel to Guido Adler. Each volume has a separate title page in Latin. The title is from page four of the cover of volume fifteen.

MorE Morehen, John. "English Church Music." In *Music in Britain: the Sixteenth Century,* pp. 94-146. Edited by Roger Bray. The Blackwell History of Music in Britain, no. 2. Oxford: Blackwell Publishers Ltd., [c. 1995].
There is a discussion of the Liturgical reform that took place following Henry VIII's formal break with Rome in 1534 until the Hampton Court Conference of 1604. The music, sources of the music, and the composers also are discussed.

MorL Morales, Cristóbal. *Lamentationi di Morales a quatro a cinque, et sei voci.* Venetiis: Apud Franciscum Rampazetum, 1564. [n.p.]: [19--]. Microfilm.
This contains five partbooks for *cantus,* tenor, *altus, bassus,* and *quintus.* Each has a special title page.

MorMA _____. *Magnificat cum quatuor vocibus: liber primus.* Venetii: Scotum, 1542. Bologna: civico Museo Bibliografico Musicale, 1986. Microfilm.
This is a facsimile of the first publication of five of Morales' eight settings of the Magnificat (in tones 1, 2, 4, 6, 7). The cycle is completed with three settings (tones 3, 4, and 8) by Jacquet of Mantua, Richafort, and Tugdual. Three additional settings appear at the end of the volume: one by Jacquet, one by Pieton, and one anonymous in tones 8, 4, and 1 respectively. All of the pieces are written for four voices, *cantus, altus,* tenor, and *bassus.* This is indexed in RISM, M3592 and Bernstein catalog, no. 27.

MorMAG _____. "Magnificat cum quatuor vocibus liber primus." Venetiis: Scotum, 1542. Ann Arbor, MI: University Microfilms International, 1963. Photocopy.
This is a photocopy of Magnificats by Morales (5), Iachet (2), Richafort, Tugdual, and Loiset Pieton (1 each). It is indexed in Bernstein catalog, no. 27.

MorME _____. *Messe. Quaeramus cum pastoribus, a 5 voix.* Anthologies des Maîtres religieux primitifs des XV., XVI. et XVII. siècles, no. 10. Paris: Éditions Musicales de la scola Cantorum, 189-.
This is a transcription of Masses by Morales. An alternative title is *Masses, book I. Missa quaeramus cum pastoribus.*

MorML _____. *Missarum liber primus.* Rome: Valerium et Ludovicum Doricum, 1544. Munich: Bayerische Staatsbibliothek, 1976. Microfilm.
This is a facsimile of Masses by Morales. The original manuscript is in the

Bibliography 83

	Bayerische Staatsbibliothek in Munich. It is indexed in RISM A/I, M3580.
MorMO	Morales, Cristóbal. *Magnificat octo tonoroum cem quatuor vocibus: liber primus*. Venetiis: [s.l.], 1545. Naples: Biblioteca Nazionale, 1975. Microfilm.

This is a facsimile of the first publication of the complete cycle of Magnificats by Morales. The editor has separated the settings into odd and even numbered verses and presents them as a collection of sixteen *alternatim* settings, instead of a complete set in the eight tones. It is indexed in RISM A/I, M3594 and Bernstein catalog, no. 55.

MorMQ _____. *Missarum quinque cum quatuor vocibus secundus liber*. Venetiis: A. Gardane, 1544. Naples: Biblioteca Nazionale, 1975. Microfilm.

This is a facsimile of the original manuscript in the Biblioteca Nazionale in Naples. It contains *Missa Aspice Domine, Missa Vulnerasti cor meum,* and *Missa De beata virgine* by Morales; *Missa quam pulchra es* by Finot; and *Missa Ave Sanctissima* by Certon. It is indexed in RISM B/I, 1544-45.

MorO _____. *Opera omnia*. Monumentos de la música española, nos. 11, 13, 15, 17, 20-21, 24, and 34. Edited by Higini Anglès. Barcelona: Consejo Superior de Investigaciónes Cientificas, Delegación de Roma, 1952.

This contains transcriptions of Masses, Magnificats, and Motets. There are eight volumes: Vol. I: *Missarum liber primus, Roma, 1544*; Vol. II: *Motetes I-XXV*; Vol. III: *Missarum liber secundus, Roma, 1544. Primera parte*; Vol. IV: *XVI Magnificat, Venecia, 1545*; Vol. V: *Motetes XXVI-L*; Vol. VI: *Missarum liber secundus, Roama, 1544. Secunda parte*; Vol. VII: *Misas XVII-XXI*; Vol. VIII: Motetes LI-LXXV.

MorP Morlaye, Guillaume. *Psaumes de Pierre Certon réduits pour chant et luth*. 1554. There is an *Introduction historique* by François Lesure. Transcriptions and commentary are by Richard de Morcourt. Luthistes. Paris: Éditions du Centre National de la Recherche Scientifique, 1957.

There are thirteen chants with lute accompaniment in both modern notation and lute tablature. These chants were originally for four voices. Words of the chants are included.

MorR Morelli, Arnaldo. "The Role of the Organ in Performance Practices of Italian Sacred Polyphony During the Cinquecento." *Musica Disciplina* 50 [1996] p.239-270.

This is an attempt to demonstrate that in Italy, at least, the organ's main function during the Renaissance was to alternate with vocal polyphony in some passages; and to fill in at a "dead" moment during the liturgy, but not to accompany polyphony.

MosF Moser, Hans Joachim, transc.; Heitmann, Fritz. *Frühmeister der deutschen Orgelkunst*. Veröffentlichungen der staatlichen Akademie für Kirchen- und Schulmusik Berlin, no. 1. Leipzig: Breitkopf & Härtel, 1930.

This contains organ music by Konrad Brumann, Hans Bucher, Paul Hofhaimer, Heinrich Isaac, Leonhard Kleber, Hans Kotter, Othmar Nachtgall, and Fridolin Sicher. The introduction is in German, English, and French.

MotC *Motetti de la corona libro quarto*. Venetia: Petrucci, 1519. [S. I.: s.n., 1977?]. Microfilm.

This is a microfilm of the *Motetti de la corona libro quarto* published by Petrucci.. The original is in the British Museum in London. It contains works for four voices by Baoulduin, Carpentras, C. Festa, Josquin, J. Le Brung, and A. Willaert. The *superius* and *altus* are on negative film and the

MotCL   *tenore* and *bassus* are on positive film. It is indexed in RISM, ser. B., v. I:I.
Motetti de la corona libro quarto. Roma: Giunta; printed by G. G. Pasoti & V. Dorico, 1526. Jena: Universitätsbibliothek der Friedrich Schiller-Universität, n.d. Microfiche.

This is a microfiiche of the *Motetti de la corona libro quarto* published by Giunta. The original is in Universitätsbibliothek der Friedreich-Schiller-Universität in Jena. It contains works for four voices by Baoulduin, Carpentras, C. Festa, Josquin, J. Le Brung, A. Willaert and anonymous. It is indexed in RISM B/I, 1526-4

MoyM   Moyer, Ann E. *Musica Scienta. Musical Scholarship in the Italian Renaissance*. Ithaca: Cornell University Press, [c. 1992].

A discussion of the process by which sixteenth century theorists divided musical knowledge into two parts, distinguishing the science of sounding bodies (later known as acoustics) from the art of music. Because of the recursive nature of the field the book begins with a survey of the classical tradition and ends with late sixteenth century thought.

MudT   Mudarra, Alonso. *Tres libros de Música en cifra para vihuela, Sevilla, 1546*. Translated by Emilio Pujol. Monumentos de la música española, no. 7. Barcelona: Consejo superior de Investigaciones Cientificas, Instituto Español de Musicología, 1949.

This is a transcription from the 1546 tablature. It includes original works and some arrangements for guitar, vihuela, voice with vihuela, harp, and organ. It is edited from a photocopy of the original edition at the Biblioteca del Escorial (15-VI-43). There are bibliographical footnotes.

MudTL   _____. *Tres libros de música en cifras para vihuela: (1546)*. Complete facsimile edition with an Introduction by James Tyler. Monaco: Éditions Chanterelle, 1980.

This is a reprint of the original published in Sevilla: DeLeo, 1546. It contains original works and arrangements for guitar, vihuela, voice with vihuela, harp, and organ.

MulA   Mulliner, Thomas. *A collection of compositions, apparently arranged for organ or virginals, and compositions in tablature...* ? 1530 1539. London: British Library Reprographic Service, 1988. Microfilm.

This contains music by Nicholas Carleton, Tallis, Newman, Redford, Allwood, Farrant, Blitheman, Tye, Taverner, Munely and others. It is described in the Catalogue of manuscript music in the British Museum/ A. Hughes-Hughes, vol. 2, p. 127; vol. 3, p. 77.

MusA   *Museo archeologico nazionale di Cividale del Friuli. Manuscript LIII.* [14 Masses]. 1540. [Cividale del Friuli: Museo archeologico nazionale, 1988]. Microfilm.

This is a choirbook manuscript from the Collegiate Church of Santa Maria Assunta, Cicidale del Friuli. It contains works by Divitis, Mouton, Janequin, Manchicourt, Morales, Gascogne, Richafort, Sermisy, and Willaert. It is indexed in the Census Catalogue of manuscript sources of Polyphonic Music 1400-1550, I, 153 (CivMA 53).

MusF   *Musiche fatte nella nozze*. Peer, Belgium: Alamire, 1984. Reprint.

This is a facsimile reprint of five sixteenth century partbooks from the Österreich Nationalbibliothek, Wien. This is music for a Medici wedding. The words are principally Italian. An index is included. It was originally published in Venice by Antonia Gardane in 1539. It contains fifteen madrigals and one motet each by Francesco Corteccia, Costanzo Festa, Mateo Rampollini and others.

MusFM   *Musiche fatte nella nozze (1539)* = *Music for a Medici wedding. Completed.* Edited by Martin Grayson, George Bate, and Rosemary Bate. [England?]: Alfredston Music, 1994.

This source was edited from the original version published in 1539 and a concordance published in 1547. It includes historical information and notes on performance and notation in English. It contains fifteen madrigals and one motet each by Francesco Corteccia, Costanzo Festa, Mateo Rampollini and others.

MusN   *Musica nova. Accommodata per cantar et sonar sopra organi, et altri strumenti*. Printed by Andrea Arrivabene, fl. 1534-1570. Venetia: al segno del pozzo, 1540. Biblioteca musicale "G.B. Martini" di Bologna, n.d.] Microfilm.

This contains works by Willaert, Julio da Modena, Nicolo Benoist, Guilielmo Golin, Hieronimo Parabsco, and Hieronimo [Cavazzoni] da Bologna. There is one partbook, the *bassus*. The original is at Bologna in the Biblioteca Musicale (1 Bc). It is indexed in RISM B/1; 1540-22 and Brown, *Instrumental music printed before 1600*, no. 1540/3, p. 65.

MusNA   _____. *Accommodata per cantar et sonar sopra organi, et altri strumenti, composta per diversi eccellentissimi musici*. Venetia, MDXL. Edited by H. Colin Slim and Edward E. Lowinsky. Monuments of Renaissance music, no. 1. Chicago: University of Chicago Press, 1964.

This contains transcriptions of twenty-one *ricercari* for *superius*, *altus*, tenor, and *bassus* by Willaert, Julio da Modena, Nicolo Benoist, Guilielmo Golin, Hieronimo Parabsco, and Hieronimo [Cavazzoni] da Bologna. The appendix on pp. 125-129 contain two ricercari by Willaert or Julio da Modena and by G. Coste. There is a Thematic index, p. [2] (3rd group).

NagF   Nagel, W., ed. "Fundamentum Authore Johanne Buchnero." *Monatshefte für Musikgeschichte*, no. 23 (1891): pp. 71ff.

This article is a study of the music and theory of Johann Buchner.

NavD   Naváez, Luis de. *Delphin de música*. Transcribed and edited by Emilio Pujol. Monumentos de la música española, no. 3. Barcelona: Consejo Superior de Investigaciones Cientificas, Instituto Español de Musicologia, 1971. Reimpresión.

This is a reproduction of the first edition of 1545. The original book was titled *Los seys libros del Delphin de música...*, (Valladolid, 1538). There are solo arrangements of ensemble music, even motets and Mass-sections, by Flemish, French, Italian, and Spanish composers.

NefD   Nef, Walter Robert. *Der St. Galler Fridolin Sicher und seine Orgeltabulatur*. Schweizerisches Jahrbuch für Musikwissenschaft, no. 7. Basel: H. Majer, 1938.

This contains a catalogue of the *Orgeltabulatur* taken from *Codex 530* der Stifisbibliothek St. Gallen, pp. 66-132; a thematic index of the *Orgeltabulatur*, pp. 159-209; and an index of the sources, pp. 151-156.

NieL   Niemöller, Klaus Wolfgang. "Listenius, Nikolaus." In *The New Grove Dictionary of Music and Musicians*, p. 28. 20 vols. Edited by Stanley Sadie. 6th ed. London: Macmillan Publishers, Ltd., [c. 1980].

This is a short biography of Listenius.

NolC I — Nola, Gian Domenico del Giovane da. *Canzone villanesche a tre voce novamente ristampate, libro primo.* Venice: Gardane, 1545. [München: Bayerische Staatsbibliothek, n.d.] Microfilm.

    This is a facsimile of three partbooks taken from the original manuscript in the Bayerische Staatsbibliothek in München. It is indexed in RISM A/1, N 0774 and the Lewis catalog, vol. 1, no. 70.

NolC II — _____. *Canzone villanesche a tre voce novamente ristampate, libro secundo.* Venice: Gardane, 1545. [München: Bayerische Staatsbibliothek, n.d.] Microfilm.

    This is a facsimile of three partbooks taken from the original manuscript in the Bayerische Staatsbibliothek in München. It is indexed in RISM A/1, N 0774 and the Lewis catalog, vol. 1, no. 71.

NolN — _____. *Nine villanelle for three voices or instruments.* Thesaurus musicus, no. 41. London: London Pro Musica edition, 1984.

    This source contains sixteenth century excerpts from *Canzone villanesche, libro 1o* (nos. 1, 3, 6, 8, 9) and *libro 2o* (nos. 4, 5, 8). There are also excerpts from *Primo libro delle villanelle alla napolitana* (nos, 2 and 7). There are Italian words with English translations printed as texts.

OstD — Osthoff, H., ed. *Desprez, Arcadelt, De Rore, Willaert, Fünf Vergil-Motetten.* Das Chorwerk, no. 54. Berlin: Kallmeyer, 1929-.

    This contains transcriptions of motets by the composers mentioned. There are two motets by Desprez and one each by the others. There is a *Vorwort* in German.

OthR — Othmayr, Caspar. *Reutterische und jegerische Liedlein...* Edited by von Fritz Piersig. Wolfenbüttel: G. Kallmeyer, 1928.

    This is a transcription of German part-songs for four or five voices.

OweI — Owens, Jessie Ann. "An illuminated manuscript of motets by Cipriano de Rore (München, Bayerische Staatsbibliothek, *Mus. Ms. B*)." 2 vols. Ph.D. Thesis, Princeton University, 1979. Ann Arbor, Mich.: University Microfilms International, 1979. Photocopy.

    Volume two of this work is a photocopy of eighty-two pages of Rore's original Latin manuscript with illuminations by H. Mielich with a text by Johannes Poullet. There is also a 1564 commentary by S. Quickelberg entitled *Declaratio picturamum imaginum.* An abstract is included.

OweR — _____. "Rore Cipriano de". L. Macy, ed.: grovemusic.com (2001), <http://www.grovemusic.com> (Accessed 1 August 2001).

    This source contains a short biography of Rore, a discussion of his works, his significance and reputation, and a bibliography.

OxfM — *Oxford, Bodleian Library, MSS. Mus. Sch. e. 376-381.* Renaissance Music in Facsimile, no. 15. 6 partbooks. New York and London: Garland Publishing, Inc., 1986.

    This is a facsimile of the partbooks of the Forrest-Heather Manuscript.

PaeF — Paesler, Carl, ed. "Fundamentbuch von Hans von Constanz 1551." *Vierteljahrsschrift für Musikwissenschaft,* 5 (1889-1892): 1-193. Superior, Wisconsin: Research Microfilm Publishers, 1952. Microfilm.

    This is a reprint of the original *Fundamentum.* It contains a Latin treatise on playing the organ, about twenty liturgical organ pieces and some teaching examples which have been transcribed

PalH — Palisca, Claude V. *Humanism in Italian Renaissance Musical Thought.* New

Haven: Yale University Press, 1985.
This book traces the path of transmission of Greek musical thought in Italy. It relies almost entirely on primary sources. There are rare and unpublished extracts from Renaissance writings on music and related subjects in the vernacular with English translations. Musical humanists from the early fourteenth century through the late Renaissance are quoted.

PaoA   Paolucci, Giuseppe. *Arte pratica di contrappunto.* 3 Vols in 2. Venezia: A. de Castro, 1765. [Rochester, N.Y.]: University of Rochester Press, 1959. Micro-opaque.
This source is a facsimile of a book on counterpoint. The book is demonstrated with examples of music by the author and with observations by various others. The original is at the Sibley Music Library of the Eastman School of Music in Rochester, New York. It is indexed in RISM B VI II, p. 635.

ParG   Partch, Harry. *Genesis of a Music.* 2nd ed. enlarged. New York: Da Capo Press, 1974.
The author makes it clear that the book is not written for musicologists, or even for musicians in the ordinary sense. It is written for those who are searching for more than intellectual openings into the mysteries of music and intonation. The book is written for composers, those who expect to compose, and for anyone who has this creative attitude. Part I is a discussion of the corporeal versus abstract music, Part II is an introduction to intonation, Part III is a discussion of the resources of monophony, and Part IV covers intonations: historic, implied, and proposed.

ParO   Parker, Robert L., ed. *Officia paschalia, de Resurrectione et Ascensione Domini: Wittenberg, 1539.* Musikdrucke aus den Jahren 1538-1545 in praktischer Neuausgabe, no. 8. Kassel: Bärenreiter, 1988.
This source contains Masses, Propers (music), Easter music, Ascension Day music, and motets for four voices with Latin words. There is a Foreword in English and German and an editorial report in English. Bibliographical references are included.

ParP   Parker, Geoffrey. *Philip II.* London: Hutchinson of London, [c. 1978]; reprint edition, 1979.
A bibliography of Philip based on new evidence, namely, the *Altamira papers*. These papers consist of some five thousand holograph letters and working papers of Philip II in two Madrid archives, plus perhaps as many again in the University Library in Geneva and in the British Library in London.

ParS   Parkins, Robert. "Spain and Portugal." In Keyboard Music before 1700. Edited by Alexander Silbiger, p. 312-359. New York: Schirmer Books, [c. 1995].
There is an introduction, a discussion of the Iberian organ, the literature and theorists, and composers, and A Guide to Literature and Editions.

PasO   Passereau. *Opera omnia.* Edited by Georges Dottin. Corpus mensurabilis musicae, no. 45. N.p.: American Institute of Musicology, 1967.
This source contains transcriptions of one motet and twenty-six *chansons* in three and four-parts, of which one may also be attributed to Janequin. There is an introduction, along with texts, notes and variants.

PedH   Pedrell, Felipe. *Hispaniae schola musica sacra.* Vol. 1: *Cristóbal de Mo-*

rales. Barcelona: J. B. Pujol y ca, 1894. Reprint ed., New York: Johnson Reprint, 1971.

This source contains unaccompanied motets for four to six voices with Latin texts: *Officium defunctorum*; *Magnificats, 8th tone*; *Emendemus in melius*; *O vos omnes* (attributed to Morales but actually composed by T. L. Victoria); *Lamentabatur Jacob*; *O crux, ave spes unica*; and *Verbum iniquum et dlorosum*. There are notes by the editor in French and Spanish.

PerMR   Perkins, Leeman L. *Music in the Age of the Renaissance*. New York: W. W. Norton & Company, [c.1999].

The time period covered is the fifteenth and sixteenth centuries. There is an attempt to focus on the historical processes as well as the general picture as it appeared at the time of writing. The intention of the author is to explain the conceptual matrix from which a particular composition emerged, and its liturgical, celebratory, and social uses. The book is written in a general chronological sequence. The emphasis is on the development of musical institutions and the musical genres and their essential characteristics.

PerS   "Perspective scenery." *Britannica 2001 Deluxe Edition CD-ROM*. Copyright © 1994-2000 Britannica.com Inc. October 5, 2001.

This is a short discussion of scenery and scene design technique in the theater that represents three-dimensional space on a flat surface in order to create an illusion of reality and an impression of distance. The technique was developed during the Renaissance.

PetP   Petraca, Francesco. *Il Petrarca*. Edited by Girolamo Ruscelli. Venetia: Plinio Pietrasanta, 1554.

This edition has a long introduction by the editor on the orthography of early writers in Italian. It contains the *Rimario* by Giovanni Maria Lanfranco. It is indexed in Fowler, M. Petrarch. p. 104. Pet N 554a.

PhaL   Phalèse, Pierre. *Liber septimus cantionum sacrarum vulgo moteta vocant, quinquw et sex vocum ex optimis quibusq: musicis selectarum*. Lovanii: Phalesium, 1558. London: British Library, n.d. Microfilm.

This is a facsimile. It contains six partbooks for *superius*, contratenor, *bassus*, quinta and *sexta pars*. There are five- and six-part motets attributed to Crécquillon and Jean Crespel. The original is in the British Library, London. It is indexed in RISM B/I, 1558-6 and Vanhulst catalog, no. 53.

PhiN   "Philosophy of nature." Britannica 2001 Deluxe Edition CD-ROM. [c. 1994-2000]. Britannica.com Inc. May 7, 2001.

This is a short summary of the history of the Philosophy of nature.

PidP I   Pidoux, Pierre, ed. *Le Psautier Huguenot du XVIe siècle: mélodies et documents*. 2 vols. Premier volume: *Les Mélodies*. Basle: Édition Baerenreiter Bâle, 1962.

This volume contains the melodies, with texts, of the Psalm melodies from 1539 to 1562. The Psalm melodies are presented in their original form, their modifications, and their final form, along with the dates of publication, in a manner which permits one to follow their evolution.

PirM   Pirrotta, Nino. *Music and Culture in Italy from the Middle Ages to the Baroque: a Collection of Essays*. Studies in the History of Music, no. 1. Cambridge, Mass.: Harvard University Press, 1984.

This volume contains twenty-two essays representing a cross-section of Pirrotta's scholarly work on Italian music and its changing cultural background from the Middle Ages through the seventeenth century.

PirMT Pirrotta, Nino. and Elena Povoledo. *Music and Theatre from Poliziano to Monteverdi*. Translated by Karen Eales. Cambridge Studies in Music. Cambridge: Cambridge University Press, 1982.
> This is a survey, based on contemporary documents, of the period leading to the rise of opera. One of the chapters, chapter six, had already been published by William Austin (*New looks at Italian Opera...*, c. 1968). The period covered is 1480 to 1607. The largest portion of the book deals with the performances of comedies occurring between the two 'Orphic' periods.

PisC Pisano, Bernardo. *Collected Works*. Music of the Florentine Renaissance, no. 1. Corpus mensurabilis musicae, no. 32. Edited by Frank A. D'Accone. [s.l.]: American Institute of Musicology, 1966.
> This source contains nineteen responsories and thirty Italian part songs for three and four voices. The thirty part-songs are from the *Musica de meser Bernardo Pisano...* published by Petrucci. They are either by or attributed to Pisano. The words for the secular songs are printed as text on pp. ix-xx. There is a list of the compositions. Uncompletable fragments are excluded.

PisM _____. *Musica de meser Bernardo Pisano sopra le canzone del Petrarch*. Forosempronii: Impressum per Octauianum Petrutium, 1520. Seville: Biblioteca Colombina, [1978]. Microfilm.
> This contains a facsimile of the *altus* and *bassus* parts of seventeen Italian madrigals with Latin words by Petrarch.

PogJ Pogue, Samuel F. *Jacques Moderne: Lyons Music Printer of the Sixteenth Century*. Travaux d'Humanisme et Renaissance 101. Geneva: Librairie Droz, 1969.
> This is an attempt to prove that Moderne was not a mere provincial printer but a man operating independently and creatively, contributing to music printing in an original and individual manner. It contains a Moderne bibliography, supporting documents, musical illustrations, and some transcriptions.

PolP "Political Philosophy." *Britannica 2002 Deluxe Edition*. Copyright © 1994-2002 Britannica.com Inc. April 14, 2002.
> This contains a discussion of political philosophy from the Greeks to the present day. It defines the political theory of each period.

PopS Popkin, Richard H. "Skepticism" *Britannica 2001 Deluxe Edition CD-ROM* [c. 1994-2000]. Britannica.com Inc. May 7, 2001.
> This is a short summary of the history and definition of the philosophy of Skepticism.

PowT Powers, Harold S. "Tonal Types and Modal Categories in Renaissance Polyphony." *Journal of the American Musicological Society* 34 (1981): 428-470.
> This is a discussion of whether polyphony of the late 15th and early 16th centuries was or should be conceived as regularly being "in" modes of the known modal system. This is thought to have been a vital question by 1525.

PraM Pratt, Waldo Selden. *The Music of the French Psalter of 1562: a Historical Survey and Analysis: with the Music in Modern Notation*. Columbia University Studies in Musicology, no. 3. New York: Columbia University Press, 1939.
> This book contains a complete rescript in modern notation of the one-hun-

	dred and twenty-five melodies found in the French Psalter of 1562. There is a considerable amount of historical or technical annotation.
PriL	Prizer, William F., ed. *Libro primo de la croce: Rome, Pasoti and Dorico, 1526: cazoni, frottole, and capitoli.* Collegium musicum (Yale University); 2nd. ser., vol. 8. Madison, Wis.: A-R Editions, 1978.
	This is a transcription of four-voice, Italian *frottole* with Italian words. The words are also printed as text with English translation. There are works by Cara, Festa, Bartolucci, and Patavino.
PriN	_____. "North Italian Courts, 1460-1540." In *The Renaissance: from the 1470s to the end of the 16th century*, pp. 133-155. Edited by Iain Fenlon. Man and Music Series. Englewood Cliffs, N.J.: Prentice Hall, [c. 1989].
	A discussion of the musical patronage of Ercole I d'Este and his children and their consorts. Ercole had set out the basic lines of musical patronage and, through the education of his children, he set patterns for later generations. He showed them the techniques and benefits of musical patronage on a large scale.
RabW	Rabelais, François. *The works of Rabelais; completely translated into English.* Translated by Sir Thomas Urquhart and Peter Anthony Motteux. Illustrations by Alfred Edward Chalon. London: 1890.
	This contains only the *Gargantua et Pantagruel*. There is a facsimile reproduction of the original title page.
RadR	Radcliffe, Philip F. "The Relationship of Rhythm and Tonality in the Sixteenth Century." *Proceedings of the Musical Association* 57 (1951): 73-97.
	This is a discussion of the changes from mode to key that took place in the sixteenth century. The thesis is that the changes did not take place as a result of experiments but due to a certain rhythmical tendency in the music. This refers to the rhythmical tendency in language and human expression that became more sharply accentuated during this period. These tendencies induce the composer to write music of a corresponding kind.
RamMU	Ramos de Pareja, Bartolomeo. *Musica practica*. Edited and translated by Clement A. Miller. Musicological studies and documents, no. 44. Neuhausen-Stuttgart: American Institute of Musicology, 1993.
	There are three parts to the treatise. Each part is divided into sections and chapters. It is an attack on those who had tried to graft the *coniunctae* upon the Guidonian system. Ramis proposes doing away with the six Guidonian "vocables" and replacing them with eight other syllables based on the octave. He also discusses *musica ficta*, intervals, simple proportions, plainsong and mensural music.
RanH	Randel, Don M., ed. *The New Harvard Dictionary of Music*. Cambridge, Mass.: The Belknap Press of Harvard University Press, 1986.
	The aim of this source is to serve as a convenient reference work for laymen, students, performers, composers, scholars, and teachers. The book mainly covers the tradition of western art music reflecting recent scholarship on all periods including more recent music.
RanM	Rankin, Susan and David Hiley, eds. *Music in the medieval English liturgy: Plainsong & Mediaeval Music Society centennial essays.* Oxford [England]: Clarendon Press, 1993.
	This is a collection of scholarly essays on medieval music, both monophonic and polyphonic, and in particular, the chant

RasN Rastall, Richard. *The Notation of Western Music: An Introduction*. London: Dent, 1983.
   This is a discussion of the underlying principles of notations. It begins with the notation of the St. Gall manuscripts and ends with twentieth century notation.

RedC Redlich, H. F. "Latin Church Music on the Continent-1. (c) Central Europe." In *The New Oxford History of Music*. Vol. 4: *The Age of Humanism: 1540-1630*, edited by Gerald Abraham, pp. 253-274. London: The Oxford University Press, [c. 1968]; reprint ed., 1974.
   This contains material on Isaac and his school, Ludwig Senfl's Masses and motets, the disciples of Isaac, and later generations of composers.

RedV _____. "Latin Church Music on the Continent-1. (d) The Venetian School." In *The New Oxford History of Music*. Vol. 4: *The Age of Humanism: 1540-1630*, edited by Gerald Abraham, pp. 275-294. London: The Oxford University Press, [c. 1968]; reprint ed., 1974.
   This is a discussion of the Venetian composers and their music in the sixteenth century. This includes Willaert, Rore, other associates of Willaert, and the Gabrielis.

ReeC Reed, Edward Bliss, ed. *Christmas carols printed in the sixteenth century, including Kele's christmas carolles newly inprynted, reproduced in facsimile from the copy in the Huntington library*. Huntington library publications. Cambridge, Mass: Harvard University Press, 1932.
   This contains facsimiles including the music of the carols. There is a bibliography of English Christmas carols, p. 93-99.

ReeD Reeser, Eduard and Sem Dresden, eds. *Drie oud-nederlandse motetten*. Vereniging voor Nederlandse Muziekgeshiedenis, no. 44. Amsterdam: G. Alsbach, 1958.
   This is a transcription of three motets for four to six voices; *Fremuit Spiritus Jesu* by Jacobus Clemens non Papa, *Gaude Virgo* by Josquin des Prés, and *Haec Deum coeli* by Jacob Obrecht. The Latin words are given.

ReeF Reese, Gustave. *Fourscore Classics of Music Literature; a guide to selected original sources on theory and other writings on music not available in English, with descriptive sketches and bibliographical references*. New York: The Liberal Arts Press, 1957.
   This book contains eighty descriptive sketches of music literature in chronological order along with bibliographical references.

ReeMR _____. *Music in the Renaissance*. New York: W. W. Norton and Co., Inc., [c. 1959].
   Part I deals with the central musical language of the fifteenth and sixteenth centuries in France, Italy, and the Low Countries. Part II covers the music of other lands.

ReiB Reichenbach, Herman. *Bicinia Germanica. Deutsche Volkslieder zu zwei gleichen oder gemischten Stimmen*. Beihefte zu "Musikanten", no. 10. Wolfenbüttel: G. Kallmeyer, 1926.
   This contains transcriptions of selections from the *Bicinia gallica, latina, germanica* published by Georg Rhau in 1545.

RenS "The Renaissance stage." *Britannica 2001 Deluxe Edition CD-ROM*. Copyright © 1994-2000 Britannica.com Inc. October 3, 2001.
   This is a summary of the developments of stage design in Rome and Fer-

rara from the end of the fifteenth century to 1585.

ResR   Resinarius, Balthasar. *Responsorium numero octoginta*. Rhau, Georg: 1543. Edited by Inge-Maria Schroder. Musikdrucke aus den Jahren 1538 bis 1545 in praktischer Neuausgabe, Vols. 1 and 2. Kassel; St. Louis: Bärenreiter; Concordia, 1955; 1957.

This is a transcription of two volumes of Responses by Balthasar Resinarius. Volume one is titled, *De Christo, et regno eius, Doctrina, Vita, Passione, Resurrectione et Ascensione*. The second volume is titled, *De sanctis, et illorum in Christe fide et cruce*. Both volumes were originally published by Georg Rhau in 1543. The Responses are written for *discantus, altus*, tenor, and *bassus* with Latin words. Volume one contains historical and editorial notes in German, with English translation plus critical commentary in German.

ReyR   Reynolds, Christopher. "Rome: A City of Rich Contrast." In *The Renaissance: from the 1470s to the end of the sixteenth century*, pp. 63-101. Edited by Iain Fenlon. Man and Music Series. Englewood Cliffs, N.J.: Prentice Hall, [c. 1989].

This is an effort to distinguish the emergent twofold Roman style: the style of local institutional practices and the regional and national styles that took shape throughout Europe during the sixteenth century.

RhaB   Rhau, Georg. *Bicinia gallica, latina, germanica...* Vitebergae: Rhaw, 1545. [Augsburg: Staats- und Stadtbibliothek, n.d.]. Microfilm.

This is a facsimile of two partbooks containing duets by A. Brumel, S. Dietrich, M. Eckel, A. Fevin, G. Forster, A. Gardane, M. Greiter, Josquin des Prez, P. de la Rue, F. Layolle, G. Le Heurteur, L. Lemlin, J. Mouton, Peletier, M. Pipelare, P. Roselli, Sampson, L, Senfl, C. de Sermisy, J. Stahel, T. Stoltzer, H. Voit, J. Walther, and others. The original is in Staats- und Stadtbibliothek in Augsburg. It is indexed in RISM B/I, 1546-06.

RhaO   _____. *Officia Paschalia, de resurrectione et ascensione Domini*. Vitebrtgae: Rhaw, 1539. Berlin: Deutsche Staatsbibliothek, n.d. Microfilm.

This is a facsimile of four partbooks for *discantus, altus*, tenor, and *bassus* containing Passion music. The original is in the Deutsche Staatsbibliothek in Berlin. It contains compositions by Galliculus, G. Forster, A. Rener, C. Rein, L. Senfl, Th. Stoltzer, P. Verdelot, J. Walther, J. Zacharias, and Anonymous. It is indexed in RISM B/I, 1539-14.

RhaOF   _____. *Officiorum (ut vocant) de nativitate, circumcisione, epiphania Domini, & purificatione...Tomus primus*. Vitebergae: Rhaw, 1545. Berlin: Deutsche Staatsbibliothek, n.d. Microfilm.

This is a facsimile of four partbooks for *discantus, altus*, tenor, and *bassus* containing Propers and Masses for Christmas and Epiphany by Bruck, Copus, Dietrich, Finck, Galliculus, Isaak, Lupi, Morales, Rener, Resinarius, Reusch, Senfl, Stoltzer, and Anonymous.. The original is in the Deutsche Staatsbibliothek in Berlin. It is indexed in RISM B/I, 1545-5.

RhaOP   _____. *Opus decem missarum quatuor vocum...* Vuitembergensi: Collectum a Georgio Rhavvo, 1541. [Kassel: Muhard'sche Bibliothek der Stadt Kassel und Landesbibliothek, n.d.]. Microfilm.

This is a facsimile of four partbooks for *discantus, altus*, tenor, and *bassus* containing Masses by Brumel, Isaak, Pipelare, A Rener, Roselli, Sampson,

	Senfl, and Stahel. The original is in the Muhard'sche Bibliothek der Stadt Kassel und Landesbibliothek in Kassel. It is indexed in RISM B/I, 1541-01.
RhaP	Rhau, Georg. *Postremum vespertini officii opus...* Wittenberg, Rhaw, 1544. [London: British Library, n.d.]. Microfilm.
	This is a facsimile of four partbooks for *discantus, altus*, tenor, and *bassus* containing Magnificat settings by Divitis, Fevin, Galliculus, Berchem, De la Rue, Morales, Pieton, Piplare, Rener, Richafort, Tudual, Verdelot, and Anonymous. The original is in the British Library in London (GB Lb1). It is indexed in RISM B/I, 1544-04.
RhaS	_____. *Symphonia jucundae, atque adeo breves 4 vocum, ab optimia quibusque musicis compositae 1538*. Edited by Hans Albrecht. Musikdrucke aus den Jahren 1538 bis in praktisher Neuausgabe, Bd. 3. Kassel: Bärenreiter, 1959.
	This source contains transcriptions of sacred part-songs written for *discantus, altus*, tenor, and *bassus*. There is a preface and editor's notes in German and English. It is indexed in RISM B/I, 1538-8.
RhaSA	_____. *Sacrorum hymnorum liber primus*. Wittenberg: Rhaw, 1542. [Budapest: Orszagos Szechenyi Konyvtar, n.d.] Microfilm.
	This is a facsimile of three partbooks for *discantus, altus*, and *bassus* containing Latin hymns by von Bruck, Breitengraser, Capellus, Cellarius, Eckel, Finck, Grefinger, Hartzer, Haugh, Isaak, Josquin, Kropstein, Obrecht, Popel, Rener, Senfl, Stoltzer, Walther, and Anonymous. The original is in the Orszagos Szechenyi Konyvtar i Budapest. The music has Latin words. It is indexed in RISM B/I, 1542-12.
RhaSAC	_____. *Sacrorum hymnorum liber primus*. Edited by Rudolf Gerber. Das Erbe deutscher Musik. 1. Reihe: Reichsdenkmale, Bd. 21, 25. Abteilung Motetten und Messen, Bd. 3-4. Lippstadt: Fr. Kistner & C. F. W. Siegel, 1961.
	This contains transcriptions of Latin hymns for four to six voices. Volume one is titled, *Proprium de tempore*. It contains a list of contents for the entire Rhau volume and transcriptions of numbers 1-74. Volume two is titled, *Proprium et communie sanctorum*.
RhaSE	_____. *Selectae harmoniae de Passione Domini... 1538*. Edited by Wolfgang Reich. Musikdrucke aus den Jahren 1538 bis 1545 in praktischer Neuausgabe, no. 10. Kassel; New York: Bärenreiter, 1990.
	This contains motets, Propers, and a Mass for three to five voices. There is a Foreword in English and German and a critical report in German. There are works by Galliculus, Compere, Issac, Walther, Senfl, and others. There are bibliographical references.
RhaSY	_____. *Symphoniae iucundae, atque adeo breves 4 vocum, ab optimia quibusque musicis compositae*. Vitebergae: Georgium Rhau, 1538. München: Bayerische Staatsbibliothek, n.d. Microfilm.
	This is a facsimile of four partbooks containing fifty-two motets by Brumel, Ducis, Eckel, Fevin, Forster, Hellinck, Isaak, Josquin, Lafage, Lapicida, De la Rue, Mahu, Mouton, Richafort, Senfl, Sermisy, Van Stappen, Unterholtzer, Verdelot, Walther, and Anonymous. It is indexed in RISM B/I, 1538-8.
RhaT	_____. *Tricina...* Wittembergae: Apud Georgium Rhau, 1542. Berlin: Deutsches Staatsbibliothek, 1961. Microfilm.

94 Bibliography

> This is a facsimile of three partbooks for *discantus*, tenor, and *bassus* containing sacred and secular trios with Latin, French, German, and Dutch words. It contains works by Agricola, Bruck, Baldwin, Billon, Compere, Dietrich, Ducis, Forster, Ghiselin, Hofhaimer, Isaak, Josquin, De la Rue, Layolle, and others. It is indexed in RISM B/I, 1542-08.

RhaV   Rhau, Georg. *Vesperarum precum officia (Wittenberg, 1540)*. Edited by Hans Joachim Moser. Musikdrucke aus den Jahren 1538 bis 1545 in praktischer Neuausgabe, no. 4. Kassel: Bärenreiter, 1955-.

> This contains four partbooks for *discantus, altus*, tenor, and *bassus*. The compositions are Psalms for Vespers by Andreas Capellus, Benedictus Ducis, Georg Foster, Johannes Galliculus, Henricus Isaak, Adam Rener, Johann Stahel, Thomas Stoltzer, and Johann Walther. There is a Preface in German and English. There are critical notes on pages 175-207.

RhaVE   _____. *Vesperarum precum officia psalmi feriarum ed dominicalium dierum tocius anni...* Vitebergae: Rhaw, 1540. Kassel: Murhard'sche Bibliothek der Stadt Kassel und Landesbibliothek, n.d. Microfilm.

> This is a facsimile of four partbooks *discantus, altus*, tenor, and *bassus* containing responses, antiphons, and hymns. The compositions are by Capellus, Cellarius, B. Ducis, G. Forster, Galliculus, Isaak, Rener, Stahel, T. Stoltzer, J. Walther, and Anonymous. The original is in the Murhard'sche Bibliothek der Stadt Kassel und Landesbibliothek in Kassel. It is indexed in RISM B/I, 1540-5.

RhaSH   _____. *Selectae harmoniae quatuor vocum de passione domini...*Vitebergae: Georgium Rhau, 1538. München: Bayerische Staatsbibliothek, n.d. Microfilm.

> This contains Holy-week music by Cellarius, Compere, Ducis, Eckel, Galliculus, Isaak, Lemlin, Obrecht, Senfl, Stahel, Walther, and Anonymous. There are four partbooks for *discantus, altus*, tenor, and *bassus*. The original publication is in Bayerische Staatsbibliothek in München (D Mbs). It is indexed in RISM B/I, 1538-1.

RhyS   Rhys, Philip ap [Aprys, Apprys, Apryce]. "Rhys, Philip ap", L. Macy, ed.: grovemusic.com(2001). (Accessed 8 August 2001).

> This contains a short biography and a discussion of Rhys' *Organ Mass*.

RicC   Richafort, Jean. *Christus resurgens*. Van Ockeghem tot Sweelinck, no. 7. Edited by A. Smijers. Amsterdam: n.p., 1949-.

> This is a transcription of the motet.

RicD   _____. *Two chansons: for four voices or instruments*. Edited by Bernard Thomas. Early Music Library, no. 93. London: London Pro Musica Edition, [c. 1991].

> The *chansons* are *De mon triste desplaisir* and *Il n'est sy doulce vie*. They are in four parts for voices or unspecified instruments. There are French texts with English translations. There are notes by Bernard Thomas.

RicF   _____. *5 chansons rustiques: for 3 voices or instruments*. Early Music Library, no. 251. [London?]: London Pro Musica edition, 1994.

> There are transcriptions of five polyphonic *chansons rustiques* by Richafort with French words that are also printed as text. There are English translations on page three of the cover and notes by Bernard Thomas on page four of the cover.

RicO   _____. *Opera omnia*. Edited by Harry Elzinga. Corpus mensurabilis musicae, no. 81. Neuhausen-Stuttgart: American Institute of Musicology, 1979. The title on an added Title page is *Collected Works*. There are three volumes of transcriptions: Volume I: *Missa O genetrix, Missa Veni sponsa Christi*, and a *Requiem*; Volume II: Motets; Volume III: Magnificats, *chansons*, and some Latin part songs. There are critical notes and bibliographical references.

RicQ   Richafort, Jean. *Quem dicunt homines*. Motetus XVI saeculi, no. 3. Bruxells: Éditions Musica Antiqua Bruxelles, 1995
This is a facsimile of the motet for four voices. Bibliographical references are included.

RicR   _____. *Requiem: zu 6 stimmen*. Edited by Albert Seay. Das Chorwerk, Hft 124. Wolfenbüttel: Moseler Verlag, 1976.
This *Missa pro defunctus* is written for six parts: *superius, altus*, canon 1 and 2, tenor, and *bassus*. There are Latin words with canon 1 and 2 partially in French.

RidM   Ridolfi, Roberto. "Machiavaelli." *Britannica 2002 Deluxe Edition*. Copyright © 1994-2002 Britannica.com Inc. April 14, 2002.
This contains material on the life and times of Machiavelli. There is also a discussion of his writings, character, and thought.

RISM B,I   *Répertoire international des sources musicales [International Inventory of Musical Sources]: Recueils imprimés XVIe-XVIIe siècles*. Series B, Volume I. Ouvrage publié sous la direction de François Lesure. Listed chronologically. München-Duisburg: G. Henle Verlag, 1960-.
This volume contains a list of collections of music published between 1501 and 1700. There is a summary of their contents along with the location of copies in major European and American libraries. There are two indexes: one of editors and printers and one of titles and authors.

RitZ   Ritter, August Gottfried. *Zur Geschichte des Orgelspiels...* 2 vols in one. Hildesheim: G. Olms, 1969.
Volume I is titled *Zur Geschichte des Orgelspiels, vornehmlich des deutschen, im 14. bis zum Anfange des 18. Jahrhunderts*. The second volume is titled *Zur Geschichte des Orgelspiels im 14. bis 18. Jahrhundert. Band II: Musikalische Beispiele*. Both were published in Leipzig in 1884. Volume I contains the history of the organ and the organists from the fourteenth century to the eighteenth century. Volume II contains transcriptions of the music of the period.

RobA   Robb, David M. and J. J. Garrison. *Art in the Western World.* New York: Harper and Brothers, [c. 1935]; reprint ed., [c. 1942].
The material is divided into general categories of architecture, sculpture, and painting. Each category begins with the Greek period and ends with the modern period.

RobW   Robbins, Harry Wolcott and William Harold Coleman, eds. *Western World Literature.* New York: The Macmillan Co., 1938; reprint ed., 1943.
A comprehensive view of the works of English and American authors together with an orientation to foreign literatures. It is a brief history of literature, with period, nationality, type, and biographical introductions preceding each group of selections. It begins with Classical Greek literature and ends with Eugene O'Neill of the twentieth century.

RocM   Roche, Jerome. *The Madrigal.* Early Music Series (London, England: 1976),

no. 11. 2nd ed., Oxford; New York: Oxford University Press, 1990.
Roche states that the purpose of this second edition is to incorporate the results of much research done in the 1970's and 1980's; in particular, the research done in regard to biographical and contextual information. Also, in this edition, Roche gives more adequate consideration to Striggio and Marco da Gagliano. There is an alphabetical index of all madrigals discussed along with the name of the composer and sources in modern editions.

RogD   Rogers, Helen Olive. *The Development of a concept of Modulation in Theory from the 16th to the Early 18th Century.* Doctoral Dissertation Series Publication, no. 14,665. Ann Arbor, Mich.: University Microfilms, 1955.
This is an investigation of treatises and the specific practice which they represent in order to determine at what point theorists give a clear recognition to modulation or the change of key in musical practice.

RokI   Rokseth, Yvonne. "The Instrumental Music of the Middle Ages and Early Sixteenth Century." In *The New Oxford History Of Music.* Vol. 3: *Ars Nova and the Renaissance: 1300-1540,* edited by Dom Anselm Hughes and Gerald Abraham, pp. 406-465. London: Oxford University Press, [c. 1960]; reprint ed., 1974.
This is a discussion of the styles, and sources of the instrumental music of Italy, France, Germany, and England.

RokT   _____. *Treize motets et un prélude pour orgue.* Publications de la Société française, 1. sér; t. 5. Paris: E. Droz, 1930.
This contains the intabulations of the motets and a prelude taken from *Orgues Espinettes et //Manicordions et telz semblables instrumentz* published by Attaingnant in 1531 with the original motets reproduced alongside. The edition of the Attaingnant print is indexed in Heartz catalog, no. 27 and (RISM 1531/5).

RorC   Rore, Cipriano de. *Cipriani Rore opera omnia.* Corpus mensurabilis musicae, no. 14. 8 vols. Edited by Bernhard Meier. [Rome]: American Institute of Musicology, 1959; 1977.
This source contains transcriptions of collected works. Volume one: Motets from the first, second, and third books of five-voice motets; Volme two: *Madrigalia 5 vocum*; Volume three: *Madrigalia 5 vocum*; Volume four: *Madrigalia 3-8 vocum;* Volume five: *Madrigalia 3-8 vocum*; Volume six: Motets; Volume seven: *Missae*; Volume eight:*Psalmi, cantica B.M.V., cantiones Gallicae,* etc.

RorM   _____. *[Motetorum celeberrimi musici Cypriani de Rore]. Declaratio picturarum imaginum, acquorumcunq[ue] ornamentorum in libro, Motetorum celeberrimi musici Cypriani de Rore.* 1559; 1563. Munchen: Bayerische Staatsbibliothek, [1983]. Microfilm.
This is a facsimile of the manuscript Munchen: Bayerische Staatsbibliothek, *Mus. MS. B* (formerly designated as *Cim. 52* and *Cim. 209*). The manuscript contains two volumes. Volume one contains twenty motets and six Latin secular pieces for four to eight voices by Cipriano de Rore, with illustrations and miniatures by Hans Mielich. Volume two is a commentary on the first volume by Samuel Quickelberg, titled *Declaratio picturarum imaginum...* The manuscript is indexed in Census-catalogue of manuscript sources of polyphonic music 1400-1550, v. 2, p. 232-233.

RorMN   Rore, Cipriano de. *Motetta nunc primum summa diligentia in lucem prodita quinque vocum.* Ventiis: A Gardane, 1545. Heilbronn: Stadtarchiv, Musiksammlung, 1978. Microfilm.
    This is a facsimile of five partbooks, *cantus, altus,* tenor, *bassus,* and *quintus.* The original is in the Stadtarchiv, Musiksammlung, Heilbronn.

RorS I   _____. *Sacrae cantiones seu moteta (ut vocant) non minus Intrumentis quam vocibus aptae, Liber unus.* Lovani: Petrus Phalesius, sibi et Ioanni Bellero Bibliopolae Antuerpiensi, 1573. London: British Library, 1976. Microfilm.
    This source contains a facsimile of four of the five original partbooks. The *altus* partbook is missing. The original manuscript is in the British Library, London.

RorS II   _____. *Sacrae cantiones quae dicuntur motecta cum quinque, sex, et septem vocibus...* Venetijs: Antonium Gardane, 1595. Kassel: Murhardische Bibliothek der Stadt Kassel und Lamdesbibliothek, 1976. Microfilm.
    This is a facsimile of the 1595 *Sacrae cantiones.* The original is in the Murhardische Bibliothek der Stadt Kassel und Lamdesbibliothek. It contains five partbooks for *cantus, altus,* tenor, *bassus,* and *quintus.* It is indexed in RISM A/I, R2478.

RosL   Rossetti, Biagio. *Libellus de rudimentis musices.* Verona: 1529. Edited by Albert Seay. Critical Texts, no. 12. Colorado Springs: Colorado College Music Press, 1981.
    This is a reproduction of the text with an emphasis on the sections appropriate to music. Mr. Seay has made an effort to trace the hidden citations from other authorities as Rossetti apparently did not feel it his duty to summarize or syntheize what they said. Mr. Seay has divided the treatises into chapters in the hope of bringing some sense of order to what would otherwise be an almost solid block of text from beginning to end.

RosLR   _____. *Libellus de rudimentis musices.* Monuments of music and music literature in facsimile, Sec. Ser., Music literature, no. 136. Verone: Stuphanum, 1529; New York: Broude Bros., 1968.
    This is a facsimile. *See* RosL.

RotI   Rotta, Antonio. *Intabolatura de lauto: di lo excellentissimo musicho Messer Antonio Rotta di recercari, motetti, balli, madrigali; Canzon francese da lui composti & intabulati, & nouamente posti in luce; Libro primo.* Venetiis: Gardane, 1546. London: British Museum, n.d. Microfilm.
    This contains lute intabulations of music by nine different composers including Gombert, Arcadelt, and C. Festa. The original publication is found in the British Museum in London.

RubF   Rubsamen, Walter H. "From Frottola to Madrigal: the Changing Pattern of Secular Italian Vocal Music." In *Chanson and Madrigal, 1480-1530: Studies in Comparison and Contrast.* Edited by James Haar, pp. 51-88. Cambridge, Mass.: Harvard University Press, 1964.
    This is a discussion of the three textures or styles of Italian vocal music set to secular texts that were popular during the period 1430 to 1480. There is also a discussion of the last decades of the fifteenth century in which the Franco-Netherlanders changed their Italian compositions to polyphony that was more consistently imitative, especially at the opening of pieces.

RuhL   Ruhnke, Martin. "Lampadius, Auctor." In *The New Grove Dictionary of Mu-*

sic and Musicians, p. 419. 20 vols. Edited by Stanley Sadie. 6th ed. Macmillan Publishers Limited, [c. 1980].
This is a short biography of Lampadius.

SalE Salmen, Walter. "European Song: 1300-1530." In *The New Oxford History of Music*. Vol. 3: *Ars Nova and the Renaissance: 1300-1540*, edited by Dom Anselm Hughes and Gerald Abraham, pp. 349-379. London: Oxford University Press, [c. 1960]; reprint ed., 1970.
This is a discussion of sacred and secular song and the composers.

SalF Salinas, Francisco de. *Francisci Salinae. De musica libri septem...* Salmanticae: Excudebat M. Gastius, 1577. Hispanic culture series; roll 552, item 4. Cambridge, Mass.: General Microfilm Co., [19--].
This contains a discussion of music theory and musical rhythm and metre. The OCLC# is 27761323.

SalSE Salminger, Sigmund, Comp. *Selectissimae necnon familiarissimae cantiones...* Augustae Vindelicorum: [M. Kriesstein], 1540. [Wien: Österreichische Nationalbibliothek, n.d.]. Microfilm.
This is a collection of motets, German, French, and Italian part-songs for two to six voices, and instrumental music. It contains works by Arcadelt, Arthopius, Balduin, Barbe, Benedictus, Benoist, Blanckenmüller, Courtois, Gombert, Heugel, Josquin, Mouton, Senfl, Verdelot, Willaert, and others. The original is in Österreichische Nationalbibliothek in Wien. It is indexed in RISM B/1, 1540-07.

SanH Sandon, Nick. "The Henrician Partbooks at Peterhouse, Cambridge." *Proceedings of the Royal Musical Association*, no. 103 (1976-1977): 106-140.
This is a summary by Sandon of the progress of his work on the Henrician partbooks.. There is an inventory of the manuscripts and some biographical information

SanML _____. "The Manuscript London, British Library Harley 1709." In *Music in the Medieval English Liturgy: Plainsong & Mediaeval Music Society Centennial Essays*. Edited by Susan Rankin and David Hiley. Oxford: Clarendon Press, 1993.
The author of this article attempts to draw attention and speculate on some topics of special interest, such as origins, sources, and functions.

SanO Sandrin, Pierre. *Opera omnia*. Edited by Albert Seay. Corpus mensurabilis musicae, no. 47. N.p.: American Institute of Musicology, [c. 1968]
This contains transcriptions of Sandrin's fifty *chansons*. There is an introduction, a list of sources, and notes on individual compositions.

SatC Satterfield, John. "A Catalogue of Tye's Latin Music." In E*ssays in the History, Style and Bibliography of Music*, 51-59. Edited by James W. Pruett. Chapel Hill: University of North Carolina Press, [c. 1969].
This is a revision of earlier catalogues by Eitner, Arkwright, and Noble as well as some corrections of errors. This study presents a catalogue of Tye's Latin music.

SatC I _____, ed. *Christopher Tye: The Latin Church Music: Part I: The Masses*. Recent Researches in the Music of the Renaissance, no. 13. Madison: A-R Editions, Inc., [c. 1972].
This contains transcriptions of Tye's Masses, *Euge Bone* and The *Western Wind*.

SatC II _____, ed. *Christopher Tye: The Latin Church Music: Part II: The Shorter*

	Latin Works. Recent Researches in the Music of the Renaissance, no. 14. Madison: A-R Editions, Inc., [c. 1972].
	This contains transcriptions of Tye's shorter works.
SatS	Sattler, Michael. *The Schleitheim confession of faith.* Edited and translated by John C. Wenger. [Goshen, Ind.: Mennonite Historical Society, 1945.
	This is a translation of the seven articles of the 1527 *Schleitheim Confession*. It is an offprint from the *Mennonite Quarterly Review* 19 (1945) [243]-253. There are bibliographic notes.
SchAN	Schreiber, Heinrich. *Ayn new kunstlich Buech welches gar gewiss und behend lernet...* Nürmberg: J. Stüchs, 1518. London: British Library, Reference Division, Reprographic Section, (1980?). Microfilm.
	This contains material on organ pipes, musical temperament, and the monochord. It is written in German. It is indexed in RISM, B VI I, p. 374.
SchFS	Schöffer, Peter. *Fünff und sechzig teütscher Lieder, vormals imm Truck nie ussgangen.* Argentorati: Schöffer & Apiarius, 1536. München: Bayerische Staatsbibliothek, n.d. Microfilm.
	This is a facsimile of five partbooks containing polyphonic *Lieder* by C. Alderinus, Arnold von Bruck, B. Arthopius, H. Brätel, G. Breitengraser, S. Dietrich, B. Ducis, M. Eckel, W. Grefinger, M. Greitter, P. Hofhaimer, St. Mahu, L. Senfl, T. Sporer, T. Stoltzer, L. Spengler, J. Wannenmacher, and P. Wüst. The original is found in München: Bayerische Staatsbibliothek (D Mbs). It is indexed in RISM B/1, [1536]-08.
SchG	Schering, Arnold. *Geschichte der Musik in Beispielen.* Leipzig: 1931.
	This is a history of music in examples. There are examples from the ninth century up through the eighteenth century. There are sacred, secular, and instrumental pieces by German, Italian, French, Spanish, English, and Polish musicians. The introduction is in German. The index lists composers by country.
SchGU	Schmeltzl, Wolfgang. *Guter, seltzamer, und künstreicher teutscher Gesang...* Faksimile-Edition; Rara; No. 5. Stuttgart: Cornetto-Verlag, 1997.
	This is a reprint of the original source published in Nürnberg by J. Petreius in 1544. It contains part-songs for four to six voices and quodlibets. It was collected and in part composed by Wolfgang Schmeltzl. There are also anonymous compositions and works by Mathias Greiter, Ludwig Senfl, Veit Schnellinger, and others. It is indexed in RISM B/1, 1544.
SchGUT	_____. *Guter, seltzsamer und kunstreicher teutscher Gesang...* Denkmäler der Tonkunst in Österreich, No. 147/148. Edited by Rudolf Flotzinger. Graz. Austria: Akademische Druck- u. Verlagsanstalt, 1990.
	This contains transcriptions of German Lieder and Italian influenced settings by Matthias, Paminger, Senfl, and others. The words are printed as text in German. One piece has Italian words.
SchH	Schmidt-Görg, Joseph. *History of the Mass.* Anthology of Music: a collection of complete musical examples illustrating the history of music, no. 30. Edited by K. G. Fellerer. English translation by Robert Kolben. Cologne: Arno Volk Verlag Hans Gerig KG, [c. 1968].
	There is an historical introduction followed by musical examples from the sixth century to the present day. The original title was *Geschichte der Messe.* There are sources, notes, and a bibliography.
SchM	Schlick, Arnolt. *Miroir des organiers et organistes: 1511...* Translation,

introduction, and notes by Christian Meyer. Paris: L'Orgue. 1979.
This is a translation of *Spiegel der Orgelmacher und Organisten*. It includes bibliographical references.

SchOF   Schmitz, Arnold, ed. *Oberitalienische Figuralpassionen des 16. Jahrhunderts*. Musikalische Denkmäler, no. 1. Mainz: B. Schott's Söhne, 1955.
This source contains Passion music for one to six voices with Latin words by Jan [Nasco], Cypriano de Rore, Jachet von Mantua, and Giovanni Matteo. There is a Foreword in German.

SchSA   Schmidt, Jost Harro, ed. *Sämtliche Orgelwerke*. Das Erbe deutscher Musik, Bd. 54-55. Frankfurt: H. Litolff's Verlag, 1974.
This contains transcriptions of the compositions of the *Fundamentum* by Johann Buchner found in two different manuscripts: Basel *Fl8a* and Zürich *S 284*.

ScoD   Scotto. *Di Girolamo Scotto i madrigali a tre voci*. Venetijs: Authorem, 1541. Jena: Universitatsbibliothek der Friedrich-Schiller-Universitat, n.d. Microfilm.
This is a facsimile of three partbooks containing fifty-six madrigals for three voices by Girolamo Scotto. They are grouped according to the mode and genre. The original manuscript is in the Universitatsbibliothek der Friedrich-Schiller-Universitat at Jena. It is indexed in RISM A/I, S 2615 and the Bernstein catalog, no. 22.

ScoDL   _____, O. *Del libro secondo de madrigali*. Venice: O. Scotum, 1534. Bologna: Civico Museo Bibliografico Musicale, 1986. Microfilm.
This contains four-part madrigals by Verdelot, Festa, Jacquet of Mantua, and Willaert.

ScoDM   _____, O. *Delli madrigali a tre voci: novamente con somma diligentia corretti*. Venice: Scotto, 1537. [Lincoln microfilm gift]. Bologna: Biblioteca Musicale, 198-. Microfilm.
There is one partbook, the *bassus*, of madrigals by Constanzo Festa, Arcadelt, Fogliano, and Anonymous. The original is in the Biblioteca Musicale in Bologna *(l Bc), R. 140, fasc. 3 (Bassus)*.. For music incipits in staff notation see: Lincoln, H. B. *The Italian madrigal and related repertories*. This is found in Chapman thesis (Ph.D)-Harvard University, 1964, no. 83, p.437. It is indexed in RISM B/1, 1537-7.

ScoEM   _____. *Exellentissimi musici Moralis Hispani, Gomberti, ac Iacheti cum quatuor vocibus missae...* Venetiis: Scotum, 1540. Microfiche. Jena: Universitats bibliothek der Friedrich-Schiller-Universitat, [n.d.].
This is a facsimile of Masses for four voices by Morales, Gombert, and Jacquet of Mantua. It is indexed in RISM B/I, 1540-4; RISM A/I, G 2973; RISM A/I, M 3576, and Bernstein catalog, no. 11.

ScoI   _____. *Il primo libro de motetti a sei voce*. Venice: Scotto, 1549. Kassel: Deutsches Musikgeschichtliches Archir, 1986. Microfilm.
This is a facsimile of six partbooks containing music by Gombert, Jacquet of Mantua, Loyset Pieton, Jean Conseil, Joannes Gallus, Morales, and Zarlino. Included are three occasional motets: *Qui colis Ausoniam glaebe* by Gombert, and *Jubilate Deo omnis terra*, and *Gaude et letare* by Morales. It is indexed in Bernstein catalog, no. 86.

ScoIP   _____. *Il primo libro di madrigali di Verdelotto novamente stampato et con somma diligentia corretto*. [Venezia: Scotto], 1537. Bologna: Civico Museo

Bibliografico-Musicale. [198-]. Microfilm.
This source contains madrigals for four voices by Jan. A. de Silva and Philippe Verdelot. It is indexed in Lincoln, H. B.: *The Italian Madrigal and related repertories;* RISM A/I, v. 1219; and RISM B/I, 1537-09.

ScoIS   Scotto. *Il secondo libro de madrigali.* [Venetijs: Scotum], 1536. [Bologna: Civico Museo Bibliografico-Musicale, n.d.]. Microfilm.
This contains the *cantus, altus,* tenor, and *bassus* part-books of madrigals by Verdelot, Willaert, Jachet de Bercham, and Costanzo Festa. The original manuscript is in the Civico Museo Bibliografico-Musicale in Bologna.

ScoISL   _____. *Il secondo libro de madrigali.* Venzia: Scotto, 1537. [Lincoln microfilm gift] Munich: Bayerische Staatsbibliothek, [198-]. Microfilm.
This contains the *cantus, altus,* tenor, and *bassus* partbooks of madrigals by Verdelot, Willaert, Jachet de Bercham, and Costanzo Festa. It is indexed in RISM B/1, 1537-10 and *The Italian madrigal and related repertories.*

ScoIT   _____. *Il terzo libro de madrigali di Verdelotto...* [Venice: O. Scotto], Nouamente stampati, [eet] con somma dilgentia corretti, 1537.
This contains four part-books of madrigals by Verdelot, C. Festa, Arcadelt, and other selections. It is indexed in RISM A/1, V 1226; RISM B/1, 1537/11, and Nuovo Vogel, no. 2882.

ScoL   _____. *Libro secondo de li motetti a tre voce da diversi eccellentissimi musici composti.* Venice: Scotto, 1949. London: British Library, [n.d.]. Microfilm.
This is a facsimile of three partbooks containing music by Claudin, Certon, Scotto, Jacotin, Gosse, Phinot, Morales, Damianus, M. Iehan, Willaert, and Verdelot. The original is in the British Library, London. It is indexed in Bernstein catalog, no. 92.

ScoM   _____. *Musica quinque vocum: motetta materna lingua vocata.* Venice: Scotto, 1543. Jena: Universitätsbibliothek, n.d. Microfilm.
This is a facsimile of five partbooks. The motets are all anonymous. But number seven is attributed to Do. Finot in another source. The original is in Jena, Universitätsbibliothek. It is indexed in RISM B/I, 1543-02 and Bernstein catalog, no. 36.

ScoMC   _____. *Missae cum quatuor vocibus paribus decantandae.* Ventiis: Scotum, 1542. Jena: Universitatsbibliothek der Friedrich-Schiller-Universitat, n.d. Microfiche.
This is a facsimile of four partbooks containing Masses by Morales (3), Jachet (1), and Ruffus (1). The original is in the Universitatsbibliothek der Friedrich-Schiller-Universitat in Jena. It is indexed in RISM B/I, 1542-3; RISM A/I, M 3577, and Bernstein catalog, no. 26.

ScoMQ   _____. *Motecta quatuor vocum, liber primus.* Venetiis: Scotto, 1544. Milan: Biblioteca del Conservatorio Giuseppe Verdi, Milan, 1975. Microfilm.
This source contains four partbooks for *cantus, altus,* tenor, and *bassus.* The original is in the Biblioteca del Conservatorio Giuseppe Verdi in Milan. There are nineteen motets by Jacquet of Mantua plus five motets with conflicting attributions. It is indexed in Bernstein catalog, no. 6. It is also found in a later edition, Bernstein catalog, no. 41.

ScoMS   _____. *Motecta quinque vocum, novissime omni studio, ac cura in lucem edita, Liber primus*. Venetiis: Scotto, 1539. [Jena: Universitäts-bibliothek der Friedrich-Schiller-Universität, n.d.]. Microfilm.

This contains motets for *cantus, altus*, tenor, *bassus, and quintas*. They are by Jacquet, Morales, Constantius Festa, and Willaert. This is indexed in RISM A/I, J 0006.

ScoP   Scotto. *Primo libro de motetti a cinque voci*. Venetiis: Hieronymum Scottum, 1549. Kassel: Deutsches Musikgeschichtliches Archiv, 1986. Microfilm.

This is a facsimile of five partbooks for *cantus, altus*, tenor, *bassus*, and *quintus*. There are three motets by Iacquet, four by Rore, one each by Silva, Billon, Baston, Claudin, Donato, Morales, Carchillion [Crécquillon], Pierison [Cambio], and Viola, and two by Zerlinus. The one by Morales is attributed to Clemens non Papa in all other sources. This is indexed in Bernstein catalog, no. 88.

ScoQ   _____. *Quinque missae liber primus cum quinque vocibus*. Venetiis: Scotum, 1540. [S.l.]: Bayerischern Staatlichen Bibliotheken, 1986. Microfilm.

This is a facsimile of five Masses for five voices; two are by Morales, two by Jacquet, and one by Jacquet Berchem. It is indexed in Bernstein catalog, no. 10.

ScoQM   _____. *Quinque missarum harmonia diapente, id est quinque voces referens...* Venetiis: Scotum, 1543. [Napoli: Biblioteca nazionale, n.d.]. Microfilm.

This is a facsimile of five partbooks containing Masses for five voices by Morales and J. Lupi. The original manuscript is in the Biblioteca nazionale in Napoli (I Nn). It is indexed in RISM A/I, M 3578; RISM B/I, 1543-01; and Bernstein catalog, no. 33.

ScoS   _____. *I sacri et santi salmi di David profeta...* Venetiis: Scotum, 1554. Microfilm. London: British Library, [n.d.]

This is a facsimile of one tenor partbook containing six psalms by Cipriano de Rore and thirteen by Jacquet of Mantua. There are also Magnificats. The music is for Vespers. It is indexed in RISM B/I, 1554-17.

ScoSL   _____, O. *Il secondo libro de madrigali d'Arcadelt*. [Venice: Scotto], 1539. Nouamente stampati, et con somma diligentia corr[e]tti.

This was published by the Scotto press in collaboration with A. Antico. It includes four partbooks containing madrigals by Arcadelt, C. Festa (5), Ihan (1), Layolle (1) and Corteccia (1). For a list of the contents see Nuovo Vogel, no. 150 and Bernstein catalog, no. 1. It is indexed in RISM A/1, A 1368 and RISM B/1, [c.1537]/6.

ScoT   _____, H. *Tutti li Madrigali del primo et secondo libro a quatro voci*. Venetiis: Scotto, 1540. Wolfenbüttel: Herzog-August-Bibliothek, n.d. Microfilm.

This is a facsimile of four partbooks containing works by J. Arcadelt (2), L. Barre, J. Berchem, C. Festa (4), Jachet, P. G. Palatio (3), P. Verdelot (48), and A Willaeret (8). The original manuscript is in the Herzog-August-Bibliothek in Wolfenbüttel (D W). It is indexed in RISM A/I, V 1228; RISM B/I, 1540-20, and Bernstein catalog, no. 14.

SeaA   Seay, Albert. "Arcadelt, Jacques." In *New Grove Dictionary of Music and Musicians*, p. 546. Edited by Stanley Sadie. London: Macmillan Publishers Ltd., 1980.

This is a short biography of Arcadelt.

SeaFC   _____, trans., ed., transc. *French Chansons: Early chansons with English*

and French texts. Evanston, Ill.: Summy-Birchard Publishing Co., [c. 1957].
This contains *chansons* by Jacotin, Pierre Certon, Morel, Roquelay, Claudin de Sermisy, Anonymous, and Mahiet

SeaT   Seay, Albert, ed. *Thirty Chansons for Three and Four Voices from Attaingnant's Collections.* Collegium musicum, no. 2. New Haven: Yale University, 1960.
This contains transcriptions of *chansons* by Certon, Sermisy, Gombert, Janequin, Willaert, and others. The transcriptions are in modern notation with the original clefs indicated. The texts are the original French.

SeaTC   _____, ed. *Transcriptions of chansons for keyboard.* Corpus mensurabilis musicae, no. 20. [N.p.]: American Institute of Musicology, 1961.
This source contains transcriptions of *Dixneuf chansons musicales reduictes en la tablature des Orgues Espinettes Manicorions et telz semblables instrumentz musicaulx...1531, Vingt et cinq chansons musicales reduictes en la tablature des Orgues Espinettes Manicordions et telz sembables instrumentz musicaulx...1531, Vingt et six chansons musicales reduictes en la tablature des Orgues Espinettes Manicordions et telz semblalbles instrumentz musicaulx...1531.* The transcriptions of the keyboard tablatures are below the original part-song versions. There is an introduction in which the music and notation are discussed. Each section has notes and a list of musical variants.

SenD   Senfl, Ludwig. *Sämtliche Werke.* Band II: *Deutsche Lieder.* I. Teil: *Lieder aus handschriftlichen Quellen bis etwa 1533.* Edited by Arnold Geering and Wilhelm Altwegg. Das Erbe Deutscher Musik, no. 10. Wolfenbüttel und Zürich: Mösler Verlag, 1962.
These compositions are transcriptions. They are principally for four to six voices. The editorial and critical notes are in German. Bibliographical references and an alphabetical index are included.

SenDL   _____. *Sämtliche Werke.* Band IV: *Deutsche Lieder,* II. Teil: *Lieder aus Johannes Otts Liederbuch von 1534.* Edited by Arnold Geering and Wilhelm Altwegg. Das Erbe Deutscher Musik, no. 15. Wolfenbüttel und Zürich: Mösler Verlag, 1962.
These compositions are transcriptions. The editorial and critical notes are in German. Bibliographical references and an alphabetical index are included.

SenL   _____. *Liber selectarum cantionum...* Augsburg: Grimm et Wyrsung, 1520. Wien: Österreichische Nationalbibliothek, nd. Microfilm.
This is a facsimile of a choirbook containing motets for four to six voices by Josquin, P. de La Rue, J. Mouton, J. Obrecht, L. Senfl, H. Isaac, and others. The original is in Österreichische Nationalbibliothek at Wien. It is indexed in RISM B/1, 1520-4.

SenM   _____. *Magnificat octo tonorum fur 6 Solostimmen und gemischten Chor.* Edited by Gabor Darvas. Eulenburg octavo edition; Nr. 10067. Budapest: Adliswil-Zürich: New York: Editio Musica; Edition Eulenburg, 1974.
This Magnificat is for two to five voices with portions edited for solo voices (*superius,* mezzo soprano, *altus,* tenor, baritone, and *bassus*) in various combinations. Plainchant settings of the uneven verses are included. There are Latin words. The Preface is in English and German.

SenS   _____. *Sämtliche Werke.* Band III: Motetten. I. Teil: *Gelegenheitsmotetten*

und Psalmvertonungen. Edited by Walter Gerstenberg. Das Erbe Deutscher Musik, no. 13. Wolfenbüttel und Zürich: Mösler Verlag, 1962.
    These compositions are transcriptions. They are principally for four to six voices. The editorial and critical notes are in German. Bibliographical references are included.

SenSM   Senfl, Ludwig. *Sämtliche Werke*. Band I: *Sieben Messen*. Edited by Edwin Löhrer and Otto Ursprung. Das Erbe Deutscher Musik, no. 5. Wolfenbüttel und Zürich: Mösler Verlag, 1962.
    This source contains transcriptions of the seven surviving Masses by Senfl. The editorial and critical notes are in German. Bibliographical references are included.

SenW   _____. *Werke*. I. Teil, edited by Theordore Kroyer and Adolf Thürlings. Denkmäler der Tonkunst in Bayern, (Jg. III, 2), vol. 5. Leipzig: Breitkopf & Härtel, 1903.
    This is a transcription of *Magnificat octo tonorum* published in Nuremberg in 1537. It is for two to six voices with Latin words. There is an introduction containing a bibliography, and biography of Senfl's life and works. There is a supplement containing material on Heinrich Isaac in Augsburg and Constance.

SerB   Serlio, Sebastiano. *The book of architecture*. An introduction by A. E. Santaniello. Architecture-Early works to 1800. London: 1611; reissued by B. Blom, 1970; reprint ed. New York: Arno Press, 1980.
    This book contains "The first booke of architecture, entreating of geometrie.-The second booke of architecture, entreaing of perspectiue...-The third booke, entreating of all kind of excellent antiquities...-The fourth booke, rules for masonry...-the fift booke of architecture, wherein there are set downe certayne formes of temples, according to the ancient maner; and also seruing for Christians."

SerI   Serlio, Sebastiano; Martin, Jean, trans. *Il primo [-secondo] libro d'architettura; lepremier [-second] liure d'architecture*. Paris: [impr.de l. Barbé], 1545. Architecture-Early works to 1800. (Fowler collection of architectural books; reel 52, no. 303). Woodbridge, Conn.: Research Publications, 1979. Microfilm.
    This contains a reprint of the original Italian edition published in Bolognois with a French translation by Lehan Martin. It is bound with Serlio's *Des antiquities* [Anvers, 1550]; his *Reigles generales de l'architecture* [Anvers], 1545; and his *Qvinto libro d'architetettvra* Paris, 1547.

SerL   *Service Book and Hymnal of the Lutheran Church in America*. Minneapolis: Augsburg Publishing House, 1958.
    This contains Lutheran Church hymns with English texts and the Lutheran Church Liturgy and ritual.

SerM   Sermisy, Claudin de. "Masses". 1959. Edited by Gaston Allaire. A part of the editor's unpublished thesis. Photolithograph.
    This contains transcriptions of Masses for four to five voices.

SerMA   _____. *Missa cum quatuor vocibus, ad imitationem moduli Ab initio*. Parisiis: du Chemin, 1556. [Paris: Bibliotheque nationale, n.d.]. Microfilm.
    This is a facsimile of a choirbook found in the Bibliotheque nationale in Paris. It is indexed in RISM A/I, S 2820 and in F. Lesure and G. Thibault, no. 54, p. 318.

Bibliography   105

SerMC   Sermisy, Claudin de. *Missa cum quatuor vocibus, ad imitationem moduli Philomena praevia*. Parisiis: Du Chemin, 1568. [Paris: Bibliotheque nationale, n.d.]. Microfilm.
     This is a facsimile of the Mass for four voices. The original publication is in the Bibliotheque nationale in Paris. This source is indexed in RISM A/I, S 2826 and in F. Lesure et G. Thibault, no. 91, p. 338.

SerMP   _____. *Missa plurium motetorum*. Twelve Franco-Flemish masses of the early sixteenth century, no. 1. [Rochester, N.Y.]: Sibley Music Library, Eastman School of Music, University of Rochester, 1941.
     The caption title is "Attaingnant 1532, tertius liber, fol. ixvii-ixxxix." It is edited by Edwin E. Stein and reprinted from his dissertation, *The polyphonic mass in France and the Netherlands, c. 1525 to c. 1560*.

SerMPD   _____. *Missa pro defunctis*. Musica liturgica, no. 1, facs. 2. Cincinnati: World Library of Sacred Music, 1958.
     This Mass is for four voices. It was published in Attaingnant's *Quartus liber viginti missarum musicalium* of 1532.

SerMQ   _____. *Missa cum quinque vocibus, ad imitationem moduli Quare fremuerunt gentes*. Parisiis: Du Chemin, 1556. [Paris: Bibliotheque nationale, n.d.]. Microfilm.
     This is a facsimile of a choirbook found in the Bibliotheque nationale in Paris. It is indexed in RISM A/I, S 2821 and in F. Lesure and G. Thibault, no. 55, p. 320.

SerMR   _____. *Missa da requiem*. Thesauri musici, no. 7. Wien: Doblinger, 1974.
     This is a reprint of the Requiem for four voices with Latin words. There is a Forward in German and English.

SerMT   _____. *Missae tres, nunc primum in lucem aedite, cum quatuor vocibus, ad imitationem modulorum, ut sequens tabula indicabit...* Lutetiae: Le Roy & Ballard, 1558. [Uppsala: Universitetsbiblioteket, n.d.]. Microfilm.
     This is a facsimile of three Masses by Sermisy: *Missa IX Lectionum, Missa Philomena praevia*, and *Missa Domini est terra*. The original publication is found in the Universitetsbiblioteket in Uppsala. It is indexed in RISM A/I, S 2824.

SerMV   _____. *Missa cum quatuor vocibus, ad imitationem cantionis Voulant honneur*. Parisiis: Du Chemin, 1556. [Paris: Bibliotheque nationale, n.d.]. Microfilm.
     This is a facsimile of a choirbook found in the Bibliotheque nationale in Paris. It is indexed in RISM A/I, S 2823, and in F. Lesure and G. Thibault, no. 57, p. 320.

SerMTP   _____. *Missa cum quatuor vocibus paribus, ad initationem moduli Tota pulchra es*. Parisiis: Du Chemin, 1556. [Paris: Bibliotheque nationale, n.d.]. Microfilm.
     This is a facsimile of a choirbook found in the Bibliotheque nationale in Paris. It is indexed in RISM A/I, S 2822 and in F. Lesure and G. Thibault, no. 56, p. 320.

SerO   _____. *Opera omnia*. 6 Vols. Edited by Gaston Allaire and Isabelle Cazeaux. Corpus mensurabilis musicae, no. 52. Neuhausen-Stuttgart: American Institute of Musicology, 1970.
     These volumes contain transcriptions of 169 *chansons* plus Magnificats and Masses. Vol. I: *Magnificats and Magnificat sections*, Vol. II: *Holy Week*

	music, Vol. III: *Chansons*, Vol. IV: *Chansons*, Vol. V: *Missa*: Attaingnant, *Viginti Missarum* 1532, and Vol.VI: *Missa II*. There are critical notes and an introduction in which the music is discussed.
SheC	Sheppard, John. *Collected Works*. Vol. 2: Hymns. Edited by David Wulstan. Voces musicales: Ser. 1, no. 8. [England]: Oxenford Imprint, 1978. This source contains facsimiles of the hymns edited by David Wulstan. The hymns have Latin words.
SheD	_____. *Te Deum laudamus*. Edited by Bruno Turner. New York Pro Musica series, no. 26. New York: Associated Music Publishers, [c.1969]. This is a transcription of the Te Deum for six voices. There are Latin words with English translation printed as text. It is edited from the manuscript partbooks (*MSS. 979-983*), Christ Church, Oxford. Pl. no.: NYPM-26-22.
SheI	_____. *I give you a new commandment: anthem for men's voices*. Church Music Society reprints, no. 18b (rev.). Croydon, England: Oxford University Press, 1965. This is a reprint of an anthem by John Sheppard. It is written for four men's voices. There is an organ accompaniment for practice only.
SheM	_____. *Masses*. Transcribed and edited by Nicholas Sandon. Early English Church Music, no. 18. London: Stainer and Bell, 1976. This contains transcriptions of the Mass compositions by Sheppard.
SheMN	_____. *Magnificat and Nunc Dimittis: from the First service for men's voices*. Edited by C. F. Simkins. Church Music Society reprints, no. 45. London: Oxford University Press, 1963. This is a reprint of music from the First Service by John Sheppard. It is for chorus (ATTB) with organ (for practice only). The text is in English.
SheMS	_____. *Responsorien*. Edited by Frank Ll. Harrison. Das Chorwerk, no. 84. Wolfenbüttel: Möseler [pref. 1960.] This source contains six Responds by Sheppard: *Audivi vocem de caelo venientem*, *Gloria in excelsis*, *In pace in idipsum*, *In manus tuas, Domine*, *Reges tharsis et insulae*, and *Spiritus Sanctus procedens a throno*. They are written for four to six voices with Latin words and German translation.
SheMV	_____. *Media vita*. Edited by Alan Thurlow. Westhampnett, Chichester, W. Sussex: Cathedral Music, 1837. This is an antiphon to the Nunc dimittis during the two weeks before Passion Sunday. There are English and Latin words. The antiphon has been edited from Oxford: Christ Church, *MSS. 979-83*. There are editorial notes in English.
SheR	_____. *I Responsorial Music*. Transcribed and edited by David Chadd. Early English Church Music, no. 17. London: Stainer and Bell, Ltd., 1977. This source contains transcriptions of the responses by Sheppard with the Latin words. There is an introduction in English and bibliographical references.
SheS	Sherr, Richard, ed. *The Susato Motet Anthologies: Liber Quintus Ecclesiasticarum cantionum quinque vocum vulgo Moteta vocant, tam ex Veteri quam ex Novo Testamento, ab optimis quibusque huius aetatis musicis compositarum omnes primi toni antea nunquam excusus. (Antwerp: Susato, 1553). Liber Sextus Ecclesiasticarum cantionum quinque vocum vulgo Moteta vocant, tam ex Veteri quam ex Novo Testamento, ab optimis quibusque huius aetatis musicis compositarum omnes primi toni antea nunquam excusus.*

(Antwerp: Susato, 1553). Sixteenth-Century Motet, no. 15. New York and London: Garland Publishing, Inc. 1995.

This source contains transcriptions of twenty motets by Johannes de Hollande, Thomas Crécquillon, Petrus Manchicourt, Cornelius Canis, Symon Moreau, Joannes Louviis, Josquin Baston, Cobrise, Eustatius Barbion, Guylle. Le Roy, Joannes Claux, and Brumen [Denis Briant]. There is a general introduction, and an introduction to the volume.

SheT Sherr, Richard. "The Performance of Chant in the Renaissance and Its Interactions with Polyphony." In *Plainsong in the Age of Polyphony*. Edited by Thomas Forrest Kelly. Cambridge: Cambridge University Press, 1992.

This source considers the aspect of chant performance in the fifteenth and sixteenth centuries that can illuminate and be illuminated by polyphony: rhythm. The author argues that there was some variety in chant performance practice.

SheV _____. "Verdelot in Florence, Coppini in Rome, and the Singer 'La Fiore'." *Journal of the American Musicological Society* 37 (1984): 402-411.

This article is a discussion of a few documents culled from the Archivio Di Stato in Florence. They concern Philippe Verdelot, Alessandro Coppini, and a female singer and her accompanying vocal ensemble.

SicS Sicher, Fridolin. *St. Galler Orgelbuch: Die Orgeltabulater des Fridolin Sicher: St. Gallen, Codex 530*. Edited by Hans Joachim with the co-operation of Thomas Warburton. Tabulaturen des XVI. Jahrhunderts, T. 3; Schweizerische Musikdenkmäler, Bd. 8 = Monuments de la musique suisse, no. 8; Veröffentlichungen der Gesellschaft der Orgelfreunde, no. 108. Winterthur, Schweiz: Amadeus, 1992.

This contains arrangements of sacred vocal compositions for keyboard. There is a Forward in English, French, and German with critical notes in German. There is an index and Bibliography, pp. 336-343.

SilI Silbiger, Alexander. "Introduction: The First Centuries of European Keyboard Music." In *Keyboard Music before 1700*. Edited by Alexander Silbiger, p. 1-23. New York: Schirmer Books, [c. 1995].

This contains a discussion of notation, accidentals, meter and note values, early repertory, genres and their contexts, organ music, harpsichord music, imitative genres, and dances.

SilK _____. ed. *Keyboard Music before 1700*. New York: Schirmer Books, [c. 1995].

This is the first of a set of four volumes offering a guide to the literature of Western keyboard music. It includes both stringed keyboard instruments and the organ. It is divided into chapters by national tradition. There is an attempt to avoid using Bach and other later masters as points of reference as is done in Willi Apel's *The History of Keyboard Music to 1700*. Composers and pieces are chosen who still have most to offer in terms of artistic interest and value. Each chapter concludes with a Guide to Literature and Editions, a bibliography, and a list of manuscript short titles.

SliG I Slim, H. Colin. *A Gift of Madrigals and Motets*. Vol. 1: *Description and Analysis*. Chicago and London: The University of Chicago Press, [c. 1972].

This volume is arranged in two parts: a section on historical and bibliographical interest and a section for musicologists.

SliG II _____, ed.. *A Gift of Madrigals and Motets*. Vol. II: *Transcriptions*. Chi-

cago and London: The University of Chicago Press, [c. 1972].
This contains transcriptions of thirty motets and thirty madrigals transcribed from four sixteenth-century partbooks in the Newberry Library (Case MS.-VM 1578.M91). The *altus* partbook is missing. The *altus* parts for four of the motets and six of the madrigals has been provided by concordant sources. The texts with their translations are given.

SliK   Slim, H. Colin, ed. *The Keyboard music at Castell' Arquato*. Vol. 2: *Masses, magnificat, liturgical works, dances, and madrigals*. Corpus of early keyboard music, no. 37. [S.l.]: American Institute of Musicology; Neuhausen-Stuttgart, West Germany: Hänssler-Verlag, 1900-.
This has been edited from mid-sixteenth century manuscripts in the archive of the Chiesa Collegiata at Castell' Arquato.

SmiM   Smijers, Albert, ed. *Missa ad modulum Benedicta es sex vocum*. Vereeniging voor nederandsche muziekgeschiedenis, no. 38. Amsterdam: G. Alsbach & Co.; Leipzig: Breitkopf & Härtel, 1920.
This contains the score of *Pleni sunt coeli* and *Osanna* from Willaert's Mass, *Missa super Benedicta es*, used to complete the Sanctus. There is also an anonymous *Benedictas es coelorum Regina* and the *Benedicta es coelorum Regina* by Josquin.

SocP   Société Français de Musicologie. *Publications, Série 1; monuments de la musique ancienne, v. 1-10*. Paris: Société Française de Musicologie, 1925-1936. Paris: Société Française de Musicologie, n.d. Microfilm.
Vols. 3-4 contain the Lute music found in *Chansons au luth et airs de cour française du XVIe siècle*.

SouP   *Souterliedekens, 1540*. Facsimile of Dutch Songbooks, vol. 2. Commentary in Dutch and English by J. van Biezen and Marie Veldhuyzen. Netherlands: Frits Knuf, 1984.
This is a facsimile of the copy of the 1540 *Souterliedekens* in the University Library of Amsterdam.

SteC   Stevens, Denis. *Tudor church music*. London, Faber and Faber [1961]
This source traces the developments and stylistic changes from 1485 to 1603 with special reference being given to the liturgical forms used principally by composers of the period.

SteE   ____, transc. and ed. *Early Tudor Organ Music II: Music for the Mass*. Early English Church Music No. 10. London: Stainer and Bell, 1970.
This contains transcriptions of music for the Ordinary and Proper of the Mass. There is an Introduction, Critical commentary, List of Sources, and two Appendices.

SteMB   ____, transc. and ed. *The Mulliner Book*. 2nd rev. ed. Musica Britannica, no. 1. London: Stainer and Bell, Ltd., 1954.
This book contains transcriptions of 120 pieces of Early English keyboard music, three-quarters of which are unique. It includes the whole gamut of sixteenth- century music, i.e., Latin motets, English anthems, arrangements of part songs, transcriptions of consort music, plainsong fantasias for organ, dance music for the clavichord or virginals, and music for cittern and gittern. The repertory includes early Tudor composers, Allwood, Taverner, Farrant, and Shelby, as well as later ones, Munday, Whyte, Heath, and Tye.

SteMBC   ____. *The Mulliner Book: a Commentary*. London: Stainer and Bell, Ltd., 1952?.

This is a description of the British Museum *Add. Ms. 30513*. The edition is limited to five hundred copies. Numbers one to ten are not for sale. There are transcriptions of music for cittern and gittern at the end of the discourse. There is a bibliography, pp. 70-74.

SteMP Stevens, John E., 1921. *Music & Poetry in the Early Tudor Court*. Lincoln: University of Nebraska Press, [c. 1961].

This is a history and criticism of English music and poetry of the early modern period of 1500 to 1700. There is a list of sources, pp. 461-468 and a bibliography, pp. 469-476.

SteN Stevenson, R. "John Marbeck's "Noted Booke" of 1550" *Musical Quarterly* 37:2 (1951): 220-234.

This source has a short discussion of Marbeck's life and a detailed discussion of Marbeck's "Noted Booke". There is a facsimile of the Title-page of the *Booke* and one of two pages taken from it.

SteP Sternhold, Thomas. *Certayne psalmes chose out of the psalter of David: and drawe into English Meter*. Ann Arbor: University Microfilms, 1976.

This is a facsimile of the 1547 edition that was published in London. It contains English paraphrases of the Psalms.

StePD _____. *Psalmes of David in metre*. [Wesel?: H. Singleton?, 1555]. Early English Books, 1475-1640; 1771:1. Ann Arbor, Mich.: University Microfilms International, 1983. Microfilm.

This is the Sternhold and Hopkins version. It contains, English paraphrases of the Psalms as well as "Certaine Christian and godly prayers, The cathechisme, A manner of examininge children before thei be admitted to the Lord's Supper, and another more briefe and shorter forme of the same." This is a reproduction of the original found in the Harvard University Library. The original is imperfect.

StePS _____. *Certayne Psalmes*. Early English books, 1475-1640; 1743:7. [London]: Excudebat Londini Edouardus Whitchurche, 1549. Ann Arbor: University Microfilms International, 1983.

The running title is, *Psalmes of David in metre*. It is dedicated to Edward VI. The date of imprint was suggested by STC (2nd edition). This is a reproduction of the original in the Henry E. Huntington Library and Art Gallery.

SteR Steigleder, Johann Ulrich. *Ricercar tabulatura*. [Stuttgart: Autor], 1624. Kassel: deutscher Musikgeschichtliches archiv, [196?]. Microfilm.

This is a facsimile of German organ music.

StrLM Straeten, Edmond vander. *La musique aux Pays-Bas avant le XIXe siècle...* Bruxelles: G. -A. van Trigt, 1867-1888.

This source contains eight volumes. There are articles on composers, theorists, luthiers, operas, motets, national airs, academies, books, portraits, plates of music, and an alphabetical index. Volume 6 has subtitle: *Les musiciens néerlandais en Italia*, and volume 7-8: *Les musiciens néerlandais en Espagne*.

StrS Strunk, Oliver, comp. *Source Readings in Music History: from Classical Antiquity through the Romantic Era*. New York: W. W. Norton and Co., Inc., [c. 1950].

This source contains extracts of the writings of theorists, composers, teachers, critics, and practical musicians. It is arranged chronologically by topic with each extract introduced with a few comments.

SusL   Susato, Tielman. *Le premier livre des chansons à deux ou à trois parties contenant trente et une nouvelles chansons, convenables tant à la voix comme aux instrumentz.* Anvers: Susato, 1544. London: British Library, n.d. Microfilm.

A microfilm of *Le premier livre des Chansons* published by Susato. It contains polyphonic *chansons* for two and three voices.

SusLDE   _____. *Liber decimus ecclesiasticarum cantionum quinque vocum vulgo moteta vocant.* Antwerpiae: Susato, 1555. [Budapest: Orszagos Szechenyi Konyvtar, n.d.]. Microfilm.

This is a facsimile. It contains motets by J. Gallus, P. Gheens, J. Bracqueniers, C. Canis, Clemens non Papa, T. Crécquillon, J. Crespel, J. Guyot, C. Hollander, J. Lupi, S. Moreau, and J. Scelutus. It is indexed in RISM B/I, 1555-08 and Meissner, vol. 2, p. 106.

SusLP   _____. *Liber primus missarum quinque vocum...* Antverpiae: Susato, 1546. Kassel: Murhard'sche Bibliothek des Stadt Kassel und Landesbibliothek, n.d. Microfilm.

This contains Masses for five voices by Crécquillon, Manchicourt, and Susato. The original manuscript is in Murhard'sche Bibliothek des Stadt Kassel und Landesbibliothek (D Kl). It is indexed in RISM B/I, 1546-3 and Meissner, Vol. 2, p. 51.

SusLPS   _____. *Liber primus sacrarum cantionum, quinque vocum, vulgo moteta vocant...* Antwerp: Susato, 1546. [Wien: Gesellschaft der Musikfreunde in Wien, n.d.]. Microfilm.

This contains motets by B. Appenzeller, P. Cadeac, Clemens non Papa, T. Crécquillon, J. Gallus, J. Guyot, L. Hellinck, C. Hollander, T. Susato, and others. There are five partbooks for *superius*, contratenor, tenor, *bassus*, and *quinta*. It is indexed in RISM B/I, 1546-06 and Meissner, vol. 2, p. 55.

SusLQ   _____. *Liber quartus sacrarum cantionum, quatuor vocum, vulgo moteta vocant...* Antwerp: Susato, 1547. [Wien: Gesellschaft der Musikfreunde in Wien, n.d.]. Microfilm.

This contains motets by Benedictus, Clemens non Papa, Conseil, Crécquillon, Geszin, Guyot, Larchier, Manchicourt, Mouton, Payen, and others. There are four partbooks for *superius*, tenor, *contratenur*, and *bassus*. The original is in Gesellschaft der Musikfreunde in Wien. It is indexed in RISM B/I, 1547-06 and Meissner, vol. 2, p. 61.

SusLS   _____. *Liber secundus sacrarum cantionum, quinque vocum, vulgo moteta vocant...* Antwerp: Susato, 1546. [Lincoln microfilm gift] London: British Museum, [198-]. Microfilm.

This contains motets for five voices by Benedictus, C. Canis, Clemens non Papa, T. Crécquillon, J. Guyot, L. Hellinck, J. Lupi, Manchicourt, N. Payen, and Anonymous. There are five partbooks for *superius*, contratenor, tenor, *bassus*, and *quinta*. It is indexed in RISM B/I, 1546-07, Lincoln, H.B., *The Latin Motet*, p. 745 and Meissner, vol. 2, p. 57.

SusLTE   _____. *Liber tertius ecclesiasticarum cantionum quatuor vocum vulgo moteta vocant.* Antwerpiae: Susato, 1553. [New York: New York Public Library, n.d.]. Microfilm.

There are motets for four voices by J. Baston, L. Hellinck, H. Hequest, J. Hollander, G. Jonckens, P. Jordanus, P. de Manchicourt, P. Massenus, J.

Vaet and Clemens non Papa. It is indexed in RISM B/I, 1553-10 and Meissner, vol. 2, p. 89.

SusLTM   Susato, Tielman. *Liber tertius missarum quatuor vocum...* Antwerp: Tylmannum Susato, 1546. [Kassel: Murhard'sche Bibliothek der Stadt Kassel und Landesbibliothek, n.d.]. Microfilm.

This contains *Missa Peccata mea domine* by L. Hellinck; *Missa, O dei genitrix* by J. Richafort; *Missa, Allemaigne* by J. Mouton; *Missa, Je prens en gre* by T. Crécquillon; and *Missa, Gris & tanna* by P. de Manchicourt. There are partbooks for *superius*, tenor, contratenor, and *bassus*. The original manuscript is in the Murhard'sche Bibliothek der Stadt Kassel und Landesbibliothek (D KI). It is indexed in RISM B/I , 1546-04 and Meissner, vol. 2, p. 54.

SusLTS   _____. *Liber terius sacrarum cantionum, quatuor vocum, vulgo moteta vocant...* Antwerp: Susato, 1547. [Wien:. Gesellschaft der Musikfreunde in Wien, n.d.]. Microfilm.

This contains motets by Clemens non Papa, Courtois, Crécquillon, de Lattre, J. Gallus, J. Guyot, L. Hellinck, Hesdin, Lupi, Manchicourt, Rocourt, Susato, Trojano, Willaert, and others. The original is in Gesellschaft der Musikfreunde in Wien. It is indexed in RISM B/I, 1547-05 and Meissner, vol. 2, p. 59.

SusP   _____. *Premier- quatoirsiesme livre des chansons.* Corpus of early music, nos. 2-15. Bruxelles: Éditions culture et civilisation, 1970-1972.

These fourteen volumes are facsimiles of the first series of polyphonic *chansons* written for one to eight voices and published from 1543 to 1555 by Susato. The fourteenth volume has *chansons* by Orlando di Lasso.

SusV   _____. Vingt et six chansons musicales & nouvelles à cinq parties... Anvers: Susato, 1543. London: British Library, n.d. Microfilm .

This source contains four partbooks with *chansons* by Baston, Canis, Crécquillon, Descaudain, J. Gallus, Gombert, Lupi, Mouton, Richafort, Susato, and anon. The original is in the British Library in London. It has the *superius*, tenor, contratenor, and *bassus*. The fifth voice is missing. It is indexed in RISM B/1, [1543]-15 and Meissner, vol. 2, p. 17.

SutC I   Sutherland, David A., ed. *The Lyons Contrapunctus: (1528).* Recent Researches in the Music of the Renaissance, no. 21. Madison, Wis.: A-R Editions, [c. 1976].

This source contains, principally, anonymous Mass Propers, for *superius, altus*, tenor and *bassus* with the Latin words. There are English translations on pp. xxiv-xxvi. There is a Preface in the 1st edition., with English on pp. xxxi-xxxiii. Bibliographical references are included. This is edited from the 1st edition. (*Lugduni: In edibus Stephani Guaynard, 1528*) which has the title, *Contrapunctus: seu figurata musica super piano cantu Missarum solennium totius anni.*

SutC II   _____, ed. *The Lyons Contrapunctus: (1528).* Recent Researches in the Music of the Renaissance, no. 22. Madison, Wis.: A-R Editions, [c. 1976].

This second volume is a continuation of the first volume and includes the motets by Francesco Layolle as well as more of the Mass Propers.

TalC   Tallis, Thomas. *Complete keyboard works.* Edited by Denis Stevens. Hinrichsen Edition, no. 1585. New York: Peters, 1953.

This contains transcriptions of keyboard music. Most of the music written

	by Tallis for keyboard was intended for the organ but would sound well on the clavichord, virginal, and harpsichord. There are some facsimilies.
TalF	Tallis, Thomas. *Five Hymns*. New York pro musica antiqua series, no 13-17. New York: Associated Music Publishers, 1961.
	The five hymns are *Sermone blando angelus, Salvator mundi Domine, Jam Christus astra ascenderat, Quod chorus vatum*, and *Deus tuorum militum*.
TalT VI	____, *(1505-1585)*. Tudor Church Music, no. 6. Edited by Percy C. Buck, Edmund H. Fellows, A. Ramsbotham, R. R. Terry, and Sylvia Townsend Warner. New York: Broude Brothers, 1923-1948.
	This contains transcriptions of the Latin music by Tallis. There are details of the manuscripts and printed books that were consulted and words of the motets. There is an Appendix containing additional notes and corrections for volumes one to ten of the series.
TavF	Taverner, John. *Five-part Masses*. Edited by Hugh Benham. Early English Church Music, no. 36. London: Stainer and Bell, 1990.
	This contains transcriptions of unaccompanied Masses. Bibliographical references are included.
TavFF	____. *Four and Five-part Masses*. Edited by Hugh Benham. Early English Church Music, no. 35. London: Stainer and Bell, 1989.
	This contains transcriptions of three unaccompanied Masses, the *Plainsong Mass*, the *Western Wind Mass*, and the *Mean Mass*.
TavJ	____. *John Taverner*. Edited by Hugh Benham. Early English Church Music, no. 25. . London: Published for the British Academy: Stainer and Bell, 1978-1990.
	This source contains transcriptions of Taverner's votive antiphons.
TavR	____. *John Taverner III: ritual music and secular songs*. Edited by Hugh Benham. Early English Church Music, no. 30. London: Stainer and Bell, 1984.
	This source contains hymns, Masses, and part songs by Taverner.
TavS	____. *Six-part Masses*. Edited by Hugh Benham. Early English Church Music, no. 20. London: Stainer and Bell, 1978.
	These are transcriptions. Editorial notes, critical commentary, and list of sources are included.
TerC	Terry, R. R., ed. *Calvin's First Psalter*. (1539). London: E. Benn, 1932.
	This is a facsimile as well as a transcription into modern notation. Twelve of the Psalms are adapted from Marot's paraphrases. The melodies are harmonized modally by R. R. Terry, together with translations of the Psalms into English verse by K. W. Simpson.
TheH	*The Hymnal of the Protestant Episcopal Church in the United States of America*. New York: The Church Pension Fund, 1940.
	This hymnal contains not only hymns but also a collection of service music. The preface has a discussion of the hymns, the music of the hymns, and the service music. There is a 1961 Supplemental Liturgical Index and Collection of Service Music.
TheM	*Thesaurus musicus*. 5 volumes. Noribergae: T. Montanus & U. Neuberus, 1564. Washington, D. C.: Library of Congress, [1991?]. Microfilm.
	Each volume has four to eight partbooks containing motets for four, five, six, seven, and eight voices. They are indexed in RISM, ser. B, v. 1, no. 1, pt. 1, p. 247.

ThoF Thomas, Bernard, ed. *Fourteen Chansons (1533) for four recorders or voices ATTB / Pierre Attaingnant*. Edited from *Vingt et sept chansons musicales (Paris: Attaingnant, 1533)*. London: London Pro Musica Edition, [c. 1972].
This contains transcriptions of the four-part *chansons* that Attaingnant indicated were suitable for recorders as well as for voices. They have been edited from *Vingt et sept chansons musicales* published in Paris by Attaingnant in 1533. There are French words and English translations. There are notes on pronunciation and incipits indicating the original clefs. The composers are Claudin, Heurteur, Passereau, Vermont, and Jacotin. There is an introduction in which the music is discussed and notes on the proper performance of the music are given.

ThoFM ____, ed. *Fifteen madrigals: for three voices or instruments*. The Italian madrigal, no. 2. [London?]: London Pro Musica Edition, 1979.
This contains eleven madrigals by Festa; one madrigal each by Pisano, Compère, and G. Fogliano; and two by Silvestro. The words are Italian with English translation at the end of each work. There are notes, a discussion of authorship, and performance suggestions. There is also an arrangement of a piece by S. Ganassi.

ThoN ____. *Neuf basse dances, deux branles, vingt et cinq pavannes, avec quinze gaillards en musique à quatre parties: 1530*. Pierre Attaingnant's Tanzbücher, no. 1. Zürich: Musikhaus Pan, 1991.
This contains transcriptions of dances for four unspecified instruments. It is edited from the first edition of *Neuf basse dances, deux branles, vingt et cinq pavannes...* published in Paris by Attaingnant in 1530. There is a transcription of twelve dances from *Six gaillardes et six pavanes avec trez chansons musicales à quatre parties* published by Attaingnant in 1530.

ThoSD ____. *6 dances from the court of Henry VIII: for four instruments*. Early music library, 57. London: London Pro Musica edition, 1989.
This is a transcription of *The emperor's pavyn, Galyard, The kyng's pavyn, The crocke, The kyng's maske*, and *Galyard*. The original manuscript, *Royal App. 58* is in the British Library. There are editorial notes by Bernard Thomas.

TinC Tinctoris, Johannes. *Concerning the Nature and Propriety of Tones. (De natura et proprietate tonorum.)* Translated by Albert Seay. Colorado College translation series, no. 2. Colorado Springs: Colorado College Music Press, 1967.
This contains a discussion of modes in plainsong and polyphony, and the length of an internal accidental.

TriM Tritonius, Petrus. *Melopoiae sive harmoniae tetracenticae: 1507*. Edited by Giuseppe Vecchi. Corpus mensurabilis more antiquo musicae, no. 1. Bologna: A.M.I.S., 1967.
This source contains four-voice settings for twenty Odes from Horace's Carmina. The text is in Latin and the Prefatory material is in Italian.

TofA Toft, Robert. *Aurol images of lost traditions: sharps and flats in the 16th century*. Toronto: University of Toronto Press, [c. 1992].
This ia an attempt to establish the parameters of sixteenth-century practices with guide lines for modern performers and scholars.

TowS Towne, Gary. "A Systematic Formulation of Sixteenth-Century Text Under-

lay Rules." Part I of II. *Musica Disciplina* 44 (1990): 255-287.
    This is a collation, restatement, and reformulation of the rules of underlay stated in a treatise by Lanfranco (1533), and elaborated by Zarlino (1558). There are related precepts by Vincento (1555), and work by Stocker (1570) and Luchini (ca. 1590). Towne has attempted to elucidate the application by singers in performance through paraphrase, collation, and summary. He has limited himself to texting Latin sacred music.

TreC   Trend, J. B. "Cristóbal Morales". *Music and Letters* 6 (1925): 19-34.
    This article contains a discussion of the life of Morales and some of his works. There is a provisional list of works and three transcriptions at the end of the article.

TyeE   Tye, Christopher. *Christopher Tye I: English Sacred Music*. Transcribed and edited by John Morehen. Early English Church Music, no. 19. London: Published for the British Academy by Stainer and Bell, 1977-1987.
    The words are in English. Historical notes and critical commentary on the music are included.

TyeM   _____. *Christopher Tye II: Masses*. Transcribed and edited by Paul Doe. Early English Church Music, no. 24. London: Published for the British Academy by Stainer and Bell, 1977-1987.
    The words are in Latin. Historical notes and critical commentary on the music are included.

TyeP   _____. *Peccavimus*. Edited by Sarah Cobbold. Voces musicales, Ser. 2, no. 9. [England]: Oxenford Imprint, 1984.
    This is a transcription of the votive antiphon, *Peccavimus*. The antiphon is written for seven voices, treble, mean, two altos, tenor, and two basses. It has the Latin words.

UlrH   Ulrich, Homer and Paul A. Pisk. *A History of Music and Musical Style*. New York: Harcourt, Brace and World, Inc., [c. 1963].
    The purpose of the book is to offer a clear, straightforward presentation of the historical developments in musical style. There is a discussion of musical style from ca. 675 B.C. through the present.

UndM   "Under the Medici." *Britannica 2001 Deluxe Edition CD-ROM*. Britannica.com Inc. October 2, 2001.
    This is a short biography of a particular period in the life of Machiavelli..

UniB   "United Kingdom." *Britannica 2002 Deluxe Edition*. Copyright © 1994-2002 Britannica.com Inc. April 9, 2002.
    This is a section of the article on the history of the Anglican church. There is a discussion of Henry VIII's break with Rome and the Act of Supremecy of 1534.

ValL   Valderrábano, Enriquez de. *Libro de Música de vihuela, intitulado Silva de sirenas (Valladolid, 1547)*. Edited by Emilio Pujol. 2 vols. Monumentos de la música española, 22-23. Barcelona: Consejo superior de investigaciones Cientificas, Instituto Español de Musicología, 1965.
    This contains transcriptions of vihuela music by F. de Layolle, Gombert, Verdelto, and others. There are some facsimiles.

ValLD   _____. *Libro de música de vihuela intitulado Silva de sirenas...* [Valladolid: Cordova], 1547. [London: British Library, n.d.]. Microfilm.
    This is a facsimile of the original publication in the British Library in London. It contains vihuela music by F. de Layolle, Gombert, Verdelot,

and others. There is music for one or two vihuelas. There are seven vols. in one.

VanR Vanneo, Stefano. *Recanetum de musica aurea*. Romae: apvd Valerium Dorcium Brixiensem, 1533. Italian Books before 1601, roll 603, item 14. Watertown, Mass.:General Microfilm Co., [19--]. Microfilm.

This book was originally written in Italian but no printed edition of the original is known. This Latin translation is by Vincenzo Rosseto of Verona. It is a treatise on music theory.

VanRD _____. *Recanetum de musica aurea*. Colorado College Music Press Texts/Translations, no. 2. Edited by Albert Seay. Colorado Springs: Colorado College Music Press. 1979.

This is an English translation of this treatise on music theory of the early sixteenth century. The Latin and English translations are on facing pages. It is edited from the first edition published in Rome by V. Dorico in 1533.

VerD Verdelot, Philippe. *De i madrigali a cinque voci libro secondo*. [Venizia: O. Scotto]: 1538. Munich: Bayerische Staatsbibliothek, 1986. Microfilm.

This contains the *cantus, altus*, tenor, *bassus*, and *quinta pars* of madrigals by Verdelot, Festa, Metre Ian, and Willaert.

VerM _____. "Madrigali a cinque: libro primo." Venezia: Scotto, 1535. Paris]: Biblioteque Nationale Service Photographique, [19--]. Photocopy.

This is a photocopy of madrigals for five voices by Verdelot. It is indexed in RISM A/I, V 1223 and Nuovo Vogel, no. 2887.

VerMN _____. *Madrigali novi de diversi excellentissimi musici: Libro primo de la Serena*. Roma: M. Valerio da Bressa, 1534. Munich: Bayerische Staatsbibliothek. Microfilm.

This contains the *superius, altus*, and *bassus* of Italian madrigals originally written for four parts. The tenor part is wanting. The *superius* and *bassus* are in the Bayerische Staatsbibliothek in Munich and the *altus* part is in the Bibliotheca Colombina in Seville.The madrigals are by Verdelot, C. Festa, J. Gallus, S. Festa, and C. Janequin. There are twenty Italian and French pieces, eight of which are by Verdelot. Two pieces are French *chansons*.

VerO I _____. *Opera omnia*. Vol. I. Edited by Anne-Marie Bragard. Corpus mensurabilis musicae, no. 28. [S. I.]: American Institute of Musicology, 1966.

This contains transcriptions of two Masses, nine hymns, and a Magnificat.

VerO II _____. *Opera omnia*. Vol. II. Edited by Anne-Marie Bragard. Corpus mensurabilis musicae, no. 28. [S. I.]: American Institute of Musicology, 1966.

This contains transcriptions of motets .

VerO III _____. *Opera omnia*. Vol. III. Edited by Anne-Marie Bragard. Corpus mensurabilis musicae, no. 28. [S. I.]: American Institute of Musicology, 1966.

This contains transcriptions of thirteen motets.

VerT _____. *Twenty-two madrigals for four voices or instruments = fur vier Singstimmen oder Instruments*. The Italian Madrigal, no 3. Edited by Thomas Bernard. London: London Pro Musica, 1980.

This contains transcriptions of madrigals with Italian words. The English translations are printed as text on pp. 6-7. There is prefatory material in German and English on pp. 2-5. Bibliographical references are included.

VesO I Vesalius, Andreas. *On the Fabric of the Human Body: a translation of De humani corporis fabrica libri septem / Book I: The bones and cartilages*. Norman Anatomy Series, no. 1 and Norman Landmarks Series, no. 1. Translated and Edited by William Frank Richardson and John Burd Carman. San Francisco: Norman Publishing, 1998.

> This is an English translation of Book I. It includes bibliographical references and indexes.

VesO II   Vesalius, Andreas. *On the Fabric of the Human Body: a translation of De humani corporis fabrica libri septem / Book II: The ligaments and muscles.* Norman Anatomy Series, no. 2 and Norman Landmarks Series, no. 2. Translated and edited by William Frank Richardson and John Burd Carman. San Francisco: Norman Publishing, 1999.

> This is an English translation. Bibliographical references and indexes are included.

VilL   "Villota." *Britannica 2001 Deluxe edition CD-ROM.* [c. 1994-2000]. Britannica.com Inc. May 19, 2001.

> This article contains a short definition of the *Villota*.

VilLA   "Villanella." *Britannica 2001 Deluxe edition CD-ROM.* [c. 1994-2000]. Britannica.com Inc. May 19, 2001.

> This article contains a short definition of the *Villanella*.

VogB   Vogel, Emil; Lesure, François; Sartori, Claudio; Il nuovo Vogel. *Bibliografia della musica italiana vocale profana pubblicata dal 1500 al 1700.* Staderini: Minkoff Editori, Nuova edizione, 1976.

> This is a bibliography of Italian secular music published from 1500 to 1700. It is augmented with indices of titles, printers, publishers and authors of the words. Also contents of collections and dedications are given.

WalSW   Walther, Johann. *Sämtliche Werke.* 6 vols. Edited by Otto Schröder. Kassel: Bärenreiter; St. Louis: Concordia Publishing House, 1953-1973.

> This is the complete works of Johann Walther.

WalW   _____. *Wittembergisch geistlich Gesangbuch von 1524.* Edited by Otto Kade. Publikationen älterer praktischer und theoretischen Musikwerke, no. 7. Berlin: Trautwein, 1878.

> This is a facsimile edition. It contains Lutheran Church hymns for three to five voices with German and Latin words.

WatT   Watkins, Glenn. "Three Books of Polyphonic Lamentations of Jeremiah." Ph.D. Thesis, University of Rochester, 1974. Rochester, N.Y.: University of Rochester Microprint Service, 1974. Microfiche.

> This is a thesis (Ph.D.) written by Glenn Watkins at the University of Rochester. There are two volumes. Volume one includes bibliographic references. Volume two contains transcriptions of *Lamentationes Hieremiae prophetae*, published by Montanus and Neuber in 1549; *Piissimae ac sacratissimae lamentationes Ieremiae prophetae*, published by Le Roy et Ballard in 1557; and *Lamentationi di Morales a 4, a 5 et a 6 voci*, published by Rampazetta in 1564.

WesK   Westphal, Kurt, ed. *Karnevalslieder der Renaissance, zu 3-4 Stimmen.* Das Chorwerk, no. 43. Wolfenbüttel: Möseler, [pref. 1936.]

> This contains Italian songs for three and four voices by Willaert, Castellino, Nola, Cimello, Perissone, Lasso, and Severino Corneti.. There are Italian and German words.

WhiE   White, Ernest. *Early German Masters: 16th century.* Masterpieces of organ music, folio no. 67. New York: Liturgical Music Press, 1952.

> There are transcriptions of six organ compositions from the *Tabulaturbuch*

of Fridolin Sicher and two Kyries for organ by Gregor Meyer.

WilA Williams, Peter. *A New History of the Organ: From the Greeks to the Present Day*. Bloomington: Indiana University Press, [c. 1980].

The history of organs has been traced briefly but comprehensively. A select bibliography is listed at the end of each chapter. There are illustrations and a glossary.

WilAE _____. *The European Organ: 1450-1850*. London: B. T. Batsford Ltd, [c. 1966].

There is a discussion of organs and organ builders in the Ntherlands, Austria, Southern Germany, Czechoslovakia, North-West Germany, Scandinavia, North-Central Germany, Silesia, Poland, France, Italy, Spain and Portugal. There are plates and maps and a glossary of stop-names.

WilAR Willaert, Adrian. *Ave regina coelorum*. Edited by Jessie Ann Owens. [S.i.: s.n., ?1900 1992.

This contains transcriptions of motets for four parts, unaccompanied.

WilC _____. *Two Chansons for Six Voices or Instruments*. Ricercate e passaggi, no. 8a. London: London Pro Musica Edition, [c. 1986].

This is a companion edition to *Divisions on chansons for treble instrument and continuo* by Girolamo Dalla Casa. This work is edited from *Canzone di diversi per sonar con ogni sorte di stromenti a quatro cinque & sei voci* published at Venice in 1588. There are two polyphonic *chansons* for six voices or unspecified instruments with French words. There is a separate section in the back containing the separate scores and parts.

WilCL _____. *Cincquiesme livre de chansons composé à troys parties*. Paris: Le Roy & Ballard, 1560. Wien: Österreichische Nationalbibliothek, n.d. Microfilm.

This is a facsimile of the original fifth book of *chansons* published by Adrian Le Roy and Robert Ballard. It contains polyphonic *chansons* for three voices composed by Adrian Willaert.

WilCV _____. *Canzon villanesche alla napolitana quatro voci: con la canzon di Ruzante: Libro primo*. Venice: Scotto, 1548. Wien: Österreichische Nationalbibliothek, [198-]. Microfilm.

This contains facsimiles of four-part Italian part-songs by Willaert, Sivestrino, and Piersson. The original manuscript is in Wien: Österreichische National-bibliothek. It is indexed in *The Italian madrigal and related repertories* by H. B. Lincoln, RISM B/1, 1548-11, and Bernstein catalog, no. 73.

WilD _____. *Del primo libro dei motetti a quattro voci*. Venetii: Scotto, 1539. Palermo: Biblioteca Nazionale, 1976. Microfilm.

This contains the *altus* and *bassus* partbooks. The *superius* and tenor partbooks are lacking. The partbooks are bound with Willaert's book two containing motets for four voices. The original publication is in the Biblioteca Nazionale in Palermo. It is indexed in RISM A/I, W1106 and Berstein catalog, no. 7.

WilDP _____. *Musica quatuor vocum (motecta vulgo appellant) liber primus*. Venice: Antonium Gardane, 1545. Vienna: Österreichische Nationalbibliothek, 1978. Microfilm.

This is a facsimile containing motets for four voices. The original is in Vienna at the Österreichische Nationalbibliothek. It is indexed in RISM A/I, W1107a.

WilF   Willaert, Adrian. *Five Double Canons for Four Voices or Instruments.* Thesaurus musicus (London Pro Musica Edition), no. 65. London: London Pro Musica Edition, [c. 1986].

These are transcriptions edited from the *Motetti novi e chanzoni franciose a quatro sopra doi* published by A. Antico in Venice in 1520. One is a Latin piece and the others are French *chansons*. There is a note on the cover stating that the texture of the pieces demands performance by balanced consorts of voices or instruments such as recorders or viols. English translations of the French texts are included.

WilFC   _____. *The Complete Five and Six-Voice Chansons.* Edited by Jane A. Bernstein. Sixteenth Century *Chanson*, no. 23. New York: Garland, 1992.

This source is edited principally from *Mellange de chansons tant des vieux autheurs que des modernes.* Paris: A. Le Roy et R. Ballard, 1572. It contains a general introduction and an introduction to this volume containing information about Willaert and his music. There are transcriptions of twenty-five *chansons*, twenty-four issued by Le Roy and Ballard and one by Kriesstein.

WilH   _____. *Hymnorum musica secundum ordinem romanae ecclesiae.* Venice: apud H. Scotum, 1550. Kassel: Deutsches Musikgeschichtliches Archiv, 1986. Microfilm.

This is a facsimile of three partbooks for *cantus, altus,* and tenor. It contains Latin hymns by Willaert and Jacquet of Mantua. It is indexed in RISM B/I, 1550-3 and RISM A/I, W 1114.

WilI   _____. *Italienische Madrigale: zu 4-5 Stimmen.* Edited by Walter Wiora. Das Chorwerk, no. 5. Wolfenbüttel: Möseler, ed. Unveränderte Neuaufl, 1930.

This contains transcriptions of eight madrigals for four and five voices by Willaert, Verdelot, Arcadelt, and Cyprian de Rore. There are Italian words with German translations.

WilM   _____. *Missa "Mente tota".* S.l.: s.n., ? 1960; 1969. Berkeley, Calif.: University of California, Library Photographic Service, 196-?. Microfilm.

This is a reproduction of a holograph. It is indexed in Llorens, J. M. Capellae Sixtinae codices...1960.

WilMA   _____. *Madrigali a quatro voci con alcune napolitane et la canzon de ruzante tutte racolte insieme.* Vinegia: Girolamo Scotto, 1563. Seattle, Washington: University of Washington, 19-. Microfilm.

This is a collection of all of Willaert's four-voice pieces, including the *canzoni villanesche alla napolitane* and "La canzone de Ruzante" (*i.e. Zoia zentil che per secreta*). These pieces were first printed in anthologies dating from 1536 to 1544.

WilMN   _____. *Musica nova di Adriano Willaert.* Venetia: Appresso di Antonio Gardano, 1559. Munich: Bayerische Staatsbibliothek, n.d. Microfilm.

This contains secular and religious motets and madrigals for four to seven voices. The title is taken from the *altus* partbook. The title page is lacking on *cantus* and tenor partbooks.

WilMQ   _____. *Musica quinque vocum...liber primus.* Venetiis: Scotus, 1539. Wolfenbüttel: Herzog-August-Bibliothek, [n.d.]. Microfilm.

This contains twenty-three motets in five partbooks for *cantus, altus,* tenor, *bassus,* and *quintus.* The title on other partbooks is *Del primo libro de i motetti a cinque voci*. It is indexed in RISM A/I, W 1110 and Bernstein catalog, no. 9.

WilO   Willaert, Adrian. *Opera omnia*. 15 vols. Edited by H. Zenck and Walter Gerstenberg. Corpus mensurabilis musicae, no. 3. Rome: American Institute of Musicology, 1950-.
Volumes I and II: *Motetta IV vocum*; Volume III: *Motetta V vocum*; Volume IV: *Motetta VI vocum*; Volume V: *Musica nova, 1559*; Volumes VI and VII: *Hymnorum Musica, 1542*; Volume VIII: *Psalmi Vesperales IV et VIII vocum, 1550, 1555, 1557, 1565, 1571;* Volume IX: *Liber quinque missarum IV vocum 1536*; Volume XIII: *Musica nova, 1559: Madrigali*; Volume XIV: *Madrigali and Canzoni Villanesche*. There is a Preface in English.

WilS   _____. *I salmi appertinenti alli vesperi per tutte le feste dell'anno...* Venetia: Apresso di Antonio Gardane, 1550. [Los Angeles: University of California, 1985?]. Microfilm.
This source contains the *cantus* and *altus* parts for Chorus I of the Vesper Psalms. Pages thirty-one to thirty-eight of the *cantus* part are missing. It is reproduced from the original in Bologna, Biblioteca Conservatorio (Liceo Musicale). It contains works by Willaert and Jachet de Mantua. It is indexed in RISM B/I, 1550-1.

WilSA   _____. *I salmi appertinenti alli vesperi per tutte le feste dell'anno...* Venetia: Apresso di Antonio Gardane, 1550. Barcelona: biblioteca central, 1974. Microfilm.
This contains only the *tenor primus* part of the Vesper Psalmes by Willaert and Jachet de Mantua. The original is in the Biblioteca central, Sección de música in Barcelona.

WilSV   _____. *I salmi appertinenti alli vesperi per tutte le feste dell'anno...* Venetia: Apresso di Antonio Gardane, 1557. Verona: Accademia filarmonica, 1975. Microfilm.
This facsimile contains the eight partbooks of the Vesper Psalms by Willaert and Jachet de Mantua. But, the first chorus lacks the *cantus* and *altus*. The original is in the Accademia filarmonica in Verona. It is indexed in RISM B/I ,1557-6.

WolN   Wolf, J., ed. *Newe deudsche geistliche Gesange für die gemeinen Schulen (Georg Rhau,1544)*. Denkmäler Deutscher Tonkunst, no. 34. Leipzig: Breitkopf and Härtell, 1892-1931.
This contains transcriptions of Lutheran church hymns by Martin Agricola, Arnold von Brück, Sixtus Dietrich, Benedictus Ducis, Lupus Hellingk, Stephan Mahu, Baltasar Resinarius, Ludwig Senfl, Thomas Stölzer, and others. There are one hundred and twenty three compositions.

WriW   Wrightson, James, ed and transc. *Wanley partbooks*. Recent researches in the music of the Renaissance, no. 99-101. Madison, WI: A-R Editions, [c.1995].
This is a collection of early Church of England liturgical music for four to five voices. It has been edited and transcribed from three manuscript partbooks found in Oxford: Bodleian Library *MS. Mus. Sch. e. 420-422*. It was most likely compiled between 1548 and 1550. The tenor partbook is lost but the missing voice parts are provided either from contemporary sources or are reconstructed by the editor. The preface includes bibliographical references.

WulT Wulstan, David. *Tudor Music*. London : J.M. Dent, 1985.
This source covers a period between 1485 and 1625. There is an emphasis on the importance of the music and the recreation of it in modern performance. It includes an index., a Bibliography (p. 356-368), and 15th, 16th, and 17th century history and criticism.

ZweO *Zwei Orgelstücke aus einer Kärntner Orgeltabulatur des 16. Jahrhunderts*. Edited by Josef Klima. Musik alter Meister, no. 9. Graz: Akademische Druck- u. Verlagsanstalt, 1958.
This is a musical score of two organ compositions: *Praeambulum 6 vocum Lud. Senfl* by Ludwig Senfl and an anonymous organ composition, *Exercitatio bona*. It is edited from Kärnter Landesarchiv in Klagenfurt, *Ms. 4/3*.

ZwiA Zwingli, ?. *Ad Carolum Romanorum imperatorem Germaniae comitia Augustae celebrantem, Fidei Hyldeychi Zuinglij ratio*. Tigvri [Zurich]: Apud Christophorum Froschouer, 1530.
This is a Latin treatise by Zwingli in which he formulates his doctrine. The place of publication and the publisher are taken from the final page.

ZwiAC _____. *Ad Carolum Romanorum imperatorem*. Zurich: Christoph Froschauer, 1530. Flugschriften des fruhen 16. Jahrhunderts; Fiche 1876, Nr. 4788. Zug. Switzerland: Inter Documentation Co., [19..]. Microfiche.
This is a facsimile of a Latin treatise by Zwingli in which he formulates his doctrine. It is indexed in Finsler 92 b.

ZwiACC _____. *The accompt and confession of the faith*. Geneva. 1555 / The English experience, its record in early printed books published in facsimile, no. 964. Translated by Thomas Cotsforde. Norwood, N. J.; Amsterdam: W. J. Johnson, Theatrum Orbis Terrarum, 1979.
This is a translation of *Ad Carolu Romanorum imperatorum Germaniae....* There is a photoreprint of the 1555 edition that was printed in Geneva and two letters by T. Cottesford that are appended on pages 65-109.

ZwiC _____. *De canone missae Hvldrychi Zvinglii epichiresis*. Zurich: Froschauer, Christoph, d. Ä, 1523. Flugschriften des frühen 16. Jarhunderts; Fiche 1191, Nr. 2989. Zug, Switzerland Inter Documentation Co., [19--]. Microfiche.
This tract contains Zwingli's revision of the Latin Mass. It is mostly in Latin except for the Lessons which are in German. It is indexed by Finsler 21.

ZwiCM _____. "The Canon of the Mass, Epichiresis." Translated by Henry Preble. New York: Union Theological Seminary, 1982. Photocopy.
This is a translation of *De Canone Missae Huldrici Zuinglii Epichiresis*. It contains the Latin Mass as revised by Zwingli.

ZwiD _____. *De vera et falsa religione*. Flugschriften des fruhen 16. Jahrhunderts; Fiches 523-527, Nr. 1346. Zurich: Froschauer, Christoph, d. A., 1525. Switzerland: Inter Documentation Co., [19..]. Microfiche.
This is a facsimile of a Latin treatise written by Zwingli in which he formulates his doctrine. It is indexed in Finsler 45a.

ZwiN Zwick, Johannes. *Nüw Gsangbüchle von vil schönen Psalmen und geistlichen liedern...* Faksimileausg edition. Zurich: Zwingli-Verlag, 1946.
This edition contains German hymns for the Reformed Church. There is a *Nachwort* by Jean Hotz.

Part II

Historical Outline and Study Guide

Theorists and Theoretical Sources

A. Pietro Aaron (Aron)

1. Introduction
   a) Aaron was born at Florence ca. 1480   MoyM, 119
      (1) He may have been a choirboy in a Florentine church   BlaC, 75
   b) He composed motets, madrigals, and Masses   BlaC, 101
      (1) There are twelve compositions written by Aaron mentioned in the *Spataro Correspondence*   BlaC, xxxviii
         (a) All of these compositions are either lost or have not been identified
         (b) The *Spataro Correspondence* is a collection of letters written between 1517 and 1543
            i) The *Spataro Correspondence*   BlaC
   c) The date of his death is uncertain   BlaC, 85
      (1) It is thought that he died ca. 1550   MoyM, 119
         (a) Most likely in Bergamo   BerLP, 1

2. Treatises
   a) *Libri tres de institutione harmonica* of 1516   BlaC, 74
      (1) This treatise was published at Bologna   LeeG, 3
      (2) It is Aaron's first published treatise
      (3) The title page includes the name of Giovanni Antonio Flaminio as the translator   BlaC, 75
         (a) Flaminio translated the treatise into Latin   BlaC, 76
            i) But, he was not a musical scholar and this created problems   BlaC, 77
            ii) He has remarks running throughout the work which include references to Greek etymologies of terms, citations of classical sources, and scholarly explanations of the material covered   MoyM, 120
            iii) As a result of his comments it is difficult to distinguish the contributions of each figure   MoyM, 120
      (4) This treatise is a progressive document   ManI, 159
         (a) It contains the first mention of composers having, in general, abandoned the successive manner of composition in favor of the simul-

			taneous or vertical method	ReeMR, 181

        i)   But Aaron treats the method used by older composers as well as the new   BlaOC, 212

   (b) Aaron moves away from ideal, abstract science toward concrete, practical art   ManI, 160

        i)   He advocates dividing tonal material into octaves rather than into hexachords   ReeMR, 182

            a - In this regard, he is following the lead of Ramis and Gallicus

(5) The treatise is divided into three books   BerLP, 58

   (a) Book I discusses plainsong as it pertains to solmization, intervals and modes

   (b) Book II discusses the differences between the solmization of counterpoint and that of plainsong along with a discussion of the Greek genera and an explanation of mensural notation

   (c) Book III is a discussion of counterpoint

(6) Facsimiles of *Libri tres de institutione harmonica*   AarLTI; AarLT

b) *Il Thoscanello de la musica*   BlaC, 4

  (1) This was published at Venice in 1523   MoyM, 120

     (a) There was a reprint in 1529, and two revised editions in 1539 and 1562

        i)   There is a supplement to the 1529 edition   BerLP, 64

            a - The main purpose of this supplement is to show the need for explicit accidentals   LocSP, 165

            b - It contains great detail about the use of accidentals in counterpoint and concludes with a discussion of the modes in plainchant

  (2) *Il Thoscanello* is written in the vernacular   MoyM, 121

  (3) It is a general manual with discussions of mensural notation, intervals, genera, counterpoint, chordal formation, etc.   ReeMR, 182

     (a) Half of the treatise is devoted to rhythm and its notation   MoyM, 121

     (b) The discussion of pitch forms a very secondary part of the work   MoyM, 121

  (4) There is a lengthy discussion on the inconsistencies in the placing of accidentals by earlier generations   LowF, 230

     (a) Aaron seems to be the first theorist to demand consistency in writing accidentals

        i)   He advocated writing out every flat and sharp   LowF, 260

     (b) He condemned the practice of conflicting signatures   LowF, 258

     (c) He sought rational application and methods in the treatment of notation and tonality   LowF, 260

  (5) There is a discussion of mean-tone temperament   ManI, 136

     (a) This discussion attempts to set forth briefly and as easily as possible that which is necessary for a player to know about tuning   LinE, 141

     (b) Aaron calls the temperament he discusses *participatio*

     (c) A letter on keyboard temperament is included in the treatise without attribution   BlaC, 939

i) The letter is thought to have been written by an organist, possibly [Marco Antonio] Cavazzoni or Giovanni da Legge BlaC, 937
- (6) A facsimile of the original *Il Thoscanello de la musica* of 1523 AarTM
- (7) Facsimiles of the 1529 reprint edition AarTD; AarTOS
- (8) A facsimile of the 1539 edition AarTO
- (9) A translation based on the supplement to the 1529 edition and the revised editions of 1539 and 1562 AarT

c) *Trattato della natura et cognitione di tutti gli tuoni di canto figurato* ReeMR, 182
- (1) This was published at Venice in 1525 BakB, 1
  - (a) A supplement to *Trattato* was issued in 1531 BerLP, 66
    - i) This appeared anonymously and without a title under the imprint of Bernardino de Vitali, the publisher of the *Trattato* BerM, 37
- (2) The 1525 edition provides criteria for identifying mode in polyphonic music ReeMR, 182
  - (a) There is also a discussion of the ethos of the modes HarW, 156
- (3) In chapters twenty-six to forty-five there is a discussion of the solmization of chromatic tones outside the normal gamut BerLP, 67
  - (a) Aaron attempts the most systematic exposition of the entire conceivable gamut BerM, 37
    - i) He states that in every place of the hand one could put all the six solmization syllables
  - (b) In the supplement of 1531, Aaron clearly implies the seventeen-step gamut BerM, 38
- (4) A facsimile of the original 1525 edition of the *Trattato*... AarTR
- (5) A facsimile of the 1531 reprint edition with an addenda AarTRD
- (6) An extract in English of the 1525 edition StrS, 205

d) *Lucidario in musica di alcune opinione antiche e moderne* BakB, 1
- (1) This was published at Venice in 1545
  - (a) It is written in the vernacular MoyM, 123
- (2) Aaron emphasizes the practical tradition MoyM, 126
  - (a) But, this is not a rejection of the larger theoretical issues of musical science
- (3) The treatise is divided into four books MoyM, 123
  - (a) Number one is a discussion of modes and solmization in plainchant; number two covers notation, use of consonance, solmization, and canon; number three covers notation; and number four is a discussion of the solmization of chromatic tones BerLP, 68
    - i) Number four is essentially a reprint of the Supplement to *Trattato*
  - (b) In chapter fifteen of the second book, Aaron states that composers are born and not made through study MoyM, 124
    - i) He thinks musicians and sculptors are similar MoyM, 125
- (4) Facsimiles of *Lucidario in musica di alcune opinione antiche e moderne* AarLM; AarLMU

e) *Compendiolo di molti dubbi, segreti et sentenze intorno al canto fermo, et figurato* BlaC, 85

        (1)   This was published in Milan by Giovanni Antonio da Castiglione, possibly in 1549 or later
            (a)   It may have been published after Aaron's death   BlaC, 86
                i)   The title page bears the inscription, *In memoria eterna erit Aron*   BakB, 1
        (2)   This treatise is curiously elementary
        (3)   It consists of two books   BerLP, 69
            (a)   Number one is a discussion of plainchant and number two, counterpoint
        (4)   Facsimiles of *Compendiolo di molti dubbi, segreti et sentenze intorno al canto fermo, et figurato*   AarC; AarCD

   3.   Letters written by or to Aaron   BlaC, 201
      a)   These are found in the *Spataro Correspondence*
          (1)   The *Spataro Cooresspondence* is comprised of one-hundred-ten letters   BlaC, 3
              (a)   These were written by fifteen correspondents between 1517 and 1543
          (2)   There are two main depositories of the letters   BlaC, 15
              (a)   The Biblioteca apostolica vaticana, *MS Vat. lat. 5318*
                  i)   An inventory of the letters from the Biblioteca apostolica vaticana, *MS Vat. lat. 5318*   BlaC, xxii
                  ii)   A facsimile of the manuscript   BibAV
            (b)   The Paris, Bibliothèque nationale, *MS. it. 1110*
                  i)   An inventory of the letters found in the Paris, Bibliothèque nationale, *MS. it. 1110*   BlaC, xxxiv
      b)   For the correspondence between Pietro Aaron, Giovanni del Lago, Marc' Antonio Cavazzoni, and Giovanni Spataro, *see*   BlaC, 201
          (1)   These are in the vernacular with English translations and commentary
      c)   For Pietro Aaron's correspondence with other musicians, *see*   BlaC, 219
          (1)   These are in the vernacular with English translations and commentary
      d)   For a substantial portion of Aaron's surviving correspondence, *see*   BerLP, Appendix B

B. Lodovico Fogliano

   1.   Introduction
      a)   He was born in Modena in the late fifteenth century   KauF, 687
      b)   He was a learned Aristotelian and a professional singer and composer   PalH, 20
      c)   He became a priest   KauF, 687
      d)   He died ca. 1539   MoyM, 141

   2.   *Musica theorica* (1529)   PalH, 235
      a)   This was published in Venice   KauF, 687
      b)   It is written in scholastic Latin   MoyM, 142
      c)   Fogliano divides the work into three sections   MoyM, 142
          (1)   Number one, musical proportions; number two, the application of those

proportions in forming consonances; number three, the division of the monochord
- d) He was the first theorist to make a complete break with the Pythagorean tradition   PalH, 20
  - (1) He establishes that the subject of the discipline of music is sonorous number, namely, the number that measures the parts of a string   PalH, 236
  - (2) But, he states that music, insofar as it consists of sound which is caused by motion, is not a mathematical but a natural phenomenon   PalH, 236
    - (a) Fogliano defines consonance and dissonance not according to ratio but in terms of how they struck his ear   PalH, 20
    - (b) He uses Aristotelian physics, psychology, and logic to defend his determination of consonance and dissonance by sense experience   PalH, 238
- e) Facsimiles of *Musica theorica*   FogM; FogMT

C. Giovanni del Lago (Zanetto)   LowAW, 686

1. Introduction
   - a) He was probably born between 1480 and 1490   BlaC, 127
     - (1) Perhaps in Venice   BerLA, 345
   - b) He was involved in a three-way debate that the theorists Giovanni Spataro and Pietro Aaron conducted by mail during the 1520s and 1530s   AtlR, 272
     - (1) The concept of the gamut and *musica ficta* had been stretched around the circle of fifths to G♭
       - (a) This stretched the concepts of gamut and *musica ficta* to their limits
       - (b) "With one more step, the descent would have reached C-flat, lying in the realm of enharmonic relationships"
     - (2) So, the controversy was over the question of whether flats could be applied to C and F
       - (a) "Could a flat (*fa*) be applied to notes that were already called *fa*?"
   - c) Del Lago died March 8, 1544   BlaC, 129

2. Treatises
   - a) *Epistole composte in lingua volgare*   BerLA, 345
     - (1) This contains a collection of letters that del Lago hoped to have published   BlaC, 130
     - (2) The letters were collected by del Lago during 1535-1538
     - (3) The collection was to consist of his letters only   BlaC, 133
       - (a) There were twenty-two   BlaC, 135
     - (4) But eleven of these letters are borrowed or even have fictitious elements   BlaC, 130
       - (a) Del Lago had fashioned parts of his own letters from bits and pieces of letters by Spataro and Aaron   BlaC, 133
       - (b) Also, the letter to Fra Seraphim may be partly fictitious
         - i) In it, del Lago enjoins composers to keep the text in mind when writing music for madrigals, barzelette, etc.   MoyM, 137

128 Theorists and Theoretical Sources

            ii)   The letter contains fourteen rules for writing a composition   HarTH, 110
                  a - A summary of del Lago's rules   HarTH, 110-113
            iii)   A copy of the letter in the vernacular   BlaC, 875
            iv)   An English translation of the letter   BlaC, 887
   (5)   There is a little dictionary of musical terms written by del Lago in a letter to Girolamo Molino   LowAW, 685
       (a)   This contains three tables of the Greek scale in the diatonic, chromatic, and enharmonic genera
            i)   There is a table showing the fifteen notes of the diatonic genus   BlaC, 912
            ii)   There is also a table showing the chromatic division of the Greater Perfect System   BlaC, 913
            iii)   Plus a table showing the enharmonic division of the double octave   BlaC, 914
       (b)   These tables contain two rows of numbers
            i)   The first row contains a large complicated set of figures according to the Pythagoreans
            ii)   The second row of figures contains the number six or multiples of it according to Aristoxenus and the practical musicians
                  a - In this table the intervals are of a well-tempered system in which each tone is divisible into two equal half tones and in which six whole tones make one octave
                  b - This row of numbers makes it evident that del Lago's theory of intervals is that of Aristoxenus   LowAW, 685
                  c - A reproduction of this row of figures   LowAW, 685
       (c)   For the letter containing the dictionary of musical terms in the vernacular, *see*   BlaC, 897
       (d)   For an English translation of the letter, *see*   BlaC, 908
   (6)   The letters, along with letters written to del Lago, and letters of Spataro and others written to Aaron, are found in the *Spataro Correspondence*   BlaC, 201
       (a)   A reprint of the letters of the *Spataro Correspondence* in the vernacular with English translation and commentary   BlaC, 201
   (7)   A reprint of the Title and Dedication of del Lago's *Epistole composte in lingua volgare* in the vernacular with the English translation   BlaC, 201
b) *Breve introduttione di musica misurata (1540)*   PalH, 340
   (1)   The object of this treatise is to instruct the reader on how to compose music that is sensitive to the text on several levels, such as the general mood, units of thought or sentences, punctuation, accentuation of words, and length of syllables
   (2)   The last section of the treatise is entitled *A Method...for composing any kind of music in parts*   HarTH, 129
       (a)   It contains eight rules covering first-species counterpoint   HarTH, 130
       (b)   Del Lago gives six more rules for joining a third voice to one of six combinations of intervals in the soprano and tenor   HarTH, 133
   (3)   There is also a compendium of his letter to Fra Seraphim
       (a)   This is a virtual treatise on the modes in composition   PalH, 339

(b) For a reprint of the letter in the vernacular, *see* BlaC, 875
(c) For an English translation of the letter, *see* BlaC, 887
(4) A facsimile of *Breve introduttione di musica misurata* LagB

D. Martin Agricola

1. Introduction
   a) He was born in 1486 GérP, 434
      (1) In Schwiebus HüsA, 166
   b) "His original name was Martin Sore or Sohr" HolM, iii
      (1) He chose the Latin surname of Agricola
   c) He was one of the first Protestant school musicians in Germany HüsA, 166
   d) George Rhau published most of Agricola's works HolM, iv
   e) Agricola died in 1556 HolM, iii
      (1) In Magdeburg HüsA, 166

2. Treatises
   a) *Ein kurtz deudsche Musica* HüsA, 166
      (1) This was published at Wittenberg in 1528
         (a) It was reprinted in 1533 as *Musica choralis deudsch*
            i) A facsimile of *Musica choralis deudsch* ColS
            ii) A translation of *Musica choralis deudsch* AgrT
      (2) An abridged Latin version of *Ein kurtz deudsche Musica* was published at Wittenberg in 1539 as *Rudimenta musices*
         (a) In this treatise, Agricola discusses the combination of modes and hexachords ManI, 180
            i) He explains the modes as B♮ *mi* in the Dorian, Phrygian, and Mixolydian modes and B♭ *fa* in the Lydian mode
            ii) Although he does not mention the hexachord species in this context, the pertinent syllables cannot be conceived without them
         (b) He also discusses the possibility of flat mutation ManI, 184
            i) He states that the notes A, D, and G can be sung as *fa*
               a - He also includes sharp mutation and goes as far as the hexachord on B with a D# *mi* ManI, 539, fn. 23
         (c) A facsimile of *Rudimenta musices* AgrR
         (d) An English translation of *Rudimenta musices* AgrRM
      (3) A facsimile of *Ein kurtz deudsche Musica* AgrE
   b) *Musica instrumentalis deudsch* GérP, 434
      (1) This was published in 1529
         (a) There were other editions in 1530, 1532, and 1542 HolM, iv
         (b) There was a revised and corrected edition published in 1545
      (2) The treatise is written in short, two-lined, rhymed couplets for young people HolM, i
      (3) The purpose of the treatise is to teach the playing of various instruments including organs, lutes, harps, viols, and pipes HolM, 1
         (a) Agricola refers to an instrument like the violin with his description of his third type of "small Geigen" HayI, 718

                i)   This is the first clear reference to the existence of a violin
        (b)   He presents a new tablature for the lute along with the old tablature   HolM, v
              i)   There were several systems of tablature used for the lute from the late fifteenth-century to the eighteenth-century   RanH, 829
    (4) This treatise is important for its enlightened presentation of material originally presented by Virdung [in his book of 1511 on musical instruments]   HolM, iv
    (5) A facsimile of the 1528 and 1545 editions of *Musica instrumentalis deudsch*   AgrMU
    (6) A facsimile of the 1529 and 1545 editions   AgrMUS
    (7) A facsimile of the 1532 edition   AgrMI
    (8) A translation of the 1528 edition   HolM
    (9) A translation of the 1529 edition   AgrMID
  c) *Musica figuralis deudsch*   GérP, 434
    (1) This was published in 1532
        (a)   It was published by George Rhau in Wittenberg   AgrM
        (b)   There is a supplement, *Büchlein von den Proportionibus*   HüsA, 166
              i)   A facsimile of *Büchlein von den Proportionibus*   AgrV
              ii)   A translation of *Büchlein von den Proportionibus*   AgrT
    (2) This treatise is a continuation of *Ein kurtz deudsche Musica*   ReeF, 41
        (a)   The study is confined to vocal polyphony
        (b)   It is a thorough study of notation and time
        (c)   Examples are taken from contemporary practice with brief explanations
              i)   Agricola composed many of the examples   GérP, 434
    (3) Facsimiles of the 1532 edition of *Musica figuralis deudsch*   AgrM; AgrMF
    (4) A facsimile of the 1534 edition of *Musica figuralis deudsch*   AgrMD
    (5) Translations of the 1532 edition of *Musica figuralis deudsch*   AgrMFD; AgrT

E. Heinrich Glarean

1. Introduction
  a) He was born in 1488   RanH, 849
    (1) "In the village of Mollis, in the Swiss canton of Glarus"   GlaD, 5
        (a)   His name was Henricus Loriti but he adopted the name of the canton early in life
  b) He taught privately at Cologne [from 1512] until 1514   CarMM, 246
  c) In 1514 he matriculated at the University at Basel   CarMM, 306
    (1) During this time he conducted a private boarding school in which he taught Latin classics and the elements of Greek   GlaD, 7
        (a)   He also taught mathematics and music   CarMM, 306
        (b)   He had thirty students in one year, which was a considerable number for that time   CarMM, 306

d) In 1517 he went to Paris where he conducted an educational institute GlaD, 8
e) While he was in Basil in 1522, he opened his own school and taught the humanities CarMM, 306
f) In 1529 he moved to Freiburg in Breisgau where he became professor of poetry at the University and later professor of theology, and teacher and writer on mathematics, geography and music GlaD, 8
g) He was becoming blind and died in 1563 GlaD, 8

2. *Treatises*
   a) *Isagoge in musicen* BakB, 568
      (1) This was published at Basel in 1516
      (2) This work is the conventional introduction dealing with music's origin CarMM, 306
         (a) It contains material on genera, intervals, and modes
      (3) It is an immature work GlaI, 105
      (4) There are ten chapters GlaI, 99
         (a) Chapter one has definitions of music and acoustics
         (b) Chapters two and three contain discussions of the Pythagorean scale and Guidonian syllables GlaI, 100
         (c) Chapter four deals with intervals and consonances GlaI, 100
         (d) In chapters five and six there is a discussion of the theory of scale construction and problems of tuning GlaI, 100
         (e) In chapters seven and eight there is a discussion of the Greek modes GlaI, 101
         (f) In chapters nine and ten there is a discussion of the church modes GlaI, 101
      (5) A facsimile of *Isagoge in musicen* GlaIM
      (6) A translation of the treatise GlaI, 109
   b) *Dodecachordon* ManI, 583
      (1) This was published in Basel in 1547
         (a) It had been completed in 1539 but Glarean was unable to find a publisher until eight years later GlaD, 9
      (2) The *Dodecachordon* represents the first critical essay on music ManI, 160
         (a) It is an attempt to subject music to historical and stylistic analysis along the same lines as writings on literature and the visual arts
         (b) Glarean promulgates new ideas about the modal system AtlR, 556
            i) He believed that the world of antiquity could be fitted into Renaissance life without overthrowing the existing order MilD, 156
            ii) He states in his opening paragraph that he wishes to show that the modal system practiced in his time is not new, but actually that of the ancients RogD, 57
      (3) The *Dodecachordon* is also valuable for other non modal reasons AtlR, 556
         (a) In it, Glarean offers a wealth of biographical information on composers of the period
         (b) He also includes an anthology of more than 120 compositions by such composers as Josquin, Obrecht, Isaac, and even Ockeghem

                i) There are eighty monophonic pieces (mostly chant) and ninety-five polyphonic compositions (twenty-nine by Josquin)
     (c) Glarean takes most of his examples from real compositions, but some notational illustrations are taken from other books   AtlR, 556
(4) There are three books with a twofold division of music (theory and practice)   CarMM, 306
     (a) The first book deals with the elements of music   CarMM, 307
                i) Glarean lists the intervals with a useful function in counterpoint illustrative of the *ars perfecta*   ManI, 148
     (b) The second book contains a discussion of the modes   CarMM, 307
                i) Glarean discusses the closes and the transposition of the twelve modes   RogD, 59
               ii) He feels that a knowledge of the octave and 4th-5th species is essential for an understanding of the nature of the modes and the way they are used in practice   RogD, 59
               iii) He derives sixteen modes by partitioning the gamut into arithmetic and harmonic divisions   ManI, 152
                   a - Four of these are rejected
               iv) He discusses *permixtio* (the combination of authentic and plagal versions of the same mode) and *commixtio* (the combination of unrelated modes)   ManI, 154
                   a - He states that the combination of the Phrygian with the Hypomixolydian mode and the Dorian with the Phrygian mode is bad as it produces frequent tritones
               v) Due to the fact that Glarean adheres to the Pythagorean tuning he limits his definition of mutation to the traditional one excluding *permutatio* (B♭ *fa* to B♮ *mi*)   ManI, 180
                   a - "But because he uses mutation to explicate modal structure, he inadvertently extends the boundaries normally created by this system"
                   b - And, in his discussion of *musica ficta*, he allows fictive hexachords outside the Guidonian gamut
               vi) He illustrates unusual mutation   ManI, 182
                   a - He includes, in an unusual mutation, *mi* on F, *sol* on E, and *fa* on A
                       1 - Therefore, he must mean F# *mi*, E♭ *sol*, and A♭ *fa*
                   b - Thus he envisages the extension of flat mutation to a surprising degree of chromaticism, *i.e.* four flats   ManI, 183
                       1 - "He contents himself with the moderate admission of one sharp"
              vii) For a discussion of the modes as presented by Glarean, *see*   RogD, 58
     (c) The third book has a discussion of rhythm and notation and includes musical examples in each of the modes   CarMM, 307
                i) There are also musical quotations from actual compositions written by many of the Netherlanders and some by Swiss and German composers
(5) A facsimile of *Dodecachordon*   GlaDO

F. Giovanni Maria Lanfranco   MoyM, 154

1. Introduction   HarW, 131
    a) He may have been born in Terenzo in the vicinity of Parma
        (1) Ca. 1490   BerLAN, 441
    b) He was an organist and chapel master
    c) He died in 1545

2. Treatises
    a) *Rimario novo di tutte le concordanze del Petrarca raccolte di maniera, che quante volte sono nel detto autore, tante per tavola ordinatissima ritrovare si potranno...*   HarW, 131
        (1) This is a rhyming dictionary with a classified index
            (a) It contains all the words at the ends of lines used by Petrarch in his sonnets and *canzoni*   LeeG, 18
            (b) The words are listed alphabetically by sounds   LeeG, 18
                i) Each word that rhymes with a basic sound is placed under the proper category along with a number indicating the number of times the word has been used in the poem
        (2) It is among the first works of its kind
        (3) It was published at Brescia   BerLAN, 441
            (a) "It was reprinted in Venice as part of Ruscelli's *Il Petrarca* in 1554"   LeeG, 18
                i) A copy of Ruscelli's *Il Petrarca* of 1554   PetP
    b). *Scintille di musica* (1533)   MoyM, 154
        (1) It was published in Brescia   BerLAN, 441
        (2) It is an introductory treatise
        (3) [In the Preface,] Lanfranco divides composers into the ancients, *i.e.*, the Franco-Flemish composers, and the moderns, *i.e.*, mostly Italian composers except for Adrian Willaert   ManI, 119
        (4) The purpose of the treatise is the training of choir boys
        (5) In part one, Lanfranco discusses notes; in part two, rhythms and mensural signs; in part three, the eight modes; and in part four, basic counterpoint, and names of instruments and their tuning   HarW, 133
            (a) He gives a set of general rules that govern the tuning of all instruments   LinE, 144
                i) A list of the rules   LinE, 149
            (b) His temperament is a regular mean-tone temperament with the major thirds larger than pure   LinE, 149
            (c) Also, he discusses a temperament that attempts to distribute the Pythagorean comma equally   RanH, 837
                i) This is the earliest source to discuss this type of temperament
            (d) [In this section], he describes a *Violetta da Arco senza tasti* or *Violetta da Braccio e da Arco* which were almost certainly

(6) A German translation of the treatise   GlaDD
(7) An English translation of the treatise   GlaD

			violins	HayI, 718
	(6)		This is the first treatise to systematize word-tone relations into a code of text underlay	HarW, 135
		(a)	A summary of Lanfranco's rules	HarW, 151
			i) These rules were designed for Masses and motets only	HarW, 152
	(7)		A facsimile of *Scintille di musica*	LanSC
	(8)		Another facsimile of the treatise	LanSM
	(9)		An English translation of *Scintille di musica*	LeeG, 50

G. Sebald Heyden

1. Introduction   BakB, 710
   a) He was born in 1499 at Nürnberg
   b) He was a writer, teacher, music theorist, and perhaps composer   MatH
   c) He died in 1561 at Nürnberg   MatH

2. Treatises
   a) *Musicae...*   HeyD, 9
      (1) This was published in 1532
      (2) This treatise presents the essential aspects of polyphony and mensural notation   MatH
   b) *Musicae, id est artis canendi libri duo*   HeyD, 9
      (1) This was published in 1537
      (2) It is an enlargement of the *Musicae...* of 1532
         (a) It contains many musical examples   MatH
      (3) A facsimile of *Musicae, id est artis canendi libri duo*   HeyMU
   c) *De arte canendi*   HeyD, 9
      (1) It was published in Nürnberg in 1540 by Petreius
      (2) It is an enlargement of *Musicae, id est artis canendi libri duo*
      (3) There are two books to the *De arte canendi*
         (a) Book I contains a discussion of the elements of music
         (b) Book II is principally a discussion of Heyden's theory of *tactus* and mensuration signs
            i) The theory of *tactus* formulated by Heyden presented the *tactus* as a single unchanging entity that should be applied to every kind of mensuration sign
            ii) This *tactus*-mensuration theory affirms that the same *tactus* is used for all of the polyphonic examples in the treatise
      (4) Facsimiles of *De arte canendi*   HeyDA; HeyDAC; ColS
      (5) A translation and transcription of *De arte canendi*   HeyD

H. Auctor Lampadius   RuhL, 419

1. Introduction
   a) He was a German composer and music teacher   LowON, 798
      (1) He was also a theorist   RuhL, 419

      b) He was born in Brunswick ca. 1500
      c) He died in 1559 at Halberstadt

2. *Compendium musices tam figurati quam plani cantus*   RuhL, 419
      a) This was published by Samuel Apiarius in Bern, Switzerland   LowON, 798
          (1) The first edition was published in 1537
              (a) There is a reprint edition of 1554
      b) *Compendium musices...* was written in Lüneburg   RuhL, 419
      c) Its purpose is to instruct   LowON, 798
          (1) The first two parts are devoted to *musica plana* and *musica figurata*
                                                                                                                                    RuhL, 419
          (2) "The third part, described in the title as an appendix (*De compositione cantus compendium*), is a significant contribution to the theory of composition in the 16th-century"   RuhL, 419
      d) The *Compendium musices...* was compiled from writings by others
                                                                                                                                  LowON, 798
      e) This may be the earliest theoretical source containing an unmistakable reference to the use of the modern score   LowON, 799
      f) A reprint edition of *Compendium musices tam figurati quam plani cantus*
                                                                                                                                                      LamC

I. Nicolaus Listenius

1. Introduction   NieL, 28
      a) He was born in Hamburg ca. 1510
      b) He gained the Master of Arts degree in 1531 at the Wittenberg University
      c) He taught at the Lateinschule in Brandenburg about 1536
          (1) He led the sacred music
          (2) He was admonished for trying to substitute the Lutheran liturgy for the Catholic liturgy without permission

2. *Musica, ab authre denuo recognita...*   ManI, 123
      a) This treatise was published in 1549
          (1) It originally appeared in 1537   LowS, 86
          (2) It was written for school boys   LowS, 85
      b) It is a corrected version of a former treatise, *Rudimenta musicae* published in 1533 by Rhau   NieL, 28
      c) Listenius is possibly the first theorist to offer a concrete example of "secret chromaticism"   LowS, 85
          (1) In his chapter on *musica ficta* he offers what amounts to clear and irrefutable evidence of the technique of secret modulation
              (a) He shows modulation consistently carried through the cycle of fifths by means of melodic progressions of fourths and fifths
              (b) By doing this he shows the existence of modulations that go as far as four steps in the circle of fifths beyond the key signature
      d) He introduced the term *musica poetica* for the first time   NieL
          (1) By this term he meant instruction in composition
      e) A facsimile of the original 1533 edition of *Rudimenta musicae*   LisR

f) A German translation of *Musica, ab authre denuo recognita* LisMN
g) An English translation of the revised edition, *Musica, ab authre denuo recognita* LisM

Musica theorica: Science of Music

A. Introduction

1. *Musica theorica* was a part of the quadrivial discipline of *musica* which was still divided between *musica theorica* and *musica practica*   MoyM, 4
   a) But [in 1537] Nicolas Listenius, wrote a treatise, [*Musica, ab authre denuo recognita...*], in which he divides the quadrivial discipline of *musica* into three branches: *theorica* (science), *practica* (performance didactics), and *poetica* (composition)   ManI, 123
      (1) He is the first in a line of German theorists to use the term *musica poetica* as an aesthetic-technical category   ManI, 209
      (2) The original title of *Musica...* was *Rudimenta musicae in gratiam studiosae juventutis diligenter comportata* [1533]   LisR
         (a) A facsimile of the original 1533 edition   LisR
      (3) A German translation of *Musica, ab authre denuo recognita...*   LisMN
      (4) An English translation of *Musica, ab authre denuo recognita...*   LisM
   b) Therefore, before 1600, writings about music were classified as *musica theorica* (*musica speculativa, musica contemplativa, and musica arithmetica*), *musica practica* (*musica attiva*), and *musica poetica*   RanH, 845
      (1) This follows Aristotle's division of knowledge ($epist\bar{e}m\bar{e}$)
         (a) He divided knowledge into $the\bar{o}r\bar{e}tik\bar{e}$, $praktik\bar{e}$, and $poi\bar{e}tik\bar{e}$
      (2) "In ths scheme, *musica theorica* (*musica speculativa*) dealt with the arithmatic foundations of music..."   RanH, 845
         (a) *Musica speculativa* has been described as music which is conceived and presented in an esoteric format for academic presentation   BraE, 48
            i) This indicates that *musica speculativa* involved something beyond compositional skill
            ii) Speculative music was reconciled with practical music by requiring a candidate for a degree to compose a piece of actual music to show his academic ability   BraMQ, 5
            iii) But, the proof of the composition was in the studying, not in the performance   BraMQ, 122
   c) Typically the discussions of *musica theorica* included the Greater Perfect System, the gamut, consonance and dissonance, and interval ratios   RanH, 845

B. Changes in Modal Theory

1. A single concept of polyphonic modality ceased to exist for sixteenth-century practicing musicians and the notion of what constituted normal modal procedure varied widely among Renaissance performers   TofA, 124
   a) But theorists who were most strongly influenced by humanistic scholarship were inclined to take a more systematic approach to the treatment of mode   PerMR, 1011
      (1) "They sought closer conformity to the models of classical antiquity"

2. Modal theory was simplified depending on the extent to which the subtleties and complexities deriving from the chant were eliminated   PerMR, 1011
   a) The ambitus, cadences, and final were not requirements of equal importance for defining a mode   GásL, 70
   b) Different scale structures (modal species) and altered pitches added elements of ambiguity   GásL, 70
      (1) Some modal species had clearly differentiated tonal types while others blended characteristic traits
   c) Melodic modes and modal fragments in polyphonic composition were crossed and interrelated   DahS, 247
      (1) This resulted in accentuating the common factor of the modes and not the specificity of each mode
      (2) Therefore, what often stood out was the autonomous diatonic system
   d) The modes changed to simply formal designations expressed by a few features and signs   DahS, 247

3. Aaron states criteria for identifying mode in polyphonic music in his of *Trattato della natura et cognitione di tutti glituoni di canto figurato* (1525)   ReeMR, 182
   a) He states that the singer should judge the mode of a piece from the tenor unless the plainsong is present in some other voice
      (1) This rather artificial procedure provides a terminology that makes it possible to comment easily on the modal character of a polyphonic piece   ReeMR, 183
   b) He also states that the mode of a work should be judged by its ending but, there are different endings   LowT, 33
      (1) Therefore, if the ending is regular (on the *finalis*) there is no problem
      (2) But, if it is irregular (on the *confinalis* [fifth above the *finalis*]) the mode is judged according to the melodic outline
         (a) The outline should follow the divisions of the mode (species)
      (3) If the ending is placed on one of the degrees of the *differentiae* [any of the various final cadences of the antiphonal psalm tones], it is that degree that determines the mode
   c) A facsimile of the original 1525 edition of the *Trattato della natura...*   AarTR
   d) A facsimile of the 1531 reprint edition with an addenda   AarTRD
   e) An extract in English of the 1525 edition   StrS, 205

4. Glarean, [in his *Dodecachordon*], states that he wishes to show that the modal system practiced in his time is not new, but actually that of the ancients   RogD, 57
   a) He thinks the ancient system is hidden in misunderstanding through the cen-

turies and he wishes to restore the system to its rightful place
- (1) He believed that the world of antiquity could be fitted into Renaissance life without overthrowing the existing order   MilD, 156
- b) So, he attempted to save medieval modal theory from the forces of disintegration, *musica ficta* and chromaticism, by broadening it   LowC, 675
  - (1) He added four new modes to the eight old church modes   AllT, 69
    - (a) The new modes were the Aeolian mode (9th), the Hypoaeolian mode (10th), the Ionian mode (11th), and the Hypoionian mode (12th)
      - i) Glareanus realized the flattening of B in the Dorian and Lydian pairs provided for the intervallic configuration of the Aeolian and Ionian pairs   ReeMR, 186
        - a - He states that the Aeolian mode is the result of the transposition of the [altered] Dorian mode a fifth higher or a fourth lower   AllT, 75
          - 1 - The Aeolian and Hypoaeolian modes are the natural minor with a final on A   ReeMR, 185
        - b - The Ionian mode is the result of the distortion of the Lydian mode, made by changing all the B♮s into B♭s   AllT, 83
          - 1 - The Ionian and Hypoionian modes are the major with a final on C   ReeMR, 185
      - ii) Glarean realized the presence or absence of the flat changed the mode, therefore he set up the independent modal pairs   ReeMR, 186
  - (2) He rejected four modes   ManI, 152
    - (a) They are the hypothetical modes XIII and XIV on B [and their plagal modes]   ReeMR, 185
    - (b) These modes are dismissed as impractical because their scales cannot be divided into a perfect fifth plus a perfect fourth or the reverse   ReeMR, 185
- c) But in reality, it is plain that only five modes actually mattered in practical polyphony   ReeMR, 186
  - (1) They were the Dorian, Phrygian, Mixolydian, Aeolian, and Ionian
    - (a) The Ionian and Hypoionian almost completely supplanted the unmodified Lydian pair
- d) Also, in polyphony, the distinction between an authentic mode and its plagal is an academic one   ReeMR, 186
  - (1) So, Glarean does not deal with the mode of a polyphonic complex as much as with the modes of individual voices
    - (a) "He realized that in such a complex the different ranges of adjacent voices will frequently tend to place them in different modes, these rather often being the authentic and plagal forms of the same pair"
- e) He discussed two positions for the modes, the *regular* position and the *irregular* position   AllT, 72
  - (1) The *regular* position is shown in figures 1a and 1b
    - (a) It makes use of the diatonic scale as exemplified by Guido of Arrezo's gamut

i) This is done by means of the interlocking of the hexachords *naturale* and *durum*

Fig. 1a. The authentic modes on the interlocked hexachords *naturale* and *durum*

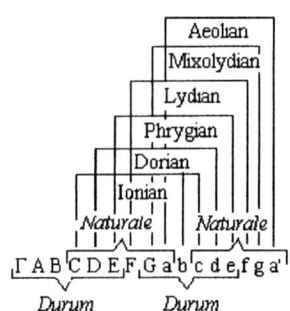

Fig. 1b. The plagal modes on the interlocked hexachords *naturale* and *durum*

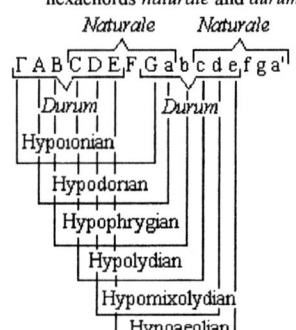

AIIT, 72

(2) The *irregular* position uses either B♭ or F#
   (a) Figure 2a shows the Ionian, Dorian, Phrygian, and Lydian modes in their first *irregular* position on the *molle* side of the hexachords
   (b) Figure 2b shows the Mixolydian and Aeolian modes in their first *irregular* position on the *Durum* side of the hexachords
   (c) The use of the B♭ or F# does not produce chromaticism, and should not be identified with chromatic practice

Fig. 2a. *Irregular* position of the Ionian, Dorian, Phrygian, and Lydian modes using B♭

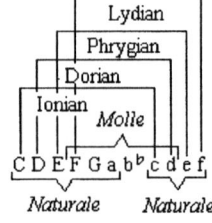

Fig. 2b. Irregular position of the Mixolydian and Aeolian modes using F#

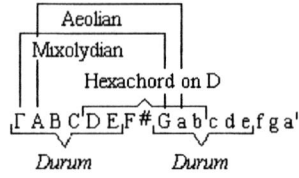

AIIT, 72, 73

f) A facsimile of the *Dodecachordon*   GlaDO
g) A German translation of the *Dodecachordon*   GlaDD
h) An English translation of the *Dodecachordon*   GlaD

C. Tonality

1. There was a quasi-tonality in the sixteenth century that was only partially comparable to the tonality of the eighteenth century   RanH, 862
   a) It was generated by the organization of pitch relationships in fifteenth and six-

teenth century music found characteristically in contrapuntal textures where harmonic functions are a byproduct
b) It was approached in a horizontal and vertical manner   LowT, 75
   (1) The beginnings of tonality in the horizontal approach are delimited as ranging roughly from 1450 to 1550
      (a) During this time, it became obvious that the modal scales do not lend themselves to polyphonic composition as they were intended to be used in plainsong   RogD, 199
         i) This becomes apparent in the attempts to adjust the modes to practice
            a - The Dorian mode comes closer to minor and the Lydian and Mixolydian modes approach major
            b - The major-minor type modes become those most frequently used   RogD, 200
         ii) It is also apparent in the technique of modulation found in the music of Willaert and his circle that expanded the limits of modality without erasing it entirely   LowT, 38
   (2) In the vertical approach, tonality is found with the expanding secularization of Western civilization   LowT, 75
      (a) It is increasingly found in strong root progressions that are not subjugated to contrapuntal motions of the bass   RanH, 862
         i) This appears increasingly during the sixteenth century and is found particularly in secular music
            a - The earliest and most mature examples of tonality are found in the dances tabulated for lute or keyboard instruments   LowT, 62
      (b) It is found also in the organization of pitch relationships in contrapuntal textures where harmonic functions are a byproduct   RanH, 862
         i) Such as the ostinato bass pattern that became an organic part of the emergence of harmony and of tonality   LowT, 6
            a - The ostinato always functioned harmonically when it was in the bass
         ii) But this quasi-tonality is only partially comparable to the tonality of the eighteenth century and since
      (c) Chordal consciousness had developed by the middle of the sixteenth century but the functional importance of each note within the chord was not fully recognized   BusC, 239
c) There are prefigurations of tonal and atonal thinking found in the music that does not fit into the traditional system of the eight modes   LowT, 1
   (1) This is found in performance through the observation of the rules of *musica ficta*
      (a) And it is found in the increasing urge toward a vivid expression of human passion that led to the exploration of a bolder use of *musica ficta* and of chromaticism in its many direct and indirect manifestations   LowT, 38
d) The most significant advance was the endeavor to emphasize the tonic through modulation to the dominant, however tentative such modulation was
          LowT, 65

D. The Current Conception of the Gamut

1. The gamut has no permanent anchor at a standard pitch level MenP-I, 89
   a) It formed the basis of discussions of pitch in the Middle Ages and Renaissance RanH, 333
   b) It has pitches from G to e" with additional pitches of b♭ and b♭' RanH, 333
      (1) Accidentals still were thought of in terms of syllables, *ie,* ♭ = *fa* and ♮ / # = *mi* BerM, 42
         (a) The sharp and flat signs were guides to solmization and did not necessarily affect the pitch of the notes they preceded AllT, 14
         (b) Therefore, the flat (♭) or sharp (#) could not additionally inflect a step which was already *fa* or *mi* BerM, 42
   c) The pitches [G to e"] are the twenty places of the hand BerM, 16
      (1) They constitute *musica recta* with the remainder pitches constituting *musica ficta*
      (2) But when it came to composition, these limits were not always observed PerMR, 979
         (a) "A considerable expansion of the musical space effectively utilized in composition and performance was one of the significant achievements of the musicians of the Renaissance"

2. *Musica recta [musica vera]*
   a) In general the term *musica recta* was thought to refer only to those steps which could be found within the twenty places of the hand and those which were solmizated with the appropriate syllables of the seven regular hexachords BerM, 16
      (1) The complete mastery of this diatonic system with letter names, range designations, and solmization syllables continued to be regarded as indispensable PerMR, 990
         (a) Solmization was useful in the performance of polyphony, both vocal and instrumental
      (2) Different forms of solmization were used, but figure 3 shows one type that seems to have gained the most generalized currency throughout Western Europe, and by some sixteenth century theorists AllT, 43
         (a) The seven regular hexachords begin respectively on G, c, f, g, c', f', g' BerM, 4
            i) They were known as the hexachord [D] *durum* (beginning on G), the hexachord [N] *naturale* (beginning on c), and the hexachord [M] *molle* (beginning on f) AllT, 16-18
         (b) Each pitch of the gamut is identified by the pitch letter and the syllable or syllables corresponding to its position in one or more hexachords such as the A *la mi re* in figure 3 RanH, 377
            i) Where the same name occurs in another octave such as the higher a' *la mi re*, the two pitches are distinguished as *acutum* (high) or *grave* (low)
         (c) Intervals beyond the range of a hexachord were defined by making a mutation (*mutatio*) within a single place from a syllable belonging to one hexachord to a syllable of the same pitch belonging to another interlocking hexachord BerM, 4

The Current Conception of the Gamut   143

Fig. 3. The seven overlapping hexachords

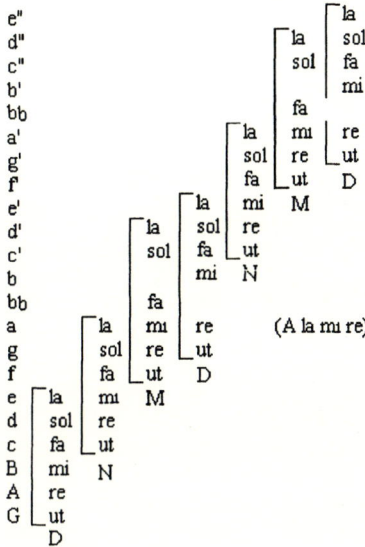

RanH, 377

(3) There were three rules used in order to pass from one hexachord to another
AllT, 47
   (a) The first rule states that the interlocking must be made between the hexachords *naturale* and *durum* and the *molle* and *naturale*
      i) As a result of their respective positions in the gamut and their respective functions in the modal system, mutual interlocking is not an attribute of the hexachords *molle* and *durum*
AllT, 47 fn

Fig. 4. The application of the three rules; taken from *Rudiments de musique* by Guilliaud

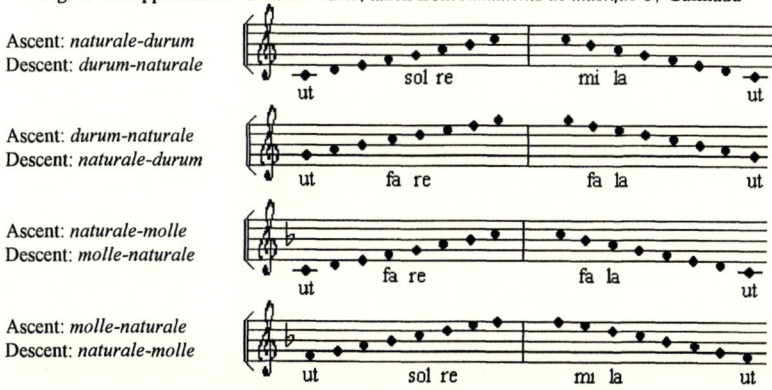

AllT, 48

(b) The second rule states that to ascend from the hexachord *naturale* into the *durum*, and from the *molle* into the *naturale*, one must sing *re* after *sol*   AllT, 48
        i) And, to ascend from the hexachord *durum* into the *naturale*, and from the *naturale* into the *molle*, one must sing *re* after *fa*

(c) The third rule states that to descend from the hexachord *molle* into the *naturale*, and to descend from the *naturale* into the *durum* one must sing *la* after *fa*   AllT, 48
        i) And, to descend from the hexachord *durum* into the *naturale*, and from the *naturale* into the *molle* one must sing *la* after *mi*

b) All steps outside *music recta* belonged to *musica ficta*   BerM, 16

c) But, a large portion of musical opinion in the sixteenth century included within the realm of true music those steps which were solmizated with the syllables appropriate to corresponding *musica recta* steps in another octave   BerM, 16

    (1) This extension of the hand is fully systemized by Stephano Vanneo in his treatise [*Recanetum de musica aurea*]   BerM, 13
        (a) His gamut goes an octave above and below the customary one
        (b) A facsimile of *Recanetum de musica aurea*   VanR
        (c) A translation of *Recanetum de musica aurea*   VanRD

3. *Musica ficta* [the extension of the hand]

    a) Theoretically, the term *musica ficta* refers to those notes outside of the gamut or Guidonian hand   RanH, 516

        (1) But, "it is important to realize that a feigned step does not have to differ in pitch from the true one found in the same place"   BerM, 13
            (a) Actually, all that is necessary is that its syllable be feigned
            (b) According to Listenius, [in his *Musica...*], feigned music is that in which the syllables are not pronounced in their correct places, such as when *ut* is sung on E, *re* on F, and *mi* on G

    b) The theory that *musica ficta* refers to those notes outside of the gamut or Guidonian hand prompted the question as to whether the flat (♭) and the ♮/♯ could be applied in all the places of the hand as well as to all the new steps resulting from such applications, or whether there is a limit beyond which one cannot go inflecting steps by means of accidentals   BerM, 30

        (1) It was thought that since the primary function of an accidental is to indicate whether the step it accompanies is *fa* or *mi*, accidentals may be applied only in those places which do not contain these syllables already
        (2) Therefore, the logic of the hand dictates that the largest conceivable gamut will contain sixteen different pitches in an octave
            (a) That is, the eight steps of the gamut plus flats at a, d, e, g and sharps at c, d, f, g
        (3) Thus, it would appear that the outer limits of *musica ficta* have been discovered   BerM, 30

    c) [In the treatise, *Trattato della natura et cognitione di tutti gli tuoni di canto figurato....*,] Aaron suggested a scheme that was quite daring in as much as its disjunct mutations resulted in forbidden flat permutations on every note except C and F   ManI, 184

        (1) He advocated that all notes in the octave could be solmizated on all six

voces musicales
    (a)   He demonstrates how each of the twenty tones of the Guidonian scale can be solmizated as *ut, re, mi, fa, sol,* and *la*   LowGM, 255
 (2)   He combined the three traditional hexachords with additional flat ones up to A♭
    (a)   For example, if he wants to show how G can be interpreted as *fa*, he changes it to G♭ and bases it on the hexachord starting on D♭   LowMG, 255
    (b)   It is odd that he uses only hexachords involvng flats   LowGM, 255
 (3)   This combination produced some inconsistencies in *proprietas*
    (a)   There was a lack of semitonal permutations on C and F   ManI, 184
        i)   The production of these would require Aaron to complete his procedure by using C♭ *fa* and F♭ *fa* based on hexachords starting on G♭ and C♭
    (b)   Due to tuning problems affecting enharmonic equivalence, Aaron decided that these two hexachords [C and F] were no good
        i)   His arguement was that a flat, for instance, would make F a comma lower than E   BerM, 40
            a -   This was due to the fact that a flat lowers a step by a major semitone but the diatonic semitone between E and F is minor
        ii)   A comma was not used in musical practice   BerM, 40
            a -   Del Lago, in a letter written to Spataro, agrees that the interval of a comma is not singable   BlaC, 660
                1 -   He states that even if you can hear it, the voice can not produce it
                2 -   Also, since the monochord and other instruments are not yet divided by commas, it can be called useless
                3 -   A reprint of del Lago's letter   BlaC, 653
                4 -   A translation of the letter   BlaC, 660
            b -   Spataro, in a letter to Aaron, disagrees with the assumption that the comma is useless   BlaC, 699
                1 -   He states that Boethius and other theorists say the comma is necessary to complete many musical intervals on the divided monochord
                      a -   Otherwise the monochord would not have the correct proportion
                2 -   He agrees that the comma may be unsingable but states that it is audible and is added to other larger intervals in the necessary places
                3 -   A reprint of the letter   BlaC, 678
                4 -   A translation of the letter   BlaC, 696
 (4)   Facsimiles of *Trattato della natura et cognitione...*   AarTR; AarTRD
 (5)   A translation of an extract   StrS, 205
d)   But, theorists in Italy had been advocating a seventeen-step gamut since the time of Prosdocimus   BerM, 42
 (1)   Aaron, in his supplement of 1531 to the *Trattato della natura...*, clearly implies the seventeen-step gamut   BerM, 38
    (a)   That is, the eight steps of the gamut plus flats at a, d, e, g and

sharps at c, d, f, g and a non-redundant A# in every octave
BerM 30 and 42
- (b) This is a revision of his exposition of the gamut in the original *Trattato...* BerM, 37
- (2) The introduction of an a# broke the barriers which, up to then, had limited the gamut
  - (a) This implied that the primary function of an accidental was to inflect
    - i) This made the syllable-indicating function secondary
  - (b) As a result, any limit to the application of an accidental, other than for practical considerations, had been removed
- (3) The addition of the A# promoted the tendency to think of b♭ and b♮ as steps identical in status with other 'black key' steps BerM, 42
  - (a) As a result the whole gamut was thought of less in terms of the hand and its syllables and more in terms of the monochord or keyboard
  - (b) But, the controlling image of the keyboard resulted in the limitation of the gamut to the seventeen steps BerM, 43
- e) Later, [in his treatise *Lucidario in musica*], Aaron revised his system to include sharp mutation as far as the hexachord on F# ManI, 184
  - (1) But, due to the same reasons as the ones he gave for the flat system, he omitted the hexachords on C# and G#, which needed E# and B#
  - (2) Facsimiles of *Lucidario in musica* AarLM; AarLMU
- f) Since the keyboard resulted in the limitation of the gamut, the gamut began to be conceived in terms of the staff notation rather than the keyboard BerM, 43
  - (1) With the conception of the gamut in terms of the staff notation the twenty-one-step gamut resulted
    - (a) Non-redundant single flats on c and f and non-redundant sharps on b and e became acceptable
    - (2) With the acceptance of non-redundant single flats on c and f, and nonredundant single sharps on b and e, the gamut of practical music could reach its fullest state conceivable BerM, 43
- g) But, not all theorists accepted the twenty-one-step gamut as being practical BerM, 43
  - (1) It created problems when used within the premises of the Pythagorean tuning system
  - (2) Three theorists, Aaron, del Lago, and Spataro, all understood that the twenty-one-step gamut was possible, but only Spataro argued that it could be used in practice
    - (a) Spataro had advocated that all notes of the gamut, without exception, could be raised or lowered by applying sharps or flats
ManI, 185
      - i) But, in addition, he advocated the unusual accidentals of double sharps and double flats
      - ii) As a result, Spataro's system entails a complete double cycle of circle-of-fifths
  - (3) Usually, the twenty-one-step gamut was thought of in theoretical terms
    - (a) Therefore, it remained the largest possible gamut of musical practice

Consonances and Dissonances   147

h) The expansion of the tonal system had brought the concerns of modal theory closer to newly composed music (polyphony)   RanH, 501

E. **Consonances and Dissonances**
1. During this period, intervallic systems arise in conjunction with historical concepts of musical style   ManI, 148
   a) This particular part of the science of counterpoint becomes increasingly allied with practice
      (1) Glarean concentrates on the intervals that have a useful function in counterpoint
         (a) These are the unison, fifth, and octave (consonances), third and sixth (imperfect consonances), and semitone, tone, fourth, and major seventh (dissonances)
         (b) All of the dissonances, except the fourth, must appear in syncopation
            i) The fourth may appear without syncopation in *faux bourdon* and cadences
         (c) Glarean gives rules explaining the limited deployment of dissonances
            i) He feels that they disturb the ear
      (2) Lodovico Fogliano, [in his treatise *Musica theorica*], states that music is not a mathematical but a natural phenomenon because it consists of sound that is caused by motion   PalH, 236
         (a) Thus, he places music as a science in an intermediate position between the mathematical and natural
         (b) He recognizes the existence of both consonance and dissonance on the grounds that if consonance is perceived, its contrary must also be perceptible
            i) He describes consonance as a mixture of two sounds separated with respect to high and low pitch that is pleasing to the ear and dissonance as a mixture of two sounds separated with respect to high and low pitch that is displeasing to the ear   PalH, 237
         (c) He defends his determination of consonance and dissonance by sense experience through Aristotelian physics, psychology, and logic   PalH, 238
      (3) As a result, Fogliano is freed from determining the limits of consonance by numerical definition   PalH, 239
         (a) He proposes a new numeration and classification for them
         (b) "He limits the consonances to seven within the octave"
            i) He limits them to the octave because after that they seem to return as if by a cyclical motion, just as numbers do after ten
               a - This happens only with the octave because, although it has two sounds, it strikes the sense as if it were a single sound
            ii) The seven consonances are the *semiditone* [a minor third], a *ditone* [a major third], a *diatesseron* [a semitone, tone, tone],

a *diapente* [a fifth], a minor *hexad* [a minor sixth], a major *hexad* [a major sixth], and a diapason [an octave]   PalH, 240
- a - Of these, the diapason, *diapente*, and *disdiapason* are perfect
- iii) All other intervals are dissonances   PalH, 240
  - a - They are the major tone (9:8), minor tone (10:9), major semitone (27:25), minor semitone (16:15), minimal semitone (25:24), and comma (81:80)
- (4) Fogliano gives a logical defense of imperfect consonances in just tuning   PalH, 235
  - (a) He shows that a string may be divided through superparticular proportions other than those accepted by Pythagoreans and thus produce consonances   PalH, 237
    - i) Thereby, consonances such as the *ditone* (5:4) and *semiditone* (6:5) may be produced
  - (b) He also shows that there are ratios of the multiple *superparticular* class that generate consonances: PalH, 237
    - i) 5:2, or *dupla sesquialtera*, the diapason-plus-*ditone*
    - ii) 10:3, the *tripla sesquitertia*, the diapason-plus-major *hexad*
    - iii) 16:5, the *tripla sesquiquinta*, the diapason-plus-minor *hexad*
  - (c) Also, he shows the *superpartient genus* of ratios generates the following consonances: PalH, 237
    - i) 5:3, the *bipartiens tertia*, major *hexad*
    - ii) 8:5, *superbipartiens quinta*, minor *hexad*
  - (d) Finally, he shows the multiple *superpartiens genus* of ratio produces the following consonances: PalH, 238
    - i) 8:3, *dupla superbipartiens tertia*, the diapason-plus-*diatessaron*
    - ii) 12:5, the *dupla superbipartiens quinta*, diapason-plus-*semiditone*
- (5) Facsimiles of *Musica theorica*   FogM; FogMT

F. Interval Ratios: Intonation

1. Ludovico Fogliano, [in his treatise *Musica theorica*], proposes a system close to just intonation   ManI, 135
   a) He applies his methodology to the tuning of the practical musical scale   PalH, 240
   - (1) He divides the monochord in a new way almost according to the sense and materially in contrast to the usual mathematical method
     - (a) He permits pure major and minor thirds as well as the pure fifths and fourths of the Pythagorean tuning
     - (b) He uses the intense or syntonic tuning of Ptolemy   KauF, 687
       - i) This results in just intonation some sixty or seventy years before Zarlino
       - ii) Actually this method goes back to Aaron
         - a - Aaron's central tetrachord is identical to Ptolemy's syntonic diatonic, 10:9, 9:8, 16-15 descending   PalH, 240

Interval Ratios: Intonation 149

iii) But Fogliano's tetrachord is based on the octave C so that there are two identical tetrachords rising 10:9, 9:8, 16:15
    a - This is the reverse of Ptolemy's descending pattern
        1 - For a discussion of Ptolemy's Intense Diatonic, *see* GanMR, 359

(c) The whole tones are not all equal   JeaS, 176
    i) Some are known as major tones with a frequency ratio of 9/8 and others are known as minor tones with a frequency of 10/9

(d) The two semitones have the same frequency ratio of 16/15
    i) But the 16/15 frequency is more than half the frequency ratio of any full tones

(e) The pitches of the notes are not fixed   JeaS, 178
    i) As a result they vary with the key in which the notes are being played
        a - Each scale has its own special characteristic quality   JeaS, 179
        b - This is true in every system of tuning other than equal temperament,   JeaS, 179

Fig. 5. Fogliano's Diatonic Division of the Monochord

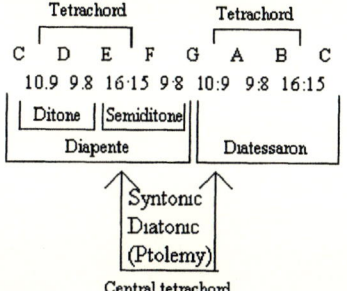

PalH, 240

(2) Fogliano's choice of the C octave has important theoretical advantages   PalH, 241
    (a) It offers a number of harmonic means to assist in the division of the monchord
        i) It is divided harmonically with the fifth [*diapente*] below and the fourth [*diatessaron*] above
            a - This yields the best sounding combination of these two intervals
        ii) The *diapente* may be divided harmonically to produce a *ditone* [major third] below and a *semiditone* [minor third] above
            a - This also provides the best sounding combination of the two thirds
        iii) Also, the *diapente* f-c' is divided harmonically by the note a

b) Fogliano's treatise is also of interest because it heralds the coming preoccupation with tuning systems for keyboard instruments   ManI, 135

(1) But, Fogliano's system is actually inferior to one previously proposed by

Ramis
- (2) Fogliano suggests double keys for D and B♭ for his keyboard
  - (a) The alternate notes were a comma apart   PalH, 241
    - i) The alternate D produces a pure minor third against F (which otherwise would be too small) and the normal D produces a perfect forth with G
    - ii) Likewise, the higher B♭ makes a just minor third with G, whereas the normal B♭ makes a perfect fourth with F
  - (b) The difference between these two notes is the syntonic comma (81:80)   PalH, 241
    - i) This division is not possible according to Pythagorean mathematics
    - ii) Therefore, Fogliano proposes a geometric solution for the required division, using Euclid's construction of Book VI, Proposition 9
      - a - [This is found in Euclid's *Elements*]
      - b - For a discussion of the geometric solution, *see*   PalH, 242
- (3) For the chromatic scale, Fogliano suggests five pure minor semitones (25:24); six pure major semitones (16:15); and one unusual one, F#-G (27:25)
  - (a) This produces six pure triads on G major, G minor, A major, A minor, B♭ major, and B minor
- c) Facsimiles of *Musica theorica*   FogM; FogMT

2. For a detailed discussion of just intonation, *see*   GanMR, 358

G. Interval Ratios: Temperament

1. Mean-tone temperament   RanH, 837
    - a) Mean-tone tuning had its origin in modal music and served, at least for tuning the organ, for some three hundred years   LloL, 223
        - (1) This temperament was used on keyboard instruments from ca. 1500 to ca. 1830   RanH, 478
    - b) The first evidence of temperament came from northern Italy
        - (1) Franchinus Gafurius had stated [in his *Practica musicae* of 1496] that organists were making fifths slightly smaller
            - (a) This was known as *participata*
            - (b) A translation of *Practica musicae*   GafPR
    - c) Arnolt Schlick was the first to articulate the temperament in his *Spiegel der Orgelmacher und Organisten* of 1511   JeaS, 173
        - (1) Actually Schlick's tuning method was an irregular system lying somewhere between mean-tone and equal temperament   BarT, 138
        - (2) He suggested tuning the fifths FC, CG, GD, and DA "as flat as the ear could endure"   JeaS, 173
            - (a) Schlick thought this should be done so that the third FA would "sound decent"   JeaS, 173
        - (3) A translation of *Spiegel der Orgelmacher und Organisten*   SchM
    - d) Pietro Aaron [in his treatise *Il Thoscanello de la musica*] described mean-

Interval Ratios: Temperament   151

tone temperament in 1523 with the same term used by Gafurius, *participata*
(1) He states that there are many ways of tempering   ManI, 136
   (a) "These range from written versions of practical methods to learned discussions based on classical authority"
(2) But, the tempering system suggested by Aaron is the most widely accepted system   ManI, 136
   (a) He described a scale with pure thirds and the fifths flattened by one-quarter of a comma   ReeMR, 530
      i) He suggested that each successive fifth be tempered by one-quarter of the syntonic comma in such a way that the comma is distributed among the intervals of the octave   ManI, 136
         a - Therefore, the fifth has a frequency ratio of 1.49527   JeaS, 172
         b - Evidence supports the one-quarter comma mean-tone temperament only insofar as the first notes C, G, D, A, and E   LinE, 139
            1 - After that ambiguities arise
      ii) The result is that four such fifths in succession (F-C, C-G, G-D, D-A) lead to a pure major third   ApeHD, 835
         a - That is, the major third from F to A has a frequency ratio of 5.00
            1 - In the Pythagorean system, the first four pure fifths produce a third that has a frequency of 5.06   JeaS, 172
      iii) Each pure major third consists of two equal sized whole tones   RanH, 478
         a - The value of the whole tones is the geometric mean of 5.4, thus the name for the scale
   (b) Two chromatic pairs of pitches in this system, the D# and E♭ as well as G# and A♭, have a difference of 41 cents, a discrepancy called the "wolf-tone"   ManI, 136
      i) Sometimes organs were built with two black keys placed between D and E   JeaS, 173
         a - One black key would sound D# and the other would sound E♭
         b - Other notes were treated the same way
      ii) This interval was called the *quinte-de-loup*, or "Wolf-fifth", wolves being howling animals

Fig. 6. The clock-face on the mean-tone scale

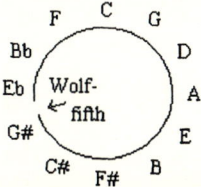

JeaS, 172

   (c) Facsimiles of *Il Thoscanelle de la musica*
    AarTD; AarTO; AarTOS; AarTM

(d) A translation of *Il Thoscanelle de la musica*   AarT
(3) Evidence supports the one-quarter comma mean-tone temperament only in so far as the first notes C, G, D, A, and E because after that ambiguities arise   LinE, 139
    (a) When the scale of fifths continued, the interval G#-E♭ proved to be three-eights of a semitone more than the exact fifth   JeaS, 173
        i) This interval was called the *quinte-de-loup*, or "Wolf-fifth", wolves being howling animals, *see* figure 6
e) It was discovered that by making slight departures from the mean-tone system it was possible to tune the notes so that music played in one key would sound harmonious, while that in a few other and nearly related keys did not sound too bad   JeaS, 173
    (1) Musicians had to avoid writing or playing in the more remote keys
        (a) They were generally limited to two flats or three sharps
f) The triads of this temperament sound purer than those of equal temperament   ApeHD, 835
    (1) But, not all triads in the plan are good   ParG, 283
g) For a detailed discussion of mean-tone temperament, *see*   GanMR, 362

2. Equal temperament
    a) Very gradually mean-tone temperament was superseded by the system of equal temperament   JeaS, 174
    b) Equal temperament consists of the equal distribution of the comma of Pythagoras over twelve intervals of the fifth   JeaS, 174
        (1) Each interval of a fifth is flattened by about a forty-eighth of a semitone
            (a) Every fifth without exception is one-eleventh of a comma, or V1 in V885, too flat and every major third is seven elevenths of a comma, or V1 in V126, too sharp.   EllO, 12
        (2) All semitones are equal with a frequency ratio of 1.05946   JeaS, 175
    c) Equal temperament had been proposed as early as 1482 by Bartolomé Ramis [in his *Musica practica*], *see*   GanMR, 233
        (1) His ratios of 5:3 and 8:5 for the intervals of the sixth along with his ratios [of 5:4 and 6:5] for the intervals of the major and minor third laid the foundation for equal temperament   CarMM, 218
    d) Henricus Grammateus [in his *Ayn new kunstlich Buech* of 1518] constructed a temperament for the organ that came close to systematizing equal tuning   ManI, 138
        (1) His system gave the octave two equal halves, C to F# and F# to C
            (a) Each was equal to 600 cents
        (2) He kept the Pythagorean semitone between diatonic half-steps (90 cents) and calculated all chromatic semitones as half of the just major tone (102 cents)
            (a) As a result, all fifths and fourths not involving E and B are pure intervals
        (3) A facsimile of *Ayn new kunstlich Buech*   SchAN
    e) Also, a temperament that attempts to distribute the Pythagorean comma equally was discussed by Giovanni Maria Lanfranco, in his *Scintille di musica* of 1533   RanH, 837
        (1) This source gives the first tuning rules that might be interpreted as equal

    temperament   BarT, 45
   (a) His method was to sharpen the fourths and flatten the fifths by minute amounts   ManI, 138
  (2) Facsimiles of *Scintille di musica*   LanSC; LanSM
  (3) A translation of *Scintille di musica*   LeeG, 50
 f) The first definite mathematical definition of equal temperament was stated by Francisco Salinas in his treatise *De musica libri VII* of 1577   BarT, 6
  (1) A facsimile of *De musica libri VII* of 1577   SalF
 g) All theorists from about the middle of the sixteenth century agreed that fretted instruments such as the lute and viol were tuned in equal temperament   BarT, 11
  (1) But theorists disliked equal temperament   ManI, 138
  (2) A few writers suggested it for keyboard instruments, and some radical theorists even dared to say that vocal music is best tuned this way   ManI, 138
  (3) But equal temperament did not become the norm for some 300 years   RanH, 837
 h) "Equal temperament turned out to be the only practical and effective answer to the problems created by chromaticism and modulation"   LowT, 47
  (1) But, equal temperament, while having unlimited possibilities for transposition, has rather poor major and minor thirds   KleE, 140

Musica practica: Performance Didactics

A. Introduction

1. *Musica practica* was a part of the quadrivial discipline of *musica* which was divided between *musica practica* and *musica theorica* MoyM, 4
   a) The term *musica practica*, or *musica attiva*, refers to the application of the ideas found in *musica theorica* RanH, 845
   b) *Musica practica* was divided into two branches, *musica mensurabilis* (*musica figuralis*) and *musica plana* RanH, 845
      (1) *Musica mensurabilis* dealt with mensural notation, discant, and counterpoint
      (2) *Musica plana* dealt with plainsong, solmization, mode, intervals, etc.
   c) But the concept of *musica practica* was enlarged during the Renaissance to encompass performance, instruments, and the art of composition as transcending the craft of counterpoint LowR, 939

2. Nicolaus Listenius, in his treatise, [*Musica, ab authre denuo recognita...* of 1549], divides the study of music into three branches: *theorica* (science), *practica* (performance didactics), and *poetica* (composition) ManI, 123
   a) The original title of the treatise was *Rudimenta musicae in gratiam studiosae juventutis diligenter comportata* [1533] LisR
      (1) A facsimile of the original 1533 edition LisR
   b) A German translation of *Musica, ab authre denuo recognita...* LisMN
   c) A translation of a revised edition of *Musica...* LisM

B. Chromaticism: *Musica ficta*

1. Introduction
   a) The theoretical definition of *musica ficta* remained constant but the degree of unwritten accidentals admitted to practice and sanctioned by theorists changed greatly over time RanH, 517
   b) Therefore, the term *musica ficta* "is now often used loosely to describe intended accidentals left unwritten in the original manuscripts or prints of music from before about 1600" RanH, 517

(1) Composers of the Middle Ages and Renaissance found it unnecessary to write all accidentals BerM, xi
   (a) This was due to the fact that there were some accidental inflections that were conventionally implied by the musical context
   (b) Performers would make them whether or not they were notated
(2) The use of unwritten accidentals arose partly from a guild secrecy perpetuated by singers WulT, 164
   (a) It was also partly due to the fact that the system of solmization did not encompass unusual inflections and because there was a desire to preserve a "modal" appearance in the music
c) The practice of adding accidentals in performance was a generally accepted practice in the sixteenth century RanH, 517
   (1) But certain melodic and vertical factors clouded the issue and as a result there was a demand for a certain degree of planning on the part of the performer TofA, 19
d) No single formula for applying accidentals to all types of music of this period has been found RanH, 517
   (1) But, there are certain guidelines for adding accidentals that are commonly used

2. The horizontal precepts of *musica ficta*
   a) The tritone and the diminished fifth are the only two non-harmonic relations (diminished or augmented intervals) which can arise in the untransposed system BerM, 79
      (1) They are usually discussed together
   b) "The melodic tritone is prohibited regardless of whether it is ascending, descending, direct, or indirect" BerM, 76
      (1) The rule states that a note above *la* ("a") should be sung *fa* (b♭), [*i.e., fa supra la*], *see* figure 4 BerM, 77
         (a) This rule was cited by Agricola, in his treatise, *Musica choralis deudsch*, and by Aaron in the *Lucidario* of 1545, as being applicable only when one wants to avoid the tritone BerM, 78
            i) A facsimile of *Musica choralis deudsch* ColS
            ii) A facsimile of *Lucidario* AarLM
         (b) This is only one of the ways in which the prohibition of the tritone was formulated
         (c) On the other hand, the *fa supra la* rule is cited without reference to the tritone by some theorists BerM, 78
            i) This was done by Stephano Vanneo in his *Recanetum de musica aurea* and by Nicolaus Listenius in his *Musica, ab authre denuo recognita...*
               a - A translation of *Recanetum de musica aurea* VanRD
               b - A translation of *Musica...* LisM
      (2) According to the *fa supra la* rule, whenever a note exceeds the six-degree syllable (*la*) by a second, the seventh note must be called *fa* without making a mutation into the next hexachord
         (a) But, if the vocal range of a part is restricted to the six notes of a given hexachord, the rule of *fa supra la* has no relevance AllT, 46
            i) Nor is it applicable in the first tetrachord of a conjunct hexa-

chord-order when the part range is contained within the limit of that hexachord-order

Fig. 7. Example of irrelevant *Fa supra la* rule

AllT, 46

(3) The *fa supra la* rule is applicable when the vocal range of a part covers a conjunct hexachord-order interlocked with a disjunct one   BerM, 77
    (a) The rule must be applied in the disjunct part of the range, provided proper solmization demands it   AllT, 46

Fig. 8. *Fa supra la* rule applied in the disjunct hexachord-order *naturale-durum*

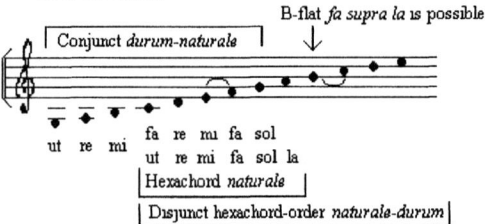

AllT, 46

    (b) The difference between the conjunct hexachord-order and the disjunct one lies in the location of the second semitone   AllT, 17
        i) Therefore, in the *durum-naturale*, the second semitone occurs between the VIth and VIIth degrees of the hexachord order
        ii) But, in the *naturale-durum* it takes place between the VIIth and VIIIth degrees
    (c) When the *fa supra la* rule is applied to the hexachords *naturale* and *molle*, it results in B-flat and E-flat respectively   AllT, 47
(4) Factors such as mode, cadential notes, and musical context condition the application of the rule, *fa supra la*   AllT, 47
c) There are exceptions to the general rule concerning the melodic tritone
        BerM, 76
    (1) The melodic tritone is acceptable if it is resolved properly
        (a) A descending tritone (b♮...F) may be resolved by E
            i) This rule may be broken when, by the rules of counterpoint, F is to be sharpened as the cadential leading tone   BerM, 74
            ii) But, if the b♮ only descends to the cadentially sharpened F, but is also reached in a progression from a natural F, then the b♮ should be flattened in spite of the resulting diminished fourth
                a - An example is F...-b♭-...F#-G

	(b)	An ascending tritone (F...b♮) may be resolved by c
		i) But, if an ascending tritone (F ...b♮) is not immediately followed by c, *i.e.*, if there is an interruption in the resolution after the F...b♮, the b♮ must be changed to b♭ BerM, 73
		a - An example is F-G-a-b♭-a-rest-a-b♮-c
(2)	An unresolved indirect tritone loses its force if it is filled with many notes (more than four) therefore it does not have to be corrected BerM, 76
(3)	There is no certain guideline as how to treat tritones which are strictly speaking not resolved, but are embedded in perfect fifths BerM, 76

- (2) An unresolved indirect tritone loses its force if it is filled with many notes (more than four) therefore it does not have to be corrected BerM, 76
- (3) There is no certain guideline as how to treat tritones which are strictly speaking not resolved, but are embedded in perfect fifths BerM, 76
  - (a) They may have been treated according to the relative structural weight of the notes involved
    - i) The more important structurally the notes of the tritone are the more offensive the tritone is found to be
      - a - That is, when it is found in notes that represent structurally central steps of the mode or notes of the underlying simple counterpoint (rather than those of the embellishing diminished one) it is found to be offensive
      - b - For example, the tritone b-F would require correction, while the tritone found in the fifth c-F would not
- (4) There is a difference of opinion concerning direct tritones BerM, 76
  - (a) Some theorists are of the opinion that they should always be corrected
  - (b) Others think they should be corrected only if they are unresolved
  - (c) Actually, the treatment of direct tritones varies according to the mode in which they are found
    - i) In the Lydian and Hypolydian modes, the tritone often has to be avoided because the tritone arises there in relation with the final
    - ii) It is fairly common to avoid the tritone in the Dorian and Hypodorian modes
      - a - A b♭ is rare in the Dorian and Hypodorian modes because the tritone produces a non-harmonic relation with the final
    - iii) The b♭ is particularly rare in the Mixolydian and Hypomixolydian modes because, unlike in the other modes, the consistent application of b♭ destroys the modal identity
      - a - It transforms the mixolydian and Hypomixolydian into the transposed Dorian and Hypodorian

d) When diminished fifths are indirect and properly resolved they are tolerable BerM, 80
  - (1) "The *diminished* fifth does not offend when it is indirect and resolved by a semitone *inward* to the perfect fourth"
e) Some theorists believe that the diminished fifth, tritone, and octave should be corrected by means of a flat BerM, 88
  - (1) But, this is not the case with diminished fifths and tritones produced by the introduction of an internal B♭
    - (a) For example, when a correction of a non-harmonic relation between F and B gives rise to another non-harmonic relation between B♭ and E, one does not proceed to flatten E in a kind of "chain reaction" involving steps a fourth or fifth apart BerM, 89

(b) Instead, the singer had to choose between the tritone and the diminished fifth
  i) Aaron, in a discussion of the circumstances, states that it is more important to preserve the perfect fifth than to correct the tritone AllT, 58

Fig. 9. The tritone and the diminished fifth

TofA, 36

(c) In discussions of the problem by one theorist after another, the possibility of using F# did not exist BerM, 80
f) Both the tritone and diminished fifth are almost never used in a leap BerM, 80
g) The direct imperfect octave and the direct chromatic semitone are prohibited BerM, 85
  (1) But, The chromatic semitone may be introduced if its use is justified by contrapuntal rules and, if it is resolved to fill the whole tone and is followed by a diatonic semitone going in the same direction BerM, 87

3. The vertical precepts of *musica ficta*: Intervals
  a) It has been concluded that all non-harmonic vertical relations which arise normally in polyphony (that is, without the use of internal accidentals) should be corrected by means of flats BerM, 115
    (1) The tritone, diminished fifth, and imperfect octave were the vertical relations most commonly prohibited BerM, 93
      (a) They were the only vertical relations which might normally require a correction by means of a *musica ficta* step BerM, 115
      (b) The prohibition against the tritone and the diminished fifth is commonly known as the prohibition of *mi contra fa* on perfect consonances
        i) *Mi contra fa* was prohibited because when *mi* is sung on b natural in the lower voice and *fa* is sung on f in the upper voice the resulting fifth will not be a consonance
          a - The resulting fifth had to be corrected
        ii) The status of the fourth, unlike that of other intervals, depends on the context
          a - By itself, the fourth is a dissonance
          b - Only in counterpoint for more than two parts can the fourth be used as a consonance
            1 - As a consonance the *mi contra fa* had to be avoided
      (c) The rules state that an octave should be kept perfect, by means of accidentals if necessary
        (a) This was true as early as the fourteenth century
    (2) There were exceptions to the prohibition of augmented and diminished intervals BerM, 113
      (a) They played as important a role in determining normal sixteenth century practices as did the precepts themselves TofA, 40

(b) Augmented and diminished intervals were tolerated if they were correctly resolved   BerM, 99
    i) They were tolerated if discords resolved to concords
        a - The tritone could be used in passing if it proceeds to an octave   TofA, 28
        b - The diminished fifth was tolerated if it resolved to a third
            1 - Also if it is followed by a perfect fifth   BerM, 101
    ii) The diminished fifth and tritone could be used if they are preceded by a perfect or imperfect consonance   TofA, 27
    iii) Also, the diminished fifth will be tolerated even in simple counterpoint provided it is preceded and followed by a consonace with at least one, and preferably both, of the dissonant notes properly resolved   BerM, 112
        a - The diminished fifth should be resolved with the *mi* step going a diatonic semitone up and /or the *fa* step going a semitone down
            1 - This should happen immediately, or after notes belonging to the diminished counterpoint, or even after a rest
    iv) The rules listed above were tolerated provided that in such cases the discord lasts no longer than a minim   BerM, 103
        a - That is, under the regular mensuration signs
(c) A passing dissonance in rapid passages was permitted   TofA, 29
    i) This was true no matter how the dissonance was resolved   BerM, 114
(d) The diminished fifth is commonly used in cadences involving a suspension figure   TofA, 28

b) Sometimes a correction of a melodic relation produced an unwanted vertical one or the reverse   BerM, 118
   (1) For example, in the following figure, for melodic reasons, in order to avoid the tritone with the preceding F, one would want to flatten the second b in the counterpoint   BerM, 119
      (a) But, a b flat at this point would create a diminished fifth with E in the tenor

Fig. 10. A non-harmonic melodic relation left uncorrected in order to prevent a non-harmonic vertical relation; indicated by an internal accidental

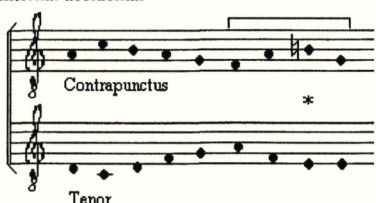

BerM, 119

      (b) Therefore, this example confronts us with three choices:
         i) Correct the melodic relation and thus produce an incorrect

vertical one;
- ii) Correct the melodic relation and then also correct the resulting non-harmonic vertical relation by making the E flat;
- iii) Or, leave the uncorrected melodic relation in order to prevent a non-harmonic vertical relation
- (c) According to Tinctoris, [in his *Liber de natura et proprietate tonorum*] the last choice is the correct one
  - i) A translation of *Liber de natura et proprietate tonorum*   TinC
- (d) As a result it is clear that "'chain reactions' in which the introduction of one accidental necessitates the introduction of another at a place a fourth or a fifth apart are not allowed"
- (e) Also, when choosing between two non-harmonic relations, one melodic and the other vertical, one should correct the latter
- (f) These two rules are also true of music notated with flats in the key signature

4. The vertical precepts of *musica ficta*: Cross-relations (false relations)
   - a) A cross-relation is the succession of a pitch in one voice by a chromatic alteration of that pitch (or its equivalent in another octave) in another voice   RanH, 215
     - (1) "A simultaneous or verticle cross-relation is the simultaneous occurrence of two pitches related in this way "
   - b) Some composers apparently liked the sound of cross-relations and composed in such a way that these harmonically rich sonorities would be included in performance   BooF, 221
     - (1) They often structured the part-writing to allow for, and virtually encourage, the cross-relation in the cadence   BooF, 253
     - (2) They seemed to choose where dissonances should be heard in a composition and then composed in such a manner that singers would be drawn towards, or away from, applying specific *ficta* accidentals
     - (3) Much chromaticism in this music is the result of what seems to be a genuine liking for the cross-relation created by the *mi-fa* clash even in the work of composers who wrote basically diatonic music   HaaF 93
   - c) Some composers would indicate that *musica ficta* was not to be applied to a note occurring in a context normally requiring it by doubling that note
     ReeMR, 297
   - d) Cross-relations usually appear as the result of leading notes in more than one voice at the approach to the cadence   BooF, 221
     - (1) As a rule one leading note will rise to the tonic (except in a phrygian cadence) while the other leading note must then move in a different direction, usually falling
       - (a) As far back as Jean de Muris the rule was to sharpen the returning leading notes   BenF, 89
         - i) They are sung as *fa mi fa*   BenF, 90
       - (b) These leading notes usually were not sharpened until the last possible moment   BooF, 222
   - e) Three possibilities of treating doubled leading notes at cadences were equally available to composers, and thus to singers, at least in the second quarter of the sixteenth century   BooF, 259

(1) They could sharpen both leading notes as *mi*
(2) They could flatten both notes as *fa*
   (a) But, in many cases, if both singers sing the same version of the leading note, one or the other would have to suspend the normal approach to *musica ficta* BooF, 222
(3) Or, they could sing both versions of the note
f) In some cases, there is a question as to whether the subsemitone should be sharpened BooF, 230
   (1) Some music seems to have been written as if to provide simple answers to such a question

Fig. 11. The *Satzfehler*, taken from the Credo of *Missa de Beata Virgine* by Arcadelt

BooF, 223

   (a) In the figure above, Arcadelt moved the fourth voice from F as if to avoid any possible conflict with the same pitch in the *cantus*
      i) As a result, the latter can be sharpened normally
   (b) The voice-leading produces the effect of sounding the suspension (g) against its resolution (f) BooF, 222
      i) This produces the so-called *Satzfehler*
   (c) This suspension-and-resolution figure was even more common in the works of composers in the next generation BooF, 229
      i) It is considerably lessened by the way in which the lower voice moves away before the upper voice resolves
   (d) A transcription of *Missa de Beata Virgine* ArcO, I, 56
g) Sometimes the composer arranged the voice-leading so that the leading note could not be sharpened BooF, 230

Fig. 12. An example of a leading note that could not be sharpened; taken from *Ave nobilissima creatura* by Josquin

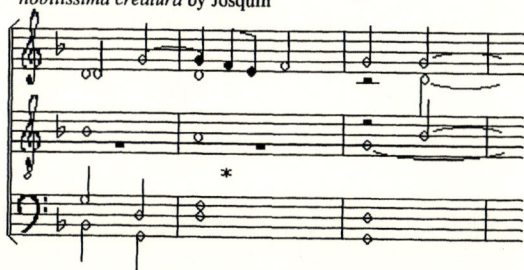

BooF, 226

  (1) A transcription of *Ave nobilissima creatura*   JosW
h) But there are other cases where the solution is even more difficult when considering *musica ficta*   BooF, 222
  (1) This is true in the following example

Fig. 13. An example taken from the final cadence of *Io che di viver* by Arcadelt

BooF, 223

  (a) It would be logical, at first sight at least, for the tenor to sing an F natural and the *quintus* to sing an F sharp
  (b) The alternative is the simultaneous sounding of *mi* and *fa*
    i) If the tenor and the *quintus* were to sing the same version of F in performance, one or the other would have to suspend his normal approach to *musica ficta*
  (c) A transcription of *Io che di viver*   ArcO
i) The examples of the *Satzfehler* and other cases with potential cross-relations usually fall into a number of distinct types   BooF, 246
  (1) There are those such as the examples just discussed and another group with most thorny problems
  (2) In this second group, two voices overlap, but the lower voice moves away before the upper voice resolves
    (a) In practice the resolution of this problem depends on the intent of the composer or scribe as to the stress of the overlap

Fig. 14. An example taken from *Sub tuum presidium* by Lhéritier

BooF, 248

    (b) A transcription of *Sub tuum presidium*   Lhé, O
    (c) As a result, this group has to be further subdivided
      i) It should be subdivided according to whether or not the composer or scribe stressed the overlap, thus making it a

significant part of the sequence of sonorities
- a - This includes a few cases where the overlap is purely the result of a decorative figure on the upper leading note, the subsemitone as in figure 14
- ii) It also includes those times when the composer seems to want the overlap of the two notes to be more noticeable
BooF, 247
- a - This usually is a function of the rate of movement of the music, especially that of the harmonic movement, whereby the subsemitone is itself sounded longer

(3) This second group also includes those cases where the lower voice slides away from its version of the leading note soon after the upper has sounded its version as in figure 15

Fig. 15. An example taken from *Missa de feria,* Agnus by Beausseron

BooF, 245

 (a) A transcription of *Missa de feria*   JosE

(4) In the third group, which is related to the second group, both leading notes sound until the resolution of the chord BooF, 248

Fig. 16. An example taken from *Repleatur os meum,* final cadence by Lhéritier

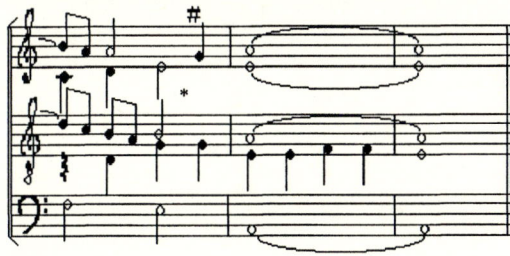

BooF, 249

- (a) In this situation the composer makes sure that the two soundings of the leading note will be clearly heard
- (b) Some situations, such as that found in figure 17, are so constructed as to require *fa* from the lower voice
- (c) A transcription of *Repleatur os meum* Lhé, O

(5) In the fourth group, the composer organizes the vocal lines so that both singers should sing the leading note as *fa* BooF. 250

Fig. 17. An example taken from *Io che di viver* by Arcadelt

BooF, 252

    (a)   A transcription of, *Io che di viver*   ArcO
(6) In the next group, two leading note pitches begin simultaneously
        BooF, 250
    (a)   This is a curious group as the potential clashes in this group clearly present a hazard to be faced by singers
    (b)   There are instances when the singer may have sharpened the falling leading note in sympathy with the subsemitone in the other voice, but in some cases this would be impossible
        i)   For example, it is clearly not possible in figure 18

Fig.18. An example taken from *Io che di viver* by Arcadelt.

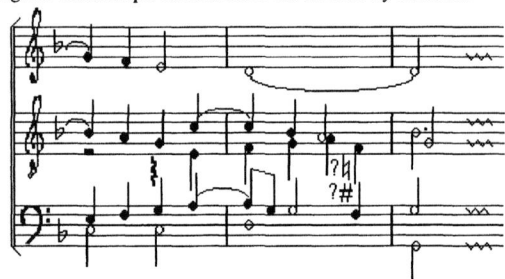

BooF, 251

        ii)   A transcription of, *Io che di viver*   ArcO
  j) All of the above possibilities of treating doubled leading notes at cadences were equally available to composers and singers by the second quarter of the sixteenth century, at least in Rome   BooF, 259
  k) There are some distinct harmonic progressions by means of which sixteenth century composers achieved a coloristic result without recourse to melodic chromaticism   HaaF, 94
    (1) Harmonic color is introduced when composers alter the third degree over a static bass particularly between the end of one phrase and the beginning of the next   HaaF, 96
        (a)   This produces an audible cross-relation
        (b)   This was often specified in prints from the middle of the sixteenth century but was seldom indicated earlier in the century
                HaaF, 119

Fig. 19. Altered third degree over a static bass; *O dolce vita mia* by Willaert

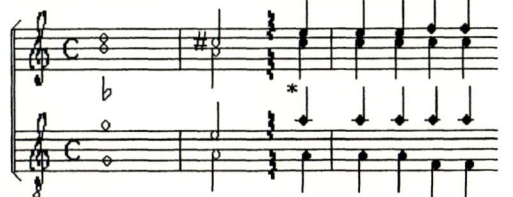

HaaF, 96

- (2) Strongly heard cross-relations occur when composers use progressions in which the bass moves by a third, major or minor, up or down   HaaF, 96
- (3) Deliberate use of this cross-relation in music with the bass moving by thirds begins to show in the *frottola* repertory   HaaF, 102
    - (a) It serves as an effective way to separate phrases
    - (b) Thus the cross-relation occasionally turns up in mid phrase

Fig. 20. Movement of the bass by a major third
Taken from *La verginella* by Ghibel.

HaaF, 98

- (c) But, the use of a bass line with many skips of a third does not necessarily need to produce cross-relations   HaaF, 101
- (4) The progression by a minor third can easily be written with diatonic voice leading in all parts   HaaF, 101
    - (a) This may make the cross-relation all the more striking

Fig. 21. Movement of the bass by a minor third; taken from
Dolcemente s'adirà by Gero.

HaaF, 100

- (b) The use of a minor third was frequent much earlier than that of the major third

5. The vertical precepts of *musica ficta*: Contrapuntal progressions
    a) There are contrapuntal progressions which require *musica ficta* steps
       BerM, 122

                (1) This refers to progressions that involve horizontal motion not between individual steps, but between intervals
            b) One such progression was the progression from an imperfect to a perfect consonance   BerM, 122
                (1) [There were two] versions of this rule that remained valid through this period [and up to ca. 1560]   BerM, 126
                    (a) There was a standard version of the rule
                        i) The voices must move in contrary motion toward the closest perfect consonance
                        ii) One voice must move a whole tone and the other a semitone   BerM, 123
                            a - Thus a minor third should contract to a unison, a major third should expand to a fifth, and a major sixth to an octave
                            b - In order to do this, one of the steps in the imperfect consonance may have to be chromatically inflected
                        iii) But there is no proper way to proceed from a minor sixth by means of this strict version in two-part counterpoint   BerM, 126
                            a - The minor sixth would have to be followed by a fourth which was considered an inadmissible interval   BerM, 127
                            b - Both Ramos and Gafurius seem to imply that they approve of the rule in its strict form but state that the minor sixth could not be followed by step in contrary motion, therefore oblique motion is allowed
                                1 - A translation of *Music practica* by Ramos   RamMU
                                2 - A translation of *Practica musicae* by Gafurius   GafPR
                    (b) There was a relaxed version of the rule   BerM, 123
                        i) Some theorists thought that imperfect intervals could move to perfect ones with one voice moving a semitone but without the contrary motion or the requirement that the other voice should move a whole tone
            c) Not all musicians considered the imperfect-to-perfect rule to be obligatory   BerM, 128
                (1) Ghiselin Danckerts, in his *Trattato sopra una differentia musicale*, thinks that if the imperfect-to-perfect rule was observed in every place, it would excessively damage the modes
                    (a) A facsimile of *Trattato sopra una differentia musicale*   DanD
            d) According to Gafurius, in his *Practica musicae*, the imperfect-to-perfect rule is obligatory only at cadences   BerM, 127
                (1) All cadences formed on a unison or an octave must be approached from the closest imperfect interval   TofA, 17
                    (a) This means that a subsemitone or the suprasemitone must be used
                        i) According to Aaron, in his *Libri tres de institutione harmonica*, all cadences which are shown to terminate by a whole tone should be sharpened   BerM, 145
                            a - But he also states that sharpening the leading tone in the upper part is not necessary if the lower part descends to the final by a half step

Chromaticism: *Musica ficta* 167

     b - A facsimile of *Libri tres de institutione...*   AarLTI
   ii) Also, Giovanni Maria Lanfranco, in his *Scintille di musica*, presents examples of cadential formulas in which the final tone has whole tones below and above and shows that in all such situations the sharp leading tone is chosen rather than the flat one   BerM, 146
     a - A translation of *Scintille di musica*   LeeG, 50
 e) According to Stephano Vanneo in his *Recanetum de musica aurea*, the above rules were true in simple counterpoint   BerM, 132
  (1) But he states that in florid counterpoint the *penultima* is preceded by a dissonant suspension
   (a) This dissonant suspension often takes the form of sounding the suspension against its resolution (the *Satzfehler*), *see* figure 11
                     BooF, 222
  (2) A translation of *Recanetum de musica aurea*   VanRD
 f) Another rule is that the third above a cadence note is raised   TofA, 23
  (1) According to Aaron, in his *Il Thoscanello de la musica*, ending on a minor tenth or third sounds unpleasant   BerM, 138
   (a) One should use the *diesis* to make these intervals major
  (2) The practice of sharpening the third in the final harmony was confirmed by other theorists such as Lanfranco and Vanneo
   (a) This was true from the 1520s
  (3) But this rule was not universally applied   TofA, 70
 g) Due to the practice of employing sharps only for cadential leading tones and for thirds of the final harmonies in cadences, only three or four sharps were used; *i.e.*, C#, F#, G#, and D#   BerM, 153
  (1) And, the normal practice of this period required no more than three flats; *i.e.*, B♭, E♭, and A♭

6. The vertical precepts of *musica ficta*: Canon and imitation
 a) The use of canon and imitation raises two questions   BerM, 155
  (1) Should one aim at preserving exact intervals of the melody at each appearance?
   (a) Theoretical evidence concerning preserving exact intervals of the melody at each appearance is too scarce to allow a certain answer
                     BerM, 156
    i) It is thought that composers dealt with the *mi* against *fa* rule and the cadential situation requiring an accidental in the usual fashion and that this was also true in canon and imitation
                     BerM, 155
    ii) But, it seems that only in canon at the fourth or fifth are accidentals used in the consequent to preserve the exact intervals of the guide   BerM, 158
    iii) Intervals in imitation at the octave should preserve their exact size   BerM, 158
  (2) When forced to introduce an inflection for harmonic or contrapuntal reasons, should it always be introduced in the non-imitative voice?
   (a) Theorists of the time offered no evidence to suggest that, when confronted with the need to correct a vertical *mi* against *fa* discord

or a penultimate cadential harmony, musicians worried about which voice to inflect

C. Chromaticism: "Chain Reactions"

1. Progressive composers of this period were seeking paths to chromaticism other than those offered by notation   LowS, 14
   a) They found it through the "chain reaction" chromaticism, or, as it is otherwise known, the "secret chromatic art"   LowS, 15
      (1) This phenomenon appears in the music of the Netherlanders   LowS, 73
         (a) It was their approach to the new musical language of the Italians
         (b) It achieved a coloristic result without recourse to melodic chromaticism   HaaF, 94
         (c) It was an occasional resource used by composers from the time of the celebrated use of the device in *Absalom fili mi* by Josquin ?   HaaF, 94
            i) It became commonly used by the middle of the sixteenth century

2. "Chain reaction" chromaticism produced a technique of modulation without the full notation of the accidentals ordinarily used to indicate the course of a modulation   LowSC, 756
   a) It is based on the practice of singing and laying unnotated accidentals according to the two famous categories of rules *causa necessitatis* and *causa pulchritudinis*
   b) It is stringent in its demand that accidentals be used to avoid imperfect intervals such as the diminished and augmented fourth, fifth, and octave

3. "Chain reactions" produced departures from the diatonic system that were not provided for by *musica ficta*   LowS, 15
   a) A♭, D♭, G♭, and C♭ were introduced
   b) Also, tones that change the character of the church modes beyond recognition were introduced
      (1) They were B♮, F#, C#, and B♭, F, and C in the transposed Dorian mode on G

4. The technique anticipates the prevalence of major and minor over the other modes   LowS, 15
   a) It is a technique that expands the limits of modality without erasing them entirely   LowT, 38
   b) It reveals a definite capacity for thinking in chords and understanding the connections and relationships of chords in the circle of fifths   LowS, 16
      (1) In the more daring advances the style could be called "floating tonality"   LowT, 38
   c) The technique has to be announced by means of voice leading, motif structure, harmonic and contrapuntal texture   LowS, 74
      (1) Motif transposition is the chief means of getting a modulation started   LowS, 75

                (a) A motif is transposed to a degree which calls for the insertion of accidentals
                (b) All motifs modulate in the direction of a fourth above or a fifth below
        d) The cadence is used to make the transition from the chromatic back to the diatonic LowS, 76
            (1) The transition is not achieved through the use of naturals
        e) Even though there is an apparent tonal "strength" of each pair of chords, the technique seems primarily a coloristic device, allowing the composer quick departure from, and easy return to, the main tonal center HaaF, 94

    5. The technique is "an attempt to create a new musical symbolism and new media of expression" LowS, 79
        a) One of the main characteristics of the secret chromatic art ("chain reaction") chromaticism) is its ambiguity LowS, 135
            (1) It allows for two readings; one literal and the other implied
                (a) The music can be sung as it stands or with the addition of accidentals LowS, 78
                (b) An example of this is found in *Fremuit spiritu Jesu* by Clemens non Papa AtlR, 400
                    1) A transcription of measures 5-13 AtlR, 401
                (c) Another example is found in Willaert's *Quid non ebrietas* AtlR, 402
                    i) A transcription of measures 11-39
            (2) The text must embody a secret significance as well as its obvious literal meaning LowS, 78
            (3) It is a musical style offering one face to the world and another to the initiated few LowS, 175
                (a) Chromaticism, frowned upon by the church, was hidden
                (b) Esoteric religious messages were hidden in texts

D. Pitch

    1. The pitch of any period before the second half of the nineteenth century cannot be established MenP-IV, 167
        a) There was no international pitch ReeMR, 530
        b) Therefore pitch varied from town to town and church to church
            (1) Even different organs were tuned at varying pitch-levels ReeMR, 350
                (a) Their pitch is impossible to determine before seventeen hundred MenP-IV, 167
                    i) All vibration frequencies are rough approximations and should be labeled "plus or minus a semitone or more"
            (2) Secular music may have varied even more as there was no anchor such as the organ
        c) The notes on the staff represented degrees that moved freely up and down according to the nature of the voices or instruments involved on any given occasion MenP-I, 89
            (1) It did not matter what the particular pitch was called as long as players

                could tune together to it   RanH, 638
            (a) Singers and instrumentalists used a standard pitch compatible with
                the organ when performing in a church
                i) But, the organ had to be tuned properly for singing, other-
                    wise singers were forced to sing too high or too low and
                    the organist had to play the chromatics   EllO, 23
            (b) Chamber music far exceeded church requirements, as a result
                church pitch was usually too high or too low   EllO, 25
                i) Chamber pitch may have differed from church pitch by a
                    semitone, a tone, a minor third, or even a fourth
        d) The pitch for a particular body of vocal music for any individual composer is
            possible to roughly establish
            (1) This can be done by analyzing the ranges of the compositions
                (a) But, different pitches may have been intended for different places,
                    or different institutions
                (b) Also, secular music may have been intended at a different pitch
                    from the sacred music

E. Text Underlay

   1. Introduction
      a) The rules are fairly clear in reference to music from 1475 to the end of the six-
          teenth century   McGM, 28
          (1) But both manuscript and printed sources often fail to make clear the
              alignment of individual syllables with individual notes   RanH, 842
              (a) Often, it is not possible to resolve these ambiguities

   2. Writings by theorists on text underlay
      a) *Libellus de rudimentis musicae* by Biagio Rossetti (Blasius Rosssettus)
          [1529]   MoyM, 150
          (1) Rossetti's major concern was the new interest in text and metrics, parti-
              cularly with the rhythms of chant texts   MoyM, 150
              (a) In the *Libellus de rudimentis musicae* he seems to be arguing for
                  the equal note theory
                  i) But his argument curiously is based on the ignorance of the
                      rules of mensural notation by most singers of chant
                                                                            SheT, 182
              (b) His argument for the equal note theory seems to imply that those
                  who did know mensural notation might have performed the chant
                  differently
                  i) Singers with polyphonic training could not have helped notic-
                      ing that the ligatures and basic note forms of chant were the
                      same as those of mensural notation
                  ii) This may have had an influence on their methods of perfor-
                      mance
              (c) Rossetti wanted to alter the melodies so that the stresses and other
                  types of musical emphasis would help to project, rather than ob-
                  scure, the source words of the texts

i) He makes it clear that one needs to observe the varying weights of long and short syllables, avoid running together syllables, and make the words clearly understandable RosL, ii
   a - If these ideas are followed, there will be an inequality in the length of the notes
(2) The precepts he forms also carry over into mensural music HarW, 114
(3) The first of Rossetti's prescriptions concerns a fitting adaptation of rhythm to long and short syllables in syllabic or neumatic writing
   (a) He advocates the differentiating of long and short syllables by commensurate rhythmic changes
      i) In one situation, a short syllable is set to a melisma (*notulae ligatae*)

Fig. 22. *Notulae ligatae.*

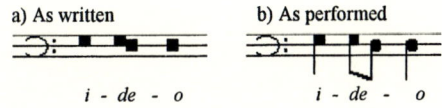

HarW, 117

   a - Rossetti states, (instead of performing two quarter notes on the short syllable *de*), "briefly utter those two notes in ligature" HarW, 117
      ii) In another situation, a short syllable is set to a single note (*sola notula*)

Fig. 23. *Sola notula.*

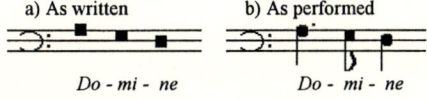

HarW, 117

(4) His inclusive statement on text placement ranks as the earliest systematic statement of its kind HarW, 116
   (a) It precedes Lanfranco's rules for mensural music by four years
(5) The following are Rossetti's rules that deal with the relation of notes to syllables: HarW, 123
   (a) "Syllables should be adapted to long or short notes according to their inherent stresses"
   (b) "The phrasing of the music should be patterned after the syntax of the text"
   (c) "Single notes carry their own syllables"
   (d) "Notes in ligature are sung to the syllable on the first of them"
   (e) "The middle notes of a ligature are sometimes set to a syllable of their own"
   (f) "Syllables or words should never be repeated"
   (g) "The last syllable may hold a terminal melisma"
(6) Rossetti also discuses the requisites of good singing HarW, 123

(a) In his discussion concerning the delivery of words, four kinds of instructions may be distinguished
(b) He gives instructions for pronunciation, breathing, tempo, and expression
    i) When discussing pronunciation, he lists six different abuses   HarW, 124
        a - Nasalizing vowels, running words together, omitting a letter from the middle of a word, adding a letter to the middle of a word, altering the ending of a word by replacing two letters by one, and compressing two adjacent vowels of one word into a single syllable   HarW, 125
    ii) He gives seven instructions for breathing   HarW, 126
        a - Never take a breath in the middle of a word unless absolutely necessary, breathe steadily in leaping a third, a fourth, or a fifth, breathe evenly in ligatures and melismas, breathe easily during rests, and never take a breath within a ligature   HarW, 127
        b - He also states two factors that bear on breathing: the capacity of the human voice to sustain a melisma in its entirety and the structure of the melodic line   Harw, 127
        c - Also, breathing should be molded to the contour of the melody (its natural rise and fall)   HarW, 127
    iii) The tempo should be moderate yet flexible and uniformly maintained for the duration of the example   HarW, 128
    iv) In the summary of his words on expression, he stated that the singer should adapt his performance to the content of the words   HarW, 129
(6) A reproduction of *Libellus de rudimentis musicae*   RosL
(7) A facsimile of *Libellus de rudimentis musicae*   RosLR
b) [*Scintille di musica*] by Giovanni Maria Lanfranco [1533]   McGM, 26
  (1) It is the first treatise to systematize word-tone relations into a code of text underlay   HarW, 135
    (a) It was followed by a treatise by Nicolo Vicentino in 1555, a set of ten rules given by Gioseffo Zarlino in 1558, and a treatise by Gaspar Stocker ca. 1570-1580   McGM, 26
    (b) A summary of Lanfranco's rules   HarW, 151
      i) Composers need to plan cadences and rests so musical and textual phrases coincide   TowS, 265
      ii) A ligature should have one syllable only
      iii) The dot of a dotted note may not be fitted to a syllable
        a - In the figure ♩. ♩ ♩ the first note may carry a syllable
        b - But if a note is necessary to accommodate a syllable where the composer has placed the dot, the dot may be replaced by a note for the syllable, but not if the pitch forms a dissonance   TowS, 277
        c - [A singer] may assign a syllable to the semiminim which follows a dotted minim and the larger note that follows the semiminim   TowS, 277

            iv) Only those notes larger than a semiminim may carry a syllable
                a - There are exceptions; sometimes a semiminim may carry a syllable of its own
                b - [Composers and singers] should assign a syllable to each minim or larger note　　　　　　　　　　　TowS, 268
            v) In a series of semiminims, only the first note may carry a syllable
                a - The syllable could begin on a larger note preceding the run　　　　　　　　　　　TowS, 271
                b - A syllable should not be placed, however, on the larger note that follows the series
                c - There is an exception in works in the style of the French *chanson*
                    1 - "Syllables are sometimes apportioned to the middle and final notes of the series as well as to the larger note that follows"
            vi) Textual repeats may occur only when the notes will accommodate them
            vii) When a melisma contains more notes than syllables, but not enough for textual repetition, the melisma should fall on the penultimate syllable　　　　　　　　　　　TowS, 271
                a - There is an exception in the case where the final syllable cannot be placed on the last note, it is then assigned to a suitable note preceding it　　　　　　　　　　　HarW, 151
            viii) The last note of a phrase should receive the [singer's] last syllable　　　　　　　　　　　TowS, 268
            ix) These rules were for Masses and motets only　　　　HarW, 152
        (2) These rules applied to all [Masses and motets] from the time of Josquin until 1570-1580　　　　　　　　　　　McGM, 28
        (3) For examples of music illustrating most of the rules, *see*　　　McGM, 29
    3. There were problems in England with liturgical settings in English　　　WulT, 287
        a) They stemmed partly from the rigid desire to make the music syllabic
        b) Also, the problems with underlay were partly a consequence of the failure to deal satisfactorily with the very short syllables of the English language
        c) For example, in a number of [sacred] works found in the Forrest-Heyther manuscripts, a borrowed melody and the new text do not fit　　　BenL, 51
            (1) At times there was a complete omission of words and phrases and on the other hand there was the placing of several syllables beneath a single note or ligature
                (a) The composer (or copyist) apparently left some of the arranging to the singer

F. Ornamentation

1. Performing conventions of the time permitted singers and instrumentalists to embellish music that had already been composed　　　　　　　　　BroE, x
    a) Almost all compositions, sacred or secular, were candidates for ornamenta-

tion   McGM, 183
   (1) But, the ornaments added to sacred music were somewhat more conservative than those for the secular repertory
  b) Both instrumental and vocal ensembles would have used discreet ornaments in order to decorate the music   BroE, 74
   (1) But ornamentation could be performed by only one of an ensemble of voices or instruments   McGM, 184
       (a) This was usually done in the top voice - occasionally in the bottom voice
  c) The ornaments were presumably practiced and learned by rote   BroE, 20
   (1) They then could be added on the spot to any composition

2. Theorists made a distinction between ornaments for single notes as opposed to ornaments for longer, freer, running passages that substitute for the slower moving basic intervals of a melody   BroE, 1
  a) The former were called *Mordanten*, that is graces and the latter were called diminutions or *passaggi*
   (1) However, the term 'graces' was never applied to *Mordanten* in the sixteenth century
   (2) The graces include mordents, trills, turns, appoggiatura, and vibrato
                                                                      McGM, 150
       (a) The grace is made with an upper or lower neighbor and the turn is made with the upper and lower neighbor   McGM, 151
       (b) The appoggiatura enters on the neighboring note either from above or below
       (c) The vibrato is a pitch variation consisting of less than a half step
                                                                      McGM, 153
   (3) Two of the graces that were used throughout the entire century were the tremolo and the *groppo*
       (a) The tremolo [trill] is a rapid alternation between a main note and its upper or lower auxiliary   BroE, 5

Fig. 24. The *tremolo*

BroE, 3

           i) The interval between the two notes may be a whole step, a half step, or a third
           ii) The tremolo seldom took up more than half the time value of the main note
           iii) The evidence points to the fact that the tremolo was added to all sorts of music between 1500 and 1600   BroE, 7
       (b) The *groppo* is a cadential trill on the subsemitone, usually starting on the tonic   BroE, 8
           i) The subsemitone could be held a time before the *groppo* actually started
           ii) The ornament usually ended with the underthird

Fig. 25. The *groppo*

BroE, 3

- (4) The graces were varied according to the speed at which the individual grace was executed McGM, 153
  - (a) They could be played at a constant or variable speed
- (5) The grace could be performed at the time of the written note, in anticipation, or slightly delayed McGM, 153
- (6) The trill and vibrato could vary in length McGM, 153
  - (a) They could last the full value of the note, just the beginning part, or just the end
- b) Graces that were combined were called diminutions or *passaggi* BroE, 1
  - (1) These were applied to ascending and descending intervals of seconds, thirds, fourths, and fifths BroE, 17
    - (a) They were also applied to scale fragments and cadences
      - i) Tables showing diminutions all include a much higher proportion of cadential formulas than simple interval formulas BroE, 20
        - a - Since cadences are invariably singled out as a special category, it is clear that *passaggi* may always be added to cadences
        - b - This does not mean that all cadences should be decorated
      - ii) For a table showing 175 diminutions (divisions) for a basic cadence, *see* GanO, 97
  - (2) The passages are mostly stepwise, but there are skips of a third which usually turn in the other direction McGM, 168
  - (3) There are no stereotyped formulas BroE, 29
    - (a) Variations involve length, note patterns, and a variety of rhythms McGM, 153
  - (4) Diminutions (divisions) fall into four groups GanO, 15
    - (a) A simple diminution
      - i) Only the same kind of notes are used and performed in one kind of time and the time signature is not changed
      - ii) Every group of notes of the melody is similar and there are several identical groups in the final cadence and also in the middle
    - (b) A compound diminution (division)
      - i) A diminution is compound when various kinds of notes are used
      - ii) A diminution also is compound when there are changes of time signature
      - iii) It is compound in melody when each diminution is different and unlike any other
    - (c) A particular or special diminution
      - i) The diminution is simple in two respects and compound in one

176 *Musica practica:* Performance Didactics

       a - An example would be a simple diminution in the development of the melody and the time signature but compound in rhythm or a simple division in time and rhythm and compound in the development of the melody
    (d) A uniform diminution
      i) This diminution is compound in all three respects, rhythm, time, and melody
  (5) For a list of the rules for graces and *passaggi* taken from various instruction books, *see*   McGM, 168

2. English ornament signs
 a) There are a few in English sixteenth-century keyboard music   WulT, 126
  (1) There are stroke signs
    (a) But, not all strokes are to be considered grace signs   WulT, 127
      i) They are often used to denote the crossing of parts, to cancel a stem, or, at times, as a scribal flourish
    (b) The single stroke is found in the *Mulliner Book*
      i) It must have meant a lower-note ornament   WulT, 129
    (c) The double stroke must have meant both an upper- and lower-note ornament   WuT, 129
    (d) In the liturgical organ music of the British Library, *MS. Add. 29996*, the double stroke, found in several passages, seems to do duty for a particular figure   WulT, 126
      i) The first occurrence of the figure is fully written, after which the sign appears to be a variety of shorthand for subsequent repetitions
      ii) This could be peculiar to this manuscript

Fig. 26. The double stroke

WulT, 126

Musica poetica: Composition

A. Writings by Theorists on *Musica poetica*

1. *De musica et poetica opusculum* by Raffaele Brandolini   MoyM, 107
   a) *De musica*... is a reworked and expanded version of an earlier work, *De laudibus musicae et poesos*, and was published shortly before 1513   MoyM, 108
      (1) The latter treatise has not survived
      (2) The *De musica et poetica*... is written in rhetorical style
   b) *De musica et poetica*... is the first independent work to examine music in the context of the poetry that music accompanies rather than in the context of mathematical consonance
   c) Brandolini's ultimate goal was to prove that both music and poetry form parts of true eloquence   MoyM, 108
      (1) He shifts attention away from scales and intervals toward the rhetorical goals of the singer-poet   MoyM, 112
         (a) He thought that while the tools for the proper practice of music lie in the realm of proportion, music's use and effectiveness is connected to the words of the text, its rhetorical goals, and the type of audience   MoyM, 113
      (2) He wished to present known authorities and information in a new light   MoyM, 109
         (a) This he wished to do in order to highlight the importance of music and poetry, both separately and, most importantly, together
         (b) In his explicit reference to the connection between music and poetry he discusses the importance of hymns   MoyM, 111
   d) The *De musica et poetica opusculum* is found in the manuscript, Rome, Biblioteca Casanatense *805 [20v-21r]*   MoyM, 298
   e) A translation of *De musica et poetica opusculum*   BraD

2. Nicolaus Listenius wrote a treatise, [*Musica, ab authore denuo recognita*... in 1537]   ManI, 123
   a) In this treatise, Listenius divides the study of music into three branches: *theorica* (science), *practica* (performance didactics), and *poetica* (composition)
      (1) It is thought that he was the first to differentiate *musica poetica* from *musica practica*   HarW, 162

- (2) He defines *musica poetica* "as the process of composition whereby the musician strives for artistic significance"   HarW, 162
  - (a) The term, *musica poetica*, meant music making that goes beyond the execution of conventional technical procedures   RanH, 698
  - (b) It meant music making whose stylistic aspect transgresses the confines of correct usage   RanH, 698
  - (c) And it meant music making that corresponds to the contrapuntally controlled dissonance transgressing the norms of consonance   RanH, 698
  - (d) The term considered more general aspects of musical composition such as rhetorical models and affective content   RanH, 845
- (3) Listenius states that the *poetici* are not content with theory and execution
  - (a) Their aim is to produce the consummate and complete art work, and after their death, to leave behind the *opus perfectum* and *absolutum*
- b) A translation of *Musica, ab authore denuo recognita...*   LisM
  - (1) The original title of the treatise was *Rudimenta musicae in gratiam studiosae juventutis diligenter comportata* [by Rhau in 1533]   LisR
    - (a) A facsimile of the 1533 edition, *Rudimenta musicae...*   LisR
  - (2) *Musica...* is a corrected version of *Rudimenta...*   NieL, 28

B. The Evolution of *Musica poetica*

1. First, *Musica poetica* means a theory of musical composition   ManI, 209
   a) The theoretical approach to polyphony changes from the abstraction of linear counterpoint to the concrete idea of compositional style   ManI, 158
   - (1) Within the latter approach, there are concepts of vertical sonorities, expressivity, and genre
     - (a) Such concepts were possible only after the development of mannerism
   - (2) Pietro Aaron, in his *Il Thoscanello de la musica* [1523], credits the moderns with the development of an integrated conception [integrated polyphony] and attributes a layered approach [linear counterpoint] to older composers   ManI, 159
     - (a) This distinction implicitly posits modern musical style as a superior refinement over the older style   ManI, 235
     - (b) A translation of *Il Thoscanello de la musica*   AarT
   b) Music shifts from the scientific *quadrivium* to the expressive *trivium* [grammar, logic, and rhetoric]   ManI, 115
   - (1) It was the stressing of the connection between music and words that naturally evolved into consideration of the question of music and grammar and music and rhetoric   HarW, 2
   - (2) The terms grammar and rhetoric are roughly equivalent to the structure of speech versus the style and effect of its content
     - (a) In music, grammar might be defined as the art of composing and performing correctly
       - i) Del Lago, in his letter to Fra Seraphin, states that since gram-

　　　　　　　　　mar requires good writing, then music requires good composition under due and lawful rules　　　　　　　HarW, 3
　　　　ii)　He cautions that composers should observe grammatical accents that have temporal quantity, *i.e.*, long and short accents
　　　　　　　　　　　　　　　　　　　　　　　　　　　　BlaC, 890
　　　　　　a - That is, a long accent should not be set to a short syllable or a short accent to a long syllable　　　　BlaC, 889
　　　　iii)　He states also that cadences are necessary in order to distinguish the parts of speech, such as the comma, colon, and period　　　　　　　　　　　　　　　　　　　　MoyM, 137
　　　　　　a - They are necessary to make clear the meaning of the text, both in prose and poetry
　　(b)　Rhetoric in music is the conscious and consistent use of patterns and formal arrangements　　　　　　　　　RanH, 698
　　　　i)　These patterns and arrangements are used to engender in an audience the sense of aesthetic satisfaction or psychological plausibility that clarifies or heightens the intended effect of the composition or the performance
　　　　ii)　Rhetoric was divided into five parts by Cicero, in his *De inventione*　　　　　　　　　　　　　　　　　RanH, 698
　　　　　　a - The five parts are invention, arrangement, style, memory and delivery
　　　　iii)　Music began to be mentioned in relation to arrangement and style with the rise of notated polyphony during the middle ages
　　　　iv)　And early writings on rhetoric usually mention music in the context of delivery
　　　　　　a- This was due to the fact that ancient music theory was allied chiefly with speculative philosophy and mathematics
　　　　v)　But, a full-fledged doctrine of musical rhetoric, including analogues for all five parts and virtually every procedure of classical rhetoric, had to wait until the Baroque era
　c)　A conflict developed between the ear and mathematics in things musical　　　　　　　　　　　　　　　　　　LowMR, 90
　　(1)　This conflict is not only openly acknowledged but often no less openly resolved in favor of the ear
　　(2)　Aristoxenus' theory, revived by the humanists, held that the ear was the decisive factor in determining consonance and dissonance and not mathematics　　　　　　　　　　　　　　　　　　LowMA, 733
　　(3)　Fogliano, [in his *Musica theorica* of 1529], states that music, insofar as it consists of sound which is caused by motion, is not a mathematical but a natural phenomenon　　　　　　　　　　　　　PalH, 236
　　　　(a)　He defines consonance and dissonance not according to ratio but in terms of how they struck his ear　　PalH, 20
　　　　　　i)　He describes consonance as a mixture of two sounds separated with respect to high and low pitch that is pleasing to the ear and dissonance as a mixture of two sounds separated with respect to high and low pitch that is displeasing to the ear
　　　　　　　　　　　　　　　　　　　　　　　　　　　　PalH, 237

      d) In order to succeed in developing the expressive vein of music, composers would have to free themselves increasingly from technical considerations blocking their free invention   LowMR, 97
          (1) This is perhaps the reason for the emancipation of Renaissance composers from such techniques as the use of a *cantus firmus*, the strictures of canonic writing, and the artifice of rhythmic proportions

  2. Secondly, *musica poetica* means more than the ordinary concept of contrapuntal craft; it actually refers to the art of composition   ManI, 209
      a) Music began to be thought of as an aesthetic experience and the human factor of creativity and enjoyment was stressed   ManI, 158
          (1) But, the idea that music should move or arouse the affections was not introduced by writers on music until the later sixteenth century   RanH, 16
              (a) This idea was not prevalent until Elizabeth's reign   SteMP, 70
                  i) It was called *musica reservata*   SteMP, 69
      b) Glarian, in the *Dodecachordon*, presented the first critical essay on music in an attempt to subject this art to historical and stylistic analysis   ManI, 160
          (1) His ideas about the structure of the modes, their ethos, and their judicious combination in counterpoint combine to form a subtle but imposing system for evaluating musical procedure and expressivity- in short- style
          (2) He affirms the expressive possibilities of modal combinations   ManI, 198
              (a) He considers the arrangement of semitones to be the source of the particular structure and character of each mode   ManI, 152
          (3) But, his system is still somewhat old-fashioned   ManI, 194
              (a) He clings to ideas of individual modal integrity and character
          (4) An English translation of *Dodecachordon*   GlaD
      c) The choice and treatment of mode determined by the text is considered   LuoR, 135
          (1) If the text determines the treatment of the mode, it also influences the shape of lines, the contrast of sonorities, the layout of textures, and the plan of cadences
              (a) These elements were considered important and expressive in the sixteenth-century
          (2) In the treatise, *Breve introduttione di musica misurata* of 1540, by Giovanni del Lago, there is a discussion on how to compose music that is sensitive to the text on several levels   PalH, 340
              (a) The composer should choose the proper mode to fit the words and thus produce the right affection   HarW, 156
              (b) Cadences should be considered important as a means of articulation   HarW, 157
              (c) Attention should be given to the location of long syllables within a line in poetic texts   PalH, 340
              (d) A facsimile of *Breve introduttione di musica misurata*   LagB
          (3) In a letter to Fra Seraphin, 26 August, 1541, Del Lago states that the first thing to do when setting a text is to find a melody that fits the words   BlaC, 888
              (a) This includes which affects are to be portrayed and therefore which mode should be chosen

    (b)   This letter is a part of del Lago's treatise, *Epistole composte in lingua volgare*   BerLA, 345
          i)   It may be partly ficticious   BlaC, 130
    (c)   Also, portions of the letter are found in del Lago's treatise, *Breve introduttione di musica misurata*   BlaC, 875
    (d)   And, the letter is a part of the Spataro Correspondence   BlaC, 201
    (e)   For a copy of the letter in the vernacular with English translation and commentary, *see*   BlaC, 875

d) Thought was given to beat and accent   WulT, 19
   (1)   Beat and accent are not the same thing
      (a)   The beat is a boundary which is not necessarily physically perceptible although felt in the mind
      (b)   Accent helps suggest the beat, or sometimes to go against it
          i)   There are several different kinds of accent; stress (loudness), length, and pitch
          ii)   The disposition of accents, either in verse or music, is crucial

e) Also, consideration is given to rhythm   LesM, 30
   (1)   It was rhythm, not chromaticism, that first brought about expression
      (a)   Aristotle [in his *Politica*] states that rhythms have a character of rest, and motion, while some have a more vulgar or nobler movement   HarW, 26

f) Aaron, in his *Il Thoscanello de la musica* [1523], stresses the aesthetic function of dissonances and states that beautiful counterpoint embodies an artful variety of intervals   ManI, 159
   (1)   Examples in his treatise are detailed enough to exemplify not only rules of correct procedure but also guidelines for artistic value   ManI, 160
      (a)   As a result, even the teaching of rudiments becomes infused with stylistic criteria
   (2)   He moves away from ideal, abstract science toward concrete, practical art   ManI, 160

g) The proper coordination of word and tone and their proper coordination in performance becomes a general aspect of composition   HarW, 7
   (1)   The coordination of word and tone means how the various levels of syntax, accentuation and general expression are related
      (a)   In order for music to reflect the content of its text, the notes and syllables were required to be set in a clear and sensible relation to one another   HarW, 8
      (b)   Therefore, the parts of vocal compositions were written to be sung and the words were accurately placed under the notes by the publisher   LesM, 16
      (c)   The practice of placing initial words only at the beginning of the composition was no longer practiced   LesM, 16
   (2)   This aspect of composition brought about new innovations   LesM, 15
      (a)   The composer began a search for literary texts which would become his principal source of inspiration
          i)   He wanted the text to condition the form of his composition and to dictate the musical laws
          ii)   He found such literary texts in the prose writings of Pierre de Ronsard who succeeded in creating a *"mystique"* of the

union of poetry and music which profoundly influenced the subsequent history of their relationship LesM, 57
- (b) Also a solution was sought for the relationships between the melody and the text which the melody was expected to support LesM, 42
  - i) Luther, [in his attempt to create a German Mass], insisted that the text, notes, accent, melody, and movement of the music must come out of the correct mother tongue and voice BluPR, 60
    - a - His artistic sense protected him from the superficiality of merely placing the German text under the customary melody of the Latin piece
- (3) Certain conventions of relating text and music required the formulation of rules HarW, 9
  - (a) The basic rules are traceable to antiquity
    - i) They were transmitted as part of an oral tradition
  - (b) Theorists, from the 1530s on, put the rules into writing HarW, 10
    - i) These rules stem from an attempt to translate the relation of word and tone into specific regulations and also to strengthen and stabilize this relation in the practice of their time
  - (c) Biagio Rossetti's major concern in his *Libellus de rudimentis musicae* [1529], was the new interest in text and metrics, particularly with the rhythms of chant texts MoyM, 150
    - i) But the precepts he forms also carry over into mensural music, such as the observance of syllabic stress, and the rule of one note to a ligature, etc. HarW, 114
    - ii) His inclusive statement on text placement ranks as the earliest systematic statement of its kind HarW, 116
      - a - It precedes Lanfranco's rules for mensural music by four years
    - iii) For a list of Rossetti's rules, *supra*, p. 175
    - iv) A facsimile of *Libellus de rudimentis musicae* RosLR
  - (d) [The *Scintille di musica* of 1533 by Giovanni Maria Lanfranco], is the first treatise to systematize word-tone relations into a code of text underlay HarW, 135
    - i) A summary of Lanfranco's rules, *supra*, p. 176
      - a - These rules were for Masses and motets only HarW, 152
    - ii) An English translation of *Scintille di musica* LeeG, 50
- h) This stress on the connection between music and words by the humanists resulted in a great war between counterpoint and the supremacy of text and music LowH, 171
  - (1) "The Netherlandish position was one of unquestioned supremacy of music"
    - (a) It aimed for ever greater refinement of rhythm, melody, and counterpoint
      - i) "Its problems were how to reconcile voice-leading with harmony, consonance with dissonance, and demands of text expression with the demands of counterpoint"
  - (2) "The humanist position was one of unquestioned supremacy of the

poetic text"
- (a) The first documents of humanistic music were found in Germany
  LowH, 156
    - i) They are found in *Melopoiae sive harmoniae tetracenticae...* of 1507 by Petrus Tritonius
    - ii) An original source of *Melopoiae sive harmoniae tetracenticae...* TriM
- (b) They consisted of nineteen poems of Horace set in the rhythm dictated by the various classical meters in simultaneous four-part declamation LowH, 156
    - i) Every syllable of the text was set to one note only
    - ii) No repetitions or parts of sentences were tolerated
    - iii) There were only two note values, a short and a long, the long having twice the duration of the short note
        - a - These notes were painstakingly adapted to the long and short syllables of the Latin meter
            - 1 - All of the voices moved in one and the same metric step
    - iv) There were no passing notes or dissonances
    - v) Sharps and flats were used sparingly in order to preserve the purity of the modes
- (c) At this point the humanists felt they had solved the problem of how to set music to words by adopting the old Greek idea of subordinating music to poetry and equating musical rhythm with poetic meter LowH, 171
- (d) But humanists failed to see that the limitations that had been imposed on every musical element of the Latin odes made it impossible for music to unfold its expressive power LowH, 172
    - i) It was discovered that melody cannot soar freely when it is tied to a text in a manner preventing even the slightest melismatic movement
    - ii) Also, rhythm is unable to speak eloquently when it is reduced to two note values
    - iii) And, harmony is unable to be expressive when dissonance is banished altogether
    - iv) A text cannot be flexible if the repetition of phrases or single words used for emphasis or climatic effect are ruled out
    - v) If the modes are painstakingly observed, the range of expression is limited
- (e) It was Glarean, in his *Dodecachordon*, who felt the need to deviate from the common metrical pattern LowH, 173
    - i) He abandons the idea of one note to a syllable
    - ii) He shows sensitivity to the meaning of the text
    - iii) He tries to enlarge the limited repertory of musical devices found in the ode composition of his day
    - iv) He stands midway between the world of the humanist and the musician LowH, 176

Notation

A. Part Arrangement

1. Partbooks were the usual format from the beginning of the sixteenth century
   a) This was true in both manuscript and print
   b) They were separately bound manuscripts, or printed books, containing the music for a single voice or instrument in an ensemble RanH, 609
      (1) The number of partbooks in a set corresponded to the number of parts of an individual work
      (2) Each partbook was named for the voice or part contained
      (3) In part-arrangement notation bar lines were used to mark off main sections of a piece RasN, 113
   c) The earliest surviving set of partbooks is in manuscript RanH, 609
      (1) It is the *Glogauer Liederbuch* of ca. 1480, *see* GanMR, 165
   d) "Printed sets begin with Ottaviano Petrucci's *Motetti C* of 1504 RanH, 60

B. Score Arrangement

1. Definition ApeN, xx
   a) "The voices of a composition are written one underneath the other, arranged in such a way that simultaneous tones appear in a vertical or nearly vertical alignment"
      (1) This notation is historically the earliest method of writing used for polyphonic music
         (a) "The practice of superimposing one voice of a polyphonic composition above the other and aligning the voices in time (even if only roughly) reaches back to the earliest notation of polyphony and extends through the late-twelfth-century *organa* of Leonin and Perotin" AtlR, 417
         (b) It was employed in the sources for the polyphonic repertories of Notre Dame and St. Martial RanH, 736
            i) It was used especially for the *conductus*
      (2) But score notation fell into disuse during the thirteenth century AtlR, 417
         (a) This was the result of the development of the motet which gave

rise to individually written parts in choirbook format
- i) As a rule, in four-part polyphony, the *superius* was copied above the tenor on the left-hand page (*verso*) of the opening, with the alto above the bass on the right-hand page (*recto*)   RanH, 157
- (b) Score notation "was abandoned for vocal music except in England, where it survived into the fifteenth century"   RanH, 736
- (3) It was resurrected in the fourteenth century in keyboard notation   AtlR, 417
- (4) There are references later in the century that attest to the use of scores as a help to study a piece or to facilitate its performance   AtlR, 417
  - (a) But, this does not indicate that composers customarily used scores to compose   AtlR, 418
    - i) Of course, it is possible that some composers may have used them in the process of composing
  - (b) In 1537, Auctor Lampadius presented a carefully aligned score, bar lines and all, of the opening of a four-voice motet by Verdelot   AtlR, 417
    - i) "He called it a *tabula*"
    - ii) This was published in his *Compendium musices...*   LowON, 798
    - iii) It is possible that the *Compendium musices...* is the earliest theoetical source containing an unmistakable reference to the use of the modern score   LowON, 799
    - iv) A facsimile of *Compendium musices...*   LamC
  - (c) Scores were definitely used for didactic purposes   AtlR, 418
- (5) Manuscript scores for vocal music are not found until the latter part of the sixteenth century   RanH, 736

2. Keyboard scores
   a) These were also known as Italian, French, and English keyboard tablatures   RanH, 833
      (1) But, these are not actually tablatures since they employ notation either on two staves with five to eight lines each or on a single staff with as many as thirteen lines
   b) Keyboard scores were used for printed keyboard music of the early sixteenth century   RanH, 736
      (1) The first printed example of keyboard score appeared in an Italian publication of 1523
         (a) The example is found in *Recerchari, Motetti, Canzoni*, by Marcantonio da Bologna [Marco Antonio Cavazzoni]   ApeN, 3
            i) The notes are tied across bar-lines

            Fig. 27. Tied notes

            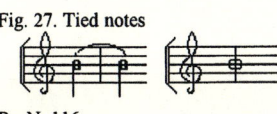

            RasN, 116

            ii) They could also be written as one complete note on the bar-

line itself until the late seventeenth century
- iii) A facsimile of *Recerchari, Motetti, Canzoni* — CavR
- c) Keyboard scores normally have an Italian six line staff — RasN, 111
  - (1) But, in 1529-1530, Attaingnant used the modern five line staff for his seven books of keyboard music for [*Orgues Espinettes et Manicordions*] — ApeN, 6
    - (a) This method was not generally accepted for keyboard scores for another one hundred years
    - (b) But, five line staves were normal for other notations — RasN, 111
    - (c) Facsimiles of six of the seven books
      - i) *Dixneuf chansons musicales...* — AttDC
      - ii) *Vingt et cinque chansons musicales...* — AttVC
      - iii) *Vingt et six chansons musicales...* — AttVSC
      - iv) *Quatorze gaillardes, neuf pavennes, sept branles et deux basses dances...* — AttQG
      - v) *Treze motetz musicaulx...* — AttTM
      - vi) *Tablature pour le jeu d'orgues espinettes et manicordions sur le plain chant de Cunctipotens et Kyrie fons...* — AttTP
    - (d) Transcriptions of three of the books
      - i) *Dixneuf chansons musicales...* — AttTR
      - ii) *Vingt et cinque chansons musicales...* — AttTR
      - iii) *Vingt et six chansons musicales...* — AttTR
  - (2) English composers clung to older traditions — ApeN, 8
    - (a) As many as eight lines were used on two staves
    - (b) Sometimes a staff of twelve or thirteen lines was used
  - (3) Also, Germany did not accept keyboard score until the early seventeenth century — ApeN, 14
- d) Clef signs indicating c' and F were used in keyboard score — ApeN, 3, 9

Fig 28. The clef signs c' and F

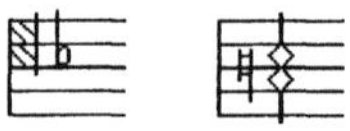

ApeN, 7, 121

- e) Dots above or below single notes indicate either a flatting or sharpening of the note and, since there was a limited number of chromatic tones in use, no confusion arose — ApeN, 4
  - (1) In keyboard music published by Attaingnant the dot was used also for a third purpose; the cancellation of the B flat in the signature — ApeN, 6

Fig. 29. The cancellation of B♭

a) As written   b) As performed

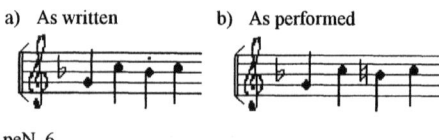

ApeN, 6

- f) Ledger lines in keyboard score are drawn for groups of notes and not separate-

ly for each note ApeN, 4
g) Each note (or rest) is equal to two, and only two notes (or rests), of the next smaller value ApeN, 3
h) The *custos,* or direct, was still in use RanH, 233
   (1) It was indicated by a mordent-like sign at the end of the staff ApeN, 3
      (a) This sign refers the player to the first note of the same part on the next staff
i) Regular bar lines were used in [keyboard] score and instrumental tablatures RasN, 113
   (1) There use was very consistent in printed sources but not in manuscript RasN, 114
   (2) English organists did not accept this innovation until the middle of the sixteenth century ApeN, 9
j) Germany was the last country to adopt keyboard score ApeN, 14
   (1) The *Ricercar Tabulatura* of Joh. Ulrich Steigleder of 1624 seems to be the earliest German example of this notation
      (a) A facsimile of *Ricercar Tabulatura* SteR
k) It is thought that some Spanish composers of organ music prior to 1550 employed a notation similar to that of the Italian keyboard score ApeN, 47
   (1) But only two printed collections and a few manuscripts of organ music have been left to us ReeMR, 626
      (a) And these two printed collections are in Spanish tablature, not score ApeN, 47
   (2) Part of the loss of printed collections and manuscripts is due to the desire of Spanish organists to keep their works for their own use ReeMR, 626

C. Tablatures

1. Introduction
    a) There are two types of tablatures: the indirect way and the direct way ApeN, 54
        (1) These two methods are known as 'pitch notation' (*Tonschrift*) and 'finger notation' (*Griffschrift*) respectively
        (2) The indirect method refers the player to his instrument through the medium of numerous elements of an intellectual character, such as pitch, intervals, tonality, accidentals, scales, etc.
        (3) In the direct method the player's fingers are referred immediately to the technical devices of his instrument, the keys, frets, holes, etc.
            (a) It is probable that the lute was the earliest instrument for which a finger notation was invented and developed

2. Keyboard tablatures
    a) The term keyboard tablature is often referred to as organ tablature RasN, 143
        (1) But the term refers to other instruments as well
    b) German keyboard tablature
        (1) There are two systems that are generally recognized RanH, 833
            (a) The Old German Tablature was used in many parts of Europe from

the fourteenth century until the late sixteenth century
- (b) It was then replaced by a New German Tablature which remained common, particularly in northern lands, until well into the eighteenth century
- (2) The Old German Tablature was usually written for two voices
  ReeMR, 659
  - (a) The upper part is notated on a staff and the lower part is notated with letters RanH, 833
    - i) The letters a to h are used ReeMR, 659
  - (b) For a detailed discussion of the Old German Tablature, *see* GanMR, 39
    - i) For variations of the Old German Tablature, see GanMR, 149
- c) Spanish [Neapolitan] Keyboard Tablature
  - (1) Spanish tablature for keyboards was based on figures HayI, 781
    - (a) Juan Bermudo, in his *Declaración de instrumentos musicales* of 1555, advocates a method of notation in which each note is numbered consecutively from the bass, 1-42, in the range shown in Figure 30
      - i) The numbers include every semitone
      - ii) There should be forty-six units, but four units are missing, [E♭, A♭, D♭, G♭], because of the 'short octave' in the bass which was common to the keyboards of the period

Fig. 30. The range of the numbered notes including every semitone

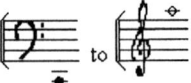

HayI, 781

- iii) There is no taking account of octaves, tuning-structure, or the subsidiary nature of black notes such as placed on the keyboard RasN, 149
- iv) The staff consists of a line for each voice with the numbers of the notes placed on the lines
  - a - The purpose is to separate the parts of a polyphonic composition RasN, 150
  - b - For a polyphonic composition with *cantus*, *altus*, tenor, and *bassus*, there would be four lines with the proper numbers reading from top to bottom RasN, 150
- v) There are no rhythm signs but there are ties between numbers for tied notes RasN, 150
- vi) For an example of this notation, *see* HayI, 781
- (b) Bermudo also gives a modification of this system in which he reduces the quantity of numbers to be memorized HayI, 781
  - i) He does this by only numbering the white notes from 1-27 and introducing signs for flats or sharps
    - a - These numbers include the small octave at the bottom of

the range, tuned and numbered as shown in Figure 31a
and 31b   RasN, 149

Fig. 31a. The short octave   Fig. 31b. The numbers for the short octave

```
D E Bb                           2 3 7
C F G A B♮                      1 4 5 6 8
```

- b - This numbering of the short octave is illogical since Bermudo uses note-names and not key-names   RasN, 149
    1 - Therefore the performer had to remember the numbers for the short octave
- c - The numbering of the short octave should have been as shown in Figure 31c

Fig. 31c. The correct numbering

```
1 2 3 4 5 6 7 8
C F D G E A Bb B♮
```

RasN, 149 and 150

- d - This numbering extended the range up to c''' as shown in Figure 32

Fig. 32. The extended range using white
notes, flats and sharps

HayI, 781

ii) A facsimile of *Declaración de instrumentos musicales* BerDI
iii) A collection and restoration of some of the compositions
                                                              GayL
iv) Transcriptions of two *tientos*   BerT
v) Transcriptions of selections from the *Declaración de instrumentos musicales*   FroO

3. Lute tablature
   a) Introduction
      (1) Several systems of tablature were used for the lute from the late fifteenth century to the eighteenth-century   RanH, 829
         (a) These systems were also applied to other plucked and bowed string instruments
            i) The tablatures for the viol, bass lute, theorbo, and chiterrone were very similar   RasN, 165
      (2) All of these systems entail some method of indicating the string on which a pitch is to be played and the fret, if any, at which that string is to be stopped   RanH, 829
      (3) There was a standard tuning for lutes and viols   HayI, 777
         (a) It was represented by denoting on which fret each string must be

190 Notation

stopped in order that it may sound a unison with that next above it
HayI, 776
    (b)   The intervals of a fourth, a fourth, a major third, a fourth, and a fourth were used
         i)   The sequence of intervals by which the standard tuning is formed is attested by a long line of writers extending from Agicola in 1529 into the eighteenth century   HayI, 711
(4)   Tablatures are unambiguous and free from doubts of the sharpening or flatting of notes by *musica ficta* that beset early texts in staff notation
HayI 773
(5)   There were Italian, French, and Neapolitan (Spanish) lute tablatures
RanH, 829
    (a)   There was also a German lute tablature   ApeN, 55
    (b)   For a discussion of Italian, French, and German lute tablatures, *see*   GanMR, 249 and 150
    (c)   For examples of Italian, French, and German lute tablature, *see*
HayI, 774-776
b)   The Neapolitan (Spanish) lute tablature   RanH, 829
    (1)   It has six horizontal lines representing the courses [sets of one, two, or three strings played as one] of the instrument
        (a)   These lines are arranged from the highest pitch down to the lowest
    (2)   Numerals indicate open and stopped courses that are plucked individually
        (a)   They start with 0 (and sometimes 1) equaling an open course, 1 equaling the first fret, 2 the second fret, etc.
            i)   The frets are placed chromatically
            ii)   Therefore the numbers represent notes a semitone, tone, minor third, major third, etc. above an open course
(3)   Juan Bermudo gives the lute tuning as $G^0\ C^0\ f^0\ a^0\ d^1\ g^1$ MarMI, 318
    (a)   This was also true for the vihuela
(4)   Note stems appear above the lines showing durations separating successive attacks

Fig. 33. Note values used in lute tablature

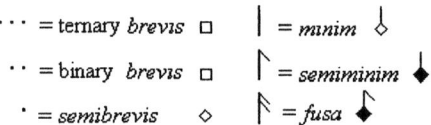

RanH, 829

    (a)   Sometimes these are given only when the note value changes
    (b)   But, even though the signs indicate the point at which each note enters, they fail to prescribe the precise duration of the notes
AtlR, 388
        i)   The duration of the note depends on the acoustical qualities of the lute (a note can neither be sustained forever, nor continue to sound after another fret on the same string is stopped)
        ii)   There are some tablatures that show held notes with an as-

Tablatures   191

terisk or other sign placed next to the affected cipher or with
a diagonal line   RanH, 829
a - These indications are rare and seldom used
(c) The prolongation of a note stem was indicated by dots   HayI, 778
   i) Also, dots placed under some individual numbers tell the
      player to pluck the string upward with the index finger
                                                                    RanH, 829
(d) A sign over a blank space represents a rest of equivalent duration
                                                                    HayI, 778
(e) The signs described above were plain enough for a single line of
    melody   HayI, 778
   i) "But the music for which tablature was needed was seldom
      simple and normally had internal parts that demanded clari-
      fication in this notation"
      a - Therefore, bars were introduced to tablature
         1- Symbols were placed within the bars so that their time
            value was obvious
         2 - These bars did not indicate accent or rhythm
(5) A facsimile of Neapolitan lute tablature   ApeN, 57
(6) An example of Neapolitan lute tablature   RanH, 830

4. The Viol tablature
   a) Introduction
      (1) The term 'Viol' refers to any of a family of fretted, bowed stringed
          instruments in use from the sixteenth century through much of the
          eighteenth century   RanH, 914
         (a) They use the basic principles of the French and Italian lute tabla-
             tures   RasN, 164
            i) "The music is written on a 'staff' whose lines correspond to
               the principal courses or strings of the instrument"
               a - Additional bass courses were notated below or above the
                   staff
            ii) "Each line bears letters or figures corresponding to the frets
                on the fingerboard"
               a - These letters or figures direct the player to stop the rele-
                   vant course at a particular fret with the left hand
            iii) "Rhythm-signs above the 'staff' show the duration of each
                 musical event"
      (2) "Terminology and tunings were often inconsistent for the viol, especially
          in the sixteenth century"   RanH, 914
         (a) The standard tuning for viols was the same as that for the lute
                                                                    HayI, 777
            i) The intervals of a fourth, a fourth, a major third, a fourth, and
               a fourth were used
            ii) Thus, there is a compass of two octaves over the open
                strings   HayI, 710
            iii) Since a tablature operates entirely by intervals, it is indepen-
                 dent of pitch   HayI, 777
   b) The viol tablature is closely related to Italian lute tablature   RasN, 165

(1) The finger-positions are shown by the numerals 0-9 for the open string, the eight frets, and the semitone above
(2) The higher positions, 10-15, are shown by symbols derived from lute tablatures

Fig. 34. Symbols showing the high positions of viol tablature

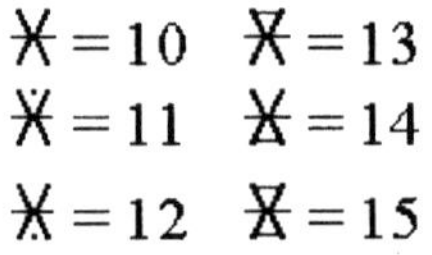

$$\text{X} = 10 \quad \text{X} = 13$$
$$\text{X} = 11 \quad \text{X} = 14$$
$$\text{X} = 12 \quad \text{X} = 15$$

RasN, 166

c) But there are several differences in viol tablature from lute tablature RasN, 165
  (1) A system of dots are used to show fingering
    (a) A dot above the line and to the left of the symbol indicates the index finger
    (b) A dot below and to the left of the symbol indicates the second finger
    (c) A dot above the line and right of the symbol indicates the use of the third finger
    (d) A dot below the line and to the right of the symbol indicates the use of the little finger
  (2) Also, a system of dots are used to indicate bowing
    (a) A dot placed well above a symbol indicates a forward bow while a dot placed well below a symbol indicates a back bow

Fig. 35. (a) An example of viol tablature with a rhythm sign as written, and (b) as played. (c) An example of viol tablature indicating the twelfth fret, to be fingered with the little finger and played with a forward bow.

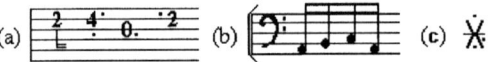

RasN, 166

5. The *vihuela de mano* tablature
  a) The *vihuela de mano* is the classical *vihuela* of Spain   MarMI, 564
    (1) It was a six-course guitar that was tuned like a lute   ReeMR, 620
      (a) But the *vihuela de mano* is related much more closely to the sixteenth century lute than with the seventeenth and eighteenth century guitar   ApeN, fn56
      (b) Six courses are typical, though printed music for five- and seven-course instruments has been preserved   RanH, 911
  b) The tablature, like that of the viol, is closely related to the Italian lute tablature   ReeMR, 620
    (1) Actually, it is a combination of the French and Italian tablatures
    GásL, 153
      (a) Luis de Milán, in his *El Maestro* uses Italian numbers to indicate each fret, but unlike the Italian tablature, he places the number representing the highest course of the *vihuela* on the top line of

            the tablature [French tablature] Gás, 153
            i) His highest fret is the tenth GásL, 154
    c) But Spanish tablature has some uniquely Spanish characteristics ReeMR, 620
        (1) There is the use of red ciphers to indicate the part to be sung
        (2) And, according to Luis de Narváez, the nominal tuning for the *chanterelle* [The highest pitched string of a stringed instrument] of six sizes of *vihuela* is c", b♭', a', g#', g', and f ' RanH, 912
            (a) Luis de Milán recommended tuning the *chanterelle* as high as it would go without breaking
    d) Luis de Milán was the first to use the Spanish system of notation GásL, 109
        (1) He used it in his *vihuela* book [*Libro de Música de Vihuela de Mano: intitulado El Maestro*] GásL, 153
            i) All other *vihuela* books use the Italian tablature ReeMR, 620
        (2) His book, *El Maestro*, is the earliest preserved book of Spanish *vihuela* music ApeN, 56
            i) It was published in Valencia in 1535
            ii) A facsimile of *Libro de Música de Vihuela de Mano:...* MilL
            iii) A transcription of *Libro de Música de Vihuela de Mano:...* MilLM
    e) A second published tablature is *Los seys libros del Delphin de música* by Luis de Narváez ReeMR, 620
        (1) It was published in 1538 AtlR, 489
        (2) In this book and the book by Milán, the tablatures contain some of the earliest known indications of tempo (*tiempo*) ReeMR, 622
            (a) Narváez provides signs for two different tempos
                i) One is Φ for *aperiessa* meaning hurried
                ii) A second sign ₵ is for *muy de espacio* meaning very slowly
            (b) Milán merely suggests tempos for most of his compositions, such as *batido o apressurado*, "with a beaten or hurried measure" and *un compas bien mensurado*, "neither too fast nor too slow, but with a measured beat"
        (3) A reprint of *Los seys libros del Delphin de música* NavD

D. Clefs Used in Sixteenth Century Polyphony

1. Early writing for three voices had often been notated for only two different clefs, and early writing for four voices had been notated with three-clef combinations ReeMR, 531
    a) But when writing for four voices became the norm, the additional voice, at first, caused congestion to reappear, especially within the area of the inner voices
        (1) As a result, it became customary to use a different clef for each part
    b) In time, the inner parts became increasingly differentiated in range, crossing less frequently

2. There were clef combinations, the *chiavi naturali, chiavette, and chiavi trasportati* RanH, 154
    a) Actually, the terms *chiavi naturali* and *chiavette* do not appear before the time of Paolucci MenP-III, 132

(1) The terms are found in his *Arte prattica di contrappunto* of 1765
MenP-III, 130
(a) A facsimile of *Arte prattica di contrappunto* PaoA
b) Clef-combinations made it possible for the composer to compose music for several voices at various pitch levels and still keep to the five-line staff
MenP-III, 132
c) The SATB [*chiavi naturali*] became more or less a standard set ReeMR, 531
d) The VMABar-T, [*chiavette*] became standard to a lesser extent ReeMR, 531
  (1) It is a coordinated collection of clefs that locates the staves of individual parts a third lower on the gamut than do the usual *chiavi naturali* clefs (natural clefs) RanH, 154
  (2) In the *chiavette*, Bar [F3] was sometimes replaced by T [C4]
e) The *chiavi trasportati* [MTBarSub-B or transposed clefs] locate most staves a third higher on the gamut than do the *chiavi naturali*
  (1) This third grouping was noted by Heinrich Bellermann in his *Der Contrapunct* of 1862 RanH, 154

Fig. 36. Clef combinations: S=*superius*, A=*altus*, T=tenor, B=*bassus*, V=violin or treble, M=mezzo-soprano, Bar=baritone, Sub=sub-bass

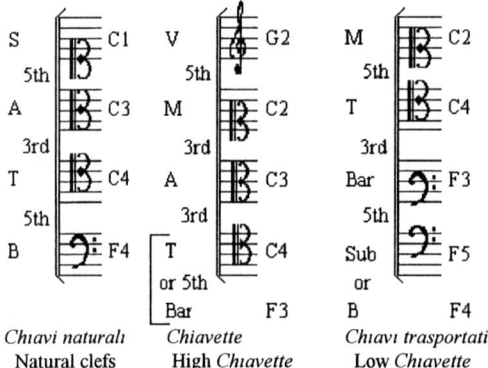

Chiavi naturali   Chiavette   Chiavi trasportati
Natural clefs   High Chiavette   Low Chiavette

MenPW, 59; RanH, 154, ReeMR, 531

f) All of the clef combinations have the same intervallic structure, *i.e.* a fifth, a third, a fifth ReeMR, 531
g) [Even though the *chiavette* and the *chiavi trasportati* move the staves of individual parts a third down or up], there is not a single reference to the use of *chiavette* for transposition by a third that has been discovered in the literature before 1847 ReeMR, 532
  (1) Therefore, the theory that the *chiavette* was a signal for such transposition must be abandoned
h) But there is considerable evidence that the use of the T clef [C4 of the *chiavette*] or Bar clef [F3 of the *chiavette*] for the lowest voice was a signal for transposition down a fourth or fifth ReeMR, 532
  (1) That is, the baritone or tenor clef in the lowest voice was a signal for the choirmaster to give the pitch a fourth or fifth lower than would be given if the lowest voice were written in bass clef

Accidental Signatures (Key Signatures)

            (a)   This would also be a signal to the keyboard accompanist, if any, to transpose accordingly
    i) Gradually clef-combinations became symbolic to identify different modes
                                                                                    MenPW, 59
        (1) In several Italian sixteenth century sources of polyphony a systematic association of modes with clef groupings and system signature are used
                                                                                         RanH, 154
            (a)   In these sources, the *chiavette* is reserved for the authentic (odd numbered) modes, and the *chiavi naturali* for the plagal (even numbered) modes
            (b) Therefore, in such sources, the first priority of the *chiavette* is to signal a feature of the modal system rather than to accommodate ranges   RanH, 155

E. Accidental Signatures (Key Signatures)

1. Introduction
    a) Accidental signatures are the round ♭ and the square ♮ that are placed at the beginning of the staff   BerM, 58
        (1) The square ♮ (*quadrum*) was the ancestor of our natural (♮)
        (2) When placed at the beginning of the staff these flats (♭ and ♭) are valid for the whole length of the staff
        (3) But, the accidental signatures usually discussed by theorists of this period are those involving the use of the round ♭   BerM, 60
            (a)   The square ♮, as a key signature, seems to be inconceivable to most theorists of the period
        (4) At times, the round ♭ was even used for complete compositions
                                                                                       PerMR, 981
            (a)   It appeared at the beginning of the staff and altered the degree so marked at every occurrence
    b) There is much disagreement over the precise theoretical significance of signatures in early music   RanH, 429
        (1) Part of the difficulty is due to the connection of accidental signatures with the use of accidentals in general (*musica ficta*)
        (2) In a signature, the flat sign usually indicates the lowering of the pitch in question by a semitone
            (a)   But, this was not always true since the flat sign was principally an instruction to the performer to sing or play *fa*
        (3) "In general, the addition of each flat can be thought of as transposing the tonal system down a perfect fifth, as is in effect the case in modern signatures"
            (a)   "The use of sharp signatures did not become common until the 17th century"

2. "In the sixteenth century the function of accidental signatures was clearly to make modal transpositions possible"   BerM, 59
    a) The accidental signature was used to transpose a melody to a different location from the one that would have been notated if there was no signature BerM, 58

(1) All of the intervals were retained unchanged, therefore the mode is retained
  (a) This justifies calling the accidental signature a 'key signature'
 b) The accidental at the beginning of the staff transposes the mode while an internal accidental does not   BerM, 61
  (1) The exception to this, during the sixteenth century, was found in the regular (untransposed) modes five and six with the final on F   BerM, 59
   (a) Unlike the other regular modes, these two are notated with a flat in the signature
 c) The addition of each flat, in general, transposed the tonal system down a perfect fifth   RanH, 429
 d) Modal transpositions were necessary in order to keep the lowest part within the gamut of the hand and to avoid the steps of *musica ficta*   BerM, 62
  (1) They were also necessary for instrumentalists accompanying a choir in order to help the singers sing at a comfortable pitch
  (2) This system of transposition by means of a signature was thought by musicians of this period as representing *musica ficta*   BerM, 59

F. Conflicting Signatures ('Partial Signatures')

1. The notating of different voices of a composition with different accidental signatures produced conflicting signatures   BerM, 65
 a) The common patterns used in conflicting signatures were - ♭, - - ♭, - ♭ ♭, and - - ♭ ♭   RanH, 195
  (1) The "-" indicates the absence of a flat
 b) During the early *cinquecento* the native Italian composers seldom used conflicting signatures   LowF, 662
  (1) There was a "tendency towards clarity and simplicity in rhythmic, melodic, harmonic, and formal structure"   LowF, 663
 c) Conflicting signatures were rejected by Pietro Aaron in the second edition of his *Thoscanello* of 1529   LowF, 663
  (1) He stated that they produce inconsistency in the solmization of identical melodic progressions
  (2) Also, they create incongruous results in octaves and double octaves
  (3) A translation of *Il Thoscanello de la musica*   AarT

2. It is thought that conflicting signatures were used in order to make diminished fifths impossible   BerM, 66
 a) During the period when parts were written separately (either in separate areas of an opening in a choirbook or even in separate partbooks) rather than vertically in score, the accidentals which musicians were most likely to miss were the ones needed because of vertical relations arising between different voices   BerM, 65

3. With the advent of simultaneous composition, conflicting signatures became obsolete   BerM, 68
 a) Simultaneous composition minimized the functional differentiation of individual parts

(1) It encouraged musicians to think about the mode of the whole, not of a single part
 (a) They thought of the species used in all parts

G. *Note nere*

Note nere was also known as *chromaticho, a misura di breve*, or *misura alla breve* CarCV, 138
a) It is thought that the term [*chromaticho*] may refer to the musical rhetoric of the madrigals HaaN, 212
 (1) It may refer to music in short, fast-declaimed values that are suitable for musical speech that moves at the speed of conversational speech HaaN, 216
 (2) It also may refer to the colorful style that moves quite fast and then with exaggerated slowness, making use of syncopations, pictorial devices, and ornamental *passaggi*
 (3) An essential feature of this music seems to be contrast between fast and slow motion HaaN, 206
b) The term *a misura di breve* has been described as music in which the motor rhythm is on the minim and the up- and down beats which comprise the tactus take place within a semibreve HaaN, 205
c) *Note nere* was characterized by an extensive use of short black notes
 (1) Such as, semiminims (♩), chrome (♪), and semichrome (♬)
d) The time signature, in pieces written in this notation, is C
 (1) Also, prints advertising their contents as *madrigali a note nere* have the mensuration sign q HaaN, 201
 (2) These signatures replace the more typical ¢
  (a) Without this sign of diminution, these values become equivalent to those of the ordinary madrigal HaaN, 201
   i) As a result, the music is unchanged; only the notation has been altered
 (3) The tempo in pieces using this notation is probably slower than the tempo in pieces using ¢ RanH, 549
  (a) But, they were not half the speed
 (4) The *tactus* is on the semibreve rather than the breve RanH, 549
e) *Note nere* was apparently a notational development seen in single compositions of the 1530s RanH, 549
 (1) The time signature C was normally used for the *villanesca* with an abundance of black notes CarCV, 138
  (a) The black notes were used by *villanesca* composers as a means of indicating a lively style characterized by rapid syllabic declamation on small values CarCV, 139
   i) This was true, but the *villanesca* books never advertised the various names given to this style notation CarCV, 138
  (b) This use of black notes was true particularly in the refrain CarCV, 138
   i) The refrain usually is characterized by declamation on minims and semiminims

                ii)   These semiminims are faster than the minims of cut time madrigals, although, most likely, not twice as fast
        (c) The mutation is characterized usually by declamation on the breve or semibreve (white notes)   HaaN, 205
    (2) The use of blackened notes in the early *villanella* indicates the possible origin for *note nere*   RanH, 549
        (a) Actually, the connection is rather slight   HaaN, 206
  f) *Note nere* was advertised in madrigal collections of the 1540s   RanH, 549
  g) This novelty was not accepted by conservative theorists   RanH, 549

2. *A Chronological List of Note Nere Prints*   HaaN, 212

3. Examples of *note nere*
    a) A composition by Thomaso Cimello   CarCV II, Plate 27
    b) A composition by Giovan Thomaso di Maio   CarCV II, Plate 28
    c) A composition by Giovanni Domenico da Nola   CarCV II, Plate 25
    d) Five volumes of anthologies of black-note madrigals   AntB

Sacred Latin Music for the Catholic Church on the Continent

A. Introduction

1. The musical style of the Mass Ordinary in the early sixteenth century was redefined as a result of the multiple borrowings from a single polyphonic model
   PerMR, 582
   a) "Models began to be chosen from the motet repertory"
      (1) This was particularly true where the popular styles of writing had been developed, thus adding a bit of evidence for a liturgical link between Mass and motet
      (2) The motet offered a substitute for the *cantus firmus* melody
         (a) Fifteenth-century composers had done some experimenting with this

2. The Mass Propers continued to attract the attention of composers until the end of the sixteenth century PerMR, 591
   a) Usually they were taken as individual texts and set in the manner of the motet
   b) There was very little indication as to whether they were actually intended for liturgical use
      (1) Sometimes they were set as motets for liturgical use, but with no explicit indication as to their intended function
         (a) They may have been written for devotional or processional use

3. The use of polyphony in the liturgy for the Office became more common during this period PerMR, 451
   a) There was an increase in settings for Magnificats, Psalms, and hymns
      (1) The increase in these three categories suggest that polyphonic performance at Vesper services on major feast days was a matter of course for musical chapels
   b) There were also other settings of canonical texts, although the number of compositions for some of these remained relatively small
      (1) They include "the Te Deum (traditionally sung at the end of Lauds but also as a hymn of thanksgiving on any special occasion), the Lamentations of Jeremiah (sung at Matins during Holy Week), and the Passions (also sung during Holy Week as Gospel lessons at Mass)"

(2) These compositional types had achieved a distinct generic identity
    (a) All of the settings were similar to motets but were generally less elaborate plainsong settings for liturgical use   PerMR, 511
        i) They became established as individual compositional types
    (b) They continued to maintain an independent existence, although not in every case a distinctive stylistic profile

4. The motet was defined as a distinct compositional genre   PerMR, 511
   a) Even so, it appears that it was being integrated ever more regularly into the liturgical services as an officially sanctioned component
     (1) There is evidence that the Mass itself was frequently embellished on important occasions by the insertion of one or more motets that were paraliturgical if not clearly nonliturgical
        (a) This was done with or without texts specified for use at a given service or particular feast

5. National schools, in the strict sense, did not exist as yet   BriL, 236
   a) But during the course of the sixteenth century, each European country began to manifest an artistic style with its own qualities

B. Polyphony for the Ordinary and Proper of the Mass

1. General style of the Mass
   a) The interest in Mass composition by the composers seems to have declined   RanH, 473
     (1) During this period, composers such as Willaert, Gombert, and Jacques Arcadelt wrote mostly motets and secular music   RanH, 474
        (a) The cyclic Mass was relegated to a small (and sometimes early and unrepresentative) part of their total output
     (2) Composers made melodies and settings the basis for church compositions, even though the original texts with which the melodies and settings were associated had nothing at all to do with the church   FelC, 86
        (a) In fact the texts were often quite profane
        (b) Thus the music became independent of the liturgical text
   b) The rise in the composition of the four-voice, imitative style motet had a pronounced effect upon the Mass   RanH, 473
     (1) In this style motet, individual phrases of the text are set as points of imitation or as homophonic passages
        (a) This creates a texture in which no one voice is a linear entity
     (2) These motets gave rise to the new type of cyclic Mass, the parody Mass (imitative Mass)   RanH, 473
        (a) The parody Mass is a cyclic Mass that is based on a polyphonic model   RanH, 609
            i) The entire polyphonic texture of a piece-sacred or secular-was used   AtlR, 407
        (b) The Mass makes use of the model's motivic construction rather than any one line and quotes more than one of its voices
            i) Thus it was based on the new style of pervading imitation

      that, as a result, lacked a structural *cantus firmus* of its own
                                       AtlR, 407
    (c) It became the overwhelming favorite of composers   AtlR, 396
  c) Composers also wrote paraphrase Masses   AtlR, 407
    (1) In these Masses, a monophonic model, sacred or secular, wound its way imitatively through all voices
      (a) This was done in such a way that the model blended into the prevailing polyphony, sometimes to the extent of almost losing its own identity
  d) There were other Mass types   AtlR, 408
    (1) One Mass type was built on a newly invented *soggetto* [theme]
      (a) In the sixteenth century, the term *soggetto* refers to the entirety of a melody forming the basis of a canon   RanH, 758
    (2) Other Mass types were those using a strict *cantus firmus* and those that were freely composed from start to finish
    (3) The plainsong Mass did not interest composers outside of Germany
                                       RanH, 474
      (a) An exception was the *Missa de Beata Virgine*
        i) In the *Missa de Beata Virgine*, each movement of the Ordinary was based on a chant of its own kind such as a polyphonic Kyrie on a Kyrie chant, and so on   AtlR, 407
        ii) This was a Mass for a special liturgical occasion AtlR, 407
      (b) Another exception was the Requiem Mass   AtlR, 408
        i) But, it did not become standardized in respect to its chants until the second half of the sixteenth century
  e) The driving stylist force of the Mass was pervading imitation which gradually grew thicker and more seamless   AtlR, 396

2. The French Mass
  a) General style of the French Mass
    (1) The characteristics of a national style in France appeared almost at once after 1521   LesF, 238
    (2) Church music was influenced by the Parisian *chanson* LesF, 238
      (a) Chordal writing in *chanson* style was favored   ReeMR, 338
        i) This trait resulted in clear text treatment; a treatment that is typical of Sermisy and of the French school
        ii) It was a taut form of art that served to outline the text
      (b) There was an obsession with the declamatory style, and yet at the same time a lack of expressiveness   FelC, 92
      (c) The melodies are short and smooth and large leaps are avoided
                                       ReeMR, 338
        i) The melodies have a lack of breadth and tension
                                       LesF, 238
      (d) Ternary rhythm is no longer in style   ReeMR, 338
    (3) There were some Josquin traits such as voice pairing and the use of canon   ReeMR, 338
      (a) Also, the French were among the first to take the decisive step in joining the imitative style of the Latin motet with the notion of polyphonic borrowing   PerMR, 582

- (4) Sermisy helped establish a distinct French Mass-tradition   ReeMR, 338
  - (a) His style included some Josquin traits such as revealed in his voice-pairing
  - (b) He introduced passages varying the predominating four-part fabric
  - (c) Occasionally there is a canon in the two upper voices answered by such canon in the two lower voices
    - i) But due to the trend toward simplicity in French writing, the voices of each pair often sound note against note
      - a - At times, the note against note was in parallel motion
  - (d) Sermisy favored chordal writing in *chanson* style
    - i) As a result there is clear text treatment
  - (e) The melodies are usually short and smooth
    - i) They usually progress stepwise rather than by leaps   UlrH, 138
- (5) The complete Ordinary of the Mass was usually written for four voices, but often included sections for two, three or five voices   LesF, 239
  - (a) The Benedictus was usually written for three voices and the Agnus was written for five
    - i) The increase of two voices for the final Agnus was frequently accomplished by the use of canonic writing   DobM, 239
  - (b) These were short works with little melismata and rudimentary imitation
    - i) This was true both in the sections where the text is of some length and also in the Kyrie and Agnus
  - (c) Most settings are parody Masses
    - i) The themes are usually borrowed from motets or *chansons*
- (6) The Proper of the Mass was at times given a polyphonic setting   LesF, 240
  - (a) These settings were alternated with plainchant found in the Gradual   DobM, 232
  - (b) There are settings for four parts with the *cantus firmus* in the tenor found in the *Contrapunctus seu figurata musica...* of 1528
    - i) This source contains Introits, Offertories, and Graduals for solemn festivals
    - ii) The *Contrapunctus...* was published by Guaynard at Lyons
    - iii) A facsimile of the *Contrapunctus...*   ConS
    - iv) Transcriptions of the *Contrapunctus...*   SutC I; II
- b) Composers of the French Mass
  - (1) Clément Janequin [b. ca. 1485]
    - (a) He wrote two Masses   LesF, 243
      - i) Both were based on themes of two of his *chansons*
        - a - The *chansons* were *La Bataille de Marignan* and *L'aveuglé diu*   ReeMR, 340
    - (b) *La Bataille*   ReeMR, 340
      - i) The material for this Mass is taken from *pars I* of the *chanson*
        - a - Material from *pars* II would have been less suitable, as in it there are attempts to duplicate the noises of battle
        - b - The selected material is kept in an easily recognizable form
      - ii) The Mass is typical of the later "parody" Masses that begin

each of the five main sections with "head-motif" reference to all four voices of the model   DobM, 235
- a - This is done with only slight rhythmic changes and successive quotes from one or more voices
- iii) A manuscript source of *La Bataille*   MusA
- iv) Facsimiles of Janequin's Masses   ModL
- v) Transcriptions of *La Bataille*   JanBA; JanB

(2) François [Francesco] de Layolle [b. 1492]   DobM, 233
- (a) He is thought to be the composer of the Masses found in the *Contrapunctus: [seu figurata musica super plano cantu missarum solennium totius anni]*
- (b) The *Contrapunctus...* contains thirteen Masses   DobM, 232
  - i) These Masses are a cycle taken from the Temporale and Sanctorale
    - a - They celebrate the most important feasts from Christmas to All Saints
    - b - They celebrate feasts of the highest rank and span the entire liturgical year   SutC I, vii
      - 1 - But, this source is not a complete liturgical book   SutC I, viii
  - ii) Most of the Masses include polyphonic settings for the Introit, Responsory verse, Alleluia, and its verse, Offertory, and Communion
    - a - The polyphony alternates with the plainchant found in the Gradual
  - iii) There are imitative entries and dovetailed syncopated cadences
  - iv) The Masses are distinguished by their melodic skill and harmonic variety
  - v) A facsimile of the *Contrapunctus...*   ConS
  - vi) Transcriptions of the *Contrapunctus...*   SutC I and II
- (c) Two of the Masses [in the *Liber decem missarum*, 1532] are by Layolle   DobM, 147
  - i) His *Missa Adieu mes amours*, is based on the *chanson* tune   DobM, 234
    - a - The *chanson* tune is by Mouton   LayM, ix
    - b - The opening motif, *re fa mi re la*, is used as an ostinato in the tenor
      - 1 - It is repeated eighty-eight times without proceeding further   ReeMR, 343
      - 2 - It is only in the third Agnus that the motive is extended to include the entire melody with the addition of a canonic fifth voice
    - c - The composition is old-fashioned in plan and in the choice of *cantus firmus*   ReeMR, 343
    - d - A facsimile of *Adieu mes amours*   ModL
    - e - A transcription of *Adieu mes amours*   LayM, 1
  - ii) Layolle's *O salutaris hostia* is the final Mass in the *Liber decem missarum*   DobM, 236

                a - This Mass seems to be a parody of an earlier motet
                b - It follows a pattern common to many contemporary four-part Masses
                    1 - The Benedictus is set for two voices, the Pleni and Agnus II are set for three, and the final Agnus III is set for five
                c - A facsimile of *O salutaris hostia*   ModL
                d - A transcription of *O salutaris hostia*   LayM, 21
        (d) Layolle's *Ces fascheux sotz* is found in the revised edition of the *Liber decem missarum* of 1540   DobM, 237
            i) This is modeled on the anonymous *chanson* published in Paris in 1529
            ii) A facsimile of *Ces fascheux sotz*   ModLD
            iii) A transcription of *Ces fascheux sotz*   LayM, 41
        (e) A facsimile of the 1532 edition of *Liber decem missarum*   ModL
    (3) Claudin de Sermisy [b. ca. 1495]   ReeMR, 338
        (a) He wrote thirteen Masses   LesF, 242
        (b) In these Masses he shows more contrapuntal sense than other Frenchmen of his day   LesF, 242
            i) He makes use of canonic writing and shows many other signs of deep musicianship   LesF, 243
            ii) His melodies are short and smooth and he avoids large leaps   ReeMR, 338
            iii) Nevertheless there is an ever-present tendency to return to syllabic treatment
                a - His tendency to return to syllabic treatment results in a clear text treatment that is typical of him and of the French school   ReeMR, 338
            iv) But his Mass, *Domine quis habitavit* is an exception to this   LesF, 243
                a - In this Mass, Sermisy follows the Netherlandish tradition   ReeMR, 338
                b - A transcription of *Domine quis habitavit*   SerO, VI, 155
        (c) Examples of his Masses
            i) *Missa plurium motettorum*   ReeMR, 338
                a - Sermisy helped to form a distinct Mass-tradition with this Mass
                b - Sometimes there is a canon for two upper voices answered by such canon in the two lower voices
                    1 - The Josquin traits are still revealed, but the voices in each pair often sound note against note
                    2 - At times, this is done in parallel motion
                c - There is chordal writing in *chanson* style
                d - A manuscript source of *Missa plurium motettorum*   MusA
                e - A facsimile of *Missa plurium motettorum*   AttTLT, fol. ixvii-ixxxix
                f - Transcriptions of *Missa plurium motettorum*   SerMP; SerO, V, 59
            ii) *Missa pro defunctis*   ReeMR, 338

a - The plainsong of this Requiem is in the third voice
  1 - It is often shorn of melismas and the initial or final notes of phrases
  2 - This is done despite the effect that the elimination of the last note has on the mode of the chant
b - Facsimiles of *Missa pro defunctis* SerMR; AttQLT
c - Transcriptions of *Missa pro defunctis*
  SerMPD; SerO, V, 85

(d) Other sources of his Masses
  i) A facsimile of *Missa cum quatuor vocibus, ad imitationem moduli Ab initio* SerMA
  ii) A facsimile of *Missa cum quatuor vocibus, ad imitationem cantionis Voulant honneur* SerMV
  iii) A facsimile of *Missa cum quatuor vocibus paribus, ad imitationem moduli Tota pulchra es* SerMTP
  iv) A facsimile of *Missa cum quinque vocibus, ad imitationem moduli Quare fremuerunt gentes* SerMQ
  v) Transcriptions of his Masses SerM; AllM; SerO, V and VI

(4) Pierre Certon [fl. 1529] ReeMR, 339
 (a) Certon uses the customary imitation technique in each of his Masses and usually has a section for two voices at the middle of each movement
   i) The section for two voices is usually drawn out by loose imitation
 (b) All of his Masses are for four voices
   i) *Sus le pont d'Avignon*
     a - This Mass is based on a fifteenth century tune, no doubt after some *chanson* setting
     b - Facsimiles of *Sus le pont d'Avignon* CerMT; CerM
   ii) *Adiuva me*
     a - Facsimiles of *Sus le pont d'Avignon* CerMT; CerM
   iii) *Regnum mundi*
     a - Facsimiles of *Regnum mundi* CerMT; CerM
     b - A transcription of *Regnum mundi* CerMR
   iv) *Missa pro defunctis cum quatuor vocibus, nunc primum in lucem aedita*
     a - In this Requiem, the *cantus firmus* is varied by being frequently reduced to its bare skeleton rather than by the addition of notes ReeMR, 340
       1 - Usually the texture is very plain and chordal
     b - A facsimile of *Missa pro defunctis cum quatuor vocibus, nunc primum in lucem aedita* CerMP

(5) Jacques Arcadelt [b. ca. 1514]
 (a) He was probably French and most likely a member of the circle around Verdelot in the early part of his life SeaA, 546
   i) But, his nearness to Josquin is much apparent
 (b) Only three Masses by him are known ArcO, I, v
   i) *Noe, Noe* and *Ave Regina Coelorum* are parody Masses
     a - The *Noe, Noe* Mass is built on a motet by Jean Mouton

and the *Ave Regina Coelorum* Mass is built on a motet by Andreas de Silva
- b - A transcription of *Noe, Noe*   ArcO, I, 1
- c - A transcription of *Ave Regina Coelorum*   ArcO, I, 24
  - ii) *De Beata Virgine* is a paraphrase Mass
    - a - It is built on material from Mass IX plus Credo I
    - b - The Credo includes the normal Marian tropes in the Gloria
    - c - A transcription of *De Beata Virgine*   ArcO. I, 56

3. The Flemish Mass   BriL, 219
   a) The general style of the Flemish Mass
      (1) This generation was oriented towards a new principle of style, namely, through-imitation   SchH, 12
          (a) They retained much of the style of Josquin   BriL, 219
              i) But, what had been occasional with Josquin became a "sovereign principle" with the composers of this period
              ii) It fertilized the art of Palestrina and Orlando di Lasso
          (b) This pervading imitation results in a full, rich sonority   UlrH, 136
              i) But, the style hinders the understanding of the words   ReeMR, 344
                 a - The text is sacrificed to purely musical considerations
          (c) Each verbal phrase has its own musical theme that is stated by each voice in free imitation   BriL, 219
          (d) The musical phrases interlock   BriL, 219
              i) They are never interrupted by a cadence
                 a - The polyphonic texture is interrupted only occasionally by rests in the several voices or by chordal writing   UlrH, 136
          (e) The two-part episodes, typical of the previous age, are almost completely absent   BriL, 219
      (2) Extreme rhythmic contrasts between voices give way completely   UlrH, 139
      (3) Motifs that are freely invented become increasingly frequent   ReeMR, 354
      (4) Basically, the Masses were *missae parodiae*
          (a) The *missae parodiae* used the entire polyphonic texture of a piece that was based on the new style of pervading imitation   AtlR, 407
              i) The *cantus firmus* technique was abandoned in favor of the newer style   BriL, 219
          (b) Therefore all of the voices were of equal importance
      (5) The forms were those of the Catholic liturgy; Masses, motets, Magnificats, and Lamentations
   b) Composers of the Flemish Mass
      (1) Jean Richafort [b. ca. 1480]
          (a) Richafort's extant sacred works include four Masses   ReeMR, 335
              i) One is a Requiem based on a canon, *Circumdederunt me* by Josquin   ReeMR, 335
                 a - It is written for six voices and is evidence of Richafort's command of complicated technique   BriL, 231

Polyphony for the Ordinary and Proper of the Mass 207

      1 - In spite of the complicated technique, this Requiem is both expressive and plastic
       a - "The Entombment is suggested by descending scales, and the words 'non timebo' are sung by men's voices only"
       b - The bass states each intonation before the other parts take it up BriL, 231
       c - Two tenors sing the canon as a *cantus firmus* while the other voices weave their counter melodies
        1 - The *superius* sings the proper liturgical text with a free treatment of Gregorian melody BriL, 231
       d - In the V*irga tua* there is a short canon based on a phrase from Josquin's *Faulte d'argent*
        1 - This canon recurs in the Offertory
       e - It is possible that Richafort wrote this Requiem upon the death of Josquin ReeMR, 336
       f - Transcriptions of the Requiem RicO, I; RicR
     ii) His *Missa Veni sponsa Christi* is found in the *Liber decem missarum* DobM, 234
       a - The four motives of the Gregorian antiphon are paraphrased in succession, ending with a canonic six-voice Agnus III
       b - A facsimile of *Missa Veni sponsa Christi* ModL
       c - A transcription of *Missa Veni sponsa Christi* RicO, I
     iii) *Missa O Dei genetrix* ReeMR, 336
       a - Richafort uses paired imitation in which he introduces double counterpoint on the words *Domine Deus rex coelestis*
       b - A manuscript source of *Missa O Dei genetrix* MusA
       c - A transcription of *Missa O Dei genetrix* RicO,I
  (b) Other sources of his Masses
     i) A facsimile of a Mass MasB
     ii) Transcriptions of *Missa O Genitrix, Missa Veni Sponsa Christi,* and *Requiem* RicO, I
(2) Nicolas Gombert [b. ca. 1490]
  (a) He wrote ten Masses BriL, 220
     i) Two are based on plainsong ReeMR, 347
      a - The *Missa tempore paschali* and *Missa da pacem*
       1 - A transcription of *Missa tempore paschali* GomO, III, 53
       2 - A transcription of *Missa da pacem* GomO, I, 1
     ii) Two are based on *chansons,* and six are based on motets
      a - These are parody Masses ReeMR, 347
      b - "Each Mass movement begins with a transformation of the borrowed material" UlrH, 136
      c - But thereafter the material is treated freely UlrH, 136
       1 - The parodied sections are separated by new material
       2 - Voices are added or subtracted from the borrowed motet

3 - At times the writing is entirely original
- iii) *Cantus firmus* treatment is found in his Masses, an example being his *Missa Forseulement*   ReeMR, 347
  - a - However, it is interesting to note that the *cantus firmus* is in the *superius* rather than in the tenor
    1 - This is also true in the final Agnus of his *Missa A la Incoronation* which was composed on *Sur tous regretz* by Richafort
      - a - This Mass is built on two models; one on an anonymous *Forseulement* that may be by Josquin, and the other on a setting by Pipelare
      - c - A transcription of *Missa Forseulement*   GomO, II, 89
- iv) His *Je suis déshéritée* is based on a *chanson* by Cadéac
  - a - The entire melody of the *chanson* is found in the first section of the Credo and the last part of the six-voice Agnus Dei   BriL, 221
    1 - The melody of the *chanson* is often recalled by quotation of its opening phrase
  - b - Once again, the *cantus firmus* is found in the *superius* rather than in the tenor   ReeMR, 347
  - c - Transcriptions of *Je suis déshéritée*
         EitC, 20; SchG, 115; GomO, I, 81
- v) His Missa *Quam pulchra es* bears only a loose relation to the motet by Bauldeweys   ReeMR, 347
  - a - Many of the motifs are new
  - b - The *cantus firmus* is in the second tenor in the seven-part Agnus
  - c - This Mass is written mainly for six voices
  - d - A transcription of *Quam pulchra es*   GomO, III, 1
- vi) His Masses usually retain a uniform texture   ReeMR, 348

(b) Other sources of his Masses
- i) A facsimile of *Je suis déshéritée*   GomMC
- ii) A facsimile of *Missa Media vita, Missa tous regretz, and Missa Philomena*   GomS
- iii) Transcriptions of his Masses   GomO, I, II, III

(3) Thomas Crécquillon (Créquillon) [b. ca. 1480 to ca. 1500]
  (a) He wrote sixteen Masses, fifteen of which are *missae parodiae*   BriL, 223
  - i) Eight are based on *chansons* and seven on motets
    - a - Three of the *chansons* and two of the motets are by Crécquillon
  - ii) The sixteenth Mass is built on a German song, *Kein adler in der Welt*
    - a - Transcription of *Missa Kein in der Welt so schön*   CreO, I
  (b) All of the Masses are written in a more or less imitative style   BriL, 223
  - i) But, they have short homophonic passages set to certain important parts of the text
  (c) They keep more or less close to the model on which they are based

Polyphony for the Ordinary and Proper of the Mass   209

- i) Sometimes Crécquillon only borrows a few short passages from the model BriL, 223
  - a - Examples are *Domine Deus omnipotens* and *Mort m'a privé*
    - 1 - A transcription of *Domine Deus omnipotens* CreO, IV
    - 2 - A transcription of *Mort m'a privé* CreO, III
- (d) His parody technique is basically a matter of variations BriL, 223
  - i) Variations occur in melody, harmony, and rhythm
  - ii) An example is the Credo of his Mass *Se dire je l'osoie*
    - a - A transcription of *Se dire je l'osoie* CreO, III
- (e) Other sources of his Masses
  - i) Facsimiles SusLP; HelL
  - ii) Transcriptions CreO, I, II, III

(4) Jacobus Clemens (Clemens non Papa) [b. ca. 1510]
  - (a) He wrote sixteen Masses of which fifteen are written according to the principle of the *missa parodia* BriL, 227
    - i) Seven are written on *chansons* and eight on motets
      - a - They are written on works by Clemens himself, and by Lupus, Gombert, Claudin, Willaert, Manchicourt, and Hellinck ReeMR, 351
    - ii) His model is seldom quoted exactly ReeMR, 352
      - a - He shows particular skill in varying the material artistically
    - iii) Clemens adds themes of his own invention in his Masses, returning to his basic material only at significant points of the text as if to emphasize their importance BriL, 228
    - iv) He uses a variation-technique to his chosen themes which is always original and interesting BriL, 228
  - (b) The sixteenth Mass, *Missa pro defunctis*, is built on the Gregorian melodies
    - i) This Mass was long thought to be partially lost but was reprinted in 1959 in the *Opera omnia* by Bernet Kempers BriL, 228
    - ii) Clemens paraphrases the chant in those movements that are set polyphonically ReeMR, 351
      - a - This is a normal procedure for its type
      - b - The *Dies irae* is not included
        - 1 - This is also a normal procedure of the period RanH,, 695
    - iii) A transcription of *Missa pro defunctis* CleO, VIII, 1
  - (c) All of his Masses are written in imitative style BriL, 228
  - (d) In his *Missa Ecce quam bonum*, a repetition of the same melodic fragment is made to symbolize the thought in the words *Deum de Deo* ReeMR, 352
    - i) This is not done necessarily in the same voice
    - ii) This Mass is built on a motet by Clemens, the words of which are the 133rd Psalm CleO, I, Part 4
      - a - The melodic material used for *qui descendit in montem*

       Syon in the motet is used in the Mass for the words
       descendit de caelis   ReeMR, 352
      b - A transcription of the motet   CleO, I, Part 4, 28
   iii) A transcription of *Missa Ecce quam bonum* CleO, Part 4, 1
 (e) The repetition technique is used also in Clemens' *Missa Miséricorde, Missa Languir my fault,* and *Missa Or combien* ReeMR. 352
   i) But his Mass *Miséricorde* shows a special concern with textual clarity   BriL, 228
      a - Most of the main sections open with a distinct statement of the words in strict homophonic style
      b - This Mass is based on a *chanson* as well as some parts of a French Psalm by Marot   CleO, I, ii
       1 - The *chanson* is written by Clemens CleO, I, Part 1
      c - A transcription of *Miséricorde*   CleO, I, Part 1, 1
   ii) The *Missa Languir my fault* is based on a *chanson* by Sermisy   CleO, V, i
      a - In this Mass, Clemens repeats the same melodic passage four times, at *Laudamus te, Benedicimus te, Adoramus te,* and *Glorificamus te*   ReeMR, 352
       1 - With each use, he modifies the passage
      b - A transcription of the *chanson*   CleO, V, 103
      c - A transcription of *Missa Languir my fault* CleO, V, 69
   iii) The *Missa Or combien* is based on a *chanson* by Claudin or Sandrin   CleO, VII, ii
      a - Clemens uses a lot of chordal writing in this Mass   ReeMR, 352
      b - He also illustrates effectively his liking for prominent bass themes   ReeMR, 352
      c - A transcription of the *chanson*   CleO, VII, 156
      d - A transcription of *Missa Or combien* CleO, VII, 131
 (f) In his *Missa Virtute magna* for four voices, he adds a second *superius* in the Sanctus, and to this combination a second bass in the Agnus   ReeMR, 352
   i) This Mass is based on a motet that has been attributed to different composers in different sources CleO, I, Part 2, i
   ii) A transcription of *Missa Virtute magna* CleO, I, Part 2
 (g) Clemens uses an extremely bold example of dissonance treatment in his *Missa Spes salutis*   ReeMR, 352
   i) This Mass is built on a motet by Lupus   CleO, V, iii
   ii) A transcription of *Missa Spes salutis*   CleO, V, 1
 (h) His only six-part Mass is *Missa A la fontaine du prez* ClEO, VII, i
   i) It is built on a *chanson* by Willaert
      a - A transcription of the *chanson*   CleO, VII, 43
   ii) A transcription of *Missa A la fontaine du prez* CleO, VII, 1
 (i) A complete list of his Masses   CleO, I, i
 (j) Other sources of his Masses
   i) A facsimile of *Missa sum quatuor vocibus ad imitationem Cantilenae Miséricorde*   CleM
   ii) Transcriptions of all his Masses CleO, I, V, VI, VII, VIII

4. The Venetian Mass
   a) The General style of the Venetian Mass
      (1) After the death of Pope Leo X (1521) and after the sack of Rome (1527), Venice became even more important as the center of European music   RedV, 276
         (a) It was during this period (late 1520s) that the greatest personality in the history of Venetian music first entered the city, namely, Adrian Willaert
            i) He helped establish the Flemish technique as part of the musical language and also the cultivation of a "modern" style that emphasized faultless declamation of the text   ReeMR, 372
            ii) He also contributed to the development of choral antiphony   ReeMR, 372
         (b) Church music takes on a secular coloring
         (c) Psalms continued to be written for double choir   RedV, 276
            i) But, unlike the predecessors, the unity of each Psalm verse is strictly preserved   RedV, 277
         (d) Harmony and color were adopted without sacrificing the northern polyphonic element   RedV, 283
      (2) Most of the Masses are parody Masses   RedV, 281
         (a) They are based on a polyphonic composition   LenS, 410
            i) They contain preexistent material consisting not only of themes but of consonances, successive entries, subjects, countersubjects, of phrases having a harmonic dimension and cadences that show an accentuated tone-color
            ii) The material is of an harmonic nature
         (b) The Masses are written for four, five, and six voices   RedV, 281
   b) A composer of the Venetian Mass
      (1) Adrian Willaert [b. ca. 1490]
         (a) He was a Flemish composer who lived mainly in Venice   ReeMR, 309
         (b) His Masses number less than ten and are written for four, five, and six voices   UlrH, 153
            i) He does not employ the antiphonal principle
         (c) He parodied works by Josquin and employs the familiar canonic devices and imitative techniques   UlrH, 153
         (d) Five of the Masses are for four voices   RedV, 281
            i) These are all parodies   WilO, IX, ix
                a - Willaert's borrowed motives usually appear in the order in which they occur in the original   WilO, IX, x
            ii) *Mussa Gaude Barbara*
                a - This Mass is found in Cambrai, Bibl. comm., *Ms. 124*   ReeMR, 371
                    1 - It is also found in Museo archeologico nazionale di Cividale del Friuli, *MS. LIII*   MusA
                b - The Mass is based on a motet by Mouton   RedV, 281
                c - A transcription of *Mussa Gaude Barbara*   WilO, IX, 108
            iii) *Missa Quaeramus cum pastoribus*   ReeMR, 371
                a - This Mass is based on Mouton's *Quaeramus cum pastori-*

                bus
            b - The beginning of the model is quoted almost literally in the initial measures
                1 - But it is varied skillfully in later section openings as well as at other points
            c - A manuscript source of *Missa Quaeramus cum pastoribus*   MusA
            d - A transcription of *Missa Quaeramus cum pastoribus*   WilO, IX, 1
        iv) *Christus resurgens*
            a - This Mass may be based on a motet by Mouton but probably one by Richafort   RedV, 281
            b - A transcription of *Christus resurgens*   WilO, IX, 34
        v) *Laudate Deum*
            i) This Mass is modeled on a motet by Mouton   RedV, 281
            ii) A transcription of *Laudate Deum*   WilO, IX, 71
        vi) *Osculetur me*
            i) A transcription   WilO, IX, 144
    (e) There is a five-part Mass *Benedicta es [coelorum Regina]* that is either by Willaert or Hesdin   RedV, 281
        i) It is preserved in eight manuscripts
            a - Two credit Willaert for the Mass, three credit Hesdin, and three are anonymous
        ii) The Mass is based on large tracts of Josquin's motet and it adheres closely to the original plainsong
        iii) Kyrie I opens with a canon on the chant between the *superius* and tenor   ReeMR, 371
            a - The rhythm configuration is different than that of Josquin's and the very first phrase ends at a different point
            b - The canon is soon abandoned and original melodic material is introduced
            c - The other three voices sing a revised version of the counter melody in imitation
        iv) A transcription of *Pleni sunt coeli* and *Osanna* from the Mass   SmiM
    (f) There are two Masses for six voices   RedV, 281
        i) *Mente tota* and *Mittit as virgmem*
            a - *Menta tota* is based on the fifth section of the motet *Vultum tuum* by Josquin
                a - The construction is completely canonic
                b - A facsimile of *Menta tota*   WilM
            b - The *Mittit as virgmem* is modeled on one of Willaert's motets
                1 - A manuscript source of the Mass   BibE
                1 - A transcription of the motet   WilO, V, 173

5. The Roman Catholic Mass
    a) General style of the Roman Catholic Mass
        (1) After the sack of Rome in 1527, Rome gradually became more a center

of church music   RedV, 276
- (2) But, the style of Roman church music is difficult to identify   ReyR, 64
  - (a) This is partially due to the many different local institutional practices
    - i) Music was arranged to suit the local practice   ReyR, 87
      - a - For example, the choir at St. Peter's sang odd verses of the Magnificat and hymns polyphonically
      - b - At S Maria Maggiore, the odd numbered verses of the Magnificat were omitted
        - 1 - This was done to satisfy the preference for even-verse polyphony
      - c - The choir at the Cappella Sistina required polyphony for all verses
      - d - Composers in the papal chapel were influenced by a mixture of papal tastes, liturgical considerations and performance practices   ReyR, 73
  - (b) The Roman style is also difficult to identify due to the compositional styles which assumed even more distinct regional identities   ReyR, 87
    - i) Few northern composers were in Rome long enough to influence compositional styles   ReyR, 73
- (3) There was a Flemish style infused with the melodiousness characteristic of Italy   ReyR, 64
  - (a) "A penchant for thoroughly imitative counterpoint, for canonic writing and for an increased number of voices in both the *Agnus Dei* of the Mass and the concluding doxology of the *Magnificat*" appeared   ReyR, 87
- (4) The Roman taste was conservative and seldom given to sensuous display   ReeMR, 362
  - (a) The difference between this music and the brilliant music of Venice became more pronounced as the century progressed
  - (b) Nevertheless, the music coming from the Holy City churches resounded with some of the most splendid music the *cinquecento* produced

b) A composer of the Roman Catholic Mass
- (1) Costanzo Festa [b. ca. 1490]
  - (a) Much of his music contains pervading imitation in the Flemish manner   ReeMR, 362
    - i) Although, he is not absorbed by the technique as Gombert is
    - ii) At times he merely suggests pervading imitation or employs non-imitative counterpoint
  - (b) He also writes chordally with equal readiness   ReeMR, 362
  - (c) His music has many parallel thirds, sixths, and tenths   ReeMR, 362
  - (d) He wrote four Masses   ReeMR, 362
    - i) *Missa se congie pris*   FesO, I, iii
      - a - This Mass is built on a secular tenor
      - b - It uses *ostinati* and a recurring "motto" theme
      - c - The Credo *Solemnitas* uses quotations and paraphrases from Credo plainchants that are woven into the contra-

puntal fabric
- d - A transcription of *Missa se congie pris*   FesO, I, 61
- ii) *Missa de Domina nostra*   FesO, I, iii
  - a - The structural basis is provided by plainchant paraphrase
  - b - Ostinato-like repetition and two canons, one of them double, also are included
  - c - A transcription of *Missa de Domina nostra*   FesO, I, 37
- iii) *Missa Et in terra pax*   FesO, I, iii
  - a - This is an unusual parody Mass
    - 1 - There are three movements based on, and apparently intended to be performed in company with a Gloria setting by Isaac
      - a - The Gloria setting is built on a chant paraphrase
  - b - A transcription of *Missa Et in terra pax*   FesO, I, 1
- iv) *Missa Carminum*   FesO, I, iii
  - a - This has an unusual structural method
    - 1 - It incorporates material from five French *chansons*
  - b - A transcription of *Missa Carminum*   FesO, I, 16

6. The Central European Mass
   a) The general style of the Central European Mass
   (1) During this period, German music was strongly influenced by Flemish music   ReeMR, 673
   (2) In Germany, a whole school of composers and disciples of Heinrich Isaac disseminated the principles of his style throughout the sixteenth century   RedC, 253
   - (a) They included Ludwig Senfl, Benedictus Ducis, Balthazar Resinarius [Harzer], Sixtus Dietrich, and Adam Rener
     - i) Four of these composers differ from Isaac by the ambiguity of their relations to the Roman Catholic Church   RedC, 260
       - a - Three of them, Ducis, Dietrich, and Rener, were definitely Protestants
       - b - Resinarius was originally a Catholic but turned Lutheran
   (3) The church music was religiously ambiguous   RedC, 260
   - (a) During the years of Luther's revolutionary activity, *i.e.* his radical alterations of the liturgy and the kind of music used in it, there is little that may be regarded as constituting a specifically Protestant musical style   ReeMR, 673
   - (b) At first, Luther derived the music from the chants of the Catholic Church and the pre-Reformation, predominantly German, religious songs   ReeMR, 674
     - i) The music from the Catholic Church consisted of hymns and other chants and melodies that were taken over bodily and incorporated into the Protestant liturgy
       - a - Luther insisted that these texts should be in the vernacular
     - ii) At the same time, he continued to use Latin Kyries and Glorias and often Latin settings of the Credo and Agnus   RedC, 260

Polyphony for the Ordinary and Proper of the Mass   215

       a - He also used Latin motets and Magnificats
   (c) German-born composers of both faiths, Lutheran and Catholic, published their religious music in an inter-confessional atmosphere
 b) A composer of the Central European Mass
  (1) Ludwig Senfl [b. 1490]
   (a) He was a pupil of Issac at Constance   RedC, 254
    i) He completed and edited the *Choralis Constantinus* [by Isaac]   RedC, 255
    ii) "As a composer of Masses he cannot compare with Isaac in fertility or with Josquin in originality"   RedC, 256
   (b) Only seven of his Masses have survived   RedC, 256
    i) There are three *Missae dominicales*
     a - The character of these three Masses is somewhat archaic
     b - *Missa dominicales* I combines plainsong and *chanson* tenors
      1 - This combination appears throughout the Mass which is remarkable, in that most composers who employ a double *cantus firmus* in a Mass usually restrict it to the Credo   ReeMR, 689
      2 - The plainsong is based on the plainsong Ordinary of the Mass   RedC, 256
       a - It is found in the *discantus* except in the Agnus where the two *cantus* exchange positions   ReeMR, 690
      3 - The *chanson* tune, *L'Homme armé*, in one voice is combined with the plainsong in another ReeMR, 689
       a - It is in the tenor except in the Benedictus where it does not appear at all   ReeMR, 690
      4 - In some passages the borrowed melody is treated freely   ReeMR, 690
      5 - A transcription of *Missa dominicales* I SenSM, 3
     c - The *Missa dominicales* II   RedC, 257
      1 - This Mass may well have required the support of wind instruments in the Kyrie
       a - "It begins with the liturgical melody in long notes in the discantus while an instrumental figure in *tuba* style...is brandied about among the other three voices"   ReeMR, 689
        1 - *Tuba* style is characterized by fanfare effects   ReeMR, 21
       b - An example of the style
      2 - Certain progressive traits may be found in this Mass
       a - There is employment of arpeggios of triads and a tendency to clear-cut diatonic tonality
      3 - A transcription of *Missa dominicales* II SenSM, 27
    ii) There are two *missae parodiae*   RedC, 258
     a - *Nisi Dominus* and *Per signum crucis*
     b - They indicate a deliberate change of style from the *cantus firmus* technique, with alternating unison sections of plain-

song, to a continuously polyphonic motet style with canonic imitation
     c - A transcription of *Nisi Dominus*   SenSM, 77
     d - A transcription of *Per signum crucis* SenSM, 92
   iii) Transcriptions of his Masses   SenSM

7. The Spanish Mass
 a) General style of the Spanish Mass
  (1) During the sixteenth century, Spain's religious polyphony of the humanistic age carries an unmistakable and typical national stamp AngS, 375
   (a) The music is distinguished by its natural and extremely simple technique and its austerity and dramatic mysticism
    i) There is a tendency towards simplicity of forms and the absence of elaborate technique AngS, 381
   (b) The music expresses moods of profound sadness to moods of tenderness and optimism
 b) A composer of the Spanish Mass
  (1) Cristóbal de Morales [b. ca. 1500]
   (a) He is perhaps the outstanding Mass composer of this generation AtlR, 408
    i) Testimonials to his fame are numerous
    ii) He was still revered as late as the eighteenth century in many circles
   (b) In his Mass settings that embody Gregorian plainsongs, Morales uses the chant strictly UlrH, 145
    i) The other voices are composed in such a way that the contour of the chant melodies are not obscured
   (c) He wrote all his Masses before the Council of Trent AngS, 383
    i) This explains his use of tropes in the *Ordinarium Missae* and his tribute to the Netherlanders, whose technical procedures he had assimilated so well, by writing Masses on French secular *chansons*
   (d) There are twenty-two surviving Masses AngS, 382
    i) Two are written on themes of Castilian songs
     a - *Decidle al cavallero* for four voices AngS, 383
      1 - This is preserved in Milan, Bibl. Ambrosiana, *MS. Mus. E46, fo. 41*
      2 - A transcription of *Decidle al cavallero* MorO, VII, 58
     b - *Tristezas me matan* is for five voices
      1 - This is preserved in the Sistine Chapel in Rome, *Capp. Sist. 17, fo. 80-96* AngS, 383
      2 - The voice singing the *Tristezas* tune sings the Spanish words while the other voices sing the liturgical text ReeMR, 588
      3 - A transcription of *Tristezas me matan* MorO, VII, 86
   (e) There are six Masses written on Gregorian themes AngS, 383
    i) Two *Missae de Beata Virgine*
     a - They are composed on the chants of Mass IX of the *Kyriale Romanum*

Polyphony for the Ordinary and Proper of the Mass 217

       1 - They preserve the well known trope *Spiritus et alme* in the Gloria
     b - One is for four voices and the other is for five voices
     c - A manuscript source of the five voice *Missae de Beata Virgine*   MusA
     d - Facsimiles of the four voice Mass   MorMQ; ScoEM
     e - Facsimiles of the five voice Mass
         ScoQ; ModCMH; ScoQM
     f - A facsimile of a *Missae de Beata Virgine*   ModCM
     g - A transcription of the five voice Mass   MorO, III, 66
     h - A transcription of the four voice Mass   MorO, I, 1
   ii) *Missa Ave Maria*   BerCA, 277
     a - This is a Marian Mass
     b - It is for four voices on the theme of the antiphon
         AngS, 384
     c - It is written in strict *cantus firmus* style
     d - A facsimile of *Missa Ave Maria*   ModCMH
     e - A transcription of *Missa Ave Maria*   MorO, III, 32
   iii) *Missa Ave maris stella*   AngS, 383
     a - This is written on the theme of the hymn
     b - It is for four notated voices with a counterpoint in the *altus* that is sung in canon almost throughout
     c - A facsimile of *Missa Ave maris stella*   ModCM
     d - A transcription of *Missa Ave maris stella*   MorO, I, 104
   iv) A *Missa pro defunctis* for five voices   AngS, 384
     a - This is very different in style from the rest of the Masses
       1 - It is lugubrious in tone
     b - A facsimile of *Missa pro defunctis*   ModCMH
     c - A transcription of *Missa pro defunctis*   MorO, III, 114
   v) A *Missa pro defunctis* for four voices   AngS, 384
     a - A transcription   MorO, III, 114
(f) There are eight *missae parodiae*   AngS, 384
   i) *Aspice Domine*
     a - This is written for four voices
     b - It is based on *Aspice Domine* by Gombert
     c - A facsimile of *Aspice Domine*   ModCM
     d - A transcription of *Aspice Domine*   MorO, I, 35
   ii) *Quem dicunt homines*   AngS, 385
     a - This is for five voices
     b - It uses the four-part motet by Richafort
     c - A facsimile of *Quem dicunt homines*   ModCMH
     d - A transcription of *Quem dicunt homines*   MorO, VII, 89
   iii) *Si bona suscepimus*   AngS, 385
     a - This is for six voices
     b - It is based on the five-part motet by Verdelot
     c - A facsimile of *Si bona suscepimus*   ModCM
     d - A transcription of *Si bona suscepimus*   MorO, I, 274
   iv) *Mille regretz*   AngS, 385
     a - This is for six voices

                      b - It is built on a *chanson* by Josquin, the *canción del Emperador* (Charles V)
                            1 - The melody is given prominence in the highest part throughout

		c - A facsimile of *Mille regretz*	ModCM
		d - A transcription of *Mille regretz*	MorO, I, 238
	v)	*Vulnerasti cor meum*	AngS, 384
		a - This is for four voices	
		b - It is based on an anonymous motet in the *Motetti de la Corona* published by Petrucci in 1514	
		c - A facsimile of *Vulnerasti cor meum*	ModCM
		d - A transcription of *Vulnerasti cor meum*	MorO, I, 70
	vi)	*Benedicta es coelorum Regina*	AngS, 384
		a - This is for four voices	
		b - It is based on Mouton's motet	
		c - A facsimile of *Benedicta es coelorum Regina*	ModCMH
		d - A transcription of *Benedicta es coelorum Regina*	MorO, III, 1
	vii)	*Gaude Barbara*	AngS, 384
		a - It is for four voices	
		b - It is based on a motet by Mouton	AngS, 385
		c - A facsimile of *Gaude Barbara*	ModCMH
		d - A transcription of *Gaude Barbara*	MorO, VI, 34
	viii)	*Quaeramus cum Pastoribus*	AngS, 385
		a - This is for five voices	
		1 - It expands to six voices in the final Agnus Dei	AtlR, 409
		b - It is built on a four-part motet by Mouton	AtlR, 409
		1 - An example showing the five motives taken from the motet on which Morales based his Kyrie	AtlR, 409
		c - Facsimiles of *Quaeramus cum Pastoribus*	ScoQM; ModCM
		d - Transcriptions of *Quaeramus cum Pastoribus*	AtlAR, 283; MorE, I; MorO, I, 148
(g)		There are three Masses built on a *cantus firmus*	AngS, 385
	i)	*Tu es vas electionis*	
		a - This is written for four voices	
		b - It uses the old strict *cantus firmus* technique	
		c - A facsimile of *Tu es vas electionis*	ModCMH
		d - A transcription of *Tu es vas electionis*	MorO, VI, 1
	ii)	There are two *L'homme armé* Masses	
		a - These are based on French *chansons*	AngS, 383
		b - The four-voice *Missa L'homme armé* retains the form of the old *cantus firmus* intact	ReeMR, 588
		1 - A facsimile of the four-voice *L'homme armé*	ModCMH
		c - The five-voice Mass is "progressive" in that the *cantus firmus* permeates all the voices	ReeMR, 588
		1 - A facsimile of the five-voice *L'homme armé*	ScoQM

     d - Transcriptions of the *L'homme armé* Masses
                  MorO, I, 193; MorO, VI, 67
  (h) There are three other Masses
    i) All three of the Masses are for four voices AngS, 385
     a - *Super ut re mi fa sol la*
      1 - A transcription MorO, VII, 36
     b - *Super fa re ut fa sol fa*
      1 - This is also known as *Missa Cortilla* ReeMR, 588
      2 - A transcription MorO, VII, 18
     c - *Missa Caça*
      1 - The *Missa Caça* is a markedly canonic Mass
      2 - A transcription MorO, VII, 1
  (i) Facsimiles of Morales' Masses ScoMC; MorML

C. Music for the Passion

1. General style of the Passion
   a) The Passion is a musical setting of Jesus' sufferings and death as told by one of the four Evangelists RanH, 612
      (1) It is called a responsorial Passion because it preserves both the traditional passion narratives and the tripartite division of its recitation [the three distinct reciting tones]
      (2) The settings of the Passion texts were traditionally intoned at Mass during the final days of Holy Week
      (3) During the period of ca. 1450 to ca. 1550, the monophonic Passion tone was either augmented or replaced by polyphony
         (a) There was a close connection between the music and the text
         (b) There were two kinds of text; those that made use of the complete account of Jesus' betrayal and suffering as given by a single Evangelist and those that combined segments from all four gospels of the events that led up to crucifixion and death of Christ PerMR, 602
      (4) It was early in the sixteenth century that a new type of Passion composition made its appearance PerMR, 602
         (a) This new type of composition is different in that the entire text is set in a manner reflecting the motet composition of the period
         (b) The north Italian repertory contains two four-voice Passions in which all direct speech, including that of Christ, is set in polyphonic textures RanH, 612
            i) These four-voice Passions, St. Matthew and St. John, were written before 1541 by Gasparo Alberti
   b) The French polyphonic Passions are of a dramatic type and may be regarded as a separate genre LesF, 240
      (1) But, in French-speaking areas of northern Europe, composers had little reason to give serious attention to the polyphonic Passion PerMR, 602

2. Composers of the Passion
   a) A French composer
      (1) Claudin de Sermisy [b. ca. 1495] ReeMR, 339

- (a) Sermisy builds his setting on the Passion Tones, which he treats as *cantus firmi* with some melismatic elaboration
- (b) There is one Passion for four parts based on the text from St. Matthew XXVI-XXVII
  - i) This is a dramatic-type Passion divided into forty little numbers
    - a - It is distinct from the motets on Passion-tide texts
  - ii) It is constructed entirely on a single melody, the *turba* [the words spoken by the crowd]   LesF, 240
  - iii) The words of the individual characters are set in polyphony
    - a - But, they are not always set for the same combination of voices
      - 1 - The words of St. Peter, Judas, or Pilate are set for two or four voices while the crowd passages are set consistently in four parts   LesF, 240
  - iv) The range is low   LesF, 240
  - v) A facsimile of the *St. Mathew Passion* in *Liber decimus: passiones dominice in ramis palmarum, veneris sancte...*   AttL
  - vi) Transcriptions of the *St. Mathew Passion*   AttTL, X; SerO, II, 14
- b) A Flemish composer
  - (1) Cipriano de Rore [b. 1516]   ReeMR, 376
    - (a) *Passion according to St. John*
      - i) This is modeled after the St. Mathew Passion by Maistre Jhan
      - ii) It is written for two to six voices
        - a - The music for the Evangelist is written for four voices and the music for the *turba* is for six voices
        - b - For the other *dramatis personae* the music is for two voices
          - 1 - Christ's passages are set for the two lowest voices and music for the others is set for the two highest
    - (b) Transcription of Passion music by Cipriano de Rore   SchOF
- c) A Florentine composer
  - (1) Francesco Corteccia [b. 1504]   PerMR, 605
    - (a) He set the Passion according to both John (1527) and Matthew (1532)
    - (b) He applied polyphony only to the introductory verses beginning with *Passio Domini nostri, Jesu Christi*, the *turba* sections, and the closing words of the Evangelist's narrative
- d) A Mantuan composer
  - (1) Jacquet of Mantua [ca. 1495]   PerMR, 605
    - (a) He set to polyphony the words of some individual speakers other than those of Christ
    - (b) He used John's account of the Passion
    - (c) Transcription of Passion music by Jacquet of Mantua   SchOF

3. It becomes obvious that in all of these responsorial Passions, the sober simplicity of the monophonic tones was set off against the relative opulence of the sections

done in polyphony PerMR, 606
- a) Even so, the polyphonic sections tend toward the syllabic and the homophonic
  - (1) This is in keeping with the character of the liturgy of Holy Week
- b) The compositional procedures show a greater affinity with the polyphony written for the chants of the Office, such as the Magnificats, Psalms, and Hymns, rather than with the more sophisticated contrapuntal motet
  - (1) Rarely were the two compositional styles brought together in the same work
    - (a) This was achieved at a much later date by Orlandus Lassus

D. Polyphony for the Office

1. Introduction
   - a) The Divine Office is "the daily series of services of the Western Christian rites, as distinct from the Mass" RanH, 559
     - (1) The practice of daily services was established early in the Christian communities of both East and West
       - (a) They derive from a Jewish custom
       - (b) The precise arrangement of the services within this series and of the series throughout the liturgical year followed one plan in the churches (the Roman cursus) and another in the monasteries (the monastic cursus)
     - (2) In the Roman Catholic Church there were eight of these daily services for each day
       - (a) They are Matins, Lauds, Prime, Terce, Sext, None, Vespers and Compline
     - (3) **The services consist of psalms, chanted with antiphons, readings, accompanied by responsories, and canticles, with the accompanying antiphons, hymns, verses, and prayers**
2. The Psalms
   - a) A Psalm is a sacred poem or song RanH, 663
     - (1) Specifically, it is one of the one-hundred fifty such poems that make up the Book of Psalms of the Bible, which is also termed the Psalter
     - (2) There needs to be a distinction stylistically and liturgically between Psalm texts and complete Psalm motets and Psalms simply arranged polyphonically for use at Vespers PerMR, 556
       - (a) The function in Christian ritual for which the Psalm motets were intended are not easy to determine, but the Mass seems to be one context in which they were frequently performed
         - i) The musical style relied on syntactically determined points of imitation PerMR, 518
           - a - This style was especially favored for motets based on texts taken from the Psalter
         - ii) These motets are in most cases indistinguishable from other compositions in the genre
       - (b) The Psalm settings for liturgical performance are tied closely to the formulaic tones of the chant

i) Therefore they are restricted melodically and harmonically by a narrow range and repetitive nature of the plainsong
ii) They are more closely akin to the polyphonic genres in which a recitation tone is an important structural element than they are to motets
iii) There are three forms of [liturgical] psalmody: antiphonal, responsorial, and direct   RanH, 664
    a - "In antiphonal psalmody, the verses of a Psalm are sung alternately by the two halves of a choir or schola seated facing one another in front of and on opposite sides of the altar"
        1 - The psalm itself is sung to a melodic formula called a psalm tone that is adapted and repeated for each verse
        2 - This is preceded and followed by the singing of an antiphon containing a brief text usually drawn from the psalm
    b - "In responsorial psalmody, one or more soloists or cantors sing one or more verses, and a choir sings a refrain or respond at the beginning and end and perhaps following each of the verses"
    c - In direct psalmody, a Psalm is sung without alternation among singers and without the additions similar to refrains found in antiphonal and responsorial psalmody
iv) While the three forms are distinguished, both medieval and modern practice often obscure the supposed differences among them   RanH, 664

(3) Venetian Psalms were written in polychoral [*coro spezzato*] style   RanH, 645
  (a) In this style, instead of each choir singing a self-contained verse in turn, the choirs interact more closely   AtlR, 413
    i) Two choirs sing individually most of the time but, one verse runs directly into the next with only the briefest of cadences
    ii) At the end, the two choirs sing together
  (b) The practice of *cori spezzati* was already well established in Venice by 1550   FenV, 114
    i) Some examples written for Ferrara date from the end of the fifteenth century
    ii) These were written for two four-voice choirs   FenV, 113

b) Composers of the Psalms
  (1) A French composer
    (a) Francesco de Layolle [b. 1492]   LayM, ix
      i) He composed *Septem psalmi penitentiales*
        a - Transcriptions of the seven psalms   LayM
  (2) Venetian composers
    (a) Adrian Willaert [b. ca. 1490]   ReeMR, 309
      i) He was a Flemish composer who lived mainly in Venice
      ii) He produced a collection of psalms called *I Salmi spezzati* of 1550   RedV, 277
        a - The original title was *I salmi appertinenti alli vesperi per*

Polyphony for the Office 223

            tutte le feste dell'anno...
        b - The collection contains compositions by Phinot, Giovanni Nasco (Maistre Jhan), and Heinrich Scaffen, plus psalms by Willaert and Jacquet of Mantua
        c - These are Vesper psalms   WilS
        d - A facsimile of a psalm in *I salmi appertinenti alli vesperi...*   WilS
        e - Facsimiles of *I salmi appertinenti alli vesperi per tutte le feste dell'anno...*   WilS; WilSA; WilSV
            1 - WilS contains the *cantus* and *altus* parts for Chorus I of the Vesper Psalms
            2 - WilSA contains only the *tenor primus* part of the Vesper Psalms
            3 - WilSV contains eight partbooks of the Vesper Psalms
        f - Transcriptions of *I salmi appertinenti alli vesperi per tutte le feste dell'anno...*   WilO, VIII
  iii) The *I Salmi spezzati* of 1550 contains three different types of antiphonal settings of the Psalms   RedV, 277
        a - *Salmi a versi con le sue Risposte*
            1 - These are psalms in which the separate verses of four-voice settings based on the Gregorian tones may be sung by one or two choirs
        b - *Salmi a versi senza Risposte*
            1 - These are psalms in which the monophonic plainsong intonation alternates with a simple four-voice harmonization of the psalm-tone
        c - *Salmi spezzati*
            1 - This group contains eight pieces by Willaert
                a - These are psalms composed for double choir
            2 - It is this group of eight pieces by Willaert which earned special fame for the composer
  iv) The technique used in the eight pieces of the last group became the chief characteristic of Venetian church music of the *seicento*   RedV, 276
        a - For many years, Willaert was regarded as the chief founder of the technique
            1 - But, research has shown that he only perfected an already existing choral practice
        b - But, Willaert's manner of treatment was new   AtlR, 413
            1 - Instead of each choir singing a self-contained verse in turn, Willaert makes the choirs interact more closely
                a - They still sing individually most of the time but, one verse now runs directly into the next with only the briefest of cadences
                b - This produces some blurring of the articulations between the choirs
                c - For an example of this *see* Willaert's *Credidi, propter quod locutus est*, Psalm 115   AtlR, 414
            2 - At the end, the two choirs sing together

                    a - An example   AtlR, 415
                3 - The choirs were situated at floor level next to the altar
                    or squeezed into one of the two pulpits that stood in
                    front of a partition separating altar from nave
                                                                AltR, 415
                4 - There was not an equal number of singers in each
                    group, therefore the psalms were not antiphonal
                                                                AltR, 415
                    a - They were sung responsorially   AtlR, 416
                    b - This explains Willaert's disposition of the voice
                        parts   AtlR, 416
                        1 - He assigns both high and low extremes to choir
                            I while bunching the other four-voice parts of
                            choir II compactly in the middle
            v) The technique used in *Salmi spezzati* is known as *coro spez-
                zato* or *coro battente*   RedV, 276
        (b) Cipriano de Rore [b. 1516]   RedV, 292
            i) There is a book of psalms [and Magnificats] published by
                Rore in 1554 in collaboration with Jacquet of Mantua

                    a - There are five psalms by Rore   BerCA, 472
                        1 - They are intended specifically for the second Vespers
                            of Christmas   BerCA, 471
                        2 - The odd-numbered verses of the text are set in poly-
                            phony with the alternating verses sung in chant
                                                                BerCA, 471
            ii) The book was published by Scotto under the title, *I sacri et
                santi salmi di David profeta...*   ScoS
                    a - A list of the contents   BerCA, 472
                    b - A facsimile of the tenor partbook of *I sacri et santi salmi
                        di David profeta...*   ScoS
    (3) A Florentine composer
        (a) Francesco Corteccia [b. 1504]   CorD
            i) There are two psalms by Corteccia, *Ecce nunc benedicite* and
                Gaudetete in Domino semper
                    a - Transcriptions of the two psalms   CorD
    (4) A Mantuan composer
        (a) Jacquet of Mantua [b. ca. 1495]   RedV, 292
            i) There is a book of psalms [and Magnificats] published by
                Rore in 1554 in collaboration with Jacquet of Mantua
                    a - There are thirteen psalms by Jacquet   BerCA, 472
                        1 - The odd-numbered verses of the text are set in poly-
                            phony, with the alternating verses sung in chant
                                                                BerCA, 471
            ii) The book was published by Scotto under the title, *I sacri et
                santi salmi di David profeta...*   ScoS
                    a - A list of the contents   BerCA, 472
                    b - A facsimile of the tenor partbook of *I sacri et santi salmi
                        di David profeta...*   ScoS

(5) A Central European composer
    (a) Ludwig Senfl [b. ca. 1490]   RedC, 259
        i) His psalms are clearly modeled on Josquin
            a - They are divided into two groups
                1 - One of free invention and another revolving around a *cantus prius factus*, sometimes taken from one of the psalm-tones
                    a - The latter is less frequent
                    b - An example is found in his *Deus in adjutorium* from the *Liber selectarum cantionum*
                        1 - An example of *Deus in adjutorium*   RedC, 259
                        2 - A transcription of *Deus in adjutorium*   SenS, 48
                        3 - A facsimile of *Liber selectarum cantionum*   SenL
        ii) Transcriptions of his psalms   SenS; GriT

3. The Magnificat
   a) Introduction
      (1) The Magnificat is used at Vespers   RanH, 464
      (2) The text is the canticle of the Virgin, Luke 1:46-55   RanH, 464
          (a) The Latin text begins with *Magnificat anima mea Dominum*
          (b) The verses are set to one of a set of psalm tones [one for each mode]
              i) "The tone of the canticle had to correspond with that of the antiphon by which it was framed liturgically, and the antiphons for the Magnificat represent all eight of the modal categories then current"   PerMR, 550
          (c) The verses are followed by the Lesser Doxology [*Gloria Patri et Filio et Spiritui Sancto*] that is treated as two additional verses
      (3) The first complete cycles of Magnificat settings were composed in the sixteenth century   PerMR, 550
          (a) They contained one setting for each of the eight modal categories used for liturgical recitation of the canticle
   b) General style of the Magnificat
      (1) The settings were often composed for *alternatim* performance
                                                                           RanH, 465
          (a) Polyphony was supplied for every other verse with plainchant used for the rest of the verses
              i) The polyphony was usually used for the even-numbered verses but at times for the odd-numbered verses
      (2) However, the papal choir sang every verse of the Magnificat in polyphony   BerCA, 278
   c) Composers of the Magnificat
      (1) French composers
          (a) Claudin de Sermisy [b. ca. 1495]
              i) He wrote ten complete Magnificats and some Magnificat sections   SerO, I, ix
              ii) Transcriptions of his Magnificats   SerO, I

  (b) Pierre Certon [Fl. 1539]
    i) A facsimile of a Magnificat   CerCD
 (2) Flemish composers
  (a) Jean Richafort [b. ca. 1480]
    i) His extant works include some eleven Magnificats
                           ReeMR, 335
    ii) In his *Magnificat quinti toni*, he alternates the sharply cut motives of the French with the longer-breathed lines of the Flemish composers   BriL, 231
      a - The two-part section, *Fecit potentiam* by Richafort, is reminiscent of similar episodes in Josquin, with the words *Dispersit superbos* set to a scale passage in the *altus* in order to emphasize them
        1 - At the same time, the upper voice recites on a monotone in syncopated rhythm
        2 - An example of the *Dispersit superbos*   BriL, 232
    iii) Facsimiles of the Magnificats   ModM
    iv) Transcriptions of *Magnificat sexti toni, Magnificat octavi toni*, and some Magnificat movements   RicO, III
  (b) Nicolas Gombert [b. ca. 1490]
    i) He wrote eight Magnificats   ReeMR, 344
    ii) He makes each verse that he sets into a little motet and each Magnificat into a motet cycle
    iii) He follows the common practice of setting the even-numbered verses, with the other verses left in chant
      a - The polyphonic plainsong is composed variously
        1 - There is a *cantus firmus* treatment disposed in long notes while the other voices move in imitation
        2 - Or, the plainsong may be bandied about from one part to another
    iv) In his Magnificat in tones three and eight, he adds one voice in setting each successive even-numbered verse
      a - For example, there are three voices in verse two with the number growing until there are eight voices in verse twelve
    v) Transcriptions of the Magnificats   GomO, IV
  (c) Jacobus Clemens (Clemens non Papa) [b. ca. 1510]
    i) He wrote fifteen settings of the Magnificat   BriL, 228
    ii) He set the even verses in polyphony, alternating them with the odd verses sung in the Gregorian manner   CleO, IV, i
      i) These settings may be a rather early work as they are less smooth and less balanced than most of his other works
    iii) Transcriptions of the Magnificats   CleO, IV
 (3) A Roman Catholic composer
  (a) Costanzo Festa [b. ca. 1490]
    i) He wrote thirteen Magnificats   ReeMR, 362
      a - They include examples of settings of all the verses polyphonically, except the opening word, with the music being based on the plainsong   ReeMR, 363

                b - There are also examples of the alternation of plainsong
                   and polyphony   ReeMR, 363
                    1 - They include both those in which the even-numbered
                        verses are set and those in which the odd-numbered
                        ones are set
                c - He uses continuous imitation with endless variety
                                                                        FesO, II, x
                    1 - This is done with motives derived from the chant or
                        freely composed motives set in contrapuntal combin-
                        ation with a *cantus firmus* in long notes
                d - He also uses strict canon   FesO, II, x
                e - He uses conflicting accentuation, paired imitation, and
                   ostinato   FesO, II, xi
          ii)   The *Magnificat sexti toni*   ReeMR, 363
                a - This Magnificat is a good example of all verses set poly-
                   phonically except for the opening word
                    1 - They are set for from two to six voices
                b - The most interesting verse is the seventh one, *Deposuit*
                   potentes, for five voices
                    1 - Four of the voices weave a web of imitation around
                      the fifth, which sings the plainsong in long notes as a
                      cantus firmus
                        a - "The imitation is based on a descriptive motif
                            (found in its most complete form in bass I), not
                            derived from the *cantus*"
                c - An extract from *Magnificat sexti toni*
                d - A transcription of *Magnificat sexti toni*   FesO, II, 58
          iii)   Other sources of his Magnificats
                a - Facsimiles   FesC; FesM; FesSM
                b - Transcriptions   FesS; FesO, II
  (4)   A Venetian composer
      (1)   Cipriano de Rore [b. 1516]
          i)   There is a book of [Magnificats] and psalms published by
                Rore in 1554 in collaboration with Jacquet of Mantua
                                                                          RedV, 292
                a - It contains one Magnificat by Rore, *Et exulavitt*
                                                                 BerCA, 472
                    1 - This Magnificat is intended specifically for a Vesper
                        service   BerCA, 471
                b - A facsimile of the Magnificats   ModM
          iii)   The book was published by Scotto under the title, *I sacri et*
                santi salmi di David profeta...   ScoS
                a - A list of the contents   BerCA, 472
                b - A facsimile of the tenor partbook of *I sacri et santi salmi*
                   di David profeta...   ScoS
  (5)   A Mantuan composer
      (a)   Jacquet of Mantua [b. ca. 1495]   RedV, 292
          i)   There is a book of [Magnificats] and psalms published by
                Rore in 1554 in collaboration with Jacquet of Mantua

                    a - It contains one Magnificat by Jacquet, *Et exulavitt*
                                                                BerCA, 472
                        1 - This Magnificat is intended specifically for a Vesper
                            service   BerCA, 471
                    b - A facsimile of the Magnificats   ModM
                ii) The book was published by Scotto under the title, *I sacri et
                    santi salmi di David profeta...*   ScoS
                    a - A list of the contents   BerCA, 472
                    b - A facsimile of the tenor partbook of *I sacri et santi salmi
                        di David profeta...*   ScoS
        (6) A Central European composer
            (a) Ludwig Senfl [b. ca. 1490]
                i) The *Magnificat octo tonorum*   RedC, 259
                    a - It was published in Nürnberg in 1537
                    b - Transcriptions of *Magnificat octo tonorum* SenW; SenM
        (7) A Spanish composer
            (a) Cristóbal de Morales [b. ca. 1500]
                i) He composed a set of eight twelve-verse settings
                                                                BerCA, 279
                    a - Every verse of each tone was set polyphonically
                        1 - This was unusual for the period   PerMR, 552
                        2 - This may reflect practice at the papal chapel where
                            alternatim performance was not usually used for this
                            particular chant   PerMR, 552
                    b - For the musical institutions where chant and polyphony
                        were sung in alternation, two complete sets were offered
                        in all eight tones   PerMR, 552
                        1 - The set for *alternatim* practice had the odd-numbered
                            verses in polyphony and the even-numbered ones in
                            chant
                ii) A facsimile of the first publication of Morales' settings
                                                                MorMA
                    a - A list of the contents   BerCA, 279
                    b - There are only five of the eight settings (tones 1, 2, 4, 6,
                        7) by Morales   BerCA, 278
                    c - The cycle is completed with three settings (tones 3, 5,
                        and 8) by Jacquet of Mantua, Richafort, and Tugdual
                                                                BerCA, 278
                iii) A facsimile of the first complete cycle of Magnificats by
                     Morales   MorMO
                    a - A list of the contents   BerCA, 332
                iv) A facsimile of the Magnificats   ModM
                v) Transcription of *Magnificat, 8th tone*   PedH, 20
                vi) Transcriptions of the Magnificats   MorO, IV

4. Lamentations
    a) Polyphonic treatment was not used as a rule for the liturgical music for the
       night Offices, Matins and Lauds   PerMR, 564
        (1) At least, there are none that have left any significant trace in the written

polyphony
b) There are exceptions found in observances of particular solemnity, especially those observances prescribed for Holy Week   PerMR, 564
    (1) These were the readings formally intoned during the first Nocturne at Matins on Thursday, Friday, and Saturday of Holy Week
        (a) This three-day period was known as *triduum sacrum*
b) The most frequent texts provided with a polyphonic setting were the *Lamentations of Jeremiah*   PerMR, 564
    (1) But in spite of the importance of the Holy Week rituals, the number of polyphonic settings for the Lamentations was not particularly significant
    (2) In the sixteenth century, settings vary significantly in the number of verses used   RanH, 435
        (a) In the earlier Lamentations, the *tonus lamentationum* is included and the settings are relatively imitative and polyphonic in texture
            i) Most later settings do not use this tone and they are more homorhythmic in texture
        (b) Spanish composers made considerable use of the Spanish Lamentation tone throughout the century   RanH, 435
    (3) "The Hebrew letter that precedes each verse in the Bible is retained in musical settings"   RanH, 435
        (a) It is often set in a more elaborate fashion than the remainder of the text
    (4) Expressive devices were used sparingly in polyphonic compositions of this period   RanH, 435
c) Composers of the Lamentations
    (1) A French composer
        (a) Claudin de Sermisy [b. ca. 1495]   LesF, 240
            i) There are three Lamentations for four voices   SerO, II
                a - There are homophonic passages which were traditionally of great importance   LesF, 241
            ii) Facsimiles: *Lamentationes Hieremiae Prophetae...*   BerCR
            iii) Transcriptions of the Lamentations   SerO, II
    (2) A Flemish composer
        (a) Thomas Crécquillon [b. ca. 1480 to ca. 1500]   BriL, 222
            i) Crécquillon's Lamentations have much dramatic vigor and great expressive power   BriL, 224
            ii) In the first Lamentation, written for five voices, the word *convertere* enters with a rising semitone in the *discantus*, a fourth in the *altus* and *primus tenor*, a third in the *secundus tenor*, and an octave in the *bassus*   BriL, 224
                a - This makes the exhortation stand out strongly
                b - For an example of the above, *see*   BriL, 224
            iii) Crécquillon's Lamentations were published in 1549 by Montanus and Neuber in [*Lamentationes Hieremiae Prophetae...*]   BriL, 224
                a - A facsimile of *Lamentationes Hieremiae Prophetae...*   BerCR
                b - A transcription of *Lamentationes Hieremiae Prophetae...*   WatT

(3) A Roman Catholic composer
   (a) Costanzo Festa [b. ca. 1490]
      i) Transcriptions of his Lamentations FesO, VI
(4) A Spanish composer
   (a) Cristóbal Morales [b. ca. 1500]
      i) Some Lamentations were published in 1549 by Montanus and Neuber in [*Lamentationes Hieremiae Prophetae...*] BriL, 224
         a - A transcription of *Lamentationes Hieremiae Prophetae...* WatT
      ii) A facsimile of *Lamentationi di Morales a quatro a cinque, et sei voci* MorL

5. Hymns
   a) Introduction
      (1) There were polyphonic settings in cycles of hymns for the whole year RanH, 385
         (a) "Significantly, the great majority of all the musicians whose liturgical hymn cycles are known to us spent a major part of their career on the Italian peninsula, and it was undoubtedly for Italian institutions that most of their work in the genre was done" PerMR, 542
      (2) The hymns in these hymn cycles usually contained polyphony for the odd-numbered strophes composed around the chant as *cantus firmus* PerMR, 542
         (a) Chant alone was implied for the even-numbered strophes
      (3) But, this pattern for the polyphonic treatment of hymns in Italy appears to have had no significant impact on the German tradition in the sixteenth century PerMR, 548
         (a) Perhaps this was because of the intervention of the Protestant Reformation
            i) The Reformation created a barrier that insulated the Lutheran communities in the north from the influence of liturgical practice in Catholic Italy
      (4) There was a collection of hymns, the *Sacorum hymnorum liber primus*, printed in Wittenberg in 1542 by Georg Rhau, containing works from a variety of German-speaking composers PerMR, 548
         (a) It is an anthology of works and is not strictly ordered according to the liturgical calendar PerMR, 543
         (b) It contains many settings that are thought to have been prepared for Catholic worship since they are found in manuscripts going back to the beginning of the century
         (c) It contains compositions that reflect the considerable variety typical of German hymn composition at the time PerMR, 549
            i) Some of the more important composers are Thomas Stoltzer, Heinrich Finck, and Johann Walther PerMR, 548
            ii) Hymns were provided for many more liturgical occasions than contemporaneous Italian cycles
         (d) Alternate settings are given for a good number of the texts PerMR, 549

i) But, as a rule, there is only a single polyphonic setting for any given hymn
- (e) A facsimile of *Sacrorum hymnorum liber primus*   RhaSA
- (f) A transcription of *Sacrorum hymnorum liber primus*   RhaSAC

(5) Only two masters currently credited with a complete cycle of polyphonic hymns were active in regions of Germanic culture around mid-century; Sixtus Dietrich and Benedictus Ducis   PerMR, 543
- (a) These composers were defintely Protestants   RedC, 253
- (b) The compositions of Dietrich were published by Georg Rhau in Wittenberg in 1545 and the collection by Ducis for the courtly chapel in Heidelberg has been lost

b) Composers of the Hymn
   (1) A Venetian composer
   - (a) Adrian Willaert [b. ca. 1490]   BerCA, 284
      i) *Hymnorum musica* (1542)
        - a - There is a 1550 reprint edition of the 1542 edition
        - b - All of these hymns belong to the Office of Vespers
        - c - There are alternating strophes of each hymn
           1 - Sometimes Willaert begins his polyphonic setting with the second strophe of the hymn
        - d - There are two settings by Jacquet of Mantua
        - e - A list of the contents
        - f - A table of the polyphonic strophes for each hymn with the textual and melodic sources   WilO VII, iv-vii
        - g - A facsimile of *Hymnorum musica* (1550)   WilH
        - h - A transcription of *Hymnorum musica*   WilO VI-VII
   (2) A Roman Catholic composer
   - (a) Costanzo Festa [b. ca. 1490]   PerMR, 545
      i) He wrote a liturgical cycle of polyphonic hymns [*Hymni per totum annum: 3, 4, 5, 6 vocibus*]
        - a - His settings of hymns have alternate strophes sung in polyphony and plainsong   ReeMR, 362
           1 - The even-numbered strophes are set to polyphony
        - b - Each polyphonic strophe has a different setting
        - c - For the hymns with an odd number of strophes, Festa either set the last two for consecutive polyphonic performance or composed in parts for the first strophe, then composed for only the odd-numbered strophes that followed
           1 - An example of the first process is *Christe redemptor omnium* which has seven strophes
           2 - An example of the second process is *Aures ad nostras...preces* which has nine strophes
        - d - In any case, the first strophe to be set was invariably written for four voices, the penultimate usually for three, and the last for five or six
           1 - The added voice was generally due to a strict canonic imitation of the part with the chant
           2 - This provided for a climatic conclusion

                    e - Concern for "correct" Latin pronunciation is discernible due to the adjustment of the declamation of the strophic text from one strophe to the next
                    f - For an example of Festa's characteristic treatment of the genre, *see*   PerMR, 546
                ii) A transcription of *Hymni per totum annum: 3, 4, 5, 6 vocibus*   FesSV
        (3) Florentine composers of the Hymn
            (a) Francesco Corteccia [b. 1504]   PerMR, 542
                i) *Hymnarium*
                    a - This was composed in the early 1540s
                    b - It contains thirty-seven Vesper hymns based on plainchant and written for three to six parts   CorE, viii
                    c - The hymns are grouped according to the four classes of the liturgical year   CorE, viii
                        1 - The four classes are: Proper of the Time, Ordinary, Proper of the Saints, and Common of the Saints
                    d - Corteccia alternates stanzas of polyphony with stanzas of plainsong   ReeMR, 365
                        1 - Only the even numbered verses are set to polyphony
                        2 - Each polyphonically sung strophe has a different setting
                ii) Sources of his hymns
                    a - A facsimile of *Himnario secondo l'uso della chiesa romana et fiorentina*   CorH
                    b - A xerographic copy of four hymns   McKF
                    c - A transcription of *Hinnario secondo l'uso de la chiesa romana et fiorentina*   CorHS
                    d - Transcriptions of some of the hymns   CorC; McKF; CorE
            (b) Philippe Verdelot [b. ?]
                i) Transcriptions of nine hymns   VerO I
        (4) A Mantuan composer
            (a) Jacquet of Mantua [b. ca. 1495]   BerCA, 681
                i) Twenty-six different hymn settings by Jacquet were published by Scotto posthumously in 1566
                    a - These were authored perhaps as early as the 1540s and no later than 1556   PerMR, 543
                    b - In these settings, Jacquet follows the sixteenth-century practice of setting only alternate strophes polyphonically
                    c - He sets the last strophe of each hymn for five voices instead of four with a few exceptions
                    d - These settings were published in *Himni vesperorum totius anni secundum Romanam curiam diligentissime recogniti...cum quatuor et quinque vocibus*
                        1 - A list of the contents of *Himni vesperorum... cum quatuor et quinque vocibus*   BerCA, 682
                        2 - A facsimile of *Himni vesperorum...cum quatuor et quinque vocibus*   JacH
                        3 - A transcription of *Himni vesperorum...cum quatuor*

		et quinque vocibus	JacHV
	ii)	A facsimile of two hymns by Jacquet	WilH

E. **The Motet**

1. The general style of the motet   RanH, 511
    a) The motet occupied the central position in the work of all the leading composers of the period
    b) It was a vocally conceived composition with all the parts provided with text
        PerMR, 514
        (1) This did not preclude the possibility of the voices being doubled instrumentally
    c) Four voices were spread across the most common ranges of the human voice from soprano to bass   PerMR, 514
        (1) Three-voice motets did not entirely disappear from the repertory
            (a) But they were written more infrequently except for internal sections of large works in contrast to the overall sonorities or in response for particular needs
    d) The motet is vast and varied
        (1) There is great variety in texts and musical structures   RanH, 512
    e) But during this period it is generally a polyphonic setting of a sacred Latin text
        (1) The Latin texts consist of traditional texts from the liturgy, passages taken directly from the Bible, and amalgamations of portions of the liturgy or of the Bible
    f) There are also settings of secular Latin texts
        (1) A significant number of such texts are taken from classical or humanist Latin poetry
        (2) Others are newly composed texts honoring a particular person or event
            (a) A motet, *Jubilate Deo omnis*, by Cristóbal de Morales lauds Paul III, Emperor Charles V, and King François I by name   ReyR, 89
                i) This was composed for the treaty-signing ceremonies in Nice in 1548
                ii) A facsimile of *Jubilate Deo omnis*   ScoI
    g) The main concern of the composer was the relationship between the music and the word   RanH, 512
        (1) The music could be fitted to the individual phrase due to the equal participation of all the voices in presenting motivic material   RanH, 511
    h) Many of the motets employ the same techniques as those used in settings of the Mass
        (1) The techniques such as imitation, canon, ostinato, *cantus firmus*, and paraphrase are used
        (2) The technique of imitation is used the most
            (a) Pervading imitation is the driving stylist force which grows even thicker and more seamless   AtlR, 396

2. The French motet
    a) The general style of the French motet

234   Sacred Latin Music for the Catholic Church on the Continent

       (1) It is in simple style with Netherlandish traits   ReeMR, 339
           (a) It contains imitative or canonic writing   DobM, 216
       (2) There are usually five or more voices   LesF, 240
           (a) But there were still many motets written for four voices DobM, 307
       (3) The melodies are based on psalms, antiphons, or sequences   LesF, 240
       (4) The texts are usually divided into two parts   LesF, 240
           (a) But occasionally they are divided into three parts   DobM, 216
       (5) The clear comprehension of the text was important to the composers
                                                                                                                     LesF, 240
           (a) They attached more importance to the comprehension of the text than to strictly musical elaboration
  b) The composers of the French motet (the Paris school)
       (1) Clément Janequin [b. ca. 1485]   LesF, 243
           (a) He wrote a volume of motets that probably have been lost
           (b) One motet, *Congregati sunt*, has survived
                i) It is in the French motet style with a natural tendency to rapid declamation
                ii) A transcription of *Congregati sunt*   JanCS
       (2) Claudin de Sermisy [b. ca. 1495]   ReeMR, 338
           (a) He wrote some seventy motets for three, four, five, and six voices
                                                                                                    LesF, 242
           (b) He used the typical form of the French motet throughout his motet compositions   LesF, 242
                i) His music follows the text closely
                      a - He attempts "to interpret accurately the saddest of liturgical texts"
                      b - The last phrase of the text is repeated as in a *chanson*
                ii) His music is constructed on a rhythmical theme
                      a - But he is careful in his treatment of the Gregorian melodies
                iii) He uses Netherlandish traits   ReeMR, 339
           (b) Examples of his motets
                i) *Praeparate corda vestra*   LesF, 242
                      a - This was written as early as 1529
                      b - It is a good example of the typical form of the French motet
                          1 - It is constructed on a rhythmical theme and has a repeat of the last phrase as in a *chanson*
                          2 - The text is followed closely
                      c - Sermisy remained faithful to this form throughout his motets
                ii) *Aspice, Domine, de sede sancta tua* is in responsory form (*aBcB*)   ReeMR, 339
                      a - There is polyphonic overlapping between the end of the first B and the opening of c
                      b - Transcriptions of *Aspice, Domine, de sede sancta tua*
                                                    AttTL, III, 72; SliG II, 24
              iii) *Clare sanctorum senate apostolorum* is for four voices and is written in two *partes*   ReeMR, 339

                a - This motet is based on fragments of the similarly named plainsong sequence
                    1 - The sequence is the basis of a free variation chain
                    2 - The fragments are presented in points of imitation
                b - A transcription of *Clare sanctorum senate apostolorum*
                                                                                AttTL, I, 1
            (c) A list of the motets attributed to Sermisy and others   BroS, 31
                i) Only *Domine Deus omnipotens* may be by some other composer
                                                                                BroS, 57
            (d) Some facsimiles of his motets   FioM; ModP; ScoL; GarI
        (3) Pierre Certon [Fl. 1539]
            (a) He is not considered a great composer in the domain of church music
                                                                                LesF, 244
            (b) There are two motets by him, following his Masses that parody them, in an Attaingnant collection   ReeMR, 339
                i) One of the Masses is *Missa Dulcis amica*
            (c) A facsimile of the Masses and motets   AttM
        (4) Guillaume Le Heurteur   LesF, 244
            (a) He wrote motets on the Antiphons of Our Lady
                i) These motets for four, five, and six voices were published in 1545
                ii) They all follow the same pattern in which there seems to be no idea of the resources of polyphony
                iii) Little vocalizations that are scattered through the compositions serve only as decorative additions as might be done in a *chanson*
                iv) In his *In te Domine speravi* he sets the text syllabically
                    a - Perhaps he did this because it is a verse of a psalm forming part of the Office for Holy Thursday
                    b - He still subordinates his music to the words even when the text calls for rejoicing such as in his *Noe, Noe, natus est Christus*
                        1 - An example from *Noe, Noe, natus est Christus*
                                                                                LesF, 245
                v) He uses more varied resources in his *Christum ascendentem*
                    a - In this piece, the choir frequently divides antiphonally
                                                                                LesF, 245
                    b - Triple time is used in the final section to indicate the Christians hope in the Holy Spirit on Ascension Day
            (b) Facsimiles of some of Le Heurteur's motets   AttO
    c) The composers of the French motet (Lyons school)
        (1) François (Francesco) de Layolle [b. 1492]   DobM, 177
            (a) He composed with a keen sense of colour and effective contrast
                                                                                LesF, 241
            (b) There are three of his motets appended at the end of the Mass Propers found in the *Contrapunctus* of 1528   DobM, 216
                i) There may be a connection between these motets and the preceding Masses
                ii) One motet is a Marian antiphon, *Salve Virgo salutaris*

     a - This antiphon presents a plainchant part in equal notes with the other three voices adding derived imitative entries or independent counterpoints
     b - Transcriptions of *Salve Virgo salutaris*
                 SutC II, 87; AmbG V, 201
    iii) A hymn, *Media vita in morte*   DobM, 216
     a - The *Media vita in morte* also presents a plainchant part in equal notes with the other three voices adding derived imitative entries or independent counterpoints
     b - Transcriptions of *Media vita in morte*
                 AmbG V, 204; SutC II, 90
    iv) An *Ave Maria*   DobM, 217
     a - This has three equal voices in a three-in-one canon at the unison
     b - A transcription of *Ave Maria*   SutC II, 94
    v) A facsimile of the *Contrapunctus*   ConS
    vi) A transcription of the *Contrapunctus*   SutC I, SutC II
    vii Transcriptions of the three motets   LayC, nos. 1, 19, and 30
 (c) Twelve of his motets are found in the British Library Tenor partbook   DobM, 215
   i) British Library, *K. 8. b. 7(5)*   DobM, 139
    a - This collection is thought to be the set of twelve motets published in Lyons and found in no. 5582 of the [Ferdinand] Columbus catalogue   DobM, 142
     1 - It was most likely printed by Moderne at a date earlier than 1531 or 1532   ChaP, 54
     2 - It is possibly identifiable with one of the six Layolle motet books that has not survived   ChaP, 53
 (d) One motet, the *Ave Virgo sanctissima,* is written for five voices
                          DobM, 216
   i) It has a series of short conventional chant-derived motives in canon at the unison between two tenor parts
   ii) Each of the above are preceded by a series of imitative entries in the other voices
    a - These are based on the same motives
   iii) A transcription of *Ave Virgo sanctissima*   LayC, no. 6
 (e) Another motet, the *Stabat mater,* is written for five voices and is divided into three sections with an ostinato *cantus firmus* of five *longae (la sol fa re mi)* in the second tenor part   DobM, 216
   i) Imitative counterpoint is woven in the other voices above and below
   ii) A transcription of *Stabat mater dolorosa*   LayC, no. 36
 (f) There are three motets appended to the 1532 Ordinaries [*Liber decem missarum*]   DobM, 217
   i) *Stephanus autem*
    a - This motet has the same mode, clefs, and melodic basis as the preceding *Missa Stephane gloriose* by Pierre Molu
    b - Facsimiles of *Stephanus autem*   ModL, ModLD
   ii) *Libera me de morte eterna*

                a - This motet has the same mode, clefs, and melodic basis as
                    the preceding *Missa Adieu mes amours* by Layolle
                b - "It is composed with an extra voice derived in canon
                    from the Superius"
                c - Facsimiles of *Libera me de morte eterna*   ModL, ModLD
            iii) A Marian antiphon, *Beata Dei genitrix*
                a - It shares the mode and clefs of the preceding *Missa Veni
                    sponsa Christi* by Richafort
                b - Facsimiles of *Beata Dei genitrix*   ModL, ModLD
        (e) Facsimiles of Layolle's motets   ModP; ModS; ModT

3. The Flemish motet
   a) General style of the Flemish motet   BriL, 219
      (1) It has been described as "the imitative syntactic style"
          (a) Each verbal phrase had its own musical theme
          (b) Each theme was stated by each voice in free imitation
          (c) The musical phrases were interlocked in a closely knit web
              i) The continuity of the musical statements was never inter-
                 rupted by a cadence
          (d) There was an almost complete absence of the two-part episodes
              that had been typical of the previous age
      (2) There was an attempt to make the music fit the words
          (a) In order to suit the words, new melodies were invented   BriL, 220
              i) Thus, the foundations of a new musical language were laid
      (3) But, the imitative syntactic style hindered the understanding of the words
          (a) The text was sacrificed to purely musical considerations
   b) Composers of the Flemish motet   BriL, 219
      (1) Jean Richafort [b.ca. 1480]
          (a) He wrote at least thirty-five motets   ReeMR, 335
          (b) His motets found much favor with his contemporaries   BriL, 232
              i) They were often chosen as models for *missae parodiae*
          (c) *Misereatur mei*   ReeMR, 336
              i) This motet resorts to symbolism
              ii) It is a five-voice motet written in imitation of Josquin's five-
                  part *Miserere mei, Deus*   LowN, 195
                  a - Richafort uses the same *cantus firmus* as did the older
                      master   ReeMR, 336
                  b - He also uses the identical melodic and rhythmic version
              iii) There is an ostinato motif that holds the three *partes* of the
                   piece together   LowN, 195
              iv) A transcription of *Misereatur mei*   LowN, 195
          (d) *Sufficiebat*   ReeMR, 336
              i) The text of this motet is drawn from the *chanson, Mon sou-
                 venir* by Hayne
                  a - It is most likely symbolically significant
                  b - The text is drawn from the speech made by the weeping
                      mother when the father sends Tobias forth to journey
                      with the angel
              ii) A transcription of *Sufficiebat*   MalTR, XVII, 33

238 Sacred Latin Music for the Catholic Church on the Continent

    (e) *Gloria, laus et honor*   ReeMR, 336
- i) This motet is composed in a variation of the normal hymn-form except a refrain is added at the beginning and after each strophe
  - a - The refrain remains unaltered
  - b - Each strophe is given a different paraphrase setting
- ii) The motet is based on the chant setting
- iii) A transcription of *Gloria, laus et honor*   AttTL, I, 25

    (f) *Quem dicunt homines*   ReeMR, 336
- i) This is possibly Richafort's most famous work
  - a - Many composers based Masses on it
- iii) A transcription of the opening *Pars II* of *Quem dicunt homines*
  - a - The words as translated are, "Peter, lovest thou me? He answering said: Thou knowest, Lord, that I love Thee."   ReeMR, 337
- iv) Facsimiles of *Quem dicunt homines*   RicQ; GarF, 41; RhaS, no. 32; ModP
- v) A transcription of *Quem dicunt homines*   LocDM, 1

    (g) *Christus resurgens*   ReeMR, 337
- i) This motet is in responsory form aBcB
- ii) It serves as a model for Masses
- iii) A transcription of *Christus resurgens*   RicC, 218

    (h) Other sources of Richafort's motets
- i) Facsimiles   ModP; GarF
- ii) Transcriptions   RicO, II

(2) Thomas Crécquillon [b. ca. 1480 to ca. 1500]
    (a) He wrote 116 motets   BriL, 222
    (b) His motets show the full measure of his talent and employ all the resources of his art in the service of the words   BriL, 225
- i) He attempts to set his opening themes to the general feeling of the words   BriL, 227
  - a - He then restates an opening theme in a varied form and prolongs it with a second phrase set to the same words
- ii) He is very attentive to text-expression and declamation   ReeMR, 350
  - a - *Domine Deus conteris bella* is an example
    - 1 - He uses a number of dissonances to depict the harshness of war

    (c) His counterpoint is transparent and best suited by long, calm, well-balanced themes   BriL, 225
- i) He uses a series of points of imitation; rarely, with short passages in chordal style   MarFV I, 79
- ii) Note-against-note counterpoint is used throughout   MarFV I, 80
- iii) His overall texture is full and uniform   MarFV, p. 81

    (d) He had a fine feeling for scale passages   BriL, 225
- i) An example is *Sed melius est*
  - a - A facsimile of *Sed melius est*   PhaL

| | | b - | A transcription of *Sed melius est* | MarFV II, 20 |

- (e) He uses octave leaps which provide the opportunity for vocal expansion   BriL, 225
  - i) An example is found in his *Parasti in dulcedine tua*
    - a - A facsimile of *Parasti in dulcedine tua*   PhaL
    - b - A transcription of *Parasti in dulcedine tua*   MarFV II, 72
- (f) At the opening of pars II of an *Ave Virgo*, the voices enter by upward leaps of a fourth (*superius*), a fifth (*altus* II), a fourth (*tenor*), a fifth (*altus* I), and a fifth (*bassus*)   ReeMR, 350
  - i) "The leaps of a fifth are tonal answers to the leaps of a fourth"
  - ii) Musicians of the first half of the century were attracted to tonal, or quasi-tonal, answers
    - a - This occurred the more the modal system veered toward major and minor
  - iii) A transcription of *Ave Virgo*   MalTR, XII, 27
- (g) Tonal answers also occur in the motets, *Carole, magnus erat* and *Quis te victorem dica*   ReeMR, 350
  - a - Both of these are motets in praise of Charles V
  - b - Transcriptions of the motets respectively   MalTR, XII, 15 and 21
- (h) A new high was reached by Crécquillon in his *Congregati sunt inimici nostri*   ReeMR, 350
  - i) In this six-voice motet, he combines *cantus firmus* style, pervading imitation, and careful matching of sonority to word
- (i) Sources of his four-voice motets
  - i) The *Opus sacrarum cantionum* of 1576   MarFV I, 22
    - a - This is a printed source containing only motets by Crécquillon
    - b - It contains sixteen motets   MarFV II
      - 1 - Texts of the motets   MarFV I, 22
      - 2 - A transcription of *Opus sacrarum cantionum*   MarFV II
  - ii) Miscellaneous printed editions containing music by various composers of the time   MarFV I, 22
    - a - There are nineteen motets by Crécquillon in these sources   MarFV III
      - 1 - Texts of the motets   MarFV I, 32
      - 2 - Transcriptions of the motets   MarFV III
  - iii) Nine of his motets are found only in manuscript   MarFV IV
    - a - Transcriptions of the motets
- (j) Other sources of his motets
  - i) A facsimile of his first motet   CanT
  - ii) A facsimile of five-voice motets   SusLDE
  - iii) Transcriptions of four-voice motets   CreO, XI, XII
  - iv) Transcriptions of motets for three, five, six and eight voices   CreO, V-IX

(3) Nicolas Gombert [b. ca. 1490]
- (a) Most of his sacred music is in the form of motets   ReeMR, 344

        i)   There are 169, eight of which are Magnificats
        ii)   The majority of his motets are written for four and five voices
        iii) Slightly over half of his motets are written in two *partes*
            a - They have simplicity and clarity without excluding elegance

(b) Gombert was the most brilliant exponent of the style of the period   BriL, 220
        i)   He avoids constructivist methods such as canon and *cantus firmus* treatment   ReeMR, 345
            a - *Cantus firmus* treatment, although found in his Masses, is rare in his motets   ReeMR, 347
            b - His plainsong melodies are not reduced to a long note *cantus firmus*, but allowed to appear in their own character by applying the same technique of variation as with a melody of his own invention   BriL, 221
        ii)   The pervading imitation found in Josquin reaches full bloom with Gombert   ReeMR, 344
            a - Imitation is found at close time-intervals
                1 - Entries vary from point to point in number and order   AtlR, 398
            b - His music is seamless   AtlR, 398
                1 - He uses very few clear-cut cadences followed by silence
            c - At times, he departs from literal imitation by means of tonal answers   ReeMR, 345
        iii) He derives form for his music from a series of imitation-points   ReeMR, 345
            a - He uses short points of imitation for small divisions of the text   DavH, 228
            b - Each point is based on a different subject
            c - A good example of this is his *Super flumina*
                1 - A facsimile of *Super flumina*   GomM
                2 - Transcriptions of *Super flumina*   DavH, 118; GomO, V, 66
        iv) But, he also employs the homophonic style for particular passages of the text   BriL, 221
        v)   The majority of the motets have religious texts   GomO, V, i
            a - But very few of the texts are strictly liturgical
        vi) He avoids literalness in repetitions   ReeMR, 344
            a - He reworks motifs several times before proceeding to a new motif
            b - He freely alters the rhythmic pattern of a phrase when it is imitated in another voice   UlrH, 136
                1 - He uses many syncopations and a variety of note values

(c) His "rich" style is shown in his *Quem dicunt homines*   AtlR, 398
        i)   The biblical text is set for six voices
            a - The voices are almost constantly busy due to the avoid-

      ance of textual contrasts between different combinations
       of voices that was a hallmark of the Josquin generation
     b - Also, there are no contrasts between imitative and homo-
      phonic sections or passages in triple and duple meter
  ii) A transcription of *Quem dicunt homines* AtlAR, 273
(d) One of Gombert's best known works is exceptional ReeMR, 345
  i) It is the Marian motet that bears the motto *Diversi diversa orant*
    a - In this motet, Gombert does not apply pervading imitation
    b - He draws on seven different Marian plainsong melodies
     1 - Four such melodies are usually sung at one time
     2 - These melodies are reshaped by rhythmic alterations, melodic interpolations, appendages, and pauses in order to make them fit together
    c - A facsimile of *Diversi diversa orant* MalTR II, 3
(f) There are two books of four-part motets and two books of five-part motets containing motets by Gombert GomO, V, I
  i) The four-part motets:
    a - *Musica quatuor vocum vulgo motecta liber primus* of 1539 [published by Scotto] contains twenty-three motets BerCA, 229
     1 - A list of the contents BerCA, 229
     2 - A facsimile of *Musica quatuor vocum vulgo motecta liber primus* GomM
     3 - A transcription of *Musica quatuor vocum vulgo motecta liber primus* GomO, V
    b - A *Musica quatuor vocum vulgo motecta liber primus* was published by Scotto in 1541 GomO, V, 1
     1 - This contains fourteen of the motets from the 1539 edition plus ten works by other composers BerCA, 262
     2 - A list of the contents BerCA, 262
     3 - A facsimile of *Musica quatuor vocum vulgo motecta liber primus* GomMQ
     4 - Transcriptions of *Musica quatuor vocum vulgo motecta liber primus* GomO, V, VIII; MorO, II
  ii) The five-part motets:
    a - The *Musica vulgo motecta quinque vocum liber primus* of 1539 BerCA, 230
     1 - A list of the contents BerCA, 231
     2 - Transcriptions of *Musica vulgo motecta quinque vocum liber primus* GomO, VII
    b - The *Motectorum quinque vocum liber secundus* was published by Scotto in Venice in 1541 and an abridged version of the first book in 1550 GomO, V, I
     1 - A list of the twenty-one motets in the 1541 edition BerCA, 267
     2 - A facsimile of the 1541 edition, *Motectorum quinque vocum liber secundus* GomMO

3 - Transcriptions of the 1541 edition
              GomO, VIII; WilO, III
4 - A facsimile of the 1550 edition, *[Motetta] cum quinque vocibus liber primus*   GomMQV
  a - Gardano published an abridged version of the 1550 edition in 1552
  iii) The writing is conservative in the four-voice settings with more advanced writing in the larger settings   UlrH, 136
 (g) Other sources of his motets
   i) Facsimiles   GarF; ModT; GarMD; ScoI
   ii) Transcriptions   GomO, V, VI, VII, VIII, IX, X
(4) Jacobus Clemens (Clemens non Papa) [b. ca. 1510]   ReeMR, 352
 (a) He composed 233 motets   PerMR, 510
   i) They are written for three to eight voices   ReeMR, 352
    a - But, the majority are for four or five voices   UlrH, 139
   ii) A large number of the motets are in two *partes*   BriL, 228
 (b) His motets are written mostly for the church and usually have short texts taken from the Bible
   i) In spite of the short texts, Clemens' motets are often long
                     BriL, 228
    a - This was due to the fact that he was fond of repeating the words to fresh musical ideas
    b - An example is *Erravi sicut ovis*
     1 - A partial transcription of *Erravi sicut ovis*   BriL, 228
     2 - Transcriptions of *Erravi sicut ovis*
                 CleO, XII, 8; CleO, XXI, 13
 (c) There are at least four ceremonial pieces with specific textual references either to the household of Charles V or to one of his greatest generals   PerMR, 537
   i) One of the motets, *O quam moesta dies*, was set for five voices   PerMR, 538
    a - The conventional rhythms of the Latin are followed
    b - But by contrast, Clemens makes the verbal syntax relatively difficult by his use of overlapping repetitions of short segments of text and an almost continuous contrapuntal fabric
    c - An example of *O quam moesta dies*   PerMR, 538
 (d) A few of his motets are bi-textual   ReeMR, 353
   i) An example is *Fremuit spiritu Jesu*
    a - One voice sings words in longer notes as a commentary to the words sung by the other voices
    b - This motet is often cited also as a claim that Clemens, though seldom using accidentals, sometimes indicates the application of *musica ficta* in such a way as to produce elaborate chromaticism
     1 - If the *musica ficta* is applied, highly charged "modulatory" harmonies are produced that express equally emotional texts
     2 - A musical example showing the music with and

		without *musica ficta*	AtlR, 401
		c - Transcriptions of *Fremuit spiritu Jesu*	
			ReeD; CleO, XIV, 32

(e) The basic method of motet technique, *i.e.*, the principle of points of imitation, was used by Clemens with great freedom DavH, 230
    i) A good example is his *Vox in Rama* DavH, 230
        a - Transcriptions of *Vox in Rama*
            DavH, 134; CleO, IX, 105
    ii) When Clemens employed imitation in all the voices, the practice of referring to one voice as the principal one, or as heavier or lighter than another, disappeared UlrH, 139
        a - His motets were particularly evenly balanced in this respect

(f) He experimented in fashioning tonal answers ReeMR, 354
    i) Examples of this are *Super ripam Jordanis* and *Mane nobiscum*
        a - Transcriptions of both motets
            ComB, II, 17; ComB, III, 20
        b - A transcription *Super ripam Jordanis* CleO, XIV, 26
        c - A transcription of *Mane nobiscum* CleO, XIV, 14

(g) His use of musical motives (shorter melodic phrases used repeatedly in different contexts) were forward-looking UlrH, 138
    i) The motives often were freely invented ReeMR, 354
    ii) At times they derive their rhythms from the metrical accents of the words ReeMR, 354
        a - This is true usually of the beginning sections of the motets
    iii) This technique was to become common later in the sixteenth century
    iv) His motet, *Vox in rama* is a good example of this
        a - A musical example of *Vox in rama* UlrH, 138

(h) He uses note-against-note in his counterpoint ReeMR, 354
    a - It contains much parallel motion and archaic fauxbourdon-like writing
    b - He makes sparing use of both canon and chordal writing
        ReeMR, 355

(i) He avoided extreme rhythmic contrast between voices UlrH, 139
    i) Similar note values were employed in all voices
        a - As a result, unified rhythmic structures resulted
    ii) But, even in such passages, the judicious use of syncopations, cross currents, and poly-rhythms provided a clear and flowing rhythm

(j) He already presents most details of Palestrina's normal voice-relation technique ReeMR, 355
    i) One exception "is the use of a tone that enters stepwise being approached as one kind of dissonance (such as an auxiliary note or passing-note) and being quitted as another (such as a suspension) provided the tone with which it clashes is stationary ", *see* ReeMR, 322, Ex. 68
    ii) Another exception is the use of passing six-three chords in

                                minims against a stationary voice   ReeMR, 355 fn. 84a
- (k) He was known for the expressiveness of his melodies, the clarity of his style, and for his advanced treatment of the harmonic idiom

                                                                       DavH, 230
  - i) He is gifted particularly in the delineation of tender and lyric moods   ReeMR, 355
    - a - He favors the *superius*   ReeMR, 354
  - ii) He uses certain melodic intervals as an expressive device

                                                                         ReeMR, 355
    - a - Such as the leap of a minor sixth in the beautiful opening motif of *Vox in Rama*
      - 1 - A transcription of *Vox in Rama*   DavH, 134
    - b - He uses the minor second with words of sorrow or pain
    - c - A leap of a fourth or fifth downward followed by a whole step upward is used as an expression of tender emotions
  - iii) His use of the authentic cadence gives the effect of finality much more than had been the custom in the past

                                                                         ReeMR, 355
- (l) His respond motets are in the typical aBcB form   ReeMR, 353
  - i) Examples are *Angelus Domini,* and *Jerusalem surge*
    - a - Transcriptions of *Angelus Domini*

                              ComB, I, 29; CleO, IX, 99; CleO, XIII, 1
    - b - A transcription of *Jerusalem surge*   CleO, XIII, 62
- (m) Other sources of his motets
  - i) A facsimile   TheM
  - ii) Transcriptions   CleO, III, IX, XII-XXI; ComB

(5) Pierre de Manchicourt [b. ca. 1510]   ReeMR, 351
- (a) Manchicourt belonged to the conservative branch of the Netherland school   BriL, 234
  - i) He remained faithful to the style of those who had gone before him
- (b) His technique in counterpoint seems to have too often served him instead of inspiration   BriL, 234
  - i) His motet *Ave Virgo Cecilia* is an example   BriL, 235
    - a - The value of this motet lies chiefly in the skill with which Manchicourt uses constant double counterpoint
      - 1 - This was done in the imitative treatment of two themes in each section
    - b - A transcription of *Ave Virgo Cecilia*   ManMV
- (c) Through imitation is employed except for a homophonic opening in *Peccantem me*   DobM, 221
  - i) A transcription of *Peccantem me*   ManMV
- (d) The motet, *Pater peccavi*, is an example of an instance using a tonal answer
  - i) It deals with the return of the Prodigal Son
  - ii) A transcription of *Pars I*   StrLM, VIII, opp. p. 62
  - iii) A transcription of *Pater peccavi*   ManMV
- (e) *Ave Virgo Cecilia* is a good example of the Netherlandish style

rather than the French ReeMR, 351
  i) It is an unusual work
    a - There are five points each involving paired imitation on two motifs
      1 - Each voice states the first motif assigned to it and then reworks the material originally stated by the voice that is paired with it
        a - This is done in all points except the second
      2 - The two upper voices of the final point, after reworking such material, enter for a third time, restating their original motifs
    b - A transcription of *Ave Virgo Cecilia* ManMV
 (f) Other sources of his motets
  i) Facsimiles GarF; ModS; ManL; ManLD; ModT
  ii) Transcriptions AttQL; ManM; ManMP; ManMV

4. The Roman Catholic motet UlrH, 144
 a) General style of the Roman catholic motet
  (1) It is likely that Rome, as the center of the Christian world, had to be conservative in attitude
    (a) This attitude remained through the entire sixteenth century
  (2) A distinct Roman style did not develop until well into the fifteen hundreds
    (a) Perhaps this was due to the presence of many eminent foreign musicians-Flemish and Spanish for the most part
  (3) "The Roman sacred style represents in a sense the amalgamation of many foreign styles"
 b) Composers of the Roman Catholic motet
  (1) Costanzo Festa [b. ca. 1490]
    (a) More than forty of his motets survive ReeMR, 362
    (b) Festa set a tradition of smoothness, euphony, and unadventurousness that was later inherited by Palestrina CoaP, 3
    (c) Many of his works use pervading imitation but he is not absorbed by the technique ReeMR, 362
      i) "He writes chordally with equal readiness or merely suggests pervading imitation or employs non-imitative counterpoint"
      ii) His works abound in parallel thirds, sixths, and tenths
      iii) An example of a chordal setting is his four-voice Te Deum
        a - This setting is tied closely to the liturgical chant which is carried throughout by the *superius* PerMR, 571
        b - The polyphony begins with the second verse, therefore it must be preceded by the initial phrase of the text sung in plainchant PerMR, 571
        c - A transcription of the Te Deum FesO, III
    (d) His *Regem Regum* incorporates part of the Litany of the Saints ReeMR, 362
      i) Each petition and acclamation throughout the work is accorded special treatment
        a - Some are set chordally and others are given duos of the

upper and lower pairs
- b - "Still others are embellished with imitative polyphony"
- ii) The entire motet is in two *partes* and is unified by a refrain
- iii) A transcription of *Regem Regum*   FesO, V
- (e) Festa uses the same contrast of textures as found in his *Regem Regum* in his *Regem archangelorum*   ReeMR, 363
  - i) A transcription of *Regem archangelorum*   FesO, V
- (f) Other sources of his motets
  - i) Facsimiles   GarMT; MotC; MotCL
  - ii) Transcriptions   FesS; FesO, III-V

(2) Cristóbal de Morales [b. ca. 1500]
- (a) Morales should be considered the Roman-Spanish musician who, in advance of his age, anticipated the spirit and liturgical-artistic ideals presented by the Council of Trent   AngS, 387
  - i) He prepared the way for Palestrina
- (b) He was a singer in the papal chapel from 1535 to 1545   AngS, 382
- (c) He took advantage of the opportunity his stay in Rome offered to show the world what he could do   AngS, 382
  - i) Some of his motets were published in Lyons and some Masses were published in Venice and Rome
- (d) For a discussion of his motets, *infra*, p. 252

(3) Jacques Arcadelt [b. ca. 1514]
- (a) Arcadelt was an Italianized Netherlander who was master of the Sistine Chapel from 1539 or 1540 to 1545 and again from 1547 to 1552   CoaP, 313
  - i) He was probably French and most likely a member of the circle around Verdelot in the early part of his life   SeaA, 546
- (b) He wrote twenty-four motets   ArcM, ix
  - i) Most of his religious music comes from early in his career
  - ii) His style was smooth, euphonious, and unadventurous   CoaP, 313
    - a - An example is his *O sacrum convivium*
      - 1 - A transcription of *O sacrum convivium*   MalTR, XX, 3
- (c) Some manuscripts in the Sistine archives and a book of motets published at Venice are probably works belonging to this period of his career   ReeMR, 364
  - i) A list of the motets in the Sistine archives   EitBQ, I, 187
- (d) Other sources of his motets
  - i) Facsimiles   GarF; ModS; ModT; GarMD
  - ii) Transcriptions   OstD; ArcM

5. The Venetian motet
   a) Introduction   RedV, 276
   - (1) After the death of Leo X in 1521 and still more after the sack of Rome in 1527, Venice became more important as a center of European music
     - (a) And in Venice, even church music took on a secular colouring

(2) In the late 1520s, Adrian Willaert, the greatest personality in the history of Venetian music, first appeared
b) Composers of the Venetian motet
   (1) Adrian Willaert [b. ca. 1490]
      (a) "His fame as a composer rests largely on his motets"   ReeMR, 371
         i) He wrote more than 170 of them   PerMR, 510
         ii) There are fewer than ten Masses
      (b) His motets are both sacred and secular   RedV, 283
         i) The sacred motets are usually based on plainsong tenors   RedV, 283
            a - The four-part *Pater noster* is typical of Willaert's insistence on the liturgical tenor and his tendency to low sonorities   RedV, 284
               1 - Transcriptions of *Pater noster*   WilO, II, 10; AmbG V, 538; SliG II, 29
      (c) It is in his motets and psalms that a polychoral medium is implied   UlrH, 153
         i) Willaert has been regarded as the chief founder, if not the actual inventor, of the so-called *coro spezzato*   RedV, 276
         ii) But, research has shown that he only perfected an already existing choral practice, particularly at home in northern Italy   RedV, 276
      (d) Willaert was especially known for his expressive declamation with marked accentuation   RedV, 283
         i) He was concerned with correct declamation not only with dramatic texts but also in works that treat words free of dramatic import   ReeMR, 374
         ii) The four-part *Pater noster* is a good example of correct declamation   ReeMR, 374
            a - For example, in the *Ave Maria* each *pars* is an elaboration of the Gregorian melody of the text
            b - And, although it is polyphonic, the elaboration is sufficiently restrained so as not to interfere with good declamation
            c - Transcriptions of *Pater noster*   WilO, II, 10; AmbG V, 538; SliG II, 29
      (e) Willaert adopted the Venetian cult of harmony and colour while keeping the northern polyphonic element   RedV, 283
      (f) Willaert would vary his treatment of each section of a sequence melody upon its repetition and thus produce what may have been called variation-chain sequences   ReeMR, 372
         1) This technique may have been a Josquin invention   ReeMR, 251
         ii) The following settings are good examples of the technique
            a - *Verbum bonum et suave*
               1 - A transcription   WilO, IV, 16
            b - *Benedicta es coelorum Regina*
               1 - A transcription   WilO, I, 78
            c - *Salve, crux sancta*

			1 - A transcription	WilO, I, 83
		d -	*Inviolata, integra*	
			1 - A transcription	WilO I, 95
		e -	*Veni, Sancte Spiritus*	
			1 - A transcription	WilO V, 88
		f-	*Victimae paschali laudes*	
			1 - A transcription of the *Prima pars*	DavH, 116

    (g) The Netherlandish technique is found in his skillful use of canon
                                                                                                    ReeMR, 372
        i) An example is a setting of *Ave Regina coelorum, Mater
            Regis* for four voices   ReeMR, 372
            a - Willaert wrote the two upper voices in skillful canon at
               the fifth below while the two lower voices sometimes
               share the thematic material of the canon, at times intro-
               ducing it in anticipatory imitation
            b - Transcriptions of *Ave Regina coelorum, MaterRegis*
                                                                        WilA; WilO, II, 34
    (h) Willaert was also influenced by the French   WilO, I, ii
        i) He incorporated the Gallic precision, sprightliness, and
            rationalism into his music
    (h) Other sources of his motets
        i)   Facsimiles   GarF; ModP; ModS; ModT; WilD; WilDP
        ii)   Transcriptions   WilO, I-IV
(2) Cipriano de Rore [b. 1516]
    (a) Rore's motets show an evolutionary curve leading from the tradi-
        tion of Flemish polyphony to a more homophonic structure
                                                                                                     RedV, 291
        i)   They occasionally contain syllabic declamation   RedV, 291
        ii) They also show a greater subjectivism in the sense of the ten-
            dencies of the Italian Renaissance
    (b) But, his motets still abound in traditional Netherland polyphony
                                                                                                     RedV, 291
    (c) Rore shows skill in illustrating the pictorial or expressive features
        of the text by so-called musical *figures*   RorC, vol. I, i
        i)   An example is *Illuxit nunc sacra dies*   RorC, vol. I, iii
            a - The words are emphasized by rapidly ascending move-
                 ment or high position
            b - A transcription of *Illuxit nunc sacra dies*   RorC, I, 152
    (d) His motets are found in three separate motet books   ReeMR, 376
        i)   Book I of 1544 [*Motectorum ...liber primus quinque vocum*],
            Book II [*Motetta... quinque vocum*] of 1545 , and Book III
            [*Il terzo libro di motetti a cinque voci*] of 1549
            a - They all contain motets for five voices   RedV, 291
            b - They were published by Gardano   RorC, I, i
            c - Only Book II contains motets by Rore exclusively
                                                                                           RorC, I, i
            d - A list of all the motets published in the three books
                                                                                          RorC, I, i
        ii) Book I contains seven of Rore's motets

					a - These seven motets are in the older Franco-Flemish style
						1 - But, there is an occasional appearance of short passages of syllabic declamation showing evidence of Willaert's Italianate modern style
					b - A facsimile of Book I GarM
				iii) Book II of 1545 is devoted entirely to Rore
					a - In this book, Rore pays more attention in a single work to grouping the voices in varying smaller combinations
						1 - An example is found in the motet, *Beatus homo*
							a - A transcription of *Beatus homo* RorC, I, 34
					b - A facsimile of Book II RorMN
				iv) Book III of 1549 shows some notably sensitive handling of the text
					a - A good example is found in *Infelix ego*
						1 - This was published in the second set of *Sacrae Cantiones* of 1595 ReeMR, 376
						2 - A facsimile of *Sacrae Cantiones* RorS II
					b - Facsimiles of four motets ScoP
						1 - Three of these motets are from Book III RorC, I, i- ii
					c - A facsimile of Book III GarI
				v) Transcriptions of Rore's three motet books RorC, I
			(e) Twenty-six of his motets are found in the Rore codex of Munich, *Cipriani de Rore et aliorum auctorum motetae* for four voices (1563) RedV, 287
				i) The codex was lavishly illustrated by the miniatures of the Bavarian court-painter Hans Mielich
				ii) A photocopy of eighty-two pages of Rore's original Latin manuscript with the illuminations OweL, vol. II
				iii) A facsimile of the original manuscript RorM
			(f) Rore's motets are also found in *Sacrae Cantiones seu Moteti ut vocant, non minus instrumentis quam vocibus aptae* (1573 and 1595) RedV, 291
				i) A facsimile of the 1573 edition RorS I
				ii) A facsimile of the 1595 edition RorS II

6. The Florentine motet
	a) General style of the Florentine motet
		(1) A similar style to that of Festa was employed in Florence during the same period CoaP, 313
			(a) The style consisted of smoothness, euphony, and unadventurousness
	b) Composers of the Florentine motet
		(1) Philippe Verdelot [b. ?]
			(a) In 1529, Attingnant printed two motets by Verdelot under the name of Philippe Deslouges, therefore, the name Verdelot was possibly a pseudonym DenS, 38
			(b) Verdelot is famous for his madrigals but most of his church music lies in oblivion RedV, 276
			(c) Some of his motets are thought to reveal his adherence to Savona-

250 Sacred Latin Music for the Catholic Church on the Continent

      rolian, and hence republican, principles   SliG I, 55
     i) One such motet is, *In te, Domine, speravi*
       a - The text was one of Savonarola's favorite psalms
       b - A transcription of *In te, Domine, speravi* SliG II, 140
  (d) One motet possibly indicates that Verdelot remained in Florence
     during the siege in 1529 to 1530   SliG I, 56
    i) *Congregati sunt inimici nostri*
      a - It "seems to be a patchwork formed from parts of Ecclesiaticus (Sirach), the close of the Antiphon for Peace, and from various psalms"
      b - It is bound together by a *cantus firmus* with the text of the Antiphon for Peace, *Da pacem Domine*
      c - The melody is a free version of the chant melody
      d - A transcription of *Congregati sunt inimici nostri*
                           SliG II, 280
  (e) In the opening of Verdelot's four-voice *Ave sanctissima Maria*, there are tonal answers between the *altus* and the *superius* and the tenor and bass   ReeMR, 365
    i) Tonal answers were increasingly used as composers abandoned the relics of the modal system and veered toward major and minor   ReeMR, 351
    ii) A transcription of the four-voice *Ave sanctissima Maria*
                           AttTL, II, 182
    iii) There is also a three voice *Ave sanctissima Maria* that was expanded into six voices and attributed to Verdelot
                          ReeMR, 269
      a - A transcription of the six-voice *Ave sanctissima Maria*
                         AttTL, III, 166
  (f) Verdelot's motet *Gabriel archangelus* has each voice enter with a descending leap of a fifth   ReeMR, 365
    i) This produces real answers
    ii) A transcription of *Gabriel archangelus*   AttTL, I, 99
  (g) Other sources of his motets
    i) Facsimiles   GarMD; FioM; GarF; ModP; ModS
    ii) Transcriptions AttTL, I, II, III, IV, X, XI; VerO II, III; AmbG, III, 293-4; MalTR, XXIII, 26; XXVIII, 8; SliG II

7. The Mantuan motet
 a) Composers of the Mantuan motet
  (1) Jacquet of Mantua (=Jachet of Mantua) [b. ca. 1495]   PriN, 151
    (a) He uses alternating points of imitation and homophony within a four-voice framework
      i) This is in the style of the Josquin period
    (b) He writes in a relatively seamless style of pervasive imitation within a five-voice framework
      (d) He employs voice-pairing and tonal answer   ReeMR, 367
    (c) He handles canon and conflict of accents with taste and skill
                           ReeMR, 367
    (d) He writes chordal passages with eloquent effect   ReeMR, 367

(e) Four of his motets were used by Palestrina for his Masses
ReeMR, 366
    i) *Aspice Domine*
        a - A facsimile of *Aspice Domine*   ScoMQ, no. 6
           1 - *Aspice Domine* is attributed to Claudin in other sources   BerCA, 237
        b - A transcription of *Aspice Domine*   MonO, XXVI
           1 - *Aspice Domine* is wrongly ascribed to Berchem in this source
    ii) *Salvum me fac*
        a - A facsimile of *Salvum me fac*   ScoMS, no. 14
    iii) *Spem in alium*
        a - A facsimile of *Spem in alium*   ScoMQ, no. 19
    iv) *Repleatur os meum*
        a - This motet consists of a canon for two in the highest voices   ReeMR, 366
        b - The melody of the canon is imitated and freely elaborated by the three lower voices
           2 - At least one of these voices always anticipates the canonic pair
        c - An example of *Repleatur os meum*   ReeMR, 367
        d - Facsimiles of *Repleatur os meum*   ScoMS, no. 20; GarMF; GarMP
        e - A transcription of *Repleatur os meum*   LewG
(f) Other sources of his motets
    i) Facsimiles   GarMT; GarPL; GarQ; GarMQ; GarMTV; ScoMS; ScoMQ
    ii) Transcriptions   MerTL; JacPL; JacPLM

8. The Central European motet
    a) General style of the Central European motet
        (1) Music in Germany in the early sixteenth century was influenced by Heinrich Isaac who founded a school of composers   RedC, 253
            (a) These composers disseminated the principles of his style throughout the sixteenth century
            (b) Many of them served as choirboys under him and members of the Imperial Court Chapel or as singers in the cathedral choir at Constance
    b) Composers of the Central European motet
        (1) Ludwig Senfl [b. ca. 1490]   ReeMR, 690
            (a) He was a part of the older group who display the psychological and religious peculiarities of the German mind at the time of Luther's advent   RedC, 253
                i) Luther was an admirer of Senfl and wrote to him on 4 October 1530, asking him to compose a motet on the tenor *In pace in idipsum*   RedC, 256
            (b) Senfl used a considerable degree of freedom in his use of quickly changing points of imitation   DavH, 228
                i) An example of this is his *Salutatio prima*

                        a - A transcription of *Salutatio prima*   DavH, 113
            (c) *Ave rosa sine spinis*
                i) This is a particularly fine motet based on the tenor of *Comme femme* [*desconfortée*, a *chanson* by Binchois] undoubtedly via Josquin's *Stabat Mater*   ReeMR, 290
                ii) A transcription of *Ave rosa sine spinis*   AmbG V, 385
            (d) Transcriptions of his motets   SenS
9. The Spanish motet
    a) General style of the Spanish motet
        (1) Spanish composers continued composing in the Flemish style   DavH, 231
        (2) But the Flemish style was colored to a certain extent by national characteristics
            (a) Spanish music was distinguished by its natural and extremely simple technique   AngS, 375
                i) It was also noted for its austerity and dramatic mysticism that evoke a higher degree of spiritual feeling than that of the *a cappella* polyphony of other European schools
            (b) Spanish composers frequently adopted a subjective, and at times even dramatic, expression   DavH, 231
    b) Composers of the Spanish motet
        (1) Cristóbal de Morales [b. ca. 1500]   ReeMR, 591
            (a) He was the first Spanish composer to succeed in giving his work an international character   AngS, 382
                i) He was able to break out of the closed circle and isolation in which Spanish musicians lived
                ii) Many of his motets were published during his Roman stay and were written presumably in Italy   ReeMR, 591
            (b) It is in his motets that he reaches the highest peaks of technique and emotion   AngS, 385
            (c) His music is surrounded by an air of mysticism, especially in works whose text express somber thoughts
                i) An example of this is the motet, *Emendemus in melius*
                    a - The four outer voices proceed with the main text while at the same time, the tenor reiterates six times on a severe, stark melodic line, "Remember, man, that thou art dust..."
                        1 - The same melody was used for these words all six times   TreC, 23
                        2 - The text of the four outer voices is the Ash Wednesday response, *Emendemus*   ReeMR, 591
                    b - A facsimile of *Emendemus in melius*   EslL, 109
                    c - Transcriptions of *Emendemus in melius*
                             PedH, 29; DavH, 138; MorO, VIII, 73
            (d) It seems that Morales liked having one voice sing a text different from but relevant to that given to the others as seen in *Emendemus in melius*   ReeMR, 591
                i) This technique is also found in the six-part *Pater peccavi*
                    a - The tenor II sings the Lord's Prayer in long notes as the other voices proceed with the words of the Prodigal Son

                    b - A facsimile of *Pater peccavi*   ElúA, 52
            ii)   Another example is found at the beginning of the mainly four
                    voice motet, *Hoc est praeceptum*
                    a - "A fifth voice twice invokes a saint to 'pray for us'"
                    b - A facsimile of *Hoc est praeceptum*   ElúA, 41
            iii)   This technique was not discovered by Morales   SteC, 17
                    a - He had learned it from a predecessor in the papal choir,
                        Jean Conseil (Consilium)
        (e) He had a tendency to have the voices sing in pairs and other small-
            er groups
            i)   Such as in the beginning of *Sancte Antoni* for four voices
                                                                          AmbG V, 595
                    a - Transcriptions of *Sancte Antoni*
                                                          AmbG V, 595; MorO, V, 86
        (f) The most celebrated motet by Morales is *Lamentabatur Jacob*
                                                                          ReeMR, 591
            i)   It has the same text in all five voices
            ii)   In this motet, Morales reaches the highest peak of technique
                    and emotion by his sense of drama   AngS, 385
            iii)   A facsimile of *Lamentabatur Jacob*   EslL, 119
            iv)   Transcriptions of *Lamentabatur Jacob*
                                                    PedH, 40; AraH, 243; MorO, II, 102
        (g) Two of his motets were published in Moderne's *Motetti del fiore* at
            Lyons in 1539   AngS, 382
            i)   A transcription of *Motetti del fiore: Quartus liber motteto-
                    rum ad quinque et six voces* (1539)   ModFI, pt. 1
        (h) A provisional list of his works   TreC, 28
        (i) Some Facsimiles of his works   ScoI; ScoL
        (j) Some Transcriptions of his works   MorO, II, V, VIII; ModT

F. **Performance Practices of Sacred Latin Music**

    1. Performance practices in Rome
        a) The papal choir normally oscillated between twenty-two and twenty-four
           singers   ReyR, 67
            (1) The *Nunc dimittis* and the antiphon *Lumen ad revelationem* on the
                Feast of the Purification of the Virgin (2 February) were sung in alter-
                nating chant and polyphony   BraT, 168
            (2) Vesper hymns were sung in alternating chant and polyphony on the ma-
                jor feasts over the whole year   BraT, 169
            (3) Lamentations were sung in alternating chant and polyphony during the
                Tenebrae services in Holy Week   BraT, 169
                (a) These are among the best known and most highly documented
                    parts of the polyphonic liturgy sung by the papal choir
                (b) Six lessons by Festa and three by Carpentras formed the core of
                    the Lamentation repertory sung by the papal choir until the late
                    1570s
            (4) All or part of the Mass Ordinary was sung in polyphony by the pontifical

    choir   BraT, 170
   (5) Motets and similar compositions were sung after the offertory   BraT, 172
  b) The charter of the Cappella Giulia called for twelve adult singers and twelve boys, a *maestro di cappella*, and a *magister puerorum*   ReyR, 68
   (1) This was a model for subsequent chapels
   (2) In practice, there were seldom the number of boys indicated
   (3) The *maestro di cappella* was most often French or Flemish
  c) The Cappella Sistina had performance traditions of long standing   ReyR, 73
   (1) They sang chordal types of improvisation such as three-voice fauxbourdon and four-voice *falsobordone*   ReyR, 74
    (a) The latter type was particularly good for reciting psalms
     i) It was usually sung in alternation with chant, such as in the Magnificat and Lamentations   RanH, 298

2. Performance practices in Venice
  a) The double-choir psalms were sung from the same place; they were not separated   FenV, 114
   (1) Both choirs sang from the octagonal structure placed to the right of the iconostasis
    (a) This structure was commonly known as the *pulpitum magnum cantorum* or *bigonzo* ("tub")
   (2) They did not sing from the choir-lofts
    i) They may have sung from organ-lofts on rare occasions when large scale ceremonial pieces for three or four choirs were sung
   (3) The differentiation of the choirs rose from the fact that one choir consisted only of soloists
   (4) The polyphony was sung unaccompanied   ReyR, 75
  b) The performance of these double-choir psalms was not an everyday affair   FenV, 114
   (1) These psalms were only sung when the *pala d'oro* (the large gold altarpiece which is the major treasure of the basilica) was opened
    (a) This was done on the major feasts of the church year
  c) Usually the psalms were sung in plainchant until the middle of the sixteenth century   FenV, 114

3. Performance practices in Paris
  a) Approximately three dozen singers were employed in the chapel at the French court during the early 1530s   FreP, 179
   (1) These singers were divided into two principal groups
    (a) About one third of the singers were called simply *chantres*
     i) These singers were responsible for plainchant during the various regular services
    (b) The remaining singers were listed according to the range of their voices, that is contratenors, tenors, and basses
     i) This suggests that they, along with the choir boys for the soprano lines, specialized in the performance of polyphonic compositions
      a - These compositions included Masses, motets, and perhaps even *chansons*

4. Performance practices in religious plays
   a) Mystères and Miracles
      (1) These were plays with incidental music   BroMF, 42
         (a) They did not employ elaborate musical numbers nor a large performing force
         (b) The music served as an adjunct to the spectacle
      (2) Motets, *chansons*, plainsong, and instrumental pieces were used to make the dramas more impressive
         (a) The musical forces required to perform the music were a choir of angels singing the plainsong, soloists for part music, an organist associated with the chorus, a few trumpets and drums, a pipe and tabor, and one or two *haut* wind instruments   BroMF, 47
            i) This combination of performers could be varied   BroMF, 50

Sacred Music for the Reformed Church on the Continent

A. Introduction

1. The Protestant Reformation did not represent a single unified movement
   PerMR, 724
   a) The efforts to reform religious practice differed from region to region according to the local circumstances
      (1) The changes sought depended on the political situation
         (a) Secular rulers often viewed religious orthodoxy as an important ingredient in maintaining the established social order
   b) And these efforts "were usually shaped by the particular views of one or more of the leading figures active there"
      (1) These leaders did not always agree on all points   PerMR, 725
         (a) Martin Luther stressed the importance of music in the training of the clergy and in the curricula of the Latin schools
         (b) Ulrich Zwingli thought the music for liturgical purposes could not be justified by the scriptures and therefore banned music in the reformed churches under his direction and even had organs removed
         (c) John Calvin followed a middle ground between Luther and Zwingli
            i) He approved monophony for religious services but only when sung in the current vernacular by the entire congregation
   c) "These divergent views produced predictably different results where the cultivation of music was concerned"   PerMR, 725
      (1) In the three areas mentioned above and in Anglican England, musical practice followed its own course, therefore the traditional compositional types were affected very little in the early Protestant movement
      (2) It was the birth and development of musical genres, due in part to the concepts of public worship and the attitudes toward music, that were characteristic of Protestant communities

B. Lutheran Church Music at Wittenberg

1. Martin Luther created a liturgical and theological climate which enabled a new musical tradition to develop within "Lutheranism"   LeaL, 263

- a) He realized there was a need for a guide for all those who desired liturgical reform but did not know how and where to begin   LeuL, 9
  - (1) He addressed this concern in his publication, *Von ordenung gottis diensts ynn der gemeyne* of 1523
    - (a) In this publication, he provides a congregation with an order for singing, praying, and reading
      - I) He expressed a desire for as many songs as possible in the vernacular which the people could sing during the Mass after the Gradual and also after the Sanctus and Agnus Dei   LeuL, 36
    - (b) A translation of *Von ordenung gottis diensts ynn der gemeyne*   LeuL, 11
- b) Luther's main concern, insofar as the musical portion of his reforms are concerned, was to modify those portions of the Catholic liturgy which conflicted with evangelical teachings   UlrH, 159
  - (1) For churches in the larger cities, which had capable choirs and schools in which children were taught singing and the rudiments of Latin, Luther advocated the retention of the Latin Mass with some alterations and improvements
    - (a) The Offices, primarily Matins and Vespers, were to be retained
    - (b) The Ordinary of the Mass was retained but the Credo and Agnus Dei were omitted
  - (2) Where musical training did not exist, such as in the smaller communities and rural areas, Luther offered other modifications
    - (a) These modifications were merely suggestions; considerable latitude was allowed
      - i) Any Latin portions of the Mass could be substituted with German prose texts or songs
        - a - Generally, any prose item, whether in Latin or German, could be replaced by a song
      - ii) Appropriate songs could be added at various places in the service

2. Luther issued a revised form of the Catholic Latin Mass in 1523   LeaL, 267
   - a) This Latin Mass was presented in his *Formula missae et communionis pro Ecclesia Wittembergensi*
     - (1) A facsimile of *Formula missae...*   LutF
     - (2) A translation of *Formula missae...*   LeuL, 19
   - b) The following parts of the Mass were retained, and in some instances, revised
     - (1) A Psalm was still sung for the introit, except, instead of singing only a few verses, it was sung in its entirety
     - (2) The use of the Kyrie eleison was continued along with the various plain chant melodies for different seasons
       - (a) A transcription and translation of the Latin Kyrie as corrected and performed (without its collects) for the Lutheran Latin Mass   LeuL, 155
     - (3) Also, the Angelic Hymn, Gloria in excelsis, which follows the Kyrie was retained
     - (4) The Gradual of two verses, or the Alleluia, was sung   LeuL, 24

    (a) These could be sung together
    (b) Any Gradual with more than two verses should not be sung
      i) German *Lieder* were to be sung after the Gradual LeaL, 267
        a - This required music for psalms that had a specific place in the liturgy BluPR, 58
  c) The polyphonic settings and the traditional plainchant of the ordinary continued to be sung LeaL, 267
    (1) But, two radical musical departures were in the Lutheran Latin Mass LeaL, 267
      (a) The priest sang the Words of Institution
        i) The Words were usually inaudible in the Catholic Mass
        ii) Luther used the same melody for the Words of Institution as for the Gospel LeuL, 59
      (b) And, congregational song was to be added to the traditional music of the Mass
        i) Vernacular song was added after the Sanctus and Agnus Dei
        ii) This was a departure from the traditional Catholic Mass in which the music was performed by the priest and his assistants, the choir, the organ, and at times other instruments GérP, 420
  d) The sequence was rejected for Christmas BluPR, 57
    (1) Occasionally the sequence was kept for Good Friday, Easter, Pentecost, and a few other feast days
      (a) But, generally, only the shorter sequences are to be sung

3. In 1525 Luther summoned Conrad Rupsch and Johann Walther to Wittenberg to assist him in producing a German Mass ReeMR, 676
  a) The resulting Mass was Luther's *Deudsche Messe* published in 1526
    (1) Luther wrote that this Mass was arranged for the unlearned lay folk LeaL, 271
      (a) It was intended for the churches in small towns and villages where Latin was virtually unknown LeaL, 271
    (2) This Mass is a vernacular reformation with congregational participation RanH, 460
      (a) Luther composed vernacular hymns for it
      (b) He insisted that the text, notes, accent, melody, and movement of the music must come out of the correct mother tongue and voice BluPR, 60
        (1) His artistic sense protected him from the superficiality of merely placing the German text under the customary melody of the Latin piece
    (3) The German Mass differed radically from Luther's Latin Mass
      (a) The service was begun by singing a hymn or a German Psalm LeuL, 69
        i) In the *Deudsche Messe* the example used is Psalm 34, *Ich will den Herrn lben allezeit* GérP, 426
          a - It is set to music throughout in the first mode
          b - The first two phrases are repeated without alteration except for a few inflections

Lutheran Church Music at Wittenberg 259

       ii)   A translation and transcription of Psalm 34 in the First Tone
                                                                                                                 LeuL, 70

(b)   Then the Kyrie eleison followed in the same tone   LeuL, 72
       i)   It was reduced to threefold instead of nine-fold   BluPR, 60
              a - It could be omitted and be replaced with the German
                   congregational hymn, *Kyrie, Gott Vater in Ewigkeit*
                                                                                                            LeaL, 271
       ii)   A transcription of the Kyrie eleison chant
       iii)   A translation and transcription of the Kyrie eleison as per-
            formed in the German Mass   LeuL, 163
(c)   The Gloria was completely omitted or was fitted in as a translation
      of the Latin text or as a German *Lied*   BluPR, 60
       i)   The German translation of the Gloria is *All ehr und lob soll*
            Gottes sein   LeuL, 186
              a - It is probably by Luther and has the structure of an anti-
                   phonal chant
                   1 - The boys' choir would sing one verse and the congre-
                       gation would sing the others   LeuL, 185
                   2 - If the organ is played, it produced three choirs
                                                                           LeuL, 185
                       a - The organ formed one choir, the boys formed the
                           second, and the congregation formed the third
                       b - The organ began the process
              b - A translation and transcription of the Gloria in excelsis
                                                                               LeuL, 187
       ii)   The German *Lied* would have been *Allein Gott in der Höhe*
            sei Ehre   LeaL, 271
              a - The composer of this hymn was Nikolaus Decius   BusO, 4
                   1 - The hymn was composed in 1525
                   2 - The melody is based on the plainsong setting of the
                       Gloria in excelsis from the Mass of 1524 by Thomas
                       Muentzer
              b - The music is written in the form of an ordinary chorale
                   with four stanzas   LeuL, 184
              c - An harmonic arrangement of the tune by J. S. Bach
                                                                                BusO, no. 6
              d - A translation of *Allein Gott in der Höhe sei Ehre* [by
                   Catherine Winkworth, 1865]   BusO, 13
(d)   A Collect is read by the priest in a monotone on F-fa-ut followed
      by the chanting of the Epistle in the Eighth Tone   LeuL, 72
       i)   An example of a chant along with the rules for its perfor-
            mance   LeuL, 72-73
(e)   A German *Lied, Nun bitten wir den Heiligen Geist,* was sung after
      the Epistle   BluPR, 60
       i)   Luther had suggested this *Lied* although others could be sung
                                                                                                LeuL, 74
       ii)   The *Lied* was sung by the choir
              a - But sometimes the congregation would sing with the
                   choir   GérP, 426

		b -	The first stanza is from the twelfth century and the second and third stanzas were written by Luther in 1524 BusO, 5
		c -	The melody is from the thirteenth century and is found in Johann Walther's *Geystliche Gesangk Buchleyn* of 1524 BusO, 5
	iii)		A translation and transcription of [*Nun bitten wir den Heiligen Geist*] LeuL, 264
(f)	The Gospel is read in the Fifth Tone		LeuL, 74
	i)		But, according to Walther, Luther stated that the Gospel should be in the sixth mode GérP, 426
		a -	Luther probably had in mind the dramatic form of the Passion texts in which the words of different personages have different tones
	ii)		For the rules regarding the performance of the chant, *see* LeuL, 74
	iii)		An example of the Gospel chant for the Fourth Sunday in Advent LeuL, 76
(g)	After the Gospel the entire congregation sang the German affirmation of faith, *Wir glauben all an einen Gott* BluPR, 60
	i)		A translation and transcription of *Wir glauben all an einen Gott* LeuL, 272
(h)	The sermon on the Gospel follows		LeuL, 78
(i)	Then follows a paraphrase of the Lord's Prayer and an admonition to partake of the sacrament LeuL, 78
	i)		The text of the paraphrase
(j)	This is followed by the Office and Consecration		LeuL, 80
	i)		This is chanted
	ii)		A translation and transcription of the chant LeuL, 80
(k)	After the consecration, the sacrament is administered		LeuL, 81
	i)		During the administering of the sacrament the German Sanctus or the hymn, [*Gott sey gelobet und gebenedeiet*], or John Huss' hymn, [*Jesus Christus unser Heiland*] could be sung LeuL, 81
		a -	The German Sanctus was Luther's *Jesaja dem Propheten das geschah* BluPR, 60
		1 -	Luther composed both text (based on Isaiah 6, 1-4) and music for the German Sanctus GérP, 427
		2 -	A translation and transcription of the German Sanctus LeuL, 82
		b -	*Gott sey gelobet* was recommended by Luther for use after communion in his *Von ordenung gottis diensts ynn der gemeyne* of 1523 LeuL, 252
		1 -	The hymn appeared in the *Geystliche Gesangk Buchleyn* of 1524 without music LeuL, 252
		2 -	It also appeared in the *Erfurt Enchiridia* without music LeuL, 252
		3 -	A translation and transcription of *Gott sey gelobet* LeuL, 253
		c -	The German text of *Jesus Christus, unser Heiland* was by

Martin Luther and the Latin text, *Jesus Christus, Nostra Salus* was written by John Huss (ca. 1369-1415) BusO, 8

          1 - This hymn appeared first in the *Geystliche Gesangk Buchleyn* of 1524   LeuL, 249

          2 - The melody is from the thirteenth century and was published in the *Erfurter Enchiridien* [the same year]   BusO, 8

          3 - A translation and transcription of [*Jesus Christus unser Heiland*]   LeuL, 250

    (l) Then during the administering of the cup the remainder of the hymns listed above or the German Agnus Dei is sung   LeuL, 82

        i) The German Agnus Dei was the canticle, *Christe, du Lamm Gottes*   GérP, 427

        ii) A translation and transcription of the Agnus Dei [*Christe, du Lamm Gottes*]   LeuL, 152

    (m) The collect and benediction follow   LeuL, 84

        i) The text of the collect and benediction   LeuL, 84

(4) In the original printing of the *German Mass*, the music is written in German or hobnail notation   LeuL, 57

    (a) There are only two notes: the punctum ◆ and the distropha in the form ◊◊ or ◊◊

(5) Luther did not attempt to impose his plan on the other communities which supported him   GérP, 428

    (a) The towns, villages, and religious institutions of the different states were in complete freedom to organize the liturgy according to their means

(6) The first completely German service was held in Wittenberg on October 29, 1525   LeuL, 60

(7) A facsimile of the *Deutsche Messe...*   LutD

(8) A translation of the *Deutsche Messe...*   LeuL, 53

4. General style of the texts and music for the reformed church
  a) Monophonic hymns
    (1) The texts of the monophonic hymns
      (a) Luther wanted vernacular songs for the congregation to sing during Mass   LeaL, 267

        i) Hymns in the vernacular had been tolerated by the church from the early Middle Ages   LeuL, 195

          a - These hymns were sung at pilgrimages and processions and for special occasions, such as, the great festivals of the church year, and sometimes at Mass

        ii) But, Luther wished to find poets who would write new hymns in a proper devotional style   LeuL, 191

        iii) He provided prototypes of what he had in mind   RanH, 158

          a - He thought the texts for congregational song should be strophic in form, metrical in style and in the vernacular

            1 - Many are in the bar form with each strophe of text consisting of two lines for each *Stollen* and three for the *Abgesang*

            b - But, some of Luther's texts sound more like prose than
                poetry   LeuL, 197
                1 - They lack metric regularity and the mellow flow of
                    words
                2 - They were meant to convey a message and not to
                    create a mood   LeuL, 197
                3 - They were a confession of the Lutheran faith and
                    were written to be sung by the congregation
            c - He adapted texts and tunes from many different sources
                and composed some of them himself
                1 - He composed thirty-four *Lieder* taken from the
                    Psalms, Gregorian seasonal hymns, antiphons, the
                    Mass Ordinary, German sacred song, and non-liturgical Latin hymns
                    a - The tunes were adapted and readapted from the
                        same sources or composed on similar models
    (2) The music of the monophonic hymns
        (a) The music used in the Lutheran Church represented in some ways
            an official recognition and intensification of practices begun spontaneously in many parts of Germany long before Luther
                                                                    ReeMR, 673
            i) Actually, the kind of music used in the liturgy produced little
                that may be regarded as constituting a specifically Protestant
                musical style
        (b) Except for the polyphonic collections, the hymnbooks offered only
            the melody line   LeuL, 202
            i)   The melody was usually in the range of the male voice
            ii) The majority of the melodies are modal in character
                                                                    LeuL, 203
                 a - But some savor strongly of the modern major scale
            iii) Sometimes the melodies contain amazingly complicated
                 rhythmical structures   LeuL, 203
                 a - They contain syncopations and rhythmical anticipations
                                                                    LeuL, 204
                     1 - This practice may have been the result of "dressing
                         up" plain melodies to serve as tenors in polyphonic
                         settings
                 b - It is very likely that congregations sang the melodies in
                     far simpler rhythms   LeuL, 204
            iv) "The beat of the music was fairly rapid"   LeuL, 205
        (c) Luther was concerned that the accents and the melody of the *Lied*
            should agree with the natural accents of the syllables MatG, 256
        (d) "Each hymn was given its own proper tune or tunes, though certain
            tunes were matched with several hymns"   LeuL, 201
            i) Some were original while others were adaptations of plainsong melodies and secular *Lieder*   HugH, 168
b) Polyphonic hymns
    (1) The texts of the polyphonic hymns
        (a) The relationship of word and music, stressed by Luther for mono-

phonic music, was nonexistent in Luther's concept of polyphonic music as he considered the music to be conceived primarily as an objective, ornamental decoration of the text   MatG, 261
- i) This was true except for the tenor voice   BluPR, 73
- ii) It was kept in the strict traditional manner required by its liturgical sense as the bearer of the divine Word   BluPR, 73

(2) The music of the polyphonic hymns
- (a) Every year more and larger [polyphonic] hymn collections were published   LeuL, 193
  - i) But, relatively speaking, there were very few polyphonic *Lied* settings   BluPR, 105
- (b) These polyphonic pieces were developed from the *Lied* melodies   HugH, 168
  - i) The *Lied* melody is given to the tenor while the other three voices may have active figuration, or may move chordally with the *Lied*
    - a - The tenor moves in basic, quiet, broad rhythmic values and the other voices move in a lively rhythm   BluPR, 73
    - b - This is true in compositions for four or more voices   BluPR, 73
  - ii) In pieces with two or three voices, the melody was placed in the middle or lower part   BluPR, 73
    - a - On rare occasions the melody was placed in the upper part
  - iii) At times there are imitative passages   UlrH, 161
    - a - This is usually found at the beginning of compositions   BluPR, 73
  - iv) The *Lieder* have free treatment of the harmony and rhythm   UlrH, 161

5. The sources used for the development of new vernacular music for the Protestant service
    a) The Latin hymn
    - (1) The most important hymns were taken over with their melodies and left in their customary place in the Liturgy   BluPR, 15
    - (2) The following are examples of hymns taken from the Catholic Church   BluPR, 15
        - (a) *Veni redemptor gentium* became *Nun komm, der Heiden Heiland*
            - i) There are pre-Reformation German translations of this Advent hymn from the fourteenth century
                - a - They are probably very much older
            - ii) *Veni redemptor gentium* was originally an Ambrosian Christian hymn   LutH, 16
                - a - Luther made a new translation of it
                    - 1 - This was done sometime between 1523 and 1524   BluPR, 41
                - b - He translates it quite literally except in the last stanza where he substitutes a doxology for the original words   LeuL, 235

			c - He made skillful changes in the melodic line	LeuL, 235

        iii)   *Nun komm, der Heiden Heiland* is in the *Erfurt Enchiridia* of 1524   LeuL, 236
            a - It is also in Walther's Wittenberg hymnal [*Geystliche Gesangk Buchleyn*]
        iv)   A translation and transcription of *Nun komm, der Heiden Heiland*   LeuL, 236
    (b) *Veni creator spiritus* became *Komm Gott Schöpfer, heiliger Geist*   BluPR, 15
        i)   *Veni creator spiritus* comes from Rhabanus Maurus who lived ca. 780-856   BusO, 7
            a - There are pre-Reformation German translations from the twelfth century or probably earlier   BluPR, 15
        ii)   It was translated by Luther   LutH, 24
            a - This was done sometime between 1523 and 1524   BluPR, 41
            b - He exchanged the third and fourth stanzas and omitted the sixth   LeuL, 260
        iii)   It was published in the *Erfurt Enchiridia* of 1524   LeuL, 261
        iv)   The melody was adapted from an ancient plainsong by Luther in 1529   BusO, 7
        v)   Two different transcriptions and a translation of *Komm Gott Schöpfer, heiliger Geist*   LeuL, 261
    (c) *A solis ortus cardine* became *Christum wir sollen loben schon*   BluPR, 15
        i)   *A solis ortus cardine* was translated by Luther in 1524
            a - The original came from Coelius Sedulius ca. 450   BusO, 7
        ii)   Luther reversed the first and second halves of the first stanza so that the name of Jesus stands at the head of the hymn   LeuL, 237
        iii)   The melody is pre-Reformation and anonymous   BusO, 7
            a - The hymn is found in Walther's *Geystliche Gesangk Buchleyn*
            b - There is a simplified version in Klug's *Geistliche Lieder* of 1529   BusO, 7
        iv)   A translation and three different transcriptions of *Christum wir sollen loben schon*   LeuL, 238
    (d) *Te Deum laudamus* became *Herr Gott, dich loben wir*   BluPR, 15
        i)   Pre-Reformation translations are documented from the ninth century
        ii)   It was also translated by Luther in 1529
            a - He published a rimed paraphrase ca. 1529 and in 1538 he offered a prose translation   LeuL, 171
        iii)   A translation, transcription, and indications for performance of the Te Deum [*Herr Gott, dich loben wir*]   LeuL, 174
  b) Chants derived from the Catholic church   ReeMR, 674
    (1) Introduction
        (a) The Latin texts were translated into German, sometimes by Luther
        (b) Sometimes the melodies remained the same and at other times a

new melody was supplied
- i) At times the old melody became so altered that it became unrecognizable
- (c) The chant was much closer to the hymn in musical style than it is today LeuL, 149
  - i) And the modal tonality and floating rhythm of the hymns were much closer to plain chant than our modern hymns
- (d) The extended intonations and mediations of the chants were more syllabic and melodious than that found in proper Gregorian psalmody LeuL, 149
- (2) The traditional sequence BluPR, 16
  - (a) It was used to a lesser degree than the hymn, mainly because of its florid melodies and complicated textual structure
    - i) Also, there was a Lutheran hostility toward the genre due to the excessive production of sequences and sequence-like pieces in the late Middle Ages for Marian and saints' feasts
  - (b) Examples of sequences taken from the Catholic Church
    - i) *Media vita in morte sumus* which Luther translated as *Mitten wir im Leben sind* ReeMR, 674
      - a - Luther translated the sequence sometime between 1523 and 1524 BluPR, 41
        - 1 - He altered the character of the hymn as a whole LeuL, 274
        - 2 - He also expanded it BluPR, 17
      - b - The melody used for this sequence was so altered from the original that it became unrecognizable
      - c - A translation and transcription of *Mitten wir im Leben sind* LeuL, 275
        - 1 - This is the tune from [the *Geystliche Gesangk Buchleyn* of 1524 by Walther]
    - ii) [*Veni, Sancte Spiritus*] became *Komm, Heiliger Geist, Herre Gott* BluPR, 17
      - a - *Veni, Sancte Spiritus* was translated in pre-Reformation times and is associated with a hymn-like melody
      - b - Luther translated it into German sometime between 1523 and 1524 BluPR, 41
        - 1 - He left the original verse practically intact, but added two stanzas LeuL, 265
        - 2 - The two extra stanzas are a free imitation and amplification of *Veni, Sancte Spiritus, reple tuorum corda fidelium* BluPR, 17
      - c - A translation and transcription of *Komm, Heiliger Geist, Herre Gott* LeuL, 266
        - 1 - This melody is found in the *Erfurt Enchiridia*
- c) The Passion
  - (1) Johann Walther adapted the Latin Passion tones to the requirements of German RanH, 612
    - (a) He set Martin Luther's translation of the Vulgate narratives (St. Mathew and St. John)

- (b) "It was customary to have the parts of the evangelist, of Christ, and of all other persons sung by different clerics and on different reciting notes" LeuL, 59
  - (a) The reciting notes were middle *c* for the evangelist's words, lower *f* for Christ, and high *f* for all other persons
- (c) Some Passion music by Walther is found in *Selectae Harmoniae quatuor vocum de passione Domini* published by Georg Rhau in 1538 LeuL, 321
- d) Non-liturgical pieces (in Latin or in a mixture of Latin and German) ReeMR, 674
  - (1) Some of these pieces were already centuries old in the time of Luther
  - (2) Some examples of these pieces are:
    - (a) *Dies est laetitiae* became *Der tag der ist so freudenreich*
      - i) It had been a Latin *Lied* since the early fifteenth or late fourteenth century BluPR, 18
      - ii) When it was translated into German, the verse *Ein Kindelein so löbelich* was added and in turn became the beginning verse of a new *Lied* with the same melody BluPR, 18
      - iii) A translation of *Der tag der ist so freudenreich* and a harmonized version of the melody BusO, no. 101
    - (b) *Puer natus in Bethlehem* became *Ein Kind geborn zu Bethlehem* ReeMR, 674
      - i) It originated in the thirteenth century BluPR, 18
        - a - It was translated from the Latin into German by Heinrich von Laufenberg in 1439
      - ii) A translation of *Ein Kind geborn zu Bethlehem* and a harmonized version of the melody BusO, no. 90
    - (c) *Resonet in laudibus* became *Singet frisch und wohlgemut* ReeMR, 674
      - i) This German version is perhaps older than the original Latin version BluPR, 18
        - a - The Latin version originated in the fourteenth century
      - ii) *Singet frisch und wohlgemut* appears as *Joseph, lieber Joseph mein* in Johann Walther's *Gesangbuch* of 1544
      - iii) Another German translation is *O Jesu liebes Herrlein mein* BluPR, 18
    - (d) *In dulci jubilo* became *Nun singet und seid froh* ReeMR, 674
      - i) This was originally a fourteenth century one-stanza dance song BluPR, 19
      - ii) In the fifteenth century, four stanzas appear in different dialect versions, *i.e.*, Low German and Dutch BluPR, 19
        - a - They appeared as a Protestant piece in Klug of 1533 [*Geistliche Lieder auffs new gebessert zu Wittemberg*] and in Bapst in 1545 [*Geystliche Lieder: mit einer newen vorrhede D. Mart. Luth.*]
          - 1 - In the latter, the order of stanzas has been changed and the words have "improved in a Christian manner" (the last stanza has the praise of Mary removed)
- e) Centuries old German religious songs ReeMR, 674

(1) The following songs had been used in many churches since the days of the *Geissler* (1349), but they had not been officially admitted as part of the liturgy
    (a) They were known as *Leisen* because of their common refrain "Kyrie eleison"   LeaL, 268
    (b) *Nun bitten wir den Heiligen Geist*
        i) Luther added three new stanzas to the original source   BluPR, 20
            a - He did this sometime between 1523 and 1524   BluPR, 41
        ii) The song was used between the Epistle and Gospel, during and after Communion; as an Introit *Lied* for Advent and Pentecost, before and after the sermon; and as a funeral song   BluPR, 20
        iii) The melody is found in Klug's [*Geistliche Lieder auffs new gebessert zu Wittemberg*] of 1533   LeuL, 263
            a - A different version of the melody is found in Walther's [*Geystliche Gesangk Buchleyn*] of 1524   LeuL, 263
        iv) Translation and transcription of *Nun bitten wir den Heiligen Geist*   LeuL, 264
            a - For the German text *see*   LutDM 35, 447-448
    (c) *Christ ist erstanden*
        i) This German folk melody was widely known by the thirteenth century and remained popular well into the eighteenth century   LeuL, 255
        ii) Luther "improved" the song in his *Lied, Christ lag in Todesbanden*   BluPR, 20
            a - This was done sometime between 1523 and 1524   BluPR, 41
            b - He used the melody of *Christ ist erstanden* as a pattern for his *Lied*
        iii) He rewrote the text, modeling it after the sequence, *Victimae paschali laudes*, making Christ's death and resurrection as one event   BluPR, 20
            a - The sequence, *Victimae paschali laudes*, had become a strong item in the Roman Easter liturgy by the fifteenth century
            b - The first three and one-half stanzas of Luther's text rehearse the Easter message and the other three and one-half give the application   LeuL, 255
            d - A translation and two transcriptions of [*Christ lag in Todesbanden*]   LeuL, 256
                1 - For the German text *see*   LutDM 35, 443-445
                2 - The first transcription appears in the *Erfurt Enchiridia* and in Walther's hymnal [*Geystliche Gesangk Buchleyn*] (his first setting of the hymn)   LeuL, 255
                3 - The second transcription forms the *cantus firmus* for the other two settings of the hymn in Walther's hymnal   LeuL, 255
    f) Centuries old songs with rewritten texts (*contrafacta*)   ReeMR, 674

(1) The old melodies were retained but the texts were rewritten to suit Protestant ideas
    (a) Several new texts could be written for the same melody   BluPR, 30
    (b) The distinction between sacred and secular music was vague and there was no hesitation in adapting sacred texts to secular melodies
    (c) The melody was usually one that was already popular and, therefore, was useful in disseminating new doctrine and in activating congregational participation in the musical service   BluPR, 29
(2) An example of *contrafactum* is *Vom Himmel hoch, da komm ich her*   ReeMR, 675
    (a) This Christmas hymn is entirely Luther's own   LeuL, 289
        i) He wrote it in 1534 or 1535
        ii) The text is based on the secular song, *Aus fremden Landen komm ich her*   ReeMR, 674
    (b) Luther intended this piece as a round dance for the Christmas manger play   BluPR, 30
    (c) It is thought that Luther also wrote the melody   LeuL, 289
        i) The melody has some of the same characteristics found in other melodies by Luther
    (d) A translation and transcription of *Vom Himmel hoch, da komm ich her*   LeuL, 290
        i) For the German text *see*   LutDM, 35, 459
(3) *Lied contrafacta* came to an end with the sixteenth century   BluPR, 34

g) Songs especially written for the Lutherans   ReeMR, 675
(1) Songs with texts by Luther
    (a) Some of these texts were original with Luther, some were translations from the Latin, and some were "parodies" of older texts
        i) The texts are based on Latin hymns and other liturgical pieces, on the Psalms and other passages in the Old and New Testament, and on pre-Reformation German sacred and secular *Lieder*   BluPR, 41
          a - Also, there are a few examples upon which the basis of the texts are still unknown
        ii) There are thirty-six texts   ReeMR, 675
    (b) Twelve of these *Lieder*, written between 1523 and 1524, are translations, *contrafacta*, paraphrases, or expansions of one-stanza pre-Reformation songs   BluPR, 41
        i) *Jesus Christus unser Heiland*
          a - This text is "improved" from a [Latin] communion hymn of John Huss, *Jesus Christus, Nostra Salus* and is in the Walther song-book of 1525 [the *Geystliche Gesangk Buchleyn*]   LutH, 30
            1 - The term "improved" refers to a complete theological revision, but as a whole, Luther's text has little in common with its Latin counterpart   LeuL, 249
            2 - The first, second, fourth, and sixth stanzas of Luther's text are reminiscent of the hymn by Huss   LeuL, 249
            3 - The hymn ascribed to John Huss had been known

              since the fifteenth century   LeuL, 249
         b - The Dorian melody is of pre-Reformation origin
                                                             LeuL, 249
         c - A translation and transcription of *Jesus Christus unser
              Heiland*   LeuL, 250
              1 - For the German text *see*   LutDM 35, 435-437
              2 - For the melody *see*   AmeK
              3 - The chorale is found in Walther's [*Geystliche Ge-
                   sangk Buchleyn*]   LeuL, 250
ii)   *Gelobet seist du, Jesu Christ*   BluPR, 41
         a - The text of the first stanza was based on the Sequence,
              Grates nunc omnes reddamus of the fourteenth century
                                                              BusO, 7
              1 - *Grates nunc omnes reddamus* is an ancient German
                   Christmas hymn   LutH, 20
         b - Six stanzas were added by Luther   LutH, 20
         c - The melody was adapted from a ca. 1400 plainsong
                                                              BusO, 7
         d - For the German text see   LutDM 35, 434-435
         e - A translation and transcription of *Gelobet seist du, Jesu
              Christ*   LeuL, 240
iii)   *Wir glauben all an einen Gott*   BluPR, 41
         a - This *Lied* was intended by Luther to be sung as the
              Creed during morning service   LutH, 46
         b - The text of Luther's hymn is based on an earlier medieval
              verse   LeuL, 271
              1 - He uses the first two lines of the original German text
              2 - But, his paraphrase of the three articles of the Creed
                   are his own
         c - The melody is the original medieval melody with a few
              significant changes   LeuL, 271
              1 - It is in this melody that the derivation from Gregorian
                   song can be clearly seen   AmeR, 7
         d - A translation and transcription of *Wir glauben all an
              einen Gott*   LeuL, 272
iv)   *Gott der Vater wohn uns bei*   BluPR, 41
         a - This was adapted from an ancient German Litany
                                                              LutH, 44
         b - It is a hymn of invocation of the Holy Trinity   LeuL, 268
              1 - It is patterned after medieval pilgrims' songs that in-
                   voked the aid of the saints
         c - Luther retained the first five lines with minor changes and
              replaced the appeal to the saints with an invocation of the
              three Persons of the Trinity   LeuL, 268
              1 - The concluding part he formed differently
         d - The melody was well known and Luther adopted it with-
              out change   LeuL, 268
         e - A translation and transcription of *Gott der Vater wohn
              uns bei*   LeuL, 270

                1 - For the German text *see*   LutDM 35, 450
                2 - The chorale is found in Walther's [*Geystliche Ge-
                    sangk Buchleyn] of 1524   LeuL, 269
      v)   *Gott sei gelobet und gebenedeiet*   BluPR, 41
          a - This was a German hymn that enjoyed great popularity
              before the Reformation   LeuL, 252
          b - Luther adopted this hymn minus the fifth and sixth lines
                                                                       LeuL, 252
              1 - He added two stanzas
          c - He retained the melody and used it as a post-communion
              chorale   LeuL, 252
          d - A translation and transcription of *Gott sei gelobet und*
              gebenedeiet   LeuL, 253
              1 - For the German text *see*   LutDM 35, 452-453
              2 - The melody is found in Klug's 1533 *Geistliche Lieder*
                                                                         LeuL, 252
      vi)   [The other seven *Lieder* have been discussed above in the
          sections on "Latin hymns"*, "The Chants derived from the
          Catholic church"**, and "Centuries old German religious
          songs"***]
          a - *Nun komm, der Heiden Heiland* *
          b - *Komm Gott Schöpfer, heiliger Geist* *
          c - *Christum wir sollen loben schon* *
          d - *Mitten wir im Leben sind* **
          e - *Komm, Heiliger Geist, Herre Gott* **
          f - *Nun bitten wir den Heiligen Geist* ***
          g - *Christ lag in Todesbanden* ***
      vii) Most of these *Lieder* retained the melodies of their pre-Re-
          formation models   BluPR, 41
  (c)   There are approximately fifty surviving melodies   ReeMR, 675
      i)   Approximately twenty of the melodies can be traced to pre-
          Reformation sources
      ii)   Twenty melodies seem to have originated in or near Luther's
          seat at Wittenberg
      iii) Others are encountered elsewhere
      iv) It is difficult to determine the melodic contribution made by
          Luther
          a - Early Lutheran melodies had turns of phrase that were
              common property of the time
          b - And, the differences between free *Lieder* melodies of the
              early Protestant Church and those based on Latin hymns
              of the Catholic Church are often scarcely discernible
                                                                        BluPR, 37
      v)   The melodies can be organized according to melodic formu-
          lation such as: BluPR, 41
          a - Those with more or less note-for-note *contrafacta*
          b - And those that are new creations characterized by the use
              of formulas and patterns
(2)   There are two *Lieder* with both text and melody by Luther   BluPR, 43

(a) *Jesaja dem Propheten das geschah*
    i)   This was written for Luther's German Mass   LutH, 50
        a - Johann Walther vouches for Luther's authorship saying, "among other [melodies] it is the German Sanctus which shows his [Luther's] perfect mastery in adapting the notes to the text"   LeuL, 60
    ii) This is the Sanctus itself in a Protestant interpretation
    iii) The text is a paraphrase of Isaiah 6:1-4   LeuL, 60
    iv) The melody is a free adaptation of *In Dominicis Adventus et Quadragesimae* in the *Graduale Romanum* (a plainchant Sanctus)   LeuL, 60
    v) A translation and transcription of *Jesaja dem Propheten das geschah*   LeuL, 82

(b) *Ein feste Burg*   BluPR, 43
    i)   This is taken from Psalm 46: *Deus noster refugium et virtus*   LutH, 52
    ii) This probably was written between 1526 and 1528
    iii) It is one of the most magnificent examples of perfect unity of word and music
        a - The melody is found in Klug's *Geistliche Lieder* of 1533   LeuL, 284
    iv) A translation and transcription of *Ein feste Burg*   LeuL, 284
        a - For the German text *see*   LutDM 35, 455-457

(3) Eleven other *Lieder*, written between 1523 and 1524, are free poems, six of which are the great *Psalm Lieder*   BluPR, 42
   (a) Definite musical models for the melodies of the eleven *Lieder* cannot be traced
   (b) Some examples of the eleven *Lieder* are:
      i)   *Wohl dem, der in Gottes Furcht steht*
          a - This was taken from Psalm 128: *Beati omnes qui timent Dominum*   LutH, 36
          b - This is a hymn in opposition to the medieval glorification of celibacy   LeuL, 242
             1 - Luther made a German and Latin paraphrase of it
          c - There are four different tunes for this hymn   LeuL, 242
          d - The earliest sources for the hymn are the *Erfurt Enchiridia* and Walther's [*Geystliche Gesangk Buchleyn*]
          e - A translation of *Wohl dem, der in Gottes Furcht steht* and a transcription of Walther's tune in its original form and in its simplified form   LeuL, 243
             1 - For the German text *see*   LutDM 35, 437-438
      ii) *Aus tiefer Not*   BluPR, 42
          a - Taken from Psalm 130: *De profundis clamavi ad te*   LutH, 10
          b - The now-common version with five stanzas is found in Walther's [*Geystliche Gesangk Buchleyn*] of 1524   LeuL, 222
          c - There is also a [four-stanza version] with a Phrygian melody in the Erfurt *Enchiridion* of [1524]   ReeMR, 675

                d - There are a number of different melodies associated with this text   LeuL, 222
                    1 - The Phrygian melody in Walther's hymnal of 1524 became the proper tune for the text
                e - A translation of *Aus tiefer Not* with two transcriptions   LeuL, 223
                    1 - For the German text *see*   LutDM 35, 419-420
            iii) *Ach Gott vom Himmel sieh darein*   BluPR, 42
                a - This is taken from Psalm 12: *Salvum me fac, Domine*   LutH, 6
                b - The proper melody for this hymn is unknown   LeuL, 225
                    1 - A Hypophrygian melody found in the *Erfurt Enchiridia* is most likely the proper one
                c - A translation of *Ach Gott vom Himmel sieh darein*   LeuL, 226
                d - A transcription of the Hypophrygian melody and a Dorian melody from Walther's [*Geystliche Gesangk Buchleyn*] of 1524   LeuL, 226-227
                    1 - For the German text *see*   LutDM *35*, 415-417

h) Freely-composed hymns for the Lutheran service   LeaL, 268
    (1) These hymns were modeled after the *Hofweisen* (the art songs of the day)
        (a) The *Hofweisen* were court songs   RanH, 447
        (b) Their melodies were syncopated and rhythmic
        (c) They were written in a basic AAB or bar-form structure
        (d) There was a built-in repetition which helped congregations memorize the songs
    (2) Examples of the *Hofweisen* style hymns are *Nun freut euch, lieben Christen g'mein* and *Ein feste Burg*   LeaL, 268
        (a) A translation and transcription of *Nun freut euch, lieben Christen g'mein*   LeuL, 217
            i) The text is by Luther and the melody is from a fifteenth century anonymous tune   BusO, 7
            ii) The first source of the hymn is found in the *Achtliederbuch*
            iii) The hymn is also in the *Erfurt Enchiridia* and Walther's [*Geystliche Gesangk Buchleyn*]
            iv) For the German text *see*   LutDM 35, 422-425
        (b) A translation and transcription of *Ein feste Burg*   LeuL, 284
            i) The melody and text are by Luther   BusO, 6
            ii) For the German text *see*   LutDM 35, 455-457
            iii) The melody is found in Klug's *Geistliche Lieder* of 1533

C. Published Sources of Vernacular Music for the Lutheran Church

1. Monophonic Hymnals
    a) The *Achtliederbuch* of 1523-24   LeuL, 192
        (1) By the end of 1523, individual leaflets, or broadsheets, containing several of Luther's hymns and those by his friends were printed and distri-

		buted			LeuL, 191

(2) By January of 1524 the broadsheets and hymns were compiled into the *Achtliederbuch* by Jobst Gutknecht in Nürnberg   LeuL, 191

    (a) This is the earliest collection of texts and monophonic melodies   RanH, 158

    (b) But half of the *Achtliederbuch* was compiled from slightly older broadsides, mostly from Magdeburg and it is full of errors   BluPR, 46

(4) The *Achtliederbuch* contains eight texts and four melodies   RanH, 158

    (a) Three of the texts are by Paul Speratus, one is by an unnamed author, and four are by Luther   LeuL, 192

        i) The anonymous one is a two-part setting of *In Jesus Namen heben wir an*   BluPR, 46

    (b) The four melodies are by Luther   BluPR, 46

        i) *Nun freut euch, lieben Christen g'mein*   LeuL, 218

            a - This melody is most likely by Luther, but as usual he made use of well-known idioms   LeuL, 217

                1 - It may have been taken from a fifteenth century anonymous tune   BusO, 7

            b - The hymn and tune are also found in Walther's *Geystliche Gesangk Buchleyn*   LeuL, 217

            c - A translation and transcription of *Nun freut euch, lieben Christen g'mein*   LeuL, 219

        ii) *Ach Gott von hymel sich dar eyn*   LeuL, 226

            a - This text is a paraphrase of Psalm 12   LeuL, 225

            b - The proper melody for the tune is uncertain   LeuL, 225

                1 - The *Achtliederbuch* uses the melody *Es ist das Heil*

                2 - But in Walther's *Geystliche Gesangk Buchleyn*, it is set to a Dorian melody and in the *Erfurter Enchiridia* it is set to a Hypophrygian melody

                    a - A translation and transcription of the Hypophrygian and Dorian melodies   LeuL, 226-227

                3 - The Hypophrygian tune is most likely by Luther

            c - A translation of *Ach Gott von hymel sich dar eyn* and a transcription of the melody, *Es ist das Heil uns kommen her*   SerL, no. 259

        iii) *Aus tieffer not schrey ich zu dyr*   LeuL, 222

            a - This text is a four-stanza version of Psalm 130 with slightly different lines from the other sources and a conflation of the second and third stanzas

            b - The melody in the *Achtliederbuch* is *Es ist das Heil uns kommen her*

            c - The proper tune for the text was published in one of the *Erfurter Enchiridia* and Walther's *Geystliche Gesangk Buchleyn*

            d - A translation of *Aus tieffer not schrey ich zu dyr* and a transcription of the melody, *Es ist das Heil uns kommen her*   SerL, no. 259

        iv) *Es spricht der unweysen mund wol*   LeuL, 229

                a - This hymn was most likely written in 1523
                b - The text is from Psalm 14
                c - The melody is *Es ist das Heil uns kommen her*
                d - A translation of *Es spricht der unweysen mund wol* and a transcription of *Es ist das Heil uns kommen her*
                                                                                                                    SerL. no. 259
        (5) A reprint edition of the *Achtliederbuch*   AmeD
    b) Two *Erfurter Enchiridion* of 1524-[1525]   RanH, 386
        (1) These two *Enchiridia* were published by two different printers in Erfurt
                                                                                                                    LeuL, 193
            (a) They are from the printing press of Jum Schwarzen Horn (Maler) and Zum Färbefass (Loersfeld)   BluPR, 46
        (2) They contain twenty-five texts   RanH, 386
        (3) There are twenty-six melodies in the first edition of 1524 and thirty-eight in the second edition a year later   BluPR, 46
        (4) Facsimile reprints of the two *Erfurter Enchiridion*   AmeE
    c) *Enchiridion* of Hans Lufft   GérP, 429
        (1) It was published at Wittenberg in 1526
        (2) This is the first Wittenberg congregational hymn-book   BluPR, 47
        (3) It offers the hymns from the *Geystliche Gesangk Buchleyn* of Walther
                                                                                                                    LeuL, 194
        (4) For a description of this publication *see*   LutDM 35, 317-318
    d) *Geistliche Lieder*   BluPR, 46
        (1) The *Geistliche Lieder* was published by Josef Klug   GérP, 429
            (a) It was the first Klug song-book of 1529   LeaL, 272
            (b) This is lost but it is possible to reconstruct it   BluPR, 46
                i) It can be reconstructed from the reprints by Rauscher in Erfurt and by Gutknecht in Nürnberg in 1531 and through altered new editions of 1533, 1535, and 1543   BluPR, 47
                    a - The 1533 edition is a reprint of the 1529 edition by Andreas Rauscher of Erfurt with little alteration   GérP, 429
                        1 - It was titled *Geistliche Lieder auffs new gebessert zu Wittemberg*
                        2 - A reprint of the 1533 edition of *Geistliche Lieder*
                                                                                                                    AmeK
            (c) Klug produced at least eight further editions of this Wittenberg hymnal over a sixteen year period LeaL, 272
                i) Many of them are revisions and expansions of the previous ones
        (2) The *Geistliche Lieder* was a new congregational hymnal   LeaL, 272
            (a) It contained fifty *Lieder*   BluPR, 46
        (3) It was authorized by Luther and he wrote a foreword for it   BluPR, 47
            (a) There is also a preface titled *A Preface for All Good Hymnals* by Luther appended to the end of Klug's 1543 edition   BluPR, 46
                i) This preface was taken from a rimed introduction to Walther's *Lob und Preis der Loblichen Kunst Musica*   LeuL, 319
                ii) A translation of Luther's *A Preface for All Good Hymnals*
                                                                                                                    LeuL, 319
                iii) A print of the 1543 edition   KluG

(4) There was a new feature developed in the subsequent editions LeaL, 272
   (a) The new feature was a section of catechism hymns
      i) Luther thought of the hymn as a means of instilling the Word of God in the people   LeuL, 277
         a - "He wanted both law and gospel to be expressed in verse to instruct the common people..."
   (b) These hymns were written by Luther on the five main parts of his *Small Catechism*
      i) Luther created two hymns on the Ten Commandments   LeuL, 277
         a - *Dies sind die heiligen zehn Gebot* was to be sung before Catechism sermons
            1 - A translation of *Dies sind die heiligen zehn Gebot*   LeuL, 278
               a - This was a pre-Reformation pilgrims' hymn
            2 - A transcription of the melody, *In Gottes Namen fahren wir*   LeuL, 278
               a - It is a thirteenth century anonymous melody   BusO, 7
            3 - For the German text *see*   LutDM 35, 426-428
         b - [*Mensch wiltu leben seliglich*] was to be sung after Catechism sermons   LeuL, 277
            1 - A translation of *Mensch wiltu leben seliglich*   LeuL, 281
            2 - A transcription of the Phrygian melody that was taken from Walther's *Geystliche Gesangk Buchleyn* of 1524   LeuL, 281
            3 - For the German text *see*   LutDM 35, 428-429
      ii) The Creed, *Wir glauben all' an einen Gott*
         a - This is found in the *Erfurt Enchiridion* of 1525   LeuL, 271
         b - A translation of *Wir glauben all' an einen Gott*   LeuL, 272
         c - A transcription of the melody found in Klug's *Geistliche Lieder* of 1533   LeuL, 272
         d - For the German text *see*   LutDM 35, 451-452
      iii) The Lord's Prayer, *Vater unser im Himmelreich*
         a - A translation of *Vater unser im Himmelreich*   LeuL, 296
         b - A transcription of two melodies, one of which is taken from an original draft in Luther's hand   LeuL, 296-297
         c - For the German text *see*   LutDM 35, 463-467
      iv) The Baptism, *Christ, unser Herr, zum Jordan kam*
         a - A translation of *Christ, unser Herr, zum Jordan kam*   LeuL, 300
         b - A transcription of the Dorian melody taken from Walther's [*Geystliche Gesangk Buchleyn*] of 1524   LeuL, 300
         c - For the German text *see*   LutDM 35, 468-470
      v) The Communion, *Jesus Christus, unser Heiland*
         a - A translation of *Jesus Christus, unser Heiland*   LeuL, 258
         b - A transcription of a melody from the *Erfurt Enchiridion*

of 1524 and one from Klug's *Geistliche Lieder* of 1533
                            LeuL, 258
    c - For the German text *see*   LutDM 35, 445

2. Polyphonic hymnals
 (a) The *Geystliche Gesangk Buchleyn*   ReeMR, 677
  (1) It was published by Joseph Klug in 1524 at Wittenberg LeaL, 272
    (a) It was also known as the *Walther Chorgesangbuch* LeaL, 269
    (b) It was reprinted in 1525, 1537, 1544, and 1551, with changes and additions in each   ReeMR, 677
      i) A 1525 [monophonic] congregational Wittenberg hymnal, 'for the laity' rather than for the choir, was modeled on the tenor partbook of the 1524 publication LeaL, 270
        a - The texts and melodies are in the same order as those found in the *Walther Chorgesangbuch*
        b - The preface is the same one Luther wrote for the part-books in 1524   LeaL, 271
      ii) The 1544 expanded edition was issued by Rhau in two different sets of partbooks with predominantly German texts
                            LeaL, 273
        a - The first set was an expansion of the fourth edition and the second set was a new work, *Newe deudsche geistliche Gesenge*
    (c) *The Geystliche Gesangk Buchleyn* was also reprinted by Rhau in 1550   LeaL, 273
  (2) It was [created] in Wittenberg by Luther and Johann Walther PraM, 5
    (a) Luther's preface in the *Geystliche Gesangk Buchleyn* states that the book is for youthful singers   ReeMR, 677
      i) It also states that the songs are arranged for four parts but, actually, some compositions are written for three voices and others for five   LeaL, 269
      ii) Translations of the preface   LutH, xxi; LeuL, 315
  (3) The *Geystliche Gesangk Buchleyn* was the earliest polyphonic collection
                            RanH, 158
    (a) It is the first systematically planned collection of German *Lieder* authorized by Luther   BluPR, 46
    (b) It became the model for all later polyphonic choral songbooks of the young church   BluPR, 46
      i) The music was for four or more voices with the melody in the tenor   BluPR, 73
        a - There were some two- or three-voice pieces with the melody in the middle or lower part
      ii) This was not a new form but Walther changed the character of the traditional one by making it simpler BluPR, 74
  (4) It is a collection of polyphonic motets based on Lutheran hymns
                            LeuL, 193
    (a) Luther asked Walther to compose choral settings of some forty Wittenberg hymns that already existed LeaL, 269
    (b) Walther was to use as his model the polyphony associated with the

		Mass	LeaL, 269
	(c)	He composed polyphonic settings of thirty-eight of the Wittenberg hymns with Luther's guidance	LeaL, 269
(5)		The 1524 edition contains forty-three pieces	ReeMR, 677
	(a)	There are thirty-eight [polyphonic] German [*Lieder*] and five Latin compositions	BluPR, 46

- i) The thirty-eight *Lieder* are all *cantus firmus* pieces   ReeMR, 677
  - a - Thirty-six have the principal melody in the tenor
  - b - The other two *Lieder* have the melody in the *discantus*
- ii) Twenty-three of the thirty-eight German *Lieder* employ texts by Luther   ReeMR, 677
- iii) Twenty-nine of the forty-three pieces are *a* 4, twelve are *a* 5, and two are *a* 3   ReeMR, 677

(b) Besides the thirty-eight polyphonic settings in five partbooks, this collection contains thirty-two texts, and thirty-five melodies   RanH, 158

(6) The settings of these hymns are in two basic styles   LeaL, 270
  (a) These styles fall into approximately equal sized groups   ReeMR, 677
  (b) The first style follows the old *cantus firmus* motet style similar to the compositions of Josquin Desprez   LeaL, 270
    i) Both Walther and Luther admired Josquin's music
    ii) The chorale melody was usually rather obvious with imitation and canonic devices in the other voices being derived from it
      a - It (the chorale melody) proceeds in long notes which are occasionally broken up into short figures   ReeMR, 677
      b - The imitation in the other voices is usually at the beginning of a section and is short-breathed with no constructive significance   ReeMR, 677
      c - A canon appears at times in the five voice *Lieder* with the second voice bearing the *cantus firmus* in canon with the tenor   ReeMR, 678
  (c) The other style used by Walther is simpler and more homophonic and similar to the settings of the older composers such as Fink, Isaac, and Hofhaimer   LeaL, 270
    i) The chorale melody is usually in the tenor and is supported by three other voices in a basically homophonic style
      a - The melody is clearly heard throughout
    ii) There is no imitation and the cadence is definite in all the parts at the end of each line   ReeMR, 678
    iii) The harmonic function of the bass is definitely audible   ReeMR, 678
    iv) For an example of this style, *see*   DavH (a), 115
  (d) The Lutheran practice of combining simple congregational song with complex polyphonic choral music was established   LeaL, 271

(7) These settings were to be used in the Wittenberg schools as part of the musical education   LeaL, 269
  (a) Once the songs were learned they were to be sung in the church

worship
- (b) It seems likely, that Luther issued this choral hymnbook before issuing a specifically congregational collection so that the choir could teach the congregation how to sing the new hymns LeaL, 270
- (c) "Thus, a double educational function was involved" LeaL, 270
  - i) Good music was taught to the pupils of the school and songs of worship were taught to the congregation
- (d) In the early stage, the *Kantorei* sang Walther's polyphonic settings in the church services as the representative of the congregation LeaL, 270
- (8) A reprint edition of *Geystliche Gesangk Buchleyn* WalW
- (9) A transcription of Walther's *Geystliche Gesangk Buchleyn* WalSW, III
- b) *Newe deudsche geistliche Gesenge... für die gemeinen Schulen* GérP, 430
  - (1) It was published by Georg Rhau in 1544 at Wittenberg
  - (2) The purpose of this publication was to make available material to be used to develop in young people an understanding of church music and the ability to perform it
    - (a) It was also intended for the church service BluPR, 95
  - (3) There are 123 pieces plus the twelve anonymous ones ReeMR, 678
    - (a) Generally, the compositions are in contrapuntal style UlrH, 162
      - i) The melody is treated in *cantus firmus* fashion in the tenor
      - ii) "In some cases bits of imitative writing introduce each phrase"
    - (b) Also, passages in chordal style occur UlrH, 163
  - (4) It is an anthology containing works by nineteen different masters and twelve anonymous pieces BluPR, 80
    - (a) But, only seventeen names of composers are given GérP, 431
      - i) Five of the most prominent of the composers were probably or certainly Catholics
      - ii) It contains settings by Catholics such as [Heinrich] Isaac, [Thomas] Stoltzer, and [Balthazar] Resinarius as well as compositions by belligerent Protestants such as [Benedictus] Ducis and [Sixtus] Dietrich RedC, 260
    - (b) It may be assumed that the majority of the anonymous pieces are by Rhau GérP, 431
      - i) They are short and simple Christmas songs GérP, 435
      - ii) It may be that Rhau thought this type of song should not be omitted and introduced them himself GérP, 435
    - (c) One of the anonymous pieces is actually by Johann Walther
      - i) It is his *In dulci jubilo* BluPR, 89
    - (d) Approximately two-thirds of these pieces are the settings of five composers LeaL, 273
      - i) The composers are Resinarius, Bruck, Senfl, Ducis, and Dietrich
      - ii) There are eleven of Senfl's compositions of varying length and structure GérP, 431
        - a - His most important composition in the *Newe deudsche geistliche Gesenge...* is *Da Jakob nu das Kleid ansah*

Published Sources of Vernacular Music for the Lutheran Church   279

       1 - A transcription of *Da Jakob nu das Kleid ansah*
                          DavH, 114
     b - Not one of Senfl's compositions is based on a really
       Protestant hymn
    iii) There are twenty-six compositions of different types by Resi-
      narius   GérP, 432
     a - About half of these are very short but their structure is
       fairly varied
    iv) There are ten melodies by Ducis, one of which is unique, the
      Nun freut euch, lieben Christen gmein   GérP, 433
     a - This hymn is written in a responsorial method
       1 - This is a method that later was used frequently
    v) Seventeen compositions are by Arnold von Bruck GérP, 433
     a - Some of his compositions are in the style of the later
       Choralmotette
       1 - In the later *Choralmotette* the melody is treated se-
        parately in imitative style with each section starting
        with a fugal treatment of the corresponding chorale
        line in diminution   GérP, 668
       2 - After the anticipatory imitation, the chorale line ap-
        pears once in each part in longer note values with the
        other parts providing a contrapuntal background
                              GérP, 668
       3 - The chorale line is stated in full chords at the end of
        the section   GérP, 688
     b - The majority of his compositions are set to texts by Lu-
       ther
     c - A transcription of *Aus tiefer Not* by Arnold von Bruck
                            DavH (b), 115
    vi) There are three of Martin Agricola's hymn-tune settings
                            GérP, 434
     a - The most developed one is *Mit Fried und Freud ich fahr
       dahin*
      i) A transcription of *Mit Fried und Freud ich fahr
       dahin*   WolN, 12
 (6) For a detailed discussion of the nineteen composers of *Lieder* found in
   this publication *see*   BluPR, 80
 (7) A transcription of *Newe deudsche geistliche Gesenge... für die gemeinen
   Schulen*   WolN
c) *Ein Sangbüchlein aller Sontags Evangelien*   HüsA, 166
 (1) This was published in Wittenberg in 1541
 (2) It contains two and three voice German Protestant songs by Martin
   Agricola
 (3) This is the oldest collection of its kind
   (a) The songs are arranged according to the church calendar
   (b) They are also divided according to educational songs, songs of
     edification, rhymed songs based on the Gospels and Histories,
     household devotional songs, and others   BluPR, 45
 (4) A facsimile of *Ein Sangbüchlein...*   AgrD

280   Sacred Music for the Reformed Church on the Continent

(5) Transcriptions of *Mit Fried und Freud, Ach Gott von Himmel,* and *Ein feste Burg*   WolN, 12, 91, 94
(6) A transcription of *Ach Gott von Himmel*   AgrA, 48

D. Published Sources of Latin Music for the Lutheran Church

1. Sources taken from the Catholic church
   a) Music for the Mass   BluPR, 115
      (1) There were complete Masses, or Proper cycles for the main feasts of the year
         (a) *Selectae harmoniae de Passione Domini*   LeuL, 321
            i) This was published by Georg Rhau in 1538   GérP, 435
            ii) It contains compositions for Passion Week
            iii) A facsimile of *Selectae harmoniae...*   RhaSH
            iv) A transcription of *Selectae harmoniae...*   RhaSE
         (b) *Officia Paschalia, de Resurrectione et Ascensione Domini*
                                                              GérP, 435
            i) This was published by Georg Rhau in 1539   ReeMR, 681
            ii) It contains Easter music   RhaO
               a - Such as motets and a psalm for Easter by Senfl   GérP, 435
            iii) There are Masses and also Offices in the strict modern sense
               a - The Latin Gradual, Creed, and Offertory of the Masses are discarded and passages in German are inserted
            iv) It is a good illustration of the gradual nature of the departure of the Lutheran liturgy from that of the Catholic Church
            v) A facsimile of *Officia Paschalia...*   RhaO
            vi) A transcription of *Officia Paschalia...*   ParO
         (c) *Officia de Nativitate*
            i) This was published in 1545 by Georg Rhau   ReeMR, 681
            ii) It contains Christmas and Epiphany music   RhaOF
            iii) There are compositions for the Propers and the Ordinary
               a - The Latin Gradual, Creed, and Offertory of the Masses are discarded and passages with German are inserted
                                                              GérP, 435
            iv) It is another good illustration of the gradual nature of the departure of the Lutheran liturgy from that of the Catholic Church
            v) A facsimile of *Officia de Nativitate*   RhaOF
            vi) A transcription of *Officia de Nativitate*   KraO
      (2) Compositions for the Ordinary
         (a) *Opus decem missarum*
            i) This was published by Georg Rhau in 1541   GérP, 435
            ii) It contains music by Catholic and Protestant composers
            iii) There are six Masses composed on tenors from secular songs
            iv) A facsimile of *Opus decem missarum*   RhaOP
   b) Music for the Vespers   BluPR, 115
      (1) *Vesperarum precum officia*   GérP, 435
         (a) This was published in 1540 by Georg Rhau

		(b)	It contains hymns, antiphons, and Magnificats in very simple counterpoint	GérP, 436

       (b) It contains hymns, antiphons, and Magnificats in very simple counterpoint   GérP, 436
          i)   There are also psalms in so-called *faux bourdon* style
       (c) A facsimile of *Vesperarum precum officia*   RhaVE
       (d) A transcription of *Vesperarum precum officia*   RhaV
  (2) *Novum et insigne opus musicum triginta sex antiphonarium*   BluPR, 114
       (a) This was published in 1541 by Georg Rhau
       (b) It contains antiphons by Sixtus Dietrich   LeaL, 273
       (c) A facsimile of *Novum et insigne opus musicum...*   DieNO
       (d) A transcription of *Novum et insigne opus musicum...*   DieN
  (3) *Sacrorum hymnorum liber primus*   RanH, 385
       (a) This was published in 1542 by Georg Rhau for the young Lutheran church
       (b) These Latin hymns are practically indistinguishable in language and style from their polyphonic contemporaries
       (c) A facsimile of *Sacrorum hymnorum liber primus*   RhaSA
       (d) A transcription of *Sacrorum hymnorum liber primus*   RhaSAC
  (4) *Responsoriorum...libri duo*   BluPR, 114
       (a) This was published in 1543 by Georg Rhau
       (b) It contains two volumes of responsoria by Balthazar Resinarius (a pupil of Isaak)   LeaL, 273
       (c) A transcription of *Responsoriorum...libri duo*   ResR
  (5) *Postremum Vespertini officii opus*   BluPR, 118
       (a) This is a Magnificat collection
       (b) It was published by Georg Rhau in 1544   BluPR, 117
       (c) A facsimile of *Postremum Vespertini officii opus*   RhaP
       (d) A transcription of *Postremum Vespertini officii opus*   BunP
  (6) *Novum opus musicum tres tomos sacrorum hymnorum continens*
       (a) This was published in 1545 by Georg Rhau   BluPR, 115
       (b) It contains three volumes of hymns by Sixtus Dietrich   LeaL, 273
       (c) A transcription of *Novum opus musicum...*   DieNOV
c) Music for diverse liturgical and non liturgical purposes   BluPR, 115
  (1) *Symphoniae jucundae atque adeo breves*   BluPR, 114
       (a) This was published in 1538 by Georg Rhau
       (b) It contains fifty-two Latin motets and a few secular ones   BluPR, 118
          i)   The fifty-two motets are for the Sundays of the church year   LeuL, 321
       (c) This is musical material for the service, the school, and the household   BluPR, 118
       (d) A translation of the preface by Luther   LeuL, 321
       (e) A facsimile of *Symphoniae jucundae atque adeo breves*   RhaSY
       (f) A transcription of *Symphoniae jucundae atque adeo breves*   RhaS
  (2) The *Tricinia...latina, germanica barbantica et gallica*   RanH, 869
       (a) This was published in 1542
       (b) It contains three-voice compositions
       (c) It has material similar to the *Symphoniae jucundae*   BluPR, 118
       (d) A facsimile of *Tricinia...latina, germanica barbantica et gallica*   RhaT

		(e)	A transcription of *Tricinia...latina, germanica barbantica et gallica*	GaiT

- (3) The *Bicinia gallica, latina, germanica*   RanH, 94
  - (a) This was published in 1545 at Wittenberg
  - (b) It contains pieces in a variety of textures
    - i) Some of the pieces are two-voice sections of larger works by Josquin and others
    - ii) The texts are both sacred and secular in several languages, some of which were newly adapted *contrafacta*
  - (c) The *Bicinia* has material similar to the *symphoniae jucundae*   BluPR, 118
  - (d) A facsimile of *Bicinia gallica, latina, germanica*   RhaB
  - (e) A transcription of *Bicinia gallica, latina, germanica*   ReiB

E. The Performance of Lutheran Church Music

1. In the early stages, Walther's polyphonic settings of the Wittenberg hymns were sung in the church service by the *Kantorei*   LeaL, 270
   a) The *Kantorei* was a voluntary group of townspeople who performed polyphonic music in church under the direction of the *Kantor*   RanH, 424

2. By 1525, the congregation had the [monophonic] congregational Wittenberg hymnal along with broadsheets   LeaL, 270
   a) As a result, the congregation began to sing hymns in unison without organ accompaniment   GérP, 436
      (1) But in some church ordinances, it was expressly mentioned that choristers must be placed among the congregation in order to help them

3. The one-stanza pre-Reformation *Lieder* had been expanded to structures with many stanzas   BluPR, 106
   a) These stanzas represented a unified thought   BluPR, 105
   b) The unity of thought could not be torn apart, therefore, the *Lied* was always sung complete   BluPR, 105
      (1) As a result, the congregation, led by the boys of the choir, would sing alternate stanzas in unison in response to the *Kantorei* singing the other stanzas of Walther's polyphonic setting of the hymn for the day   LeaL, 270
         (a) This practice occurred especially for the main liturgical hymn which was sung between the Epistle and Gospel after the Gradual
      (2) At times, the stanzas were portioned out among congregation, choir, and organ   BluPR, 106
         (a) In Wittenberg, each verse of the Te Deum was sung in Latin by the *Kantorei* with the congregation responding by singing the same verse in Luther's German translation   LeaL, 271
            i) This performance was punctuated by improvisations on the basic melody by the organist
               a - The organist would introduce the hymn, and, after each stanza was sung, repeat it with embellishments   UlrH, 161

                    b - Although Luther encouraged the use of the organ in the service, no appropriate repertoire yet existed UlrH, 161
        (b) At Christmas, the German hymn *Gelobet seist du, Jesus Christ* was sung by the congregation while the choir and organist inserted the Latin sequence *Grates nunc omnes* between the stanzas LeaL, 271
            i) A translation and transcription of *Gelobet seist du, Jesus Christ* LeuL, 240
        (c) The same pattern was followed at Easter with the sequence *Victimae paschali laudes* and *Christ ist erstanden* LeaL, 271
            i) A translation and transcription of *Victimae paschali laudes* TheH, 97
            ii) A translation and transcription of *Christ ist erstanden* LeuL, 256
        (d) The *Lied* could be sung by the choir accompanied by the organ
    c) At times there was alternation between the pastor and the choir in the performance of non-congregational liturgical texts BluPR, 110

4. "Instruments could have been added to strengthen all the voices" BluPR, 78
    a) Instruments such as lutes, fiddles, recorders, crumhorns, bass shawms, and dolcians were used for this purpose BluPR, 106

5. Instruments could have replaced individual voices BluPR, 106
    a) They could have been added to the *cantus firmus*
        (1) Instruments such as cornetts, trumpets, and trombones were most likely used for this purpose
    b) Or, they could have been added just to the non-*cantus firmus* parts BluPR, 78
        (1) But it is doubtful that adding instruments to the non-*cantus firmus* parts was used in the service except for an especially festive Introit BluPR, 106

6. The *Lieder* could have been transcribed for organ BluPR, 106
    a) But, most Lutheran regulations paid no attention to the organ BluPR, 107
        (1) The independent performance of *Lieder* in the service by the organ was assailed in theory
            (a) Virtuoso or soloistic performances by organists were regarded as objectionable
            (b) The use of secular melodic material for organ gave offense
        (2) But actually the organ played a large role BluPR, 106
            (a) As a soloist and also in vocal-instrumental combinations

F. Lutheran Church Music at Leipzig

1. There were two principal churches in Leipzig LeaL, 274
    a) They were the Nicolaikirche and the Thomaskirche
        (1) Each church had a school with a *Kantorei* made up of boys' voices
        (2) Polyphony was sung as a supplement to the traditional liturgical chant on which it was based
    b) In 1518, Georg Rhau from Wittenberg was appointed to the Thomaskirche and Thomasschule as Kantor LeaL, 275

(1) He left Leipzig in 1520, most likely because of the hostility towards any who sympathized with Luther
(2) In spite of this hostility, Michael Blum published a Lutheran hymnal, *Enchiridion geistlicher gesenge und Psalmen für die leien* in 1530
    (a) The hymnal was modeled on the Wittenberg collections

2. By 1539 the Reformation had been introduced officially into the churches of the city and area, as well as into the university   LeaL, 276
    a) The liturgical provisions of the service closely follow the practices of Wittenberg in general and Luther's two liturgies in particular
    b) The hymns that were sung were presumably sung from the new hymnal published by Valentin Schumann (Leipzig, 1539)
        (1) This publication followed [Klug's] Wittenberg model, *Geistliche Lieder auffs new gebessert und gemehrt zu Wittemberg*
    c) Also, the publication of the Wittenberg hymnal [*Geistliche Lieder...*] was transferred from Klug in Wittenberg to Valentin Bapst in Leipzig
        i) The new publication was called *Geystliche Lieder...[und] Psalmen.. [Geystliche Lieder: mit einer newen vorrhede D. Mart Luth.]*
        ii) It was published in Leipzig in 1545 with a new preface by Luther

G. Published Sources of Lutheran Music at Leipzig

1. *Enchiridion geistlicher gesenge und Psalmen fur die leien*   LeaL, 275
    a) This was published in Leipzig by Michael Blum in 1530
    b) It was modelled on the Wittenberg collections
    c) A facsimile of *Enchiridion geistlicher gesenge und Psalmen fur die leien*   BluE

2. *Geystliche Lieder...[und] Psalmen: [Geystliche Lieder: mit einer newen vorrhede D. Mart. Luth.]*   LeaL, 276
    a) It was published by Valentin Babst in 1545   RanH, 158
        (1) It was published In Leipzig   LeaL, 276
    b) This is a reprint of Klug's [*Geistliche Lieder auffs new gebessert zu Wittemberg*] hymnal with a new preface by Luther
        (1) A translation of Luther's preface   LutH, xxvi
        (2) A translation of the preface and the verse preceding the preface that first appeared on the title page of the Klug hymnal of 1543   LeuL, 332
    c) This hymnal is the most complete and carefully edited hymnal to appear in Luther's lifetime   LeuL, 332
        (1) It is considered the finest hymnal of the Reformation period   LeuL, 194
        (2) It contains eighty texts with tunes arranged in sections   RanH, 158
            (a) There are 128 pieces in all   BluPR, 46
            (b) Texts by Luther come first followed by those of other authors and concludes with pre-Reformation German and Latin texts
            (c) In the section with texts by Luther, the material was arranged for the convenience of liturgical or instructional use
                i) Such as *de tempore Lieder* for the church year, Catechism, Psalm paraphrases, Litanies, and miscellaneous chorales
    d) It was the last hymnal to appear under the auspices of Luther   GérP, 429

  e) For a description of *Geystliche Lieder...*, see   LutDM 35, 332-333
  f) A facsimile of *Geystliche Lieder...*   LutG

H. Lutheran Church Music at Augsburg

 1. The beginnings of the Reformed church in Augsburg
  a) Editions of Luther's writings, including collections of the Wittenberg hymns, were published beginning in 1523 with Augsburg imprints of Wittenberg broadsheet hymns   LeaL, 280
  b) In 1525, the Annakirche formally adopted Lutheran doctrines and practice   LeaL, 280
   (1) A Eucharist was celebrated for the first time following the practice established in Wittenberg
  c) In 1526, Luther's *Deutsche Messe* was published within weeks of the original Wittenberg publication   LeaL, 280
   (1) After this, Augsburg was second only to Wittenberg for the dissemination of Lutheran views

I. Published Sources of Lutheran Music at Augsburg

 1. *Concentus novi trium vocum*   GérP, 430
  a) This is by Johann Kugelmann and was published at Augsburg in 1540
   (1) It was published by Kriesstein   BluPR, 49
  b) It was most likely used in the Annaschule since most of the settings were in three parts   LeaL, 280
  c) *Concentus novi...* is a collection of thirty-nine settings of Latin and German liturgical prose and German hymns   LeaL, 280
   (1) It contains mainly three-part hymn arrangements   GérP, 430
    (a) But, there is an appendix of four- to eight-voice pieces   BluPR, 96
   (2) Some of the melodies appear here for the first time
   (3) "Most of the compositions are by Kugelmann and Stoltzer"
    (a) There are some lesser-known and anonymous composers
  d) *Concentus novi...* was limited to a peripheral local area   BluPR, 49
   (1) Duke Albrecht of Prussia had commissioned it   LeaL, 280
    (a) Therefore, it may have been intended for church use in East Prussia   BluPR, 96
  e) A facsimile of *Concentus novi trium vocum*   KugC
  f) A translation of *Concentus novi trium vocum*   KugCO

J. Calvinist Music in Southern Switzerland

 1. Protestantism arose in 1518 in German-speaking Switzerland   ReeMR, 358
  a) It was led by Zwingli   ReeMR, 358
   (1) He had developed a strong opposition to Catholic teachings   UlrH, 163
    (a) He thought they interfered with individual freedom
   (2) He frowned on the performance of music in the church and had the

            organs in Swiss churches destroyed   ReeMR, 683
    b) After the death of Zwingli in 1531, Swiss Protestantism was without vigourous leadership for several years   ReeMR, 358

2. In 1536, Calvin was invited to align himself with Zwingli's followers   UlrH, 163
    a) Calvin stood closer to Zwingli than to Luther in terms of music and its role in the liturgy   AtlR, 520
       (1) But, his reforms and austerity brought him temporary banishment from Geneva

3. In 1538, Calvin took refuge in Strasbourg   GérP, 438
    a) He observed that singing was well organized in all the churches of the town
    b) He accepted the direction of the community and determined to introduce congregational singing of psalms in the church as soon as possible
    c) His authority concerning appropriate texts for congregational singing was St. Paul who had advocated the singing as well as the reciting of the psalms
                                                                     ReeMR, 359
       (1) Calvin permitted no other texts to be used for this purpose
    d) "In keeping with his belief that the psalms should be understood by the congregation, he adopted the use of French translations, in verse"   ReeMR, 359
       (1) He versified a few psalms and in 1539 was able to produce a small collection under the modest title of *Aulcuns pseaulmes et cantiques mys en chant*   GérP, 438
       (2) He also used translated texts of psalms by Marot who had been supplying metrical psalm translations into French for the court of Frances I
          (a) Marot had translated thirty psalms into metrical form (1533-1539)   BakB, 192
            i) His texts were translations of great fidelity
            ii) He used successive stanzas that were alike in structure
                                                                ReeMR, 360
            iii) As a result, nonmetrical, unrhymed, nonstanzaic psalms were turned into verse with meter, rhyme, and stanzas of equal length   AtlR, 523
            iv) Also, each pair of stanzas was sung to the same melody in the manner of a strophic song   AtlR, 523
            v) For an example, *see*   AtlR, 522

4. In 1541, Calvin returned to Geneva and Swiss Protestantism was provided with a new leader   ReeMR, 358
    a) He subordinated the state government to a church government   UlrH, 163
       (1) He made the Bible the source of all law
    b) Two months after his return to Geneva, he obtained permission from the Council to introduce psalms into public worship   GérP, 441
       (1) "He immediately resumed work on the organization of religious music"
                                                                      GérP, 440
          (a) "He advocated the employment of selected schoolboys to teach the tunes to the congregations"
          (b) He had a new Psalter printed by Girard   GérP, 441
          (c) Only unison, unaccompanied congregational singing in the verna-

cular was allowed in the service   BluPR, 517
- i) Even though polyphonic complexity and chordal innovation were prevalent during this period, Calvin remained hostile to part-singing   ReeMR, 359
- ii) He thought polyphony would too easily distract worshipers from the meaning of the word   AtlR, 520
    - a - Therefore it should be relegated to the home, although even there it should be limited to music of a religious nature
- (d) German melodies, borrowed from the Lutherans, were given French psalm translations   BluPR, 517
    - i) Calvin's main stipulations were that the melody should be equal to the text in majesty and should be proper for singing in the church   ReeMR, 359

5. In 1547, Louis Bourgeois published *Pseaumes cinquante de David roy et profète, traduictz en vers françois par Clément et mis muique par Loys Bourgeoys à quatre parties à voix de contrepoinct égal consonante au verbe*   GérP, 441
    a) The melody was given to the tenor with the other voices providing note-against-note counterpoint

6. Bourgeois published another Psalter through the same printers and in the same year   GérP, 441
    a) *Le premier livre des Pseaulmes de David, contenant XXIV Psaulmes, composé par Loys Bourgeois en diversité de musique: à scavoir familière, ou vaudeville: aultres plus musicales: & aultres à voix pareilles, bien convenable au instrumentz*   GérP, 442
        (1) The music was in *chanson* style and the words were taken from the previous Psalter
        (2) "This was hardly the type of composition to win the approval of Calvin"

7. Calvin also used texts by Bèze (or Beza)   ReeMR, 359
    a) Bèze's translations have been described as paraphrases, tending toward diffusion
        (1) Yet in many respects he followed in the footsteps of Marot
    b) He did not contribute any versifications until 1551   GérP, 442
        (1) He versified thirty-four psalms which were immediately set to music by Bourgeois
            (a) A publication of versifications by Bèze   BèzP

8. Calvinism penetrated into France, the Netherlands, Spain, and England   BaiR, 160
    a) In France the Calvinists were called Huguenots   BaiR, 161
        (1) They maintained a sturdy independence from the papacy   BaiR, 160
        (2) They were either loyalist or revolutionary depending on whether the monarchs veered for or against Reform   BaiR, 161
            (a) None of the French ruling powers were deeply religious, so when it became apparent that the attempt to enforce one religion was an impediment to stability, they were ready to expouse toleration   BaiR, 161

                (3) Under Francis I (1515-1547) the lines were not sharply drawn in the
                    religious situation   BaiR, 162
                    (a) But this was to change under Henry II (1547-1559)

    9. Three volumes of original works and transcriptions for voice and lute were produced by Morlaye which included works by Janequin, Arcadelt and the first book of *Psaumes* by Certon   ReeMR, 554
        a) The first book of *Psaumes* was printed in Morlaye's voice-and-lute transcriptions of 1554, the original of which is lost
            (1) But the transcriptions had already been published two years earlier in Le Roy's *Tiers Livre de tablature de luth*
                (a) A transcription of *Tiers Livre de tablature de luth*   LeRoP
        b) A facsimile of *Premier livre de psalmes mis en musique*   CerLP
        c) A transcription of *Premier livre de psalmes mis en musique*   MorP

    10. There were Catholic settings of the Protestant psalms   BriL, 251
        a) Non-Huguenot musicians did not hesitate to set the psalms from the Marot-Bèze Psalter to music
            (1) "Here there was still no clear distinction between Catholic and Calvinist music"
        b) As early as 1542 there was great demand for the psalms at court
            (1) Musicians occupying the most strictly official posts vied with each other in setting the psalms of the Marot-Bèze Psalter to music
                (a) This was done by Certon, Janequin, Thomas Champion, Mornable, Arcadelt, and others who do not appear at any time to have attached themselves to the new religion
        c) Since both Francis I and Henry II had a great liking for these psalms, the act of translating them into the vulgar tongue was not an offense in itself

K. The Published Psalters in Southern Switzerland

    1. Monophonic Psalters
        a) *Aulcuns pseaulmes et cantiques mys en chant*   BluPR, 517
            (1) During the period of his exile from Geneva, Calvin published this Psalter containing eighteen psalms translated into French   UlrH, 163
                (a) It was published at Strasbourg in 1539   BluPR, 517
                (b) It was printed by Knobloch   GérP, 438
            (2) Some of these psalms were by Calvin and others were adapted from translations by Clément Marot, a French court poet   UlrH, 163
                (a) There are six texts translated by Calvin and twelve by Marot
                                                                                      ReeMR, 359
            (3) The Psalter also contains the Song of Simeon, the Creed, and the Ten Commandments   ReeMR, 359
            (4) The music for Marot's psalms came with the psalms   GérP, 438
                (a) But Calvin had to search for music for the others   GérP, 439
                    i) He found it among the religious compositions of Strasbourg musicians
                    ii) The melodies are mostly by Greiter

                a - Matthias Greiter was the principal singer at the Cathe-
                    dral in Strasbourg, which at that time was in the posses-
                    sion of Protestants   ReeMR, 683
                b - Greiter had composed some original melodies for the
                    Cathedral   ReeMR, 683
        (b) Calvin showed discernment in his choice of the music   GérP, 439
            i) But due to his French verses being shorter than those of the
                German verses [sung in Strasbourg], Calvin did not repeat
                the melody of the first four lines and he omitted a few notes
                of the penultimate line of the second half in order to fit the
                melody to the words
            ii) As a result, the union of music and poetry for these psalms is
                far from appropriate   LesM, 46
                a - French accentuation is mauled
        (c) There are eighteen melodies   BluPR, 517
            i) They are written as single-line melodies   LesM, 45
    (5) A facsimile of *Aulcuns pseaulmes et cantiques mys en chant*   AulP
    (6) A transcription of *Aulcuns pseaulmes et cantiques mys en chant* with
        texts   PidP
    (7) A transcription of *Aulcuns pseaulmes...* with modally harmonized melo-
        dies   TerC
b) *La Manyere de faire prières aux églises françoyses...ensemble pseaulmes et
    cantiques...1542*   PraM, 15
    (1) This was published in Geneva   BakB, 192
    (2) It contains thirty-eight psalms, some by Marot in altered form
        (a) Thirteen psalms are taken from the *Aulcuns pseaulmes et cantiques
            mys en chant* plus seventeen added psalms by Marot   PidP I, 264
            i) Transcriptions of the melodies of the seventeen added
                psalms   PidP I, nos. 4c, 5b, 6c, 7b, 8b, 9, 10b, 11b, 12b,
                        13b, 14b, 22b, 24b, 37b, 38b, 104d, and 113d
        (b) There are also five of Calvin's psalms, and his versions of the Song
            of Simeon and Décalogue [the Ten Commandments]   BakB, 192
            i) The texts and melodies of Calvin's psalms
                PidP I, nos. 25b, and 36b with the music of 36d and text
                of 36a, 46b, 91b, and 113b
    (3) A facsimile of *La Manyere de faire prières aux églises francoyses...*
            ÉglF
    (4) Transcriptions of some of the melodies   PraM, 15
        PraM, 81, 82, 84, 85, 86, 88, 89, 93, 94, 99, 102, 104, 118, 177
    (5) An English translation and a transcription of *La Manyere de faire pri-
        ères aux églises françoyses...ensemble pseaulmes et cantiques...1542*
            CalLM
c) *La forme des prières et chants ecclésiastiques*   BluPR, 518
    (1) This was published in Geneva in 1542 under the direct influence of Cal-
        vin
        (a) Calvin thought music was a gift from God and he acknowledged
            the power of song in the preface   DobM, 259
            i) A translation of an excerpt from the preface
    (2) *La forme des prières et chants ecclésiastiques* was based on the *Aulcuns*

pseaulmes et cantiques mys en chant of 1539
- (a) But Calvin's songs were reduced by two (Psalm 113 and the Credo) and Marot's were increased from thirteen to thirty-two
- (3) A facsimile of *La forme des prières et chants ecclésiastiques*   CalL

2. Polyphonic Psalters
   a) Bourgeois was largely responsible for the melodic settings of the [Genevan] Psalter   ReeMR, 360
      (1) He composed new melodies and revised old ones by improving the melodic lines   LesM, 46
         (a) Secular melodies were drawn upon to a greater extent than the sacred melodies   ReeMR, 360
      (2) The four-part settings are mostly chordal and syllabic in style   ReeMR, 362
         (a) But none of these harmonic settings found permanent acceptance
            i) The melodic settings were perpetuated with harmonizations of other composers
         (b) A transcription of a four voice setting (*Qui au conseil*)   DavH, 144
   b) Bourgeois rectified the accentuation of the text and modified the rhythm of some of the psalms   LesM, 46
      (1) After Marot's departure [from Geneva], Calvin tried to find someone who could continue to versify the Psalter   GérP, 442
         (a) He engaged Théodore de Bèze to undertake the translation
         (b) In 1551, Bèze sent [to Calvin] thirty-four psalms which Marot had not versified
         (c) Bourgeois immediately set them to music
   c) By composing, compiling, and editing the psalms, Bourgeois gave the final and accepted form to about eighty-five of the melodies   ReeMR, 360
      (1) "The remaining tunes were devised in the same manner though with less inspiration, by more than one of his minor successors"
      (2) The complete form of the Psalter was not achieved until 1562   ReeMR, 360
   d) Bourgeois' Psalters
      (1) *Pseaulmes cinquante de David roy et profète, traduictz en vers françois par Clément Marot et mis en musique par Loys Bourgeoys à quatre parties à voix de contrepoinct égal consonante au verbe*   GérP, 441
         (a) This collection by Bourgeois was the first to introduce four-part homophonic writing to church music as a whole   BluPR, 532
            i) But it was intended as music for the home   BluPR, 533
         (b) It was published in Lyons in 1547   BluPR, 532
            i) It was published by Godefroy and Marcelin Beringen   GérP, 441
         (c) These settings are chordal with one note to each syllable   BluPR, 532
            i) This type setting became, in general, the most characteristic manifestation of Calvinist music   BluPR, 533
         (d) The melody is in the tenor with the other voices providing note-against-note counterpoint   GérP, 441
            i) The melodies were often adapted from a popular source

      (e)   Facsimiles of *Pseaulmes cinquante de David...*   BouLP; CerC
- (2) *Le premier livre des Pseaulmes de David, contenant XXIV Psaulmes, composé par Loys Bourgeois en diversité de musique: à scavoir familière, ou vaudeville: aultres plus musicales: & aultres à voix pareilles, bien convenable au instrumentz*   GérP, 442
  - (a) This is another collection by Bourgeois   BluPR, 533
    - i) It was published by the same printers as the *Psaulmes cinquante...*   GérP, 441
  - (b) The texts are taken from the previous Psalter   GérP, 442
  - (c) This collection is dated 1547 and contains twenty-four four-part arrangements   BluPR, 533
    - i) Some of the pieces are homophonic although somewhat ornamented while others contain imitations line by line, frequently in pairs
      - a - In the motet-like settings one frequently finds stretches of a declamatory nature
    - ii) Some of the pieces could be played on instruments   GérP, 442
  - (d) These may have been composed for the meetings often held in the castles of the nobility or the houses of rich bourgeois   GérP, 441
  - (e) A facsimile of *Le premier livre des Pseaulmes de David...*   BouL
  - (f) A transcription of *Le premier livre des Pseaulmes de David...*BouV

L. Protestant Music in Northern Switzerland

1. Singing in the service was promoted by Johannes Oecolampadius in Basel   BluPR, 513
   a) He thought that singing helped prayer and devotion much more than senseless ceremonies
   b) The congregation sang Psalm *Lieder* but the organ remained intact

2. In Constance, Reformer Zwick thought that no music other than congregational singing should be heard in church   GérP, 438
   a) He stated that the psalm-tunes should be developed first, but that other types of song should not be neglected

M. Published Sources of Protestant Music in Northern Switzerland   BluPR, 513

1. The first Protestant hymnal in Switzerland was published in St. Gallen
   a) This was done under the leadership of Dominik Zili in 1533

2. Another hymnal was commissioned in the city of Constance
   a) It was published around 1533-1534 in Zurich by Christoph Froschauer
   b) It was compiled by the poets Ambrosius Blaurer and Johannes Zwick
3. There was a second printing not later than 1537

4. The third printing was the so-called Constance songbook of 1540
   a) The title was *Nüw gsangbüchle von vil schönen Psalmen und geistlichen*

  liedern
- (1) This was written by the Constance Reformer Zwick   GérP, 438
  - (a) It was published by Christoph Froschauer
- (2) There are sixty-seven versifications based on fifty-five psalms (with thirty-five melodies), some sacred pieces, and sixty Christian songs (with thirty melodies)   BluPR, 514
  - (a) There are a group of twenty-three songs based on Scripture (with six melodies) that are not designated for use in the service
  - (b) Complete information about the poets of individual songs is given
- (3) In the second part of this Psalter there are important clues for the position of congregational singing in the service in the regions where this collection was distributed   BluPR, 515
  - (a) There are children's songs for church festivals, catechismal songs, canticles based on the New Testament, the German Sanctus, songs about the Holy Spirit and the Trinity, and songs for certain times of day
- (4) Most of the melodic material is in mensural notation, but there are a few isolated cases of *Hufnagel* notation   BluPR, 515
  - (a) *Hufnagel* (*Nagelschrift*) notation is a type of neumatic notation, so called because some individual neumes resemble horseshoe nails   RanH, 526
    - i) It was employed in Germany in the fourteenth and fifteenth centuries
    - ii) The neumes are also termed Gothic
    - iii) For examples of *Hufnagel* neumes, *see*   RanH, 538
- (5) A facsimile of *Nüw gsangbüchle von vil schönen Psalmen und eistlichen liedern...*   ZwiN

N. The Bohemian-Moravian Brethren (*Unitas fratrum*)   BluPR, 593

1. There were two branches of the main line of Czech songbooks   BluPR, 594
   - a) There was one branch in Poland with three editions
     - (1) A 1541 edition in large format with artistic adornments [*Piesne Chwal Bozskych...*]
       - (a) It was edited by Johannes Horn (Jan Roh in Czech)   BluPR, 593
       - (b) It contains 481 songs and 300 melodies   BluPR, 593
       - (c) A facsimile of *Piesne Chwal Bozskych...*   BohP
     - (2) There are also 1569 and 1589 editions   BluPR, 593
   - b) The other branch was German
     - (1) This branch helped the song repertory of the Bohemian Brethren to attain its real significance
     - (2) It originated with the publication of *Ein New Gesengbuchlen* in Jungbunzlau in 1531   BluPR, 594
       - (a) The *Ein New Gesengbuchlen* was edited by Michael Weisse, a minister of the congregations of Brethren in Landskron (Bohemia) and Fulneck (Moravia)
         - i) Weisse's only purpose was to create songs for the congregation   BluPR, 595

  (b) *Ein New Gesengbuchlen* was based on earlier editions of Czech songbooks   BluPR, 595
    i) Also, it shows evidence of being influenced by Johann Walther's Wittenberg *Geystliche Gesangk Buchleyn*
  (c) It is more comprehensive than any German hymnal of the period   BluPR, 595
    i) It contains 157 songs
     a - Some of the songs do not have their own tunes
  (d) It has a detailed division by title and begins with the seasons of the church year   BluPR, 595
  (e) The texts of the *Ein New Gesengbuchlen*   BluPR, 595
    i) The historical significance of Weisse rests on the poetic strength of his texts and translations
     a - Sixteen texts are German translations from the Czech
     b - The rest are original with Weisse
      1 - These are characterized by their syllable-counting, rhymed poetry, which takes no notice of the pleasing smoothness of verse meters   BluPR, 597
      2 - Therefore, it is almost impossible to sing one of his texts to a strictly metered melody   BluPR, 597
    ii) Weisse added the new texts to existing melodies without changing the melodies for textual reasons   BluPR, 597
  (f) The music of the *Ein New Gesengbuchlen*   BluPR, 595
    i) There is ample use of medieval liturgical tradition, accomplished indirectly by building on the melodic material of earlier Czech Brethren hymnals
     a - This includes the use of folk songs
     b - Also, there are arrangements of hymns, *Leisen*, antiphons, tropes, sequences, and Lamentations
  (g) A facsimile of *Ein New Gesengbuchlen*   AmeG
 (3) There was a new version of Weisse's songbook published by J. Horn at Nuremberg in 1544   BluPR, 598
  (a) There were thirty-two new songs added
    i) Some of these were from Horn's songbook of 1541 and the rest were from Wiesse

O. Dutch Psalm Books

1. The *Souterliedekens*   ReeMR, 355
 a) This Dutch psalter, complete with monophonic melodies, appeared even before the French-speaking counterpart   AtlR, 525
 b) It was entitled *Souterliedekens* and was published in 1540   AtlR, 525
  (1) It became popular immediately   ReeMR, 355
    (a) There were at least thirty-three editions between 1540 and 1613
  (2) There are 159 texts translated into rhymed verse of the 150 Psalms, the *Te Deum*, and five of the Canticles   ReeMR, 356
    (a) Psalm CXVIII (119) is divided into four items
      i) The Catholic number for each psalm is given

        (b) Incipits of the former folk or art text and those of the basic sacred text, in Latin, are given in all instances
            i) "All but twenty-five of the former secular texts have been recovered"
        (c) There are questions as to the literary value of these translations
            i) But their author showed sensitive musical feeling in fitting at least some of them to the melodies
   (3) The *Souterliedekens* contains monophonic settings printed by Symon Cock at Antwerp
        (a) These monophonic settings are drawn from folk or popular melodies, mainly Dutch, that were current in the sixteenth century
            i) These consist of love songs, drinking songs, dance tunes, and religious songs
            ii) On rare occasions, they also draw upon art music   ReeMR, 356
                a - Such as a chant or French *chanson* melody   AtlR, 525
        (b) There is a difference of opinion as to how the melodies should be accented in conjunction with the Dutch Psalm texts   ReeMR, 356
   (4) The *Souterliedekens* differed from the contents of the Genevan Psalter in at least two respects   ReeMR, 356
        (a) It was not used in the church service, but was designed for the home and at social gatherings   ReeMR, 357
        (b) Also, in the *Souterliedekens*, the words were fitted chiefly to folk or popular melodies   ReeMR, 357
            i) In the Genevan Psalter, the melodies were fitted by trained musicians to the words of a gifted poet and his successor
   (5) The probable collector of the melodies and the translator of the texts was Willem van Zuylen van Nyevelt   ReeMR, 357
        (a) He was a nobleman of the province of Utrecht
   (6) A list of the contents of the *Souterliedekens*   MeiD, 137-142
   (7) A facsimile of the *Souterliedekens*   SouP
   (8) A transcription of the *Souterliedekens*   BruS, leaves 129-568

Sacred Latin and Vernacular Music in England

A. **The Pre-Reformation Period in England from ca. 1521 to ca. 1547**

1. The invasion of Lutheran ideas in England was under way by 1521   HarH, 465
   a) Lutheranism had its groups of proponents at the universities and its martyrs to Henry's orthodoxy in matters of faith and ritual
      (1) It was less radical than Wycliffism which had survived into the early sixteenth century
   b) Lutheranism was strong, but its proponents and leaders of the English Reformation never took up Luther's explicit direction that choral music, along with the new congregational hymns, should be cultivated in the reformed churches and schools
      (1) It was the influence of Calvinist ideas that resulted in the printing of the *Psalms in English Metre* [in 1547] and ensured that the congregational music of the English reformed church would follow the German model
         (a) A facsimile of the 1547 edition of *Psalms in English Metre*   SteP
      (2) So, "from the point of view of the musical heritage, the closest analogy is with Lutheran practice, though the Anglican tradition was subsequently enriched by the adoption of a Calvinist style of psalmody"   CalO, 271
   c) But Lutheran opinions were repugnant to Henry VIII   CalO, 267
      (1) His policy was to preserve the outward forms and doctrinal essence of Catholicism as he saw it

2. The pre-Reformation period from 1534 to 1547 saw rapid changes in belief and in liturgy following the rise of Lutheranism and the limited reform under Henry VIII   BenL, 6
   a) The formal break between England and the papacy occurred in 1534   ReeMR, 781
      (1) The *Act of Supremacy* was passed   BaiR, 191
         (a) This Act declared the King head of the Church of England which was called *Anglicana Ecclesia*
         (b) As a result, England embraced a form of Catholicism without the Pope   ReeMR, 781
            i) This helped to create a liturgical *impasse*   SteC, 16
         (c) But things were not actually resolved until the *Act of Uniformity*

      of 1662   SteC, 16
- b) The Royal Injunction of 1536 required every parish to possess a copy of the Bible in English   LonM, 19
    - (1) The Bible was a translation by [Myles] Coverdale
    - (2) Although the Bible was authorized in 1536, it wasn't until 1543 that it was appointed to be used in the Services, after the Te Deum and Magnificat   WulT, 279
- c) In 1538 the King's Vicar-General, Thomas Cromwell, issued further injunctions directing that a Bible in English be set in some convenient place in every church   LonM, 19
    - (1) But the Bibles were not issued until 1539
    - (2) Also, Cromwell ordered that the Creed, Lord's Prayer, and Ten Commandments should be taught in English
- d) The Catholic monasteries were dissolved   LucH, 131
    - (1) The smaller monasteries were dissolved in 1536 and the larger ones in 1539
- e) The Suppression of 1540-1541 closed abbeys such as Bury St. Edmund's and Glastonbury   HarME, 466
    - (1) St. Albans and Waltham were reduced to being parish churches
    - (2) Forthwith, the secularized communities adopted the Sarum rite
        - (a) As a result, the Suppression was less serious than sometimes supposed
- f) After about 1540, it is difficult to distinguish between English Catholic and Protestant music   UlrH, 168
    - (1) One sacred piece in contrapuntal style, whether set to Latin or English words, was in general similar to another
        - (a) Many composers wrote sacred music to English texts while remaining Catholic
        - (b) Latin texts were kept in the English service even after a definite turn to a Protestant form of worship had taken place
- g) The vernacular had been introduced in 1543 for the Litany and for a lesson at Vespers and Matins   HarME, 466
    - (1) But, this affected only a small part of the rite   HarME, 466
        - (a) The main edifice was left untouched
- h) It was about 1543 that the first music directly connected with the English Reformation was printed   HarME, 498
    - (1) It was the *Goostly psalmes and spirituall songes drawen out of the holy Scripture, for the comforte and consolacyon of soch as love to rejoyse in God and his worde*   LeHM, 370
        - (a) It was printed about 1543 [by Myles Coverdale]   HarME, 498
        - (b) It contains fifty-one melodies   ReeMR, 781
            - i) The melodies were not harmonized   LeHM, 371
                - a - They drew on Gregorian chant and German chorales   ReeMR, 781
            - ii) There are thirteen metrical psalms, some metrical versions of Magnificat, Nunc dimittis, the Lord's Prayer, Creed, Commandments, and a dozen or so German and Latin hymns   LeHM, 371
                - a - The psalms are probably the earliest metrical ones in

		English to be printed with melodies	ReeMR, 781

(c) *Goostly Psalmes and Spirituall Songes* draws heavily on Lutheran originals for the words, music, prefatory material, and title   LeHM, 371
    i) This proved to be the undoing of the work   HarME, 498
    ii) These Psalms and songs along with Coverdale's 'Great' Bible were among the 'heretical' books burned at Paul's Cross four months before Henry VIII's death [1546]   HarME, 498
(d) A reprint of *Goostly Psalmes and Spirituall Songes*   FroE, 293
(e) A facsimile of *Goostly Psalmes and Spirituall Songes*   CovG

B. The Pre-Reformation Rite

1. Introduction   BenL, 8
   a) There was no complete liturgical uniformity
      (1) The Sarum Use was followed by the great majority of churches, except monastic ones
      (2) There were a few other independent Uses but in the most important aspects they were very similar
   b) The music for the pre-Reformation rite [was developed] before the introduction of the first English Prayer Book [1549]
      (1) Most of the music sung in church was plainchant
         (a) Polyphony was usually reserved for important services and feasts
            i) It was used also for liturgical texts of particular interest and for important devotions

2. Worship in the pre-Reformation church may be divided into three main parts; the Office, the Mass, and the extra-liturgical devotions   BenL, 9
   a) The Divine Office   BraM, 30
      (1) Sources of the music for the Divine Office   BenL, 15
         (a) The plainsong of the Divine Office was contained in the *Antiphonale*
         (b) The music for the hymns was in the *Hymnal*
         (c) The psalm-tones were contained in the *Tonale*
         (d) The psalms and their ferial antiphons were in the *Psalter*
         (e) The Lessons, antiphons, responds, and other items were found in the *Breviary* without music
      (2) Polyphonic music for the Office was mainly settings of the Magnificat, responds, and hymns   BenL, 15
         (a) All of the music for the Divine Office is written in plainsong-polyphony alternation
         (b) But in most settings of the Magnificat, the polyphonic settings do not normally replace the proper plainsongs altogether
            i) They incorporate the plainsong as *cantus firmi*, usually in equal notes
      (3) Vespers attracted most of the music, but some was sung at Matins and Lauds, and a little at Compline   BenL, 15
         (a) Vespers comprised an opening versicle, psalms with their anti-

phons, a reading with its respond, a hymn, the Magnificat, and final prayers   BraM, 30
- i) The choir may have performed the respond and hymn framing the reading
  - a - The opening line of the hymn was sung by one or more soloists   BenL, 16
    - 1 - The verse was continued by one side of the choir and then the verses were alternated by both sides of the choir (soloists and chorus)
- ii) The Magnificat was sung at Vespers on greater festivals   HarEP, 307
  - a - It was always "framed" by an antiphon   BenL, 15
    - 1 - The antiphon varied according to the season or feast
  - b - The choir may have performed the Magnificat   BraM, 30
    - 1 - It may also have been performed on the organ

(b) Compline was almost identical to Vespers except the Nunc dimittis was sung instead of the Magnificat   BraM, 30

(c) Lauds followed the same form as Vespers and Compline with the Benedictus used in place of the Magnificat or Nunc dimittis   BraM, 32

(d) Matins was an extended form of Vespers and Compline   BraM, 31
- i) It comprised the Introit and Venite [Invitatory], a hymn, as many as nine psalms and their antiphons, nine lessons and their responds, and the Te Deum
  - a - There were polyphonic settings of some of the responds and the Te Deum   BraM, 32

b) The Mass   BraM, 32
  (1) The English Masses may be divided into two types that correspond to the Great and Short Services of the Anglican Church music at a later date   ReeMR, 773
  - (a) There was nothing peculiarly English about this division
  (2) The Short Service type Mass was for ordinary purposes   ReeMR, 773
  - (a) It was of smaller dimensions than the Great Service and the music had fewer voices   ReeMR, 774
    - i) "Diversity might be considered its chief trait"
      - a - There are Masses built on a *cantus firmus*, those built on a special plan, and those that are freely composed
  - (b) Before the Mass actually began there was the Blessing, Aspersion [baptism by sprinkling] and Procession   BraM, 32
  - (c) The Mass began with the Introit [*Officium*], the Kyrie, and the Gloria   BraM, 33
    - i) The Kyrie had a normal pattern   BenL, 12
      - a - A plainsong or square was used for the odd-numbered invocations
      - b - Polyphony was used for Kyrie II, Christes I and III, and Kyrie V
      - c - The Kyrie was almost part of the Proper, since in the Sarum rite it often had a seasonal or festival trope   BenL, 9
    - ii) During Advent and Lent the Gloria was omitted

(d)		This was followed by the chanted Collect and Epistle	BraM, 33
(e)		The Gradual, Alleluia, and sequence came next	BraM, 33
	i)	The Gradual was sung in responsorial palmody	RanH, 345
		a - It was sung between soloists and the choir	
	ii)	The Alleluia was replaced by the Tract during Lent	
	iii)	The sequence was performed in simple alternation between the two sides of the choir	BenL, 14
		a - Sometimes the sequence was omitted	BenL, 9
(f)		Next was the Gospel, Credo, and Offertory	BraM, 33
	i)	In English settings before 1540, the Credo almost certainly used the practice of "telescoping" the text	BenL, 13
		a - The "telescoping" consisted of having two sets of words from the Credo sung simultaneously	
	ii)	Some Masses had Credos with true omissions	BenL, 13
		a - Omissions vary considerably, but after ca. 1525 a cut might be made before *Et in spiritum Sanctum* and resume at *Et exspecto*	
	iii)	A few Masses have a complete Credo, or in *alternatim* set tings, one in which only a single sentence has to be supplied between one polyphonic section and the next	BenL, 13
(g)		Next was the Sanctus, which included the *Pater noster*, followed by the Canon	BraM, 33
	i)	The *Pater noster* may have been sung to polyphony at this time in the Mass	
(h)		This was followed by prayers, the Agnus Dei, and the Communion	
	i)	The Communion may have been set to polyphony	
(i)		Some examples of the Short Service that are built on a special plan are the Lady Masses	ReeMR, 774
	i)	Music was provided for the Introit, Kyrie, Gloria, sequence, Credo, Offertory (organ), Sanctus, and Agnus Dei	BraM, 33
		a - The Kyrie was untroped	BenL, 10
		b - And, it is in these Masses that most complete settings of the Credo are found	BenL, 13
	ii)	The Alleluia and sequence were always available in the Lady Mass, even when excluded from the Mass of the day	BenL, 14
		a - The Alleluia began with a short solo phrase in plainsong on the word Alleluia	
		1 - This was repeated by the choir along with a newer phrase, the *jubilus*, on the final syllable	
		2 - The verse was then sung by the soloists with the last couple of words or so being sung by the choir to the melody of the Alleluia with *jubilus*	
		3 - This was followed by a repeat of the solo Alleluia if a sequence was to follow, but with the *jubilus* as well, sung by the choir, if there was no sequence	
		b - The plainsong sequence was performed in alternation between the two sides of the choir	
		1 - One side would take the odd-numbered verses and the	

                    other the even-numbered verses
                    a - In Ludford's settings, polyphony is provided for
                        the latter and plainsong for the former which was
                        sung by a soloist
        (3) The Great Service type Mass was for ceremonial occasions ReeMR, 773
            (a) It was sung on Sundays and festivals   BenL, 9
            (b) It was extremely long, even when the Kyrie and portions of the
                Credo text were omitted   ReeMR, 773
            (c) The Ordinary of the Mass presumably was set to polyphony
                                                                    BraM, 33
                i) The polyphony was usually for five or six voices with the
                    cantus firmus in the tenor   ReeMR, 773
                ii) Where it is not set to polyphony it is sung in plainsong
                                                                    ReeMR, 774
            (d) The Kyrie was usually troped and regarded as part of the Proper in
                England   BraM, 33
                i) Settings of Propers were extremely rare
                ii) When the Kyrie was not set polyphonically, it was sung in
                    plainsong   ReeMR, 774
            (e) "Excisions in the Credo...are particularly numerous in English
                Masses"   ReeMR, 774
    c) Extra-liturgical devotions
        (1) The votive antiphon was used to conclude Compline in the Roman rite
            and in most English monastic liturgies although it is not mentioned in
            the Sarum books   BenL, 19
            (a) Statutes of many foundations indicated that an antiphon was wide-
                ly sung as a separate and very important devotional act
        (2) Most votive antiphons were Marian antiphons, but there were antiphons
            to the Trinity and to St. William of York
            (a) There was also the Jesus-antiphon which was sung in the course of
                additional devotions later in the evening
        (3) There were many polyphonic settings of the votive antiphon written on
            an even grander scale than individual movements from larger Masses

C. The Establishment of Distinctive Music for the Pre-Reformation Liturgy

    1. "Thomas Cranmer became the first Protestant Archbishop of Canterbury"
                                                                    AtlR, 544
        a) He produced his *Letanie with Suffrages* to a "devout and solemn note" in
            1544   HarME, 498
            (1) He may have done this in collaboration with Merbecke ReeMR, 795
            (2) The *Letanie* was published by Thomas Berthelet in plainsong notation
                                                                    FelE, 7
                (a) Cranmer adopted the available range of note-shapes and rearranged
                    the notes to fit the changed accentuation of the English text
                                                                    CalO, 272
                    i) But as to whether they were intended by Cranmer to be given
                        precise durations is debatable

ii) These note-shapes are those used later by Merbecke in his *Booke of common praier noted*
a - Merbecke explained their meaning and added the dotted punctum
(3) Cranmer strove for an entirely natural setting of the English text
CalO. 272
(a) The chant was modified so that there was only one note to a syllable
ReeMR, 795
(4) The *Letanie* replaced the [Latin] processions of the Sarum Use
(a) The English procession was a combination of several existing Latin forms of procession, each involving a movement towards a "station"
LeHM, 5
i) The station was made before the Rood for festal and Sunday processions
ii) It was made at some altar within the church during Lent
iii) It was once again made at an altar in times of need and on Rogation days
a - This involved the celebration of Mass
iv) "The procession then returned to the original point of departure, halting at the steps of the choir to sing a versicle, respond and collect"
(5) A facsimile of *Letanie with Suffrages* HunC
b) There was also a setting [of Cranmer's Litany] harmonized for five voices which appeared in the same year [1544]
ReeMR, 795
(1) This setting is mentioned in a copy of Maunsell's *Catalogue of English Books* (1595) as having been published by Richard Grafton in 1544
FelE, 23
(a) "But no trace of this seems to have been discovered"
c) Some four-part arrangements [of *Cranmer's First Litany*] appeared soon afterwards
WulT, 283
(1) Three partbooks found in the Wanley manuscript contain two harmonized settings of the plainsong of the Litany
ReeMR, 796
(a) The fourth partbook is missing
(b) Transcriptions of the two harmonized settings
FelE, 36

2. After producing the *Letanie*, Cramner set about translating the processions before Mass on some festivals
HarME, 498
a) This included their *Salve festa dies* and verses
(1) Cranmer stated that if music was set to them, there should be just one note to a syllable
ReeMR, 795
(a) He thought the plainsong "sober and distinct enough... Nevertheless, they that be cunning in singing can make a much more solemn note thereto"
HarME, 498
b) He thought the other processional items, the antiphons and responds, also should be set as near as possible "for every syllable a note"
c) Cranmer did not fulfill his intention to set the text to notes
CalO, 273

3. In 1545, Cranmer and Henry VIII were projecting a complete English Processional on the lines of the Latin *Processionale*
FelE, 24

- a) Cranmer stated, in a letter to the King, that he had adapted a number of Latin processions and in one case (or some cases-the text is not clear) he had written entirely new words   FelE, 25
  - (1) He thought these texts should be set to syllabic chants
- b) But, this project advanced no further   FelE, 25
- c) "In the first Book of Common Prayer (1549) all processions were abolished..."   HarME, 498

D. The Reformation Period in England from ca. 1547 to ca. 1550

1. In 1547 Edward VI came to the throne and the tide of reform swept on faster than ever   LonM, 20
   - a) The Chantries Act of 1547 resulted in many choral foundations being dissolved   BenL, 6
     - (1) St. Steven's (Westminster), St. Mary Newark, Fotheringhay, Tattershall, and Higham Ferrers were suppressed or deprived of their musical establishment   HarME, 466
       - (a) But, some places such as Windsor, Eton, and St. George's Windsor were exempted from the provisions of the Chantries Act
     - (2) The suppression of chantries [a chapel in or attached to a church] together with the injunctions of Edward's reign against organs and florid polyphony were significant for the musical life of the church   HarME, 466
   - b) "The first major public occasion at which a vernacular liturgy was used seems to have been the service which marked the opening of Edward's first session of Parliament, held in Westminster Abbey on 4 November 1547"   WriW I, xi
     - (1) A Mass with Gloria, Credo, Sanctus, Benedictus, and Agnus was sung in English

2. The first official liturgical publication was the *Order for Communion* published in March of 1548   WriW I, xi
   - a) It was a brief supplement to the Latin Mass
   - b) The opening proclamation made it clear that further reforms were to be expected

3. Versified translations of the psalms without music were provided   CalO, 284
   - a) The *Psalms in English Metre* was printed   HarME, 465
     - (1) It was published without music in 1548 or 1549   CalO, 284
     - (2) It was influenced by Calvinist ideas
     - (3) It contained nineteen psalm translations in verse by Thomas Sternhold   ReeMR, 796
       - (a) Seventeen of the psalms were in common metre and two were in short metre   LeHM, 372
       - (b) Like Marot's psalms, these were intended for court circles, but they are not comparable to those by Marot in poetic quality
     - (4) A reprint of *Psalms in English Metre*   SteP
     - (5) A reproduction of a 1549 edition   StePS
   - b) After Sternhold's death in December of 1549, an enlarged edition of thirty-

seven psalms, together with an appendix of seven by John Hopkins, was published   CalO, 284
     (1)   A facsimile of the enlarged edition   StePD

4.   The basic Anglican liturgical text was developed   RanH, 453
    a) *The Book of Common Prayer* was first issued in 1549 under Edward VI   RanH, 453
     (1)   It was printed by Grafton and Whitchurch   SteC, 19
         (a)   It was issued without a Psalter   CalO, 270
     (2)   The text was set to the traditional chant but was modified so there was only one note to each syllable   UlrH, 168
     (3)   It was an amalgam of traditional elements   LeHM, 18
         (a)   It contained all that was necessary for the performance of the services as laid down by authority except for the Holy Scriptures   CalO, 270
         (b)   It contained the services of Baptism, Confirmation, Marriage, Purification, and Burial which were very much direct translations of the originals
             i)   The Litany was Cranmer's English procession of 1544
     (4)   The *Book* was substantially affected by the Sarum Use   RanH, 727
         (a)   It criticized the diversity of liturgical observance which may have greatly contributed towards conditions which produced a lack of uniformity   SteC, 23
             i)   It suggested that only one Use should be used in the whole realm
                 a - The suggestion was that the Use of Salisbury, Hereford, Bangor, York, and Lincoln should be discarded
     (5)   The English form of Matins was first set out in this Prayer Book   FelE, 13
         (a)   It does not differ greatly from what is in use today in regard to the opportunities for musical treatment
         (b)   The service began with the Lord's Prayer, followed by "O Lorde, open thou my lippes", and ended with the third collect
             i)   "The opening section of Matins did not yet exist"
     (6)   *The Book of Common Prayer* was not well received by church dignitaries who thought it should be reformed before being adopted   SteC, 19
         (a)   This left composers in an awkward state of not knowing whether the liturgy would survive
     (7)   A detailed discussion of this Prayer Book   LonM, 22
     (8)   A reprint of *The Book of Common Prayer* [1549]   ChuF
    b) *An Act for the Uniformity of Service...* was passed through both Houses of Parliament in January of 1549   MorE, 94
     (1)   This was a statutory introduction of services in English
         (a)   It directed that after June 9 *The First Book of Common Prayer* be used, and none other   ReeMR, 796
             i)   This was met with armed resistance   HarME, 466
             ii)   But, the rebellion was suppressed   HarME, 466
    c) An act of 1550 called for the surrender and destruction of all old service books in order to insure universal adherence to the new English Prayer Book   BenL, 6

(1) But, a large number of service-books as well as a few musical manuscripts survived

5. When the liturgy became English, there was a change from the dominance of Latin church music within a Latin liturgy to a limited position under Edward VI and Elizabeth   BenL, 162
   a) Compline was sung in English in the Chapel Royal, the Mass was invaded, and the Epistle and the Gospel were read in English   HarME, 466

E. The Development of the Music for the Early Anglican Rite

1. "The chief effects of the Reformation on English church music were, first and foremost, a drastic curtailment of what was required; and, second, the adoption of the English language and with it the search for a simple and intelligible style"   CalO, 270
   a) The new Anglican Church needed less music   AtlR, 545
      (1) A Lincoln Cathedral injunction dated April 15, 1548 stated that the choir would henceforth sing no anthems of our Lady or other saints
      (2) Only anthems of our Lord would be sung, and "them not in Latin"
         (a) These would be sung in English set in a plain and distinct note for every syllable
         (b) But Liturgical settings of Latin texts were never entirely abolished
            i) Such music could be performed in the privacy of the home
   b) Due to *An Act for the Uniformity of Service...* of 1549, musical settings of the Mass and all other sacred music wedded to the Latin language were completely ruled out   FelE, 7
      (1) It became necessary at once to provide music for the Anglican Use in cathedrals and similar establishments
         (a) This included a need for music for Versicles and Responses, the Psalms, the Litany, the canticles (both for Matins and Evensong), as well as anthems
      (2) This demand for musical services in English had already been anticipated to some extent such as in Cranmer's *Litany* of 1544, the *Primer of Henry VIII* issued in 1545, and the music in the Wanley partbooks of 1546-1547   FelE, 7-8
         (a) And even before 1549, the Holy Communion was celebrated in English with music for the complete Office similar to the Latin Mass   FelE, 27
            i) The Holy Communion still retained the same six sections as the pre-Reformation Mass: the Kyrie (Responses to the Commandments), Gloria, Credo, Sanctus/Benedictus, and Agnus Dei   MorE, 95
   c) The liturgical curtailment [by *An Act for the Uniformity of Service*] may be assessed by comparing the requirements of the first Prayer Book with those of the Salisbury missal and breviary   CalO, 271
      (1) Antiphons, responds, Alleluias, Tracts, Graduals, and Sequences were gone
      (2) "The Introit becomes a complete psalm without antiphon, the Offertory

and Communion a small selection of 'sentences'"
- (a) Gradually, even the Introit and Communion (called post Communion in the first Prayer Book) disappeared
- (3) All processions except the Litany were abolished
  - (a) Also, many feasts and all the special ceremonies connected with Holy Week and Easter, Candlemas, and Ash Wednesday were abolished
- (4) "The eight fold Office was reduced to Matins and Evensong"
  - (a) The canticles for Morning and Evening Prayer were taken over from the pre-Reformation Offices as laid down in the 1549 Prayer Book MorE, 95
    - i) This included the Venite and Te Deum from Matins, the Magnificat from Vespers, and the Nunc dimittis from Compline

2. In 1549, a *Psalter of David newely translated into Englysh metre* by Robert Crowley was published LeHM, 371
   a) It was published in London HarME, 500, fn. 3
   b) It was the first complete English metrical Psalter and the first to contain harmonized music
      (1) It contained translations of the psalms by Robert Crowley with a single setting for four voices applicable to all one-hundred-fifty psalms
      ReeMR, 796
      (2) The music consists of no more than a single chant-like tune with a single harmonization of tone 7 which is placed in the tenor CalO, 284
         (a) It imitates the reciting notes of prose psalmody
      (3) A transcription of the harmonization LeHM, 372
   c) It was not destined to live ReeMR, 796
      (1) It seems that this Psalter was little used, perhaps because of the austere and restricted nature of the music CalO, 284

3. Monophonic music for the English liturgy was provided by the *Booke of common praier noted* by John Merbecke CalO, 273
   a) It seems clear that Merbecke may have worked in fairly close collaboration with Cranmer in the production of it LonM, 29
      (1) But Cranmer's *Litany* is not included HunC, 19
   b) The *Booke* was published in 1550 by Richard Grafton MorE, 98
   c) It was originally intended to supply simple plainchant for the priest's and clerks' parts of the 1549 Prayer Book CalO, 273
      (1) The simplicity of the music was meant to make the words intelligible to the hearer, not to enable the music to be sung by the congregation
      (2) There is measured monophonic music for Morning and Evening Prayer, the Communion and the Burial services HarME, 499
   d) The *Booke* contains monophonic music in conformity with the requirements of *The Book of Common Prayer* MorE, 98
      (1) The music is partly adaptations from the traditional chant and partly the original work of Merbecke ReeMR, 796
         (a) Merbecke used simplified forms of the Sarum chants for the Te Deum and *Pater noster* HarME, 499

                    i) The Te Deum is a condensed form of the Ambrosian melody
                                                                    BluPR, 699
            (b) The rest of the music seems to be Merbecke's own except for the
                psalms and canticles
                    i) The *Gloria in excelsis,* the Creed, the Offertory sentences,
                        and the post Communion are by Merbecke   BluPR, 699
        (2) There is virtually no genuine plainsong   FelE, 48
            (a) The melodies are a compromise between plainsong and mensural
                music   ReeMR, 797
                    i) The music departs from plainsong by maintaining the principle
                        of one note to a syllable and also by using leaps BluPR, 699
                        a - Also the notation gives rhythmic indications ReeMR, 797
                    ii) But the monophonic settings are not mensural, "as the shape
                        of the semibreve is sometimes used in recitation passages
                        where it was unnecessary to indicate strict time-values"
            (b) The melodies are modally conceived   SteN, 225
        (3) Time values are adjusted to the accentuation of English   ReeMR, 797
            (a) Merbecke accommodated the prose rhythms of the language to a
                free musical rhythm and, in order to do this, he devised something
                like a mensural notation   BluPR, 699
                    i) He uses notes of four different time values (*breve, semy
                        breve, mynymme,* and as he states it, a "close")   LonM, 29
                    ii) The *breve* is a strene note [♩], the *semy breve* is a square
                        note [■], and the pycke [♦] is a *mynymme*   HunC, 22
                        a - The fourth note is a "close" [♮] which is only used at
                            the end of a verse
                    iii) A prycke by the square note indicates half as much time as
                        the note that goes before it [■♦]   HunC, 22
                        a - In his preface he states that he wants the relative note
                            lengths to be carefully observed and the music sung in
                            tempo   LonM, 29
            (b) Merbecke reveals much skill in adjusting his time-values to the
                normal accentuation of English   ReeMR, 797
    e) It is doubtful that Merbecke's book was ever used   LonM, 29
        (1) With the revision of *The Book of Common Prayer* of 1549 [with the
            second *Book of Common Prayer* of 1552], changes were made that
            resulted in Merbecke's settings no longer fitting the words LonM, 29
            (a) Merbecke made no effort to make revisions
        (2) But in time, the decisions made in the second *Book of Common Prayer*
            became reversed, and Merbecke came into his own again through the
            Oxford Movement [1850], which was the great Catholic Revival in the
            Church of England   HunC, 27
    f) Merbecke produced no more music after the *Booke of Common Praier noted*
                                                                        ReeMR, 798
    g) A list of the extant copies of The *Booke of common praier noted* HunC, 27
    h) Facsimiles of the *Book of Common Praier Noted*
                                                    HunC, 121; ChuB; ChuC; LeaB

4. Besides Merbecke, the chief composers to make important early contributions to

English church music were Tye and Tallis   ReeMR, 798
    a) These two composers continued to compose music into the reign of Elizabeth

5. English church music was halted in Mary's reign and the writing of church music did not really flourish until the cultural revival in the latter half of Elizabeth's reign   FelE, 7

F. The Sacred Latin Music for the Reformed English Church

1. Introduction
    a) It is almost impossible to tell whether a piece of Tudor church music with Latin text was intended for the Roman Catholic service or for the Anglican service   ReeMR, 781
        (1) Even after the formal break between England and the papacy, England continued to have a form of Catholicism
            (a) The Six Articles enacted in 1539 reaffirmed the main points of Catholic doctrine
        (2) English did not become the official language of the service until after 1542   ReeMR, 781
            (a) And it was not until *An Act for the Uniformity of Service...* of 1549, that musical settings of the Mass and all other sacred music wedded to the Latin language were completely ruled out   FelE, 7
    b) During the Tudor period, English polyphony did not include "motets"   HarEP, 307
        (1) That is, pieces which were not an integral part of the liturgy but could be inserted into the service at certain points
            (a) There were some exceptions to this
                i) Such as two settings of texts from the Psalms found in a 1516 manuscript, British Museum, *MS. Royal 11 E. xi*, which do not fit into any particular place in English liturgical practice   HarM, 340
                ii) They are motets in the sense of that word which was normal on the continent but not in England   HarM, 340
        (2) Therefore, the term "motet" actually has no useful application in English music of this period
            (a) But, there are settings of prayers that have been termed "prayer-motets"   RanM, 379
                i) These are settings of prayers that have been extracted from their liturgical environment for use in a devotional context   RanM, 375
                ii) They were possibly designed as a last item in a devotion replacing the customary chanted prayer   RanM, 379
                iii) An example is Ludford's composition, *Domine Jesu Christe*   RanM, 376
                    a - The text is a lengthy prayer to Our Lord
                    b - A transcription of *Domine Jesu Christe*   LudD
            (b) The "prayer-motets gained favor as the votive antiphons decreased after the 1520s   BraS, 84
            (c) Both the "prayer-motets" and the votive antiphon gave way to re-

sponds and hymns in the 1530s and 1540s　　　　　　　　BraS, 84
- (3) The term "motet" did not become customary in English usage until after the Reformation
  - (a) It seems not to have been current before Thomas Morely defined it in *A Plaine and Easie Introduction*　　　　HarME, 478

2. The general style of the sacred Latin music
   a) The techniques of imitative, antiphonal, and homophonic writing increasingly played a part in English settings of shorter liturgical forms　　HarEP, 304
      (1) But. the fully imitative style was delayed until the mid-sixteenth century
          (a) This was due to the persistence of the florid style and *cantus firmus* method
          (b) Also there was a tendency on the part of the English composer to exploit individual vocal tone-color which was partly responsible for the late adoption of more advanced imitative techniques from the Continent　　　　WulT, 192
      (2) Imitation was usually more decorative than formal and therefore did not have the structural significance it was to assume in the latter part of the sixteenth century　　　　LonM, 45
          (a) Short musical phrases (points) were announced first by one voice-part, then taken up by a second while the first voice continued to sing a counter-melody
              i) Then other voices entered with the point
   b) The vocal lines were related to an underlying harmonic framework　LonM, 45
      (1) They involved a good deal of thematic repetition
          (a) These repetitions were often rhythmically varied
   c) The music was rhythmically free as a result of the fact that Latin is a language in which verbal stresses are comparatively weak and unimportant　　LonM, 50
      (1) The text was often divided into short clauses　　　　LonM, 45
          (a) Some of these clauses were set to block harmony
   d) Words or even individual syllables were set to a group of notes and at times an extended phrase or series of phrases　　　　LonM, 47
      (1) As a result, the words lost their significance and identity
   e) Sections for full chorus were often contrasted with passages for two, three, and four solo voices　　　　LonM, 45

3. The votive antiphon, the Magnificat, and the Mass, were most commonly set to polyphony during the early Tudor period　　　　BraS, 54
   a) The votive antiphon
      (1) The general style of the votive antiphon　　　　HarEP, 307
          (a) The votive antiphon was the same in liturgical form with the Mary-antiphons
              i) But it differed in its ritual position and treatment
              ii) It was sung during devotions which followed evening Compline　　　　HanJ, 75
          (b) It was not limited to the four seasonal texts of the Roman Use
              i) Texts were sometimes specified in Statutes, but more frequently they were left to choice　　　　BenL, 20
                 a - They could consist of verse or prose settings which could

			be liturgical or otherwise	HanJ, 75
		ii)	The texts were usually of a petitionary nature and, in the majority of cases, were expressed in the name of the Blessed Virgin Mary	HanJ, 75
	(c)	The chief formal feature of the votive antiphon was the alternation of ornate passages for reduced choir with simpler passages for full choir written around a *cantus firmus*		BraS, 83
		i)	This pattern was followed until about 1530	
	(d)	"The large votive antiphon resembled a single movement of a festal Mass in scale and design"		
		i)	Its use of a plainsong *cantus firmus* had a structural function only	
			a - The *cantus firmus* was not intended to secure liturgical appropriateness	
		ii)	The large votive antiphon was written in a florid style	HarEP, 306
		iii)	Composition of the large votive antiphon continued into the last decade of Henry VIII	HarME, 474
	(e)	Lengthy continuous polyphony was used for settings of the antiphon for much of the pre-reformation period		BraS, 55
(2)	Composers of the votive antiphon			
	(a)	Hugh Aston [b. ca. 1480]		
		i)	General style of his antiphons	WulT, 269
			a - They evince signs of modernity in their technique and bridge the gap between the votive antiphons of an earlier period and those of the Marian period by composers such as William Munday	
		ii)	*Gaude virgo mater Christi*	WulT, 269
			a - This antiphon for five voices shows an imaginative and technically accomplished handling of the florid style	HarEP, 332
			1 - It is a fine work culminating in a splendid "Amen"	CalO, 243
			2 - It uses a text taken from an anonymous composer in the Ritson manuscript	CalO, 243
			b- It is Aston's only complete antiphon	CalO, 243
			1 - But it is imperfectly preserved	BenL, 156
			c - A transcription of *Gaude virgo mater Christi*	BucT X, 85
		iii)	*Ave Maria [divae matris Annae]*	WulT, 269
			a - This is imperfectly preserved	BenL, 156
			b - Transcriptions of *Ave Maria*	BucT X, 127; AstA
		iv)	*Te matrem Dei laudamus*	HarEP, 332
			a - This antiphon is for five parts and also shows an imaginative and technically accomplished handling of the florid style	
			b - The setting has a Marian adaptation of the Te Deum text	CalO, 242
			1 - This is fragmentary	BenL, 156
			c - It was later provided with a non-Marian text, *Te Deum*	

                laudamus   CalO, 242

                      1 - A translation of *Te Deum laudamus*   BucT X, 99

      v)   *Ave Maria ancilla Trinitatis* and *O Baptista vates Christi* are
            fragmentary   BenL, 156

          a - A transcription of *Ave Maria ancilla Trinitatis*
                                                                             BucT X, 114

          b - A transcription *O Baptista vates Christi*   BucT X, 138

(b)   Nicholas Ludford [b. ca. 1485]   BenL, 126

      i)   All of the works listed below are imperfectly preserved

      ii) *Ave cujus conceptio*

          a - A transcription   LudD

      iii) *Ave Maria ancilla Trinitatis*

          a - The opening phrase of this antiphon was used by Ludford
              as the opening phrase of his Mass, *Inclina*   BenL, 132

      iv) *Domine Jesu Christe*

          a - This is a Jesus-antiphon   BenL, 19

          b - It was most commonly sung after Compline as a separate
              and very important devotional act   BenL, 19

              1 - It is a lengthy prayer to Our Lord   RanM, 376

          c - A transcription of *Domine Jesu Christe*   LudD

      v)   *Salve regina pudica mater* and *Salve Regina* are fragmentary

(c)   John Taverner [b. ca. 1495]

      i)   General style of his antiphons

          a - He established relationships in length between various
              sections and types of textures   BenFD, 193

              1 - This technique is found in *Gaude plurimum, Christe
                  Jesu, Mater Christe,* and *O splendor gloriae*
                                                                 BenFD, 198

          b - He uses antiphonal writing with the top two (boys')
              voices answered by the lower three (men's) voices
                                                                  BenL, 142

          a - Some antiphonal writing is chordal   BenL, 143

      ii) Taverner wrote three large-scale festal settings   HanJ, 75

          a - *Ave Dei Patris filia*   ReeMR, 780

              1 - It is possible that this piece was a product of the
                  second decade of the sixteenth century   HanJ, 76

              2 - It is probably the longest single-movement work
                  written by Taverner   JosJ, 123

              3 - It is based on the Te Deum chant and is a rather dull
                  piece   CalO, 238

                  a - The Te Deum is used for the opening theme
                                                                          ReeMR, 780

              4 - Fragments from all five verses of the Te Deum are
                  used as a *cantus firmus*   JosJ, 151

                  a - They are given to the tenor in long note values

                  b - The use of a *cantus firmus* is most unusual for an
                      early sixteenth century votive antiphon   HanJ, 77

              5 - The Amen of the antiphon is based on the last verse
                  of the Te Deum, *In te Domine speravi*   HarM, 331

The Sacred Latin Music for the Reformed English Church 311

      6 - The antiphon is scored in five parts   JosJ, 123
         a - A treble, meane and three men's voices
         b - There are passages for full choir and other passages for reduced voices   HanJ, 77
            1 - The style of the full sections is basically non-imitative   HarM, 331
      7 - A detailed discussion of the text and music   JosJ, 150
      8 - Manuscripts with partbooks containing *Ave Dei Patris filia*   HanJ, 114-118
         a - Cambridge: St. John's College, *MS. K. 31*; University Library, *MS. Dd. 13. 27*; Peterhouse, *MSS. 40, 41, 31, 32*
         b - London: British Museum, *MS. Harley 1709*; Royal College of Music, *MS. 2035*
         c - Oxford: The Bodleian Library, *MSS. Music School, e. 1-5*; The Bodleian Library, *MS. Music School, e. 423*; Christ Church, *MS. 979-83*
         d - Tenbury: St. Michael's College, *MSS. 354-58*
      9 - A facsimile of the beginning of the bass part   JosJ, Plate 4
     10 - A transcription of *Ave Dei Patris filia*   BucT III, 61
  b - *Gaude plurimum*   HarEP, 339
      1 - It is possible that this piece is a product of the second decade of the sixteenth century   HanJ, 76
      2 - The text is a piece of prose in honor of the Blessed Virgin   JosJ, 151
         a - It was later adapted for use in the English [service]   HanJ, 39
      3 - It is long and elaborate and has been treated with a generally syllabic treatment   HanJ, 77
         a - Melismatic writing is reserved for the final 'Amen'   HanJ, 78
      4 - There are frequent imitative entries with a number of voices involved in the point   JosJ, 152
      5 - A detailed discussion of the text and music   JosJ, 151
      6 - Manuscripts containing partbooks of *Gaude plurimum*   HanJ, 114-119
         a - Cambridge: King's College, *Rowe Music Library, MS. 316*
            1 - This source is an adaptation to the English words, *I will magnify Thee*
         b - *Cambridge: Peterhouse, MSS. 40,41,31,32*; St. John's College, *MS. K. 31*
         c - Chelmsford: Essex Record Office, *MS. D/DP. Z. b/1*
         d - London: British Museum, *MS. Harley 1709*; British Museum, *MS. Add. 34191*; British Museum, *MSS. Add. 18936-9*
            1 - The latter manuscript is an excerpt and is

                        incorrectly labeled a Sanctus
                    e - London: British Museum, *MS. Add. 29246*
                        1 - This is a lute transcription
                    f - London: British Museum, *MS. Add. 34049*; British
                        Museum, *MSS. Add. 41156-8*; British Museum,
                        MS. Royal Music Library 24. d. 2; Royal College
                        of Music, *MS. 2035*
                    g - Oxford: The Bodleian Library, *MSS. Music
                        School, e. 1-5*; The Bodleian Library, *MS. Music
                        School, e. 423*; Christ Church, *MS. 979-83*
                    h - Tenbury: St. Michael's College, *MSS. 341-44*;
                        MSS. 354-58; *MSS. 1469-71*; *MS. 1486*
                    i - Worcester: Worcestershire Record Office, *The
                        Wilmott MS*
                7 - A transcription of an excerpt labeled Sanctus
                                                            BucT III, 58
                8 - A transcription of *Gaude plurimum*   BucT III, 78
            c - *O splendor gloriae*   HarEP, 339
                1 - This antiphon is the most mature of the three large-
                    scale antiphons   HanJ, 78
                    a - It is thought to be the latest of the three major
                        antiphons   JosJ, 154
                    b - It is a fine, closely knit work, part of which is
                        elsewhere attributed to Tye   CalO, 238
                2 - It is a Jesus-antiphon   BenL, 19
                    a - The text is an account of the Lord's role in crea-
                        tion, his conception and birth, Passion, resurrec-
                        tion, ascension, and his gift of the Holy Spirit
                                                            BenL, 152
                3 - The text is treated syllabically except for some phrase-
                    ending melismas and the final "Amen"   JosJ, 152
                    a - In the "Amen", Taverner allows his polyphony to
                        flower in well-contrived melismatic phrases of
                        great beauty   HanJ, 78
                4 - There is extensive imitation   HanJ, 78
                    a - At times it is the controlling factor in the entire
                        musical structure
                5 - A detailed discussion of the text and music   JosJ, 152
                6 - Manuscripts containing partbooks of *O splendor
                    gloriae*   HanJ, 116-119
                    a - Chelmsford: Essex Record Office, *MS. D/DP. Z.
                        b/1*
                    b - Oxford: The Bodleian Library, *MSS. Music
                        School, e. 1-5*; Christ Church, *MS. 979-83*
                7 - A transcription of *O splendor gloriae* BucT III, 99
    iii) There are six short votive antiphons   HanJ, 75
         a - *Mater Christi*
             1 - This is the only one of the short votive antiphons to
                 come down to us complete   HanJ, 78

The Sacred Latin Music for the Reformed English Church 313

    2 - It is written in a restrained, syllabic style which gives way at the cadences to melismatic embellishments   JosJ, 154
    3 - This antiphon was later adapted for use in the English [service]   HanJ, 39
    4 - Manuscripts containing partbooks of *Mater Christi*   HanJ, 116-117
      a - Cambridge: King's College, *Rowe Music Library, MS. 316*
        1 - This source is an adaptation to the English words, *O most Holy and Mighty Lord*
      b - Oxford: The Bodleian Library, *MSS. Music School, e. 420-22*; Christ Church, *MS. 979-83*
    5 - A transcription of *Mater Christi*   BucT III, 92
  b - *Christe Jesu pastor bone*   HarEP, 339
    1 - It is written for five voices in point-against-point style
      a - The tenor voice is lost   BenL, 153
    2 - There is antiphonal writing with one group repeating the text previously sung by the other
    3 - The text has come down to us in an altered form   JosJ, 154
      a - It contains a prayer for Henry VIII   ReeMR, 781
    4 - The entire choir is employed at various points and at the close
    5 - Manuscripts containing partbooks of *Christe Jesu pastor bone*   HanJ, 117
      a - Cambridge: Peterhouse, *MSS. 40,41,31,32*
      b - Oxford: Christ Church, *MS. 979-83*
    6 - A Facsimile of the treble part of *Christe Jesu pastor bone*   JosJ, Plate 16
    7 - A transcription of *Christe Jesu...*   BucT III, 73
  c - *Ave Maria*
    1 - There are short homophonic passages alternating with polyphony   HanJ, 80
    2 - There is a limited use of imitation   HanJ, 80
      a - The chordal fabric is interrupted only briefly by simple points of imitation   JosJ, 155
    3 - There are two interruptions stipulated for the ringing of bells   JosJ, 155
    4 - The manuscript Cambridge: Peterhouse, *MSS. 40,41, 31,32* contains the partbooks of *Ave Maria*   HanJ, 117
    5 - A transcription of *Ave Maria*   BucT III, 134
  d - *Sancte Deus*
    1 - This is a short and simple setting   HanJ, 80
    2 - It was supposed to be sung after *Ave Maria* in front of the Crucifix in the nave   BenL, 153
    3 - Only three of the original voice-parts have survived   JosJ, 155
      a - The treble and tenor voices are lost   BenL, 153

                    4 - The rich chordal setting is interrupted only briefly by simple points of imitation   JosJ, 155
                    5 - The manuscript Cambridge: Peterhouse, *MSS. 40,41, 31,32* contains the partbooks of *Sancte Deus*   HanJ, 117
                    6 - A transcription of *Sancte Deus*   BucT III, 139
            e - *Sub tuum praesidium*
                  1 - This setting of a Marian antiphon is in an incomplete state   JosJ, 15
                      a - Only three of the five original voice parts have survived
                      b - The treble and tenor voices are lost   BenL, 153
                  2 - The words do not appear in the Sarum liturgy   BenL, 153
                  3 - The manuscript Cambridge: Peterhouse, *MSS. 40,41, 31,32* contains the partbooks of *Sub tuum praesidium*   HanJ, 117
                  4 - A transcription of *Sub tuum praesidium* BucT III, 141
            f - *Fac nobis*
                  1 - This antiphon has come to us in an incomplete state   JosJ, 155
                      a - Only three of the original five voice-parts have survived
                      b - The treble and tenor voices are lost   BenL, 153
                  2 - It has gracefully shaped phrases   HanJ, 80
                  3 - It is longer than some of the other settings and the most florid   HanJ, 80
                  4 - Imitation is a regular feature of the style   HanJ, 80
                  5 - The manuscript Cambridge: Peterhouse, *MSS. 40,41, 31,32* contains the partbooks of *Fac nobis*   HanJ, 117
                  6 - A transcription of *Fac nobis*   BucT III, 135
    iv)   There are two settings which are probably excerpts from larger works   HanJ, 76
            a - *Prudens Virgo*
                  1 - This is a Marian setting for three voices   HanJ, 82
                      a - It is set for two tenors and a bass   JosJ, 155
                  2 - It is thought that it is an extract from a lost five-part antiphon of the Blessed Virgin   JosJ, 155
                  3 - The manuscript London: British Museum, *MS. Royal Music Library 24. d. 2* contains the partbooks of *Prudens Virgo*   HanJ, 115
                      a - This is an early seventeenth century commonplace book
                  4 - A transcription of *Prudens Virgo*   BucT III, 124
            b - *Virgo pura*
                  1 - This is a Marian setting for three voices   HanJ, 82
                      a - There are two tenors and a bass   JosJ, 155
                  2 - It is thought that it is an extract from a lost five-part antiphon of the Blessed Virgin   JosJ, 155

		3 - It is written in melismatic style	HanJ, 83

             4 - The manuscript London: British Museum, *MS. Royal Music Library 24. d. 2* contains the partbooks of *Virgo pura*   HanJ, 115

             5 - A transcription of *Virgo pura*   BucT III, 131

    v)   Transcriptions of Taverner's votive antiphons   TavJ

(d)   Christopher Tye [b. ca. 1495]   BenL, 206

    i)   Tye most likely did not write much Latin church music after the death of Henry VIII   BenL, 207

         a - He may well have been strongly Protestant

    ii)   *Peccavimus cum patribus*

         a - This is for seven voices

         b - The opening lines are from a psalm, but the composition seems to be another Jesus-antiphon   BenL, 209

         c - This is found in Oxford: Christ Church, *MSS 979-983*   SatC, 56

         d - A transcription of *Peccavimus cum patribus*   TyeP

    iii)   *Ave caput Christi*   BenL, 206

         a - This is written for six voices

         b - It is now fragmentary   BenL, 209

         c - It has a text of four-line stanzas each hailing some aspect of Christ's Passion   BenL, 209

         d - This is found in Oxford: Library of Christ Church College, Christ Church Mus., *MS 45*   SatC, 53

         e - A transcription of *Ave caput Christi*   SatC II

    iv)   *Sub tuam protectionem*

         a - This begins by following a Marian antiphon from the feasts of the Virgin's Conception and Nativity   BenL, 208

             1 - It even refers to the opening of the proper plainsong   BenL, 209

             2 - But it commences as an independent Jesus-antiphon   BenL, 209

         b - It is written for four voices   BenL, 206

             1 - It is not in *alternatim*

         c - This is found in London: British Museum, *MSS. Add. 17802-5* (the 'Gyffard' partbooks)   SatC, 57

         d - A transcription of *Sub tuam protectionem*   SatC II

(e)   Thomas Tallis [b. ca.1505]

    i)   Tallis' antiphons were written for the Sarum Use   BenL, 180

         a - Since the Sarum liturgy was finally outlawed in 1559, they were most likely written before that date   BenL, 163

    ii)   He wrote four large votive antiphons   DoeT, 12

         a - *Salve intemerata*

             1 - The text of this antiphon is in prose

                 a - It is rather rambling and long   BenL, 180

                 b - There is far too much text for its content and interest, even with limited melisma   BenL, 180

             2 - The music is divided into two sections, each consisting of two solo sections followed by one full section

          a - This antiphon has the final *tutti* relieved by two very brief solo passages
     3 - The texture is seldom imitative but there is much use of melodic formulae   DoeT, 15
     4 - Manuscripts containing *Salve intemerata*
          a - Chelmsford: Essex Record Office, *MS. D/DP. Z. b/1*   FelT, 6
          b - Oxford: Christ Church, *MSS 979-983*   BraP, 184
          c - Tenbury: St. Michael's College, *MSS. 1469-1471*   FelT, 8
          d - Tenbury: St. Michael's College, *MS. 1486*   FelT, 5
          e - Worcester: Worcestershire Record Office, *The Willmott MS.*   FelT, 5
     5 - A transcription of *Salve intemerata*   BucT VI, 144
  b - *Ave rosa sine spinis*
     1 - This is fragmentary and was most likely written during the Henrician period   BenL, 181
     2 - This has a verse text of seven stanzas and is similar to *Ave Dei Patris filia*
          c - The text is a troped form of the *Ave Maria*   BenL, 180
     3 - The music is divided into two sections, each consisting of two solo sections followed by one full section
          a - There are extended melismas   BenL, 180
     4 - This is Tallis' most old-fashioned piece   BenL, 180
     5 - Manuscripts containing *Ave rosa sine spinis*
          a - Chelmsford: Essex Record Office, *MS. D/DP. Z. b/1*   FelT, 6
          b - Oxford: Christ Church, *MSS 979-983*   BraP, 184
     6 - A transcription of *Ave rosa sine spinis*   BucT VI, 169
  c - *Ave Dei Patris filia*
     1 - This is most likely from the Henrician period   BenL, 181
     2 - It has a verse text of seven stanzas
          a - This number is widely associated with the Virgin
          b - It is found typically in the Feasts of the Seven Joys and Seven Sorrows
     3 - The music is divided into two sections, each consisting of two solo sections and followed by one full section
          a - It is in duple rhythm throughout   DoeT, 15
               1 - This is a feature that became increasingly common from about 1540 onwards
     4 - Manuscripts containing *Ave Dei Patris filia*
          a - Chelmsford: Essex Record Office, *MS. D/DP. Z. b/1*   FelT, 6
          b - Tenbury: St. Michael's College, *MS. 1464*   FelT, 8
          c - Tenbury: St. Michael's College, *MSS. 1469-1471*   FelT, 8

The Sacred Latin Music for the Reformed English Church 317

                d - Tenbury: St. Michael's College, *MS. 1486* FelT, 5
                e - Worcester: Worcestershire Record Office, *The Willmott MS.* FelT, 5
                f - The manuscripts are fragmentary BenL, 181
           5 - A transcription of *Ave Dei Patris filia* BucT VI, 162
        d - The antiphon, *Gaude gloriosa*, was written during Mary's reign BraS, 85
     iii) Tallis also wrote one short votive antiphon DoeT, 11
        a - *Sancte Deus*
           1 - This small antiphon is marvelously effective with its ringing invocations DoeT, 15
           2 - It is most likely from the Henrician period BenL, 181
           3 - A transcription of *Sancte Deus* BucT VI, 98
(d) John Merbecke [b. ca. 1510] HarME, 474
     i) His two antiphons are written in a competent and craftsman-like manner, but are of little positive interest BenI, 160
        a - They are of a kind which he presumably would not have wished to see preserved CalO, 240
     ii) They were most likely written for post-compline LeaJ, 50
        a - It is thought they were written about 1530
     iii) They are written for five voices LeaJ, 50
        a - *Ave Dei Patris filia*
           1 - This is a Mary antiphon CalO, 240
           2 - It is found in Cambridge: University Library Peterhouse, *MSS. 471-4* [The Peterhouse partbooks] BucT X, 162
           3 - A transcription of *Ave Dei Patris filia* BucT X, 215
        b - *Domine Jesu Christe*
           1 - This is a Jesus antiphon CalO, 240
           2 - It is found in Oxford: Bodleian *MSS. Mus. Sch. e. 1-5* BucT X, 162
           3 - A transcription of *Domine Jesu Christe* BucT X, 200
(e) John Sheppard [b. ca. 1515] BenL, 196
     i) He sets the texts of his votive antiphons complete BenL, 202
     ii) Since he was probably not active before 1540, it is not surprising that there are, apart from fragments, only two votive antiphons by him BenL, 203
        a - *Gaude virgo christipera* BenL, 196
           1 - This is written for six voices
              a - It has a rhyming text BenL, 203
           2 - It is imperfectly preserved
              a - The treble voice is lost BenL, 203
        a - *Gaudete coelicolae omnes*
           1 - This is written for four voices
           2 - It is an antiphon for All Saints
     iii) There are three fragments of antiphons, all for three voices
        a - *Igitur O Jesu*
        b - *Illustrissima omnium*
        c - *Singularis privilegii*

b) Canticles: The polyphonic Magnificat
   (1) General style of the polyphonic Magnificat
      (a) It was set in *alternatim*   BraS, 54
         i) Polyphony was provided for every other verse   RanH, 465
            a - This was done usually for the even-numbered verse but sometimes for the odd-numbered one
         ii) The rest was sung to plainchant   RanH, 465
      (b) The verses were sung to one of a set of psalm tones determined by the mode of the accompanying antiphon   RanH, 465
         i) But following the Reformation, when English was substituted for Latin, the English Magnificat was no longer based on the psalm tones
      (c) The florid style was invariably used   HarEP, 306
   (2) Composers of the polyphonic Magnificat
      (a) Nichoas Ludford [b. ca. 1485]
         i) *Benedicta* for six voices   BenL, 126
            a - This Magnificat shows a mastery that is astonishing by a composer of whom virtually nothing was known until modern times   CalO, 219
            b - It has two bass parts   BenL, 130
            c - The first eight bars serve as the Mass' head-motive   BenL, 130
            d - The full sections are based on the same plainsong as the Mass, *Benedicta et venerabilis'* verse from the eighth respond at Matins of the Assumption, *Beata es virgo Maria*   BenL, 130
                1 - The fact that this Magnificat is based on a Mass-style *cantus firmus* is exceptional and makes it almost certain that the Magnificat was written after the Mass
                2 - Since the *cantus firmus* is the same as that of the Mass, the Magnificat effectively becomes a fifth movement   CalO, 219
            e - The *Et incarnatus* is scored for high voices and the *Crucifixus* for low   CalO, 219
                1 - An example showing the *Et incarnatus* and *Crucifixus*   CalO, 220
            f - Transcriptions of *Benedicta*   LudC II; DoeE
      (b) John Taverner [b. ca. 1495]
         i) A Magnificat on the first Tone for six voices   HarEP, 339
            a - This is written in *alternatim*   HanJ, 84
                1 - The odd-numbered verses are sung to plainchant and the even verses are treated polyphonically   JosJ, 155
                2 - Each pair of polyphonic verses is treated as a major section
            b - There is contrast in the texture by the use of adjacent passages for full and reduced choir   HanJ, 86
                1 - There is audacious vocal acrobatics in the reduced sections and rich sonorities in the full sections   JosJ, 157

The Sacred Latin Music for the Reformed English Church   319

                a - The full sections have the first Tone with a little elaboration in places   BenL, 154
          c - The Magnificat is built on a *cantus firmus* taken from the psalm tones   HanJ, 85
              1 - The *cantus firmus* is in the tenor voice in long-note values
              2 - It is treated with considerable freedom
                a - Taverner has abandoned the traditional elaborated faburden tenor   BenL, 154
          d - Much of the top part of this Magnificat is missing   CalO, 234 fn.117
          e - Manuscripts containing the six voice Magnificat   HanJ, 115-118
              1 - London: British Museum, *MSS. 18936-9*
              2 - Oxford: Christ Church, *MS. 45*; The Bodleian Library, *MS. Music School, e. 423*
              3 - Tenbury: St. Michael's College, MSS. 354-58; MSS. 807-811
          f - A transcription of the Magnificat on the first Tone for six voices   BucT III, 3
    ii) A Magnificat on the second Tone for five voices   HarEP, 339
          a - This is based on the faburden and is in *alternatim*   CalO, 234
          b - There is contrast in the texture by the use of adjacent passages for full and reduced choir   HanJ, 86
              1 - The florid duos are harnessed by strong motives in sequence treatment   JosJ, 156
              2 - The full sections are more restrained and only occasionally integrated by imitation   JosJ, 156
          c - The polyphony follows the English tradition of basing an elaborate faburden of the plainchant in the tenor voice   JosJ, 155
              1 - But the tenor voice is missing   BenL, 154
          d - The Magnificat is found in Cambridge: Peterhouse, *MSS. 40, 41, 31, 32*   HanJ, 117
          e - A transcription of the Magnificat on the second Tone for five voices   BucT III, 9
    iii) A Magnificat on the sixth Tone for four voices   HarEP, 339
          a - This is written in *alternatim*   HanJ, 84
          b - This is the only setting that has survived in its complete form   HanJ, 84
          c - The setting is built on a *cantus firmus* taken from the psalm tones   HanJ, 85
              1 - In this setting, Taverner has abandoned the traditional elaborated faburden tenor   BenL, 154
          d - This is perhaps the most advanced of the Magnificats   JosJ, 156
              1 - The contrapuntal texture is integrated by imitation
                a - But, most of these points are free of the repeated

320 Sacred Latin and Vernacular Music in England

        cantus firmus
      e - There is contrast in the texture by the use of adjacent
        passages for full and reduced choir   HanJ, 86
      f - The Magnificat is found in London: British Museum,
        MSS. Add. 17802-5   HanJ, 114
      g - A transcription of the Magnificat on the sixth Tone for
        four voices   BucT III, 17
  (c) Christopher Tye [b. ca. 1495]   BenL, 206
    i) There are two settings for six voices
    ii) Both of these are fragmented
  (d) John Sheppard [b. ca. 1515]
    i) A six-part Magnificat   BenL, 196
     a - This is fragmentary
    ii) A four-part Magnificat   BenL, 196
     a - The plainsong and faburden appear occasionally
        BenL, 202
      1 - The first half of Tone I is in the bass at *Sicut erat*
      2 - The plainsong, in decorated form, appears at *Fecit*
        potentiam
 c) Canticles: The Te Deum laudamus
  (1) General style of the Te Deum
   (a) This is a song of praise to God that was sung at the end of Matins
     on Sundays and Feast days   RanH, 836
    i) "In the Anglican rite, it is a canticle at Morning Prayer"
    ii) There are polyphonic settings from the late Middle Ages and
      Renaissance   RanH, 837
   (b) There are a variety of styles in the texts and they quote the Sanctus
     of the Mass and several Psalms   RanH, 836
  (2) Composers of the Te Deum
   (a) Hugh Aston [b. ca. 1480]
    i) *Te Deum laudamus*   BucT X, 99
     a - The words of *Te Deum Laudamus* are not those of the
      normal Te Deum from Matins, the title of which is *Te*
      matrem Dei laudamus   BenL, 158
      1 - *Te matrem Dei laudamus* is a Marian adaptation of
       the Te Deum text   CalO, 242
      2 - *Te Deum laudamus* contains a non-Marian text
        CalO, 242
     b - Manuscripts containing the music of *Te Deum laudamus*
      1 - London: British Library, *Harley 1709* BucT X, xviii
       a - This contains the medius only
      2 - Cambridge: University Library, *MS. Dd.13.27*
        BucT X, xviii
       a - This contains the bassus only
      3 - Oxford: Bodleian Library, *MSS. Music School, e 1-5*
        BucT X, xviii
      4 - Cambridge: St. John's College Library, *MS. K31*
       (James 234)   BucT X, xviii
     c - A transcription of *Te Deum laudamus* BucT, 99

(b) John Taverner [b. ca. 1495]
    i) He wrote a five voice Te Deum   HanJ, 84
        a - It is for men's voices only   CalO, 235
            1 - "The tenor is missing from the only source, but can be reconstructed as it carried the plainchant"
        b - The Te Deum is florid in style with a festal mood and a controlled expression of praise
        c - It is written in *alternatim* with the even-numbered verses set in polyphony and the odd-numbered verses sung to plainsong
            1 - The chant is handled quite liberally   JosJ, 157
                a - There is alteration of several cadences
        d - The *alternatim* structure creates self-contained sections
            1 - Some begin imitatively and end with a melisma on the final word
        e - Imitation is close and is scored for all voices throughout
            1 - This differs greatly from his other pieces which usually have equal-note *cantus firmi*   BenL, 156
        f - There is text repetition at the end of phrases   JosJ, 157
        g - The Te Deum is found in Oxford: Christ Church, *MSS. 979-83*   HanJ, 117
        h - Transcriptions of the five voice Te Deum   BucT III, 26; TavR, 53
            1 - The latter transcription has plainchant insertions and a superior reconstruction of the tenor CalO, 235 fn. 118
(c) Christopher Tye [b. ca. 1495]   BenL, 206
    i) *Te Deum laudamus*
        a - This was originally written for six voices
            1 - But, only a single voice has survived   BenL, 209
        b - It must have been an antiphon of the Trinity or a motet   BenL, 209
        c - It has the complete text of the hymn   BenL, 209
(d) John Sheppard [b. ca. 1515]
    i) There is one setting of the Te Deum for six voices BenL, 196
        a - It is a work of great grandeur   CalO, 307
    ii) A transcription of *Te Deum laudamus*   SheD

d) The Mass
  (1) The Tudor Mass proved itself as a vehicle for splendid and reverent musical adornment from the beginning of the sixteenth century, or the last decade of the fifteenth, until the abbeys and monasteries were being despoiled (1536-1541)   SteC, 23
    (a) After rising to great heights, it suddenly vanished
    (b) It reappeared with Byrd
  (2) General style of the Mass
    (a) Most Masses had the text set in continuous polyphony with contrast between full and reduced texture   BraS, 54
        i) These Masses usually were confined to settings of the festal Mass and antiphon   BraS, 55
    (b) Texts were seldom compressed into a small musical space SteC, 27

	i)	This was due to the opulent and melismatic style of the music
(c)		But, composers, such as Taverner, and Ludford, went to some trouble to make the four sections of the polyphonic Mass fairly equal in length SteC, 27
	i)	As a result, the Credo, which has the longest text of the sung portions of the Ordinary, was curtailed in order to match the other sections
	ii)	But omission of certain phrases was frequent and not confined to one composer or period SteC, 26

- a - "There are at least ten different Credo omissions, some long and some short, but it is significant to note that composers do not adhere to any single pattern of omission"   SteC, 27
- b - The usual place for omissions was in the latter part of the Credo from *et resurrexit tertia die* to the end

(d) The Lady-Masses and a few very early Tudor Masses were written in *alternatim* with phrases of the text alternating between polyphony and plainsong or squares   BraS, 54
    i) This included the Kyrie, Gloria, and Credo   HarEP, 307
        a - It was also true for the Alleluia and sequence   BenL, 12
    ii) There was divergence in thought as to which phrases were given to polyphony and which phrases to the singers of plainchant   SteC, 28

(e) The Mass and antiphon, at times, were linked to each other by a shared *cantus firmus,* a structural relationship, or common musical material   BraS, 55
    i) "The cantus firmus, when liturgical, gave the work its *raison d'être*, since the feast for which the Mass was intended was usually represented by an antiphon or respond from the Office of the day"   SteC, 29
        a - This tradition of liturgical relevance was a factor in the prolonging of the *cantus firmus* Mass in England   HarEP, 306
        b - But, the *cantus firmus* was no longer a major formal influence on the structure of the composition   BraS, 78
    ii) Some but not all passages were based on a *cantus firmus*   BraS, 78
        a - The *cantus firmus* usually appeared only during the sections for full choir   SteC, 30
            1 - Pieces written before the 1530s have a substantial number of passages for reduced voices that are not written on a *cantus firmus*   BraS, 56
                a - Sections in duo or trio use independent motives   SteC, 30
        b - The normal position of the *cantus firmus* was in the tenor part   SteC, 29
    iii) There are a small number of works based on a secular or para-liturgical *cantus firmus*   SteC, 32
        a - Four-part Masses on *The Western Wynde* by Sheppard,

                    Taverner, and Tye are examples
            iv) In the last years of the Sarum rite composers had lost interest in writing large-scale *cantus firmus* Masses HarME, 473
                a - The *Per arma justitiae* by Merbecke was almost the only example from this generation
                    1 - It may have been written as early as 1531
                    2 - A transcription of *Per arma justitiae* BucT X, 165
                b - The Sarum rite was officially abolished in England in 1559 RanH, 727
        (f) Some Masses written on a particular theme are either choral variations, *missa paradia*, or those referring to a unifying theme but not used in the orthodox *cantus firmus* method HarME, 473
            i) A piece of unifying structural aid was a short phrase common to the beginnings of all four sections of the Mass SteC, 30
                a - This has become known as a head-motive, which is quite suitable provided it is clearly understood that the motive is a polyphonic segment, and recurs at the beginning of Gloria, Credo, Sanctus and Agnus Dei
(3) Composers of the Mass
    (a) Thomas Ashwell [b. ca. 1478]
        i) He is a much more important figure than has been generally recognized BraS, 68
            a - He has not been recognized, no doubt, due to the misfortune in the survival rate of his music
            b - Also, his Masses are immensely complex in construction and, as a result, they may have created problems for singers no longer able to cope with an older tradition which made use of three colors of notes showing different mensurations
            c - But the anxiety of the contemporary arrangers to avoid using multicolored notation has led to other problems almost as great as those being avoided BraS, 69
                1 - In the Mass, *Ave Maria*, there is an excessive use of dots of either perfection or addition
                2 - Also, there are annotations attempting to clarify the proportions which are not always accurate
        ii) Two complete Masses have survived BraS, 68
            a - *Jesu Christe*
                1 - This Mass is written for six voices CalO, 241
                2 - It is based on the short respond from Prime in Easter week BenL, 159
                3 - The plainsong, *Jesu Christe*, is so monotonous that it presented a challenge to the composer BraS, 73
                    a - Therefore, Ashwell devised a complex rhythmic layout [for the plainsong] which could not be made into the basis for the imitative writing
                        1 - The *cantus firmus* is laid out as a study in proportions CalO. 241
                4 - There is imitation based on Ashwell's own material

                        that is fully worked out in all voices   BraS, 73
                5 - This is found in Oxford: Bodleian Library, *MSS.*
                    Arch. f. e. 19-24 (The Forrest-Heather partbooks)
                         BraS, 69
                6 - A facsimile of *Jesu Christe*   OxfM, 76v
            b - *Ave Maria*
                1 - This is in six parts and is based on an antiphon at
                    Commemorations of the Virgin in Advent   BenL. 159
                2 - It is noteworthy for its rhythmic qualities and the
                    brilliance of its scoring   CalO. 241
                3 - In this Mass, Ashwell shows a greater interest in imitation   BraS, 73
                    a - "The opening of each movement is imitative and
                        based on the first few notes of the 'Ave Maria'
                        plainsong"
                    b - These first few notes are set in a different way in
                        each movement   HarEP, 333
                4 - The plainsong pervades the Mass in all voices, not
                    just the tenor
                    a - The complete *cantus firmus* is also used as the
                        basis of some of the solo sections
                5 - The Mass contains a rare example of double gymel in
                    the Gloria   SteC, 30
                    a - The trebles and altos are both divided at one point
                    b - This gives a complete and rich harmonic effect of
                        high tessitura
                6 - This is found in Oxford: Bodleian Library, *MSS.*
                    Arch. f. e. 19-24 (The Forrest-Heather partbooks)
                         BenL, 25
                7 - A facsimile of *Ave Maria*   OxfM, 102v
        iii) There is also a fragmentary Mass
            a - *Sancte Cuthberte*
                1 - This was evidently written as part of Ashwell's obligations at Durham which specified that every year
                    he had to compose a four- or five-part Mass "in
                    honor of God, of the Virgin Mary, and of St. Cuthbert"   BraS, 68
                2 - This is found in London: Brit. Lib., *Add. 30520*, fos.
                    3ʳ⁻ᵛ   CalO, 240, fn. 137
                    a - It is possibly based on the Salisbury respond
                        Sancte N. Christi confessor
(b) Hugh Aston [b. ca. 1480]
    i) The general style of his music   Buc I, xxii
        a - His part writing is vigorous and his climaxes are sustained
        b - His two large-scale Masses are powerful works prefiguring the vigor of Sheppard's style   WulT, 269
        c - His works show an imaginative and technically accomplished handling of the florid style   HarEP, 332

ii) His two large-scale Masses have survived BraS, 68
    a - *Te Deum*
        1 - This Mass is written for five voices HarEP, 332
        2 - It and Aston's antiphon both use the Marian adaptation, *Te matrem Dei laudamus*, for their settings
                                                                    CalO, 242
            a - Both use parts of the Te Deum plainsong as a *cantus firmus* and have a common opening phrase
                                                                    BenL, 159
        3 - The Mass is based on a *pot-pourri* of three or more tunes from the Te Deum plainsong BraS, 74
            a - It makes almost continuous use of a *cantus firmus* that is the chant of the second verse of the Te Deum HarEP, 333
                1 - The chant appears twenty-six times in various voices
                2 - As a result, the Mass approaches variations in form
        4 - The Sanctus verse of the Te Deum is the *cantus firmus* of the Sanctus of the Mass HarEP, 333
            a - It is also tonally contrasted with the other movements CalO, 243
                1 - It cadences in G while the other movements cadence in C
            b - The first verse of the Te Deum is the basis of the common opening of the other three movements
                                                                   HarEP, 333
                1 - That is, the opening of the Gloria, Credo, and Agnus CalO, 243
            c - The *cantus firmus* of the Agnus is not from the Te Deum at all BraS, 74
        5 - Manuscripts containing the music of *Te Deum*
            a - Cambridge: University Library Peterhouse, *MSS. 471-4* [The Peterhouse partbooks] BucT X, xviii
                1 - This was formerly *MSS. 40, 41, 31, 32*
                                                                    BraS, 50
            b - Cambridge: University Library, *MS. Dd.13.27*; St. John's College Library, *MS. K31 (James 234)*
                                                                   BucT X, xviii
            d - Oxford: Bodleian Library, *MSS. Arch. f. e. 19-24* (The Forrest-Heather partbooks) BucT X, xviii
                1 - This was formerly *Mus. Sch. e. 376-81*
                                                                    BraS, 50
        6 - A facsimile of *Te Deum* OxfM, 53
        7 - A transcription of *Te Deum* BucT X, 1
    b - *Vitete manus meas*
        1 - This is written for six voices HarEP, 332
            a - It is based on the Magnificat antiphon for Tuesday in Easter Week

		b - It is massively scored and motivically conceived CalO, 241
		2 - It omits the first three notes of the *cantus firmus* for several statements BraS, 74
		3 - It bases some points of imitation on extraneous *cantus firmi* rather than totally free material
		4 - This is found in Oxford: Bodleian Library, *MSS. Arch f. e. 19-24* (The Forrest-Heather partbooks) BucT X, xviii
		a - There are several mistakes in this source BraS, 74
		5 - A facsimile of *Vitete manus meas* OxfM, 107v
		6 - Transcriptions of *Vitete manus meas* BucT X, 39; BerE II
	iii)	A third work survives in fragmentary form (the bass part only) BraS, 68
		a - This is written on the same ground bass as an instrumental piece called *Aston's Maske*
		1 - This may be a mistake for Aston's Mass
(c)	Nickolas Ludford [b. ca. 1485] BraS, 77
	i)	He is a very accomplished composer BenL, 127
	ii)	His output is varied BenL, 126
		a - It contains some six-voice writing and the set of three-voice Lady Masses
	iii)	His Masses are among those that combined *cantus firmus* with a head-motive SteC, 30
		a - The *cantus firmus* of the Mass was usually presented in equal notes BenL, 131
		1 - This was a favorite procedure with Ludford
	iv)	His music is seldom very florid BenL, 126
	v)	Ludford often went to some trouble to make the four sections of the polyphonic Mass fairly equal in length SteC, 27
		a - But he is noted for setting the entire text of the Credo without any omissions
	vii)	There are six large-scale festal Masses that have survived as well as fragments of a seventh
		a - Four of these large-scale festal Masses have survived complete HarEP, 330
		1 - The *Benedicta* Mass
		a - This is linked structurally and melodically with his Magnificat of the same name BraS, 77
		b - It has six voices and is unusual in that it is based on the verse of a respond, *Beata es* for the Assumption
		1 - The plainsong is *benedicta et venerabilis* BenL, 130
		c - Ludford sets the *Et incarnatus* for high voices and the *Crucifixus* for low CalO, 219
		1 - This was unusual at the time
		2 - An example of *Et incarnatus* and the *Cruci-*

     fixus   CalO, 220
  d - In this Mass, Ludford has a great feeling for florid
    detail and a tendency toward rapid declamation
                BenL, 130
  e - There is a passage at the end of the Credo which
    has a little bell-like theme worked in imitation
                BenL, 130
    1 - It is always off the beat in the bass parts
  f - A transcription of the *Benedicta* Mass LudC II
2 - The *Christi virgo* Mass
  a - This is written for five voices on a respond for the
    Annunciation
    1 - Ludford indulges in brilliant and florid voice-
      writing which must have taxed the powers of
      the singers severely   SteC, 31
  b - This Mass has some interesting antiphonal effects
    in the *Et incarnatus* and at *Et in Spiritum Sanctum*   BenL, 132
    1 - These are the parts of the Credo that are not
      normally set in large-scale English Masses
    2 - The antiphony does not involve any repetition
    3 - An example of the *Et incarnatus*
  c - A transcription of the *Christi virgo* Mass LudC II
3 - The *Lapidaverunt [Stephanum]* Mass
  a - This is in five parts on an antiphon for the feast of
    St. Stephen
  b - Manuscripts that contain *Lapidaverunt Stephanum*   BenL, 125
    1 - Cambridge: Gonville and Caius College, *MS. 667*
    2 - London: Lambeth Palace, *MS. 1*
  c - A transcription of the *Lapidaverunt* Mass LudC II
4 - The *Videte miraculum* Mass
  a - This is for six parts with two interweaving treble
    voices
    1 - In the solo passages involving the two trebles,
      the music is more florid than that found in the
      Benedicta Mass   BenL, 130
    2 - The scalic writing is tight and imitative
                BenL, 131
    3 - An example of the above BenL, 131
  b - The Mass is based on the respond at first Vespers
    of the Purification   BenL, 130
  c - It is a brilliant testimony of Ludford's powers as a
    contrapuntist   SteC, 31
  d - It has some special features in the treatment of the
    cantus firmus   HarEP, 330
    1 - It has one statement in each movement based
      on the respond for the feast of the Purification

        2 - The statement is divided according to the three sentences of its text
        e - A transcription of *Videte miraculum*   LudC II
    b - The *Inclina cor meum* [*Deus*] Mass has strutural links with the antiphon *Ave Maria ancilla*
        1 - It is based on an Epiphany respond   BenL, 132
           a - It lacks its tenor part
        2 - It is found in the Cambridge: Peterhouse, *MSS 471-474*   SanH, 137
        3 - A transcription of the *Inclina cor meum* Mass   LudC II
    c - The *Regnum mundi* Mass   BenL, 126
        1 - This mass is fragmentary
        2 - It is found in the Cambridge: Peterhouse, *MSS 471-474*   SanH, 138
        3 - A transcription of the *Regnum mundi* Mass   LudC II
    d - *Leroy* is a fragmented Mass and is unique in surviving festal repertoire in having a square as its *cantus firmus*
        1 - In the surviving fragment from the Benedictus, the *Leroy* square retains its own rhythm at *Osanna* but not in the immediately following *in excelsis*   BraS, 77
        2 - A transcription of *Leroy*   LudC II
viii) There are seven small-scale Lady-Masses   BenL, 126
    a - These Masses are the only complete system of daily votive Masses of the Virgin remaining in English music   BerL, 35
        1 - They cannot be any earlier than 1509 nor later than 1533
    b - They exist in four presentation books   WulT, 259
        1 - There are three partbooks for the three voices and a fourth partbook containing those parts of the Ordinary destined to be sung alternately with the polyphony or even played by an elaborating organist   SteC, 28
           a - The elaborate interplay of vocal and organ polyphony for the weekday Masses is notable because the normal practice was for polyphony to be provided by the organ when the choir was not present   WulT, 260
        2 - 'Squares' and other measured monodies for the *alternatim* parts of the Kyrie, Gloria, Sequence and Credo, and for the whole of the Offertories and Communions are found in the fourth book   WulT, 259
           a - These squares retain either the exact rhythm or the approximate rhythmic shape of their fragmented *cantus firmus*   BraS, 77
           b - Only the incipits for the words are provided except in the Kyries   WulT, 259
               1 - Therefore, it seems clear, that these squares are

mostly *cantus firmi* upon which the organist could improve
- c - The fourth book also contains the plainsong of the solo parts of the Alleluias, and of alternate verses of the Sequences   HarEP, 336
- c - Each Mass is allocated to a different day of the week   BenL, 127
    - 1 - *Dominica* (Sunday), *feria ii* (Monday), *feria iii* (Tuesday), *feria iv* (Wednesday), *feria v* (Thursday), *feria vi* (Friday), and *sabbato* (Sunday)   BenL, 126
- d - They contain a Kyrie, Gloria, Alleluia, Sequence, Credo, Sanctus, and Agnus settings   CalO, 223
    - 1 - The Offertories and Communions are given in plainchant
- e - The Masses are noteworthy liturgically since many of the variable parts of the Mass, *i.e.*, the Propers, are set alongside the invariable Ordinaries   WulT, 259
    - 1 - They each contain the Ordinary with Kyrie, plus an Alleluia and sequence   BenL, 127
- f - All are written for three voices
    - 1 - But the ranges and clefs are for various combinations of voices   WulT, 259
- g - All of the Masses contain movements written in *alternatim* as well as movements set in polyphony throughout   BerL, 35
    - 1 - The Sanctus, Agnus and Credo are set in full polyphony with the rest of the music in *alternatim*   CalO, 223
- h - The Offertory and Communion were played by the organ   WulT, 259
    - 1 - The chants for three Offertories and Communions are given in the soloist's book
        - a - They are for Advent, Christmas to the Purification, and Purification to Advent
    - 2 - There is a fourth Communion for use in Easter tide
        - a - It is also found in the soloist's book
- i - There were variations in the performance of the different parts of the Mass on different days of the week   WulT, 259
    - 1 - The Gloria and Credo were entirely vocal on Wednesday and Friday
        - a - As a result, the Kyrie perhaps was sung with an organ *alternatim*
- j - The Lady-Masses are found in London: British Museum, *Royal Appendix 45-48*   BraS, 50
- k - Transcriptions of the Lady-Masses   LudC I

ix) Ludford's music is prominent in the London: Lambeth Palace, *MS 1* and the Cambridge: Gonville and Caius College, *MS 667*   BraS, 49

(d) John Taverner [b. ca. 1495] BraS, 75
   i) General style of his Masses
      a - A *cantus firmus* disposed in equal note values is an important part of Taverner's style BraS, 75
         1 - But it seldom appears in other than the full-choir sections BenFD, 190
            a - An exception is found in the *Western Wynde* Mass where the *cantus firmus* is found continuously throughout the work
      b - The borrowed melodies in his festal Masses are set several times to a movement BenFD, 190
         1 - One complete statement of the melody is found in each major section
      c - In all of his Masses there is an attempt to establish relationships in length between various sections and types of texture BenFD, 193
         1 - Length relationships are found in Mass-movements, major sections, *cantus firmus* and non-*cantus firmus* texture BenFD, 194
      d - The two Masses, *Gloria tibi trinitas* and *Corona spinea* mark a turning point not only in Taverner's work but in that of Tudor music as a whole CalO, 230
         1 - In one sense, while they belong to the florid tradition of the Eton composers, they, however, opened up new possibilities in the realms of vocal scoring, structure, and harmonic manipulation
      e - In his Masses, Taverner uses frequent changes in vocal registration and repetitions of melodic fragments by varying voice-groups ReeMR, 779
      f - He was the first great English exponent of the extensive use of imitation together with a clear feeling for harmonic propriety ReeMR, 773
   ii) Taverner wrote three large-scale [festal] Masses
      a - *O Michael*
         1 - This Mass is considered an early work JosJ, 134
            a - It is a six-voice Mass built on a liturgical *cantus firmus* JosJ, 129
         2 - The *cantus firmus* is derived from part of the respond *Archangeli Michaelis interventione* HanJ, 52
            a - It is in the tenor and is a more integral part of the overall structure than found in the other two festal settings HanJ, 54
            b - Phrases of the *cantus firmus* often move rhythmically; similar to the other five parts rather than in long notes
            c - Several times the *cantus firmus* is freely composed JosJ, 134
               1 - It begins as a free voice and then returns to quoting the chant

3 - A countertenor figure (an opening motto) opens each movement and is followed after three or four breves by the *cantus firmus* JosJ, 134
	4 - Taverner explores experimental techniques in this Mass HanJ, 40
		a - He uses canons in all four movements HanJ, 54
		b - There are five canons which are extended and assured JosJ, 134
			1 - They possess a natural flow without a feeling of being forced HanJ, 54
			2 - They are placed at the extremities of the pitch range
	5 - Passages for full choir alternate with ones for a reduced choir HanJ, 54
	6 - The closing phrase is written in seven-part polyphony HanJ, 55
		a - This is the only time that Taverner writes for this many voices
	7 - Partbooks of *O Michael* are found in Oxford: The Bodleian Library, *MSS. Music School, e. 376-381* (The Forrest-Heyther partbooks) HanJ, 116
	8 - Facsimiles
		a - The beginning of the Mass, tenor part JosJ, Plate 13
		b - The canon at *filium Dei unigenitum*, treble part in gymel JosJ, Plate 14
		c - A portion of Agnus Dei, second countertenor part JosJ, Plate 15
		d - The complete *Missa O Michaell, a 6* OxfM, 113
	9 - Transcriptions of *O Michael* BucT I, 194; TavS
b - *Gloria tibi Trinitas*
	1 - This Mass may justifiably be regarded as Taverner's best work HanJ, 46
		a - It is a six-voice Mass JosJ, 129
		b - It is built on the antiphon of the same name JosJ, 137
	2 - The Mass is unusual in that it presents not one but several *cantus firmi* passages in equal, or regular, rhythm BraS, 76
		a - The chant is written generally in longs and breves, though not monorhythmically JosJ, 138
			1 - However, the last statement in each movement is usually in semibreves and virtually monorhythmic in the last three movements
		b - The *cantus firmi* are all in the meane BraS, 77
	3 - Taverner has combined imitation with writing around the *cantus firmus* BraS, 75
		a - He borrows brief chant-derived motives in other voices, at the beginning of their parts, and uses

    them to anticipate the *cantus firmus* itself
                    JosJ, 138
   b - Such treatment makes a *cantus firmus* become an integral part of the texture while still providing a framework upon which to build HanJ, 48
  4 - The *In nomine* passage from the Benedictus began to be circulated as a detached piece RanH, 395
   a - It is written in the style described above and became a show piece and progenitor of a form in its own right, *i.e.* the *In nomine* BraS, 75
   b - "It is a passage of wonderful beauty" CalO, 227
  5 - Manuscripts containing the partbooks of *Gloria tibi Trinitas* HanJ, 115-118
   a - London: British Museum, *MS. Add. 29246*
    1 - This is a lute book from the early seventeenth century
   b - London: British Museum, *MS. Royal Music Library 24 d. 2*; Royal College of Music, *MS. 2035*
   c - Oxford: The Bodleian Library, *MSS. Music School, e. 376-381* (The Forrest-Heyther partbooks); Christ Church, *MSS. 979-83*
   d - Tenbury: St. Michael's College, *MSS. 341-44*; St. Michael's College, *MS. 1464*; St. Michael's College, *MSS. 1469-71*
  6 - Facsimiles
   a - Beginning of the Mass, meane part JosJ, Plate 6
   b - Beginning of the Mass, first countertenor part
                    JosJ, Plate 7
   c - Beginning of the Mass, second countertenor part
                    JosJ, Plate 8
   d - Beginning of the Mass, bass part JosJ, Plate 9
   e - Beginning of the Mass, tenor part JosJ, Plate 10
   f - The *In nomine* from the Mass JosJ, Plate 20
   g - The complete *Missa Gloria tibi Trinitas*, *a* 6
                    OxfM, 5
  7 - Transcriptions of *Gloria tibi Trinitas*
                BucT I, 126; TavS
 c - *Corona spinea*
  1 - This Mass was probably composed to celebrate an old Feast of the Holy Crown of Thorns HanJ, 41
   a - The Feast has now been discontinued
  2 - It is a six-voice Mass JosJ, 129
  3 - It is a highly complex work BraS, 75
   a - It is built on an unidentified *cantus firmus* placed in the second countertenor JosJ, 135
    1 - The *cantus firmus* is disposed in unornamented long note values but not monorhythmically, with longs, breves and occasional semibreves to fit syllables and words of the text

b - The *cantus firmus* is built on the contour of the
first phrase of six notes HanJ, 42
  1 - The first phrase is expanded to produce the
  second phrase
  2 - The third phrase is a decorated version of the
  original six notes in inversion
  3 - And, the melody ends with an abbreviated
  recapitulation of the initial phrase
  4 - Therefore, the whole chant embodies the
  sonata-form principle of statement, development, and restatement
    a - An example of the melody HanJ, 42
  5 - The text of the chant is unknown
c - Different groupings of voices are used; often accompanied by a change in musical style HanJ, 43
  1 - There is an antiphonal use of two groups of
  voices
  2 - There are several passages displaying a more
  elaborate melismatic treatment than the rest of
  the composition
    a - This suggests that the more ornate passages
    were possibly intended for solo voices in
    order to contrast with other passages for
    full choir
d - Also a voice part may be divided HanJ, 43
4 - Imitation is brief but there are many wonderful passages using sequence JosJ, 136
5 - Manuscripts containing the partbooks of *Corona
spinea* HanJ, 115-118
  a - London: British Museum, *MS. Add. 29246*
    1 - A lute book from the early seventeenth century
  b - London: Royal College of Music, *MS. 2035*
  c - Oxford: The Bodleian Library, *MSS. Music
  School, e. 376-381* (The Forrest-Heyther partbooks)
  d - Tenbury: St. Michael's College, *MSS. 341-44*
6 - Facsimiles
  a - Beginning of the Mass, tenor part JosJ, Plate 11
  b - Beginning of the Mass, countertenor part
    JosJ, Plate 12
  c - The complete *Missa Corona spinea, a 6*
    OxfM, 93v
7 - Transcriptions of *Corona spinea* BucT I, 157; TavS
iii) There are three small-scale Masses BraS, 76
  a - Two are parody Masses; *Mater Christi* and *Sancte
  Wilhelmi* or *Small Devotion*
    1 - Actually, the term "parody" has been shown to have
    no currency in the sixteenth century DoeT, 17f
      a - But, these Masses were derived from their parent

        antiphons   BraS, 76

2 - *Mater Christi*
  - a - This Mass is written for five voices   JosJ, 129
  - b - The first and last sections of each of the four movements are an adaptation of the opening and closing passages of the antiphon, *Mater Christi*   HanJ, 62
    - 1 - The tenor part is missing but it is fortunate that the antiphon on which it is based survives complete   CalO, 234
      - a - Since the adaptation of the opening and closing passages is fairly close, a good part of the Mass can be reconstructed with confidence
  - c - The transfer, at times, involves little more than substituting a new text, *contrafac*tum fashion   CalO, 234
    - 1 - But note values and rhythmic stress, in some cases, are changed in order to accommodate different words
  - d - In the course of transfer, the polyphonic parts acquire a few decorative passing-notes   HanJ, 62
  - e - Some passages from the middle of the antiphon are used, but the part writing has often undergone major change
    - 1 - Sometimes only the general outline of the original quotation is retained
  - f - Taverner uses imitation, canonic treatment, sequence, and ostinato   HanJ, 63
    - 1 - Imitation is used extensively and effectively, often in a very close form
      - a - Sometimes the imitation is carried some distance and provides a certain thrust to the polyphonic writing
    - 2 - Sometimes the writing becomes a near canon
  - g - Sections in homophonic style are used throughout the work and often involve the antiphonal use of upper and lower voices   HanJ, 64
  - h - Mater Christi is found in Cambridge: Peterhouse, *MSS. 40, 41, 31, 32*   HanJ, 117
  - i - A transcription of *Mater Christi*   BucT I, 99

3 - The Mass, *Small Devotion* is a parody of Taverner's antiphon *Christe Jesu Pastor bone*   BraS, 76
  - a - But it relies very little on parody-techniques   HanJ, 65
    - 1 - It quotes only a few passages from its parent antiphon   JosJ, 145
    - 2 - Therefore, *Christi Jesu* played a very small part in the writing of the composition

The Sacred Latin Music for the Reformed English Church 335

      b - The title is thought to be a corruption of an abbreviated form, *S. Will. Devotio*   HanJ, 64
          1 - It is thought that the original title was *Sancti Wilhelmi Devotio*
      c - It is a retexted version of an antiphon in honor of St. William of York
          1 - "The statutes of Cardinal College specified that an antiphon in honour of this Saint...should be sung every evening"
      d - The Mass is written for five voices   JosJ, 129
          1 - There are antiphonal groupings of two boy's voices and three men's parts   JosJ, 144
          2 - Unfortunately, the tenor part is missing from both the Mass and the antiphon   CalO, 234
      e - Taverner uses strongly articulated imitation and homophony   JosJ, 144
      f - Manuscripts containing partbooks of *Small Devotion*   HanJ, 116-117
          1 - Cambridge: Peterhouse, *MSS. 40, 41, 31, 32*
          2 - Oxford: The Bodleian Library, *MSS. Music School, e. 420-22* (The Wanley Manuscripts)
      g - A transcription of *Small Devotion*   BucT I, 70
  b - The *Meane Mass*   BraS, 76
      1 - This Mass is the shortest of Taverner's eight complete settings   HanJ, 66
      2 - It is called the *Meane Mass* because it dispenses with the treble voices, leaving the uppermost voice a high meane part   HanJ, 66
      3 - It also has the name, *Sine nomine* which is a title used to denote a Mass composed upon original material rather than a *cantus firmus*   HanJ, 66
      4 - It is in imitative style and not based on a plainsong   BraS, 76
          a - Imitation occurs in various forms throughout the Mass   HanJ, 66
              1 - One unique feature is the writing of imitation in pairs of voices   HanJ, 67
          b - Another type of imitation, previously described as "internal", occurs regularly   HanJ, 68
              1 - Brief chant-derived motives in other voices, at the beginning of their parts, are used to anticipate the *cantus firmus* itself   JosJ, 138
              2 - Thus, imitation begins to play a primary role in the structural scheme of the Mass   HanJ, 69
      5 - There are opening and closing passages common to all four movements   HanJ, 66
      6 - There is a transferal of a network of passages and sections from the Gloria to the other movements   JosJ, 146

       7 - The style of writing throughout the Mass is very consistent   HanJ, 66
          a - There is a refined quality about the polyphony
             1 - Individual parts have smooth, graceful curves of predominantly conjunct movement
          b - Contrast is used but it depends more on regular mensural change than varied scoring of adjacent passages
       8 - There is a high regard for appropriate word setting   HanJ, 66
          a - A more direct mode of expression and an articulate rendering of the words has been achieved by a mainly polyphonic texture in which the individual lines are separated into clear-cut phrases with short melismas on important words and syllabic treatment elsewhere   HanJ, 69
       9 - This Mass shows a close relationship to the principles and practices of the late Renaissance and clearly shows those aspects of Taverner's technique that were to influence later English composers   HanJ, 69
      10 - Manuscripts containing partbooks of The *Meane Mass*   *HanJ, 115-119*
          a - Cambridge: Peterhouse, *MSS. 40, 41, 31, 32*; Peterhouse, *MSS. 44, 43, 37, 35*
          b - Chelmsford: Essex Record Office, *MS. D/DP. Z. b/1*
          c - London: British Museum, *MS. Add. 29246*
             1 - This is a lute book of the early seventeenth century
          d - London: Royal College of Music, *MS. 2035*
          e - Oxford: The Bodleian Library, *MSS. Music School, e. 420-22* (The Wanley Manuscripts)
          f - Tenbury: St. Michael's College, *MSS. 354-58*; St. Michael's College, *MS. 1464*
      10 - Transcriptions of the *Meane Mass*   BucT I, 50; TavFF
iv) There are two short Masses   BraS, 68
    a - *Western Wynde*
       1 - Stylistic traits seem to indicate an early date for this Mass   JosJ, 141
       2 - It is the earliest known English Mass to be built on a secular *cantus firmus*   JosJ, 139
       3 - The melody is treated as a theme for a set of variations   CalO, 230
          a - There are nine variations in each of the four movements
          b - Therefore, the composition is not a structure based on a *cantus firmus*   JosJ, 139
       4 - The melody is virtually unchanged throughout but achieves variety by the different contrapuntal contexts

in which it is placed   CalO, 233
- a - But, the *cantus firmus* poses problems because its melodic shape differs substantially from the courtly song upon which the Mass is supposedly based   HanJ, 55
- b - There are certain features, though, common to both, including the style and some of the rhythmic figuration   HanJ, 57
5 - The tune migrates freely between the voices   BraS, 79
- a - Even though the statement transfers from one voice to another, there are no breaks between one statement and the next   HanJ, 59
6 - There is imitation throughout the Mass but it is not carried beyond the first two or three notes   HanJ, 60
7 - The techniques of repetition and imitation are easily grasped due to the use of only four voices   JosJ, 140
8 - Manuscripts containing the partbooks of *Western Wynde*   HanJ, 114-116
- a - London: British Museum, *MSS. Add. 17802-5* (The 'Gyffard' partbooks)
- b - Oxford: The Bodleian Library, *MSS. Music School, e. 1-5*
9 - Transcriptions of *Western Wynde*   BucT I, 3; TavFF

b - *Playn Song* Mass
1 - The title is rather puzzling as there is no plainsong melody   HanJ, 69
- a - The suggestion has been made that the title derives from the fact that the composition has a very limited number of notes, namely the breve and semibreve in company with a dotted semibreve and an occasional minim
2 - The four movements have a vague similarity between the initial phrases, but there is no sign of a conscious effort to link them through a common opening passage   HanJ, 70
3 - The first two movements are built on a sequence of adjacent phrases   HanJ, 70
- a - These phrases employ contrasting styles and techniques
4 - Unity is achieved through the exploration of the structural potential of imitative counterpoint   JosJ, 148
- a - Imitation mainly occurs at the beginning of a section   HanJ, 70
5 - Unity is achieved also through the use of homophony for contrast and articulation of structure and through the harnessing of text and music for clarity of expression   JosJ, 148
6 - The Gloria and Credo are written in a predominantly syllabic style   HanJ, 70

        7 - The Sanctus and Agnus Dei are written in a more polyphonic style with long rhapsodic passages sung to single syllables   HanJ, 70

        8 - The *Playn Song* Mass is found in London: British Museum, *MSS. Add.17802-5* (The 'Gyffard' partbooks)   HanJ, 114

        9 - Transcriptions of the *Playn Song Mass*   BucT I, 30; TavFF

v)   Miscellaneous movements for the Lady Mass

    a - *Kyrie Leroy*

        1 - This is a four-part Kyrie   HanJ, 71

        2 - It is built on a *cantus firmus* which was derived from a fifteenth-century collection of non-liturgical melodies known as squares   HanJ, 72

           a - The square from which this *cantus firmus* was derived is for the Sunday Lady Mass   JosJ, 149

              1 - Its title is *Leroy*   HanJ, 72

              2 - It is possible that *Leroy* refers to Henry IV or V   JosJ, 149

           b - The practice of using these squares for the composition of Lady Masses continued until the middle sixteenth-century   HanJ, 72

        3 - The *cantus firmus* is given to the treble voice   HanJ, 72

           a - It is ornamented and transposed up an octave   JosJ, 149

        4 - The texture is florid throughout the composition with long rhapsodic phrases sung to single syllables   HanJ, 72

        5 - It is thought that this piece was sung in *alternatim*   HanJ, 72

           a - A solo voice would sing the basic melody or square, followed by the choir singing the polyphonic setting built upon the square

        6 - *Kyrie Leroy* is found in London: British Museum, *MSS. Add. 17802-5* (The 'Gyffard' partbooks)   HanJ, 114

        7 - A transcription of *Kyrie Leroy*   BucT III, 54

    b - *Christe eleison*   HanJ, 72

        1 - There are three short settings of the *Christe eleison*

           a - They are all based on the second square for the Tuesday Lady Mass

        2 - All three settings have three voices

           a - The accompanying two voices sing florid, independent lines against the *cantus firmus*   HanJ, 73

        3 - In the first two settings the square appears in the middle voice and in the third it is given to the trebles

        4 - The square has been transposed up a twelfth in all three settings   JosJ, 149

5 - Transcriptions
    a - A transcription of *Christe eleison* I   BucT III, 56
    b - A transcription of *Christe eleison* II   BucT III, 53
    c - A transcription of *Christe eleison* III BucT III, 57

c - *Alleluia Salve virgo*
  1 - This is a four-part setting of the choral parts of the responsorial chant   JosJ, 149
    a - It is built upon a *cantus firmus* of which the origin is unknown   HanJ, 73
      1 - The *cantus firmus* has been tentatively identified as the Alleluia with verse *Salve virgo* for the Friday Lady Mass   JosJ, 150
      2 - It is in the tenor   JosJ, 150
  2 - Taverner uses a reverse procedure of the general practice of opening the respond and its verse in polyphony and the choral parts in plainsong   HanJ, 73
    a - Therefore, the procedure would be: HanJ, 74
      1 - The word *Alleluia* was sung by the soloist in plainchant
        a - This is repeated [in polyphony] by the choir with a *jubilus* added on the last syllable   JosJ, 149
      2 - Then, the first half of the verse was sung by the soloist in plainchant
        a - The second half of the verse would be sung by the choir using the same music as that of the polyphonic *Alleluia* [with its *jubilus*]
      3 - Then, the whole would be rounded off with a final *alleluia* sung to plainchant by the soloist, but omitting any *jubilus* which might have been present initially
    b - This reverse procedure began to find favor in the early sixteenth century
  3 - The polyphony is written in florid style   HanJ, 74
    a - There is a hint of imitation by pairs of voices at the beginning of the composition and also at the beginning of some of the phrases
  4 - *Alleluia Salve virgo* is found in London: British Museum, *MSS. Add. 17802-5* (The 'Gyffard' partbooks)   HanJ, 114
  5 - A transcription of *Alleluia Salve virgo*   BucT III, 52

d - *Alleluia Veni electa mea*
  1 - This is a four-part setting of the choral parts of the responsorial chant   JosJ, 149
    a - It is built on a *cantus firmus* based on the melody *Veni electa mea*   HanJ, 74
      1 - This was the *Alleluia* and verse for the Thursday Lady Mass   JosJ, 149
    b - The *cantus firmus* is placed in the treble voice and

340 Sacred Latin and Vernacular Music in England

       transposed up a fourth   JosJ, 149
     2 - Taverner uses the reverse procedure of the general
      practice of opening the respond and its verse in poly-
      phony and the choral parts in plainsong HanJ, 73
      a - He follows the same procedure as that found in
       his *Alleluia Salve virgo*
     3 - The polyphony is written in florid style HanJ, 74
      a - It opens canonically with the tenor and bass voices
       anticipating the *cantus firmus* in the treble
     4 - Manuscripts containing the partbooks of *Alleluia*
      Veni electa mea   HanJ, 114-115
      a - London: British Museum, *MSS. Add. 17802-5*
       (The 'Gyffard' partbooks; British Museum *MS.*
       Add. 4900
     5 - A transcription of *Alleluia Veni electa mea*
               BucT III, 53
    e - *Agnus Dei*   HanJ, 75
     1 - The authenticity of this composition has been ques-
      tioned by scholars on stylistic grounds
     2 - It has gracefully shaped phrases in which conjunct
      movement is predominant
     3 - Strict imitation is a regular feature
     4 - It is fragmentary   HanJ, 74
     4 - This is found in London: Royal College of Music, *MS.*
      2035   HanJ, 116
     5 - A transcription of *Agnus Dei*   BucT III, 60
  vi) Transcriptions of the four- and five-part Masses TavFF
  vii) Transcriptions of the five-part Masses   TavF
  viii) Transcriptions of the six-part Masses   TavS
(d) Christopher Tye [b. ca. 1495]   ReeMR, 782
  i) General style of his Masses
   a - His Masses show him to be a skillful technician
   b - His aim seems to have been simplicity of harmonic and
    contrapuntal effect
  ii) *Euge bone*
   a - This is probably Tye's most important work BenL, 207
   b - It is scored for six voices and therefore the use of the
    Mass on an important occasion is implied BenL, 207
    1 - But the Mass is fairly compact which led, obviously,
     to the employment of only six chords for *Sanctus,*
     Sanctus, Sanctus
   c - There are some imitative points that are loosely derived
    from the plainsong *Euge serve bone*   BraS, 78
    1 - It is also thought that the Mass is musically related to
     a motet, *Quaesumus, omnipotens*   CalO, 303
     a - The text is in the form of a prayer for the reigning
      monarch
     b - It is possible that the Mass and motet were com-
      posed to celebrate Edward VI's accession

2 - Imitation is applied consistently   BraS, 78
d - The structure of the Agnus seems to indicate that it is an extra section that may have been added in 1545   BraS, 78
  1 - It is written in four canonic parts
  2 - The Agnus may have been added when Tye supplicated for the Cambridge Mus.D. degree
e - The Mass is found in Oxford: Bodleian Library, *MSS. Arch. f. e. 19-24* (The Forrest-Heather partbooks)
                                           BraS, 78
f - A facsimile of *Euge bone*   OxfM, 120v
g - A transcription of *Euge bone*   SatC I, 17
iii) The *Western Wynde* Mass   BraS, 79
  a - This Mass is written for four parts with the tune in an ostinato manner
  b - Tye anchors the tune firmly in the meane at all times
    1 - This causes him interesting harmonic problems
      a - The *cantus firmus* dictates the structure   BraS, 79
      2 - The tune appears no less than twenty-nine times and is often elaborated and rhythmically varied   LonM, 67
  c - There is a common opening for the various movements
                                           LonM, 67
    1 - This gives the Mass some overall unity
  d - There is a very limited use of sequence and a lack of triplets   BenL, 208
  e - This Mass is found in London: British Museum, *MSS. Add. 17802-5* (the 'Gyffard' partbooks)   SatC, 52
  f - A transcription of *Western Wynde*   SatC I, 69
iv) Transcriptions of his Masses   TyeM

(e) Thomas Tallis [b. ca. 1505]
  i) Two of Tallis' Masses were written during the [latter part of Henry VIII's reign]; a five-part Mass, *Salve intemerata* which is a parody Mass on one of his antiphons and a short four-part *Playnsong* Mass that is written in an homophonic style
                                           BraS, 79
    a - The former Mass was written ca. 1540
  ii) *Salve intemerata virgo*   DoeT, 17
    a - This Mass is derived from his antiphon of the same name
      1 - Apart from the common opening, he did not use any section of the antiphon twice, but all of it is transplanted except for one passage from *Tu nimirum* to the double bar
    b - Only about a quarter of the Mass is newly composed
      1 - There is a disparity between the new material and the old   BenL, 180
        a - The newly composed sections are better and more modern than the borrowed ones
        b - But "the Mass is more successful than the antiphon"
    c - Verbal repetition is frequently used, mostly in the Sanctus

              and Agnus   BenL, 180

                  1 - From this time on, this practice becomes accepted

           d - This Mass is found in Tenbury: St. Michael's College,

              MS. 1464   FelT, 8

           e - A transcription of *Salve intemerata virgo*   BucT VI, 3

      iii)   An unnamed Mass for four voices [*Playnsong* Mass]

                                                                        DoeT, 19

           a - This Mass is syllabic, being an almost perfect embodiment of Cranmer's express wish for music "not full of notes, but, as near as may be, for every syllable a note, so that it may be sung distinctly and devoutly"

              1 - The chordal and other straight-forward full-choir textures ensure clear text projection   BenL, 182

              2 - There are only three or four passages with protracted melisma and a modest melisma at the cadence

              3 - What imitation Tallis uses provides a contrast and is very simple

           b - Four parts are used throughout with only brief reductions to two or three voices   DoeT, 20

           c - There are some repetitions of phrases, but the repeat is always slightly varied   DoeT, 20

              1 - The repeat could be extended, in sequence at a higher pitch, or simply more fully scored

           d - This Mass is either of a late Henrician or Marian date

                                                                    CalO, 296

           e - A transcription of the Mass   BucT VI, 31

      iv)   Tallis' Mass, *Peur natus* [*est nobis*] is thought to have been written during Mary's reign   BraS, 79

(f)   John Merbecke [b. ca. 1510]

      i)   *Missa per arma Iustitiae*   BucT X, 162

           a - This Mass shows Merbecke's thorough but conventional musicianship   CalO, 240

           b - It is the most important of his extant polyphonic compositions   LeaJ, 51

              1 - It is based on a Latin antiphon

              2 - The *cantus firmus* is mainly in the tenor

           c - The Mass is found in Oxford: Bodleian Library, *MSS. Arch. f. e. 19-24* (The Forrest-Heather partbooks)

              1 - This was formerly *Mus. Sch. e. 376-81*   BraS, 50

           d - A facsimile of *Missa per arma Iustitiae*   OxfM, 21

           e - A transcription of *Missa per arma Iustitiae*   BucT X, 165

(g)   John Sheppard [b. ca. 1515]

      i)   He wrote five Masses   CalO, 304

           a - *Western Wynde* Mass   BraS, 78

              1 - This is probably the least accomplished of Sheppard's major works   BenL, 204

              2 - The *cantus firmus* is no longer the major formal influence on the structure of the composition

                  a - The tune is placed at the top of his texture, thus

The Sacred Latin Music for the Reformed English Church 343

                treating it as a melody with the harmony underneath   BraS, 79
           3 - It is written for a four part choir and is in ostinato manner   BraS, 79
      b - One Mass was written for the English rite with a vernacular text, *Be not afraid*
      c - The other three Masses by Sheppard were likely written during Mary's reign   BraS, 79
      d - Sources of his music
           1 - Oxford: Bodleian Library, *MSS. Arch. f. e. 19-24* (The Forrest-Heather partbooks)   BraS, 78
           2 - London: British Museum, *MSS Add. 17802-5* (The 'Gyffard' partbooks)   BraS, 79
      e - Transcriptions of his Masses   SheM

e) The Processional
  (1) The processional is a work performed during a procession at the beginning of the ceremony   RanH, 656
      (a) Processions gradually came to be frowned upon as superstitious and unnecessary   SteC, 18
          i) Only rarely was the Litany sung in procession (as at Rogationtide)
          ii) Therefore, the Sarum *Processionale* came to nothing
  (2) Processional antiphons
      (a) Christopher Tye [b. ca. 1495]   BenL, 206
          i) *Salve regina...Ad te clamamus*
            a - This is a five-part composition
            b - It is found in Oxford: Christ Church, *MSS. 984-88*   SatC, 52
  (3) Processional psalms with antiphons
      (a) John Sheppard [b. ca. 1515]   BenL, 197
          i) *In exitu Israel*
            a - This is on Psalms 114 and 115 for Easter
            b - It was composed jointly with William Mundy and Thomas? Byrd
               1 - This is Thomas Byrd who was Gentleman of the Chapel Royal from 1546 to 1548   BenL, 25
            c - The faburden of the psalm tone is in the bass   BenL, 202
            d - Each even-numbered verse is set in simple functional style with a single Alleluia appended
          ii) *Laudate pueri*
            a - This is for four-parts on Psalm 113 for Easter
            b - As in *In exitu Israel*, Sheppard has set each even-numbered verse in simple functional style with a single Alleluia appended   BenL, 202
  (4) Processional hymns
      (a) Christopher Tye [b. ca. 1495]
          i) *Gloria laus et honor* for Palm Sunday   BenL, 206
      (b) John Sheppard [b. ca. 5115]
          i) *Salve festa dies...* for Easter   BenL, 197

4. The votive antiphon, Magnificat, and Mass were joined by the respond, hymn and ritual antiphon, toward the end of Henry VIII's reign BraS, 54
   a) Introduction BraS, 84
      (1) The writing of the votive antiphon had decreased from the 1520s in favor of "prayer-motets"
         (a) But, both gave way to responds and hymns in the 1530s and 1540s
            i) The responds and hymns began to be written in much larger quantities in order to fill different liturgical requirements
            BraS, 85
      (2) As the votive antiphon temporarily disappeared, the *cantus firmus* reappeared in even stricter form in the responds and hymns BraS, 85
         (a) It moved in equal notes in one or other of the voices, usually in the tenor in the responds and in the highest voice in the hymns
            i) This required skill and imagination from the composer in order to weave a contrapuntal web within such an inflexible framework
      (3) The responsories are a type of liturgical chant common to the Gregorian and other Western chant repertories RanH, 696
         (a) The great responsories (*responsoria prolixa*) are a part of Matins in the Office for a few important feasts where they are associated with lessons or readings from Scripture
            i) They are also sung in processions and at Vespers on solemn feasts
         (b) The texts are taken from a variety of books of the Bible
            i) This includes the Psalms and some non-Bibical sources
            ii) In the sixteenth century, these texts were often set as elaborate motets in two sections
               a - The first section was the respond (R) and the second section the verse (V) and repeated section of the respond (R')
                  1 - The (R'), *repetendum*, is the last part of the respond
            iii) Sometimes the first half of the lesser Doxology (D) may be added
               a - The scheme is as follows: R V R' D R'
               b - There are other schemes
         (c) The verses and the lesser Doxology were usually sung to one or another of a set of eight psalm tones
            i) This was done according to the mode of the respond
      (4) The rich and highly decorated style that is so characteristic of Aston, Ludford, and Taverner began to give way in the 1530s and 1540s to a leaner, sparer, idiom characterized by bolder melodic lines, a freer use of dissonance, a predominance of duple time over triple, and a tendency to write in a smaller number of voices CalO, 244
   b) The respond
      (1) The composition and performance of the respond
         (a) The polyphonic respond was set in *alternatim* BraS, 54
            i) Before Taverner, the opening of the respond and its verse would be sung in polyphony [by soloists] with the choral

parts sung in plainsong   HanJ, 73

Fig. 37. The older setting of the respond.

Respond	Polyphony
	Plainsong
Verse	Polyphony
Respond	Plainsong
Verse	Polyphony
Respond	Plainsong

CalO, 235

        a - In this performance of the respond, the [polyphonic] setting of the music was allotted in the rubrics to the cantors   CalO, 235
            1 - *In pace* by Taverner is a typical specimen
                a - A transcription of *In pace in idipsum* BucT III, 48
  ii) But in the early sixteenth century just the reverse of the above procedure was beginning to find favor   HanJ, 73
        a - The polyphony usually was provided for the choral parts and the plainsong was sung by the soloists

Fig. 38. The reverse order of setting the respond.

Respond	Plainsong
	Polyphony
Verse	Plainsong
Respond	Polyphony
Verse	Plainsong
Respond	Polyphony

CalO, 236

        b - Taverner appears to have been the first to introduce this reverse procedure into a respond   HanJ, 89
            1 - The two settings of *Dum transisset sabbatum* by Taverner appear to be the earliest extant examples of this type of respond   CalO, 236
                a - Transcriptions of *Dum transisset sabbatum*
                                           BucT III, 37, 40, 43
(2) Composers of the respond
  (a) John Taverner [b. ca. 1495]
      i) *Dum transisset Sabbatum*   BenL, 146
        a - "This is the Respond to the third lesson at Matins on Easter Sunday"   HanJ, 88
            1 - It was used also daily during Easter Week and on subsequent Sundays until Ascension
        b - There are two settings for five voices and a version of one of these for four voices   HarEP, 339
        c - Both five voice settings of this respond are in *cantus firmus* style with the chant in the tenor   HanJ, 88
            1 - But, Taverner had to abandon his usual practice of setting the *cantus firmus* in long notes due to the length of the chant which was far longer than that

of the *incipit* and verse together   JosJ, 160
    2 - Therefore, he set the *cantus firmus* in semibreves
                                                          JosJ, 160
d - There is a balance of syllabic and melismatic treatment of the words   HanJ, 89
    1 - There is also a remarkable textual clarity
e - These settings are examples of the new method of setting responds   HarEP, 340
    1 - They are the earliest of this type of setting   BenL, 154
    2 - First, the *incipit* is left in chant followed by the body of the response and Alleluia in polyphony   JosJ, 160
    3 - Then, the verse is chanted followed by a polyphonic repetition of the latter part of the response and Alleluia   JosJ, 160
    4 - This is followed by the Gloria Patri in chant and then a repetition of the polyphonic Alleluia   JosJ, 160
f - Manuscripts containing the partbooks of *Dum transisset Sabbatum*   HanJ, 115-117
    1 - London: British Museum, *MS. Add. 31390*
    2 - Oxford: Christ Church, *MSS. 979-83*; Christ Church, *MSS. 984-88*
g - Facsimiles
    1 - A facsimile of the countertenor part of a lost setting   JosJ, Plate 21
    2 - A facsimile of *Dum transisset Sabbatum*   JosJ, Plate 19
h - Transcriptions
    1 - A transcription of *Dum transisset Sabbatum* I [for five voices]   BucT III, 37
    2 - A transcription of *Dum transisset Sabbatum* I [an alternative version for four voices]   BucT III, 40
    3 - A transcription of *Dum transisset Sabbatum* II [for five voices]   BucT III, 43
        a - This setting does not include clean breaks at the points from which partial repetitions would be made in performance   CalO, 236, fn. 124
ii) *Audivi vocem de caelo*   HanJ, 86
    a - This is the eighth respond at Matins on the Feast of All Saints
    b - It is scored for four voices; two trebles and two meanes
        1 - This was due to the fact that boys voices were used at this point in the Office on All Saints' Day
        2 - The first meane is thought to have been added by William Whythbroke, a chaplain at Cardinal College at the same time as Taverner   HanJ, 87
    c - Five boys, facing the altar and holding candles to represent the virgins with their oil lamps, would begin the response with the *cantus firmus* in the treble   JosJ, 159
    d - Then, the response was completed by the choir in plain-

The Sacred Latin Music for the Reformed English Church 347

              chant   JosJ, 158

          e - Following this, a verse was sung by the soloists in polyphony with the choir then repeating the latter portion of the response in plainchant   JosJ, 158

          f - *Audivi vocem* is a good example of florid counterpoint on the plainsong   HarEP, 342

          g - It is found in London: British Museum, *MSS. Add. 17802-5* (the 'Gyffard' partbooks)   HanJ, 114

          h - A transcription of *Audivi vocem*   BucT III, 35

     iii) *In pace in idipsum*   HanJ, 87

          a - This respond was sung at compline between the first Sunday in Lent and Passion Sunday

          b - It is scored for three men and a child   HanJ, 88

              1 - It is tightly controlled by imitation and sequence   JosJ, 159

          c - The *cantus firmus* is always in the treble supported by three florid parts   HanJ, 88

              1 - It is written in longs   JosJ, 159

          d - *In pace in idipsum* is found in London: British Museum, *MSS. Add. 17802-5* (the 'Gyffard' partbooks)   HanJ, 114

          e - A facsimile of the treble part of the beginning   JosJ, Plate 17

          f - A transcription of *In pace in idipsum*   BucT III, 48

     iv) *Hodie nobis caelorum rex*   HanJ, 89

          a - This is the first respond at Matins on Christmas day

          b - Taverner set only the verse, *Gloria in excelsis Deo* to polyphony

              1 - It is written for four-part boys voices with two trebles and two meanes   HanJ, 89

                  a - It was sung by five boys   JosJ, 160

                  b - During this Office, the boys represent the angels referred to in the respond and stand in an elevated position near the altar holding lighted candles

              2 - The *cantus firmus* is disposed in dotted breves in the second treble part   JosJ, 160

                  a - Long melismatic phrases accompany the *cantus firmus*   HanJ, 89

              3 - There is occasional imitation   HanJ, 89

          c - *Hodie nobis caelorum rex* is found in London: British Museum, *MSS. Add. 17802-5* (the 'Gyffard' partbooks)   HanJ, 114

          d - A transcription of *Hodie nobis caelorum rex*   BucT III, 46

(b)   Thomas Tallis [b. ca. 1505]

     i)   There are three small responds by Tallis   DoeT, 29

          a - It is possible that these responds belong to the Marian period   CalO, 299

          b - *Audivi media nocte*

              1 - This respond has the usual structure   DoeT, 30

                  a - The first half is the response which is all choral

                except for the incipit
                  1 - The incipit is set to polyphony
              b - The second half is the solo verse which is set to polyphony
              c - Then the solo verse is followed by a shortened repeat of the response
              d - This produces an ABA structure
            2 - Imitation is used as the chief structural principle   DoeT, 30
              a - The points are not superimposed on the texture as in the early antiphons
              b - They become part of the music, interweaving and overlapping cadences, and dictating the shape of the phrases and the form of the whole
            3 - A transcription of *Audivi media nocte*   BucT VI, 90
        c - *Hodie nobis caelorum*
            1 - This respond has the same structure as *Audivi media nocte*   DoeT, 30
            2 - And again, Tallis has set the solo sections in polyphony   DoeT, 30
              a - But it is almost completely syllabic with wide melodic intervals that were to become a prominent feature of Tallis' late style   DoeT, 32
            3 - There is hardly a trace of plainsong   DoeT, 32
            4 - A transcription of *Hodie nobis caelorum*   BucT VI, 92
        d - *In pace si dedro*
            1 - This respond has an unusual structure   DoeT, 30
              a - It has a second verse which is the *Gloria patri*
              b - The *Gloria patri* is sung to the same chant as the beginning of the verse and is followed by the complete response again
            2 - Otherwise, *In pace si dedro* has the same ABA structure as the two previous responds   DoeT, 30
            3 - This respond also has the solo sections set in polyphony and uses imitation as the chief structural principle   DoeT, 30
              a - That is, the points are not superimposed on the texture as in the early antiphons
                1 - They become part of the music, interweaving and overlapping cadences, and dictating the shape of the phrases and the form of the whole
            4 - Every phrase of the chant has been paraphrased   BenL, 185
            5 - A transcription of *In pace si dedro*   BucT VI, 94
    ii) There are six large responds by Tallis   DoeT, 32
        a - General style of the large responds
            1 - They are all festal works   DoeT, 33
            2 - They are set in the layout established by Taverner for this form and are textually incomplete at the beginning

The Sacred Latin Music for the Reformed English Church 349

    unless the plainsong is supplied   CalO, 301
   3 - They have the choral part of the respond set to polyphony
    a - This consists of the response only
    b - The incipit, in square brackets, is left to the soloist
    c - There is a partial repeat of the polyphonic response following the solo verse
   4 - The full chorus is almost constant but with some variation of texture or material to suit succeeding phrases of text   DoeT, 33
    a - Rhythmic and melodic contrasts are used to offset any effect of monotony
   5 - Another departure for Tallis is the presence, in all of the settings, of the choral plainsong itself   DoeT, 32
    a - The plainsong is sung as a *cantus firmus* in equal semibreves throughout   BenL, 186
     1 - This imposes a regular rate of chord change against which Tallis uses expressive suspensions   DoeT, 32
     2 - This procedure was just beginning to crystallize in England   DoeT, 33
    b - The plainsong is set in the tenor in all except the [*Homo*] *quidam fecit coenam* and the [*Dum transisset*] *Sabbatum*
     1 - The [*Homo*] *quidam fecit coenam* has it in the countertenor
     2 - The [*Dum transisset*] *Sabbatum* has it in the treble
   6 - Ostinato-type procedures are found particularly in closing sections   BenL, 186
 b - [*Videte*] *miraculum* is written for six voices and is sung at the Feast of Purification
   1 - It is found in Oxford: Christ Church, *MSS. 979-983*
                BraP, 188
   2 - A transcription of [*Videte*] *miraculum*   BucT VI, 293
 c - [*Loquebantur*] *variis linguis* is written for seven voices and is sung at the Feast of Whitsun
   1 - It is found in Oxford: Christ Church, *MSS. 979-983*
                BraP, 186
   2 - A transcription of [*Loquebantur*] *variis linguis*
                BucT VI, 272
 d - [*Honor*] *virtus et potestas* is written for five voices and is sung at the Feast of Trinity
   1 - A transcription of [*Honor*] *virtus et potestas*
                BucT VI, 237
 e - [*Homo*] *quidam fecit coenam* is written for six voices and is sung at the Feast of Corpus
   1 - It is found in Oxford: Christ Church, *MSS. 979-983*
                BraP, 186

350 Sacred Latin and Vernacular Music in England

      2 - A transcription of *Homo] quidam fecit coenam*
                      BucT VI, 282
     f - [*Dum transisset*] *Sabbatum* is written for five voices and
      is sung at the Feast of Easter
      1 - It is found in Oxford: Christ Church, *MSS. 979-983*
                      BraP, 184
      2 - A transcription of [*Dum transisset*] *Sabbatum*
                      BucT VI, 257
     g - [*Candidi*] *facti sunt Nazarei* is written for five voices and
      is sung at the Feast of the Apostles
      1 - A transcription of [*Candidi*] *facti sunt Nazarei*
                      BucT VI, 186
 (c) John Sheppard [b. ca. 1515]
   i) General style of his responds
     a - His responds and hymns contain much of the best poly-
      phony of the pre-Reformation period   BraS, 86
      1 - Sixteen are choral responds and twelve have texts not
       previously set to music   BenL, 197
     b - He perfected a style based on short imitative points
                      BraS, 86
      1- This brought all of the voices in quickly and achieved
       a thick texture with frequent audible imitation
     c - His responds were written around a *cantus firmus* moving
      in equal notes in one or another voice BraS, 85
      1 - Usually in the tenor
   ii) *Gaude, gaude, gaude Maria*   BenL, 198
     a - This is Sheppard's best respond
     b - Most of the composition is exciting, densely textured
      six-part writing, and usually with the tune in the tenor
     c - The verses three to eight are for divided trebles, and
      divided meanes, with a supporting lower part BenL, 198
      1 - The melody alternates between the first and second
       meane
     d - There is harmonic color and wide spacing at the end of
      the respond
     e - "It incorporates the prose 'Inviolata', assigned to the
      second Vespers of the Purification (2 February) in the
      Salisbury ritual"   CalO, 306
     f - A table outlining the scheme of the respond CalO, 306
   iii) *Dum transisset sabbatum* I for Easter and *Dum transisset*
    sabbatum II   BenL, 196
     a - One has the melody in the tenor while the other has it in
      the meane   BenL, 198
     b - Both of these are fine works, but the Alleluia of the first
      one is especially good   BenL, 198
     c - Number I is imperfectly preserved BenL, 197
   iv) *Non conturbetur cor vestrum I*   BenL, 200
     a - This is for the Eve of the Ascension BenL, 196
      1 - It is imperfectly preserved

		b - It has the melody in the treble	

- b - It has the melody in the treble
- c - The closing Alleluia has rhythmic variety and melisma
- v) *Non conturbetur cor vestrum II*   BenL, 196
  - a - This is imperfectly preserved   BenL, 197
- vi) *In pace* [*in idipsum*]   BraM, 30
  - a - This is for Compline in Lent
  - b - It is a solo respond written for four voices   BenL, 200
  - c - It is a small-scale piece without equal note *cantus firmus*   BenL, 200
- vii) *In manus tuas I, II, and III*   BraM, 30
  - a - These small-scale pieces form a pair with *In pace* [*in idipsum*]   BenL, 200
    - 1 - They are for Compline in Lent and are linked musically by common scoring, similarity of general method, and by sharing an important musical phrase
  - b - Each of these is imitative with paired entries and a few points that paraphrase the plainsong   BenL, 200
- viii) A list of all of Sheppard's responds   BenL, 196
- ix) Transcriptions of some responds   SheMS
- x) Transcriptions of his responsorial music   SheR

(3) Composers of the verse
  (a) John Taverner [b. ca. 1495]
    i) *Ecce mater*   HanJ, 91
      a - This is the verse of the processional respond, *Ecce carissimi*
        1 - It was sung at High Mass on the three Sundays before Lent
      b - It is the only surviving two-part work by Taverner
        1 - The two freely composed lines are florid lines employing points of imitation
        2 - They are disposed so as to produce a remarkable fullness of sound
      c - Traditionally *Ecce mater* was scored for two clerks, therefore, Taverner scored it for a countertenor and a bass
      d - It is found in Oxford: Christ Church, *MSS. 979-83*   HanJ, 118
      e - A transcription of *Ecce mater*   BucT III, 122
    ii) *Jesu spes poenitentibus*
      a - It is thought that this is an excerpt from a complete *alternatim* setting   HanJ, 91
      b - It is the third verse of the sequence, *Dulcis Jesu memoria* for the Mass of the Holy Name of Jesus   HanJ, 92
      c - It is written for a treble, countertenor, and treble   HanJ, 92
        1 - The monorhythmic *cantus firmus* is in the middle voice and is treated decoratively at the cadence
        2 - The other two parts move in a simple and rather undistinguished manner
      d - *Jesu spes poenitentibus* is found in London: British Museum, *MS. Royal Music Library 24 d. 2*   HanJ, 115

     e - A transcription of *Jesu spes poenitentibus*   BucT III, 123
   iii) *Traditur militibus*
     a - It is thought that this is an excerpt from a complete *alternatim* setting   HanJ, 91
     b - This is the sixth verse of the sequence, *Coenam cum discipulis,* for the Mass of the Five Wounds of Jesus
       HanJ, 92
     c - It is written for three parts, meane, tenor, and bass
       HanJ, 92
       1 - The *cantus firmus* is in the middle voice in semibreves
       2 - The other two parts are written in simple, steadily moving curves around the monorhythmic chant
       3 - There is slightly increased activity in the cadential phrase
     d - *Traditur militibus* is found in London: British Museum, *MS. Royal Music Library 24 d. 2*   HanJ, 115
     e - A transcription of *Traditur militibus*   BucT III, 132
   iv) *Tam peccatum*
     a - It is thought that this is an excerpt from a complete *alternatim* setting   HanJ, 91
     b - This is the fourth verse of the tract, *Dulce nomen Jesu Christe* for the Jesus Mass sung during Lent   HanJ, 92
     c - It is written for three voices, treble, tenor, and bass
       HanJ, 92
       1 - There is a *cantus firmus* built on a short musical phrase in the highest voice
        a - It is stated first in breves, then in semibreves, and then in minims
       2 - The lower parts are freely composed with simple points of imitation
     d - *Tam peccatum* is found in London: British Museum, *MS. Royal Music Library 24 d. 2*   HanJ, 115
     e - A transcription of *Tam peccatum*   BucT III, 126
 (b) Thomas Tallis [b. ca. 1505]
   i) *Euge caeli porta*   DoeT, 36
     a - This is a solitary verse from the sequence, *Ave praeclara*
     b - Tallis probably set all the even-numbered verses
     c - A transcription of *Euge caeli porta*   BucT VI, 179
       1 - The text in this source is defective   DoeT, 36, fn. 19
   ii) *Alleluya [ora pro nobis]*   DoeT, 36
     a - This has a number of features that are unusual for Tallis
       1 - There are four very widely spaced voices with some long rests
     b - *Alleluya* is performed in the same manner as the large responds
       1 - The incipit *Alleluya* is solo
       2 - The remainder of the response is sung to polyphony with the plainsong in the alto

The Sacred Latin Music for the Reformed English Church 353

      3 - "The verse 'Ora pro nobis' is not set"
     c - *Alleluya* is found in London: British Museum, *MSS. Add. 17802-5* (the 'Gyffard' partbooks)   HanJ, 114
     d - A transcription of *Alleluya*   BucT VI, 88
 (4) The prose was an insertion into a respond that was sung at first Vespers on the feasts of certain saints   HarEP, 343
  (a) General style of the prose
    i) Its form was the same as a sequence
    ii) It usually was performed by a small group with the choir repeating the music of each line to its final vowel
    iii) The prose of the Office was set to polyphony   HarEP, 307
  (b) Composers of the prose
    i) John Taverner [b. ca. 1495]
     a - *Sospitati dedit aegros*   HanJ, 89
      1 - This is a polyphonic work of festal proportions   JosJ, 163
      2 - It is an interpolation into the respond, *Ex eius tumba*
       a - *Ex eius tumba* is the ninth respond at matins on the Feast of St. Nicholas sung on December 6   JosJ, 162
      3 - *Sospitati dedit aegros* is in choral polyphony throughout   HanJ, 91
       a - There is a different setting for each of the eight verses with the final phrase of the respond added at the end
       b - Some of the verses are written in five-part polyphony for full choir and others are in three or four parts
      4 - The *cantus firmus* is moved back and forth in successive double versicles between the meane and tenor voices   JosJ, 162
       a - It is written with unusual freedom in the first six verses   JosJ, 164
       b - The *cantus firmus* is not in the last double versicle
      5 - *Sospitati dedit aegros* is found in London: British Museum, *MS. Add. 29246* (a lute book from the early seventeenth century)   HanJ, 115
      6 - A transcription of *Sospitati dedit aegros*   BucT III, 110
    ii) John Sheppard [b. ca. 1515]
     a - *Inviolata*   BraS, 86
      1 - This is a part of *Gaude, gaude, gaude Maria virgo*
      2 - It is assigned to the second vespers of the Purification in the Salisbury ritual   CalO, 305
      3 - It is performed in plainsong   CalO, 306
      4 - The untransposed chant   SheR, 99
c) The ritual antiphon
 (1) The ritual antiphon was designed to replace part of the plainsong of the ritual   HarEP, 307

       (a) Such as the settings of the antiphons that followed the Psalms at Matins   BraM, 31
            i) Antiphons that were sung with the Psalms of the Office are the most numerous type   RanH, 43
       (b) They are unlike two types of antiphon which are not associated with psalmody at all   RanH, 43
            i) Namely, the processional antiphons that sometimes include verses after the fashion of responsories and the Marian antiphons which are more elaborate than the antiphons of the Psalms and canticles
       (c) Ritual antiphon texts appeared in the same Primers as the Psalm texts   BraS, 54
  (3) The composers of the ritual antiphon
       (a) John Sheppard [b. ca. 1515]
            i) It is thought that if Sheppard had written nothing else, the next two settings would remain objects of wonderment   WulT, 273
            ii) *Libera nos sava nos* I (Trinity)   BenL, 197
                a - This is written for seven voices and is imperfectly preserved
                b - The plainsong is in breves in the bass   BenL, 201
            iii) *Libera nos sava nos* II   BenL, 197
                a - This is written for six voices and is imperfectly preserved
                b - It has a faburden bass in semibreves   BenL, 201
                c - The six upper voices form a delicate filigree that evokes a votive fervor unequaled in any other sixteenth-century work   WulT, 273
            iv) *Media vita*   BraM, 30
                a - This is an antiphon to the Nunc dimittis
                b - It is the most masterly six-part setting of this antiphon   BenL, 201
                    1 - It also has some rambling and often crude passages   WulT, 273
                c - It has a *cantus firmus* in breves which encourages a spacious harmonic rhythm   BenL, 201
                d - It was used during Lent and is imperfectly preserved   BenL, 197
                e - A transcription of *Media vita*   SheMV
d) The hymn
  (1) The polyphonic hymn was set in *alternatim*   BraS, 54
       (a) The choir's texts were provided with polyphony and the soloists sang the plainsong
       (b) Also, hymn verses alternated between the organ and the choir   SteC, 69
            i) In a hymn with five verses the organ would play verses 1, 3, and 5
            ii) The choir would sing verses 2. and 4
       (c) The hymn generally was tied strictly to a *cantus firmus*
  (2) Composers of the hymn

(a) Thomas Tallis [b. ca. 1505] DoeT, 34
    i) It is possible that these hymn settings belong to the Marian period CalO, 299
    ii) General style of his hymns
        a - All of Tallis' hymns are written for five parts
        b - They were set for *alternatim* performance with the polyphony beginning with the second verse HarME, 476
        c - The first one or two verses are in triple time except in *Deus tuorum militum*
            1 - The rhythm of the *cantus firmus* is treated rather freely in the triple time verses
        d - The other verses are in duple rhythm DoeT, 35
            1 - In these verses the chant is set out in regular semibreves
                a - It is always clearly recognizable
                b - This is similar to the chant of the responds
        e - The melody was usually in the treble set in monorhythm or with a consistent rhythmic scheme HarME, 476
            1 - The added parts are usually loosely imitative and enter in quick succession, often in pairs DoeT, 35
        f - Occasionally there was ornamentation, particularly at the cadence HarME, 476
    iii) Tallis wrote eight hymns BraM, 30
        a - *Salvator mundi Domine* BraM, 30
            1 - The last verse of this hymn has significant ornamentation DoeT, 35
            2 - It was sung on Christmas Day to octave of Epiphany DoeT, 34
        b - *Deus tuorum militum* BraM, 30
            1 - It was sung at the Common of one martyr DoeT, 34
            2 - One voice is missing DoeT, 66
            3 - This is of uncertain authorship, but probably by Tallis DoeT, 66
        c - *Iam Christus astra ascenderat* BraM, 30
            1 - It was sung at Pentecost DoeT, 34
            2 - There is a strict canon between the treble and countertenor DoeT, 34
            3 - The same music is used for more than one verse DoeT, 36
        d - *Jesu salvator saeculi* BraM, 30
            1 - This was sung on the Sunday after Easter employ the same vocal forces DoeT, 34
        e - *Quod chorus vatum* BraM, 30
            1 - This was sung at the Feast of Purification DoeT, 34
        f - *Sermone blando angelus* BraM, 30
            1 - More than one verse uses the same music DoeT, 36
                a - All the themes may be seen as derivatives of the one used at the beginning BenL, 187
            2 - The anticipations in verse two are developed into

                    brief imitations   BenL, 187
                        a - But, the breaks between the lines are never total
                        3 - The texture is continuous in verse six with imitation
                            against an equal-note *cantus firmus*   BenL, 187
                        4 - This was sung on Low Sunday to Ascension
                                                                        DoeT, 34
                g - *Te lucis ante terminum*
                    1 - This is the simplest hymn of all   BenL, 186
                    2 - It has only three verses, therefore, Tallis has set only
                        the second verse   DoeT, 36
                    3 - It is set to the second tune that was normally used
                        at the time   DoeT, 36
                        a - It is set in slightly decorated homophony
                                                                        BenL. 186
                    4 - It was sung at Compline   DoeT, 34
                h - Facsimiles of five of these hymns   TalF
    (b) John Sheppard [b. ca. 1515]
        i)   The general style of his hymns
             a - His hymns are written around a *cantus firmus* moving in
                 equal notes in one or other of the voices   BraS, 85
                 1 - They are usually written around the highest voice, but
                     sometimes in the tenor or even the bass   BenL, 200
             b - "The subdivision of the standard vocal ranges often yields
                 textures of seven or eight parts"   CalO, 305
             c - Sheppard usually sets the even numbered verses to poly-
                 phony   CalO, 304
        ii) *Sacris solemniis*   BenL, 201
             a - The trebles and meanes divide from time to time making
                 possible eight-part writing
                 1 - Although more than six parts are seldom sounding
        iii) *A solis ortus cardine*   BenL, 201
             a - This hymn is for Christmas   BraM, 32
             b - The outer verses are for seven parts
             c - The inner two verses have divided trebles making eight
                 parts
             d - "Each pair of verses is musically the same, apart from the
                 usual but not invariable practice of having the two coun-
                 tertenors exchange parts for the repeat"
        iv) *Jesu salvator saeculi, Redemptis*   BraM, 30
             a - This hymn, along with the respond, *Laudem dicite*, form
                 a kind of pair   BenL, 201
                 1 - Both works belong to first Vespers of All Saints and
                     employ the same vocal forces
        v)   *Ave maris stella*   BenL, 201
             a - This is linked with the respond, *Christi virgo dilectis-
                 sima*
        vi) *Hostis herodes impie*   BenL, 201
             a - This is linked with the respond, *Reges Tharsis*
        vii *Salvator mundi Domine*   BraM, 30

		a -	This is written for six voices and is imperfectly preserved	BenL, 197

	viii)	*Christe redemptor omnium*	BraM, 31
		a - This is written for five voices and is imperfectly preserved	BenL, 197
	ix)	A complete list of the hymns	BenL, 196
	x)	Facsimiles of the hymns	SheC

G. The Sacred Vernacular Music for the Reformed English Church

1. Music for the English liturgy, written between the accession of Edward VI in 1547 and the *First Book of Common Prayer* of 1549, survives in two sets of incomplete partbooks   HarME, 498
   a) One is a set of Edwardian partbooks found in London: British Museum, *Roy. App. 74-76* [The 'Lumley' partbooks]   SteC, 20
      (1) There were originally four partbooks but the bass partbook is now missing   LeHM, 181
      (2) The greater part of the manuscript was compiled between ca. 1547 and ca. 1552   BleT, vii
         (a) It "consists of mostly anonymous simple vocal settings of English sacred texts"
         (b) The two composers named are Tallis and Tye   BleT, viii
            i) There is a *Benedictus* for men's voices by Tallis with the text from Henry VIII's Primer of 1545   CalO, 276
               a - A transcription of the *Benedictus*   BleT, 104
            ii) There is a psalm, *O God br merciful unto us (Deus misereatur)* by Tye   BleT, 39
      (3) There is a later addition containing anonymous untitled dances set in score for from two to seven instruments in a simple chordal style   BleT, vii
      (4) The sacred music is confined to prose and metrical psalms and canticles, two anthems, a Litany, a doxology, and a 1552 Kyrie   HarME, 499
         (a) The music is mainly homophonic in texture with none of the highly melismatic adaptations from Latin originals found in the Wanley manuscript   LeHM, 181
      (5) A transcription of London: British Museum, *Roy. App. 74-76*   BleT
   b) The second set of partbooks is the Wanley books found in Oxford: Bodleian Library *Mus. Sch. e, 420-2*   HarME, 498
      (1) These partbooks were probably compiled between 1549 and 1552 for a parish church or private chapel   CalO, 279
         (a) But the repertory reflects a wider chronology and may well embrace works written for a larger institution such as the Chapel Royal
      (2) Three partbooks have survived, two countertenor and one *bassus*
         (a) Restoration of the tenor partbook is often possible due to the fact that it frequently carried the plainchant or faburdun   CalO, 273
      (3) The music is anonymous, but through concordances with later sources, names of the composers have been revealed   LeHM, 176

                (a) There are compositions by Tallis, Tye, Sheppard, Johnson, and
                    Okeland   FelE, 9
                    i) Other composers who have been identified are Thomas
                       Causton and Whytbroke   FelE, 39
                (b) Most of the compositions are in four parts and scored for men's
                    voices   LeHM, 173
                    i) There are one or two settings for four and five parts
                       a - These are set for men and boys
        (4) There are ninety anonymous musical compositions [set to English words]
            of which nearly three-quarters are unique to the Wanley manuscript
                                                                              WriW I, xiii
        (5) These partbooks contain a wide range of compositions that demonstrate
            how composers not only adapted older works and structural formulae to
            serve new purposes but also developed new structural techniques
                                                                              WriW I, xii
                (a) They contain morning and evening canticles, two harmonized set-
                    tings of the plainsong of the Litany, a large number of anthems, and
                    ten English settings of the Office for Holy Communion with Kyrie,
                    Credo, Gloria in excelsis, Sanctus, Benedictus, and Agnus Dei
                                                                             ReeMR, 796
                (b) There is a preponderance of settings of the Magnificat, Nunc dimit-
                    tis and Te Deum   CalO, 276
                    i) Some are based on modified plainchant and others on the
                       faburden
                       a - One setting of the Te Deum makes use of both plainchant
                           and faburden
                           1 - This setting has the added interest of being adapted
                               for antiphonal singing in the Lumley part-books
                (c) There are anthems which have prose texts from the Psalms or Gos-
                    pels and also a few metrical psalms   HarME, 499
                    i) The anthems and metrical psalms include compositions by
                       Tallis, Tye, Sheppard, Johnson, and Okeland
                (d) The Communion services, except for the Taverner adaptations and
                    an anonymous setting, are syllabic in style   HarME, 499
                    i) The term "Communion" was the term used for the Mass of
                       the Anglican liturgy   AtlR, 548
                    ii) The Taverner adaptations are the *Small Devotion* and *Meane
                        Masses*
                    iii) An Agnus Dei, in English as *O Lamb of God*, by John Heath
                         is an example of the style of the music of the Communion
                         service   AtlR, 548
                         a - A transcription of *O Lamb of God*
        (6) A table of the contents of the Wanley partbooks   LeHM, 173
        (7) A transcription of the Wanley partbooks   WriW
   2. The early solution for developing a repertory was to adapt a new text to a pre-
      existing composition (*contrafactum*)   MorE, 104
      a) Of the known *contrafacta*, the majority appeared for the first time in seven-
         teenth century sources   DanC, 101
         (1) Only two or three of these date from the formative years of the Anglican

Church
- (2) It is possible that some of the earliest examples of *contrafacta* have not survived, or that some of the early anthems are *contrafacta* but that their earlier forms have not been identified or have not survived
- b) There are some pre-Reformation Latin compositions that were adapted to English texts
  - (1) The earliest unquestionable examples occur in the first printed collection of English church music, John Day's *Certaine Notes* of 1560   DanC, 101
    - (a) A facsimile of *Certaine Notes*   DayC
  - (2) Examples [found in Day's *Certaine Notes*] are *In trouble and adversity* and *O give thanks unto the Lord*
    - (a) Both of these are based on the famous "In nomine" passage in the Benedictus of *Gloria tibi Trinitas* by Taverner
      - i) *In trouble and adversity* is attributed to Thomas Causton in the *medius* partbook, but acknowledges "In nomine of Master Taverners" in the bass partbook   DanC, 101
      - ii) Also, Causton is named as the composer of *O give thanks unto the Lord* in the *medius* and tenor partbooks   DanC, 101
      - iii) Therefore, Causton must have been the one responsible for the adaptations   DanC, 101
    - (b) Manuscripts containing *In trouble and adversity* and *O give thanks unto the Lord*
      - i) London: British Museum, *Add. 15166* contains the treble part of *In trouble and adversity*   DanC, 101
      - ii) London: British Museum, *Add. 30480-84* contains *O give thanks unto the Lord*   DanC, 102
        - i) This manuscript also contains a Tallis *contrafacta* that is the earliest example of an adaptation for church use of a secular piece   DanC, 103
          - a - It is *Purge me, O Lord* based on *Fond youth is a bubble*
            - 1 - A keyboard arrangement of *Fond youth is a bubble*   SteMB, 21
    - (c) Facsimiles of *In trouble and adversity* and *O give thanks unto the Lord*   DayC
    - (d) A transcription of *In trouble and adversity*   BucT I, 199
    - (e) A keyboard arrangement of *In nomine*   SteMB, 30
  - (3) Other examples of *contrafacta* are found in Cambridge: King's College Rowe Music Library, *MS. 316*   DanC, 102
    - (a) This is a set of manuscript partbooks that was compiled ca. 1580
      - i) Only the *cantus* partbook has survived
    - (b) The manuscript is the only unified collection of *contrafacta* encountered
    - (c) The first thirty-one folios contain largely Latin works and motets with English words substituted
      - i) The remainder of the manuscript contains a miscellany of vocal and instrumental pieces
        - a - This part is in a different and later hand
    - (d) The first four items are Taverner's *I will magnify thee* taken from

Mene gaude plurimum, Sheppard's *I cried unto the Lord* from *Voce mea ad dominum*, Taverner's *O most holy and mighty Lord* taken from *Mater Christi*, and an anonymous setting of *Wipe away my sins*
- i) The latter piece has been identified as an adaptation of Tallis' *Absterge Domine*
- ii) The first three adaptations have not been found elsewhere
   (e) Adjacent to the above *contrafacta* is one of four examples of an anthem by Robert Johnson in which both Latin and English words are used
- i) It is Johnson's *Benedicam Domino...O Lord with all my heart*
  - a - This had previously appeared in a set of partbooks during the 1540s
  - b - A keyboard arrangement of the bass part   SteMB, 62
  (4) Some other manuscripts containing pre-Reformation Latin *contrafacta*   DanC, 102
- (a) Chelmsford: Essex Record Office, *MS. D/DP. Z. b/1*
- (b) London: British Museum, *Add. 22597*

c) Some early anthems were derived from secular part songs such as *I will give thanks unto the Lord* by Sheppard
  (1) This is a *contrafactum* of *O happy dames* taken from *The Mulliner Book*
- (a) A keyboard arrangement of *O happy dames*   SteMB, 81

d) But, since there are only about thirty instances of *contrafactum* that have reached us from the first century of the English anthem, the obvious conclusion to be drawn is that the substitution of texts played a very insignificant role in the development of the form   DanC, 106
  (1) "The only significance of this small by-path of music history lies in the fact that the Anglican repertory has been immeasurably enriched by masterworks that would otherwise have been excluded"

3. A craving for simplicity in Edwardian church music precluded a rational and ambitious approach to form   MorE, 105
  a) But the range of forms and styles in this period was wide   LeHT, xii
- (1) The forms include simple monodic chant, homophonic chant, short four-part anthems, and the more elaborate polyphonic anthem
- (2) The general style of the anthem during this period was polyphonic, based on free imitation interspersed with chordal passages   ReeMR, 798
  - (a) The anthem is simply a motet with English words
  - (b) The imitative points are rather rigidly developed and the melodic motives used conform to easily immutable archetypes   LeHT, xiii
  - (c) A good example of this style is found in a *Benedictus* by Tallis in the Lumley manuscript
    - i) A transcription of the *Benedictus*   BleT, 104
- (3) There were settings of paired morning and evening canticles, and settings of the ordinary of the communion service   LeHT, xix
- (4) The very early compositions for the English rite, to some extent at least, must be regarded as experimental   LeHT, xiii

4. The text was given pride of place and to some extent governs the rhythm and the melodic shape of the music   LonM, 48
   a) The general practice was to give every syllable a note
   b) The verbal rhythm is strongly marked due to the fact that English is a particularly accentual language   LonM, 50
      (1) Thus, conflicting rhythms for expressive purposes were exploited   LonM, 51

5. The chief composers besides Merbecke to make important early contributions to English church music were Tye and Tallis   ReeMR, 798
   a) Tye's anthems contain many chordal passages in the midst of basically contrapuntal texture   UlrH, 169
      (1) They are somewhat variable in quality   CalO, 290
         (a) But three settings from the Office of the Dead in the 1545 Primer are perfectly controlled
            i) An example is *Deliver us good Lord*
               a - This piece is a little masterpiece of balanced feeling
               b - A transcription of *Deliver us good Lord*   TyeE
      (2) Tye's mixture of styles did not entirely conform to the Royal Injunction of 1548 which prescribed the content and style of the anthem
         (a) According to the Injunction, the style of the anthem was to be syllabic throughout, concerned only with Our Lord and not with the Saints, and to be in English only
            i) A good example of this style is Tye's *I will exalt thee*   UlrH, 169
               a - There is striking contrast in *pars II* after *pars I* has presented a constant flow of polyphony using much imitation
                  1 - "Tye resorts to clear-cut sections, at the ends of which all the voices not only reach their cadences together, but sustain rests together"
               b - The original second edition of *Cathedral Music* by William Boyce contains *I will exalt thee*   BoyC II, 10
               c - A facsimile of the second edition of *Cathedral Music* by William Boyce containing *I will exalt thee*   BoyCA II, 10
         (b) Tye's composition, *Lord, let thy servant now depart in peace*, is an illustration of the change in style that gradually took place in English liturgical polyphony during the second third of the sixteenth century   AtlR, 549
            i) This composition is an English translation of the New Testaments's Nunc dimittis, known as the Canticle of Simeon found in Luke 2:29-32
               a - The Nunc dimittis is a part of Evensong in the Anglican liturgy
            ii) The composition most likely dates before the publication of the *Book of common Prayer* of 1549, as the translation does not square precisely with it
               a - It may have been written for private use before the accession of Edward VI   CalO, 289

iii) The style of the composition is noteworthy in its liberal use of imitation
    a - Almost every phrase begins with a point of imitation in all four voices
        1 - There is one example of paired imitation
    b - But, the composition is predominantly syllabic
    c - Each phrase comes to a cadential full stop without the elided cadences and interlocking phrases so prominent in the music of the Netherlanders
        1 - And due to the fact that each verse is set as a musically separate section with a full close in all but one instance, the composition is somewhat disappointing   CalO, 289
    d - A reprint of the original, *Lord, let thy servant now depart in peace*   WriW I, 16
    e - A transcription of *Lord, let thy servant now depart in peace*   AtlAR, 82

b) Tallis has eleven anthems that can be definitely attributed to him   EllT 12, xi
  (1) It is thought that most of them were composed during the experimental years from 1546 to 1549
    (a) The texts are all drawn from Coverdale's Great Bible of 1539   EllT 12, xii
  (2) Most of these early anthems are basically homophonic in style EllT 12, xii
    (a) *Remember not, O Lord God, our old iniquities* is declamatory and very simple but impressively so   CalO, 291
      i) It is rigidly chordal, consisting almost entirely of 5/3 chords   DoeT, 52
        a - The small amount of melisma used is very effective because it is almost unique in the piece
      ii) In the earliest version of the composition, there is no repetition of text   DoeT, 53
      iii) Transcriptions of *Remember not, O Lord God, our old iniquities (Ne reminiscaris)*   BleT, 52; EllT 12, 43
  (3) There are three anthems by Tallis in the Wanley manuscript ReeMR, 799
    (a) The following anthems illustrate what may be called the standard procedure of the early anthem   DoeT, 51
      i) They are predominantly imitative in texture, but often have a sustained chordal opening with lighter homophonic phrases intermixed for contrast
      ii) There is very little text repetition and melisma amounts to little more than ornamental voice-extension that produces a simultaneous cadence
    (b) One of these is the four-part *Heare the voyce and prayer*
      i) This anthem is notable for an opening point of imitation in which there is an ascending leap of a diminished fourth which figures prominently in the composition
      ii) The source of the text is I Kings viii   DoeT, 50
      ii) A facsimile of *Heare the voyce and prayer*   BurG III, 27
      iii) A transcription of *Heare the voyce and prayer*   EllT 12, 11

(c) Another composition from the Wanley manuscript is *If ye love mee*   ReeMR, 799
    i) This anthem illustrates a common Anglican practice of having the *decani* and *cantoris* sides of the choir sing antiphonally and at other times jointly
        a - This method of singing is different from the standard Italian polychoral practice
            1 - In English music, the basic number of parts usually is not increased when the choir sings together
            2 - Both sides are SATB groups and, in general, in full passages, the voices of the same type sing the same notes
        b - There are exceptions to the above
            1 - In *If ye love mee*, the trebles of both sides of the choir sing different notes at the same time, although due to the disposition of the rests, genuine writing for five voices is never actually heard
        c - Transcriptions of *If ye love mee*
                                                     EllT 12, 16; WriW, Vol.. 100, 127

(4) Tallis wrote a Dorian Service for four voices   ReeMR, 800
    (a) This is most likely an early work assignable to the reign of Edward VI
        i) It is possible that this is the very first of a "complete" Anglican service   CalO, 290
            a - It consists of Venite, Te Deum, Benedictus, Responses to the Commandments, Creed, Sanctus, Gloria, Magnificat, and Nunc dimittis
        ii) Actually, the dating of the music is difficult to determine because of the variants occurring in the texts and because of the late date of many of the manuscript sources   EllT 13, vii
    (b) The Service contains music for the Morning, Communion, and Evening Services
        i) The Communion Service contains a Gloria which is contributory evidence of the work's early date
        ii) The Credo contains a slightly free canon at "Begotten not made" and runs through "who for us men,...came down from Heaven, And was incarnate by the Holy Ghost of the Virgin Mary"
            a - There was no break in the music at this point as there had been after *descendit de coelis* in the Roman service to correspond to the kneeling of the congregation before the *Et incarnatus*
                1 - This was possible due to the fact that in the Anglican service the congregation remains standing after "Who for us men, and for our salvation, came down from Heaven"
        iii) Also, the Nunc dimittis contains a canon, but in the main the writing is chordal and syllabic
    (c) The Dorian Service   BoyC I, 1

                (d) A facsimile of the Dorian Service   BoyC I, 1
                (e) A transcription of the Dorian Service   EllT 13, 1
    5. John Sheppard's English music is of considerable interest although not as extensive [as his Latin music]   LeHM, 206
        a) There are three complete anthems for men: *Christ rising again, I give you a new commandment*, and *Submit yourselves*
            (1) Of these three anthems, *Christ rising again* is the most distinguished
                                                                     LeHM, 207
                (a) The text is based on the 1549 Prayer Book
                (b) The music is in a solemn liturgical style with a harmonic richness that characterizes the best of Sheppard's work
                    i) There is little obvious attempt at expressive word setting
            (2) A reprint of *I give you a new commandment*   SheI
            (3) A transcription of *Submit yourselves*   Wriw, Vol. 99, 109
        b) The First Service by Sheppard dates from the Edwardian period   LeHM, 207
            (1) It consists of Venite, Te Deum, Benedictus, Creed, Magnificat, and Nunc dimittis   LeHM, 206
            (2) It is possible that Sheppard intended it for men and boys as it covers the usual two octaves and a sixth range
                (a) It is basically in four parts, but there are *divisi decani* and *cantoris* sections in five or more parts
            (3) A reprint of the Magniicat and Nunc dimittis from the First Service
                                                                     SheMN

H. Performance Practices

1. The English Reformation produced two quite separate, yet complimentary, streams of church music, the parish church tradition and the cathedral tradition
                                                                     LonM, 31
    a) These traditions are most clearly differentiated in the choir offices of Matins and Evensong
        (1) The aim of the service in the parish church was to allow the congregation whole-hearted participation   LonM, 37
            (a) There was less music than found in the cathedral and it was much more simple
        (2) Cathedral music is offered on behalf of the people by a highly trained all-male choir and by boys who have been carefully selected and thoroughly musically trained   LonM, 39
            (a) The men were usually professional singers
    b) Performance of English church music In the Cathedral
        (1) Before the Reformation   LonM, 39
            (a) Services on weekdays as well as Sundays were fully choral
            (b) Settings of prescribed services were fully composed, some of them being highly elaborate
            (c) The psalms of the day were sung in *toto*
                i) It was the custom to sing them antiphonally
            (d) The Te Deum and Beneticius in Matins and the Magnificat and

Nunc dimittis of Evensong were sung to full settings in the style of anthems
                    i) These canticles are confusingly called 'Services'
                       a - In such a 'Service' all settings are normally set in the same key   LonM, 40
                    ii) The anthems are usually long and elaborate   LonM, 40
                (e) The organist accompanied the choir when an independent accompaniment was needed   LonM, 39
            (2) After the Reformation   BluPR, 697
                (a) The English religious reformers objected to the organ and disliked choir music
                (b) Music was admitted to the Cathedral as long as the words remained clear
        c) Performance of English church music in the parish church   LonM, 37
            (1) The music is more simple and there is less of it than in the cathedral
            (2) The main purpose of the organist in the parish church was to encourage, guide, and often lead the singing of the people   LonM, 39
            (3) The purpose of the choir was to lead the congregation   LonM, 39

2. Choral Practice in England
    a) Professional liturgical choirs
        (1) By 1520, where the strength of forces permitted, the performance of liturgical music had become truly choral   BowC, 33
            (a) Instruments would have served no useful purpose   BenL, 30
        (2) It was normal for the polyphonic chorus to consist of clerks and boys as well as a high proportion of priests   BowC, 33
            (a) But there was some degree of variety in the practical disposition of the vocal forces available
        (3) Four out of the five parts of polyphony composed in the standard five-part style (treble, alto, tenor, bass) were allocated to the men and the top part to the boys   BowC, 34
            (a) A satisfactory balance consisted of twenty men and eight boys
            (b) The three men's voices above the bass could cover a compass of fifteen or sixteen notes   BowC, 35
        (4) But, at times this disposition was not suitable and as a result the three lowest voices were allocated to the men and the two upper parts were allocated to the boys   BowC, 35
            (a) Then, the vocal parts were labeled treble, meane, countertenor, tenor, and bass   HanJ, 40
                i) In modern notation the treble had a range of d' to g", the meane g to c", the countertenor c to g', the tenor c to d' (sometimes extended to e' and down to A), and the bass from F to b flat
            (b) A satisfactory balance for this disposition could be sixteen boys and five to ten men
                i) The number of men and boys varied according to the resources available
        (5) But early in the Reformation period most composition of church music was in four parts   BowC, 39

Secular Vocal Music

A. **The French *Chanson***

1. Introduction
   a) The *chanson* was clearly in a transitional period as a genre at the approach of the sixteenth century   PerMR, 607
      (1) The transformation was a gradual one with a number of different influences at work to bring about these changes
      (2) The influences that had the greatest impact appear to have varied as well from one region to another
   b) The once homogeneous Franco-Flemish song style shattered decisively in the second quarter of the sixteenth century   AtlR, 421
      (1) A stylistic gulf developed between the settings of serious poetry by Pierre de la Rue and the lighter, more airy approach of the three-part popular arrangements of the French royal court of Louis XII
      (2) By the 1520s the split hardened along geographic lines with one style of *chanson* in the Low Countries and another in France
         (a) The labels generally attached to the above are "Netherlandish" and "Parisian" respectively
      (3) The Netherlandish *chanson* was a direct offspring of the Franco-Flemish central tradition of thick, imitative counterpoint   AtlR, 421
         (a) The music was composed by many French-speaking composers who were born beyond the borders of the French kingdom   DobO, vii
            i) Most of these composers were born in the area now known as Belgium
            ii) They often worked in Italy, Germany, Spain, and elsewhere
            iii) They were often hampered by very poor poems and would avoid difficulty by setting these verses in ready-made musical forms such as the *pavane,* [a court dance of Italian provenance]   BorF, 16
         (b) Examples of the Netherlandish *chanson*   AtlR, 422-423
   c) It was in France, during this period, that the decisive steps were taken in the stylistic transformation of the polyphonic *chanson*   PerMR, 618
      (1) An enormous role was played by the printers of music

    (a) Pierre Attaingnant published the first of more than seventy books of *chansons* in 1528
    (b) Jacques Moderne initiated his eleven collections of *chansons, Le parangon des chansons,* in 1538
  (2) The poets of sixteenth-century France had their part to play
    (a) The practitioners of the day understood that the *chanson* was a short simple verse, sometimes popular in character, that was capable of being sung or at least did not preclude a musical setting
                            HeaCH, 194
  (3) The *chanson* was defined in terms of text   HeaCH, 194
    (a) During this period the term refers to texts not in one of the *formes fixes*   RanH, 148
      i) "By the 1520s the fixed forms and conventional diction of medieval tradition were beginning to give way once and for all to the freer formal structures and topical innovations of such gifted authors as Clément Marot"   PerMR, 618
    (b) The texts run the gamut from refined courtly eroticism to earthy expressions reflecting urban and country life   PerMR, 626
  (4) The music varies in polyphonic style from homophony to imitative counterpoint, at times within a single piece   PerMR, 626
    (a) A subspecies of the genera, possibly unique with Clément Janequin, is the unmistakable feature of onomatopoetic imitation, both verbal and musical, of natural sounds
      i) This was made a part of the compositional fabric
      ii) It appears to have had little impact on the subsequent development of the genre
 d) The *chansons* supplied melodic and harmonic material for much new sacred music   DobO, vii
  (1) They supplied material for the imitation or parody Masses and Magnificats, as well as for the vernacular psalms and chorales
 e) Also, *Chansons* were arranged for instrumental ensemble or solo   DobO, vii
  (1) This inspired new forms such as the *canzona*, fantasia, and variations
  (2) It led to the creation, in Italy, of the *canzon francese*   BorF, 1
    (a) This is an instrumental form which in turn was the original of the seventeenth-century *sonata da chiesa*

2. The *chanson* in France [The Parisian and Provincial styles]
 a) General style of the poetry
  (1) The *chanson*, in freeing itself from the servitude to poetic structure, did not submit to any arbitrary form   BorF, 3
  (2) The change in poetic form was due, somewhat, to Clément Marot (1496-1544)   ReeMR, 288
    (a) Clément Marot was the most famous and widely imitated French poet of the time   AtlR, 425
      i) He was a special favorite of Claudin de Sermisy and Clément Janequin as well as other composers, both French and Netherlandish
    (b) He followed in his father's footsteps by attempting to revive the classical ideas in poetry

            (a) The duplication of the tenor part was abandoned
            (b) The parts above the tenor were named 'countertenor' and 'meane'
            (c) Therefore, the singers of the 'meane' part in any given choir were just as commonly boys as men BowC, 39
                i) The 'meane' voice was as much that of a boy alto as of an adult
                ii) As a result, after the Reformation, the term 'meane' became that by which the single standard boy's voice was known
        (6) In some chapels the term 'tenor' referred to those who sang the plainsong BowC, 36
            (a) In this case, the countertenors were listed in sufficient strength of numbers to perform two parts
        (7) There is a special body of Lady Mass music specifically designed for the voices of the boys and their Master BowC, 38
            (a) The weekly cycle of three-part *alternatim* Lady Masses by Nicholas Ludford is characteristic of this repertory
            (b) The lowest part was sung by the Instructor and the upper parts were sung by the boys
        (8) Fully polyphonic compositions have some sections scored for the full number of parts, others for smaller groups BenL, 30
            (a) The complete body of singers would have taken the full parts
            (b) Soloists, or possibly sometimes a semi-chorus would sing the reduced passages BenL, 31

3. Pitch depended on vocal scoring BraM, 41
    a) Some scholars think the close relationship between staff limits and vocal ranges in manuscript sources of this period indicate that the points of reference which the singer needed in order to pitch the voice were supplied by the extremities of the stave itself WriW I, xix
        (1) Staff limits must have represented approximately the same actual pitches for singers regardless of the clefs used since different clef combinations would have enlarged the range of available keys by making available a scale pattern at one pitch level which could be notated only at another
            (a) Therefore the main function of the clef would have been to indicate the location of diatonic semitones, not to specify exact pitches
    b) Other scholars think that if the two top voices are boys (treble and meane) the pitch should be transposed upwards
        (1) Others contend that the male voice is the meane and therefore upward transposition is not appropriate
        (2) But the pre-Reformation pitch standard is assumed to have been the same as the pitch standard of the Jacobean [organ] pitch standard BraM, 42
            (a) The Jacobean transposing organ is tuned to a pitch standard that requires choral parts today to be transposed up a minor third

The French *Chanson* 369

    (c) He reconciled two opposing traditions: the courtly and the popular
                                         BroG, 28
      i) He preferred short anecdotal pieces written on day-to-day occurrences LesM, 23
      ii) Vernacular elements came to the fore HerT, 8
      iii) Most of his best poems deal with love BroG, 28
    (d) In spite of Marot's use of a certain rigidity, he did not adopt any stereotyped scheme
      i) Many of his poems are strophic but seldom is the arrangement of strophes exactly the same BroG, 29
    (e) He and Mellin de Saint-Gelais introduced the sonnet and the epigram into the French language during the 1530s HeaCH, 197
      i) Mellin de Saint-Gelais wrote French sonnets chosen by Janequin and Arcadelt for their musical settings LesM, 23
      ii) He composed music to his own poems, sang them, and played them on instruments LesM, 22
    (f) The *chansons* written after 1525 have texts by Clément Marot, Mellin de Saint-Gelais, and perhaps Claude Chappuys AdaF I, viii
  (3) Basically, the form of the French poem was a four- or eight-line strophe with verses of eight or ten "feet" LesM, 25
  (4) The alternation of masculine and feminine rhymes became established ReeMR, 288
    (a) This practice was favorable to musical phrasing HerT, 8
  (5) At times, the texts are sentimental, humorous, or erotic UlrH, 185
    (a) They always appeal to the general audience
    (b) The language is simple and direct BroG, 35
  (6) The connection between word and music is very strong HerT, 10
b) General style of the music
  (1) The *chanson* is a highly original form BorF, 1
    (a) It is essentially in miniature FreC
      i) "Unlike the Italian madrigals, which were sometimes composed in sequences of three, four, or more sections, French chansons tend to remain individual in the sense that they are self-contained, epigrammatic, and brief"
  (2) The music incorporated Italian and Netherlandish elements ReeMR, 290
    (a) Contrapuntal textures were used UlrH, 185
      i) Most of the *chansons* contain a mixture of contrapuntal and homophonic writing AdaF I, vii
        a - Narrative settings often have a simplified imitative style with prominent homorhythmic sections BroG, 32
        b - Lyrical settings often have a chordal texture enlivened by lightly imitative counterpoint BroG, 33
    (b) Rich harmony was used along with swinging syncopations, and imitative entries CroH, 185
    (c) The Italian folk like spirit became characteristic UrlH, 185
    (d) French grace and wit were added
  (3) Toward the beginning of the sixteenth century composers lost interest in the three-part *chanson* and began writing for four voices AdaF I, vii
    (a) The vocal range of the compositions and the relationship of the two

upper parts help date them
- i) In the early *chansons* the bass range is common for the third voice and, at times, the upper voices are in the tenor range
  - a - There is some crossing of parts
- ii) Later *chansons,* such as those published by Attaingnant in 1535, keep the upper lines separate and contain parallel writing at the interval of a sixth
- iii) By 1550 the bottom voice had risen from the bass register to the tenor and sometimes even to the alto

(4) There is a restricted use of repetitions of words and phrases   BorF, 3
- (a) But, there is often a repetition at the end of a piece
  - i) The usual form is AA (with different texts) BCC (with the same text)
  - ii) Other forms containing this repetition are ababcdEE and ababcDD   ReeMR, 294
- (b) Also, there are purely musical repetitions at the beginning of *chansons*
- (c) Sometimes the first phrase returns as the last phrase of the *chanson* with new text   UlrH, 186

(5) The music comments on the text   LesM, 30
- (a) The musician, while being respectful of the text he had chosen, often took the liberty of clarifying it whenever he found it obscure or if the allusion bothered him   LesM, 27
- (b) At first, this was done by rhythm and melodic invention

c) The Parisian *chanson*
- (1) The term "Parisian" does not fix the genre geographically   AtlR, 424
  - (a) Many of the *chansons* with this label were composed outside Paris in the French provinces and not all *chansons* composed in Paris necessarily wear the Parisian stylistic label comfortably
    - i) Also, not all the *chansons* that came off the presses of the music publisher, Pierre Attaingnant, can be automatically attached to the label
  - (b) But most of the Parisian pieces were by composers at the royal court   BerP, 212
  - (c) "In sum, what we call the Parisian chanson was composed both in and outside Paris, and both its music and its poetry embraced multiple styles"   AtlR, 428
  - (d) There is one constant that unifies this rich and wonderful repertory   AtlR, 428
    - i) It is its stylistic differentiation from the Netherlandish *chanson*
- (2) The general style of the Parisian *chanson*
  - (a) It was written for four voices in homophonic style with the melody in the upper voice   UlrH, 185
    - i) French composers seldom used a larger number of parts   ReeMR, 295
    - ii) But the *altus* is a filler voice and may be omitted without removing anything essential to the composer's conception   BroG, 33

               a - It is possible that some of the *chansons* were written for only three voices
          iii) The tenor was still important and often moves in parallel motion with the *superius*   BroG, 3
               a - It frequently states more than an equal share of the significant melodic material
     (b) The musical phrases are molded upon each single line, the declamation of words is syllabic, and part-to-part imitations are short
                                                                         LesM, 20
          i) There is a clear division of music according to the text
                                                                        HelSC, 241
          ii) There are strong, definite cadences   HelSC, 241
     (c) There is a characteristic opening rhythm deriving from the syllabic treatment of the four syllables that precede the caesura of the ten-syllable poetic line   RanH, 149

          Fig. 39. The characteristic opening rhythm of the "Parisian" *chanson*

BroG, 31

     (d) The Parisian *chanson* has a light, ornamental quality   HelSC, 241
(3) There were three basic Parisian *chanson* styles in the late 1520s and early 1530s   AtlR, 425
     (a) The lyrical *chanson*
          i) The opening rhythmic motive is virtually always dactylic
                                                                         AtlR, 426
          ii) There is a lyrical melody in the *superius*
          iii) There are clear-cut, balanced phrases
          iv) The tonal scheme is tight knit, at times progressing i-i-III-v-i-i
          v) There are clearly discernible sections, with repetition at the beginning and/or at the end
          vi) There is a full triad at the final cadence   AtlR, 426
               a - This was becoming increasingly popular in the second quarter of the century
          vii) All voices are fully texted   AtlAR, 290
          viii) The syllabic declamation is at the level of the semibreve and minim
          ix) A good example of the style is *Je n'ay point plus d'affection* by Sermisy   AtlR, 425
               a - A transcription of *Je n'ay point plus d'affection*
     (b) The program style *chanson*   ReeMR, 295
          i) This style *chanson* is also known as a descriptive *chanson*
                                                                         BorF, 6
          ii) It contains realistic tone-painting in a distinctive manner
                                                                        ReeMR, 295
               a - There are drum-rolls, military or hunting fanfares, and chirping birds   BorF, 6
          iii) Nonsense syllables set in short notes and repeated many times

        provide rhythmic animation and a humorous tone UlrH, 186
     iv) The chordal style is replaced by rapidly moving, rhythmically diverse styles with short phrases appearing in several voices in turn UlrH, 186
     v) The supreme master of the descriptive *chanson* was Janequin BorF, 6
       a - An example of a program *chanson* by Janequin is *Les cris de Paris* AtlR, 427
        1 - A transcription of *Les cris de Paris* AtlAR, 295
   (c) The narrative *chanson*
     i) It is a setting of a humorous narrative poem RanH, 149
       a - The texts are more or less on the obscene side with double meanings and, at times, they have outright vulgarities AttTT, i
     ii) Musically, this style *chanson* is distinguished from the sentimental *chanson* by much shorter values and fewer melismas AttTT, I
     iii) Even though lines usually begin with a point of imitation, the *chansons* are a long way from the typical Netherlandish *chanson* AtlR, 426
       a - The texture is often chordal AtlR, 427
     iv) The recurring refrain along with clear-cut cadences impart a sense of distinct sections AtlR, 427
     v) A good example of the above is *Il est bel et bon* by Pierre Passereau AtlR, 426
       a - A transcription of *Il est bel et bon* AtlAR, 292
 d) The provincial style of the *chanson*
  (1) The provincial masters are stylistically different from the Parisian counterparts BerP, 212
   (a) Composers used fewer homorhythmic passages MilT, x
     i) They relied on voice pairs, part exchange, systematic imitation, free counterpoint, sweeping melismas, and uneven phrase structure BerP, 205
   (b) In the 1540s, provincial composers began favoring longer texts BerP, 231
   (c) They used more word-painting MilT, x
   (d) They did not keep a clear relationship between the text and the musical superstructure BerP, 205
   (e) There is greater musical extension-text repetition MilT, ix
  (2) There were, however, similarities between the provincial and Parisian *chansons* MilT, x
   (a) They use the same type of texts
   (b) Cadences usually mark the ends of poetic lines
   (c) They both use a tripartite musical form
     i) This is shown in the pattern of musical repetition MilT, xi
     ii) Sectional repeats occur at the beginning and the close
       a - In the former there is always a change of text upon the repetition of the music MilT, xii
        1- These sectional repeats at the beginning of a piece

serve as a means of accommodating extra poetic lines
              b - In the latter the music is always sung with the same
                    words   MilT, xii
            iii)   Between the two repetitions there is a central unrepeated
                    passage   MilT, xii
      (d) Both the Parisian and provincial styles avoid involved rhythmic and
          contrapuntal devices   ReeMR, 294
            i)   Complexity was avoided
      (e) The *chanson* rhythm appears in both types
      (f) Triple meter is rare
            i)   A change in the time signature rarely occurs   ReeMR, 294
              a - When it does, it is found in all voices simultaneously

3. The Netherlandish style *chanson*
   a) The composers of the Franco-Netherlandish *chanson* were the true heirs of
      Josquin   LesM, 21
      (1) They wrote *chansons* with five or six parts   BorF, 13
      (2) Composers favored flowing motifs and through composition
                                                                       ReeMR, 301
      (3) They used a strong melismatic style with no text-illustrating significance
                                                                       ReeMR, 309
      (4) They used contrapuntal techniques   UlrH, 187
          (a) Such as continuously imitative polyphony in four or more parts
                                                                       RanH, 149
          (b) And canonic writing and imitation in pairs of voices
                i)   Sometimes strict double canons were written   ReeMR, 309
          (c) They laced their contrapuntal fabric with Parisian clichés such as
              repeated notes, medial caesuras, and stereotyped rhythms BerP, 212

              Fig.40. A stereotyped rhythm of the Netherlandish *chanson*

              BerP, 199

4. Composers of the *chanson*
   a) The Paris School   ReeMR, 291
      (1) Clément Janequin [b. ca. 1485]
          (a) 286 examples of large *chansons* by Janequin survive   ReeMR, 298
                i)   These include many phases of the *chanson*
                  a - They are not limited to program pieces or to the chordal
                      type
                  b - Some *chansons* are graceful works in a conventional style
                ii) The texts are by Francis I, Marot, and Ronsard
                  a - Janequin continued to write *chansons* after the death of
                      Marot with the verses of Pierre de Ronsard   HeaCH, 203
          (b) Janequin shows virtuosity in controlling rhythmic effects, along
              with an attention to the sense of the text, often conveyed in an
              ingenious and effectively witty way   HeaCH, 203
          (c) Realistic tone-painting appears in a distinctive manner in Janequin's

			program *chansons*	ReeMR, 295

            i)   But, extreme expression of the text is avoided   BerC, 35
            ii)   Rhythmic aspects of the text are used to color the text rather
                   than harmony and chromaticism   BerC, 35
    (d)   His program *chansons* are written in a well-balanced form BorF, 8
            i)   Sometimes a piece is divided into two, three, or four sections
            ii)   And sometimes, the introduction is repeated in the course of
                   the work or at the end
            iii)   Transcriptions of some of his program *chansons*   JanCA
                   a - *Le Chant des Oiseaux, La Guerre, La Chasse*, and *Las,*
                       povre coeur
    (e)   His *chansons* include settings of humorous narrative poems
                                                                                    RanH, 149
            i)   They are known as *chansons grivioises*   BerC, 41
                   a - These are lighthearted licentious *chansons*
    (f)   Transcriptions of Janequin's *chansons*
            i)   Three of his *chansons*   AttT
            ii)   Ten of his *chansons*   JanCZ
            iii)   Five of his *chansons*   AttTT
            iv)   All of his polyphonic *chansons*   JanC
(2)   Claudin de Sermisy [b. ca. 1495]   ReeMR, 291
    (a)   About 160 of his *chansons* were printed in the collections of the
            period
    (b)   He wrote mostly for four voices on texts by Clément Marot
                                                                                 SerO, III, xi
            i)   He used twenty-two of Marot's texts
            ii)   He also used texts by Francis I, Marguerite de Navarre,
                   Mellin de Saint-Gelays, Octovien de Saint-Gelays, an uncle,
                   and others
    (c)   The dactylic pattern becomes prevalent   SerO, III, xi
    (d)   The initial rhythmic figure [Fig.40], which historians have associ-
            ated with the *chanson* of this period, is found in Claudin's music
                                                                                  ReeMR, 292
            i)   It is found with the typical rhetorical pause after the first
                   four syllables   HeaL, 108
            ii)   An example of this is found in *Allez souspirs*   BroC, 8
                   a - This *chanson* is from a volume of music published by
                       Attaingnant in 1533 [*Vingt et sept chansons musicales...*]
                                                                               BroC, 2
                       1 - A facsimile of *Vingt et sept musicales*   AttVS
                   b - The *chanson* was specifically marked as being particularly
                       suitable for recorders   BroC, 2
                   c - A transcription of *Allez souspirs*   SerO, III, 1
    (e)   The *chansons* often follow a repetition scheme that is their out-
            standing feature   ReeMR, 294
            i)   In a seven-line poem, the music for lines three and four of
                   the text are a repetition of that for lines one and two
            ii)   The music for the last line may be the same as that for lines
                   two and four

		iii) "Both the text and the music of the last line are repeated"	
		iv) There is a diminution and repetition of the opening motto at	
		the point of *reprise*	HeaL, 108
		a - For an example of this *see Tant que vivrai*	DobO, 38
		1 - A transcription of *Tant que vivrai*	AttTR, II, 10
	(f)	The prosody and musical form are in agreement in his music	
			HeaL, 107
		i) The structure of the text is brought out by separating the	
		phrases with rests in all the parts	UlrH, 186
	(g)	Often a section, no more than a phrase in length, is set in triple	
		meter in contrast to the prevailing duple meter	UlrH, 188
	(h)	Some of his *chansons* are chordal and song-like, with syllabic	
		treatment of the text	ReeMR, 292
		i) Syllabic and homophonic beginnings broaden into slight	
		ornamental passages before the cadence	HeaL, 108
		ii) These *chansons* are often homorhythmic	BroMF, 129
		a - The same or very similar rhythm is found in all parts	
			RanH, 380
		b - Usually displayed in vertical writing in ornamented or	
		slightly ornamented chord progressions	BorF, 3
	(i)	Some *chansons* have rapidly repeated notes that produce a de-	
		clamatory effect	ReeMR, 292
		i) They have a dance-like quality	
	(j)	There are hints of imitation	HeaL, 108
		i) Imitation is found in the subsidiary phrases	
	(k)	Semisy's *chansons* always indicate an advanced degree of tonal	
		planning	HeaL, 107
	(l)	He seldom drew upon preexistent melodies	ReeMR, 295
	(m)	A good example of Sermisy's *chanson* style is *Pour ung plaisir*	
			SeaFC, 20
		i) This *chanson* is found in Attaingnant's second book of *chan-*	
		sons published in 1536	
		a - A transcription of the *Secund livre contenant xxxi chan-*	
		sons musicales	AttS
		ii) A transcription of *Pour ung plaisir*	SerO, IV, 60
	(n)	Transcriptions of his *chansons*	SerO, III and IV
(3)	Pierre Certon [Fl. 1529]		ReeMR, 299
	(a)	He composed over 290 *chansons*	CerCC, xi
		i) Some are especially witty and are often based on narrative	
		texts	ReeMR, 299
		a - An example is *Frere Thibault, sejourné gros et gras*	
		b - A transcription of *Frere Thibault, sejourné gros et gras*	
			BerC, 27
		ii) Some *chansons* are in chordal style	ReeMR, 299
		iii) Some are characterized by homorhythm	BorF, 12
		iv) Many of his *chansons* are of the Parisian style of the 1530s	
		and 1540s	CerCC, xi
		a - But his later *chansons* are written in the forms of the	
		mid-sixteenth century	

(b) Certon was a friend of Sermisy and pays homage to his friend by including quotations from three different *chansons* by Sermisy in the *superius* of his *Vivre ne puis content sans ma maistresse*
                BerC, 26
  i) The three *chansons* by Sermisy are *Vivre ne puis content sans ma maistresse*, *Languir me fais sans t'avoir offensé*, and *Contentez vous, amy, de la pensée*
  ii) The first four notes and words of the first two Sermisy *chansons* are used and the melody of the entire first line of *Contentez vous, amy, de la pensée* appears intact at the end of Certon's setting
  iii) This *chanson* can best be compared to the *fricassée*
    a - The *fricassée* is a type of *quodlibet* occurring among *chansons* of the first half of the sixteenth century
                RanH, 326
      1 - Quotations from sources that include polyphonic *chansons*, folk tunes, and street cries are mixed for humorous effect
  iv) A transcription of *Vivre ne puis content sans ma maistresse* by Certon   BerC, 27
(c) Transcriptions of ten of Certon's *chansons*   CerCZ
(d) Other transcriptions of Certon's *chansons*
            CerC I, CerC II, CerC III
(4) Pierre Regnault (nickname, Sandrin) [fl. 1539-1560]
 (a) Sandrin used homophonic texture, clear cadences, limited imitative entries, and few melismatic passages   SanO, x
  i) Some of his *chansons* have a strong emphasis on rhythmic contrast with strophic texts   SanO, x
  ii) His texts are sentimental
 (b) He wrote homophonic *chansons* in the conventional mold of the Parisian *chanson*   BerC, 58
  i) That is, the Parisian *chanson* of the late thirties and early forties   SanO, x
  ii) One trait, found in the Parisian *chanson* that Sandrin used, is the use of one specific rhythmic pattern for every musical phrase of the work   BerC, 58
    a - *Sy mon travail vous peult donner plaisir* is a good example of this
      1 - Transcriptions of this *chanson* BerC, 56; EitC, no. 52
 (c) Other *chansons* show an Italian influence from the *frottola* and madrigal   SanO, x
 (d) He wrote *chansons* in pairs   AttV, i
  i) His *Reveillez vous* and *En reveillant* are characterized by a unity of poetic theme
    a - They have a unity of subject and poetic structure
    b - They most likely should be performed in alternation ending with the third strophe of *Reveillez vous*
    c - Transcriptions of the two *chansons* AttV, 18 and 20
 (e) Transcriptions of his fifty *chansons*   SanO

The French *Chanson* 377

b) Composers from the provinces   RanH, 149
  (1)   [Pierre] Passereau [fl. 1509-1547]   ReeMR, 299
        (a)   He is best in humorous or bawdy pieces written in close imitation and nearly devoid of melisma
               i)   His style included close imitation, quick syllabic declamation, and running melodic figures   BerC, 47
        (b)   His favorite texts are those in a rustic vein
              i)   An example of this *is Au joly son du sansonnet*   BerC, 43
                   a - This is in *chanson rustique* style   BerC, 47
                         1 - The *chanson rustique* has as its main characteristic its variety and flexibility   BroCR, 19
                         2 - The poems are strophic and have a wide variety of strophe arrangements with direct and colloquial language   BroCR, 19
                         3 - There is no stereotyped scheme in the short strophes and refrains are an important element   BroCR, 19
                         4 - The subject matter is wide ranging   BroCR, 19
                         5 - It is entertainment music rather than sober, learned music (*chanson musicale*)   BroCR, 18
              ii)   This *chanson* is noted for the delightfully childlike freshness and grace of its contrapuntal devices   BorF, 10
              iii)   Transcriptions of *Au joly son du sansonnet*
                                                    BerC, 43; EitC, no. 47
        (c)   Transcriptions of his *chansons*   PasO
  (2)   François (Francesco) de Layolle of Lyons [b. 1492]   ReeMR, 300
        (a)   There are thirteen French pieces by Layolle   DobM, 257
              i)   Some, using texts from old monophonic *chansonniers*, were probably old pieces
              ii)   The three *bicinia*, found in the fourth book of the *Parangon des Chansons*, are new and up to date
        (b)   Transcriptions of some of his *chansons*
              i)   *La fille qui n'a point*   AlbZ, 10
                   a - This is one of the old pieces   DobM, 257
              ii)   *Ce me semblent choses perdues*
                   a - This appears in Book IV of the *Parangon* of 1538 published by Moderne in Lyons   ModP II; ModQ
              iii)   *Donna si raro*   ModC, 70
              iv)   *Pour avoir paix avecques mon desir*   ModP, 1
  (3)   Guillaume le Heurteur of Tours [fl. 1530-1545]   BerP, 205
        (a)   He wrote twenty-three *chansons*   BerN
        (b)   His music was typical of the provincial composers
              i)   He relied on voice pairs, part exchange, systematic imitation, free counterpoint, sweeping melismas, and uneven phrase structure   BerP, 205
              ii)   He used a tripartite musical form   MilT, x
              iii)   He did not keep a clear relationship between the text and the musical superstructure   BerP, 205
              iv)   His cadences usually mark the ends of poetic lines   MilT, x
        (c)   One of his *chansons, Amour partes,* is an unaccompanied contra-

378   Secular Vocal Music

				puntal duo for voice or instruments	BelS, ix
			i)	It was most likely extracted from a longer composition written for four or more parts	BelS, x
			ii)	Such compositions were known as *bicinium* in Germany	BelS, ix
				a - They appeared in the second third of the sixteenth century	
			iii)	A transcription of *Amour partes*	BelS, 130
		(d)	Transcriptions of some of his *chansons*		
			i)	Two *chansons*	EitC, nos. 28 and 29
			ii)	Three chansons	ThoF, nos. 4, 5, and 7
			iii)	*Troys jeunes bourgeoises*	ThoF, no. 11; BroC, 6
			iv)	*Ma dame ung jour*	MilT, nos. 43, 45, and 50
			v)	*Helas! Amour*	ThoF
			vi)	*Amy, souffrez que je vous aime*	AdaF I
			vii)	Transcription of another *chanson*	ModC
			viii)	Transcriptions of two *chansons*	GarC
	c)	A "French composer" in Italy			BerC, 66
		(1)	Antoine Gardane [b. 1509]		
		(a)	From 1557 on, he was known as [Antonio] Gardano		ReeMR, 314
		(b)	He called himself a French musician		
		(c)	His music is from the mature period of the Parisian *chanson*		AttV, i
			i)	Two of his *chansons* are written as a pair	
				a - His *Vostre cueur je supply* and *Amy chercher vostre fortune* involve a dialogue between a lover and his lady	
				b - These two *chansons* are to be sung in alternation with the final word going to the lover	
				c - Transcriptions of these two *chansons*	AttV, 41 and 42
		(d)	He made arrangements of popular *chansons* for fewer than four voices		BerC, 66
			i)	An example of this is the two-part *chanson, Jouyssance vous donneray,* in which Gardano elaborates the bass part of Claudin's *chanson*	
				a - This is possibly an arrangement for instruments as the *chanson* has highly patterned figuration	
				b - A transcription of *Jouyssance vous donneray*	BerC, 64
				c - A transcription of Claudin's *chanson*	DobO, 36
			ii)	Another example is *Content desir*	BelS, 130
				a - This is an unaccompanied contrapuntal duo for voice or instruments [a *bicinium*]	BelS, ix
				b - This was most likely extracted from a longer composition written for four or more parts	BelS, x
		(e)	Some transcriptions of his *chansons*		
			i)	Three *chansons*	AttV, 5, 11, and 14
			ii)	*O doulx regard*	AntCP, 54
			iii)	*N'avons point veu mal assenée*	AdaF II
			iv)	Sixteen *chansons* by Gardano	GarC
	d)	The Netherlandish School			ReeMR, 301
		(1)	Jean Richafort [ca. 1480]		
		(a)	He writes in the Netherlandish *chanson* style		ReeMR, 301

i) But he also wrote some *chansons* in the Sermisy-Janequin style   ReeMR, 302
    a - *De mon triste deplaisir* is an example
        1 - A transcription of *De mon triste deplaisir*   RicD
(b) His early *chansons* are in the three-voice form   BerC, 69
    i) A borrowed tune is placed in the tenor with the outer voices written in imitation
        a - Each phrase begins in the outer voices followed by the tune in the tenor
    ii) An example of the later stages of this style is *Tru, tru, trut avant il fault boire*   BerC, 67
        a - Transcriptions of *Tru, tru, trut avant il fault boire*   BerC, 67; DobO, 20
(c) An example of his four-voice style is *Sur tous regrets le mien plus piteux*   EitE II, 213
    i) In this *chanson* the motifs are flowing rather than declamatory   ReeMR, 301
    ii) "Through composition and imitation are much favored"   ReeMR, 301
    iii) A transcription of *Sur tous regrets le mien plus piteux*
(d) After ca. 1540 he produced *chansons* in five or more parts   ReeMR, 301
(e) Transcriptions of his *chansons*
    i) Transcriptions of nine *chansons*   BerCL
    ii) Transcriptions of four *chansons*   BerMM I
    iii) Transcriptions of five *chansons rustiques*   RicF
        a - The original state of the *chansons rustiques* is monophonic   BroMF, 108
            1 - But, they are often arranged in part settings
    iv) Transcriptions of two *chansons* for voices or unspecified instruments   RicD
    v) Transcriptions of other *chansons*   RicO, III

(2) Thomas Crécquillon [b. ca. 1480-ca. 1500]
  (a) He wrote music with great sensibility and elegance   BorF, 14
    i) He was a master of refinement   BorF, 18
        a - He was also an admirable interpreter of humor
    ii) His best music was written for four parts
  (b) He used imitative counterpoint, vocal pairings, and a chordal middle section in triple time   BerC, 110
    i) An example of this is *Ung gay bergier prioit une bergiere*   BerC, 106
        a - A transcription of *Ung gay bergier prioit une bergiere*
  (c) After ca. 1540, Crécquillon produced *chansons* in five or more parts   ReeMR, 301
  (d) He often emulated the clear, precise style of the Parisian *chanson*   BerC, 110
  (e) Facsimiles
    i) A book of polyphonic *chansons* composed by Crécquillon and published by Susato   CreL

    ii) *Dame D'honneur vives en sperace* for four voices MilC, 37v
     a - Thought to be by ?Crécquillon
   (f) Transcriptions of some of his *chansons*
    i) Three *chansons* EitE II, 222, 225, and 228
    ii) Fifteen *chansons* BerCP
    iii) Twelve *chansons* ForC
 (3) Nicolas Gombert [b. ca. 1490] BorF, 13
   (a) He was the supreme virtuoso of the imitative style and in the arrangement and interrelationship of words in grammatical constructions
    i) He had great skill in treating the music polyphonically so as to deploy the expressive powers to their full
   (b) But his early *chansons* have very little phrase repetition and imitation ReeMR, 304
    i) The imitation that is used is not always strict and the voices often enter after time intervals which, for the period, are extraordinarily brief
    ii) He uses clear-cut cadence formulas
    iii) A good example of this style *chanson* is *Vous êtes trop jeune* DobO, 86
     a - A transcription of *Vous êtes trop jeune*
   (c) His later *chansons* for five and six parts show his gift for the invention of original melodies and his skill in treating them polyphonically in order to deploy their expressive powers to the full
    i) A good example of his six voice writing is *Jouissance vous donneray* BerC, 87
     a - A transcription of *Jouissance vous donneray*
    ii) Other good examples are a six voice *chanson*, *En l'o,bre d'umg buissonet*, written in triple canon and *Qui ne l'aymeroit* in quadruple canon ReeMR, 304
     a - A transcription of *Qui ne l'aymeroit* MalTP XI, 16
   (d) He wrote some program *chansons* ReeMR, 305
   (e) Transcriptions of his *chansons* GomO, XI
 (4) Pierre de Manchicourt [b. ca. 1510]
   (a) He seems to favor the elaborate contrapuntal *chanson* ManT, xi
    i) But, a few of his pieces resemble the Parisian *chanson*
     a - They are written in the authentic French manner, using syllabic declamation to quick notes, with light and fluid counterpoint BorF, 18
     b - An example is *J'ay veu le cerf*
      1 - It was published in Attaingnant's *Tresiesme livre* of 1543
      2 - A transcription of *J'ay veu le cerf* ManT, 72
   (b) He was noted for the tenderness and melancholy in his music BorF, 18
   (c) A facsimile of a book of *chansons* composed by Manchicourt and published by Susato (*Le neufiesme livre des chansons à quatre parties*) ManN
   (d) Transcriptions of twenty-nine *chansons* ManT

                    (e) Transcriptions of six *chansons*   ForC
          (5) Jacobus Clemens (Clemens non Papa) [b. ca. 1510]
                (a) He wrote music for three parts with imitation used throughout
                                                                              BerC, 73
                      i)   An example of this style is *Au joly boys je rencontrary
                           m'amye*   BerC, 70
                           a - All three voices share in the presentation of the melody
                                                                              BerC, 73
                           b - This piece is built on a borrowed melody   BerC, 73
                           c - While this is a good example of Clemens' musical style,
                               and while it has been attributed to him, it is doubtful that
                               it is his   BerC, 73
                           d - A transcription of *Au joly boys je rencontrary m'amye*
                                                                              CleO, XI, 1
                (b) He was able to combine a boisterous popular verve with unusual
                     inventive power   BorF, 14
                (c) He wrote some *chansons* with Middle Dutch texts   ReeMR, 308
                      i)   Transcriptions of these *chansons*   CleO, XI
                (d) A catalogue of his *chansons*   KemJ
                (e) A facsimile of *Je prens en grey la dure mort* for four voices
                                                                              MilC, 38v
                (f) Transcriptions of his *chansons*   CleO, X, XI
                      i)   This publication uses the chronological order found in the
                           catalogue
          (6) Jehan Le Cocq (=Gallus) [fl. 1534-1541]
                (a) He was a very good craftsman   BorF, 20
                (b) He used quick repeated notes and wide intervals   BerC, 116
                      i)   This style is particularly conducive to an instrumental consort
                           performance
                      ii) An example of this is *Le bergier et la bergiere* BerC, 111
                           a - A transcription of *Le bergier et la bergiere*
                (c) Transcriptions of three of his *chansons*   ForC
          (7) Jean Guyot (Castileti) [b. 1512]   BorF, 19
                (a) He wrote *chansons* in mosaic-like counterpoint, singularly rich in
                     charming effects
                (b) His *chansons* are found in the Susato collections
                      i)   Facsimiles of his *chansons*   SusLT
                      ii) Transcriptions of five *chansons*   ForC
     e) A Flemish composer who lived mainly in Italy   ReeMR, 309
          (1) Adrian Willaert [b. ca. 1490]   WilO, ii
                (a) He was the creator of the new Italianized Netherlandish style
                      i)   His *chansons* have both Netherlandish and Italian influences
                                                                              ReeMR, 309
                           a - They contain the Flemish polyphonic conception with the
                               Italian tonic style   WilO, i
                           b - They reflect the changes in the two styles in the course of
                               his *chanson* production
                      ii) He also incorporated the Gaelic style of precision, sprightli-
                           ness, and rationalism in his music after his visit in Paris

(b) His Netherlandish style
    i) The early *chansons* consist mostly of strict double-canons with the two upper voices paired against the two lower voices
        a - Transcriptions of these double canons   WilF
    ii) The later *chansons,* from 1530 to 1536, have a *cantus firmus* treatment in the tenor with the other voices written in melismatic style
        a - Willaert continues to develop this style after 1540
        b - An example of this style is *Baises moy tant, tant*   BerC, 74
           1 - A transcription of *Baises moy tant, tant*
    iii) Some of his *chansons* were "paraphrase *chansons*" in which the borrowed melody is presented in either its original or elaborated form in a number of voices   BerC, 79
        a - An example of this is his *Joissance vous donnerai*
           1 - A transcription of *Joissance vous donnerai*
(c) His *chansons* in Italian style can be traced through three periods of development   ReeMR, 310
    i) In the first period, he uses a concise and predominantly syllabic style
        a - Even the canonic settings tend to a more chordal style with a more lively rhythmic precision and a closer relationship of words and music
    ii) In the second period, he has a tendency toward a more lively rhythmic precision
    iii) And in the third period, he develops a closer relationship of the text to the music
(d) Facsimiles of *chansons* for three voices   WilCL
(e) A reprint of five double canons   AntM
(f) Transcriptions of some of his *chansons*
    i) Transcriptions of five double canons   WilF
    ii) Transcriptions of the complete five and six voice *chansons*   WilFC
    iii) Transcriptions of two *chansons* for six voices and instruments   WilC
    iv) Transcriptions of twenty *chansons*   BerMM I

5. Performance of the *chanson*
    a) The *chanson* of this period has definite accentuation and pulse   SeaFC, 2
        (1) Therefore, the entries of each voice ordinarily should be strongly indicated
        (2) Style should be used to achieve contrast as much as possible
            (a) Contrast should not be achieved by dynamics
    b) Performance practice varied according to the availability of the singers and players   AdaF I, viii
        (1) *Chansons* were performed either vocally or instrumentally
            (a) But, the most authentic mode of performance was vocal, usually with one voice *per* part   DobO, viii
                i) Extra voices were used occasionally
        (2) *Chansons* were performed with both voices and instruments

                (a) But there were very few indications as to which instruments should be employed   MeyC, 552
                    i) Often, players used whatever instruments happened to be at hand
                (b) The upper parts might have been sung and the two lower parts played
            (3) *Chansons* were often arranged for solo voice and lute or other instrument   BroE, 74
                (a) Sometimes they were arranged for two or three voices and lute, and also for other combinations of voices and/or instruments
            (4) *Chansons* may have been performed by instruments only   MeyC, 551
        c) Performance conventions of the time permitted singers and instrumentalists to embellish music that had already been composed   BroE, x
            (1) Both instrumental and vocal ensembles would have used discreet ornaments in order to decorate the music   BroE, 74
                (a) The decision as to when to use the ornaments depended more on the number and kinds of musicians rather than with the nature of the music
                    i) As a result, instrumentalists were more inclined to use ornaments than singers
                (b) Sixteenth century authors made a distinction between specific ornaments applied to single notes (graces) and to longer, freer running passages used to substitute for slower-moving basic intervals (*passaggi*)   BroE, 1
                    i) The term 'graces' was not used during the sixteenth century
        d) Texts of unrequited love and other misfortunes should not be sung at too slow a tempo   AdaF I, viii
            (1) The character of the music suggests a more lively interpretation

6. The *chanson* in the theater
    a) The only emotions and situations that demand music in the plays are happy ones   BroMF, 107
        (1) The music occurs chiefly to enliven moods, feasts, and celebrations
    b) There was a clear discrepancy between the kind of music most often described in the secular theater and that of the more sober "learned" style   BroMF, 107
        (1) The term for the former is *chanson rustique* and the term for the latter is *chanson musicale*
            (a) The term *chanson rustique* is almost exactly synonymous with theatrical *chanson*   BroMF, 111
    c) The texts for the *chanson rustique* are distinguished from those of the *chanson musicale* by the repetition schemes and content   BroMF, 109
        (1) "Strophic construction may be considered the norm for the chanson rustique"
        (2) There are refrains that often punctuate the strophic structure
            (a) The specific form of the refrain is not rigidly prescribed
                i) There are short refrains which may be repeated after every line of text
                ii) And longer refrains of more than one line may recur after each strophe

(b) The refrains contain nonsense syllables at times
- d) The texts for the *chanson rustique* differ from those of the *chanson musicale* in their variety and flexibility   BroMF, 110
    - (1) They cover many topics
    - (2) But, what ever the topic, all *chansons rustiques* deal with the everyday world, and show a profound lack of interest in an ideal world
- e) The early collections of *chansons rustiques* supports the idea of unaccompanied solo singing in the plays   BroMF, 115
    - (1) But, every performer had a different conception of the details of the music, and in time the original version was buried under an impenetrable mass of alternate versions   BroMF, 116
        - (a) The monophonic melodies led an independent existence once they were circulated   BroMF, 118
            - i) "They reappear again and again in different polyphonic arrangements, each time with details changed"
        - (b) Some of the polyphonic settings are elaborate arrangements of the melodies made by leading composers of the day   BroMF, 118
            - i) The melodies are usually found as tenor parts   BroMF, 119
            - ii) Most settings are for three voices   BroMF, 130
- f) The homorhythmic *chanson* became very popular in the second quarter of the sixteenth century   BroMF, 129
    - (1) It was a part song in which the *superius* had the melody and the lower voices accompanied it in more or less note against note
        - (a) This style *chanson* was rare before 1530   BroMF, 131
    - (2) Examples of the homorhythmic *chanson* are found in the *Farce de deulx amoureux* by Clément Marot which contains three four-part *chansons* by Sermisy in the new style
        - (a) One of the *chansons* is *Languir me fais* with a text by Marot
            - i) A transcription of *Languir me fais*   AttTR Part 2, 12
        - (b) The other two *chansons* are *Content desir* and *Puysqu'en amours*
            - i) Transcriptions of *Puysqu'en amours*   AttTR Part 3, 14; AttT, 95
        - (c) These have some characteristics of the *chanson rutique*
    - (3) Some composers, other than Sermisy, whose *chansons* were associated with the theater and have the same characteristics, are Sandrin, *Doulce memoire* and Bouteiller, [a seventeenth century composer], *Laissez moy planter le may*   BroMF, 132
        - (a) A transcription of *Doulce memoire*   EitC, 50
- g) There were *chansons* in which arranged melodies were borrowed from the *rustique* repertoire   BroMF, 132
    - (1) The *superius* was ornamented in order to smoothly incorporate it into the texture   BroMF, 133
        - (a) The device of ornamenting a *cantus prius factus* is called the paraphrase technique by Reese   BroMF, 133
    - (2) The *superius* of *Il estroit une fillette* by Janequin may be such a borrowed melody
        - (a) A transcription of *Il estroit une fillette*   AntCP, 19
- h) There is some evidence of the parody technique in the polyphonic *chansons* found in the theater   BroMF, 134

The French *Chanson* 385

    (1) An example is Janequin's *My levay par ung matin*   BroMF, 135
     (a) A transcription of *My levay par ung matin*   AttT, 9
    (2) All parts of the polyphonic *chanson* are borrowed
  i) Almost all *chansons* found in plays fall into one of the categories listed above
                             BroMF, 136
    (1) They are usually based on a monophonic model of popular character
  j) A catalogue of theatrical *chansons*   BroMF, 183

7. Some of the printed sources of the *chanson* [ca. 1520 to 1550]
  a) Sources published by Andrea Antico   BroMF, 287
    (1) Antico had been established as a music publisher at Rome since about
      1510   RokI, 443
     (a) He was a brilliant engraver   AtlR, 260
    (2) *Motetti novi e chanzoni franciose a quatro sopra doi*   AntM
     (a) This was published in Venice in 1520
     (b) It is in Firenza: Biblioteca Marucelliana   RISM B,1, 99
     (c) A reprint of *Motetti novi e chanzoni franciose...*   AntM
     (d) A transcription of *Motetti novi e chanzoni franciose...*   WilF
    (3) Sources published by Andrea Antico and Ottaviano Scotto
     (a) This was a partnership in which Scotto financed the publication
       and was in charge of sales and distribution of the pressrun and
       Antico prepared the woodcuts and edited the music   BerCA, 111
     (b) *Primo libro de le canzoni franzese*. S.I., 1535
      i) This is thought to be the first Italian print devoted entirely to
        sixteenth-century style *chansons*   ReeMR, 314
      ii) It contains twenty-three *chansons*   RISM B,1, 113
      iii) It is in Paris: Bibliothèque Nationale   RISM B,1, 113
      iv) A facsimile of *Primo libro de le canzoni franzese...*   AntP
    (4) Sources published by Andrea Antico and A. de Brebate   BroMF, 287
     (a) *La Couronne et fleur des chansons à troy* (Venice, 1536)
      i) It is in Rouen: Bibliothèque Municipale   RISM B,1, 114
      ii) A list of the contents, concordances, modern editions, and
        related settings.   BerMF, 61
      iii) A list of manuscripts containing *La Couronne et fleur des*
        chansons à troy   BerMF, 59
      iv) A list of recent literature and modern editions of *La Cour-*
        onne et fleur des chansons à troy   BerMF, 60
      v) A commentary on the contents   BerMM II
      vi) A transcription of *La Couronne et fleur des chansons à troy*
                            BerMM I
    (5) A chronological bibliography of Antico's publications   RISM B,I
     (a) This contains a summary of the contents and lists locations of
       copies in major European and American libraries
  b) Moderne, Jacques [=Grand Jacques]   BroMF, 290
    (1) Moderne was a bookseller and publisher in Lyons from ca. 1523 to
      1560   ModP I, xi
     (a) His *chanson* anthologies may have been edited by P. de Villiers
                            DobL, 208
    (2) *Le Parangon des chansons. Premier(-Dixieseme) livre*

(a) There were originally eighteen volumes of *Le Parangon* HeaP, 151
    i) Only ten have survived.
    ii) The majority of the pieces are courtly *épigrammes*, being mostly *quatraines* or *huitains* DobM, 247
    iii) There are single strophes of strophic poems or rustic *chansons* with refrain DobM, 247
    iv) The repertoire is dominated by twenty texts by Marot, ten by Frances I, and six by Mellin de Saint-Gelais DobM, 247
        a - There are some texts in Italian set to music by Layolle and P. de Villiers

(b) Sources published in Lyons in 1538
    i) *Le Parangon des chansons: Premier livre...* ModP I
        a - This is found in Munich: Bayerische Staatsbibliothek RISM B,1, 121
    ii) *Le Parangon des chansons: Deuxiesme livre contenant xxxi chansons...* ModP I
        a - This was published in Lyons in 1540 but it is a reprint of a 1538 publication
        b - It is found in Munich: Bayerische Staatsbibliothek RISM B,1, 130
    iii) *Le Parangon des chansons: tiers livre contenant xxvi chansons...* ModP II
        a - It is found in Munich: Bayerische Staatsbibliothek RISM B,1, 121

(c) Sources published in Lyons in 1539
    i) *Le Parangon des chansons: quart livre contenant xxii chansons à deux et à troys parties* ModP II
        a - It is found in Lüneburg: Ratsbücherei und Stadtarchiv RISM B,1, 122
        b - A transcription of *Le Parangon des chansons: quart livre...* ModQ
    ii) *Le Parangon des chansons: cinquiesme livre contenant xxviii chansons...* ModP III
        a - It is found in Munich: Bayerishe Staatsbibliothek RISM B,1, 126
        b - A transcription of *Le Parangon des chansons: cinquiesme livre contenant xxviii chansons...* ModC

(d) Sources published in Lyons in 1540
    i) *Le Parangon des chansons: sixiesme livre contenant xxv chansons nouvelles...* ModP III
        a - This is found in Munich: Bayerische Staatsbibliothek RISM B,1, 131
    ii) *Le Parangon des chansons: septiesme livre contenant xxvii chansons...* ModP IV
        a - It is found in Munich: Bayerische Staatsbibliothek RISM B,1, 131

(e) Sources published in Lyons in 1541
    i) *Le Parangon des chansons: huytiesme livre contenant xxx chansons...* ModP IV

			a - This is found in Munich: Bayerische Staatsbibliothek

                            a - This is found in Munich: Bayerische Staatsbibliothek
                                                                    RISM B,1, 133
                    ii)   *Le Parangon des chansons: neufuiesme livre contenant xxxi
                           chansons...*   ModP V
                            a - This is found in Munich: Bayerische Staatsbibliothek
                                                                    RISM B,1, 134
            (f)   One source published in Lyons in 1543
                    i)   *Le Parangon des chansons: dixiesme livre contenant xxx
                           chansons...*   ModP V
                            a - This is found in Munich: Bayerische Staatsbibliothek
                                                                    RISM B,1, 142
            (g)   Facsimiles of the ten books of *chansons*   ModPC
            (h)   Transcriptions of twelve *chansons* from *Le Parangon des chan-
                  sons*   AlbZ
            (i)   Transcriptions of the ten books of *chansons*   ModP I-V
      (3)   *Le Difficile des chansons*   HeaP, 152
            (a)   The two books of the *Difficile* series were published in 1540 and
                  1544   ModC, i
            (b)   *Le Difficile des chansons: Premier livre contenant xxii chansons
                  nouvelles à quatre parties en quatre livres*   ModDD
                    i)   Thirteen of these had already been printed by Attaingnant in
                           his eighth book of *chansons*   DobM, 247
                    ii)   A facsimile of *Le Difficile des chansons: Premier livre...*
                                                                           ModDD
            (c)   *Le Difficile des chansons: Second livre contenant xxvi chansons
                     nouvelles à quatre parties en quatre livres*   ModD
                    i)   This book contains a novel repertoire consisting almost en-
                           tirely of narrative pieces   DobM, 247
                    ii)   A facsimile of *Le Difficile des chansons: Second livre...*
                                                                            ModD
      (4)   A chronological bibliography of Moderne's publications   RISM B,I
            (a)   This contains a summary of the contents and lists locations of
                  copies in major European and American libraries
c) Some sources published by Pierre Attaingnant   BroMF, 287
      (1)   Pierre Attaingnant was one of the earliest to use single-impression
            printing   AttPI
            (a)   He developed it (1527-1528)   RanH, 655
            (b)   He used it in a book of *chansons* (*Chansons Nouvelles* of 1528)
                                                                            AttPI
      (2)   His *chanson* books were quite influential in Antwerp, Bruges, and Lou-
            vain before 1542   BerP, 202
            (a)   He printed several dozens of *chansons* between 1529 and 1549
                                                                           BorF, 9
      (3)   Books published in Paris in 1528
            (a)   *Chansons nouvelles en musique à quatre parties*   BorF, 2
                    i)   There are thirty-one *chansons*   RISM B,1, 103
                    ii)   Only the *altus* and tenor voices remain   HeaP, 210
                            a - The contents [of the other voices] can be reconstructed
                                from later sources   ReeMR, 290

          iii)   A facsimile of *Chansons nouvelles en musique...*   AttC
    (b) *Trente et sept chansons...*   ReeMR, 293
          i)   This is actually undated but is thought to have been published ca. 1528-30
               a - It may have been published in 1529   HeaP, 220
          ii)   A listing of *Trente et sept chansons...* in a thematic catalog   AttTSC
          iii)   A facsimile of *Trente et sept chansons...*   AttTS
(4) Books published in Paris in 1529
    (a) *Trente et une chansons musicales à quatre parties*   BorF, 2
          i)   This is in Paris: Bibliothèque Nationale   HeaP, 227
          ii)   A reprint edition of *Trente et une chansons musicales...*   AttT
    (b) *Trente et quatre chansons musicales à quatre parties*   BorF, 2
          i)   A facsimile of *Trente et quatre chansons musicales...*   AttTQ
    (c) *Trente et huyt chansons musicales*
          i)   It is in Paris: Bibliothéque National   HeaP, 214
          ii)   A facsimile of *Trente et huyt chansons musicales*   AttTH
    (d) *Quarante et deux chansons musicales à troys parties*
          i)   A facsimile of *Quarante et deux chansons musicales...*   AttQ
    (e) *Trente chansons musicales à auatre parties nouvellement et tres correctement imprimés*   AttTC
          i)   A facsimile of *Trente chansons musicales...*   AttTC
(5) Books published in Paris in 1530
    (a) *Vingt et neuf chansons musicales à quatre parties*
          i)   This is in Paris: Bibliothèque Nationale   HeaP, 232
          ii)   A facsimile of *Vingt et neuf chansons musicales...*   AttVN
    (b) *Trente et six chansons musicales*
          i)   This is in Paris: Bibliothèque Nationale   HeaP, 233
          ii)   A facsimile of *Trente et six chansons musicales*   AttTSCM
(6) Books published in Paris in 1531
    (a) *Vingt et huit chansons nouvelles*
          i)   This is in Munich: Bayerische Staatsbibliothek   HeaP, 244
          ii)   A facsimile of *Vingt et huit chansons nouvelles*   AttVH
    (b) *Trente et sept chansons musicales*
          i)   This is a reprint of *Trente et sept chansons musicales* published by Attaingnant in 1529   HeaP, 245
          ii)   This is in Munich: Bayerische Staatsbibliothek   HeaP, 245
          iii)   A listing of *Trente et sept chansons musicales* in a thematic catalog   AttTSE
          iv)   A facsimile of *Trente et sept chansons musicales*   AttTSEP
(7) Books published in Paris in 1532
    (a) *Trente et trois chansons nouvelles*
          i)   This is in Munich: Bayerische Staatsbibliothek   HeaP, 243
          ii)   A facsimile of *Trente et trois chansons nouvelles*   AttTTC
(8) Books published in Paris in 1533
    (a) *Vingt et quatre chansons musicales à quatres parties composées par Clément Jennequin*   HeaCH, 202
          i)   This is in Munich: Bayerische Staatsbibliothek   HeaP, 250
          ii)   A facsimile of *Vingt et quatre chansons musicales...*   AttVQ

(b) *Vingt et sept chansons musicales à quatre parties desquelles les plus convenables à la fleuste d'allemant...* AttVS
    i) This is in Munich: Bayerische staatsbibliothek   HeaP, 252
    ii) A facsimile of *Vingt et sept chansons musicales...*   AttVS
(9) Books published in Paris in 1534   BroMF, 288
   (a) *Trente chansons musicales*
    i) This is in Munich: Bayerische Staatsbibliothek   HeaP, 254
    ii) A facsimile of *Trente chansons musicales*   AttTCM
   (b) *Trente et une chansons musicales*
    i) This is in Munich: Bayerische Staatsbibliothek   HeaP, 266
    ii) A facsimile of *Trente et une chansons musicales*   AttTU
(10) Books published in Paris in 1535   BroMF, 288
   (a) *Vingt et six chansons musicales*
    i) This is in Munich: Bayerische Staatsbibliothek   HeaP, 274
    ii) A facsimile of *Vingt et six chansons musicales*   AttVSCM
(11) Books published in Paris in 1536   AttS
   (a) *Second livre contenant xxxi chansons musicales*
    i) This is in Paris: Bibliothèque Mazarine   HeaP, 281
    ii) A facsimile of *Second livre...*   AttSLC
    iii) A transcription of *Second livre...*   AttS
(12) Books published in Paris from 1538 to 1543   BerP, 211
   (a) *Livre premier(-trentesixiesme) de chansons*   BroMF, 288
    i) The first four books were published in 1538   HeaP, 292-295
    ii) The following are reprints of the second and third books
         HeaP, 307-308
       a - *Second livre contenantXXVI chansons*   HeaP, 307
         1 - This is a reprint published in 1540   HeaP, 308
           a - It contains five *chansons* by Sermisy, two by Certon, six by Sandrin, three by Clemens, and one by Janequin
           b - This is in Munich: Bayerische Staatsbibliothek
         2 - Another reprint of *Second livre...* was published in 1549   HeaP, 363
           a - A facsimile of the 1549 edition   AttSC
       b - The *Tiers livre contenant XXIX chansons nouvelles... 1540.*   BerP, 211
         1 - This is in Munich: Bayerische Staatsbibliothek
            HeaP, 309
         2 - A facsimile of The *Tiers livre...*   AttTLC
    iii) The fifth, sixth, and seventh books were published in 1539
         HeaP, 296 and 302
    iv) The *Huitiesme livre contenant XIX chansons nouvelles à quatre parties, de la facture et composition de Maîstre Clement Jennequin, en deux volumes...*   FloD, I,iii
       a - This was published in Paris in 1540
       b - A list of the contents   HeaP, 305
       c - This is in Oxford: Christ Church Mus.   HeaP, 305
       d - A facsimile of the *Huitiesme livre...*   AttH
    v) The *Tresiesme livre contenant XIX chansons nouvelles à*

                quatre parties, en deux volumes...   FloD, I, iii
                a - Published in 1543 by Attaingnant and Hubert Jullet
                b - This is in Munich: Bayerische Staatsbibliothek   HeaP, 323
                c - A facsimile of *Tresiesme livre*...   AttTLCN
            vi) For the contents of the thirty-six books *see*   RISM B,I
        (13) Books published in 1545   AttD
            (a) *Dixseptiesme livre contenant xix chansons legères très musicales nouvelles à quatre parties*
                i) There was a second printing of this source in the same year
                                                                      AttD, i
                ii) This is in Munich: Bayerische Staatsbibliothek   HeaP, 334
                iii) A facsimile of *Dixseptiesme livre*...   AttDL
                iv) A transcription of *Dixseptiesme livre*...   AttD
        (14) Books published in 1547
            (a) *Vingt deuxiesme livre*   AttV
                i) This source contains twenty-six *chansons*   RISM B,1, 160
                ii) It is in Munich: Bayerische Staatsbibliothek   RISM B,1, 160
                iii) A facsimile of *Vingt deuxiesme livre*   AttVD
                iv) A transcription of *Vingt deuxiesme livre*   AttV
        (15) Books published in 1549
            (a) *Trente et ungyesme livre contenant XXX chansons nouvelles à quatre [parties] en deux volumes. De la facture et composition de maîstre Clément Jannequin*...   FloD, I,17
                i) This was published in Paris
                ii) It is in Munich: Bayerische Staatsbibliothek   HeaP, 360
                iii) A list of the contents   HeaP, 360
                iv) A facsimile of *Trente et ungyesme livre*...   AttTUL
            (b) *Trente troysiesme livre contenant xx chansons nouvelles à quatre en deux*   AttTT, i
                i) This is in Munich: Bayerische Staatsbibliothek   AttTT, ii
                ii) A facsimile of *Trente troysiesme livre*...   AttTTL
                iii) A transcription of *Trente troysiesme livre*... AttTT
        (16) A catalogue of Attaingants' publications   HeaP, 210
            (a) This contains the contents of each source, the text incipit and the name of the composer
        (17) A chronological bibliography of Attaingnant's publications   RISM B,I
            (a) This contains a summary of the contents and lists locations of copies in major European and American libraries
            (b) It also contains an index of editors and printers, and of titles and authors
    d) Antoine Gardane (Antonio Gardano)
        (1) He flourished from 1538 to 1569   ChaH, 458
            (a) "He reprinted many current publications as well as important novelties, and compositions of his own"   BakB, 536
        (2) *Canzoni francese a due voci di Ant. Gardane et di altri autori*   BerC, 212
            (a) This was published in Venice in 1539
                i) It was one of the first prints made by Gardane after he arrived in Venice   GarC, i
            (b) It contains twenty-eight *chansons*, of which twelve are taken from

Moderne's *Quart livre*... (*Le Parangon*), and of which sixteen are
new *chansons* by Gardane   GarC, i
      (c)   This is in Bologna: Biblioteca del Conservatorio (*Liceo Musicale*)
                                                                                                                             RISM B,1, 126
      (d)   A transcription of *Canzoni francese a due voci*...   GarC
      (e)   Other transcriptions
            i)   Six *chansons*   FloD, VIII, 1, 4, 13, 16, 19, and 22
  (3)   *Canzoni francese a due voci d'Antonio Gardane insieme auquel de altri
        autori, libro primo*   BerC, 212
      (a)   This was published in Venice in 1544
      (b)   There were three more editions in 1552, 1564, and 1568   GarC, i
           i)   These last versions were the same as the first edition except
                 for an added *chanson, Amy souffrés* by Gardane   GarC, ii
      (c)   This is found in Eichstätt: Staatliche Bibliothek   RISM B,1, 146
      (d)   A transcription of *Canzoni francese a due voci*...   GarC
e)   Nicolas du Chemin (ca. 1510-1576)   ReeMR, 290
  (1)   He published music in Paris from 1540 to 1576
      (a)   This included a seventeen-volume *chanson* collection
      (b)   Two of the books were published in 1549
           i)   *Premier Livre de chansons à quatre parties*   DuCP
                a - It contains twenty-five *chansons*   RISM B,1, 175
                b - It is found in Firwnze: Biblioteca del Conservatorio
                                                                                               RISM B,1, 175
                c - A facsimile of *Premier Livre de chansons*...   DuCP
           ii)   *Second Livre de chansons à quatre parties*   DuCS
                a - It contains twenty-six *chansons*   RISM B,1, 170
                b - This is found in Paris: Bibliothèque Nationale
                                                                                                RISM B,1, 170
                c - A facsimile of *Second Livre de chansons*...
  (2)   A bibliography of the music editions published by Nicolas du Chemin
                                                                                                                               LesB
f)   Kriesstein, [Melchior] at Augsburg   ReeMR, 300
  (1)   *Selectissimae...cantiones* of 1540
      (a)   This is the earliest large *chanson* collection offering a majority
             of pieces *a* 5 and *a* 6   ReeMR, 304
      (b)   There are 104 compositions   RISM B,1, 129
      (c)   It is found in Munich: Bayerische Staatsbibliothek   RISM B,1, 129
      (d)   A summary of the contents and lists of locations of copies in major
           European and American libraries   RISM B,I, 129
      (e)   A facsimile of *Selectissimae...cantiones* of 1540   SalSE
g). Susato, Tielman   BroMF, 292
  (1)   Susato was an Antwerp publisher who issued an imposing series of col-
          lections of *chansons* over a period of about ten years   BorF, 9
      (a)   He published in Antwerp from 1543 to 1560   BroMF, 292
  (2)   He published twenty-two books of *chansons*   ForC, xi
      (a)   They were published in two series   ForC, xii
           i)   The first series included sixteen books
                a - The *Premier livre-Le treziesme livre* plus a fourteenth
                    book and two additional books that appeared later

                 b - These were published between 1543 and 1555
          ii)   The second series: *Fleur de chansons* included six books
               all published in 1552
  (3) Eleven books of the first series were published between [1543-1549]
      (a) Books published in Antwerp in 1543   MeiD II
          i)   *Premier livre... à quatre parties*   ForC, xvii
               a - It was apparently the first collection of polyphonic *chan-
                   sons* to be published in the Netherlands   ReeMR, 308
               b - It contains thirty-one *chansons*   RISM B,1, 142
               c - It is found in London: British Museum   RISM B,1, 142
               d - Transcriptions of some of the *chansons*   ForC
      (b) Books published in Antwerp in 1544   MeiD II
          i)   *Le second livre... à quatre parties*   ForC, xvii
               a - It contains thirty-one *chansons*   RISM B,1, 145
               b - It is found in London: British Museum   RISM B,1, 145
          ii) *Le tiers livre de chansons à quatre parties*   CreL
               a - This third book is devoted to the *chansons* of a single
                   composer, Thomas Créquillon   BorF, 16
                   1 - But, one *chanson* is by J. Le Cocq   RISM B,1, 146
               b - There are thirty-seven chansons   RISM B,1, 146
               c - It is found in London: British Museum   RISM B,1, 146
               d - A facsimile of *Le tiers livre de chansons...*   CreL
          iii) *Le quatriesme livre des chansons à quatre parties auquel
              sont contenues trente et quatre chansons nouvelles* BerC, 212
               a - It is found in London: British Museum   RISM B,1, 146
      (c) Books published in Antwerp in 1545   MeiD II
          i)   *Le cincquiesme livre... à quatre et six parties*   ForC, xvii
               a - It contains thirty-two *chansons*   RISM B,1, 146
               b - It is found in London: British Museum   RISM B,1, 146
          ii) *Le sixiesme livre contenant trente et une chansons nouvelles
              à cincq et à six parties*   BerC, 212
               a - It contains thirty-one *chansons*   RISM B,1, 151
          iii) *Le septiesme livre... à cincq et six parties*   ForC, xviii
               a - It was devoted entirely to Josquin   ReeMR, 300
               b - It is found in London: British Museum   RISM B,1 152
          iv) *Le huitiesme livre... à quatre parties*   ForC, xviii
               a - There are thirty-two *chansons*   RISM B,1, 152
               b - This is found in London: British Museum RISM B,1, 152
          v)   *Le neufiesme livre des chansons à quatre parties, auquel
              sont contenues vingt et neuf chansons nouvelles, convenables
              tant à la voix comme aux instrumentz...*   ManN
               a - The ninth book is devoted to the *chansons* of Pierre de
                   Manchicourt   BorF, 16
               b - It is found in Wien: Österreichische Nationalbibliothek
               c - A facsimile of *Le neufiesme livre des chansons...*   ManN
          vi) *Le dixiesme livre... à quatre et cincq parties*   ForC, xviii
               a - This source contains sixteen *chansons*   RISM B,1, 152
               b - This is found in London: British Museum RISM B,1, 152
      (d) One book published in 1549   MeiD II

i) *L'unziesme livre... à quatre parties* ForC, xviii
   a - It contains twenty-nine *chansons* RISM B,1, 171
   b - This is found in London: British Museum RISM B,1, 171
(e) A catalog of the eleven books with a list of the contents of each
   MeiD II
(f) Facsimiles of these eleven books of *chansons* SusP

B. The Italian *Canzone*

1. Introduction
   a) The *canzone* is a poetic form that was defined by Dante and made popular by Petrarch RanH, 138
   b) It was covered by the designation *frottola* from ca. 1470 to 1530 ReeMR, 156
      (1) The term *frottola* was applied as a generic designation and not in a specific sense
   c) But, many *canzone*, from 1520 to 1530, in effect were almost madrigals
      ReeMR, 156
      (1) Therefore the term was gradually used as a general term for the serious madrigal RanH, 138
         (a) It was also used for the lighter forms, with words such as *villanesca* attached

2. The poetry of the *canzone*
   a) The *canzone* has almost the least structural regularity of all the generic *frottola* forms ReeMR, 164
      (1) The number of strophes is constant in a single *canzone* but varies from piece to piece
      (2) The *canzone* is distinguished by an irregularity of the rhymes, its rhythmic variety, and a high standard of literary content
   b) There is, at times, a *commiato* at the end of the poem ReeMR, 164
      (1) This is a short envoy containing the author's parting words to his poem, or something similar
   c) The use of a combination of seven- and eleven-syllable lines is the only standardizing feature
      1) These iambic lines of seven and eleven syllables are freely mixed
         RanH, 138
   d) The *canzone* was made popular by Petrarch RanH, 138
      (1) His *canzoni* have five to seven strophes of identical scheme and often end with a shorter final strophe
      (2) Each strophe has a *fronte* of several groups of lines with shared rhymes and a longer *sirima* metrically distinct from the *fronte*
      (3) Petrarch's *canzoni* are love lyrics
      (4) They were imitated by many sixteenth century poets

3. The music of the *canzone*
   a) The *canzoni* found favor among musicians RanH, 138
      (1) Composers wrote compositions written mainly with a chordal texture and with the melody in the tenor PirMT, 100

          (a) The compositions are homophonic in declamatory style and are based on simple repetitive tenor tunes   CarA, xiv
     (2) The same melodic phrase was often used for a different line of text   CarA, xiv
          (a) This sets the *canzoni* apart from the *villanesche*
     (3) The vocal *canzone* was characterized by free musical form   CanZ
          (a) It showed free adaptations of the Petrachan form   RanH, 138
     (4) This style composition contributed to the formation of the early madrigal style
          (a) Sixteenth century madrigalists set whole *canzoni* as cycles, or more often, they chose individual strophes   RanH, 138

4. The *canzone* [madrigal] in the theater
   a) The terms *canzone* and madrigal were both used for the *intermedio*   PirMT, 145
     (1) The *intermedio* was a vocal or instrumental work performed between the acts of a play   RanH, 398
          (a) It appeared quite early and generally in four-part block harmony   DenS, 41
          (b) It is not an anticipation of opera but simply a prologue, entr'acte, and epilogue
     (2) The primary purpose of the *intermedio* was to give information about the play   DenM, 787
          (a) Therefore it was essential that the words of the *intermedio* be understood as clearly as possible   DenS, 41
          (b) As a result the music was extremely simple   DenM, 787
     (3) Music was generally restricted to the *intermedi*   PirMT, 82
          (a) Dancing and singing within plays did occur but they represent the exception rather than the rule   PirMT, 81
     (4) The *intermedi* of some kind were always necessary for the performance of a comedy   PirMT, 123
          (a) They were as necessary as a stage setting
   b) Four *canzoni*, written by Verdelot on texts by Machiavelli, were written as *intermedi* for production in Machiavelli's plays, *La Mandragola* and *La Clizia*   FenI, 42
     (1) These *intermedi* represent the starting point of a new concept of *intermedi*   PirMT, 124
     (2) The *cantus*, tenor, *bassus*, and *quintus* parts of these *canzoni* are found in Chicago: Newberry Library, Case *MS-VM 1578. M91*   PirMT, 153
          (a) The incomplete *altus* part is found in Sutton Coldfield: Oscott College *MS Case B No. 4*
     (3) A list of the contents and concordances of the third series of pieces [madrigals and *canzoni*] in the Chicago: Newberry Library, Case *MS-VM 1578. M91*   FenI, 155
          (a) [The four *canzoni* by Verdelot on texts by Machiavelli are nos. 6, 9, 10, and 11]
     (4) A reprint edition of some of Verdelot's *canzoni*   ScoI
   c) *La mandragola* by Machiavelli may have been presented for the first time in 1518   PirMT, 124

(1) It was first entitled *Commedia di Callimaco e di Lucrezia* and later renamed *La Mandragola*   UndM
(2) It is a comedy in which the wickedness and corruption of men, particularly the clergy, are the subject of laughter   UndM
    (a) The laughter is a bitter and painful laughter that is never an end in itself
(3) The music, performed before the comedy, is missing as is that of the *canzone* after Act II   PirMT, 144
(4) Transcriptions of the *intermedi*
    (a) A transcription of the song by Verdelot that was sung after the first act   PirMT, 135
    (b) A transcription of a song after the third act   PirMT, 138
    (c) A transcription of the song by Verdelot that was sung after the fourth act   PirMT, 142
(5) The play also contains a two-line song in Act IV scene 9   PirMT, 78
    (a) The singing is accompanied by a lute
d) *La Clizia* by Machiavelli was first presented in 1525   PirMT, 121
  (1) A *canzone* was sung preceding the beginning of the play
    (a) It was sung by a nymph and three shepherds   PirMT, 122
      i) This was an attempt to mediate between the audience and the fictitious world of play
  (2) Transcriptions of the *intermedi*
    (a) A transcription of the *canzone* by Verdelot sung at the beginning of the play   PirMT, 131
    (b) A transcription of the song by Verdelot following the first act   PirMT, 135
    (c) A transcription of the song by Verdelot sung after the fourth act   PirMT, 138
e) *Il marescalco* by Pietro Aretino was composed between 1526 and 1527   PirMT, 78
  (1) It opens with a song
    (a) The song characterizes the place and theme of the play   PirMT, 79
  (2) A character is portrayed in three other songs sung in Act II scene 3   PirMT, 79
  (3) Aretino wrote five comedies   AreP
    (a) They are acutely perceived pictures of lower-class life and are free from the conventions that burdened other contemporary dramas

C. The Italian Madrigal

1. Introduction
  a) The etymology of the word "madrigal" is unknown   RocM, 1
    (1) The source of the term could be *matricalis,* meaning "in the mother tongue"
      (a) This reputed definition of the word dates from the fourteenth century
      (b) It refers to the fourteenth century madrigal with its distinctive rhyme scheme and strophes of eight to eleven lines

b) The term "madrigal" is thought to have first appeared in sixteenth century music in the collection *Madrigali de diversi musici libro primo* of 1530
ReeMR, 314
   (1) This collection is possibly the first printed volume of music to be called *Madrigali* RanH, 462
      (a) Actually, the *Madrigali* had already been represented in manuscript sources of the 1520s
   (2) The collection is an early edition of the famous *Madrigali novi de diversi excellentissimi musici* of 1533
      (a) The 1533 edition was published by Valerio Dorico
      (b) The parts are printed separately with the complete text under each part
         i) This is a departure from the usual choirbook arrangement where the complete text is under the *cantus* only
      (c) A facsimile of the 1533 edition DorM
c) A genre of secular music began to emerge in Italy, especially in the Florentine circles, during the second decade of the sixteenth century that was distinguishable in essential ways from the *frottola* and the *canto carnascialesco*
PerMR, 649
   (1) A new technique of rhythmic animation (*note nere*) was used ManI, 289
      (a) This was achieved by the use of small rhythmic values resulting in a plethora of black notes
      (b) This technique was entirely foreign to traditional polyphony
   (2) Written accidentals appear at odd moments within a predominately diatonic framework ManI, 289
      (a) Early madrigalists went beyond the legitimate use of B♭, E♭, F#, C#, and G# by using A♭
         i) These written accidentals are always associated with key words in the text
      (b) This deployment of chromatic harmonies was used to paint Petrarchist poetry
   (3) Titles found in madrigal publications often refer to the music as *nuovo modo* and *musica nova* ManI, 289
d) The new genre took important characteristics from both the *frottola* and *canto carnascialesco*, deriving the vital development of lyric verse in the Italian vernacular from the *frottola* and the musical style from the declamatory vocal homophony of the carnival songs PerMR, 649

2. The early madrigal (1520s)
   a) Introduction
      (1) The early madrigal occupied a special position as private entertainment music to Italian texts FenI, 46
         (a) It was essentially a regional specialty, cultivated mostly in Florence, and to a limited extent, in Rome
      (2) It is thought that Florence is the city in which the new genre was nurtured during the 1520s RocM, 6
         (a) It is in the early manuscript sources that Florence is shown to be the center of the repertory and the composer Verdelot to be the principal musical figure

                        i)   These early manuscripts contain the new music   FenI, 20
                        ii) A number of them predate the prints containing the same
                             music   FenI, 21
                        iii) Verdelot set the tone of the new song form   FenI, 46
                             a - He set the tone in its stylistic aspects, and to some extent,
                                 in its social character and function
                  (b) Florence is also where Bernardo Pisano worked   RocM, 3
                        i)   He worked at the baptistery and cathedral in Florence
                        ii) He is the first Italian composer to have a complete printed
                             volume devoted entirely to his work   FenI, 27
                        iii) His work is published in *Musica di meser Bernardo Pisano
                             sopra le canzone del Petrarcha*
                             a - The *Musica* could be considered the prototype of the
                                 new genre
                                 1 - The *canzoni* [madrigali] show experimentation with
                                     freer types of poetry and imitative writing
                             b - But, due to the limited appeal and currency of this publi-
                                 cation, it is doubtful that it had a strong formative influ-
                                 ence on the madrigals of such composers as Festa, Arca-
                                 delt, and Verdelot   FenI, 28
                             c - A list of the contents   FenI, 200
                             d - A facsimile of *Musica di meser Bernardo Pisano
                                 sopra le canzone del Petrarcha*   PisM
                             e - A transcription of *Musica di meser Bernardo Pisano
                                 sopra le canzone del Petrarcha*   PisCW
            (3) Rome was the secondary center for the madrigal   RocM, 6
                  (a) Its connections with Florence were ensured by the occupancy of
                       the Papacy by members of the Medici family
                        i)   Bernardo Pisano worked under the Medici Pope Leo X in the
                             Papal Chapel at Rome   RocM, 3
                             a - But, he is said to have written no music of any kind after
                                 settling permanently in Rome during the spring of 1520
                                                                                      FenI, 28
                        ii) Costanza Festa was an important figure in the development
                             of the madrigal and he was a member of the Papal Chapel
                                                                                      FenI, 21
                             a - He became a member sometime during 1517
      b) The poetry of the early madrigal (1520s)
            (1) The most serious type of composition within the *frottola* group, namely
                 the *canzone*, merged directly into the madrigal   ReeMR, 313
                  (a) Actually most pieces from 1520 to 1530 were printed under the
                       designation *canzone*
                        i)   These were in effect almost madrigals
            (2) The texts of the early madrigal were more decorous and sentimental than
                 the texts of the *frottola* although mainly amorous   DenS, 39
                  (a) They everlastingly complain of unrequited love   ReeMR, 313
            (3) Not all of the texts were of high caliber   ReeMR, 313
                  (a) Many display a profusion of exaggerated, high-flown metaphors
            (4) The poetry of Petrarch was widely adopted in Rome by composers asso-

ciated with Leo X   FenI, 29
- (a) This was done at a time when composers working elsewhere were showing comparatively little interest in Petrarch
- (b) Petrarch's poems usually contain five to seven strophes of identical scheme   RanH, 138
  - i) Each of the strophes ends with two rhyming lines   DenS, 44
- (c) The number of lines is free with anywhere from six to twenty, with a mixture of seven or eleven syllables   DenS, 44
- (d) All of Petrarch's *canzoni* end with a coda of three lines   DenS, 44
  - i) Their metrical scheme varies but remains uniform for any one *canzone*
- (e) His poems include some of the most elegant and refined love poems in the literature   UlrH, 177

(5) Pietro Bembo was the leader and dictator of the literary movement in Italy   DenS, 36
- (a) He wished to restore to the Italian tongue the prestige it had lost following the passing of Dante and Petrarch and to place it again on a level with Latin   ReeMR, 312
- (b) Bembo supplied the models for poetry   UlrH, 176
  - i) The form he chose was free
    - a - It consisted of a single strophe containing lines of seven or eleven syllables in any desired rhyme scheme
      - 1 - The length of the line became a standardized feature
    - b - The strophe was usually ten lines long, but strophes that were both shorter and longer were used
- (c) Bembo's theories had more to do with the sound of words rather than with subject matter or imagery   HaaO
- (d) His theories were fully elaborated in his *Prose della volgar lingua* of 1525   BemPI
  - i) A facsimile of *Prose della volgar lingua*   BemO

c) The music of the early madrigal (1520s)
- (1) The essential feature of the early madrigal is a four-voice texture in a primarily chordal style   UlrH, 177
  - (a) It is chordal but, at times, bits of imitation are interspersed in the homophonic texture
  - (b) Imitation appears, particularly, at the openings of pieces   RubF, 58
- (2) In style, it is close to the French *chanson* with its four fully texted voices   RanH, 463
- (3) The principal melody is in the top line while the lines of the inner voices have a lesser degree of melodic integrity   UlrH, 177
  - (a) But all the voices share in a more or less declamatory style   HaaO
- (4) The beginnings and ends of phrases are often clearly marked   ReeMR, 315
  - (a) The phrases generally end together with pauses often separating them   UlrH, 177
  - (b) But, 'this feature often gives way to passages in which phrase endings overlap in motet style"   UlrH, 177
- (5) There is note repetition and repetition of the last line of text to virtually the same music   ReeMR, 321

d) The composers of the early madrigal (1520s)
  (1) Philippe Verdelot [b. ca. 1480?]
    (a) He came from northern France but he was different from the
        northerners who had come to Italy previously   RocM, 7
      i)   He was used to the Italian way of doing things
      ii) He was acclimatized to an Italian art-form, the madrigal
      iii) He cultivated the Petrarchan values of charm and dignity
    (b) He arrived in Florence in 1521   HaaO
    (c) Most of his madrigals were written before 1530   RocM, 7
    (d) His style contains an eclectic combination of *frottola, chanson,*
        and northern counterpoint   ManI, 290
      i) He uses four-voice imitative texture with homophonic style
         while stressing the highest voice
         a - His *Madonna qual certezza* is a good example
           1 - Facsimiles of *Madonna qual certezza*   GarT; ScoT
           2 - A transcription of *Madonna qual certezza*   VerT
    (e) He uses vocal color and texture   RocM, 9
      i) He uses harmonic coloring   ManI, 290
      ii) He constantly uses changing voice groupings or bottom
          heavy scoring (ATBBB) to produce effects
         a - His *'Dormend' un giorno* is a good example
           1 - This is found in Florence: Biblioteca Nazionale Cen-
               trale *MSS Magl XIX. 122-5,* no. 44   FenI, 172
           2 - A facsimile of *'Dormend' un giorno*   VerM
           3 - A transcription of *'Dormend' un giorno*   HarmO
    (f) Word and mood are portrayed   RocM, 9
      i) Some of his harmony underscores a kind of rhythmic contrast
          that can only be justified by the words   ManI, 290
      ii) He uses sighing figures and pauses   ManI, 290
    (g) His five-part madrigals are more contrapuntal than the four-part
        madrigals   RocM, 9
      i) In these madrigals the opening would bring in two or three
          voices in quick succession   RocM, 10
      ii) A good example is *Madonna non so dir*   RocM, 10
         a - A transcription   VerT
    (h) But, many of his madrigals are chordal   RocM, 10
    (i) Facsimiles of Verdelot's madrigals
      i)   Facsimiles of a 1533 and 1534 collection of madrigals con-
           taining eight madrigals by Verdelot   DorM; VerMN
      ii) A facsimile of seven madrigals by Verdelot   VerM
      iii) A facsimile of madrigals for four voices
                                               ScoIP; ScoDL; ScoIS; ScoISL
      iv) A facsimile of madrigals for five voices   VerD
    (j) Transcriptions of Verdelot's madrigals
      i) Transcriptions of twenty-two four-voice madrigals VerT
      ii) Transcriptions of Verdelot's madrigals for six voices AmaI
  (2) Bernardo Pisano [b. 1490]
    (a) Pisano was an Italian composer, singer, and classical scholar
                                                             D'AcP

- (b) His settings of single strophes from Petrarchan *canzoni* were probably meant to serve for the entire poems   HaaO
- (c) His compositional style seems to be a mixed one rather than a firm synthesis   HaaO
  - i) It was during the mid 1520s that such a synthesis was on the way to being achieved
    - a - This was being done by several composers but particularly by Verdelot
- (d) A facsimile of Pisano's music   PisM
- (e) Transcriptions of some of Pisano's music   PisCW
- (f) A transcription of *Una donna*   ThoFM

(3) Costanzo Festa [b. ca. 1490]   ReeMR, 320
- (a) Festa was a native Italian   RocM, 7
- (b) He wrote approximately one-hundred madrigals   HaaFC
  - i) They were probably written between 1525 and 1540
  - ii) They were for three, four and five voices   RocM, 12
    - a - His three voice madrigals were very popular
- (c) Festa's four-voice madrigals share the idiom established by Verdelot   HaaFC
  - i) But, his multi-voice madrigals show a hesitancy of technique
- (d) Many of his madrigals are predominantly chordal with phrases clearly marked
  - i) In these madrigals, the voices are not equal in importance
- (e) Other madrigals are polyphonic throughout with paired imitation
- (f) Many of his madrigals are in the *note nere* style
- (g) Festa begins some of his madrigals with the "narrative" formula and has the last line of text repeated to the same music
  - i) The "narrative" formula is the initial rhythmic figure associated with the *chanson* of the period shown in figure 39
    - a - It is generally a special mark of narrative compositions in secular vocal polyphony   ReeMR, 293
    - b - This style is virtually a *chanson* with Italian text
- (h) In the 1540s and later he used word painting   RocM, 12
- (i) Facsimiles of Festa's madrigals
  - i) Facsimiles of three madrigals   GarT; ScoT
  - ii) Madrigals for three voices   ScoDM; FesV
  - iii) Twenty-two madrigals for four voices, two for five voices, and one for six voices   FesML
  - iv) Six madrigals for four voices   ArcI
- (j) Transcriptions of Festa's madrigals
  - i) *Quando ritrova*   DavH, 140
  - ii) Eleven madrigals for three voices or instruments   ThoFM
  - iii) All of his madrigals   FesO, VII; VIII

(5) François (Francesco) de Layolle [b. 1492]
- (a) His music epitomizes the marriage of Italian and French cultures, old and new   DobM, 257
- (b) There are two books of Italian *Canzoni* written for four and five voices   DobM, 254
  - i) These were published by Moderne ca. 1540   DobM, 307

                    a - Possibly as a tribute to the composer after his death
                                                                        DobM, 254
                    b - Although these collections were published around 1540,
                        for the most part, they must have been composed in Ly-
                        ons during the 1520s and 1530s   DobM, 255
            ii) The use of the term *canzoni* for his two madrigal collections
                may be due to his Petrarchan bent, or perhaps to the influence
                of Pisano   FenI, 280
            iii) The texts of the two books are drawn from a number of
                poets   D'AcL
                    a - Some of the poets are Petrarch, Alamanni, Machiavelli,
                        and the brothers Strozzi
        (c) The first book contains fifty four-part madrigals   DobM, 255
            i) These are short *chanson* settings with clear homorhythmic
                declamation
            ii) There are rare imitative snatches with little or no word-paint-
                ing
            iii) The vocal parts are simple with a limited range and brief
                codas based on inverted pedal-points
            iv) The last lines are repeated
            v) A facsimile of the four voice madrigals   LayCC
            vi) A transcription of the four voice madrigals   LayCSW
        (d) The second book contains five-voice madrigals   DobM, 256
            i) There are twenty-three madrigals and two French *chansons*
            ii) These pieces are through composed and use more imitative
                counterpoint than the four-part madrigals found in the first
                book
                    a - The entries are dovetailed for each poetic line
            iii) A facsimile of the five voice madrigals   LayV
            iv) A transcription of the five voice madrigals   LayCS
    e) Some manuscript sources of the early madrigal (1520s)
        (1) There are three distinct groups of Florentine manuscripts from the 1520s
                                                                FenI, 22
            (a) There are two manuscripts containing pieces current both in Flor-
                ence and Rome during the pontificate of Leo X
                i) Florence: Biblioteca del Conservatorio di musica Luigi Cher-
                    ubini, *MS. Basevi 2440*   FenI, 156
                    a - This is the last secular manuscript to be arranged in choir-
                        book form   FenI, 23
                    b - It is divided into a strophic section and a non-strophic
                        section
                            1 - The strophic section is thought to have been written
                                about 1515 and the non-strophic section, containing
                                proto- and early madrigal compositions, was added
                                in the following decade   FenI, 157
                            2 - There is music by Costanza Festa, Michele Pesenti,
                                and late works by Pisano
                    c - Inventory of the contents with concordances FenI, 158
                ii) Florence: Biblioteca Nazionale Centrale, *MS. Magl XIX.*

                        164-7   FenI, 23
                    a - This may have been copied during the decade of 1530 to
                        1540   HamCC I, 228
                    b - This manuscript contains Italian songs, French *chansons*,
                        and motets   FenI, 25
                        1 - There is one Te Deum, twelve motets, twenty-four
                            French secular pieces, and forty-nine Italian secular
                            pieces   HamCC I, 228
                    c - Thirteen of the first nineteen Italian songs have been attri-
                        buted, through concordances with the *Musica*, to Pisano
                                                                    FenI, 26
                        1 - It is thought that the remaining pieces are his also
                    d - Five other pieces, out of a series of seven, have been at-
                        tributed to Sebastiano Festa through concordances with
                        Libro primo de la Croce   FenI, 26
                        1 - It is thought that the other two also were written by
                            him
                    e - An inventory of the contents with concordances FenI, 175
        (b) There are two sets of partbooks that contain the earliest pieces in
            the new style that can be securely attributed to Verdelot, and a
            great deal of music by Costanza Festa   FenI, 22
            i) Bologna: Civico Museo Bibliografico Musicale, *MS. Q 21*
                                                                    FenI, 23
                    a - This manuscript was copied ca. 1526   FenI, 31
                    b - It contains seventy-one Italian secular pieces, one textless
                        piece, and four puzzle canons   HamCC I, 75
                    c - This is a major source of Verdelot's madrigals
                        1 - There are seven   HamCC I, 75
                    d - An inventory of the contents with concordances FenI, 139
            ii) New Haven: Yale University, John Herrick Jackson Music
                Library, *Misc. MS. 179*   FenI, 23
                    a - This source was copied ca. 1525   FenI, 35
                    b - It contains the alto parts for [fifty-eight] settings of early
                        sixteenth-century Italian secular songs   FenI, 34
                        1 - Six pieces are attributed to Sebastiano Festa, by way
                            of concordant sources, and three pieces are by Con-
                            stanzo Festa with another two thought to be by him
                        2 - Nine pieces can be securely attributed to Verdelot
                    c - There are also two French secular pieces   HamCC II, 250
                    d - An inventory of the contents with concordances FenI, 182
        (c) The Newberry-Oscott set of partbooks   RocM, 8
            i) Chicago: Newberry Library Case, *MS-VM 1578. M91*
                                                                    FenI, 23
            ii) Sutton Coldfield, Oscott College: Old Library, *MS. Case B
                No. 4*[24]   FenI, 23
            iii) These were compiled ca. 1526-1529
            iv) Both manuscripts were copied in Florence   HamCC I, 151
                    a - They were presented to Henry VIII as a gift from Flor-
                        ence

  v) The Chicago manuscript contains thirty motets and thirty Italian secular pieces   HamCC I, 151
   a - The Sutton Coldfield manuscript contains twenty-nine motets (three instrumental), and thirty Italian secular pieces (three instrumental)
  vi) They contain twenty-two pieces by Verdelot   FenI, 31
   a - These have been attributed to him through concordances
   b - There are a number of five- and six-part madrigals
    RocM, 8
  vii) Some of the pieces are settings of texts from plays by Machiavelli
  viii) An inventory of the contents with concordances   FenI, 155

3. The early madrigal (1530s)
 a) Introduction
  (1) This was a transitory period for music printing and the madrigal FenI, 58
   (a) The new music was circulated mostly in manuscript
   (b) But, the issuance of Verdelot's music by [Ottaviano] Scotto in 1533 marks the beginning of the printed life of the madrigal
    FenI, 71
    i) This was followed by the collected works of Arcadelt by Antonio Gardano in 1538
  (2) This second phase of the development of the madrigal was delineated by the recovery from the Sack of Rome, and in particular, its relationship to Venetian music printing in the period between the Sack and the sustained adoption of single-impression printing at the end of the following decade
    FenI, 49
   (a) Valerio Dorico was the only music printer working in Rome from ca. 1531 to ca. 1543   FenI, 50
    i) From 1534 to 1536 Dorico changed from double to single-impression music printing
    ii) In his *Madrigali novi de diversi excellentissimi musici*, Dorico printed the parts separately, each with complete text
     ReeMR, 314
     a - He thus departed from the practice, usually applied to collections of this sort in the past, of printing the voices in choirbook arrangement with the complete text only under the *cantus*
     b - A facsimile of the 1533 edition of *Madrigali novi de diversi excellentissimi musici*   DorM
    iii) Part-music in separate partbooks made reading the music much easier and the production much cheaper DenS, 35
     a - Notes could be more widely spaced and, as a result, words could be printed under them more accurately
    iv) But, the overall impression of reportorial conservatism, technical crudity, and economic uncertainty characterizes the Roman music printing business during the 1530s FenI, 54
   (b) More favorable conditions prevailed in Venice   FenI, 54
    i) Ottaviano Scotto the younger began, in 1533, a series of pub-

lications devoted to the music of Verdelot   FenI, 55
        a - He also published three books of four-voice madrigals
            1 - There were two books for five voices, and one book of intabulations of madrigals from the first of the four-voice books
    ii) Antoine Gardane came from southern France to Venice and began printing music as early as 1538   PerMR, 679
        a - He published Arcadelt's popular *Libro primo* (1538) and Willaert's *Musica nova* (1559) along with dozens of other collections of madrigals featuring the leading masters of the day
    iii) Girolamo Scotto began publishing music in 1539   PerMR, 679
        a - He produced a continuous stream of madrigal prints
  (3) "With the 1530s came wider dissemination of the madrigal as a genre and its cultivation by a younger generation of composers"   PerMR, 670
    (a) These composers were primarily northerners, but the majority of them were apparently in some sense in the orbit of Verdelot
b) The poetry of the early madrigal (1530's)
  (1) The madrigal is usually the setting of a one-strophe poem or of a single strophe from a *ballata, canzone, sestina* or poem in *ottava rima*   HaaO
    (a) Therefore, it lacks the verse-refrain scheme
  (2) The *canzoni* of Petrarch, which were long poems with several strophes, were set as a sequence of madrigals   DenS, 44
    (a) These single strophes were free in the number of lines
        i) Some have six lines while others have twenty
    (b) The lines are a mixture of eleven or seven syllables
    (c) Each strophe ends with two rhyming lines
  (3) There were ceremonial madrigals that can almost always be identified with certainty from the words   DenS, 41
    (a) They were needed for weddings, receptions, and elegies on deceased persons, as well as incidental music to plays
        i) Poetic allusions to places, rivers, armorial bearings, and so forth give clues to the families concerned in the madrigals for weddings
        ii) The incidental music to plays consists of prologues, entr'acts, and epilogues, in which it is necessary that the words should be understood as clearly as possible
        iii) [In the plays *Cliza* and *La mandragola* by Machiavelli] the songs to be sung after the acts were well suited to the term madrigal   PirMT, 145
            a - They have free form, without a predetermined metrical scheme that is most typical of the sixteenth century madrigal
            b - The term, madrigal, is less suitable when applied to the songs sung before the comedies, as they are strophic
c) The music of the early madrigal (1530s)
  (1) After 1530 the term "madrigal" remains a generic term for polyphonic concerted and solo music throughout the sixteenth and early seven-

teenth centuries ManI, 287
- (2) The madrigal developed as the result of the contact of Netherlandish composers with Italian poets DenS, 35
- (3) The style of the genre never became too rigid PirMT, 145
  - (a) The emphasis probably should be on an entirely vocal polyphony in a particularly refined musical style
- (4) Musicians set the strophes of the *canzoni* as a sequence of madrigals DenS, 44
  - (a) They composed different music for each strophe, generally obtaining variety by alternating between five, four, and three voices
    - i) They alternated time-signatures also
  - (b) "Arcadelt was the first to adopt this plan..."
- (5) The music was through composed ReeMR, 315
  - (a) This was based on the principle that the same music could not suffice to set the varying content of the different strophes
  - (b) It was composed to a text of literary quality and was intended to express the content of the text
- (6) The natural and effortless recitation of the words dictated the shaping of the musical phrases DenS, 44
  - (a) Cross-rhythms and syncopations fell into place quite spontaneously

d) The composers of the early madrigal (1530s) RocM, 7
- (1) Adrian Willaert [b. ca. 1490]
  - (a) His first four-part madrigals belong to the 1530s RocM, 20
    - i) These early examples were printed in Verdelot's Book II of 1536 ReeMR, 323
    - ii) They are predominately chordal ReeMR, 323
      - a - The upper voice is melodically prominent but the other voices are also independently conceived
      - b - There is no clear imitation or homophony RocM, 22
    - iii) He does not use pair alternation or contrast RocM, 22
    - iv) He emphasizes color and is therefore much interested in harmonic experiments evidenced by his treatment of the bass which abounds in leaps ReeMR, 323
    - v) He occasionally used rudimentary chromaticism ReeMR, 323
    - vi) A facsimile of the 1536 edition of Book II ScoIS
- (2) Jacques Arcadelt [b. ca. 1514]
  - (a) He came from the north RocM, 7
    - i) But, he was different from the northerners who had come to Italy previously
      - a - He was used to the Italian way of doing things and he cultivated the Petrarchan values of charm and dignity
  - (b) He chose Petrarchist verse but comparatively few poems by Petrarch himself HaaO
    - i) He chose poems from many writers now forgotten but including poems by Bembo, Sannazaro, and Michelangelo
    - ii) Many of the poems show a relationship to the *ballata* and forms of the *canzone*
    - iii) Other poems are free madrigals
  - (c) Arcadelt was practiced in the art of the French *chanson* and the

			Latin motet	RocM, 15

    i) This may have affected his madrigal style
      a - This was true of his five-part madrigals
  (d) He uses canon   RocM, 17
  (e) He also uses dactylic rhythm and repeated notes   RocM, 18
  (f) There is a feeling for modality   RocM, 18
  (g) His four-part madrigals are wholly indigenous, lyrical, and in Italianate "song style"   RocM, 15
    i) The top voice asserts its superiority
      a - It carries the bulk of the cadential suspensions that were ornamented by the composer and decorated in performance
      b - It is detached from the contrapuntal activity confined to the lower voices
      c - It is kept in a high register well above the alto
    ii) *Il bianco e dolce cigno* is a good example of the song style
      a - A facsimile of *Il bianco e dolce cigno*   ArcD, no. 1
      b - A transcription of *Il bianco e dolce cigno*   HarmO
    iii) A facsimile of *Da bei rami scendea dolce* for four voices
                       MilC, 30v
  (h) Facsimiles of other madrigals by Arcadelt   ArcD; ArcIP
  (i) Transcriptions of Arcadelt's madrigals   ArcO, II-VII
    i) A transcription of *Voi ve n'andat' al cielo*   DavH, 141
e) Some manuscript sources (1530s)
 (1) There are four main manuscript sources of the four- and five-voice madrigal   FenI, 58
  (a) Florence: Biblioteca Nazionale Centrale, *MSS. Magl XIX. 122-5*
                       FenI, 169
    i) This was copied between ca. 1530 and 1537 FenI, 59
    ii) It is a set of four partbooks   FenI, 58
      a - The partbooks contain forty-eight Italian secular pieces
                       HamCC I, 227
    iii) The principal composers are Arcadelt and Verdelot FenI, 59
      a - Other composers are Costanzo Festa, and Willaert
                       HamCC I, 227
    iv) An inventory of the contents with concordances FenI, 171
  (b) Florence: Biblioteca del Conservatorio di musica Luigi Cherubini, *MS. Basevi 2495*   FenI, 60n
    i) This is known as the Strozzi partbooks   FenI, 59
      a - Three of the four partbooks have survived
      b - They contain seventy-seven Italian secular pieces
                       HamCC I, 236
        1 - There are seventy-five madrigals, all unattributed
                       FenI, 60
    ii) The first layer may have been copied ca. 1530 FenI, 60
      a - Numbers one to forty-five comprise the first layer
                       HamCC I, 236
      b - The pieces in this layer are mainly by Verdelot
        1 - There are some pieces by Costanzo Festa

iii) The second layer was probably added in the second half of the decade   FenI, 60
       a - This includes numbers forty-six to seventy-seven   HamCC I, 236
       b - The pieces in this layer are mainly by Arcadelt
iv) An inventory of the contents with concordances   FenI, 161
    (c) Brussels: Bibliothèque du Conservatoire Royal de Musique, *MS. 27731*   FenI, fn 63
         i) This manuscript was copied during the second half of the 1530s   FenI, 64
             a - There are additions to it from ca. 1545 to 1550   HamCC I, 103
         ii) It contains a single incomplete *canto* partbook   FenI, 63
         iii) It has ninety-six Italian madrigals   FenI, 63
             a - Most of the pieces are by Arcadelt, but there are also five pieces by Layolle, six by Costanzo Festa, and eight by Corteccia
         iv) An inventory of the contents with concordances   FenI, 150
    (d) Florence: Biblioteca Nazionale Centrale, *MSS. Magl XIX 99, 100, 101bis, 102*   FenI, fn. 64
         i) This source was copied in Florence during the second half of the 1530s   FenI, 64
             a - It contains fifty-six Italian secular pieces   HamCC I, 222
                 1 - Some pieces were added later
         ii) Almost three-fourths of the pieces are by Arcadelt   FenI, 64
         iii) Other composers are Costanzo Festa, Layolle, and Corteccia   FenI, 64
         iv) An inventory of the contents with concordances   FenI, 165

4. The late madrigal (1540s)
   a) Introduction
      (1) The late madrigal began to appear at the beginning of 1540   RanH, 463
      (2) There was much change in it at this time   RocM, 25
         (a) The madrigal began to be more serious   RanH, 463
            i) It became more like a motet rather than a *chanson*
         (b) This change was started by Adrian Willaert and Cipriano de Rore
      (3) Venice became the center of madrigal printing and composition from 1545   RocM, 25
   b) The poetry of the late madrigal (1540s)
      (1) Petrarch's sonnets were particularly popular   RanH, 463
         (a) They were set in two sections or *partes*
      (2) Also, the epic poem, *Orlando furioso*, by LudovicoAriosto was drawn upon by composers   ReeMR, 313
         (a) It taught composers to express passion and ardor
         (b) A translation of *Orlando furioso*   AriO
   c) The music of the late madrigal (1540s)
      (1) Contrapuntal textures often replace chordal writing   UlrH, 177
         (a) Overlapping phrases became common and the texture of the madrigal came close to that of the motet

408 Secular Vocal Music

        (b) Imitation is used more frequently   UlrH, 178
            i) When imitation is used, it does so because it enhances the rhythmic independence of the voices or illustrates the text rather than because it is intrinsic to the madrigal   ReeMR, 315
            ii) But when chordal writing is used, it is used for expressive purposes   UlrH, 177
    (2) All voices are melodic and textually conceived   RubF, 58
        (a) The musical accentuation and phraseology match that of the poetry   RubF, 58
        (b) And there is declamation in a more individual and less stereotyped manner   RanH, 463
        (c) Normally, there are five voices   RanH, 463
    (3) Word painting became increasingly prominent   UlrH, 177
        (a) The madrigal became a composition of descriptive music
        (b) A mood of depression was suggested by rapid rhythmic motion, the use of low tones, and agitation
    (4) Considerable use of syncopation is used in the melodies and there is a faint beginning of chromaticism   UlrH, 178
    (5) Composers set the strophes of long poems as a sequence of madrigals, with different music for each strophe   DenS, 44
        (a) Variety was achieved by alternating between three, four, and five voices and by alternating time signatures
        (b) Sometimes five voice groups were divided into two semi-groups singing in alternation   UlrH, 178
  d) The composers of the late madrigal (1540s)   RanH, 463
    (1) Adrian Willaert [b. ca. 1490]
        (a) His later madrigals were written around 1540 and after   RocM, 20
        (b) In these madrigals, Willaert departs from the style of his early period   ReeMR, 323
            i) His phrases are sharply defined and the end of one phrase and the beginning of the next overlap in motet fashion
            ii) All of the voices are of equal importance
            iii) His emphasis is more on line rather than color
            iv) His chordal passages are used mostly for the purpose of expression
            v) His madrigal *Quanto più m'arde* is a good example
                a - A transcription of *Quanto più m'arde*   HarmO
            vi) Some of his madrigals follow the *note nere* trend   ReeMR, 324
        (c) His five-part madrigals   RocM, 26
            i) He writes in the modes but avoids any severity of modal feeling by specifying many accidentals which produce a harmonic feeling   RocM, 20
                a - This includes false relations
            ii) Some of his madrigals are contrapuntal to the core   RocM, 20
                a - But they do not rely on the linear dissonance of the northern motet
                    1 - They have a strong sense of vertical euphony
            iii) A good example of his five-part madrigals is *Qual dolcezza*

                    giamai   RocM, 21
                a - In this madrigal he employs five voices in a changing ka-
                    leidoscope of four higher and four lower groupings
                                                                          ManI, 292
                b - There is imitative texture and refined declamation
                                                                          ManI, 292
            iv) Willaert uses rich scoring
                a - There are seldom long rests
            v) He uses lush harmony and angular part-writing   RocM, 27
            vi) Declamation was very important   RocM, 27
                a - *Mentre che 'l cor'* is a good example   RocM, 28
                    1 - A translation of *Mentre che 'l cor'*   WilI, 5
            vii) Transcriptions of the five-voice madrigals   WilI
    (d) In his six-part madrigals the words are the master of the music
                                                                 RocM, 28
            i) A good example of this is Willaert's *Aspro core*   AtlR, 435
                a - Willaert expresses the meaning of the words in almost
                    graphic terms
                b - This is done in spite of the fact that the composition is a
                    six-way debate on how to read the poem [by Petrarch]
                    1 - "The counterpoint of words is dense, as voices rarely
                        initiate--or even pronounce--the same syllable at the
                        same time"
                    2 - Willaert interprets the meanings of the text with biting
                        tritone cross-relations which eventually melt down the
                        same melody with root position triads and a little im-
                        plied triple meter to express the sweetness of the line
                                                                 AtlR, 438
                    3 - He indicates bright day to dark night by having the
                        top voice plummet an octave and then continue down
                        another third   AtlR, 438
                c - Willaert's texture varies from full six voices to various
                    combinations of trios and quartets
                d - The polyphony is both imitative and nominative as well
                    as chrodal
                e - Thus, Willaert devised a new way of interpreting
                    vernacular poetry through music   AtlR, 439
                f - A transcription of *Aspro core*   WilO XIII, 54
    (e) In the seven-part works, Willaert uses a secular dialogue RocM, 28
            i) There are two choirs of three plus four high-low disposition
                                                                 RocM, 29
                a - Sometimes he adds one voice of the lower group to the
                    upper group to produce a four plus four effect
            ii) A facsimile of *Quando nascesti amor?* for seven voices
                                                                 MilC, 209v
            iii) A transcription of *Quando nascesti amor?*   WilO XIII, 103
    (f) A facsimile of three madrigals   GarT
    (g) Transcriptions of Willaert's five-, six- and seven-part madrigals
                                                                 WilO, XIV

(h) The 1540s style of his madrigals reached its apex with the twenty-five madrigals of the *Musica nova* FroS
  i) These, as well as thirty-three motets, were composed around 1540 ReeMR, 324
  ii) The *Musica nova* was published in 1559 ReeMR, 324
    a - It is apparently a printing of an earlier collection published about fifteen years earlier that has not survived
    b - It was edited by Willaert's pupil, Francesco Viola
    c - It is the only known collection of this period containing madrigals by Willaert to the exclusion of other composers
  iii) Willaert set complete sonnets (with the exception of one) from Petrarch's *Canzoniere*
    a - The meaning, syntax, and the sonorous beauty of the poetry were conveyed with skill
      1 - Sonorous nuances of individual phrases, words, and syllables are brought out by manipulating subtle but kaleidoscopic shifts of rhythm, texture, and vocal color
  iv) He created large-scale musical structures that matched the form of each sonnet
    a - He did this by presenting the first eight verses in the *prima parte* and the closing *sestet* [the last six lines of the sonnet] in the *seconda parte*
    b - But, individual contrapuntal sections were constructed so as to draw attention to striking poetic images, important phrases or self-sufficient syntactic units which might not coincide with the poetic versification
    c - The contrapuntal idiom is no longer restricted to conventional positions in the soprano and tenor parts
      1 - It roams freely and unpredictably among diverse vocal combinations
  v) Declamation is made even more audible in these madrigals than was evident in the earlier madrigals
    a - This is done by the coincident articulation in multiple voices of important or stressed syllables of text
    b - The declamatory character approaches the recitative style ReeMR, 324
      1 - This is partly the result of many note-repetitions
  vi) A facsimile of *Musica nova* WilMN
  vii) A transcription of the madrigals of *Musica nova* WilO, XIII
(2) Francesco Corteccia [b. 1504]
  (a) He went to Florence early in his career where he published two books of madrigals for four voices in 1544 and 1547, and one book of madrigals for five and six voices in the same year ReeMR, 325
  (b) He set poetry by poets such as Michelangelo, Petrarch, A. F. Grazzini (Il Lasca), Lorenzo Strozzi, and Lorenzo the Magnificent among others D'AcC
  (c) His madrigals show a firm grasp of the priniciples underlying the

new genre and a sensitive approach to the nuances of text   D'AcA
- i) He composed attractive melodies that unfold within a slightly imitative texture and clearly directed harmonic progressions
- ii) He uses a formulaic declamation and relies on a *cantus-bassus* compositional framework
- iii) He also uses traditional compositional devices   D'AcC
  - a - Such as canon in *Perch'io veggio et mi spiace*
    - 1 - A facsimile of *Perch'io veggio et mi spiace*   CorLPM
  - b - In the top voice of *Se vostr'occhi lucenti*, Corteccia has written a melodic subject derived from vowels corresponding to solmization syllables   D'AcC
- iv) In many of his other works, he adopted the faster note values, choppy rhythms, and abrupt textural changes typical of the *note-nere* style of the early 1540s   D'AcC

(d) His *Io dico e dissi e dirò* is of special interest   ReeMR, 325
- i) The text is from [Ariosto's] *Orlando furioso*, Canto 16, strophe 2
  - a - The *Orlando furioso* imparted new impetus to the practice of singing the strophes to an improvised instrumental accompaniment
  - b - The accompaniment was improvised on preexistent patterns
    - 1 - The patterns were applied with changes that the improviser considered appropriate to the text of individual strophes
- ii) *Io dico e dissi e dirò* features repeated melodic reciting formulae in the top voice   D'AcC
  - a - This was done above the ever-changing polyphony in the lower voices
  - b - Some of the formulas were named after the localities with which they were associated   ReeMR, 325
    - 1 - Corteccia presents a formula from Florence four times in the *superius* while the other voices sing fresh counterpoint against it
- iii) A printing of the complete piece   EinI III, 49

(e) Facsimiles of Corteccia's madrigals
- i) Facsimiles of four-voice madrigals   CorL; CorLS
- ii) A facsimile of five- and six-voice madrigals   CorLPM

(f) Transcriptions of Corteccia's madrigals
- i) Transcriptions of wedding music   CorM
- ii) Transcriptions of four-voice madrigals   HarN, II, nos. 1, 10, 12, and 35
- iii) Transcriptions of two books of four-voice madrigals   CorF; CorS
- iv) A transcription of five- and six-voice madrigals   CorFB

(3) Cipriano de Rore [b. 1516]
- (a) Rore is thought to have been a student of Willaert   RocM, 29
  - i) The evidence of this is scanty   OweR
  - ii) But, it may have been under the aegis of Willaert that Rore

acquired his initial training and experience with the madrigal
    PerMR, 680
- (b) Rore concerned himself with serious and noble texts   ReeMR, 330
  - i) His texts were taken from Petrarch and from tragedies that were presented at the court of Ferrara
  - ii) Therefore his madrigals take on a dramatic aspect
    - a - With his passionate utterances, the "age of innocence" of the madrigal draws to a close
    - b - The utterances point the way to the future
- (c) Rore interpreted the new ideas of Willaert and took them to new heights in madrigal composition   RocM, 30
  - i) "Since it became important in the madrigal to illustrate every idea and every image and all the emotional value of the text as sharply and directly as possible, the construction of the madrigal underwent a change"   ReeMR, 330
  - ii) Rore was indifferent to the form of the poem or the structure of its lines
    - a - He did not feel that it was necessary that the musical line should correspond to the poetic one   ReeMR, 330
    - b - Therefore the structure of the line as well as the rhyme and line division were often disregarded   ReeMR, 330
  - iii) The form of the music became more dependent upon the expressive needs of the poetry and less upon its form than it had been in the early madrigal with its fairly constant mood and technique from the beginning of a piece to the end   ReeMR, 330
    - a - Rore set each word as expressively as possible
    - b - He was much concerned with delineating the changing mood of the text
    - c - But although his music is delicately attuned to the sense of the text, most of his madrigals maintain a closely knit contrapuntal texture that recall the motet technique   ReeMR, 331
  - iv) Rore used chromaticism in an interesting way, though only occasionally   ReeMR, 330
    - a - His madrigals as a whole are not particularly chromatic   DenS, 48
      - 1 - He becomes more chromatic in his later years   DenS, 49
  - v) A certain amount of chromaticism appears in the collection, *Il primo libro de madrigali cromatici a cinque voci*, published by Gardane in 1544   ReeMR, 330
    - a - But, the word "*cromatici*" does not refer to chromaticism but to *note nere*
      - 1 - This collection of Rore's madrigals is significant as one of the early books *a note nere*
    - b - A facsimile of *Il primo libro de madrigali cromatici a cinque voci*   GarIP
- (d) A good example of Rore's style is found in his *Da le belle con-*

			trade	DavH, 231

    i) It has exciting exclamations, daring change of harmony, word panting, and prophetic use of chromaticism
    ii) A transcription of *Da le belle contrade* DavH, 142
  (e) His four-part pieces are his earliest RocM, 30
    i) They belong to the time around 1540 in Venice
    ii) They represent the style of Arcadelt
     a - They contain melodic poise and occasional use of *note-nere* crotchet movement
    iii) *Ancor che col partire* is a good example
     a - This piece was the subject of countless arrangements and embellishments on ornamentation
     b - It is by far his most famous madrigal ReeMR, 332
     c - A transcription of *Ancor che col partire* RorC, IV
    iv) There are also collections of his madrigals for four voices in 1550, 1557, and posthumously in 1565 PerMR, 681
  (f) The five-part texture in free polyphony with imitative regularity lacking became the norm RocM, 30
  (g) Transcriptions of the madrigals for three to eight voices RorC, IV; V
  (h) Transcriptions of the madrigals for five voices RorI, II; III

5. The performance of the madrigal
   a) Madrigals were sung in small circles of connoisseurs who wanted to cultivate the arts in an agreeable social context, that is, in *accademie* FenI, 77
      (1) Groups, sometimes called academies, were formed in various places such as in Venice and Verona DenS, 44
         (a) These groups were highly cultivated amateurs who met regularly to study madrigals
            i) They were most likely familiar with the poetry of Petrarch and Ariosto as well as other poets
            ii) Therefore it follows that the natural and effortless recitation of the words would dictate the shaping of the musical phrases
      (2) But, the middle-class public had by this time learned to read music at sight and wanted a more frivolous type madrigal DenS, 36
   b) Except for the madrigals intended for ceremonial purposes, madrigals were composed for the enjoyment of the singers DenS, 36
      (1) Each singer wanted to contribute his part to the intensification of the poet's words
         (a) This was the reason for the elaborate contrapuntal treatment of the madrigals
   c) Madrigals were usually sung with voices on all the parts AtlR, 429
      (1) But, occasionally Madrigals were performed by a singer on the top voice with instrumental accompaniment AtlR, 429
      (2) Willaert arranged some of Verdelot's madrigals for voice and lute
   d) There were madrigals sung [in a variety of ways] at the wedding of Duke Cosimo I and Lenora of Toledo in 1539 DarI, 140
      (a) A madrigal for four voices was sung by a soprano accompanied by a harpsichord and a positive organ

- (b) A madrigal for six voices was sung by six voices and repeated with the voices doubled or perhaps replaced by crumhorns
- (c) A madrigal for six voices was accompanied by three lutes
- (d) A madrigal for four voices was sung by a tenor accompanied by himself playing the other three parts on a large viol
- (e) A madrigal for four voices was sung by eight voices
- (f) A madrigal for five voices was sung by one voice accompanied by four trombones
- (g) A madrigal for four voices was sung and danced by eight people with various accompanying instruments

6. The madrigal [*canzone*] for the theater
   a) Madrigals were used in *intermedi*, plays, and on other ceremonial occasions
       RanH, 464
   - (1) The terms *madrigali* and *canzoni* were both used for the *intermedi*
       PirMT, 145
      - (a) The term 'madrigal', as yet, had not been clearly defined
   - (2) A group of six *intermedi* became the norm   PirMT, 126
      - (a) One *intermedio* precedes the prologue, one precedes each act, and at times there is a final *intermedio*
      - (b) *Intermedi* acted as a frame for the comedy's re-presentation of past events   PirMT, 127
         - i) "The frame helped to create...the illusion of a temporal perspective"   PirMT, 128
   - (3) *Intermedi* rapidly became more popular than the plays themselves   MajT
      - (a) They were often performed as independent entertainments at weddings and banquets at the courts
   - (4) Many of Corteccia's black-note madrigals were written for the *intermedi*
       D'AcC
      - (a) The distinguishing features of these madrigals are frequent change of pace, variety of texture, motivic repetition within a given phrase, strategically placed cadences to enhance the rhetoric of the text, and a clearly articulated declamation essential to project words, especially on stage
   - (5) The madrigals were usually conceived with instrumental accompaniment
       D'AcC
      - (a) For example, with only one exception, Corteccia's madrigals of 1539 call for various combinations of wind, string, and keyboard instruments
         - i) His madrigals of 1544 used a consort of viols
      - (b) "Corteccia's choice of accompanying instruments shows both a sensitive approach to color and an attempt to evoke the mood and meaning of the text"
         - i) A good example of this is *Vientene almo riposo*, the last piece of his 1539 set
            - a - This was sung by the personification of Night accompanied by four trombones
            - b - A facsimile of *Vientene almo riposo*   CorLPM
   b) Singing and dancing within plays did occur but they represent the exception

rather than the rule   PirMT, 81
(1) Madrigals [*villotte*] in the Paduan dialect were used in *La pastorale* and *La vaccaria by* [Angelo Beolco] Ruzante   PirMT, 84
   (a) Beolco was nicknamed 'Ruzante' after the part he performed in the performance of *La pastorale,* a rustic comedy, written by him   PirMT, 94
      i) He used everyday situations and distinctly Italian character types and as a result introduced a more natural style of acting, drawn from life and the observation of people   MajT
      ii) He wrote lyric poems that are multistrophic and dialectal although they were often reduced to one strophe   CarA, xiv
         a - They have combinations of paired and unpaired rhyming lines in verse lengths of odd numbered syllables
   (b) Both comedies, *La pastorale* and *La vaccaria*, contained singing and dancing
      i) Some of the songs sung by Ruzante and his colleagues were most likely *canzoni*   PirMT, 99
      ii) Both comedies closed with dances   PirMT, 84
      iii) It is not known whether Ruzante wrote the music   PirMT, 84
   (c) Ruzante has become known as the most powerful dramatist of the sixteenth century   DraB

c) Madrigals were written for performances at ceremonial occasions
(1) A comedy was sponsored by Ferrante Sanseverino, the prince of Salerno, in 1536 in honor of the visit of Charles V to Naples   PirMT, 106
   (a) Many good musicians performed in the comedy
(2) There were madrigals written for the festivities at Florence for the marriage of Cosimo I de' Medici to Eleonora da Toledo in 1539   DenM, 788
   (a) There are two songs by Festa   RocM, 13
      i) *Come lieta si mostra* (How joyful [your Arrezo] shows herself)
      ii) *Più che mai vaga* (Prettier than ever)
      iii) These are in chordal style and were most likely sung by heart and performed by one voice with instrumental accompaniment
   (b) There was also music by Corteccia
      i) As the bride entered Florence, a madrigal, *Ingredere* by Corteccia, was sung in eight parts by twenty-four voices accompanied by four *cornetti* and four trombones
         a -Facsimiles of *Ingredere*   TheM; MusF
         b - A transcription of *Ingredere*   MusFM
      ii) This was followed by the madrigal, *Sacro e santo Imeneo* for nine voices
      iii) Seven madrigals by Corteccia were sung in a pageant at the wedding banquet
   (c) Several days later, after supper, a play, *Il commodo* by Antonio Landi, was performed with *intermedii* invented by Giovambattista Strozzi   DenM, 788
      i) The music for the prologue and *intermedii* was by Corteccia

                a - For a list of the music, *see*   DenM, 788-89
        ii)   The music was published by Gardano in the first book for five and six voices in 1547   D'AcC
                a - A facsimile of *Corteccia Libro primo de Madrigali a cinque e a sei voci...*   CorLPM
                b - A transcription of *Corteccia Libro primo de Madrigali a cinque e a sei voci...*   CorFB
  d) Performance of the madrigals in the theater
      (1) The Florentine *intermedi* used choruses   PirMT, 154
          (a) One final chorus consisted of eight singing dancers (two to a part), an equal number of instrumentalists with a drum, a whistle, two *cornetti,* two *storte* [krummhorns], a harp, and one *ribechino* [Rebec]   PirMT, 158
      (2) There were madrigals for solo voices and contrasted groups of men and women, with different kinds of instruments   DenM, 789
      (3) Some *intermedi* were sung accompanied by the *violone da gamba*   PirMT, 156
          (a) The organ, flute, and *grave cembalo* were also used   PirMT, 163
      (4) Some *intermedi* were performed by instruments only   PirMT, 160
      (5) The musicians were usually concealed   DenM, 787
          (a) "The sudden entry of invisible music was a notable factor in the general effect of magic and mystery"
  e) A manuscript containing madrigals for the theater
      (1) Brussels: Bibliothèque du Conservatoire Royal de Musique, *MS. 27731*   FenI, fn. 63
          (a) This was copied in Florence ca. 1535-1540 with later additions ca. 1545-1550 and ca. 1569   HamCC I, 103
              i) It contains ninety-six secular pieces   HamCC I, 102
          (b) There is a sequence of six theatrical pieces by Alessandro Striggio, a Medici court composer   FenI, 64
              i) Five of these are settings of *intermedi* written for G. B. Cini's comedy, *La Vedova*
              ii) One of these is a *mascherata*
  f) Some printed sources of the madrigals found in the theater
      (1) Books published by Antonio Gardano
          (a) *Il vero secondo libro di madrigali d'Archadelt*   PirMT, 151
              i) This was published in Venice in 1539
                  a - There were reprints in 1541, 1543, 1552, and 1560   FenI, 249
              ii) An inventory of the contents with concordances   FenI, 252
              iii) A facsimile of the 1539 edition of *Il vero secondo libro di madrigali d'Arcadelt...*   ArcIV
              iv) A transcription of *Il vero secondo libro di madrigali d'Archadelt*   ArcO, III
          (b) *Il terzo libro de i madrigali novissimi di Archadelt*   PirMT, 152
              i) This was published in Venice in 1541
              ii) A transcription of a madrigal
              iii) A transcription of *Il terzo libro de i madrigali novissimi di Archadelt*   ArcO, IV

(2) Books published by Girolamo Scotto in Venice
   (a) *Il primo libro de madrigali di Verdelotto*   PirMT, 131
      i) This was published in 1537
      ii) A facsimile of *Il primo libro de madrigali*   ScoIP
   (b) *Il Terzo libro de i madrigali novissimi d'Archadelt a quattro voci*
                                                                                    PirMT, 124
      i) This was published in 1539
         a - There are reprints in 1541, 1543, and 1556   FenI, 253
            1 - These are the work of Gardano
      ii) In spite of the term *novissimi*, the madrigals in this publication were probably older than those of the two books published by Gardane in 1539   PirMT, 151
      iii) *Il Terzo libro...* contains forty-eight madrigals   BerCA, 225
         a - Six of the madrigals are ascribed to Festa   FenI, 255
      iv) There is a cycle of madrigals resembling the ones found in *Cliza* and *La mandragola*
      v) An inventory of the contents with concordances   FenI, 255
      vi) A list of the contents   BerCA, 226
      vii) A facsimile of *Il Terzo libro de i madrigali novissimi d'Archadelt a quattro voci*   ArcI
      viii) Transcriptions of *Il Terzo libro de i madrigali...*
                                                          FesO, VIII; ArcO, IV

7. Other printed sources of the madrigal
  a) A source printed by Petrucci
    (1) *Musica di messer Bernardo Pisano sopra le canzone del Petrarcha*
                                                                    RanH, 462
      (a) This was published in 1520
      (b) The publication of *Musica...* broke new ground   RocM, 3
         i) It was the first Italian publication of secular music to be issued in separate partbooks with full textual underlay
         ii) It was conceived vocally throughout with correct verbal accentuation in all parts
         iii) It was also the first Italian publication of secular music to be devoted to a single composer
      (c) An inventory of the contents with concordances   FenI, 200
      (d) A transcription of *Musica di messer Bernardo Pisano sopra le canzone del Petrarcha*   PisC
  b) Some sources printed by Valerio Dorico
    (1) *Madrigali novi de diversi eccellentissimi musici libro primo de la serena*   FenI, 51
      (a) This was published in Rome in 1533 by Dorico   FenI, 220
         i) There are eight compositions by Verdelot   FenI, 54
            a - Two of these pieces are unique
         ii) There are two pieces by Constanzo Festa and one by Sebastiano Festa   FenI, 54
         iii) There is a *chanson*, *Résveillies vous*, by Janequin and two French *chansons* by Sermisy   FenI, 54; 220
      (b) This source is a reprint of the 1530 edition   FenI, 220

418 Secular Vocal Music

      i) Only a single *altus* partbook of the 1530 edition has survived
                                  FenI, 53
      ii) The contents of the 1530 edition are the same as those of the 1533 edition with the exception of the two French *chansons* by Sermisy
      iii) The term madrigali is considered more a novelty rather than real   FenI, 54
        a - But these sources are more madrigalistic than any previous sources
    (c) An inventory of the contents with concordances FenI, 221
    (d) A facsimile of *Madrigali novi de diversi eccellentissimi musici libro primo de la serena*   DorM
  (2) *Madrigali novi de diversi eccellentissimi musici libro primo de la serena*   VerMN
    (a) This was published in Rome in 1534
      i) It is another reprint of the 1530 edition FenI, 220
    (b) There are three partbooks remaining of this edition
      i) The contents are the same as the first edition with the exception of the addition of two French *chansons*
    (c) A facsimile of *Madrigali novi de diversi eccellentissimi musici libro primo de la serena*   VerMN
 b) Some of the sources published by Ottaviano Scotto between 1533 and 1538
                                      FenI, 55
  (1) Scotto published a series devoted to the music of Verdelot
    (a) The series was published in Venice and consists of six publications
      i) There are three books of four-voice madrigals, two of five-voice madrigals, and a volume of intabulations of madrigals taken from the first of the four-voice books
        a - The intabulations are reputedly made by Adrian Willaert
      ii) After the first book, pieces by other composers were included
                                  FenI, 56
        a - There are pieces by Costanzo Festa, Maistre Jhan, and Arcadelt   FenI, 57
  (2) *Libro primo a 4 [Il primo libro de madrigali di Verdelotto. Novamente stampato, et con somma diligentia corretto]*   FenI, 296
    (a) This was published in 1533
      i) All that survives is a single bass partbook
      ii) There is no title-page
    (b) There was a reprint in 1537
    (c) An inventory of the contents with concordances FenI, 297
    (d) A facsimile of the 1537 edition   ScoIP
  (3) *Il secundo libro de madrigali di Verdelot, novamente stampati...*
                                      FenI, 299
    (a) This was published in 1534
      i) It was reprinted in 1536 as *Il secondo libro de madrigali di Verdelot insieme con alcuni altri bellissimi madrigali di Adriano, et Constantio Festa...*   FenI, 301
      ii) It was reissued in 1537   FenI, 301
        a - The contents are the same in the 1534 and 1537 editions

The Italian Madrigal 419

  (b) This contains the *cantus, altus,* tenor, and *bassus* part-books of madrigals by Verdelot, Willaert, Jachet de Bercham, and Costanzo Festa. ScoISL
    i) It contains Willaert's earliest known madrigals FenI, 57
  (c) An inventory of the contents with concordances FenI, 300
  (d) Facsimiles
    a - A facsimile of the 1534 edition ScoDL
    b - A facsimile of the 1536 edition ScoIS
    c - A facsimile of the 1537 edition ScoISL
(4) *Il terzo libro de madrigali di Verdelotto insieme con alcuni altri bellissimi madrigali di Constantio Festa...* FenI, 301
  (a) It was published in 1537
  (b) There are only a small number of pieces by Verdelot FenI, 301
    i) It is more of an anthology rather than a Verdelot collection
  (c) An inventory of the contents with concordances FenI, 303
  (d) A facsimile of *Il terzo libro de madrigali di Verdelotto insieme con alcuni altri bellissimi madrigali di Constantio Festa...* ScoIT
(5) *Madrigali a cinque Libro primo* FenI, 304
  (a) This was published ca. 1536-1537
  (b) Two part-books survive
    i) There are two *altus* books; one is in Berkeley, University of California Music Library, and the other is in Paris, Bibliothèque Nationale *Rés. Vm^d 30*
    ii) The *bassus* book is in Bologna, Civico Museo Bibliografico Musicale
  (c) Only seven of the twenty-one pieces have been ascribed to Verdelot elsewhere
  (d) An inventory of the contents with concordances FenI, 305
  (e) A facsimile of *Madrigali a cinque Libro primo* VerM
(6) *Delli madrigali a tre voci* FenI, 224
  (a) This was published in 1537 by O, Scotto
  (b) The title is most likely an abbreviated one and is found on the *bassus* partbook (the only partbook that has survived)
    i) The full title is usually on the *cantus* partbook
  (c) Judging from the contents, it is possible the name of Costanzo Festa was included in the full title
    i) Therefore, this print could be Festa's *Primo Libro* in its first edition
    ii) Of the twenty-eight compositions, there are thirteen attributed to Festa, one to Arcadelt and one to Fogliano
      a - The others are anonymous
      b - A number of the anonymous compositions are attributed to Festa in later prints HaaFC
  (d) An inventory of the contents FenI, 225
  (e) A facsimile of *Delli madrigali a tre voci* ScoDM
(7) *Dei madrigali di Verdelotto et de altri eccellentissimi auttori a cinque voci, libro secondo* VerD
  (a) This was published in 1538 FenI, 306
  (b) This edition has a full set of partbooks FenI, 306

                (c) An inventory of the contents with concordances FenI, 307
                (d) A facsimile of *Dei madrigali di Verdelotto et de altri eccellentissimi auttori a cinque voci, libro secondo* VerD
            (8) *Il secondo libro de madrigali d'Archadelt* FenI, 57
                (a) This was published in 1539 (by Ottaviano Scotto ?) FenI, 246
                    i) There are eight pieces by composers other than Arcadelt FenI, 247
                        a - The composers are Festa, Layolle, Corteccia, and Maistre Ihan
                (b) An inventory of the contents with concordances FenI, 248
                (c) A facsimile of *Il secondo libro de madrigali d'Archadelt* ScoSL
    c) Some printed sources by Girolamo Scotto
        (1) *Primo libro di madrigali a quatro voci* BerCA, 259
            (a) This was published by Girolamo Scotto in 1541
            (b) It was by far the most popular music book of the sixteenth century
            (c) There are no attributions
            (d) Scotto published another edition in 1553 BerCA, 261
                i) This edition has attributions BerCA, 440
                    a - There are madrigals by J. Berchem, C, Festa, F. Layolle, and Arcadelt
            (e) Two facsimiles of a 1543 edition of *Primo libro di madrigali a quatro voci* ArcD; ArcIP
        (2) *Scotto. Di Girolamo Scotto i madrigali a tre voci* (1541) ScoD
            (a) A list of the contents BerCA, 271
            (b) A facsimile of *Scotto. Di Girolamo Scotto i madrigali a tre voci* ScoD
        (3) *Cantus Libro primo de Madrigali a quattro voci di Francesco Corteccia...* FenI, 265
            (a) This was published in 1544 with a reprint in 1547
            (b) It was dedicated to Cosimo I, duke of Florence BerCA, 300
                i) For a copy of the original dedication, see BerCA, 301
            (c) An inventory of the contents with concordances FenI, 267
            (d) A list of the contents BerCA, 302
            (e) A facsimile of *Cantus Libro primo de Madrigali a quattro voci...* CorL
            (f) Some transcriptions from *Cantus Libro primo de Madrigali a quattro voci...* HarN, II, nos. 1, 10, 12, and 35
            (g) A transcription of *Cantus Libro primo de Madrigali* CorF
    d) Some of the sources published by Gardano
        (1) There is a series devoted to the music of Arcadelt
            (a) *Cantus il primo libro di madrigali di Archadelt a quatro voci...* FenI, 240
                i) This was published in 1539
                    a - The first edition of this source is lost and the date of it is unknown
                        1 - But according to Thomas Bridges in his "The Publishing of Arcadelt's First Book" the date was 1538
                ii) The 1539 edition contains the classic form of the early madrigal RanH, 463

The Italian Madrigal 421

        iii) Ten madrigals have been added to the original contents
            a - It is not clear which ones are the new madrigals
        iv) An inventory of the contents with concordances   FenI, 242
        v) A facsimile of the 1539 edition of *Cantus il primo libro di madrigali di Archadelt a quatro voci...*   ArcP
        vi) A transcription of *Cantus il primo libro di madrigali di Archadelt*   ArcO, II
   (b) *Il quarto libro di Madrigali d'Archadelt a quatro voci...*   FenI, 258
        i) This was published in 1539 with reprints in 1541 and 1545
                                                                      FenI, 257
        ii) An inventory of the contents with concordances   FenI, 259
            a - Some of the pieces are by composers other than Arcadelt
                1 - Morales, Festa, Corteccia, Verdelot, and Layolle are some of the composers represented
        iii) A facsimile of the 1545 edition of *Il quarto libro di Madrigali d'Archadelt a quatro voci...*   ArcP
        iv) A transcription of *Il quarto libro di Madrigali d'Archadelt*   ArcO, V
   (c) *Cantus primo libro di Madrigali d'Archadelt a tre voci...*   FenI, 238
        i) It was published in 1542 in Venice with reprints in 1543, 1559, and 1587
        ii) This contains six madrigals by Arcadelt, one anonymous madrigal, five madrigals by Festa, and six motets and twelve *chansons*, none of which are by Arcadelt
        iii) Gardano dropped the Festa madrigals in the reprint of 1543
            a - He included nine motets and thirteen *chansons*
                1 - These include the previous six motets and twelve *chansons*
        iv) An inventory of the contents with concordances   FenI, 239
        v) A facsimile of the 1543 edition of *Cantus primo libro di Madrigali d'Archadelt a tre voci...*   GarPM
   (d) *Il Vero Libro di Madrigali a tre voci di Constantio Festa*   FenI, 234
        i) This was published in 1543 by Gardano
        ii) There are five madrigals ascribed to Festa that are of doubtful origin
            a - They are numbers 1, 13, 21, 27, and 28
        iii) An inventory of the contents   FenI, 235
        iv) A facsimile of *Il Vero Libro di Madrigali a tre voci...*   FesV
   (e) *Arcadelt il quinto libro di Madrigali di Archadelt a quatro voci...*   FenI, 261
        i) Published in 1544 and reprinted in 1550
        ii) Nineteen of the thirty-one pieces are unique
        iii) An inventory of the contents with concordances   FenI, 263
            a - There are pieces by other composers other than Arcadelt
        iv) A facsimile of *Arcadelt il quinto libro di Madrigali di Archadelt a quatro voci...*   GarQL
        v) A transcription of *Arcadelt il quinto libro di Madrigali di Archadelt a quatro voci...*   ArcO, VI

                (f) *Corteccia Libro primo de Madrigali a cinque e a sei voci...*
                                                                            FenI, 272
                    i)   Published in 1547
                    ii) An inventory of the contents with concordances   FenI, 273
                    iii) A facsimile of *Corteccia Libro primo de Madrigali a cinque
                         e a sei voci...*   CorLPM
                    iv) A transcription of *Corteccia Libro primo de Madrigali a
                         cinque e a sei voci...*   CorFB
                (g) *Corteccia Libro secondo de Madrigali a quattro voci...* FenI, 269
                    i)   This was published in 1547
                    ii) Inventory of the contents with concordances   FenI, 270
                    iii) A facsimile of *Corteccia Libro secondo de Madrigali a
                         quattro voci...*   CorLS
        e) Some sources published by Jacques Moderne
            (1) There are two sources devoted to the music of Layolle   FenI, 280
                (a) *Cinquanta Canzoni a quatro voci...*
                    i)   This was published ca. 1540
                    ii) An inventory of the contents with concordances   FenI, 281
                    iii) A facsimile of *Cinquanta Canzoni a quatro voci...*   LayCC
                    iv) A transcription of *Cinquanta Canzoni a quatro voci...*
                                                                            LayCSW
                (b) *Venticinque Canzoni a cinque voci...*
                    i)   This was published in 1540
                    ii) An inventory of the contents with concordances   FenI, 284
                    iii) A facsimile of *Venticinque Canzoni a cinque voci...* LayV
                    iv) A transcription of *Venticinque Canzoni a cinque voci...*
                                                                            LayCS

D. The Italian *Villotta*

1. Introduction
    a) The *villotta* is a type of vocal music that was popular in Venice and Padua
        during the early sixteenth century   RanH, 913
        (1) The term is usually associated with Venetian dialect songs   CarCV, 25
    b) *Villotte* often reveal their local origin by regional identifications such as *villote
        alla paduana* (Padua), *alla veneziana* (Venice), or *alla mantovana* (Mantua)
                                                                            VilL

2. The poetry of the *villotta*   RanH, 913
    a) The *villotta* is a secular song similar to the *villenella* but has its origins in folk
        music   VilL
        (1) The *villanella* was not a folk form but rather a reaction against the more
            refined madrigal   VilLA
            (a) It often parodied well-known madrigal texts and music
    b) Throughout its history the *villotta* has had a common feature   ReeMR, 164
        (1) It in some way incorporates a popular or street song into its texture
        (2) It contains street cries full of nonsense syllables   RocM, 92
            (a) These nonsense syllables were called *lilolela*   RanH, 913

i) Before or after the *lilolela* is a refrain called *nio*
c) The poetry possesses no structural regularity at all   ReeMR, 164
    (1) It consists of one or more strophes that vary in length and form
                                                             RanH, 913
d) It is of a rustic, unsentimental character
    (1) An example is the poetry sung by Ruzante, a Paduan actor   CarCV I, 36
    (2) He and his companions stressed the attractive quality of the various northern rustic languages   CarCV I, 36
        (a) For example, they performed at banquets, parties, and other court functions and on February 4, 1524 in Venice, while carrying peasant's tools, they sang Venetian dialect songs (*villotte*)
                                                                        CarCV I, 35

3. The music of the *villotta*   RanH, 913
    a) It is for four voices, often with a popular tune in the tenor
    b) Some *villotte* are quodlibets containing popular song texts and tunes
    c) "The texture is basically chordal, although there are points of imitation"
    d) The music is dance-like and often has sections in contrasting duple and triple meter   ReeMR, 164
        (1) A section called the *nio* is often found in the more developed *villotta*   ReeMR, 164
            (a) The *nio* contrasts with the main body by means of a more rapid pace and often is in triple meter   RanH, 913
    e) The *villotta* later became simplified into the *mascherata*   RocM, 92

4. Manuscripts containing *villotte*
    a) Florence: Biblioteca del Conservatorio, *MS Basevi 2440*   FenI, 23
        (1) This is the last secular manuscript to be arranged in choirbook form
        (2) It is divided into two separate reportorial sections
            (a) A strophic section and a non-strophic section
            (b) The strophic section is thought to have been written about 1515
        (3) There are five *villotte* at the end of the non-strophic pieces   FenI, 24
        (4) An inventory of the contents with concordances   FenI, 158
    b) Florence: Biblioteca Nazionale Centrale, *Magl XIX. 164*   FenI, 24, fn. 27
        (1) A copying date of no later than ca. 1522-3 is suggested   FenI, 173
        (2) This source contains a group of four *villotte*
        (3) An inventory of the contents with concordances   FenI, 175
    c) Venice: Biblioteca Marciana, *MSS It. Cl. IV, 1795-8*   FenI, 20, fn. 22
        (1) There are four *villotte* in Venice, Biblioteca Marciana *MSS It. Cl. IV, 1795-8;* numbers 9, 13, 94, and 98
        (2) An inventory of the contents with concordances   FenI, 192
        (3) A facsimile of Venice: Biblioteca Marciana, *MSS It. Cl. IV, 1795-8*   LuiA

5. Some published sources containing *villotte*
    a) The early V*illotte* are found in the eleven books of *frottole* published by Petrucci during the first two decades of the sixteenth century   HelS, 393
        (1) The books were printed between 1504 and 1514   DenS, 34
        (2) No complete copy of the tenth book has been found   HelS, 396
            (a) But, there are fragments of the alto and bass parts preserved in Se-

ville: Bibiloteca Colombina   HelS, fn. 1
- (3) In the books preceding the eleventh one, poetry of a literary nature are found only in isolated instances
- (4) But, Petrucci's eleventh book is rivaled in literary splendor only by *Musica de messer Bernardo Pisano sopra le canzone de Petrarca* of 1520   HelS, 397
- b) *Fior de motetti e canzone novi*   FenI, 17
  - (1) This was published in 1523
    - (a) Perhaps by Pasoti and Dorico   FenI, 207
  - (2) It contains four *villotte*   FenI, 20
    - (c) Three partbooks, the *cantus, altus,* and tenor, survive   FenI, 207
      - i) The *bassus* is missing
      - ii) The *altus* partbook is the third of the four *altus* books bound together as *R 141* in Bologna: Civico Museo bibliografico Musicale   FenI, 207
  - (3) The pieces in this source are found in Venice, Biblioteca Marciana *MSS It. Cl. IV, 1795-8* but in a different order   FenI, 20
  - (4) An inventory of the contents of *Fior de motetti e canzone novi* with concordances   FenI, 209
    - (a) The *villotte* are nos. [11], [12], [13], and [14]
  - (5) A facsimile of *Fior de motetti e canzone novi*   DorF
- c) *Libro primo de la Croce*   RocM, 4
  - (1) This was printed by Pasoti and Dorico   FenI, 211
    - (a) Only a reprint of 1526 is extant   RocM, 4
  - (2) This source is actually a collection of *frottole* but one piece has all the hallmarks of a *villotta*
    - (a) It is *L'ultimo di de maggio* by Sebastiano Festa
    - (b) It is labeled a *villotta* in a Venetian manuscript source
  - (3) An inventory of the contents of *Libro primo de la Croce* with concordances   FenI, 214
    - (a) The *villotta, L'ultimo di de maggio,* is no [21]   FenI, 215
  - (4) A list of the contents   CusV, 156
  - (5) A facsimile of *Libro primo de la Croce*   CarF
  - (6) A transcription of *Libro primo de la Croce*   PriL
- d) *Il primo libro delle villotte* a 4   CarCV I, 13
  - (1) It was published by Gardane in 1541
  - (2) It contains music by Alvise Castellino (Il Varoter)
  - (3) A facsimile of *Il primo libro delle villotte* a 4   CasI

E. The Italian *Villanella* of ca. 1530-1550   RanH, 913

1. Introduction
   - a) The term *villanella* is a noun meaning country girl
     - (1) The term refers to a form of music that was popular in Italy from ca. 1530 to the end of the sixteenth century
   - b) The earliest repertory of the *villanella* was called *canzone villanesche alla napolitana*
     - (1) It consisted of strophic songs for three voices with the uppermost part

              dominating the texture   CarCV I, 121
    (2)   The term *canzone villanesca alla napolitana* could be translated as
          "peasant songs in the Neapolitan manner"   CarCV I, 33
          (a) The word *villanesca* is an adjective meaning countrified
                                                                    RanH, 913
    (3)   Later, in 1544, the *canzone villanesca alla napolitana* was taken up by
          Willaert and other Venetian composers
          (a) They paraphrased the original *villanesche,* added a fourth voice,
              moved the tune to the tenor, and smoothed out the counterpoint
              i)   "Placing the *cantus prius factus* in the *tenor* allowed the four-
                   voice pieces to be no longer considered merely as revisions
                   of three-voice models"   PirM, 191
                   a - They may have been classified, by Renaissance standards,
                       under the concept of *imitatio*
          (b) An example of this is Willaert's *O dolce vita mia* taken from Nola's
              piece by the same name   PirM, 188
              i)   A transcription of Nola's piece   PirM, 187
              ii) A transcription of Willaert's arrangement   PirM, 188
  c) In the 1550's, the term *villanella* began to replace the term, *villanesche*

2. The early *villanella* [*canzone villanesca*: ca. 1537-1546]
   a) Introduction   RanH, 913
    (1)   The *Canzone villanesca* developed along side the early madrigal
                                                                    ReeMR, 332
          (a) But, the *villanesche* were more folk-like and less polished than the
              madrigal   RocM, 92
              i)   They were like "pop" music rather than "classical"
                                                                    CarCV I, 91
    (2)   The *canzone villanesa* came from the south, from Naples PirM, 175
          (a) Therefore, for some time it was called *canzone villanesca alla
              napolitana*
              i)   The *canzone villanesca alla napolitana* (and later related
                   forms) initially depended on popular traditions (oral and
                   written) and later were somewhat influenced by the learned
                   style   CarCV, 91
          (b) The early dialectal texts were the popular poetry of Naples
                                                                    PirMT, 111
          (c) The style of the music was popular in Italy from ca. 1530 to the
              end of the sixteenth century   RanH, 913
    (3)   The *canzone villanesa alla napolitana* soon started to mingle with
          pieces whose dialect and musical language were rooted in northern Italy
                                                                    PirM, 175
          (a) These later texts are often rustic when written by non-Neapolitans
                                                                    PirMT, 111
          (b) There are two kinds of rustic poetry   CarCV I, 33
              i)   There are poems written for the purpose of satirizing the
                   peasant with his rough mannerisms
              ii) And there are poems describing the habits of the peasant so
                   realistically that often caricature was the result

b) The poetry of the *canzone villanesca*
   (1) The *canzone villanesca* is a strophic poem   CarCV I, 91
      (a) It is usually composed of four strophes
         i) They vary in length from three to seven lines   CarCV, 67
            a - But, in any one poem the strophes are equal in length and syllable count
               1 - This was for the sake of the strophic musical setting
      (b) Each strophe contains an introductory couplet   CarCV I, 68
         i) This is called a mutation
         ii) The couplet is a constant factor in length and meter
         iii) But, it changes content from strophe to strophe   CarCV I, 38
      (c) The *canzone villanesca* is actually a *strambotto* expanded by the addition of a refrain after each couplet   CarCV I, 38
         i) The theory of the *strambotto* origin is indeed plausible   CarCV I, 40
            a - But, the relationship was gradually obliterated through the individual efforts of new versifiers   CarCV I, 91
      (d) The texts are love poems   ReeMR, 333
         i) Some outdo the madrigal in bewailing lovers' woes
         ii) There are double meanings as well as instances of unequivocal obscenity
   (2) The versification pattern has a series of couplets with an unchanging refrain in all strophes or sometimes a modified refrain in the final strophe in order to make a rhyme connection with the final couplet   CarCV, 91
      (a) Therefore the poetic form is ab+refrain, ab+refrain, ab+refrain, cc+-refrain and the musical form is the same except that cc repeats the music of ab   ReeMR, 333
         i) There are frequent departures from this pattern   ReeMR, 333
            a - At times, there are immediate repetitions of *a* and of the refrain
         ii) Also, this formula does not account for a wide variety of rhyme and syllable count in the refrain   CarCV, 39
         iii) Nor does it account for possible deviations in the mutation   CarCV, 39
      (b) The refrains were of various lengths in which the texts, with few exceptions, remain basically the same within any one poem   CarCV I, 38
         i) The refrains vary in length from one to four lines   CarCV I, 39
            a - A three line strophe had a refrain of one line and a four line strophe had a refrain of two lines   CarCV I, 68
         ii) They may have shorter lines than the couplets   CarCV I, 68
      (c) The texts of the refrains often have a rhyme connection to the introductory couplet, even though there is a contrast in terms of content, style, or metrics   CarCV I, 46
         i) The first line of the refrain and the last line of the introductory couplet share the same rhyme, except in the final strophe   CarCV, 68
            a - But, there are variations to this pattern
c) The music of the three-voice *canzone villanesca alla napolitana*

(1) It consists of two types; simple chordal pieces and soulful lovers' laments   RocM, 94
  (a) The latter have more independence in the vocal writing plus poise and balance in the melodies   RocM, 95
(2) The three-voice *canzone villanesca* was written in homophonic style   RanH, 913
  (a) The top voice carries the melody
    i) The melody has a flavor which sets it apart from both art music and from the examples of northern popular song   PirM, 177
      a - It consists of well-rounded melodic periods, each of which has a strong cadential orientation   CarCV I, 121
        1 - Each period corresponds to one line of the poem
        2 - These periods are often split into small parts by means of melodic repetition
      b - At times the drive to the cadence is interrupted by the truncation of words and phrases   CarCV I, 121
    ii) The melody is free from extensive melodic or rhythmic involvement with the other two parts   CarCV I, 122
      a - The melodic and rhythmic patterns are closely connected to the accentuation of the words
  (b) The tenor has no melodic independence of its own and is little more than a duplication of the uppermost part   CarCV I, 122
    i) Quite often the two voices move in parallel thirds   PirM, 183
      a - The exception to this was a fourth followed by a second and its resolution at the cadence
        1 - An example is found in Nola's *O dolce vita mia* in the second and third measures after the first repeat   PirM, 187
          a - A transcription of *O dolce vita mia*
  (c) The bass line moves in disjunct motion settling on harmonically decisive tones such as the tonic, dominant, and subdominant   CarCV I, 122
  (d) The soprano part sings in a medium range and the bass and tenor parts have a range about one fifth higher than usual   PirM, 183
    i) "The three parts... normally move within a small range, seldom exceeding two octaves"   CarCV I, 122
    ii) An example is *Madonn'io non lo so* by Nola   PirM, 190
      a - A transcription of *Madonn'io non lo so*
(3) The trio contains conjunct melodic patterns, lack of harmonic variety, and simple note-against-note counterpoint   CarCV I, 62
  (a) The note-against-note counterpoint occasionally gives way to simple imitative patterns   CarCV I, 121
    i) Usually at the unison or fifth at the beginnings of phrases
  (b) Consecutive fifths were an important part of the *napolitana*   PirMT, 112
    i) They were used mainly in cadential areas   CarCV I, 122
    ii) The use of consecutive fifths may have been a deliberate rusticity and possibly was intended to imitate the effect of a

428 Secular Vocal Music

                strumming instrument   RanH, 913
        iii)   Transcription of a *napolitana* with fifths   PirMT, 112
  (4) The music is simple and rhythmically lively and contains dance like syncopations   RanH, 913
      (a) There is sudden slowing and brisk acceleration of tempi   PirM, 177
      (b) An example is *Io dich' è sturno* by Nola   PirM, 177
          i)   A transcription of the melody of *Io dich' è sturno*
  (5) "The musical form of the *canzone villanesca* is based on the principle of strophic repetition"   CarCV I, 92
      (a) The form adheres line by line to the metrical structure of the poetic text
          i)   But, a repetition of rhyme in the text seldom suggests a musical repetition within the strophic unit
          ii) Therefore the poetic form ab/b or abb may have the following musical form, :A: B :C:
                a - This is true with or without a refrain
                b - An example of this form is found in *Chi cerca de vedere donne belle* (no. 5 in *Canzone villanesche alla napolitana* of 1537 published by Johannes Colonia)
                      1 - An example of *Chi cerca de vedere donne belle*   CarCV I, 57
      (c) The musical and textual repetition of a section within a strophic unit is usually indicated by the conventional repeat signs, :|| or :||:
          i)   Both signs call for a repeat of the musical material which precedes it
          ii) The repeat is to begin at the beginning of the piece or from a previous repeat sign or from a vertical line drawn from the top to the bottom of the staff
                a - The vertical line limits the extent of the repetition prescribed by the repeat sign
                b - It does not in itself indicate a repeat
                c - This same vertical line is used also to separate the music of the refrain from the rest of the piece
      (d) For a list of musical forms from 1537 to 1559 *see*   CarCV I, 94
  (6) *Note nere* is used as a vehicle for emphasizing rapid declamation   CarCV I, 140
      (a) There is declamation on the minim and semiminim   CarCV I, 139
          i)   It is seldom found on flagged semiminims
          ii) An example of declamation on the semiminim is found in a piece by Nola, *see*   CarCV II, Plate 25
d) There were composers of the three-voice *villanesche* of Neapolitan origin, who were actually a part of the Neapolitan scene   PirM, 178
  (1) Giovan Tomaso di Maio [b. ca. 1490]   RanH, 913
      (a) The style of his music
          i)   Maio liked simple and complex (insofar as the style permits) imitative counterpoint   CarCV I, 129
                a - He preferred the simple type of imitation at the unison or octave between two voices
                      1 - The remaining voice doubled in thirds

The Italian *Villanella* of ca. 1530-1550   429

      b - The more complicated type consists of three entries in close succession that produce rhythmic conflicts
    ii) Actually, his imitative style is so harmonically oriented that it can scarcely be called counterpoint
      a - He decorated chordal passages with passing tones
                        CarCV I, 130
      b - He used an excessive number of consecutive fifths
                        CarCV I, 130
    iii) Passages in imitative style have melismas on expressive words
                        CarCV I, 129
      a - Such passages are found in settings of the more literary texts
      b - Maio is the only Neapolitan *villanesche* composer to use melisma
  (b) Maio's music was published in *Canzone vilanesche di Giovan Thomaso di Maio musico napolitano libro primo a tre voci* by Gardano in 1546   PirMT, 112
    i) This is the largest collection of Neapolitan dialect songs for three voices published in Venice before 1560 CarCV I, 105
      a - It contains thirty *villanesche* by Maio
    ii) A transcription of a *Napolitana by Maio*   PirMT, 112
(2) Giovanni Domenico da Nola [b. ca. 1510-1520]   RanH, 913
  (a) The style of his music   CarCV I, 133
    i) The notorious succession of three-five chords in parallel motion were never too conspicuous in the pieces by Nola
                           PirM, 182
    ii) But many phrases begin with triadic outlines
    iii) His melodies cover a small interval in disjunct patterns
    iv) He uses contrasting refrains
  (b) Publications of his music
    i) *Canzoni villanesche de Don Ioan Dominico del Giovane de Nola. Libro primo et secondo...*   CarCV II, 1
      a - This was published in Venice in 1541 by Scotto
        1 - The only extant copy of this manuscript was destroyed during World War II   PirM, 178
      b - It was later reprinted by Antonio Gardano [1545]
                           CarCV II, 2
        1 - It was published in two separate books, *see* ii) and iii) below   PirM, 178
      c - A list of the contents   BerCA, 275
    ii) *Canzone villanesche de Don Ioan Domenico del Giovane de Nola, a tre voci novamente ristampate. Libro primo 1545*
                           CarCV II, 2
      a - This is the reprint of the first book of the 1541 edition by Scotto   PirM, 178
      b - It was published in Venice by Antonio Gardano
                           PirM, 178
      c - A facsimile of *Canzone villanesche de Don Ioan Domenico del Giovane de Nola,...Libro primo*   NolC I

430   Secular Vocal Music

                d - Transcriptions of excerpts from *Canzonei villanesche...*
                Libro primo (nos. 1, 3, 6, and 9)   NoIN
          iii)   *Canzone villanesche de Don Ioan Domenico del Giovane de Nola, a tre voci novamente ristampate Libro secundo 1545*
                                                      CarCV II, 2
                a - This is a reprint of the second book of the 1541 edition by Scotto   PirM, 178
                b - It was published in Venice by Antonio Gardano
                                                            PirM, 178
                c - A facsimile of *Canzone villanesche...Libro secundo*
                                                              NoIC II
                d - Transcriptions of excerpts from *Canzonei villanesche...*
                Libro secundo (nos. 4, 5, and 8)   NoIN
   (3)   Tomaso Cimello [b. ca. 1510]   PirM, 178
       (a)   The style of his music   CarCV I, 130
           i)   He uses very little imitation and avoids parallel fifths
           ii)   His melodies are in disjunct motion with strong changes of direction
           iii) He inserts passages in triple time
           iv)   He consistently uses short note values   CarCV I, 139
       (b)   His music was published in *Canzone villanesche al modo napolitano a tre voci di Thomaso Cimello da Napoli con una bataglia villanescha a tre del medesimo autore novamente poste in luce. Libro primo 1545*   CarCV II, 4
           i)   This was published in Venice by Gardano
           ii)   A facsimile of *Canzone villanesche al modo napolitano a tre voci di Thomaso Cimello da Napoli...*   CimC
           iii) A transcription of *Canzone villanesche al modo napolitano a tre voci di Thomaso Cimello da Napoli...*   CimCH
   (4)   Vincenzo Fontana [fl. 1545-1555]   PirM, 178
       (a)   It is not certain that he was a Neapolitan   CarCV I, 105
       (b)   The style of his music   CarCV I, 132
           i)   He liked imitative devices
                a - He pairs two voices in thirds answered by the remaining voice at the fifth
                b - Some of his imitation is at the unison
                c - He used imitation at the beginning of all phrases except the first
           ii)   He avoided parallel fifths
       (c)   His music was published in *Canzone villanesche di Vicenzo Fontana a tre voci alla napolitana novamente poste in luce. Libro primo. Villote di V. Fontana a 3.*   CarCV II, 4
           i)   This was published in 1545 by Gardano in Venice
           ii)   A facsimile of *Canzone villanesche...Libro primo*   FonC
       (d)   A transcription of some of his *villanesche*   FonN
       (e)   Other transcriptions of some of his music
                                   CarCV II, nos. 7, 8, 15, 18, 19, 23, 29, 33
  e)   The performance of the *canzone villanesa alla napolitana*
     (1)   The upper part becomes more conspicuous than in earlier Italian vocal

                    forms   CarCV I, 62
                    (a) The soloistic manner of performance is therefore appropriate to the
                        style
            (2) At times, the *villanesche* were sung to the accompaniment of instruments
                                                                           ReeMR, 333
                    (a) This is true particularly with the lute

    3. The non-Neapolitan, four-voice *villanella* (ca. 1544-1550)
        a) The general style of the four-voice *villanella*
            (1) New arrangements of previous works by Neapolitan composers were
                made by Willaert and other Venetian composers   PirM, 178
                    (a) These *canzone villanesche* were for four-parts and were a parting
                        of the ways between the rustic regional type and the more respec-
                        table composition with leaning toward art-music   RocM, 96
                    (b) The composers attempted to preserve fully the most typical features
                        of the polyphonic pieces such as the brisk irregular rhythms and the
                        spirited utterance of the dialectal texts   PirM, 182
                        i) But they reduced the amount of imitation and thus eliminated
                            a procedure of the three-voice model which was considered
                            irregular
                        ii) They kept the basic chordal structure and expanded it in the
                            fuller sonority of four voices
                    (c) They added new harmonizations to a melody of a previous work
                                                                           CarCV I, 180
                        i) But they used the original vertical cross sections at cadential
                            points where it is impossible to avoid them
                            a - This was done to preserve the essential qualities of the
                                stylized Neapolitan cadence
                                1 - Such as the 2-1 melodic descent and the 4-3 suspen-
                                    sion
                        ii) They quoted the bass line literally or, for reasons of harmonic
                            variety, altered it
                        iii) They also drew upon other voices without manipulating them
                            extensively
                    (d) The borrowed melody was kept in the upper part in Willaert's early
                        villanesche of 1542 and in two or three *villanesche* by Corteccia
                                                                           PirM, 181
                        i) An example is Willaert's *O bene mio fam'uno*   PirM, 184
                            a - Transcriptions of *O bene mio fam'uno*
                                                                  PirM, 184; CarA, 20
                        ii) In his later *villanesche*, he sets the *superius* tune intact in the
                            tenor   CarCV I, 182
        b) The non-Neapolitan composers who wrote four-voice *villanesche* and some
            sources of their music   PirM, 178
            (1) Adrian Willaert [b. ca. 1490]
                    (a) The style of his music   CarCV I, 182
                        i) He initiated the idea of adapting the three-voice tunes from
                            Naples
                        ii) He sets the *superius* tune intact in the tenor, transposing it in

432 Secular Vocal Music

                order to accommodate the wider compass required by a four-voice texture
- iii) He preserves the identity of the three-voice Neapolitan tune at phrase endings including the customary 4-3 suspension
  - a - The 4-3 suspension is transferred from the tenor to the *superius*
- iv) He repeats some units that were only presented once in the original
  - a - This makes Willaert's arrangements longer
- v) He removes the parallel fifths and adheres strictly to the correct rules of contrapuntal practice   CarCV I, 187

(b) Publications containing his music
- i) *Canzone villanesche alla napolitana di M. Adriano Wigliaret a quatro voci...con la Canzona di Ruzante*   CarCV II, 35
  - a - This was published in Venice by Scotto in 1544
    - 1 - For reprints of this source, *see* ii) and iii) below
  - b - There are only a few pages of the *altus* part still extant   PirM, 181
  - c - This fragment contains six *villanesche* by Willaert   PirM, 196
  - d - The madrigals by Willaert and the *villanesche* by Corteccia are missing
  - e - The manuscript is in Pistoia: Archivio Capitolare, *B.7.7.*   CarCV II, 35
- ii) There were two reprints of *Canzone villanesche alla napolitana di M. Adriano Wigliaret a quatro voci... con la Canzona di Ruzante* by Scotto in 1548 and 1563   CarCV II, 3
  - a - A list of the contents of the 1548 edition   BerCA, 371
  - b - A list of the contents of the 1563 edition   BerCA, 638
  - c - A facsimile of the 1548 edition   WilCV
    - 1 - This contains *La Canzone di Ruzante: Zoia zentil*
      - a - A transcription of *Zoia zentil*   CarA, no. [20]
  - d - Transcriptions from the 1548 edition
       WilO XIV, nos. 1-8, 10, 11, 13, 14
- iii) *Canzone villanesche alla napolitana di M. Adriano Vvigliaret a quatro voci la Canzona di Ruzante...*   PirM, 196
  - a - This was published in Venice in 1545 by Antoni[um] Gardane   CarCV II, 36
  - b - It is a reprint of Scotto's 1544 edition   CarCV II, 3
    - 1 - The contents are reordered and more stanzas of certain poems are printed   CarCV I, 18
    - 2 - This contains the *villanesche* by Corteccia   PirM, 181
      - a - But the *Canzone di Ruzante is missing*   PirM, 197
    - 3 - There were two other reprints by Gardane in 1548 and 1553   CarCV II, 3
      - a - These editions contain *La Canzone di Ruzante: zoia zentil*   PirM, 197
    - 4 - This manuscript is found in Wolfenbüttel: Herzog-August-Bibliothek   CarCV II, 36

                    5 - A list of the contents of the 1545 edition
                                                             CarCV II, 36
                    6 - A list of the contents of all the editions   PirM, 196-7
(2)   Francesco Silvestrino [fl. ca. 1540-1550]
        (a)   The style of his music   CarCV I, 186
                i)   He preserves a very strict relationship to the model
                        a - The tenor takes the *superius* as it is
                            1 - The two voices are exchanged
                        b - "The bass line is quoted verbatim except for a few octave transpositions"
                ii)   The alto is added as a filler
                iii)   A transcription of three of his compositions CarA, 23, 32, 39
        (b)   A publication containing his music
                i)   *Canzone villanesche alla napolitana di M. Adriano Vvigliaret a quatro voci la Canzona di Ruzante...*   PirM, 196
                        a - This is the 1545 publication by Antonio Gardano
                                                             CarCV II, 36
                        b - It contains *villanesche* by Willaert, Silvestrino, and Corteccia   CarCV II, 36
                            1 - There are three *villanesche* by Silvestrino
                        c - The manuscript is found complete in Wolfenbüttel: Herzog-August-Bibliothek   CarCV II, 36
                        d - A list of the contents   CarCV II, 36
(3)   Perissone Cambio [b. ca. 1520]
        (a)   The style of his music
                i)   He used various techniques for the borrowed melody in his arrangements   CarCV I, 191
                        a - The borrowed tune is placed in the tenor at the original pitch with no alterations
                        b - At other times, the borrowed tune is either partially or completely transposed and subjected to slight changes in rhythmic and melodic structure
                        c - Units of the tune are expanded by means of repetition, often with variations
                            1 - He does not alter the design of the tune
                ii)   He strengthened the cadential scheme of the model by strengthening its tonal structure with more coherent progressions   CarCV I, 192
                iii)   He changed homophony to polyphony   CarCV I, 192
                        a - He created points of imitation based on motives from the borrowed tune
                iv)   His *villanesche* are ornate in a decorative, variation style
                                                             CarCV I, 192
                        a - He ornaments the melodic line with nervous dotted figures, rapid scales and syncopations
                v)   An example of his music   CarA, 3
        (b)   One publication of his music is *Canzone villanesche alla napolitana a quatro voci di Perissone novamente poste in luce....* CarCV II, 26
                i)   It was published in Venice by Gardano in 1545   CarCV II, 4

ii) There are ten pieces that are recognizable as arrangements
with the borrowed tune in the tenor   CarCV I, 191
- a - Three of the *villanesche* are arrangements of music by
Nola (*Fontana che dai acqua a dui valluni, Na volta me
gabasti o lusinghera,* and *Oime dolente ca ne nivino*)
- b - One arrangement is of music by Fontana (*O vita mia s'io
v'amo anzi v'adoro*)
- c - And one arrangement is of music by Cimello (*Par Deo
cha te conosco*)

4. Some other printed sources of the *canzone villanesca* and the later arrangements
  a) *Canzoni villanesche alla napolitana...libro primo*   PirMT, 108
    (1) Published by Joanne de Colonia at Naples in 1537   PirMT, 110
      (a) This is the only surviving example of his work   CarCV I, 6
    (2) The original must have contained three partbooks   CarCV I, 7
      (a) Only two partbooks remain; the *cantus* and tenor
    (3) There are no attributions in this collection of pieces   CarCV I, 8
    (4) This is found at Wolfenbüttel: Herzog August Bibliothek   CarCV I, 7
    (5) An inventory of the contents with concordances   FenI, 230
    (6) A transcription of *O vecchia, tu che guardi*   PirMT, 110
      (a) "The bass part is missing in the only known copy"
  b) *Madrigali a tre et arie napolitane*   CarCV I, 10
    (1) The date of publication is thought to be ca. 1537
    (2) It was published in Rome with the types of Dorico   CarCV II, 1
      (a) No copy of the *bassus* partbook survives   FenI, 227
    (3) It contains three-voice madrigals and Neapolitan songs
      (a) There are no attributions but most of the madrigals have been identified through concordances
        i) There are eleven madrigals by Festa, one by Arcadelt, and one unidentified piece [J. Gero]
      (b) There are ten anonymous settings of Neapolitan dialect poems, the *arie napolitane*
    (4) An inventory of the contents with concordances   FenI, 228
    (5) A list of the contents   CusV, 170
    (6) This is found in Wolfenbüttel: Herzog-August-Bibliothek
    (7) A facsimile of *Madrigali a tre et arie napolitane*   MadT
  c) *Madrigali a quatro voci di Geronimo Scotto con alcuni alla misura di breve*   PirM, 179
    (1) Published in Venice by Scotto in 1542   CarCV II, 2
    (2) It contains two of Willaert's *villanesche a voci pari,* but they are not labeled as such
      (a) *O bene mio famme uno favore*   PirM, 196
        i) The melody is in the *cantus*
        ii) Transcriptions of *O bene mio famme uno favore*
            PirM, 184; CarA, 20
      (b) *A quando a quando haveva una vicina*   PirM, 196
        i) The melody is in the *cantus*
        ii) Transcriptions of *A quando a quando haveva una vicina*
            PirM, 186; CarA, 1

            (3) These are thought to be re-elaborations of Neapolitan *villanesche* for
                 three voices
            (4) They are the only known *villanesche* printed between 1541 and 1544
                                                                                       CarCV I, 18
                 (a) Also, these are the only known ones ever printed with all the
                     strophes of the poem placed directly under the musical notes
            (5) The rest of the compositions are by Scotto   CarCV I, 18
            (6) This source "was one of the earliest publications to advertise another
                 novelty, that of music *a misura breve*, also called *a note nere*" PirM, 179
            (7) A list of the contents   BerCA, 283
            (8) Transcriptions of the Willaert *villanesche*   WilO, XIV, nos. 32-35
        d) *Elletione de canzone alla napoletana a tre voci di Rinaldo Burno con altre
            scielte da diversi musici. Novamente poste in luce. Libro primo 1546*
                                                                                       CarCV II, 4
            (1) This was published in Venice by Scotto
        e) *Canzonj vilanesche napolitane nove scelte et di varij autori 1547* CarCV II, 5
            (1) This was published in Città di Capua by Sultzbach

5. The *canzone villanesca* on the stage
    a) The *villanesche* appeared on the Italian musical stage at the time of the first
       visit of Emperor Charles V to his recently secured domain of Naples in 1536
                                                                                       PirM, 175
        (1) This performance appeared in *Gli ingannati*, a Sienese comedy
                                                                                       PirMT, 106
            (a) This was an anonymous comedy of the Sienese Accademia degli
                Intronati (1531)   PirMT, 81
            (b) Actors from Siena were most likely employed to perform the parts
                                                                                       PirMT, 106
    b) The *commedia alla villanesca, farsette*, and *farse cavaiole* were popular in
       the decades before the printed debut of the *canzone villanesca*
                                                                                       CarCV I, 35-36
        (1) The *commedia alla villanesca*   CarCV I, 35
            (a) This type comedy was performed by a famous stage *villano*, the
                Paduan actor, Angelo Beolco (Ruzante)
            (b) Ventian dialect songs were sung (*villotte*)
        (2) The *farsette* (short plays)   CarCV I, 36
            (a) These were attributed to Antonio Caracciolo from the area around
                Naples
        (3) The *farse cavaiole* (farses)   CarCV I, 36
            (a) These included burlesques of the bumbling *Cavese* (a worker from
                the town of La Cava)
            (b) They were presented at carnivals
    c) The published [*villanesche*] were used in lively entertainments at Italian courts
       and academies   CarCV I, 34
        (1) They were also found on the Italian musical stage   PirM, 175
        (2) They were written by well educated, but not very elegant, versifiers
        (3) Colloquial and commonplace dialect expressions, and awkward and un-
             complimentary images and metaphors were stock items for the Italian
             lyric poet

F. The Neapolitan *Mascherata*

1. Introduction
   a) The term *mascherata* refers to a masked Carnival performance in Renaissance Italy　　　　　　　　　　　　　　　　　　　　　　　　　RanH, 470
   b) The *mascherata* composition may have been conceived as an occasional piece for outdoor festivals or carnivals　　　　　　　　　　CarCV I, 149
      (1) Some of the festivals or carnivals were partially outdoor shows with a procession and a decorated vehicle　　　　　　　　DenS, 804
   c) Contemporary documents also indicate that the *mascherate* were sung at banquets and other festivities　　　　　　　　　　　　　DenS, 55
      (1) They were always sung by three people dressed in costume
   d) Some *mascherate* allude to specific feast days　　　　　　CarCV I, 149
      (1) One such *mascherata* alludes to Candlemas Day
         (a) This celebration was traditionally devoted to torchlight parades in Naples
   e) Some of the pieces have texts with theatrical implications　CarCV I, 149
      (1) "There is a complete stock of disguises"　　　　　　CarCV I, 148
         (a) Such as Gypsies, Candlemakers, Spindle Makers, Doctors, Beggars, Soldiers, and Pilgrims
      (2) It is possible that the *mascherate* played a part in the development of the *commedia dell'arte*　　　　　　　　　　　　　CarCV I, 151
   f) The *mascherate* compositions appeared in *villanesche* prints between 1541 and 1545　　　　　　　　　　　　　　　　　　　　　CarCV I, 148
      (1) They were all contributed by Cimello and Nola
      (2) The *mascherate* differ from *the villanesche* only slightly both in the music and the poetry　　　　　　　　　　　　　　CarCV I, 148
         (a) In the Neapolitan *mascherate*, there is a recurrent refrain but, unlike the *villanesche*, the refrain is a vehicle for humorous or proverbial comment on an activity of a trade, the action of which is often reiterated in onomatopoetic terms　　　CarCV I, 149
         (b) There is a tendency toward settings of long strophes which lack the traditional division between mutation and refrain　CarCV I, 150
            i) But, these settings are exceptional
         (c) There is greater use of truncation technique in the *mascherate* of Cimello and Nola than in the *villanesche*　　　CarCV I, 150
         (d) The poetry is distinguished by its text incipit and content
            i) It usually begins with the expression *Nui siamo* or *Noi siamo* or some other form of self-introduction to the ladies, for whom it was presumably sung

2. The poetry of the *mascherata*　　　　　　　　　　　　　　　　　CarCV I, 148
   a) The *mascherate* usually begin with some convenient form of self-introduction to the ladies, for whom they were presumably sung
      (1) They nearly always begin with "we are" this or that and then proceed with the usual obscene impertinences　　　　　　DenS, 55
   b) The first strophe usually consists of a general statement identifying the maskers or their trade
   c) The remaining strophes contain descriptions extolling the various activities

involved in the pursuit of said occupations
- (1) Actually this was an excuse for bragging about masculine expertise in blunt double meanings or in clever plays on words
- d) "The recurrent refrain is a vehicle for humorous or proverbial comment on the activity of the trade" CarCVI, 149

3. The music of the *mascherata*   CarCV I, 150
   - a) The *mascherate* resemble northern carnival songs
     - (1) They sometimes contain contrasting sections in triple time
     - (2) They are written syllabically in order to make them comprehensible with clear articulation
   - b) They are written much like that of the chordal madrigals *a note nere* ReeMR, 334
   - c) They are similar to the *villanesche* in that they contain parallel fifths
     - (1) Although, some *mascherate* do not have parallel fifths
   - d) They were composed with the utmost simplicity in order to facilitate memorizing   ReeMR, 334
     - (1) This was done because *mascherate* were sung in costume, presumably without written music available
     - (2) But points of imitation were assigned to maskers in an attempt to distinguish them   CarCVI, 151
   - e) There is a dramatic juxtaposition of phrases with markedly different rhythmic patterns   CarCV I, 151

4. The composers of the three-voice *mascherate*   CarCV I, 148
   - a) [Tomaso] Cimello [b. ca. 1510]
     - (1) His music was published in *Canzone villanesche al modo napolitano a tre voci di Thomaso Cimello da Napoli con una bataglia villanescha a tre del medesimo autore npvamente poste in luce. Libro primo 1545*   CarCV II, 4
       - (a) This was published in Venice by Gardano
       - (b) It contains four *mascherate* by Cimello   CarCV I, 148
       - (c) A facsimile of *Canzone villanesche al modo napolitano a tre voci di Thomaso Cimello da Napoli*   CimC
       - (d) A transcription of *Canzone villanesche al modo napolitano a tre voci di Thomaso Cimello da Napoli*   CimCH
   - b) Giovanni Domenico da Nola [b. ca. 1510-1520]
     - (1) His music was published in two volumes   CarCV I, 148
       - (a) *Canzone villanesche de Don Ioan Domenico del Giovane de Nola, a tre voci novamente ristampate. Libro primo 1545*   CarCV II, 2
         - i) This is a reprint of the first book of the 1541 edition by Scotto   PirM, 178
         - ii) It was published in Venice by Antonio Gardano   PirM, 178
         - iii) There are seven *mascherate* in this source   CarCV I, 148
         - iv) A facsimile of *Canzone villanesche...Libro primo*   NolC I
       - (b) *Canzone villanesche de Don Ioan Domenico del Giovane de Nola, a tre voci novamente ristampate Libro secundo 1545*   CarCV II, 2
         - i) This is a reprint of the second book of the 1541 edition by Scotto   PirM, 178

		ii)	It was published in Venice by Antonio Gardano	PirM, 178
		iii)	There are four *mascherate* in this source	CarCV I, 148
		iv)	These compositions are for three voices	PirM, 178
		v)	A facsimile of *Canzone villanesche...Libro secundo*	NolC II

5. The Neapolitan *mascherate* for three voices by Nola were arranged by Willaert, Donato, and Perissone   CarCV I, 151
    a) Adrian Willaert [b. ca. 1490]
        (1) There is one *mascherata* in [*Canzone villanesche alla napolitana di M. Adriano Wigliaret a quattro voci...*]   CarCV I, 150
            (a) This was published by Scotto in 1544   CarCV II, 2
            (b) The piece is an arrangement of *Cingari simo* by Nola
                i) A transcription of the Willaert arrangement   CarA, no. 3
            (c) A facsimile of the 1548 edition of *Canzone villanesche alla napolitana di M. Adriano Wigliaret a quattro voci...*   WilCV
    b) Baldassare Donato [b. ca. 1529]
        (1) There is one *mascherata* in [*Di Baldissera Donato il primo libro di canzon villanesche alla napolitana a quatro voci...*]   CarCV I, 150
            (a) This was published by Gardane in 1550   CarCV II, 6
            (b) The piece is an arrangement of *Chi la gagliarda* by Nola
            (c) A facsimile of *Di Baldissera Donato il primo libro di canzon villanesche alla napolitana a quatro voci...*   GarDI
    c) Perissone Cambio [b. ca. 1520]
        (1) Nine of the twenty-one pieces in [*Canzone villanesche alla napolitana a quatro voci di Perissone novamente poste in luce...*] are *mascherate*   CarCV I, 150
            (a) They were published in Venice by Gardano in 1545   CarCV II, 4
            (b) Five of the pieces can be traced to three-voice compositions by Nola   CarCV I, 191
                i) *Madonna noi sapimo ben giocare*
                ii) *Medici noi siamo o belle donne*
                iii) *O anime devot'in caritate*
                iv) *Tri ciechi siamo povr'inamorati*
                v) *Veniteve a pigliare la candelora*

G. English Secular Music

1. Introduction
    a) During this period, in England, music was remarkably difficult to define in terms of time and place   CarSV, 147
        (1) There was a flexible approach to context, function, genre, and medium
            (a) The tendency was to adapt and arrange, even to translate pieces from one setting to another
            (b) Part songs may be mixed in with pieces for lute and keyboard, as well as favorite poems, recipes, and anecdotes   CarSV, 148
        (2) Pieces that can be limited to specific contexts are surprisingly few
            (a) Such instability was partly due to the absence of print
            (b) Music printing in England was relatively insignificant until the late

                1580s
            (c) Written part-music could only be afforded by the few until Eliza-
                bethan times   SteMP, 8
        b) By 1530 the carol and secular song were more widely cultivated as household
            music   HarEP, 348
            (1) But with the onset of the Reformation, the medieval carol died out
                                                                    SteMP, 8
                (a) "The last collection of 'medieval' carols appeared in the mid-six-
                    teenth century"   SteMP, 47
                    i) This is the only printed set to survive
        c) Secular court polyphony in forms other than the carol began to appear during
            the early Tudor period   HarEP, 346
            (1) "The royal court in London nurtured an international French style"
                                                                    JosJ, 167
                (a) The roots of this style lay in medieval chivalry and courtly pas-
                    times
                (b) The French style remained the mark of elegant breeding and gen-
                    tility until the 1540s at which time it was superseded by Italian
                    artists and ideas
                (c) But a few Franco-Flemish *chansons* with only the opening words
                    have been found   HarEP, 347
                    i) During the 1540s and 1550s, continental *chansons* seem to
                        have reached England with some regularity   CarSV, 163
                        a - Their influence on the English *song* is evident in the four-
                            part writing and in the use of both clear homophony and
                            imitation   CarSV, 164
                    ii) There are two sources available that help trace the *chanson*
                        through the 1540s and 1550s   CarSV, 164
                        a - London, Public Record Office, S.P.1 (Henry VIII), vol.
                            246
                            1 - This was copied ca. 1540-1550   HamCC II, 117
                            2 - It contains one motet, two anthems, one English Latin
                                sacred piece, twenty English secular songs, and one
                                French secular song   HamCC II, 117
                        b - *The Mulliner Book* (British Library, *MS. Add. 30513*)
                                                                    CarSV, 10
                            1 - This was copied ca. 1545 and 1560
                            2 - It contains mostly pre-Reformation liturgical organ
                                works but also some keyboard arrangements of
                                secular vocal music that are *unica*
                            3 - A facsimile of *The Mulliner Book* MulA
                            4 - A transcription of *The Mulliner Book* SteMB

    2. The general style of secular vocal music in England
        a) It is possible to say many obvious and important things about the style of the
            music without much reference to the words   SteMP, 100
        b) But, in one fundamental respect, the words and notes of the early Tudor
            songs cannot be considered separately   SteMP, 101
            (1) This is due to the fact that the musical form is derived from the poem

(a) Composers were mostly interested in the poetic shape and only occasionally in the physical qualities of the words   SteMP, 116
c) The texts and music
- (1) Only a small fraction of the texts that were written are found with music   SteMP, 8
- (2) There are three main groups of poems that were set to music   JosJ, 167
  - (a) Carols
    - i) The texts of the carols deal with religious and moral subjects
      - a - Texts might be contemplative, courtly, or political   RanH, 141
    - ii) The music of the carol, in the early sixteenth century, was composed in elaborate polyphony and in increasingly varied forms   RanH, 141
      - a - New music often was composed for successive verses
    - iii) Some of the music was set in strongly accented triple meter, with syncopated treble voices supported by harmonies of thirds and sixths
      - a - But some of the music has greater rhythmic variety and contrapuntal complexity in prevailing duple meter, with the texts treated with considerable sensitivity
    - iv) At the time of the Reformation in England, motet-like compositions began to replace the polyphonic carol   RanH, 141
  - (b) Political and topical poems   JosJ, 167
    - i) Poems written for specific occasions or as poetic trivia
    - ii) Judging from the surviving verses [and music], the poet, and doubtless the musician also, did his best to make an excellent contribution in his own art   SteMP, 110
      - a - There was not too much regard for his companion craftsman
  - (c) Love lyrics   JosJ, 167
    - i) They contain chivalric subjects such as absence, parting, and service to the lover
      - a - These texts are often in the rhyme royal strophe (ababbcc) derived from the *ballade*
        - 1 - Rhyme royal verses are usually short and feature the foot and syllable system   JosJ, 168
      - b - Some love lyrics follow an older tradition of prosody
    - ii) The music is shaped by the poem   JosJ, 168
      - a - It features equal voices, balanced phrases, and strong duple meter
    - iii) The music follows the poet's conception of style as adornment and decoration
      - a - One distinctive musical pattern predominates
        - 1 - A line of text begins on a simple "point"
        - 2 - The "point" is introduced by the voices in imitation   JosJ, 168
        - 3 - The imitation is developed in rhythmic intensity until it breaks out in a contrapuntal melisma leading to a cadence   JosJ, 168

English Secular Music   441

3. Manuscript sources of secular songs
   a) London, Public Record Office, S.P.1 (Henry VIII), vol. 246   CarSV, 164
      (1) This is a bass partbook that can be reconstructed, more or less, from concordances in other fragmentary sources
      (2) It contains twenty-five songs, many of which are *unica*
      (3) Some of the pieces have texts throughout while others have only text incipits
   b) British Library, *MS Add. 30513* (*The Mulliner Book*)   CarSV, 10
      (1) This source was copied mainly between ca. 1545 and 1560
      (2) It contains keyboard transcriptions of part songs   CarSV, 164
         (a) Four such pieces show clearly the styles of the English part song
            i) *Benedicam Domino* by Robert Johnson
               a - A transcription   SteMB, 62
            ii) *My friends the things that do*
               a - A transcription   SteMB, 50
            iii) *O happy dames* by John Sheppard
               a - A transcription   SteMB, 81
            iv) *The bitter swete that straynes my yeldid hart*, also by John Sheppard
               a - A transcription   SteMB, 83
         (b) It also contains transcriptions of many other pieces by English composers of the period such as Tallis (18), and Sheppard (8)
            SteMBC, 19
            i) Four of these by Tallis are secular part songs   DoeT, 69
            ii) There is also a transcription of music by Taverner (1)
               SteMB, 30
   c) London: British Museum *MS. K.1.e.1.*   HanJ, 119
      (1) This manuscript contains a bass partbook from a set of four
      (2) It contains secular vocal polyphony by a group of early Tudor composers
      (3) It was printed in London in 1530 under the title *XX Songes*
   d) London: Westminster Abbey Library   HanJ, 119
      (1) This contains three fragments of the treble and meane partbooks of London: British Museum, *MS. K.1.e.1.*
   e) New York: New York Public Library, Drexel MSS. 4180-5   SteMP, 426
      (1) This is a set of seventeenth-century partbooks
      (2) In the binding are several fragments of early Tudor songs and instrumental pieces
      (3) There are words and music to *The bella, the bella* by Taverner in a flyleaf preceding the main body of NYpl, *Drexel 4184*   JosJ, 181
         (a) NYpl *4184/1* and *NYpl Drexel 4184/2b* have words and music for the meane voice
         (b) NYpl, Music Division, *Drexel 4184/2a* has words and music for a treble voice
   f) New York: New York Public Library, *Drexel 4143 (Quintus)*   SteMP, 426
      (1) The flyleaf contains fragments of the treble voice of *The bella, the bella* by Taverner   JosJ, 181

4. Printed sources of secular music
   a) *XX Songes ix of iiii partes and xi of thre partes*   HarEP, 348

(1) This is a printed copy of London: British Museum *MS. K.1.e.1.*
    HanJ, 119
    (a) It was printed in London in 1530   HanJ, 95
    (b) This was the first attempt at printing mensural polyphony in
        England   JosJ, 189
(2) This source originally comprised four small partbooks   HanJ, 95
    (a) All that has survived is the bass partbook   SteMP, 7
        i) It is found in the British Museum, *MS. K. 1. e. 1.*
                                                      HarEP, fn. 1, 348
    (b) The *tenor* part-book has been lost altogether DarI, 135
    (c) Only the title pages of the *triplex* and *medius* are known DarI, 135
        i) The first page of the *triplex* is found in the British Museum,
           MS. K. 1. e. 1.   HarEP, fn. 1, 348
        ii) The first and last pages of the *medius* are in the Westminster
            Abbey library   HarEP, fn. 1, 348
    (d) There is one piece from this book found complete in a contem-
        porary manuscript   DarI, 135
(3) The list of composers and repertory indicates that it was a compilation
    of music composed during the period ca. 1505-1520   JosJ, 194
(4) For facsimiles of the contents *see*   ReeC
(5) An example of the opening bass part of one song   RokI, 421

H. Solo Song

1. Introduction
    a) A typical solo song would be an arrangement with the top part sung as a solo
       to an instrumental accompaniment consisting of two or all three of the lower
       parts   ForS, 125
    b) The solo song also was an art of improvisation ForS, 125
        (1) Since improvised music rarely survives, the music discussed here repre-
            sents perhaps not even a half of that known at the time
    c) There were not a large number of songs composed expressly as solos until the
       end of the century except for the songs of the Spanish *vihuelistas* ForS, 125

2. German solo song
    a) The German *Meistergesang*
        (1) It contained no independent musical meters, but rather free declamation
            based on speech rhythms   RanH, 479
            (a) Both the melodies and poetic strophes of the *Meistergesang* are
                typically in bar form
                i) Together they constitute a model, or *Ton*, for the production
                   of other songs
        (2) The *Meistergesang* was used as a means of educating lower- and middle
            class audiences in matters both religious and secular RanH, 479
            (a) Scholars have found similarities between the *Meistergesang* melody
                and bar form on the one hand and Lutheran chorales on the other
        (3) The *Meistergesang* gradually moved eastward from the Rhine during the
            fifteenth and sixteenth centuries   SalE, 365

    (a) "The Slavs did not adopt it, however, and even in central Germany it was confined to a few of the larger cities, among which Strasbourg, Augsburg, Nuremberg, and Ulm became important centres"
      i) So the *Meistergesang* remained historically insignificant
    (b) Hans Sachs was one of the most outstanding figures of this period
      i) He composed all his thirteen *Töne* before 1530   RanH, 479
        a - After that, his preoccupation was the faithful propagation of Luther's Bible in *Meistergesang* and drama
  (4) But due to the fact that mannerism and spiritual barrenness of the form spread so widely, the *Meistergesang* may be considered to have died out by the middle of the sixteenth century   SalE, 365

3. Spanish solo song
 a) Introduction
  (1) Music printing in Spain during the sixteenth century was not the flourishing trade found in France and Italy   ForS, 126
    (a) There was no printer who devoted himself exclusively to the printing of music
  (2) Seventeen volumes of music are known to have been published during the entire century   ForS, 126
    (a) Seven of the surviving volumes of music include songs for solo voice   ForS, 127
      i) They were published between 1536 and 1576
      ii) The songs were accompanied by the *vihuela de mano*
    (b) Four of the seven volumes were published before 1550   ForS, 127
      i) *Libro de música de vihuela de mano intitulado El Maestro*
        a - This was by Luis Milán and was published in Valencia in 1536
        b - It consists of music by Milán only   ForS, 128
        c - It is secular and Spanish in character and it set the pattern so far as secular song is concerned
        d - "Apart from the sonnets, the solo songs consist of twelve *villancicos* and four *romances,* two of the principal Spanish song-forms"   ForS, 128
        e - In Milán's sonnets, musical and poetic phrases do not always coincide   ForS, 129
          1 - Musical phrases to new lines are repeated in no particular order
        f - A facsimile of *Libro de música de vihuela de mano intitulado El Maestro*   MilL
        g - A transcription of *Libro de música de vihuela de mano intitulado El Maestro*   MilLM
      ii) *Los seys libros del Delphin de música*
        a - This was by Luis de Narváez and was published in Valladolid in 1538
        b - A reprint edition of *Los seys libros del Delphin de música*   NavD
      iii) *Tres libros de música*
        a - This was by Alonso de Mudarra and was published in

Seville in 1546
- b - This includes a handful of Latin songs, Spanish and Italian sonnets and *canciones* ForS, 128
  - 1 - The *canciones* are through-composed and are the closest parallels in the *vihuela* books to early Italian madrigals ForS, 129
- iv) *Libro de música de vihuela intitulado Silva de Sirenas*
  - a - This was by Enrique Enríquez de Valderrábano and was published in Valladolid in 1547
  - b - It contains sacred and secular music, original and arranged, and is completely cosmopolitan ForS, 128
- (c) The four volumes contain vocal music as well as music for instruments
  - i) The last three sources include solo arrangements of ensemble music, motets, and Mass-sections by Flemish, French, Italian, and Spanish composers
  - ii) Many of the apparently original songs in these books are possibly arrangements of no longer extant polyphonic, or even instrumental, originals ForS, 128
    - a - This is true except in Milán's and Mudarra's books
- b) The music of the Spanish solo song ForS, 129
  - (1) The vocal lines of the songs are divided into well-defined phrases that correspond to the lines of the text
    - (a) They are in long note values against polyphonic, instrumental backgrounds
      - i) The backgrounds are occasionally chordal or decorative
  - (2) *Villancicos*
    - (a) Introduction
      - i) It was in this group of songs that court and city art met in a form that charmed all classes ForS, 135
      - ii) The poetry could be of an historical nature ForS, 135
        - a - "They might pay homage to a city or important personage or comment upon trivial incidents at court"
        - b - But love was the most popular subject of all
    - (b) The poetry of the *villancico*
      - i) It consists "of a refrain (*estribillo*) that alternates with one or more strophes (coplas or pies), each of which is made up of a *mudanza* (change, *i.e.*, of rhyme) and a *vuelta* (return, *i.e.*, to the rhyme of the refrain)" RanH, 912
      - ii) The number of lines and the number of syllables to a line in the traditional scheme vary from song to song ForS, 136
    - (c) The music of the *villancico* ForS, 135
      - i) It is typically Spanish in feeling
      - ii) It is of a popular vein rather than folk music
      - iii) The *estribello* (the first section) is sung to a melody that is modified for the *vuelto* (the second section) ForS, 136
      - iv) The last section carries the original melody with the last line being in the nature of a refrain ForS, 136
      - v) This pattern often results in monotony ForS, 136

                    a - Sometimes the first phrase of the *vuelta* is sufficiently
                        different in order to appear as the logical continuation
                        of what has gone before, giving the song greater momentum
            vi) An example of elements of both styles is found in *Agora
                viniesse un viento*, see   ForS, 136
    (3) The *Romance*
        (a) The melodies are usually somber, solemn, and a little remote
                                                                            ForS, 130
            i) They are seldom lyrical
        (b) Melodic fragments found in Spanish folk music are included
                                                                            ForS, 130
        (c) The most common practice was to write music for only one verse
            of a *romance* such as those found in *Los seys libros del Delphin de
            música*   ForS, 131
            i) In *Tres libros de música*, accompaniments are provided for
                two verses
                a - In *Durmiendo yva el Señor*, the verses are linked by polyphonic treatment of the melody on the *vihuela*
                    1 - A transcription of *Durmiendo yva el Señor* MudT, 53
                    b - A transcription of *Tres libros de música*   MudTL
        (d) The *cantus-fermus*-like treatment of the popular melodies in *Tres
            libros de música* and *Libro de música de vihuela intitulado Silva
            de Sirenas* are rounded off with long, expressive cadences on the
            vihuela under pedal points in the vocal parts   ForS, 131

4. French solo song
    a) There is a collection of music for lute combining an opening group of five
        preludes with intabulations of pieces from the primarily secular vocal repertory
                                                                            PerMR, 782
        (1) It is found in *Tres breve et familiere introduction pour entendre &?
            apprendre par soy mesmes a jouer toutes chansons reduictes en la
            tabulature du lutz* (Paris 1529)   PerMR, 782, fn. 13
        (2) Forty of the compositions are for lute alone and twenty-four have been
            arranged for voice with lute accompaniment   PerMR, 782
            (a) The twenty-four compositions were transcribed by an anonymous
                musician from contemporary *chansons*   ReeMR, 557
                i) Eight originals have been identified as by Claudin
                ii) These are only slightly altered in the transcriptions except
                    for the occasional addition of slight figuration in one part or
                    another
            (b) An embellished style of playing governed in large measure the treatment of the vocal models   PerMR, 819
                i) Chordal sonorities of the vocal version are linked with a continuous filigree of running passage work
                ii) The polyphonic fabric is thinned, generally reducing four
                    parts to three
                    a - This was done except when the slower strumming of
                        full chords made fuller sonorities easier to manage

iii) For an example of this *see* Claudin's *Tant que vivray*
                           PerMR, 821
 (c) A transcription of the works for voice and lute   AttCL
 (d) A transcription of *Tres breve et familiere introduction...* HeaPC

I. Art Song

1. Introduction
   a) The art song is different from most folk and popular songs in that it includes an accompaniment that is specified by a composer rather than being improvised or arranged by and for the performer   RanH, 56
      (1) The texts of these songs are of high literary quality   RanH, 56

2. The metrical ode
   a) Introduction
      (1) Toward the end of the fifteenth century, humanism was introduced into Germany   ReeMR, 705
      (2) One of its chief founders was Konrad Celtes   ReeMR, 705
         (a) "To help his pupils learn the nineteen meters of Horace's odes and epodes and other Latin metrical patterns, Celtes had one of his students, Petrus Tritonius (=Peter Treibenreif), set representative Latin poems to music"
            i) Tritonius' setting was written in four parts, moving in block chords, with the note-values faithfully reflecting the longs and shorts of the text meters
   b) So a branch of the Latin lyric poetry, *i.e.* the metrical ode, was brought into being in the sixteenth century for didactic reasons   SalE, 370
      (1) Its sphere of influence was almost entirely restricted to the universities
         (a) "The odes were taken up in the Latin school-dramas that were presented throughout the German-speaking countries during the sixteenth century"   ReeMR, 705
            i) It has been thought that they may have served as a connecting link between the polyphonic songs of the beginning of the century and the chordal pieces of the end
      (2) The ode is a lyric poem of considerable length and complexity
                                    RanH, 558
         (a) The Latin odes of Horace consist of regular strophes in a few meters
      (3) The music was written in note-against-note chordal style SalE, 371
         (1) The melody was usually in the treble
         (2) The music was composed with deliberate simplicity with the emphasis placed on good declamation and pregnant themes
      (4) The odes were set polyphonically in four-voice settings by several Renaissance composers   RanH, 558
         (a) Some of the well known composers were Ludwig Senfl, Paul Hofhaimer, Wolfgang Greffinger, and Joachim Burck SalE, 371
            i) They composed during the first half of the sixteenth century
            ii) "Their influence extended as far as Cracow and Transylvania"

3. Court songs (*Hofweisen*) in Germany
   a) After 1500, well-known composers began to show their skill in writing court tunes and popular songs of an urban character SalE, 374
      (1) The songs were developed in four- and five-part polyphony in a style showing them to be a product of the cultured class SalE, 374
      (2) Most of the tenors in the polyphonic songs are so-called *Hofweisen* GudG, 99
         (a) The words of *Hofweisen* are different from those of the popular song
            i) They are restricted to a few subjects which lean to the didactic and moralizing
            ii) But they have spontaneity and a wealth of content
            iii) The verse structure is formal
         (b) The music of *Hofweisen* is distinguishable from the popular song by a wide melodic range, a certain melodic formality such as specific modes or keys, and by a preference for the Bar form [AAB] GudG, 100
      (3) An example of the *Hofweise* is the tenor, *Ohn Ehr und Gunst,* used and perhaps invented by Forster GudG, 100
         (a) A transcription of *Ohn Ehr und Gunst* ForF, 27

4. The tenor-song [*Gesellschaftslied*]
   a) Introduction
      (1) The German song was a decisive part in German music in the sixteenth century GudG, 98
      (2) It consisted almost exclusively of either polyphonic treatments of existing melodies or of free polyphonic compositions GudG, 96
         (a) More than 1,500 examples of polyphonic songs on tenor *canti firmi* have come down to us GudG, 98
      (3) Songbooks were issued between 1534 and 1556 by printers, publishers, and collectors GudG, 98
         (a) Between 1534 and 1545 there were two collections published by Johann Ott (236 songs); the first two parts of the *Frische teutsche Liedlein* published by Georg Forster (380 songs); the song books of Egenolff, Formschneider, and Schöffer-Apiarius; *bicinia* and *tricinia* published by Georg Rhaw; and quodlibets by Wolfgang Schmeltzl GudG, 99
   b) The tenor-song was perhaps the most essentially German creation GudG, 97
      (1) It was a peculiarly German form SalE, 373
         (a) It was influenced by Netherland imitation as well as the Italian *frottola* GudG, 97
         (b) It reached its culmination ca. 1530 GudG, 96
            (a) But it remained current until after 1550 SalE, 373
      (2) It was a song for the educated classes--the nobility, the clergy, and members of the learned professions ReeMR, 636
   d) The tenor-song was "often indistinguishable in style and idiom from the Protestant *Lieder* written during the same period and by many of the same composers" ReeMR, 707
      (1) But the large majority of these songs are love songs

e) There are chordal pieces, found at all stages of the development of the tenor-song GudG, 101
    (1) Only the tenor was underlaid with text GudG, 101
        (a) Two or more instruments played around it SalE, 373
            i) As a solo song, it was usually characterized by expressive, vigorously individual and fluid rhythm
        (b) After 1530, the instruments were sometimes replaced with voices SalE, 373
            i) These voices were provided with words and occasionally reshaped in order to make them suitable for singing GudG, 101
f) The *cantus firmus* is either a popular song or art song SalE, 373
    (1) Only a minority are taken from popular song GudG, 99
        (a) The most prominent collection of popular songs is found in the second book of *Liedlein* by Forster GudG, 100
            i) This contains a repertoire of students' songs
            ii) A transcription of the second book of *Liedlein* by Forster ForFT
        (b) Senfl showed a marked preference for popular song GudG, 100
            i) Examples are found in Hans Otts' *Liederbuch* of 1534 SenDL
            ii) A transcription of the *Lieder* by Senfl SenDL

5. Free polyphonic compositions in Germany [song motets]
    a) Introduction
        (1) The tenor song reached its culmination ca. 1530 GudG, 96
            (a) Song-production by native composers decreased considerably and the Netherlanders in Germany took over GudG, 97
                i) As a result, the tenor song was greatly influenced, in regard to polyphonic texture, by the first and second generation of Netherlanders, who, through Heinrich Isaac made an impact on German song SalE, 374
            (b) The Netherlanders employed not only the technique of the motet, but also elements of the *chanson*, madrigal, and *villanella* in the setting of German texts GudG, 97
                i) This new style was foreshadowed before the end of the tenor-song period GudG, 102
        (2) From about 1530 onward, pieces in more than four parts begin to appear GudG, 101
            (a) Four-part writing remains the general rule, but in Senfl and Brandt the number of parts is often increased
                i) This is particularly notable in the simultaneous quodlibets which combine several tunes
                ii) But, the successive quodlibets, where the same text is used in all voices, keep generally to four voices
        (3) A more homogeneous texture produced by means of imitation gradually replaced the free handling of the added parts in tenor songs GudG, 101
            (a) This was also accomplished by the pairing of voice parts
        (4) After 1536, all voices were provided with words and occasionally reshaped in order to make them suitable for singing GudG, 101

- b) At first, with this change of style, tendencies foreign to the *Lied* proper predominated   GudG, 97
  - (1) One such tendency was the adoption of procedures derived from the motet
    - (a) The song melody is completely broken up in the manner of the motet, the melody and phrases are repeated, sometimes with transposition, and free interpolations are made   GudG, 102
  - (2) But actually the motet and song are opposed in principle   GudG, 97
    - (a) The very essence of the motet is the repetition of phrases or single words which disturb the symmetry
      - i) While "the essential features of the 'song' (in the narrowest sense) are the formal coincidence of the melody with a symmetrically designed text and the setting of a number of strophes to a single melody"
    - (b) Also, a continuously composed text is far more suited to the motet than the strophic principle
  - (3) This transition from a song with *cantus firmus* to a song motet was effected not in the field of *Hofweise* arrangements but on the basis of the popular song   GudG, 102
    - (a) Composers of the *Hofweise* were conservative
      - i) They were careful to maintain the congruence of text and *cantus firmus*
    - (b) It was the composers of the popular song who treated the material much more freely
  - (4) An example of a free polyphonic composition [song motet] is *Wohl auf* found in the second part of Forster's *Frische teutsche Lieden*
    - (a) A transcription of *Frische teutsche Lieden*   ForFT

6. The German polyphonic *Lied* reached its highest point and its end with Senfl
    ReeMR, 708
  - a) Senfl had a wide range of styles from the simple note-against-note setting to fully developed imitations from three to six parts   SalE, 375
    - (1) But syllabic setting based on verbal stress is most marked in his work
    - (2) As a composer who could add parts according to the laws of art, he is distinguished by fullness of sound and delight in color
  - (a) He also had a masterly treatment of ornamentation
    - (3) At times, he used quodlibet-like combinations of several basic tunes
  - b) His secular *Lieder* are noteworthy   ReeMR, 707
    - (1) They show his mastery of the Franco-Netherlandish contrapuntal style along with a gift for a warm, flowing melody
    - (2) A good example is Senfl's setting of *Wol kumpt der May* for four voices   ReeMR, 708
      - (a) The main melody is in the tenor and is anticipated a fifth lower in the bass while fragments of the melody appear in the other voices
      - (b) Toward the end there is a melisma
      - (c) A transcription of *Wol kumpt der May*   SenDL
    - (3) Another good example is Senfl's *Das gleut zu Speier*
      - (a) It is one of the strongest dominant-tonic monuments of the sixteenth century

        (b) Senfl paints a delightful picture of pealing bells
        (c) A transcription of *Das gleut zu Speier*   SchGUT
    (4) Transcriptions of Senfl's German *Lieder*   SenD; SenDL

7. Sources of German *Lieder*
    a) Johann Ott's first collection is titled *121 neue Lieder*   ReeMR, 706
        (1) This was published at Nuremberg in 1534 by Formschneider
        (2) It contains music by three composers--Senfl, Arnoldus de Bruck, and Wilhelm Breitengraser as well as a few anonymous pieces
            (a) There are eighty-two songs by Senfl   GudG, 99
        (3) The text is provided only for the parts that are presumably meant to be sung   ReeMR, 707
        (4) A transcription of *Lieder* by Senfl taken from *121 neue Lieder*   SenDL
    b) The *Gassenhawerlin und Reutterliedlin* was issued from the press of Christian Egenolff at Frankfurt on the Main in 1535   ReeMR, 706
        (1) In this collection, the text is supplied presumably only for those voices that are meant to be sung   ReeMR, 707
        (2) A facsimile of *Gassenhawerlin und Reutterliedlin*   EgeG
        (3) A transcription of a collection of songs from three publications of 1535, 1536, and 1544 by Egenolff   EgeA
    c) *Fünff und sechzig teütscher Lieder, vormals imm Truck nie ussgangen* was published by Schöffer & Apiarius in 1536 at Strasbourg   ReeMR, 706
        (1) A facsimile of *Fünff und sechzig teütscher Lieder*   SchFS
    d) The *Frische teutsche Liedlein* brought out by Georg Forster from 1539 to 1556 has five parts   ReeMR, 706
        (1) All the voices in these collections are furnished with text   ReeMR, 707
        (2) There are 380 songs in the first two collections [1539 and 1540]   GudG, 99
        (3) The first part of *Frische teutsche Liedlein* contains many of the same composers as found in Ott's collections
            (a) There are also compositions by Lorenz Lemlin, Othmayr, Jobst vom Brandt, Stephan Zirler, and Forster himself   ReeMR, 707
                i) These composers were members of the "Heidelberg school"
            (b) A facsimile of *Frische teutsche Liedlein* (1st part)   ForE
            (c) A transcription of *Frische teutsche Liedlein* (1st part)   ForF
        (4) Popular song is most prominent in the second collection of the *Liedlein*   GudG, 100
            (a) But the *Liedlein* belongs to a different category since it presents a repertoire of students' songs
            (b) More than half of the compositions are anonymous   GudG, 99
            (c) This collection, in many respects, is the most modern collection of the period   GudG, 102
            (d) A transcription of *Frische teutsche Liedlein* (the 2nd part)   ForFT
    e) Johann Ott's second collection, *Mehrstimmiges deutsches Liederbuch* was published in 1544   EitE II
        (1) This second set contains 115 compositions   ReeMR, 706
        (2) It contains works in French, Latin, and Italian   ReeMR, 706
            (a) These are by Crécquillon, Gombert, Richafort, and Verdelot
        (3) There are a few religious pieces   ReeMR, 706

(4) The German *Lieder* are by Senfl, Isaac, Stolzer, Bruck, Dietrich, and others ReeMR, 706
    (a) There are sixty-four by Senfl GudG, 99
(5) A transcription of *Mehrstimmiges deutsches Liederbuch* EitE II
f) The *Liederbuch* by Wolfgang Schmeltzl of 1544 [*Guter, seltzamer, und künstreicher teutscher Gesang...*] ReeMR, 707
(1) This contains the first considerable collection of quodlibets in Germany
(2) A facsimile of *Guter, seltzamer, und künstreicher teutscher Gesang...* SchGU
(3) A transcription of one of the quodlibets SchG, 110
(4) Transcriptions of most of the quodlibets EitD
(5) A transcription of *Guter, seltzamer, und künstreicher teutscher Gesang...* SchGUT
g) The earliest example of a collection comprising only works by a single composer is *Reutterische und Jegerische Liedlein* by Caspar Othmayr GudG, 99
(1) It was published in Nuremberg in 1549
(2) Othmayr's songs are more advanced in some respects than most ReeMR, 707
    (a) He is perhaps the first composer to publish a complete cycle of songs as an independent work
(3) A transcriptin of *Reutterische und Jegerische Liedlein* OthR

J. The Ceremonial Motet

1. Introduction
   a) During this period the motet witnessed a remarkable flowering RanH, 511
      (1) The repertory is so vast and varied that it has not been catalogued
   b) It was generally understood to be a polyphonic setting of a sacred Latin text RanH, 511
   c) But, there were settings of secular Latin texts drawn from Classical poetry or newly composed texts to honor a person or event RanH, 511
      (1) In these motets, greater attention is given to the intelligibility of the text PerMR, 531
         (a) This may have been due to the fact that the verses expressly written to mark occasions of state were necessarily unfamiliar to the intended audience, yet they depended to a degree for their effect upon a fundamental grasp of their meaning
         (b) They are often characterized by clear declamation of individual words, careful observance and articulation of syntactic units, changes in rhythm and/or texture to give declaratory emphasis to key elements of the text

2. Composers of the ceremonial motet
   a) Adrian Willaert
      (1) *Quid non ebrietas designat* LowAW, 681
         (a) This was written ca. 1519 ManI, 285
         (b) The composition is a secular, humanistically inspired motet
            i) It may be considered as an example of mannerist striving for

| | | bizarre rhetoric in music | ManI, 287 |
| | ii) | It circulated for years as a "chromatic duo" | ManI, 285 |

(c) It is a setting of an Epistle by Horace, Book I, 5; verse 16: "What a miracle cannot the wine-cup work" — ReeMR, 369
   - i) But the text is humorous — ManI, 286
(d) It was described by Spataro, in a letter to Aaron in 1524, as a puzzle piece — ManI, 286
   - i) In its notated form, the duo ends on a seventh
     - a - The seventh has been preceded by an enigmatic series of dissonant intervals
   - ii) In performance, the composition ended on an octave — ReeMR, 369
(e) The key to the composition lies in the tenor part — ManI, 286
   - i) The tenor part begins in the Dorian mode once transposed
   - ii) It then starts down the familiar path of flat mutation
     - a - In order to be sure there will be no mistake, Willaert writes in the cumulative accidentals from E♭ to C♭
       - 1 - This last *fictum* was unheard of even in the most progressive hexachord systems of the time (except for that of Spataro)
   - iii) The *ficta* rule that leaps of fourths and fifths must be perfect forces the tenor first to f-flat and then into the realms of double flats — AtlR, 402
   - iv) At this point, the written accidentals suddenly disappear
     - a - The singers are supposed to take C♭ as a signal to continue the circle-of-fifths by applying even more abnormal *ficta* to the last half of the tenor, *i.e*, F♭, B♭♭, and so on up to C♭♭
     - b - Thus Willaert has gone through the full circle back to the B♭
     - c - As a result, the final note in the tenor, which appears to be e, is in fact an e-double-flat and sounds as a d, making the two voices end on an octave — AtlR, 402
   - v) Willaert needed a double flat at a time when the sign was not yet in existence — ReeMR, 370
     - a - So, without a double flat, he wrote certain notes a semitone higher than they were to be performed — ReeMR, 370
(f) It is thought that Willaert based his duo on the Aristoxenian doctrine — LowAW, 690
   - i) That is, Aristoxenus' theory that each tone is divisible into two equal half tones and six whole tones make one octave — LowAW, 685
   - ii) Only if Willaert's duo is performed in a tuning of equal temperament will the end of the composition circle back to the beginning
(g) This motet helped set tonal expansion in motion — AtlR, 402
   - i) It was revolutionary on three counts
     - a - The gamut was extended until it was bent into a circle
     - b - It produced questions concerning tuning and tempera-

ment
- 1 - Enharmonic equivalents were incompatible with Pythagorean tuning
- c - It brought into question the meaning of accidental signs
  - 1 - Accidental signs no longer functioned only as signals for the solmization syllables *mi* and *fa*
  - 2 - They were beginning to be used as they are used today, *i.e.*, indications to raise or lower a note's pitch
- (h) This duo is probably a clever jest ReeMR, 370
  - i) Willaert probably was trying to tease and confuse musicians who were much occupied with the measuring of intervals
  - ii) His reference to Horace was undoubtedly intended to accuse performers of being befuddled because they had partaken too freely of the wine-cup
  - iii) An example of a few measures of *Quid non ebrietas* AtlR, 402
- (i) Finally, it has been concluded that the famous duo was actually a quartet LowAW, 697
  - i) An alto part has been found that matches the two parts of the discant and tenor LowAW, 693
    - a - This produces a three-part version clearly in need of a fourth part which is missing LowAW, 694
    - b - With help from the alto part it is possible to reconstruct the bass
  - ii) Therefore, there is little doubt that Willaert originally intended *Quid non ebrietas* to be a quartet
- (j) The composition is an ingenious harmonic invention that Willaert contrived in order to cushion shock of the continued false relations resulting from the tenor's circumnavigation of the circle of fifths while the other voices stay "at home" LowAW, 697
- (k) A transcription of *Quid non ebrietas* LowAW, 694

(2) The *Musica nova*
- (a) It is thought that the *Musica nova* was written in a period previous to 1545 CarMN, 201
  - i) Some of the pieces were written in the 1540s AtlR, 406
- (b) It was published in 1559 WilO, V
  - i) By Antonio Gardano AtlR, 406
- (c) It is a collection of motets and madrigals CarMN, 200
  - i) Both are represented by four, five, six, and seven voice compositions
  - ii) There are thirty-three motets ManI, 291
    - a - They are rife with pro-republican sentiments AtlR, 406
    - b - They may have been written primarily for the colony of Florentine exiles residing in Venice AtlR, 406
- (d) It is in the motet writing that the changing musical climate of Venice in the sixteenth century becomes noticeable RedV, 285
  - i) Some are for S.A.B.T., some are for two altos or two tenors, and a few point towards chromaticism and expressiveness in the sense of Cipriano de Rore

              ii) The music has a dark and melancholy color
                  a - This is a contrast to the music of the younger Venetian composers
              iii) "The theoretical substructure of the *Musica nova* is decidedly formed of progressive elements"   CarMN, 205
                  a - The roots of strict diatonicism are cut and the ground for straight-forward chromaticism is prepared
          (e) Transcriptions of the motets   WilO, V
     b) Ludwig Senfl
          (1) A photocopy of some motets   SenS
          (2) Transcriptions of occasional motets   SenSM
     c) Clemens non Papa (Jacobus)
          (1) There are three secular motets with texts in praise of music   ReeMR, 352
              (a) An example of this is *Musica Dei donum*
                  i) An example of *Musica Dei donum*   ReeMR, 353
                  ii) A facsimile of *Musica Dei donum*   SusLTE
     d) Cipriano de Rore
          (1) He was known above all as a madrigal composer, but he also was one of the finest motet composers of the century   LowCR, 576
          (2) The *Venus Motet*   LowCR, 576
              (a) The text of this motet is one of several poems in a collection by Girolamo Falletti titled, *In pictura Annae principis Estensis* ("On a painting of Anna, Princess of Este")   LowCR, 585
                  i) It is a poem in praise of a Venus painting by Girolamo da Carpi, a great music lover
                  ii) The printed text of the poem   LowCR, 585
              (b) The musical setting of the poem is for five voices
                  i) It was published in Venice by Antonio Gardane, in the third book of his motets, in 1549
                      a - A facsimile of *Il terzo libro di motetti a cinque voci*   GarI
              (c) A transcription of *Hesperiae cum laeta* (the *Venus Motet*)   RorC I, 127
          (3) There are six Latin secular pieces by de Rore found in Munich: Bayerische Staatsbibliothek, Handschriften-Inkunabelabteilung. *Musica MS. B* (*olim Cim. 52*; = MaiM 128)   HamCC II, 232

Instrumental Music

A. Keyboard Music: Musical Forms

1. Imitative keyboard music
   a) At the beginning of the sixteenth century the evolution of instrumental motets or *chansons* for keyboard instruments began   ApeH, 165
      (1) These compositions appeared under the names of ricercar, canzona, *tiento* and fantasia
      (2) The Ricercar (Fr., It. *ricercare*; and Fr. *recherché*; It. *ricercata*; Ger. *Ricercar*; Sp. *recercario, recercada*)   RanH, 706
         (a) The term is derived from the Italian *cercare* meaning search   ApeH, 166
         (b) It was used in the sixteenth and seventeenth centuries to designate various species of composition that seem to have nothing in common with each other   ApeH, 166
            i) But all of these species represent various manifestations of a common principle which may be described by the concept of "examination" or "study" which corresponds to the literal meaning of the word ricercar
            ii) The study could have various goals such as being anticipatory, in the sense of a technical and spiritual preparation for the playing of an instrument
               a - "This seems to have been the original meaning of the ricercar"
            iii) Examples are found in the ricercars by Marco Antonio Cavazzoni (1523)
         (c) There were two varieties of ricercar existing concurrently   RanH, 706
            i) There was a rhapsodic type in homophonic texture and a polyphonic type that exploited learned contrapuntal artifices
            ii) During the sixteenth century, both types appear in German, English, Spanish, and French sources
               a - These pieces were titled respectively prelude, fancy, *tiento*, and fantasia
                  1 - These have sometimes served as etudes or studies

iii) The homophonic ricercar was a thin textured piece lacking formal organization and thematic unity
    a - Chords were mingled with running passage work as in an improvisation
    b - The homophonic ricercar was a more or less improvisational preparation or introduction   ApeH, 166
        1 - It was often attached to a following intabulation or dance   RanH, 706
        2 - But it does not always appear directly before the piece it was intended to introduce   RanH, 706
        3 - Nevertheless, it was often arranged and identified by mode or key   RanH, 706
    c - Examples of the homophonic ricercar are found in the works of Marco Antonio Cavazzoni   RanH, 706

iv) The polyphonic ricercar has been described as an instrumental counterpart to the motet
    a - It is found, generally, in organ music   ApeH, 167
    b - And it does resemble the motet in that it is genuinely polyphonic   ReeMR, 535
        1 - But it goes somewhat farther than the average motet in the extent to which the imitation reworks the motivic material
        2 - And the thematic material is generally more animated rhythmically and more angular melodically, with the melodic lines being more sweeping
        3 - It is in this style that the ricercar assumes the meaning that became standard
    c - This style dominated the ricercar composition from about 1540   JudI, 252
        a - It was the main type of ricercar   RanH, 706
    d - Examples of the polyphonic ricercar are found in the ricercars of Girolamo Cavazzoni
        1 - His ricercars started an evolution which was nourished by ever new ideas and continued into the seventeenth century

(3) Canzona (It. *canzona*)
  (a) The instrumental genre, *canzona*, was often spelled *canzon* in the sixteenth century   RanH, 136
    i) This term refers to early keyboard prints by Marco Antonio Cavazzoni and his son Girolamo of 1523 and 1543
  (b) Imitative clavier music was often called *canzona francese*   ApeH, 196
    i) This title indicated a connection with the *chanson*
        a - The earliest examples of this are by Jacob Obrecht who titled his compositions, *carmen*
            1 - This was apparently the humanistic translation of *chanson*
        b - The earliest *chansons* appearing in keyboard music under the title *carmen* were those of Paul Hofhaimer and the

"Paulomines"
- 1 - This was done in the first decades of the sixteenth century, but the episode was brief
- 2 - The frivolous and light character of the French *chanson* did not suit the German organists long

    (c) It was in Italy that the process of developing the *canzona* was more consistent   ApeH, 196
- i) "The Italian *canzona d'organo* became one of the most important types of keyboard music, one that Bach still knew and cultivated"
- ii) It was with the print of Marco Antonio Cavazzoni of 1523 that the documented history of the *canzona d'organo* began
- iii) The second stage is represented by Girolamo Cavazzoni   ApeH, 196
  - a - He produced the features that remained standard for the entire subsequent development of the *canzona d'organo*

    (d) "The keyboard canzona, along with the ricercar, laid a foundation for the fugue"   RanH, 136

(4) The *Tiento* (Sp., Fr. *tentar*; Port. *tento*)   RanH, 857
- (a) This was a composition for harp, *vihuela*, or keyboard dating from the sixteenth century to the early eighteenth century
- (b) The style and function of the *tiento* has at times resembled the ricercar, fantasia, toccata, or prelude
  - i) In Spain it corresponds to the Italian ricercar   ApeH, 188
- (c) The term, in a general sense, means to touch "intellectually", that is, to examine or scrutinize   ApeH, 188
  - i) The *tiento* for the organ acquired the character of a study in contrapuntal-imitative texture
- (d) *Tientos,* notated in parts, are found in Juan Bermudo's treatise, *Declaración de instrumentos musicales*   RanH, 857
  - i) They illustrate the contrapuntal foundations of sixteenth century solo instrumental music
  - ii) A facsimile of *Declaración de instrumentos musicales*   BerS

(5) The fantasia (Eng. fantasia, fantasy, fancy; Fr. *fantaisie*; Ger. *Fantasie, Phantasie*; Sp. *fantasia*)   RanH, 299
- (a) During the sixteenth century, the terms fantasia and ricercar are often substituted for one another
  - i) This is true particularly in music for lute and instrumental ensembles
- (b) But, in clavier music, there can be no thought of equivalence   ApeH, 166
- (c) The fantasia has often simply meant to improvise
  - i) But it may also be applied to a composition that tries to give the impression of flowing spontaneity
  - ii) It may also be an esoteric work evolving from a composer's technical manipulation and mental abstractions
- (d) Actually, it "is just what its name implies-a free or freer handling of musical invention or inspiration"   ApeH, 204
  - i) But, the "free" invention is free only within the framework

of the conventions of the time, *i.e.*, "in relation to the more firmly structured forms and types of the period" ApeH, 205
- (e) The fantasia appears sporadically in keyboard music ApeH, 205
  - i) It appears for the first time (around 1520) in connection with clavier compositions
    - a - It is found in the tablatures of Kotter and Kleber
  - ii) These fantasias, particularly those by organists, have always tended toward learnedness RanH, 300

2. Free music
   a) Prelude (Fr. *prélude*; Ger. *Präludium, Preambel, Vorspiel*; It., Sp. *preludio*; Lat. *preambulum*) RanH, 653
      (1) The prelude is a composition used to establish the pitch or key of a following piece
          (a) Works that seem to share this preludial purpose are often very different in style and scope, and they are also identified by a wide variety of terms
              i) In Germany they are also known as *Praeambulum* (or *Priambel*), in Italy as *ricercar*, in Spain as *tiento*, and in all these countries as *fantasia* (in some form) PerMR, 849
      (2) 1500 is an important and essential line of demarcation between keyboard music of the fifteenth century and keyboard music of the sixteenth century ApeH, 213
          (a) This line is particularly clear in the history of the prelude
      (3) During the sixteenth century the prelude acquired new characteristics ApeH, 213
          (a) There was a trend toward clarifying an idea, solidifying a structure, and regularizing a technique
          (b) This trend began with two German manuscripts, the tablatures of Kleber and Kotter ApeH, 213
              i) The Kotter tablature uses humanistically learned titles such as *Prooemium* or *Anabole*
                 a - The latter title means "beginning" in Greek
              ii) The preludes of the Kleber tablature still show a connection with the earlier style prelude
                  a - They contain monophonic passages, mostly at the beginning and ending of a composition
                      1 - These passages were important in the preludes of the fifteenth century
              iii) But the preludes of the Kleber tablature manifest a newer characteristic with the replacement of the free, rhapsodic lines of the fifteenth century with a more ordered motion in regular note values using the scale as the structural basis
                   a - For an example of this *see* ApeH, 214
              iv) In the Kotter tablature, the toccata-like passages disappear entirely
          (c) The evolution represented by the Kleber and Kotter tablatures was continued in Poland under the influence of German organists ApeH, 217

3. Dance music
   a) Keyboard music of the sixteenth century represents a basic change in comparison with the preceding century   ApeH, 228
      (1) This is particularly striking in dance music
      (2) "A marvelous richness suddenly unfolds, and a steady stream of varied and colorful new phenomena appear"
      (3) New dances that are in the prevailing fashion replace the *basse danse*
         (a) The most important new dances are the *pavane* and the *gagliarda* of 1510 and the *pass'e mezzo* and *saltarello* of about 1520
            i) "The saltarello was also called *alta danza* or simply *alta*"   ApeH, 229
               a - But the designation, *alta danza*, may be preferable for the fifteenth century type in order to avoid confusion with the sixteenth century *saltarello*
         (b) These dances were followed by the *branle* and the *tourdion*, the hornpipe and the dompe, the *piva* and the *calata*, and the *Hoftanz* and the *zeunertanz*
   b) The earliest sources containing keyboard dances are found in the manuscripts of Kotter and Kleber   ApeH, 228
      (1) There are two manuscripts containing two volumes of music skilfully arranged by Kotter   RokI, 435
         (a) They are the Basle: Basle University Library, *MS. F. IX. 22* and *MS. F. IX. 58*
         (b) This music was assembled between 1513 and 1532 for Boniface Ammerbach of Basle
            i) This is the first time dances have been found in a German tablature   ReeMR, 665
      (2) There is one manuscript: Berlin: *40026 (Z.26)* containing the tablature of Kleber   ReeMR, 986
         (a) This tablature was written between 1520 and 1524 by Leonard Kleber of Goppingen in Wüttemberg   RokI, 437
      (3) These three manuscripts contain nine dances   ApeH, 229
         (a) Six of the dances are based on the same melody, the S*pagna* tune (*Il re di Spagna* = the King of Spain)
            i) The six compositions are arranged in the meter of the *alta danza*
            ii) They are notated as monophonic pieces in long notes of equal value, not as dance tunes in the real sense
               a - The notes were usually breves
               b - They were probably accompanied by a trumpet or trombone, with shawm players performing livelier counterpoints that provided the melody and rhythm of the dance
            iii) For a figure showing the *Il re di Spagna* tenor, *see*   ApeH, 229
               a - Such a tenor could be used for four metrically different dances
                   1 - The *saltarello* would have three beats for each note, the *quaternaria* four, the *piva* four but at a faster tempo, and the *basse danse* would have six

(b) The *alta* dance was favored by the composers of the sixteenth century　　　　　　　　　　　　　　　　　　　　　　　ApeH, 230
    i) Perhaps this was because the progressions of the *alta* dance move twice as fast as those of the *basse danse*
    ii) For an example of the meters of the two dances, *see*　　　　　　　　　　　　　　　　　　　　　　　　　　　　ApeH, 229
    iii) For a transcription of an *alta* dance, *see*　　DavH, no. 102a
(c) A transition from a purely functional dance to a stylized type of purely musical significance takes place in these compositions　　　　　　　　　　　　　　　　　　　　　　　　　　　　　　ApeH, 230
    i) This is shown in the different treatments of the counterpoints that are added to the *cantus firmus*
        a - The *Spaniol Kochersperg* has archaic features such as elements of ancient organum in parallel fifths along with *faux bourdon* of the Dufay period
            1 - A transcription of *Spaniol Kochersperg*　　MerD, 46
        b - The *Spania in re* from the Kleber tablature has the *cantus firmus* in the middle voice supported by a harmonically oriented bass with a richly ornamented upper voice in mostly scale like figures
            1 - This is found in [Berlin: *40026 (Z.26)*], fol.29v　　　　　　　　　　　　　　　　　　　　　　　　　　　　　　　　ApeH, 229
        c - The *Spanieler* by Kotter and the *Spaniol* by Buchner have the *cantus firmus* in the middle voice with the bass line being as lively as that of the discant
            1 - Transcriptions of the *Spanieler* by Kotter and the *Spaniol* by Buchner　　MerD, 44; 50
        d - The *Spania in re* by Buchner has a richly ornamented *cantus firmus* and two introductory groups to the composition that have the character of a fore-imitation that stand outside the metric scheme　　ApeH, 231
            1 - The counterpoints are full of rich, freely changing figurations
            2 - This composition shows a much greater artistry and command of compositional technique then the pieces discussed above
            3 - This is found in [Berlin: *40026 (Z.26)*], fol.60v　　　　　　　　　　　　　　　　　　　　　　　　　　　　　　　　ApeH, 229
        e - The *Spanyöler Tancz* by Hans Weck represents as high a level of artistic formulation as the work of Schlick in his liturgical organ music　　ApeH, 231
            1 - The *cantus firmus* is transformed into a new melody that has a life of its own　　ApeH, 232
            2 - The voices are increased from three to four with a harmonic foundation that stresses the rhythm　　　　　　　　　　　　　　　　　　　　　　　　　　　　　　　　ApeH, 232
            3 - This dance type remained standard throughout the subsequent evolution of dances in the sixteenth century　　ApeH, 232

Keyboard Music: Musical Forms 461

                      4 - A transcription of *Spanyöler Tancz*   MerD, 48

d) The earliest collection containing only dances for keyboard is found in Venice: *I-Vm MS Ital. IV. 1227*   JudI, 250
   (1) The music dates from ca. 1530
   (2) This manuscript contains thirty-nine short pieces which are all anonymous
   (3) It includes dances such as the *pass'e mezzo* (duple meter), the *pavane* (duple meter), and the *saltarello* (triple meter)
      (a) They employ harmonic patterns upon which performers improvised, not unlike modern jazz bass patterns
   (4) "Most of the largely anonymous keyboard dances from the sixteenth century... are rather simple settings"   SilI, 15
      (a) They are settings of popular dance tunes and basses
      (b) The right hand usually plays the tune or stereotypical divisions while the other hand provides an accompaniment often with parallel block chords
   (5) This collection represents a turning point, not only with respect to types but also in the field of style   ApeH, 236
      (a) The contrapuntal, linear texture is completely gone
         i) It is replaced by a purely homophonic texture with accentuating chords and a figural upper voice
         ii) Passages in which two or more triads follow one another in parallel motion are found in almost every dance
         iii) These features are characteristic of the Italian (and the French) clavier dance throughout the 16th century

e) Another manuscript containing dance music is found in Castell' Arquato: *I-CARc*   JudI, 250
   (1) It was copied ca. 1540
   (2) This contains thirteen compositions that show the tradition of suites, variations, and passacaglias in Italy in the early stages
   (3) They are very simple in style and retain the character of functional dance music   ApeH, 237
   (4) A transcription of the dances, liturgical music, and madrigals   SliK

f) A published source of dance music is the *Quatorze Gaillardes neuf Pavennes sept Branles et deux Basses Dances le tout reduict de musique en la tabulature du jeu d'Orgues...*   ApeH, 239
   (1) It was published by Attaingnant ca. 1530 O.S.; [A.D. 1531]
   (2) The number of dances stated in the title is not quite correct as there are actually fifteen galliards and eight *pavane*
   (3) It is thought that the words, *reduict de musique en la tabulature*, probably should be interpreted to mean that the dances were originally written for instrumental ensemble and then transcribed into clavier tablature and ornamented with the usual figurations
   (4) The words, *jeu d'Orgues*, surely do not refer to a church organ but to a small house organ, possibly the so-called bible regal
   (5) These dances are similar in style to the Italian dances from the Venice and Castell' Arquato manuscripts   ApeH, 241
      (a) "The contrapuntal texture is predominantly replaced by homophony, in which parallel motion of fifths and octaves is not at all rare"

            (b) But, the left hand does not consist of block chords exclusively, but is also intrusted with contrapuntal fragments
        (6) A facsimile of *Quatorze Gaillardes neuf Pavennes sept Branles et deux Basses Dances le tout reduict de musique en la tabulature du jeu d'Orgues...* AttQG
        (7) A transcription of *Quatorze Gaillardes neuf Pavennes sept Branles et deux Basses Dances le tout reduict de musique en la tabulature du jeu d'Orgues...* HeaK
    4. Intabulations
        a) "The CLAVIER MUSIC of the sixteenth century includes innumerable intabulations, which occupy a much larger space than they deserve relative to their historical and artistic significance" ApeH, 288
            (1) There are examples of intabulations in the very earliest manuscript of clavier music, the *Roberstbridge fragment,* from the beginning of the fourteenth century
            (2) Intabulations are absolutely without number in the sixteenth century
                (a) This was a sign "of the increasing importance of the keyboard instruments and the growth of a class of music lovers for whom the intabulations of a Josquin motet or a Lassus chanson possessed the same value as four-hand arrangements of Classical symphonies had for the amateurs of a later epoch"
            (3) Technically satisfactory keyboard texture was created from vocal models such as the motet, *chanson,* or madrigal with stereotyped figurations added
            (4) A detailed study of the technique is found in some new editions
                                                                                                    ApeH, 289
                (a) *Dixneuf chansons (Vingt et cinq chansons, Vingt et six chansons) musicales reduicts en la tabulature des Orgues espinettes Manicordions...,* 1530, by Attaingnant
                    i) A transcription of *Dixneuf chansons...* SeaTC
                (b) *Trez Motetz musicaulx avec ung Prelude le tout reduice...,* 1531, by Attaingnant
                    i) A transcription of *Trez Motetz musicaulx...* RokT
                (c) These editions are particularly valuable because the vocal models are reproduced alongside the intabulations

B. Keyboard Music: Liturgical Organ Music

1. Organ music in England
    a) Introduction
        (1) Monastic, cathedral, or collegiate churches of any size and importance commonly had as many as three organs ElcK, 211
            (a) At times there were more
            (b) Each had its own particular function
                i) In the choir, the organ was used for the monastic offices
                ii) The one near the nave altar was used for lay services
                iii) A third organ was used in the Lady Chapel

(2) "The supremacy of the organ, and indeed of organ music, dates from the middle of Henry VIII's reign and extends to 1547, the year in which John Redford died" SteC, 67
    (a) The liturgical use of the organ was temporarily curtailed in 1549 as a result of Edward VI's Act of Uniformity, but was resumed in 1553 with the accession of Mary ElcK, 219

(3) The surviving keyboard music is almost exclusively liturgical organ music ElcK, 210
    (a) Both Propers and the Ordinary of the Mass were set frequently WulT, 104
        i) The Kyrie, Alleluia, Sanctus, and Agnus Dei were the most usual items, as well as the Offertory, *Felix namque*
            a - This Offertory seems to have had a vogue as an independent piece WulT, 105
        ii) There is a Mass Ordinary for Trinity Sunday and an incomplete Proper for Easter Sunday ElcK, 216
            a - A transcription of the Mass Ordinary for Trinity Sunday SteE, 1
            b - A transcription of the Proper for Easter Sunday SteE, 20
    (b) There is music for Matins, Lauds, Vespers, and Compline CalMO, ix
        i) This music consists of canticles, antiphons, hymns, and the Te Deum
        ii) A Magnificat also has survived ElcK, 216
            a - A transcription of the Magnificat CalMO, 23

(4) There is no evidence that organ music was published during this period SteC, 67
    (a) The music was passed on in manuscript form

b) General style of English organ music
  (1) During this period, liturgical organ music may be defined as that which is based on a *cantus firmus* CalMO, viii
    (a) The *cantus firmus* could be used in any voice ReeMR, 855
    (b) Sacred *cantus firmi* were usually kept intact ReeMR, 855
        i) They are usually present in uniformly long notes ElcK, 214
    (c) But quite often the identity of the chant will be disguised ElcK, 214
        i) This was done by elaborating the chant so as to partake of the nature of the other parts ("breaking")
    (d) Ornamented chant was especially found in the music of the Office CalMO, viii
  (2) The organ music replaces the vocal performance of the portion of the chant that is set CalMO, viii
  (3) Previously, it had normally been improvised CalO, 249
  (4) But, English keyboard music for the liturgy took a new turn with Redford and his contemporaries AtlR, 541
    (a) A whole school of composition emerged centering around John Redford and Thomas Preston CalMO, viii
  (5) Church organists began to compose and notate music of greater complexity AtlR, 541
    (a) Sometimes a composer would choose a chant, write a counterpoint

beneath it, then discard the original chant and use the counterpoint [the faburden] as a *cantus firmus*
  i) The organist would use the faburden as both bass and basis of his contrapuntal superstructure   SteC, 68
      a - The harmonic implications of the faburden were stronger than that of the chant
  ii) Thus, the organ faburden was different from the choral faburden   SteC, 68
  iii) This device was used in hymns and the *Te Deum* in order to avoid near-repetition of the chant previously sung by the choir (*in alternatim*)   ElcK, 214
      a - It was also used in the Magnificat   CalMO, viii
  iv) But the greater part of the surviving organ music for the Mass relies on the chant itself and not on the faburden of the chant   SteE, xii
(b) Monophonic melodies notated in mensural fashion were drawn upon as *cantus firmi* for liturgical works   Atlr, 542
  i) They were known as squares
  ii) They were separate from the plainsong repertory
      a - Some were extracted from polyphonic compositions
  iii) They were used in votive Masses for the Virgin Mary
  iv) A transcription of a Kyrie and Christe on a square   SteE, 16
(c) Compositions were essentially contrapuntal   CalMO, ix
  i) Each voice part leads an independent life of its own
  ii) Occasionally an extra voice is added
  iii) Imitation was absorbed into English music by the latter part of Henry VIII's reign   AtlR, 542
(d) There was much rhythmic and contrapuntal play   ElcK, 215
  i) Cross-rhythms and proportions are used
      a - But proportions, used to mark off a section of a piece, were not as popular in the 1540s and 1550s as composers preferred to keep a constant beat in extended pieces such as Offertories
(e) A distinctive instrumental manner was developed   CalMO, ix
c) Music for the Daily Offices   ApeH, 140
  (1) The organ hymn verse   SteC, 69
      (a) The organ would alternate with the choir
          i) Verses one, three and five were played by the organ and verses two and four were sung by the choir
      (b) The melody would always be present but not exactly recognizable
  (2) The organ antiphon   SteC, 70
      (a) It was based strictly on the chant and was set in a more or less elaborate polyphonic texture   ElcK, 212
          i) But, it was not always set in elaborate polyphony
              a - The occasion and the skill of the player decided this
              b - Therefore, antiphons were less frequently performed by organists   SteC, 70
              c - Sometimes a monk would simply play the chant alone
      (b) Usually the antiphon was performed before and after a canticle or

                        before and after a group of four psalms   CalMO, ix
                    i) But, since the opening words of an antiphon were usually
                        sung beforehand, the organ settings were most likely played
                        after the canticle or psalms concerned
                (c) Antiphons did not require the participation of the choir   ElcK, 212
        (3) The *Te Deum*   SteC, 71
                (a) The *Te Deum* was always set in alternating fashion
                    i) The organ and the choir alternated the chant by half-verses
                                                                              ElcK, 212
                (b) Proportion was used in order to achieve a variety of mood and
                    texture   SteC, 71
                (c) The *cantus firmus* and the number of parts were subject to change
                    i) This produced a kaleidoscopic range of color and expression
        (4) The Magnificat
                (a) The Magnificat was most likely set by many organists but only one
                    for organ and chant has come down to us   SteC, 71
                    i) It is based on a highly elaborated and extended version of a
                        faburden   CalMO, viii
                        a - It is set on the faburden of the eighth tone transposed to
                            C   SteC, 71
                    ii) The odd-numbered verses are set   CalMO, xi
                    iii) It is anonymous
                    iv) A transcription of the Magnificat   CalMO, 23
        d) Music for the organ Mass   SteC, 72
            (1) The organ offertory   SteC, 67
                (a) The offertory was not sung *alternatim*   ElcK, 215
                (b) Offertories were essentially organ solos, but it was required that
                    the "beginner" in the choir should sing the first word   ElcK, 211
                    i) Or as the earliest custom demanded, the priest or celebrant
                        would intone the opening of the Offertory   SteC, 67
                        a - There were exceptions to this with the priest's intonation
                            being set for organ   ElcK, 211
                (c) It was one of the principal tasks of the organist "to play a more or
                    less elaborate solo based on the *cantus firmus* of the Offertory..."
                                                                              SteE, x
                (d) At the point where the choir would ordinarily enter, the organist
                    would play an embellishment of the chant, or a variant such as a
                    faburden, with a constantly changing pattern of counterpoint and
                    imitation   SteC, 67
                    i) But, music for the Mass usually relied on the chant itself and
                        not the faburden   SteE, xii
                        a - This was particularly true of the offertory due to its
                            melodic character which stands out due to its florid and
                            fluent aspects
                    ii The melodic character of the chant generates enough har-
                        monic interest and moves in such a way that the free parts
                        have complete independence   SteE, xii
        e) Composers of English organ music
            (1) John Redford [b. ca. 1480-d. 1547]   ElcK, 217

(a) There are about fifty of his compositions extant   ApeH, 77
    i)   Most of these are liturgical organ music
    ii) He wrote two *Te Deum*, twenty-five hymns, seven antiphons, five offertories, and an Agnus   ElcK, 217
        a - He may have written a Magnificat

(b) His music has the characteristics of the mature style   ElcK, 217
    i)   It is characterized by the freedom and energy of the counterpoint   CalO, 250
    ii) A strict *cantus firmus* is found in only six pieces   ApeH, 141
        a - The six pieces are *Eterne rerum, O lux, Agnus Dei* and three short *Miserere*
            1 - A transcription of *Eterne rerum*   SteMB, 52
            2 - A transcription of *O lux on the faburden*   SteMB, 23
            3 - A transcription of *Agnus Dei*   SteE, 18
            4 - Transcriptions of two *Miserere*   CalMO, 41, 42
    iii) An occasionally ornamented chant is found in other pieces   ApeH, 141
        a - Notes of the chant are paraphrased by additional notes or figures
            1 - "But in the embroidered passages the chant notes also occur in their regular distribution, each occupying the time of a semibreve"
        b - An example of this is found in the third *Lucem tuam*
            1 - A transcription of *Lucem tuam*   SteMB, 34
    iv) In some of his compositions, Redford embroiders the entire chant melody   ApeH, 142
        a - An example is *Christe qui lux*
            1 - A transcription of *Christe qui lux*   SteMB, 34
    v)   The two *Te Deum* are written on a faburden   ApeH, 142
        a - Transcriptions of the *Te Deum*   CalMO, 10, 17

(c) His two-part textures, in particular, show a sensitivity to the possibilities of an unfettered melodic line   ElcK, 217
    i)   The melodic line is controlled by extension, repetition, sequence, or contraction with a clear, although irregular, phrase structure
        a - The broken plainsong in the left hand supports, is contrasted with, or interacts with a freely evolving rhapsodic right hand
    ii) There is a subtle interplay of rhythmic units of unequal length

(d) His typical three-part style is the "mean style"   ElcK, 217
    i)   It is called "mean style" because the middle of three equal parts is distributed variously between the hands
        a - There is free imitation with the broken plainsong in mean or bass taking part in the imitation
        b - Even though there is shared imitation, the melodic quality of the treble tends to predominate
        c - An example is his hymn, *A solis ortus cardine*   CalMO, 48
            1 - A transcription of *A solis ortus cardine*
    ii) In a hymn-verse such as *Eterne rex altissime*, the thematic

material, which may be derived from the plainsong, may remain monothematic
- a - A transcription of *Eterne rex altissime*   SteMB, 22
- iii) In a large scale composition such as the Offertory *Precatus est Moyses*, the texture consists of a series of overlapping points
  - a - The points are freely related to and evolving out of each other in a seemingly spontaneous manner
    - 1 - Actually, they are controlled by a finely considered sense of pitch
  - b - A transcription of *Precatus est Moyses*   SteE, 100
- (e) His other three-part style has the left hand with two parts that support a more independently melodic melody
  - i) A good example is Verse six of the hymn, *Aeterne rerum Conditor*   SteE, 53
    - a - A transcription of *Aeterne rerum Conditor*
- (f) Settings for four voices are the exception in Redford's music   ApeH, 144
  - i) An example of a four-voice piece is his *Glorificamus*   SteMB, 44
- (g) Most of his music is found in Brit. Mus. *Add. 30513*, the *Mulliner Book*, and Brit. Mus. *Add. 29996*   ApeH, 77
  - i) A facsimile of the *Mulliner Book*   MulA
  - ii) A transcription of the *Mulliner Book*   SteMB
- (h) Transcriptions
  - i) Transcriptions of some of Redford's music for the Office   CalMO
  - ii) Transcriptions of some of his music for the Mass   SteE
  - iii) A transcription of *Veni redemptor* (an organ hymn)   DavH, 128
  - iv) A transcription of *Lucem tuam* (an organ hymn)   DavH, 128

(2) Philip Ap Rhys [fl 1545-1560]   ElcK, 217
- (a) His surviving music consists entirely of liturgical organ music   RhyS
  - i) Most of it is in a three voice texture with the chant in the middle or lowest voice
- (b) He wrote the only surviving Mass Ordinary for Trinity Sunday [*Missa in Die Sanctae Trinitatis*]
  - i) It is thought to have been written before 1549
  - ii) It has a troped Kyrie, [*Deus creator omnium*] and an extended Offertory, *Benedictus sit pate*
    - a - The last movement of the Kyrie is unusual in that "the Gregorian tune (from Kyrie XIV) appears in the discant in an uninterrupted series of quarter notes (minims), supported by two low-lying voices that progress in the same note values"   ApeH, 155
      - 1 - A transcription of the last movement of the Kyrie   SteE, 2
    - b - Also, it was unusual for the offertory to be a part of an organ Mass as it is a part of the Proper rather than the

468 Instrumental Music

       Ordinary   RhyS
       1 - But the fact that it was included tells us that the work was composed for the feast of the Holy Trinity
                     SteC, 72
       2 - The opening phrase of the offertory is omitted in the setting because it was intoned by a cantor
       3 - A transcription of the offertory   SteE, 7
    iii) There is also a Gloria, a Sanctus, and an Agnus Dei RhyS
      a - These, along with the Kyrie, consist of organ verses played in alternation with parts of the chant
    iv) The Creed, [*Credo in unum Deum*] is missing
      a - There are staves ruled in the manuscript for the Credo but if composed it is not entered   RhyS
    v) This is found in London: Brit. Mus. *Add 29996* (fol.28v)
                     ApeH, 154
    iv) A transcription of *Missa in Die Sanctae Trinitatis* SteE, 1
  (c) Rhys also wrote an offertory on *Felix namque* and an antiphon, *Miserere*   SteE, x; CalMO, 42
    i) Both are found in London: Brit. Mus. *Add. 29996*; the *Felix namque* is in (fol.41) and the *Miserere* is in (fol.6v)
                     ApeH, 155
    ii) A transcription of *Felix namque*   SteE, 92
    iii) A transcription of *Miserere*   CalMO, 42
(3) Thomas Preston [b. ca. 1500]   ElcK, 219
  (a) During this period he wrote large scale offertories, one antiphon and a Mass Proper for Easter Day
  (b) There are twelve offertories of which eight are written on *Felix namque*   ApeH, 152
    i) *Felix namque I* has the chant written in the bass ElcK, 219
      a - A transcription of *Felix namque I*   SteE, 62
    ii) The other seven *Felix namque* offertories are thought to constitute a weekly cycle for the Lady-Mass ElcK, 219
      a - They are all written for four parts
      b - The plainsong is presented in unbroken breves in the first four of these
        1 - The other parts are written principally in minims in a freely imitative contrapuntal texture and enlivened with crotchet movement
        2 - Transcriptions of these four offertories SteE, 67-78
      c - The plainsong is written in broken semibreves in the other three settings
        1 - There is a faster rate of harmonic change, a more fluid texture and more crotchet movement than in the other four settings
        2 - Transcriptions of these three offertories SteE, 82-86
      d - *Felix namque VI* and *VII* do not have a recognizable *cantus firmus*   ApeH, 153
        1 - Therefore they are probably transcriptions of motets
        2 - Transcriptions of the two offertories SteE, 82, 84

Keyboard Music: Liturgical Organ Music   469

               e - Transcriptions of the seven offertories   SteE, 67-86
       iii) Two offertories are in a different style and in an idiom derived from the keyboard [*Reges Tharsis* and *Diffusa est gratia*]   ElcK, 219
            a - The chant is written in unbroken notes with two other parts having figurative patterns which increase in rhythmic complexity
               1 - Both offertories are in triple time
            b - The *Diffusa est gratia* offertory presents the chant in the right hand with the left hand playing two figurative parts in rhythmic and digital virtuosity
               1 - A transcription of *Diffusa est gratia*   SteE, 45
       iv) The "*Benedictus* has four voices and a *cantus planus* in breves in the discant; and the *Confessio* is in four parts with a *cantus planus* in semibreves in the alto"   ApeH, 153
            a - A transcription of the *Benedictus*   SteE, 38
            b - A transcription of the *Confessio*   SteE, 42
   (c) The antiphon is a setting of *Beatus Laurentius*   ApeH, 152
       i) The chant lies in the upper voice and is generally presented as a *cantus planus*   ApeH, 154
            a - "But here and there it is paraphrased simply"
       i) A transcription of *Beatus Laurentius*   CalMO, 29
   (d) The Mass Proper contains an Introit, Gradual, Alleluia, and Sequence   ElcK, 219
       i) The offertory and communion have been left out   ApeH, 154
            a - This may be due to some folios of the manuscript being lost
       ii) This is the only known comprehensive Mass proper for organ   ApeH, 154
            a - It has a curious conglomeration of styles and a varied treatment of chant tunes
       iii) A transcription of *Proprium Missae in Die Paschae*   SteE, 20
   (e) Preston's hymns are thought to have been written during Mary's reign   ElcK, 221
 f) Manuscripts containing English organ music
   (2) London: British Museum, *Roy. App. 56*   ApeH, 140
      (a) This source dates from the 1530s or 1540s   WulT, 109
          i) This is probably the earliest source to preserve English liturgical organ music   BroAL, 30
      (b) The repertory is almost equally divided between Mass music and Office services   BroAL, 30
          i) There are a set of faburdens for the Magnificat that are arranged according to the eight tones as a single tenor part   CalMO, viii
          ii) There are the even-numbered verses of the *Te Deum* in plainsong   CalMO, 137
          iii) And there is a setting of the Ordinary by Philip Ap Rhys and a Mass Proper for Easter Day by Thomas Preston   BroAL, 30
      (c) The chant of a setting is usually carried by one voice in a texture

with a fixed number of voices   BroAL, 30
      i)   It is used in its entirety with the notes usually in equal value and without rests
      ii)   But, it may be decorated to a greater or lesser extent by a process known as "breaking the plainsong"
          a - This is usually done with two-voice textures

(2) London: British Museum, *Add. 15233*   ApeH, 140
   (a) This was copied around 1530   RokI, 458
   (b) There are four hymns, a *Te Deum* and an Offertory   RokI, 458
   (c) There are several pieces by Redford along with some of his literary efforts   WulT, 106

(3) London: British Museum, *Add. 29996*   ApeH, 140
   (a) This was copied by Richard Wynslate, *informator* at Winchester, in the late 1540s   BraM, 11
      i)   But "internal evidence shows that most of this music was copied from an earlier source, or sources, now lost" SteE, ix
      ii)   The manuscript contains pre-Reformation keyboard music
          a - There are some works from the first decade of the century   SteMBC, 14
      iii) There are three main composers, John Redford, Thomas Preston, and Philip Ap Ryce   RokI, 458
   (b) This source, unlike the foregoing sources, preserves a systematic repertory of liturgical organ music   WulT, 106
      i)   There are antiphons, hymns, and canticles in the first section   SteE, ix
          a - The hymn settings are arranged liturgically starting with Advent and continuing to the first Sunday in Lent   BroAL, 28
      ii)   Following this is a larger section of Mass settings and a large collection of offertories   SteE, ix
   (c) Thomas Tomkins added to the manuscript at a later date BraM, 11
      i)   He wrote a large portion of the music in this part   CalMO, xii
      ii)   He also made corrections of supposed errors to the music of the original sections   ElcK, 251
          a - And, he added 'bar lines' to aid the performer when parts were poorly aligned
   (d) A facsimile of *MS Add. 29996*   BriM

(4) London: British Library, *MS. Additional 30513* (The *Mulliner Book*)   BraM, 10
   (a) This was copied by Thomas Mulliner of St. Paul's (later of Corpus Christi College, Oxford)
      i)   It was copied between ca. 1545 and 1560
   (b) The manuscript has no original index made by the compiler himself   SteMBC, 18
      i)   But, there are lists made in 1913 and 1951 that contain a list of the composers and the number of compositions by each
   (c) There are 120 pieces of early English keyboard music   LowE, 841
      i)   Three-quarters of these compositions are unique
      ii)   Most are written for the organ although they are applicable to

                the virginal
- (d) The principal contents are pre-Reformation liturgical organ works
  - i) These are not in liturgical order   BroAL, 29
  - ii) More than half of the contents are based on plainsong melodies   SteMBC, 23
    - a - There are many variations in the use of these melodies   LowE, 842
- (e) There are keyboard arrangements of both sacred and secular vocal music
  - i) This includes transcriptions of compositions from the Mass, the anthem, psalm, and hymn   SteMBC, 47
    - a - Some are free from all instrumental influences while others diverge considerably from the vocal partbooks
  - ii) The secular partsongs make up about a sixth of the total number of compositions   SteMBC, 55
- (f) The manuscript also includes intabulations of a lute fancy, a consort pavan, and three French masque dances
- (g) Two ballad songs, a galliard with variations, and a group of pieces for cittern and gittern were added ca. 1570
- (h) The repertory begins with early Tudor composers such as Allwood, Taverner, Farrant, and Shelby and continues with later ones, such as Munday, Heath, Tye, and Whyte   LowE, 841
  - i) There are thirty-five compositions by Redford   SteMBC, 19
    - a - This is the main source of his compositions
  - ii) There are eighteen compositions by Tallis and eight by Sheppard
- (i) A facsimile of the *Mulliner Book*   MulA
- (j) A transcription of the *Mulliner Book*   SteMB

g) Performance of the organ music in the service
  - (1) The function of the organs was to musically enhance the liturgy   ElcK, 212
  - (2) The organ was principally used on occasions on which a polyphonic choir would not have been present   CalO, 249
    - (a) It was used also in establishments which did not rise to vocal polyphony at all
    - (b) Sometimes the chant was played alone at matins and midnight services   ElcK, 212
      - i) But, a common practice was to improvise counterpoints around it
  - (3) Both Propers and Ordinary were frequently set for organ   WulT, 104
    - (a) The Kyrie, Alleluia, Sanctus, and Agnus Dei were the most usual items to be set
    - (b) Office hymns, responds, and antiphons were treated in the same way
      - i) Antiphons were less frequently played by the organists   SteC, 70
  - (4) The music was rarely complete on its own   SteC, 69
    - (a) It was always arranged so that intervening verses could be sung in unison by a choir

                i)   The choir would consist of men's voices alone or of boys and men singing in octaves
       (b)   The organ, in *alternatim* performance, would take over the chant otherwise sung by the choir   ElcK, 212
                i)   Or. the organ provided the polyphonic verses while the choir sang alternate verses in plainchant   WulT, 104
                ii)   This was done in hymns and Magnificats verse by verse
                iii)   In the *Te Deum*, it was done by half-verses
    (5)   The part marked *solus tenor* would be taken by the organ as it had no breathing spaces   SteC, 66
       (a)   The *solus tenor* was found in Mass sections and motets
       (b)   This kind of performance was fashionable probably up to 1525 or 1530
    (6)   Some form of transposition must have been necessary   WulT, 153
       (a)   The normal English keyboard compass had a high note of a″
       (b)   But, many early organ compositions have upper notes of c‴, d‴, or e‴
                i)   These notes are well outside the normal keyboard compass
       (c)   It is possible that only one part would need to be transposed
                i)   For example, those parts that are written too high should be played an octave lower
    (7)   Transposition of a fourth was necessary in certain circumstances   WulT, 153
       (a)   The organ had to conform to the pitch comfortable for the voices singing chanted passages
                i)   Some organs had two keyboards, one a fourth apart from the other
h)   The organ in England
    (1)   There was some dismantling of organs under Edward VI   BicH, 44
       (a)   This was due to the Act of Uniformity which resulted in the temporary curtailment of the liturgical use of the organ   ElcK, 219
       (b)   But organ building survived in the southwest of England better than in other parts of the country   BicH, 50
       (c)   The desire to remove organs completely did not occur until Elizabeth's reign   BicH, 44
       (d)   By the fourth quarter of the century, organs had been removed or destroyed across large parts of the country   BicH, 43
    (2)   It is known that fifteen organs were built in the 1530s   ElcK, 223
       (a)   There is much information concerning the cost of various organs in cathedral and parish records   GeeO, 275
    (3)   No organ contracts have yet come to life for the period between 1526 and 1600   BicH, 43
       (a)   But, it is thought that English organs of this period were small standardized instruments having one chest which contained a chorus in Dutch or Italian manner   WilA, 132
                i)   It may be that the earliest two-manual organs developed from the addition of a Chair organ at the old pitch (F) with a Great organ at the new pitch (C), each with its own keyboard   ElcK, 256

(4) Little is known about specifications for the instruments   GeeO, 275
   (a) "The earliest English organ specifications which have come down to us are for the organ built by Thomas Dallam in 1613 for the Cathedral Church of Worcester..."   GeeO, 276
   (b) An hypothetical scheme for an organ most likely would include a principal chorus of 8', 4', 2 2/3', 2', 1 1/3', and 1'   ElcK, 255
      i) This is a mixture chorus of which only the very lowest ranks could be drawn separately
   (c) The principal was a five foot pipe which sounded approximately A♭ at modern pitch   ElcK, 256
      i) It had the 'old' high pitch for organs with a compass of F-a″
         a - It sounded our modern A♭-c‴
      ii) Some organs had two ranks of principals, one being louder than the other   WulT, 155
   (d) It is thought that the principal chorus was gradually replaced from the beginning of the sixteenth century by a new low pitch   ElcK, 256
      i) There were twenty-seven natural keys from C to probably a″
         a - This would have sounded as AA♭-f″
         b - This compass of the keyboard was similar to those of many organs in Europe ca. 1520   WilA, 132
      ii) This was called a diapason and was a ten foot pipe
   (e) The bottom notes of the diapason and the principal (C and F) appear to be a fourth apart but they sound an octave apart (AA♭ and A♭)   ElcK, 256
      i) This "effectively converted the principal into a 4' rank"
      ii) There were no sixteen-foot stops   GeeO, 281
   (f) There were no reeds or mixtures   GeeO, 275
   (g) And there is no evidence that English organs of this period had pedals   WulT, 154
      i) Pedals were not introduced to English organs until 1720   FerK, 2

(5) The pitch of the English organ
   (a) The pitch was nominally a fourth above vocal pitch which was a minor third higher relative to our own nominal pitch   WulT, 154
      i) As a result, organ scores are often a fourth lower or a fifth higher than the vocal parts   WulT, 200
   (b) Some organ scores are at vocal pitch in which case the organist had to transpose by using a system of clef substitution   WulT, 200
      i) This often resulted in the need to regain the correct octave
   (c) In order to do this, there were two choices for the organist
      i) The organist could make a simple shift of an octave
         a - Directions might be "play this viij notes lower"
            1 - This could refer to one or both hands
      ii) Or, the organist could draw the 10 foot stop
   (d) For a working of the clef convention *see*   WulT, 208
      i) This example explains the choice of clefs associated with the various transpositions

(6) Organs were tuned in just temperament   HayI, 730

(a) As a result, organ builders were faced with the problem of the wolf notes
   i) Separate keys for d# and eb and for g# and ab were provided in order to avoid the wolf notes
(7) For a discussion of English keyboard notation, *infra*, p. 185

2. Organ music in Germany
   a) General style of the organ music in Germany
      (1) "Indigenous keyboard music was developing along lines conditioned by the instrumental medium rather than merely by mimicking vocal practice" ButG, 152
         (a) Borrowed songs and motets were adapted for the keyboard with the addition of the customary ornaments RokI, 434
         (b) But it is the qualities found in Schlick's music of 1512 that are characteristic of German organ music until the late sixteenth century GeeO, 261
            i) Schlick's works for organ show a new conception of polyphony ButG, 154
               a - There are multiple independent lines, a predilection for linear, conjunct motion, and imitation between the free voices
               b - "Ornamental figures...are kept to a minimum, imparting a sense of a "pure" contrapuntal idiom"
            ii) The music is designed to be played on two keyboards so that the crossing of parts may be heard and the *cantus firmus* kept distinct
            iii) Large forms are lacking
   b) The notation of the music is fundamentally the same as that in the fifteenth century German tablatures ReeMR, 663
      (1) Old German keyboard tablature was used throughout the fifteenth and most of the sixteenth century ReeMR, 659
         (a) For a discussion of this tablature *see* GanMR, 39
      (2) But there are exceptions found in the notation of the following composers ReeMR, 663
         (a) Kotter employs six lines while Buchner, Sicher, and Kleber use five
         (b) Kotter and Kleber write the lowest part as the highest row of letters in their compositions for four voices
            i) As a result, the order results as discant, bass, alto, and tenor
            ii) Buchner recommends this order but generally does not follow it in his compositions
   c) Composers of German organ music
      (1) Introduction
         (a) German organ music had a promising start in the early part of the sixteenth century under Schlick, Hofhaimer, and Hofhaimer's pupils ApeSI, 617
         (b) There is a large quantity of organ music in manuscript by Hofhaimer's pupils, *i.e.* Buchner, Kotter, Sicher, and Kleber, the so-called "Paulomimes" ReeMR, 662

i) Actually, Kleber may not have been a "Paulomime" as he may have been a pupil of Schlick rather than Hofhaimer
ReeMR, 663
(2) Hans or Johann Buchner (Hans von Constanz) [b. 1483]
   (a) Buchner wrote a *Fundamentum, sive ratio vera, quae docet quemvis cantum planum...* ca. 1520   ApeH, 77
      i) The *Fundamentum* is one of the most important documents of the age   ButG, 156
         a - Not only does it show a far wider range of topics than earlier examples but it also illuminates many of the important changes in taste and methology
         b - For example, Buchner outlines his rules for the subject at hand before he gives his examples
         c - And, his "liturgical music is remarkable for its thorough provision of pieces for the Ordinary, Propers, and Offices"
ButG, 157
            1 - This music was added to demonstrate the practical demonstration of the contrapuntal treatment of a *cantus firmus*   ApeH, 91
      ii) Buchner is known for his development of the art of treating a liturgical theme as a *cantus firmus*   RokI, 439
         a - He draws material for his counterpoints from the *cantus firmus* itself
            1 - He gives the composition unity by stating the material in the different voices
         b - He uses fugal entries of the chosen theme at the beginning of the piece in all the parts
            1 - They are treated in different ways
            2 - An example of his fugal handling of a *cantus firmus* is his *Kyrie eleison angelicum sollemne*
               a - A transcription of *Kyrie eleison angelicum sollemne*   PaeF, 123
      iv) The *Fundamentum* is divided into three parts   ApeH, 91
         a - *Ars ludendi* (a discussion of fingering, the scale, note values, and an explication of the tablature)
            1 - This is one of the earliest tutors on keyboard performance   ButG, 156
            2 - Buchner stresses that his rules are only guide lines
ButG, 156
            3 - He was the first German composer to give rules for fingering   ReeMR, 663
               a - He states that each finger should be chosen with the demands of the next note in mind   ButG, 156
               b - "He designates the thumb as 5 and the index finger as 1, thus: left hand, 4,3,2,1,5; right hand, 5,1,2, 3,4"
               c - For an example of his fingering, *see*   AtlR, 382
         b - *Ars transferendi*: (this contains arrangements of vocal works)

                1 - This section deals with the method of intabulation
                                                                ButG, 157
                2 - It is a collection of fifty liturgical compositions which
                    apply the theory of the *Ars ludendi* section   ApeH, 92
                3 - A Kyrie, Gloria, Sanctus, and Agnus are connected to
                    form a complete Mass   ApeH, 92
                4 - Almost all of the compositions indicate the *alternatim*
                    practice   ApeH, 92
            c - The *Fundamentum* proper: (a brief guide for treating a
                cantus firmus for two, three, or more voices)
                1 - This section, historically perhaps, is the most impor-
                    tant as it provides the first extant rules for composing
                    with a *cantus firmus* for keyboard   ButG, 157
                2 - It begins with rules of consonance, dissonance, and
                    correct voice leading   ButG, 157
                3 - It contains a theoretical recognition of imitation with
                    a table showing various ways of using it   ReeMR, 664
                4 - Scales, intervals, and sustained notes are arranged in
                    various settings   ApeH, 92
        v) A manuscript, Zurich: Staatsbibliothek, *MS. 284* containing
            the *Fundamentum*   BucF
        vi) A study of the music and theory found in the *Fundamentum,
            sive ratio vera*   NagF
        vii) Transcriptions of the compositions of the *Fundamentum*
             found in Basel: *MS. Fl8a* and Zürich: *S 284*   SchSA
        viii) A transcription of the music in the *Fundamentum*   PaeF
    (b) The musical style of the *Fundamentum* seems to be more pedantic
        than artful   ApeH, 95
        i) Buchner's figuration freezes into a mechanical routine with a
            pre-determined recipe which is applied according to a rule
    (c) But there are three of Buchner's compositions, found in Kleber's
        and Sicher's tablatures, that are on a higher artistic level ApeH, 96
        i) They are *Recordare, Maria zart,* and *Sancta Maria*
            a - The *Sancta Maria* has been wrongly ascribed to the Kle-
                ber tablature   ApeH, 785
                1 - It is found in the Sicher tablature under the name of
                    Johann Schrem   ApeH, 785
            b - The *Maria zart* is probably the earliest known example of
                a fully developed chorale motet   ApeH, 96
                1 - It has a four-part texture and systematically explores
                    canonic imitation
            c - A transcription of *Recordare* and *Sancta Maria*   MosF
(3) Johannes Kotter [b.ca. 1485]
    (a) There are two volumes of music [a tablature] skilfully arranged by
        Kotter in Basle: Basle University Library, *MS. F. IX. 22* and *MS. F.
        IX. 58*   RokI, 435
        i) This music was assembled between 1513 and 1532 for Boni-
            face Ammerbach of Basle
        ii) There are a total of sixty-seven pieces   ReeMR, 662

iii) The manuscripts contain arrangements of music by Issak, Hofhaimer, Josquin, Moulu, Rousée, and Sixtus Dietrich
iv) There are versets, ten pieces of free construction, and dances of Kotter's own composition
    a - There are also dances by Buchner, and Hans Weck
    b - The ten pieces are styled *praeambulum, preludium, prooemium, harmonia, fantasia,* or *carmen*
v) This is the first time dances have been found in a German tablature   ReeMR, 665
    a - But the style of the dances seems to point to a stringed instrument rather than to the organ
        1 - "Several are described as "Spanish"- homophonic pieces in triple time with ornamented upper voices and, in some cases, a hemiola structure in the bass"   ButG, 158
            a - One is attributed to Buchner
        b - Transcriptions of the dances   MerD

(b) In Kotter's arrangements, he usually intabulates only three parts of a four-part original by omitting the alto   ReeMR, 664
(c) He employs coloration deliberately   ReeMR, 664
    i) "This is a form of elaboration consisting of more or less stereotyped, repeated figures"
(d) Kotter was unable to find a true instrumental style but the embellishments and passing-notes put life into the music   RokI, 435
    i) An example of this is his "Ἀναβολή" (*prooemium*)
        a - A transcription of "Ἀναβολή"   DavH, no. 84g
(e) Also, in this tablature, Kotter explains the rudiments of music for beginners   RokI, 436
    i) He shows the shapes of the different notes, the marking of accidentals, ornaments, etc.
    ii) It was quite unusual for organists to give instructions of this kind
(f) A thematic catalog of the tablature, prints of all the dances and preludes collected by Kotter, plus three complete song transcriptions   MerD

(4) Fridolin Sicher [b. 1490]
(a) His tablature was probably written over a period of years, from ca. 1503 to ca. 1531   ReeMR, 663
    i) It has 167 pieces including transcriptions of works by composers of the late fifteenth century as well as Hofhaimer, Senfl, Buchner, Kotter, Grefinger, and Fuchswild
(b) Most of the pieces in this tablature are arrangements of polyphonic vocal and instrumental works   ReeMR, 664
    i) They are often intabulated note for note and are seldom altered to suit the organ
    ii) But, there is one rare specimen of Hofmaimer's organ music   RokI, 436
        a - It is a series of versets for the *Salve Regina*
    iii) There is also one anonymous composition, *In dulci iubilo,*

which differs from the rest in its brevity and simplicity

ApeH, 97

    a - This piece does not contain a single ornament
    b - The melody is folk-like in the key of *F* major and moves in 6/8 time such as a Christmas cradle song, *pastorale*, or *siciliano*
     1 - This is a new type that is realized for the first time
    c - A transcription of *In dulci iubilo*   WhiE
  (c) This tablature is found at St. Gall: Staatsbibl. *MS. 530*   RokI, 436
  (d) A catalog and thematic index of the *Orgeltabulatur*   NefD
  (e) A transcription of the *Orgeltabulatur*   SicS
(5) Leonhard Kleber [b. ca. 1490]
  (a) His tablature is dated 1524 and includes compositions by late fifteenth century composers as well as some by Hofhaimer, Buchner, Nachtgall (Luscinius), Finck, and Senfl   ReeMR, 663
    i) It is found in Berlin: *40026 (Z.26)*   ReeMR, 986
  (b) There are 112 compositions   ReeMR, 663
    i) If Kleber's *coloraturae* were removed one would easily recognize the originals he borrowed from Brumel and Finck, Senfl and Josquin, Isaac, Obrecht, Agricola, and Loyset Compère   RokI, 438
  (c) The first part of the tablature contains fifty-one pieces to be played on manuals alone   RokI, 438
  (d) The second part contains sixty-one pieces and is headed *pedaliter*

RokI, 438

  (e) There are fourteen preambles in this tablature   ApeH, 213
    i) They are apparently freely invented   ReeMR, 664
    ii) They are not all by Kleber   RokI, 438
    iii) The function of the preambles seems to be the introduction of the tone for a set of intabulations or *cantus frmus* pieces

ButG, 158

     a - The first pieces are ordered in sequence, *ut-re-mi-fa-sol-la*
    iv) The organ's special powers are exploited in the preambles

RokI, 438

     a - This is true especially in the long scale-passages and dreamy chords which give a rhapsodical air to them
     b - It is particularly noticeable in *Praeambulun in re* and *Praeambulum in sol b moll*
     c - Transcriptions of *Praeambulum in re* and *Praeambulum in mi*   DavH, nos. 84f, 84e
     d - Two transcriptions of *Praeambulum in sol b moll*

FroG I, 115; RitZ, no. 60

    v) The *Finale in re seu preambalon* is probably the highest achievement among Kleber's preludes   ApeH, 214
     a - It is the longest of the preludes and is divided into three sections separated by fermatas
     b - There is a four-part beginning and ending with a shorter two-part passage in the middle

                    c - The practice of the time would have been to perform the first and last sections on the full organ with the middle one played on solo stops   ApeH, 215
                    d - "This is one of the earliest pieces to demand a change of registration in its structure, even though it was not yet prescribed"
                    e - It is found near the end of the tablature
            (f) There are two postludes that are designated as *finale*   ApeH, 213
            (g) Kleber helped to create the instrumental type of motive that was capable of rapid and concise developments   RokI, 438
                i) Short sections of music repeated in different registers are attempts at instrumental 'conversation'
                ii) An example of this is Kleber's *Fantasia in re*
                    a - A transcription of *Fantasia in re*   RitZ, no. 62
                        1 - This is attributed to "A.T.D. Card. Sal"   RokI, 438
            (h) A facsimile of *In dulci jubilo* showing the notation found in Kleber's tablature   ApeN, 32
            (i) A transcription of Kleber's *Orgeltabulatur*   KleD
    (6) Ludwig Senfl [b. 1490]   ApeH, 216
        (a) A tablature of ca. 1550 was discovered at Klagenfurt
            i) It contains intabulated motets and two genuine organ pieces
            ii) "The tablature is written entirely in letters; it is the earliest instance of the so-called new German organ tablature"
                   ApeH, 792, n.5
                a - For an example of new German organ tablature, *see*   RanH, 833
            iii) One of the organ pieces is by Senfl
                a - It is the *Praeambulum 6 vocum Lud. Senfl*
                    1 - This is a prelude of high rank intended for four-part playing on the manual and two-part playing on the pedals
            iv) The other organ composition is an anonymous *Exercitatio bona*
            v) This tablature is found in Kärntner Landesarchiv in Klagenfurt, *Ms 4/3*   ChaH, 125
            vi) A reprint of *Praeambulum...* and *Exercitatio bona*   ZweO
  d) Manuscript sources of German organ music
    (1) Zurich: Stadtbibl. *Cod. 284*   ApeH, 784
        (a) This contains Buchner's *Fundamentum*
    (2) Basel: Basel University, *Bibl. F. 1. 8.*   ApeH, 784
        (a) This manuscript contains *Abschrift M. Hansen von Constanz* (Johannes Buchner) 1551   ApeH, 77
            i) This is a copy of the *Fundamentum, sive ratio vera...*
                a - It contains teaching examples and some twenty liturgical organ pieces
            ii) There are also about thirty additional pieces
    (3) Basle: Basle University Library, *MS. F. IX. 22* [Kotter]   RokI, 435
    (4) Basle: Basle University Library, *MS. F. IX. 58* [Kotter]   RokI, 435
    (5) St. Gall: Staatsbibl. *MS. 530* (Sicher)   ReeMR, 663

- (6) Berlin: *40026 (Z.26)* (Kleber)   ReeMR, 986
- (7) Kärntner Landesarchiv in Klagenfurt, *Ms 4/3*   ChaH, 125
- e) The German organ
  - (1) The development of organ building in Germany shows an interchange with Holland   GeeO, 263
    - (a) An organ was installed in Johanniskirche in Lüneburg in 1549 with specifications that are very similar to those of Sweelinck's large organ
      - i) The Sweelinck organ was installed in 1539 to 1542 at Amsterdam in the Oude Kerk   WilAE, 32
        - a - For the specifications of the Sweelinck organ, *see*   WilAE, 32; WilA, 81
    - (b) The Lüneburg organ had a *Hauptwerk* containing the *Prinzipal* chorus, an *Oberwerk* containing a secondary *Prizipal*, flutes, *Nasard*, *Tierce*-rank and reed, and a Rückpositiv with color stops-Quintatön, Sifflöte, regals and short reeds   WilAE, 100
      - i) The pedal had a row of pulldowns with 8′, 2′, and 1′ stops
        - a - The three ranks of the pedal can be played only if no *Hauptwerk* stops are drawn
      - ii) The specifications of the Lüneburg organ   WilAE, 100

3. Organ music in Italy
   - a) Introduction
     - (1) The impetus for most keyboard music in Italy was provided by the use of the organ in the church   JudI, 245
       - (a) The term "Church" refers to the Roman Catholic church since Protestantism and other Reformation movements had little impact on Italian Christianity at this time
       - (b) The liturgy falls into forms according to the time of year and day
         - i) Within the liturgical year, the use of the organ was restricted during Christmas and Easter   JudI 246
         - ii) "Within the liturgical day, the organ was employed primarily in mass and vespers"   JudI, 246
         - iii) Usually only the services of feast days and Sundays used organ music   JudI, 246
       - (c) The appreciation for organ performance is shown by a Venetian decree of 1546 providing that no canons or priests should interrupt performing organists   ReeMR, 544
         - i) They should remain quiet and patiently await the end of a piece
     - (2) Italian keyboard music developed both in quantity and in a steady flow from the comparatively late date of 1517   ReeMR, 528
       - (a) This is the date of the publication of the *Frottole intabulate da sonar organi* by Andrea Antico   RokI, 443
         - i) The words *da sonar organi* in the title were not meant to confine performance to the organ   RokI, 443
           - a - They were meant generically to indicate that the music was intended for all keyboard instruments and that their system of tablature had been adopted

		ii)	A facsimile of *Frottole intabulate da sonar organi*	AntFI

        ii)   A facsimile of *Frottole intabulate da sonar organi*   AntFI
        iii)   A transcription of *Frottole intabulate da sonar organi*   AntF

(3) In Italy, the organ's main function during the Renaissance was to alternate with vocal polyphony in some passages   MorR, 241

   (a) This was true especially in those passages containing alternating verses, as in hymns, psalms, the Magnificat and other canticles

(4) It was also used to substitute for the singing of a polyphonic piece during the Mass, at the Gradual, the Offertory, the Elevation, or at Vespers   MorR, 241

   (a) This was done when the antiphons to the psalms were repeated, and to fill in at a "dead" moment during the liturgy, such as processions, censing, the display of relics, vesting for the Mass, etc but not to accompany polyphony

   (b) Instrumental works, sometimes based on secular songs, were substituted for items of the Proper in both Mass and Vespers   JudI, 246

      i) Canzonas and ricercars may have been used at the Gradual, Offertory, Elevation, Communion, and at the end of Mass

      ii) They were also used in place of Magnificat antiphons and psalms of Vespers   JudI, 247

      iii) Dance music was used in ceremonials, indicating that it, too, formed a part of liturgical usage   JudI, 247

(5) Keyboard players had to be acquainted with "tablature", open-score, partbooks, and choirbooks   ReeMR, 529

   (a) There is evidence that organists used a bass partbook alone to accompany vocal music

      i) The organist most likely improvised the upper parts or added notations to the bass part

         a - These notations later developed into the figured bass

b) Several manuscripts containing valuable material for the history of Italian keyboard music from about 1530 to 1550 were discovered in the main church of Castell' Arquato in the 1540s   ApeH, 111

   (1) The church is not far from Piacenza

   (2) The liturgical repertoire includes three Masses, two single Credos, and settings of *O gloriosa Domina*, *Assumpta est Maria* and others   ApeH, 112

      (a) The Masses are arranged in alternation style

      (b) The *Messa de la Dominica* is probably by Jacques Brumel, a composer and organist at the court of Ferrara from 1533 to 1564

         i) The versets are basically cast in a four-part setting but vary from three parts to seven

         ii) Of special interest is Brumel's treatment of the *cantus firmus*   ApeH, 113

            a - At times the liturgical melody is divided into single notes, one of which may appear in the highest voice, the next one in the middle voice, and another at the bottom of a chord   ApeH, 114

            b - An example of this treatment   ApeH, 114

         iii) A transcription of *Messa de la Dominica*   JepI, 82

      (c) A transcription of the liturgical music, dances, and madrigals   SliK

c) The first printed example of keyboard score appeared in an Italian publication of 1523   RanH, 736
   (a) It was *Recerchari, motetti, canzoni, Libro I* by Marcantonio da Bologna [Marco Antonio Cavazzoni] published in Venice   ApeN, 3
      i) A facsimile of *Recerchari, motetti, canzoni, Libro I*   CavR
d) General style of Italian organ "tablatures"
   (1) They are not actually tablatures since they employ notation on two staves with five to eight lines   RanH, 833
      (a) The upper staff has either five or six lines and the lower staff has from five to eight   ReeMR, 528
   (2) The notation is ordinary mensural notation similar to the kind of notation in use today, *infra*, p. 185   ReeMR, 528
e) Composers of Italian organ music
   (1) Marco Antonio [Cavazzoni]da Bologna [b. ca. 1490]   GeeO, 235
      (a) His music has "real instrumental significance and musical interest"
      (b) There is a volume of his music, published in 1523, titled *Recerchari, motetti, canzoni, Libro I*   ReeMR, 534
         i) This is one of the most interesting and significant documents of organ music from the early sixteenth century
         ii) It is the first printed example of keyboard score   RanH, 736
         iii) It contains two *ricerchari*, two transcriptions of motets and four of *chansons*
            a - One of the *chansons* is a reworking of *Plusieurs regretz* by Josquin   PerMR, 825
               1 - The models of the other *chansons* are yet to be found
         iv) The *ricerchari* are quasi-improvisational pieces   ReeMR, 535
            a - They are the earliest surviving examples of the organ *ricercare*   GeeO, 235
            b - They bear melodic resemblance to the two motet transcriptions and were clearly intended as preludes to them
               1 - This procedure anticipates the prelude and fugue relationship   GeeO, 235
               2 - "In terms of balance they outweigh the motets in length and substance"   JudI, 252
            c - These *ricercari* are not of the imitative type   GeeO, 235
               1- The imitation is combined freely with chordal sections and with passages which anticipate certain aspects of the toccata   RokI, 445
               2 - The toccata-like movements have no relation to vocal polyphony   ReeMR, 535
            d - The passage-work groups and characteristic motifs are developed in a modest fashion
            e - The sequence has an important structural role   JudI, 252
         v) The motets are written in free style and are idiomatic keyboard paraphrases with a pure instrumental style   GeeO, 235
            a - They obviously point to a relationship with liturgical music   ApeH, 109
               1 - They may be intabulations of vocal motets but, on the other hand, they may have only the general meaning

of church music in contrast to the secular *canzoni*
- a - If so, they may be arrangements of liturgical melodies, most probably hymns
- b - The music contains imitative duos and a motet style which is not carried through systematically ApeH, 110
  - 1 - The latter is mixed with purely clavieristic style elements
- c - The mixture of styles and the freedom of treatment place these works far above the average ApeH, 110
vi) The writing in all of the pieces is basically chordal ReeMR, 535
vii) A list of the contents ApeH, 109
viii) Facsimiles of *Recerchari, motetti, canzoni, Libro I* CavR; CavRE
ix) A transcription of *Recerchari, motetti, canzoni, Libro I* JepI

(2) Girolamo Cavazzoni [b. ca. 1520-1560] GeeO, 235
- (a) The organ music by Girolamo is by far the most significant liturgical organ music in sixteenth century Italy ApeH, 115
- (b) His books of music "make him appear as one of the most astonishing examples of youthful achievement in the history of music, perhaps without parallel except for Mozart and Mendelssohn" ApeSI, 602
  - i) One stylistic peculiarity that is worthy of note is his free-voice writing entailing free change in the number of voice parts DavH, 229
    - a - Other stylistic peculiarities are the omission of rests in places where they would be required from the point of view of strict counterpoint and the use of five-voice chords within a four-voice texture
- (c) His first book was *Intavolatura cioè Recercari, Canzoni, Hinni, Magnificati* of 1542 ReeMR, 535
  - i) It contains four *ricercari*, two *canzoni*, four hymns, and two Magnificats ApeH, 115
  - ii) This organ music is highly original GeeO, 235
    - a - There are forms and devices not found in previous examples of keyboard music
    - b - All of the forms and devices are employed with complete mastery
  - iii) Girolamo has composed *ricercari* which are legitimate forerunners of the fugue GeeO, 235
    - a - Motivic material is reworked in imitation
    - b - "Several themes are treated in successive points of imitation" ApeSI, 603
    - c - These short points of imitation "are frequently extended into lengthy sections, each of which presents its subject in numerous statements" DavH, 229
    - d - There are full cadential endings and added passages in free toccata style ApeSI, 603
    - e - A transcription of a *ricercare* DavH, 121

484   Instrumental Music

        iv) Girolamo also composed "polyphonic canzonas which, though derived from vocal works, foreshadow the independent instrumental form"   GeeO, 235
           a - They are not intabulations but independent works with thematic allusion to popular tunes   JudI, 256
           b - They are rather thorough compositional reworkings of the material offered by the models   PerMR, 825
              1 - They contain a sectional structure, a contrapuntal texture, and a dactyllic rhythm of the opening figure   PerMR, 829
              2 - This "represents an important step between mere arrangements of *chansons* and entirely independent keyboard *canzoni*"   ApeSI, 604
           c - For an example, *see* Girolamo's setting of *Falte d'argens* compared with the vocal setting by Josquin Desprez   PerMR, 826
           d - A transcription of Girolamo's *canzone*, *Falte d'argens*   DavH, 126
        v) Also, there are complete sets of versets (short interludes) for the Mass and Magnificat   GeeO, 235
           a - Cavazzoni converts the plainsong into new formations by selecting motives from them, then adding or discarding notes and modifying the intervals   ApeSI, 605
           b - The *cantus firmus* is frequently divided into two phrases   ApeSI, 605
              1 - The first phrase is presented in a short point of imitation and the second phrase is presented in a single statement in the soprano or another part
           c - These plainsong settings were substituted for the singing of alternate verses of the Psalms, the Magnificat, and other liturgical numbers   GeeO, 235
        vi) There are hymn melody settings in which the plainsong is developed with ingenuity, skill, and taste   GeeO, 235
           a - Some of these settings were written in motet style with imitation used in anticipation of the *cantus firmus*
           b - Others are divided into several sections with each treating the chant in a particular way   ApeH, 119
        vii) The two Magnificats, *primi toni* and *octavi toni* consist of five movements   ApeH, 116
           a - All verses are based on the same melody, the repeated Magnifat tone
        viii) Facsimiles of *Intavolatura cioè Recercari, Canzoni, Hinni, Magnificati* of 1542   CavI; CavIC
        ix) Transcriptions of *Intavolatura cioè Recercari, Canzoni, Hinni, Magnificati* of 1542   CavD; CavO
    (d) A second book of Girolamo's keyboard music appeared in 1543   ApeSI, 602
        i) It is titled *Intavolatura d'organo cioè Misse Himni Magnificati...libro secondo*   ApeSI, 602

      ii)   It contains three Masses, eight hymns, and two Magnificats
ApeH, 115
            a - These organ works are not so much arrangements but are bold and independent paraphrases on the various chants of the Mass and the Offices   ApeH, 118
      iii)   The Masses all have the same structure   ApeH, 116
            a - There are three versets for the Kyrie, nine each for the Gloria and Credo, two for the Sanctus, and one for the Agnus
                1 - There is one exception, the troped Gloria of the Marian Mass has twelve movements
            b - All of the Credos and Glorias are comprised of even-numbered verses   ApeH, 117
            c - The Agnuses have only a single organ section which was probably used for the first and third Agnus   ApeH, 117
            d - Each Mass has a Sanctus which consists of a *Sanctus primus* and a *Sanctus secundus*   ApeH, 117
            e - The performance of these Masses was not purely instrumental   DavH, 229
                1 - They consisted of an alternation of organ music and plainsong
            f - A transcription of *Missa Apostolorum*   DavH, 123
      iv)   These hymn settings are similar to those found in *Libro I*
ApeH, 119
            a - Some of the settings were written in motet style with imitation used in anticipation of the *cantus firmus* GeeO, 235
            b - Others are divided into several sections with each treating the chant in a particular way   ApeH, 119
      v)   The Magnificats have a Gregorian chant tune presented in five settings or variations   ApeH, 120
            a - The chant tune is divided into its two natural phases
                1 - Each is treated as a separate *fugato*, i.e., the imitation is frequently not limited to a single point of imitation but is extensively developed
      vi)   A list of the contents   ApeH, 115
      vii) A facsimile of *Intavolatura d'organo cioè Misse Himni Magnificati...libro secondo*   CavIC
      viii) Transcriptions of *Intavolatura d'organo cioè Misse Himni Magnificati...libro secondo*   CavD; CavO
d) The Italian organ
   (1)   It basically retained its fifteenth century structure   ReeMR, 529
      (a)   It remained essentially the same until the middle of the eighteenth century   GeeO, 231
   (2)   It had one manual and lacked the large mixture which was the main fixture of the German organs   GeeO, 231
      (a)   Each rank of the principal chorus was drawn independently
JudI, 240
   (3)   In northern Italy, in the period around 1500, the average or large organ most likely would have a chorus of ten separate stops, mostly or all

				single-rank WilA, 68
				(a) The upper ranks may have been duplicates in some organs
			(4) The instruments were quite limited being primarily founded on principals and flutes JudI, 240
				(a) Usually there was only one solo stop which was a flute

				 ReeMR, 529
				(b) Ca. 1530, registers began to be added ReeMR, 529
					i) "Reeds were introduced ca. 1540"
			(5) "Pedals were used to some extent, but not all organs had them"

				 ReeMR, 529
				(a) Some organs might have a few pull-down pedals JudI, 240

	4. Organ music in Spain
		a) Introduction
			(1) By mid-sixteenth century it is clear that the art of improvisation and composition for organ had reached a rather high level ParS, 316
			(2) The earliest treatise to discuss keyboard playing was published in [1549] ParS, 316
				(a) This is the *Declaración de instrumentos musicales* by Bermudo
			(3) The free, noncontrapuntal style of contemporaneous foreign keyboard literature appeared at times ParS, 313
				(a) But there was no equivalent to the toccatas of the Italian and German composers
			(4) Four-voice polyphony was the norm ParS, 312
			(5) The predominant genre was the *tiento* which evolved from little more than a simple intabulation of a motet to highly idiomatic subgenres by the end of the sixteenth century ParS, 313
				(a) The term *tiento* was first seen in homophonic pieces for the lute

				 ParS, 318
				(b) It was later adopted for keyboard works with imitative polyphony becoming a dominant texture ParS, 318
		b) Composers of Spanish organ music
			(1) Juan Bermudo [b. ca. 1510] ApeSI, 616
				(a) *Declaración de instrumentos musicales*
					i) This was published in 1549 followed by an enlarged edition in 1555
					ii) In the 1549 publication, Bermudo discusses and recommends a system of notation for organ music, *infra*, p. 188 HayI, 641
					iii) The music in this treatise is instructional music designed to illustrate points in the text, but much of it has independent value as an example of sixteenth-century Spanish organ style
						a - It consists of five hymn settings and four free compositions (*tientos*) ApeH, 138
							1 - These were placed in the treatise due to requests from friends, "particularly several from the New World"
						b - All of the compositions are printed in single voices in choirbook format ApeH, 138
							1 - But Bermudo states that they are to be played and not sung

  iv) The five hymns and four free compositions (*tientos*) are remarkable for their low range, the frequent use of open fifths, Lydian cadences, and numerous other strange formations
    a - The hymns are short four-voice pieces except for *Vexilla regis prodeunt* which is in five parts   ApeH, 138
    b - Each one of the hymns begins with a fore-imitation of three or four measures   ApeH, 138
    c- Then the upper part presents the liturgical melody in semibreves in *Ave maris stella* and *Vexilla regis prodeunt* and in breves and semibreves in *Conditor alme siderum* or in a freer rhythm in *Veni creator Spiritus*   ApeH, 138
      1 - *Pange lingua* is given in semibreves and minims, but with the augmenting effect of the *prolatio perfecta* it appears to be in alternating breves and semibreves
    d - The hymns are: *Ave maris stella, Conditor alme siderum, Vexilla regis prodeunt, Veni creator Spiritus,* and *Pange lingua*   ApeH, 138
      1 - A transcription of *Conditor alme siderum*   BerT
      2 - A transcription of *Veni creator Spiritus*   BerT
  v) These compositions indicate a composer of great individuality and ingenuity
  vi) A facsimile of *Declaración de instrumentos musicales*   BerS
  vii) A collection and restoration of some of the compositions   GayL
  viii) Transcriptions of two *tientos*   BerT
  ix) Transcriptions of selections from the *Declaración de instrumentos musicales*   FroO

c) The Spanish organ
 (1) Barcelona was the most important center for organ development in Spain in the early sixteenth century largely due to several German itinerant organ builders who settled in the area   WilAE, 237
 (2) The scheme of the Barcelona, *Nuestra Señora del Pino* organ of 1540 was the most advanced   WilAE, 238
  (a) It was designed by Pedro Flamench (Peter the Fleming)
  (b) It had one manual of fifty-four notes (FF-C'''), but no FF# or GG#   WilAE, 237
  (c) There was a *Flautado, Octava, Flautado de roure de Flanders* (a Flemish *Rohrflöte*), a *Forniment de la mixtura...* (a *Fournature* or Mixture 15.19.22.22.22 or 15.19.22.26.29), a *Per més Forniment...* (a further Mixture 12.15.19. breaking in the top octave), and a *Simbalet* (*Zimbel* III)   WilAE, 237
 (3) The Toledo Cathedral, *Organo del Emperador* is an essentially conservative organ   WilAE, 238
  (a) This organ is one of several organs in the church during this period
  (b) It was built by Gonzalo Hernandéz de Córdoba and completed by Juan Gaytan in 1543 to 1549
  (c) The main chorus is the most important element
    i) This is also true of the Barcelona instrument
  (d) The organ does not contain any of the French, Dutch or German

variety common in the 1540s, nor are the chorus ranks separated in order to provide the versatility of the Italian *ripieno*
- (e) There were two chests and possibly two manuals
  - i) The main chest of fifty-seven notes CC-a″ (no g#″) had a Blockwerk consisting of a 16′ Principal (*Flautado* 8′ + a stopped rank from CC), with an Octave rank, and eight or nine other ranks in the treble
    - a - There was a further Mixture of eight to twenty-eight ranks
  - ii) The second chest, with probably forty-five notes, had a Principal 8′ and a Mixture
- (f) There was a pedal of thirteen keys that played the lowest chromatic octave of the Principal 16′ (*Flautado* 8′ from CC)

5. Organ music in France
   - a) Introduction
     - (1) The underlying spirit of the French composers of keyboard music has a real affinity only with the music of Italy   RokI, 448
       - (a) French and Italian keyboard composers did not reproduce vocal polyphony exactly with the addition of a few ornaments, rather they aimed at a synthetic reflection of the polyphony
         - i) Ornamentation is thoroughly integrated into the musical thought, not merely applied on the surface   RokI, 449
       - (b) French and Italian composers conceived their instrumental music in terms of the keyboard   RokI, 449
         - i) There was no marked difference between music for the organ and the music for stringed keyboard instruments   ReeMR, 559
         - ii) Composers made full use of the range and power of the instruments they possessed
       - (c) The tablature consisted of ordinary mensural notation and differed from its Italian equivalent in having only five lines in each of the two staves
     - (2) No name of a French composer can be inscribed in the annals of organ music   RokI, 449
       - (a) None of the composers names appear in the publications of Pierre Attaingnant in 1531
   - b) General style of French organ music
     - (1) Four-part writing plays a very subordinate role in French organ music of this period   ApeH, 107
       - (a) This is very unlike the well developed writing treated as routine by Buchner
       - (b) "Although in this respect French organ music lags considerably behind the German, it is more progressive in the frequent application of added voices"
     - (2) There is no pervading imitation   ApeH, 108
     - (3) Counterpoints are created in regularly flowing scale figures above a *cantus firmus*   ApeH, 108
       - (1) There are also held chords, homophonic progressions, and sequences which often succeed each other rather abruptly

c) Sources of French organ music
  (1) There are two books which contain liturgical versets, used when the organ alternated with the choir in the Mass, Magnificat and *Te Deum* RokI, 452
    (a) The two books are:
      i) *Tabulature pour le jeu d'Orgues espinetes et Manicordions sur le plain chant de Cunctipotens et Kyrie fons, Avec leurs Et in terra, Patrem, Sanctus et Agnus Dei...* RokI, 449
        a - This was published in 1530 O.S.; [A.D. 1531] by Attaingnant
        b - A facsimile of *Tabulature pour le jeu d'Orgues espinetes et Manicordions...* AttTP
        c - A transcription of *Tabulature pour le jeu d'Orgues espinetes et Manicordions...* AttDLD
      ii) *Magnificat sur les huit tons avec Te deum laudamus et deux Preludes, le tout mys en la tabulature des Orgues Espinettes et Manicordions...* ApeH, 105
        a - This was published in 1530 O.S. [A.D. 1531] by Attaingnant
        b - A transcription of *Magnificat sur les huit tons...* AttDLD
    (b) Basically the chant in these two books was used as a *cantus firmus*, usually with one note of chant for each bar of music
      i) This was modified by considerable variety in application and by liberties taken in successive versets on the same theme
        a - This was particularly true in both the Magnificat and the *Te Deum* ReeMR, 560
      ii) The chant is usually stated in a straightforward fashion first and then broadened, interpreted, transferred from voice to voice, cut up by interludes, or replaced by ornamental figures
    (c) The ornaments in this music are not mechanical
      i) They are used as light touches and are placed here and there to mark a cadence or to fill out a long note-value
    (d) The music is usually in three parts but is sometimes simplified by the use of two parts
    (e) The two preludes in the second book use the characteristic feature of syncopated suspensions to mark either a discord or an imperfect concord RokI, 454
      i) But their melodic intensity is the most noteworthy feature in these preludes
      ii) The *Prélude sur chacun ton* has short melodic figures that act as a scaffolding for a musical structure RokI, 454
        a - The melodic figures appear on all degrees of the scale which results in the overstepping of the limits of the hexachord
          1 - This indicates that the octave was the basis for the organists of 1531
        b - The figures generally move in a tonality similar to the modern major
        c - The prelude is conceived so as to be playable from each

of the four finals associated with the Magnificat in all
eight of its plainsong tones   PerMR, 854
- 1 - This is done by a judicious selection of clefs used to construe the notes
- 2 - Therefore, the prelude could be used to introduce the liturgical Magnificat whatever the tone in which it was sung
     d - An example of *Prélude sur chacun ton*   PerMR, 855
- (2) *Treze Motetz musicaulx avec ung Prelude...*   RokI, 450
  - (a) This was published in 1530 O.S.; [A.D. 1531] by Attaingnant   RokI, 449
  - (b) It is an entire volume of motet arrangements   PerMR, 785
    - i) But, the compositions are not mere literal reproductions with clustered decorations   ReeMR, 559
      - a - There was a definite effort made to realize the special capabilities of keyboard instruments, particularly of the organ
  - (c) There are thirteen motets and one prelude   RokI, 455
    - i) The motets are arrangements with some famous works as their vocal source
      - a - There is one on a composition by Obrecht and one by Compère with the others being drawn from the brilliant group of composers between the death of Ockeghem and the second generation of pupils of Josquin
      - b - The oldest of the musicians was probably Antoine Brumel and Antoine de Févin with the youngest being Pierre de Lafage and Pierre Moulu
        - 1 - The most fashionable composer was Claudin de Sermisy
        - 2 - An example of *Sancta Trinitas* by Fevin showing the original motet along with the keyboard arrangement   PerMR, 814
      - c - Two of the compositions are transcriptions of anonymous Italian songs
    - ii) The prelude has one long melodic thought of thirteen bars without a break or repetition
      - a - The melody has mostly conjunct intervals in even notes
      - b - The ecclesiastical mode of D is still perceptible with the final on G with a B♭ in the key signature
  - (d) A facsimile of *Treze Motetz musicaulx avec ung Prelude...*   AttTM
  - (e) A transcription of *Treze Motetz musicaulx avec ung Prelude...*   AttTMP
- (3) There are seventy songs contained in the next three volumes   RokI, 450
  - (a) These were published by Attaingnant   PerMR, 785
    - i) They contain intabulations of *chansons*
    - ii) They show a respect for the original structure which is given fragments of scales, rapid embroideries, and figures of various kinds used to replace a sustained vocal note   RokI, 450
      - a - These embellishments are usually embroidered on the

               treble line with the tenor line taking an occasional turn as well   PerMR, 813
- (b) The titles of the three books do not mean that they were intended indifferently for organ or spinet   RokI, 450
  - i) They were meant to indicate that the system of notation was that used for keyboard instruments
  - ii) There is little doubt that it was the spinet and its successors, and not the organ, which were more often used to play these songs
- (c) *Dixneuf chansons musicales reduictes en la tablature des Orgues Espinettes Manicorions et telz semblables instrumentz musicaulx... 1530* O.S.; [A.D.1531]   ApeH, 289
  - i) The music is chiefly by Claudin de Sermisy
  - ii) In this source the intabulations are treated routinely in respect to the added figurations
  - iii) Facsimiles of *Dixneuf chansons musicales reduictes en la tablature...*   BerCT, I; AttDC
  - iv) A transcription of *Dixneuf chansons musicales reduictes en la tablature...*   Seatc
- (d) *Vingt et cinq chansons musicales reduictes en la tablature des Orgues Espinettes Manicordions et telz semblables instrumentz musicaulx...1531*   RokI, 449
  - i) Facsimiles of *Vingt et cinq chansons musicales reduictes en la tablature...*   BerCT, II; AttVC
  - ii) A transcription of *Vingt et cinq chansons musicales reduictes en la tablature...*   Seatc
- (e) *Vingt et six chansons musicales reduictes en la tablature des Orgues Espinettes Manicordions et telz semblables instrumentz musicaulx...1531*   RokI, 449
  - i) Facsimiles of *Vingt et six chansons musicales reduictes en la tablature...*   BerCT, III; AttVSC
  - ii) A transcription of *Vingt et six chansons musicales reduictes en la tablature...*   Seatc
- (4) The last book [of seven books for keyboard published by Attaingnant in 1531] is a book of dances intabulated once again for keyboard   PerMR, 785
  - (a) This contains *pavannes, gaillardes,* brawls, and *basse danses*
  - (b) A facsimile of *quatorze gaillardes, neuf pavanes, sept branles et deux basses danses...*   AttQG

e) The French organ
- (1) The organs in France were so uniform that registration rules could be formulated   WilAE, 169
  - (a) Organists had publications telling them how to use the organ and obtain the best sounds
  - (b) This was particularly necessary for the organs with a set of single-rank pipes   WilA, 77
    - i) For an example of the rules for a one manual organ with single-rank pipes, *see*   WilA, 78
  - (c) But directions were also given for registrations of a two manual

organ   WilA, 79
- i) An example is the directions given for the organ at Trier in 1537, see   WilA, 80

(2) There were two organ types: the small Italian organ with a single manual and separate ranks and the Flemish organ with full *Blockwerk* or *Grand Orgue* and *Bourdons* or *Trompes* and a second manual that was perhaps a *Rückpositiv*   WilAE, 169
- (a) The Italian organ with many single stops did not need a *Rückpositiv*   WilAE, 170
  - i) The stops were combined in different ways to imitate extra-liturgical sounds
  - ii) An *Instruction pour le jeu de l'orgue* lists registrations without listing the stops   WilAE, 173
    - a - But recent research has explained the *Instruction*...
    - b - Many tone-colors are listed that could be derived from a *ripieno* from F 12′ of 16′, 8′, 4′, 2 2/3′, 2′, 1 1/3′, and 1′, *Flûte* 8′, and *Flûte* 4′
      - 1 - For an example: *Le grand jeu*: 8+4+22/3+2+11/3+1+ both flutes
    - c - There are twelve different tone-colors, see   WilAE, 173
- (b) The two chests of the Flemish organ gave a variety of sound without needing many separate ranks   WilAE, 170
  - i) But, there were only about twenty known French organs with a *Rückpositiv* between 1480 and 1580

(3) The organ music of the Attaingnant collections of 1531 would have been intended for an instrument similar to the following: GeeO, 243
- (a) The *Grand Orgue* manual would have a *Grand Jeu* consisting of one to three ranks which might be available separately, a *Cymbale*, a series of flute stops, a *Cornet*, a *Régale* or *Voix humaine*, a Trumpet, and *Rossignol*   GeeO, 242
  - i) The lowest note was often FF, therefore the original specifications would identify the stop pitches as 12', 6', and 3', etc. rather than 16', 8', and 4'   GeeO, 242 fn. 67
- (b) The *Positif* manual would have similar resources, reduced, with the basic pitch an octave higher
  - i) Or it is possible that some of the special stops might be assigned to this manual
- (c) The *Pédale* had a very small range duplicating the manual keys
  - i) An independent 32′ rank was rare
- (d) Even though the Attaingnant collection would have been intended for such an instrument, the use of two manuals is nowhere implied, nor is there any occasion for the use of pedals

(4) A 1549 organ at Beaune in Burgundy had in addition to a Principal and Octave, two kinds of Flute, *Nasard, Cymbales, Douzaine* (Dulzian), Fife, *Hautboy-cornet, Trompette de guerre*, and twelve pedal pipes in towers (*Trompes*)   WilAE, 173
- (a) Due to a variety of stops, the organist was able to imitate sounds heard outside church as well as instruments heard within
  - i) Such as *Un jeu de Musettes sonnant comme un berger étant*

aux champs which was a combination of stops to imitate the bagpipe of a sheppard in the fields

C. Music for the Lute

1. Introduction
    a) The first book devoted to musical instruments was Virdung's *Musica getutscht* of 1511 which contains instructions for the lute and depicts one with six courses [a course is a set of one, two, or three strings played as one] and seven frets   MarMI, 318
        (1) The highest string, the *chanterelle*, was tuned as high as it would go
            (a) It was usually a single string   RanH, 458
        (2) The paired strings of the other courses were tuned in unison, the lower ones in octaves   RanH, 458
            (a) But string making technology and national practice were responsible for much variation
        (3) During this period, the six courses were commonly tuned Adgbe'a' or Gcfad'g'   ReeMR, 520
            (a) These pitches were relative
        (4) By 1500, the lute had a piriform body with flat wooden top and bulging body composed of very thin ribs
            (a) In Italy in the early sixteenth century, Hans Frei and Laux Maler are known for slender lutes, half-round in rear profile, with narrow shoulders and nine or eleven ribs of hardwoods such as maple or ash   RanH, 458
    b) By the sixteenth century, lutinists were plucking the strings with the thumb and fingers of the right hand   RanH, 460
        (1) As a result, they were able to play two or more voices at once in imitation or vocal polyphony
    c) "Virtually no attributed lute music written before 1500 survives"   RanH, 460
    d) Almost all of the music for lute after 1500 was written in tablature   RanH, 458
        (1) For a discussion of Italian, and French lute tablature, *see*   GanMR, 249
        (2) For a discussion of German lute tablature, *see*   GanMR, 150
        (3) For examples of Italian, French, and German lute tablature, *see*   HayI, 774-776

2. Lute music in France
    a) The musical forms for the lute
        (1) The *basse danse*   PerMR, 783
            (a) The *basse danse* is of courtly origin dating back into the fourteenth century
                i) It is a sedate dance performed by couples   RanH, 82
                ii) It reflects its origin in its aristocratic steps and stately striding movements along with its rhythmic complexity   PerMR, 783
            (b) The music has a compound mensuration with binary breves and ternary semibreves
                i) There is frequent use of hemiola in the musical settings
            (c) The titles of many of the pieces in Attaingnant's *Dixhuit basses*

           dances...avec dixneuf branles... seem to indicate a derivation from popular songs   ReeMR, 553
- i) "The melody is sometimes written out in mensural notes above the tablature and designated as the *subjectum*"
- (d) The dances were often grouped, forming a *basse-recoupe-tourdion* set   ReeMR, 553
  - i) The *recoupe* was the first after-dance [the second of a pair of dances]   RanH, 687
    - a - It was for a second sequence of steps that were shorter than the first but in the same tempo   PerMR, 783
    - b - It usually would be composed on the same melodic-harmonic materials as the preceding dance
      - 1 - But, in the *Dixhuit basses dances...* published by Attaingnant, all of the *recoupes* are independently conceived
  - ii) The *tourdion* was the second after-dance [the third dance of a three dance suite]   RanH, 865
    - a - Apparently, it was done at twice the speed but without the leaps characteristic of the *gaillarde* or even the higher steps of the *sauterelle*
- (2) The *Pavenne*   PerMR, 783
  - (a) This dance was modeled on the more courtly *basse danse*
    - i) But it was simplified some as a result of its urban origins
  - (b) It was performed in duple meter with the feet kept close to the ground
    - i) It was usually followed by a rapid, leaping dance in triple meter, most commonly a *gaillarde*
      - a - It is difficult to say whether the dances were played in sequence
    - ii) Both the *pavenne* and *gaillarde* were derived from the same material   MeyC, 555
    - iii) Sometimes a *sauterelle* was used to form a short suite with the preceding *Pavenne*
- (3) The *branle*   PerMR, 784
  - (a) This dance was of popular origin with a surprisingly long history
  - (b) By the sixteenth century there were several different varieties, all of them characterized by movement from side to side
    - i) They were distinguished by the meter (duple or triple) and the rapidity by which they were executed
    - ii) They were identified by name:
      - a - *Branle gay* (in quick triple time)
      - b - *Branle simple* (more sedate in duple time)
      - c - *Branle de Poictou* (in triple meter)
      - d - *Branle du Haulberroys* (in duple time)
    - iii) Other types appear in publications at a later date
- (4) The performance of this music could have been with loud consorts to accompany many dancers, but a soft instrument such as the lute could have been used for a small group
  - (a) It seems more likely that they were performed simply for the

entertainment and pleasure of the player and whoever might have been present
- b) Some of the sources of lute music in France
  - (1) A substantial repertory of music specifically for instruments was published in Paris by Pierre Attaingnant starting in 1529   PerMR, 782
    - (a) He initiated a series containing a collection of music for lute
    - (b) The series was printed in French lute tablature
  - (2) *Tres breve et familiere introduction pour entendre &? apprendre par soy mesmes a jouer toutes chansons reduictes en la tabulature du lutz* (Paris 1529)   PerMr, 782, fn. 13
    - (a) This is a collection of music for lute combining an opening group of five preludes with intabulations of pieces from the primarily secular vocal repertory   PerMR, 782
    - (b) Forty of the compositions are for lute alone and twenty-four have been arranged for voice with lute accompaniment
    - (c) This publication must have been intended as an instruction book as it contains a detailed explanation of lute tuning and tablature   ReeMR, 553
    - (d) A facsimile of the lute music   SocP
    - (e) A transcription of *Tres breve et familiere introduction...*   HeaPC
  - (3) *Dixhuit basses dances...avec dixneuf Branles..*   ReeMR, 553
    - (a) There were actually nineteen *basses dances*
    - (b) This was published by Attaingnant in 1529 O.S.; [A.D. 1530]
    - (c) Transcriptions of *Dixhuit basses dances...*   AttDB; HeaPC
  - (4) A set of four partbooks were published a month or so after the *Dixhuit basses dances garnies de Recoupes et Tordions...*   PerMR, 784
    - (a) They are titled *Six Gaillards et six Pavanes avec Treze chansons musicales a quatre parties*   PerMR, 784, fn. 21
      - i) They were published in Paris in 1530
    - (b) They contain *chansons* to be sung or played and a dozen dances for instrumental consort
    - (c) A transcription of *Six Gaillardes et Six Pavanes...*   ThoN
3. Lute music in Italy
   - a) Introduction
     - (1) "Italy has left us one of the most important bodies of instrumental music produced by the Renaissance"   ReeMR, 519
       - (a) In the first half of the *cinquecento*, the Italians outstripped the northerners in the field of instrumental music
     - (2) The most widely used instrument in Italy was the lute   ReeMR, 520
     - (3) One of the high points in the literature for the lute in Italy comes from Francesco Canova da Milano as well as many other noted lutenists   ReeMR, 522
   - b) The musical forms of lute music
     - (1) There are intabulations of *chansons* called *canzoni francesi*   UlrH, 199
       - (a) These transcriptions are taken from the *chansons* of Claudin de Sermisy, Clément Janequin, Pierre Certon, and Sandrin   RanH, 136
       - (b) They began in Italy in 1536 and continued sporadically until the peaking of the lute prints by some of the composers listed below

of 1546 to 1548   RanH, 136
- (c) They are written in contrapuntal style
  - i) They have "animated chordal textures, casual imitation, simple harmonies, and rhythmic vitality"   RanH, 136
  - ii) An example of the music is Willaert's *Con lagrime e sospir*
    - a - A transcription of *Con lagrime e sospir*   EinI III, 319
- (d) For a list of intabulations of vocal music for solo lute or keyboard, see   BroES, 52
(2) "Dance pieces, mostly simple, occupy an important place in the lute repertory"   ReeMR, 523
- (a) It is in the dances that greater independence of instrumental performance from vocal practice was first achieved   MeyC, 553
(3) *Ricercari* were of a decidedly instrumental character and were sometimes called *fantasie*   ReeMR, 526
- (a) But the term *fantasie* was not as common as the term *ricercari* in the earlier lute collections
- (b) "The composer of the first known imitative *ricercare* for lute and also the person through whom this type of composition reached its artistic zenith in lute music was Francesco Canova da Milano..."

c) The composers of lute music
  (1) Some of the best local lutenists [of this period] were scattered throughout Italy   BroES, 53
  - (a) Melchiore de Barberiis [b. ?]
    - i) He came from Padua
    - ii) In his lute tablatures there are a few compositions for two lutes   ReeMR, 528
      - a - "In the performance of these pieces, the accompanying lute was often tuned a degree higher than the first lute, to gain greater sonority through an increase in the total number of open strings"
      - b - In *Libro decimo* there is a *Fantasie per sonar a due laute*
        - 1 - A facsimile of selections *from Libro decimo*   BarOI
    - iii) A facsimile of *Libro sesto*   BarID
    - iv) A facsimile of *Libro nono*   BarIL
  - (b) Simon Gintzler [b. ca. 1490]
    - i) Gintzler was a German lutenist of Italian leanings   ApeSI, 694
      - a - He worked for the Cardinal of Trent   BroES, 53
    - ii) His *Intabolatura de lauto, Primo libro* was published at Venice in 1547   ApeSI, 694
      - a - It represents a technical highpoint of the imitative lute *ricercar* of the sixteenth century
    - iii) A facsimile of *Intabolatura de lauto...*   GinI
    - iv) A reproduction of six *ricercari*   GinR
  - (c) Antonio Rotta [b. ca. 1495]
    - i) He taught the lute to foreign students from the university
    - ii) His lute-book of 1546 contains *passamezzi*, and an early instance of the substitution of the *gagliarda* for the *saltarello*, and the introduction of the *padovana*   ReeMR, 524
    - iii) A facsimile of *Intabolatura de lauto...libro primo*   RotI

(d) Francesco da Milano [b. 1497]
  i) He enjoyed an international reputation
  ii) His original compositions include pieces in free style, imitative *ricercari* or *fantasie*, and some in which there are toccata-like sections with rapid scale-passages, trills, and turns, which alternate with contrapuntal sections   ReeMR, 527
    a - The latter are particularly suited to the lute, but part-writing is very clear in some of his pieces
  iii) There are eight books of *Intavolaturo di liuto* by him published at Venice from 1536 to 1563   ApeSI, 691
    a - They contain mostly *ricercari* and *fantasie*
      1 - The *ricercari* consist mainly of chords and scale fragments
      2 - The *fantasie* are mainly imitative with two themes introduced in separate sections
    b - A facsimile of the 1536 edition: *Intavolatura e viola o vero lauto* (books I and II)   FraI
    c - A facsimile of *Intavolatura di lauto, libro 3*   FraID
  iv) Transcriptions of his complete works for lute   FraO
(e) Domenico Bianchini (Rossetto) [b. ca. 1510]
  i) He is among the earliest composers of imitative *ricercari*
      ReeMR, 527
  ii) A facsimile of his *Intabolatura de lauto...*   BiaI

4. Lute music in England
 a) Introduction   HarEL, 315
  (1) During the reign of Henry VIII the lute displaced the harp
  (2) As a solo instrument, the lute was best for playing chords, arpeggio figures, and rapid passage work
    (a) It was not suitable for polyphonic textures and could not sustain harmonies
  (3) It was best suited for dance music and variations on dance music   HarEL, 316
    (a) Dance music contains the rhythmical periods of the dance that serve from this period on to define the purely musical structure   HarEL, 316
      i) But the music of ca. 1530 was not meant to be danced   ReeMR, 523
    (b) The dance music is of great importance in the development of idiomatic writing for the lute   ApeSI, 702
  (4) There are arrangements of vocal or ensemble music found in many manuscripts that do not differ in style from the hundreds of similar ones in continental sources   ApeSI, 702
    (a) "The music is transcribed either as it stands or else with a number of somewhat stereotyped embellishments"
  (5) English lute music cannot be dated earlier than 1540   SteMP, 7
    (a) Also, there are no instrumental tutors or books of that sort before this date
    (b) But lutenists would have had little need for musical scores during

                this period   HarEL, 315

                    i)   Their skills enabled them to transform polyphonic models into idiomatic instrumental music, or to improvise on grounds and melodies
            (c)   The identities of the composer and arranger often became blurred   HarEL, 316
      b)   The composers of English lute music
          (1)   "Many of the best lute-composers are hardly known elsewhere"   ApeSI, 703
              (a)   There were composers such as Bacheler, Cutting, Brewster, Newman, Collarde, Bulman, Robinson whose names occur in few reference books, if any
              (b)   Some of the more familiar names found in lute sources are Holborne, the Johnsons, Pilkington, Rosseter, and Phillips (probably Philippe Van Wilder)
          (2)   Philip Van Wilder [b. ca. 1500]
              (a)   He was a purchaser of instruments [at King Henry's court]   HarEL, 279
              (b)   He was also a lutenist and composer   AtlR, 528
              (c)   He was a tutor to the royal children and Gentleman of the Privy Chamber   HarEL, 279
              (d)   Transcriptions of his music   BerCO, Pt. 2
      c)   The sources of English lute music
          (1)   "Most English lute-music survives only in manuscript sources"   ApeSI, 703
              (a)   The sources are similar in their layout and contents and were personal books belonging to professional or amateur players
              (b)   They were compiled over a long period of time and constantly replenished with new music
              (c)   They were primarily intended for use
          (2)   London: British Library, *MS Royal Appendix 58*   HarEL, 299
              (a)   This is a vocal partbook with some additions   HarEL, 316
              (b)   It contains a small group of six dances as well as keyboard and lute music
                    i)   These dances are from the last years of the reign of Henry VIII   HarEL, 299
                  ii)   There are eight modest lute pieces that were inserted around 1550   HarEL, 316
          (3)   London: British Library, *MS Stowe 389*   HarEL, 316
              (a)   This is a book of statutes containing [two] modest lute pieces on some spare pages

D. Music for the Viol

1. The earliest comprehensive tutors for the viol ever published were two books by Silvestro Ganassi   ApeSI, 705
    a)   They were *Regola Rubertina* and its sequel, *Lettione Seconda*
        (1)   The former was published in Venice in 1542 and the latter in Venice in

1543
- (2) These books take the learner through every stage of handling the instrument
  - (a) They have discussions of "such subjects as tuning, testing strings, fretting, bowing, fingering, reading from tablature and from notes, scale-practice, cadenzas, arranging a madrigal for voice and solo viol, and the invention of improvised solo *ricercari*"
  - (b) The chapters on bowing and fingering are particularly significant ReeMR, 548
    - i) Ganassi gives advice on various ways of using the bow ReeMr, 549
      - a - Using the bow in different ways produces effects appropriate to different types of pieces
    - ii) He shows six different ways of fingering a passage
  - (c) There are also discussions of transposition, diminution, the art of accompanying a song, and such matters as the correct way to hold the instrument ReeMR, 548
2. The development of solo instrumental music took a decisive step forward with Ganassi's books, and it was the viol that led the way ReeMR, 549
   - a) One chapter in Ganassi's tablature has an explanation on how to transfer mensural music to viol tablature ReeMR, 548
     - (1) This is evidence that compositions were common property of all media on which they could be performed
     - (2) For a discussion of viol tablature, *infra,* p. 191
   - b) Both volumes of Ganassi's books contain *ricercari* in tablature
     - (1) There is also one *ricercari* written in ten-line mensural notation found in *Regola Rubertina*
     - (2) All of these pieces are in the early prelude style and are for solo viol
       - (a) There is a generous use of double stops and some genuine writing for two voices
       - (b) These pieces are among the earliest known compositions written especially for the viol
   - c) The only extant Italian viol-tablatures are Ganassi's *ricercari* along with a few examples in Scipione Ceretto's *Della Prattica Musica vocale e strumentale* of 1601 ReeMR, 549
   - d) A facsimile of *Regola Rubertina*
   - e) A facsimile of *Lettione Seconda*
   - f) Transcriptions of two Ricercars by Ganassi DavH, 127

E. Music for the Vihuela

1. Vihuela music in Spain
   - a) Introduction
     - (1) "The vihuela was the Spanish counterpart to the lute" AtlR, 488
       - (a) It had six courses tuned at intervals of 4th-4th-3rd-4th-4th and the music was notated in a tablature system
       - (b) It differed from the lute in its shape

     i) It had a flat back, slightly indented waist, and a pegbox that angled back only slightly
  (2) The publication of repertories of music for instruments in Spain was more the province of performer-composers than of printers PerMR, 786
    (a) Beginning in 1536, Spanish vihuelists turned out six great collections of music for the vihuela AtlR, 488
     i) They contain some of the earliest examples of tempo indications such as *apriesa* (hurried), and *espacio* (slowly)
 b) Collections of music for the vihuela
  (1) *Libro de Música de Vihuela de Mano intitulado El Maestro* of Luis de Milán GásL, 153
    (a) His book, *El Maestro*, is the earliest preserved book of Spanish *vihuela* music ApeN, 56
     i) It was published in Valencia in 1535
    (b) Milán was the first to use the Spanish system of notation, *see also*, p, 192 GásL, 109
     i) All other *vihuela* books use the Italian tablature ReeMR, 620
    (c) Milán combines vocal music such as *villancicos* and *romances* as well as settings of poems by Petrarch and Sonnazaro with six *pavane*, forty *fantasías*, and four *tientos* PerMR, 786
    (d) A facsimile of *Libro de Música de Vihuela de Mano...* MilL
    (e) A transcription of *Libro de Música de Vihuela de Mano...* MilLM
  (2) *Los seys libros del Delphin de música* of 1538 AtlR, 489
    (a) This was compiled by Luys de Narváez and published by Valladolid in 1538 PerMR, 786
    (b) It is indicative of future trends PerMR, 786
     i) It is presented in tablature very similar to that in use in Italy PerMR, 787
     ii) Narváez includes arrangements of vocal works by such composers as Josquin (six), Gombert (two), and Richafort
     iii) There are eight *fantasías* (one for each of the eight modes)
      a - This indicates their preludial function
     iv) There are also variation sets identified as *diferencias*
    (c) *Diferencias*, or variations, make what is thought to be their first full-fledged appearance in this book AtlR, 489
     i) There is one well-known set of *diferencias* in this collection that is based on the ground that was known in Spain as *Guárdame las vacas* or, as it came to be known in Spain and elsewhere, the *romanesca*

Fig.41. The *Guárdame las vacas* ground (*romanesca*)

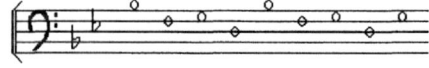

AtlR, 489

    (d) Narváez wrote four self-enclosed variations on the underlying *Guárdame las vacas* ground AtlR, 489
     i) Each successive variation increases in intensity
      a - "The rhythm activity increases; the range expands; the

ii) A transcription of *Cuatro diferencias sobre Guárdame las vacas*   AtlAR, 326
(e) A reprint of *Los seys libros del Delphin de música*   NavD
(3) *Tres libros de música en cifras para vihuela*   PerMR, 787
   (a) This was compiled by Alonso Mudarra and published in Seville in 1546
   (b) There are intabulations of Mass sections by Josquin and Févin, motets by Gombert and Willaert, accompaniments for *villancicos, romances*, and songs in Latin and Italian
   (c) There were also twenty-seven *fantasías*, eight *tientos*, a few dances, and several sets of variations
   (d) A reprint edition of the original publication   MudTL
(4) *Libro de música de vihuela, intitulado silva de serenas...*   PerMR, 787
   (a) This was compiled by Enríquez de Valderrábano and published in Valladolid in 1547
   (b) The seven "books" of this publication contain intabulations for vihuela and voice, vihuelas in pairs, and vihuela alone
   (c) There are arrangements of vocal works, sacred and secular, by composers from northern Europe, Italy, and Spain
       i) The composers were Josquin, Gombert, Layolle, Morales, Willaert, Ruggo, Sepúlveda, and others
   (d) Compositions by Enríquez de Valderrábano consist of a set of *pavane* and thirty-three *fantasías*, nineteen of which are based on musical material from other composers
   (e) A facsimile of *Libro de música de vihuela...*   ValLD
   (f) A transcription of *Libro de música de vihuela...*   ValL

F. Music for Ensemble

1. Introduction
   a) "The tremendous growth of independent instrumental music during the sixteenth century was a system of secularization"   MeyC, 550
      (1) "Instrumental music in general, had been of secondary importance compared with vocal music"
         (a) This was due to the preoccupation of the Church with the latter
      (2) It was brought about by the great social changes of the era
      (3) Purely instrumental works played at musical gatherings were intended mainly for pleasure and entertainment
   b) Much of the vocal music that was published in the sixteenth century was clearly intended for instrumentalists as well   AtlR, 486
      (1) The refrain repeated on many a title page of the period was, "Suitable for voices as well as instruments"
   c) There were very few principles laid down for the employment of any particular instruments in preference to others   MeyC, 551

(1) "As a general rule the more powerful types of wind instrument were used wherever instrumental music served the purpose of display in the open air, large halls, or churches"
(2) The use of strings and recorders was preferred for domestic entertainment
(3) But the players most likely used whatever instruments happened to be available MeyC, 552
d) Two main types of music can be discerned from the beginning of the sixteenth century; dances and "free" compositions MeyC, 553
   (1) "Greater independence of instrumental performance from vocal practice was first achieved in the dances, but it was in the "free" forms that the typically instrumental style developed most strongly"
   (2) The instrumental dance forms
      (a) The melody, counterpoint, rhythm, and metrical structure in instrumental music have great clarity MeyC, 554
         i) The principal melody predominates all the time in the top part
         ii) There are few syncopations as the accents fall on the main beat
            a - Metrical regularity is derived from the requirements of the dance
         iii) Block harmonies replace the intricate work of polyphony
      (b) The above characteristics were popular in the dance music of all countries from England to Italy and from Spain to Poland
            MeyC, 554
   (3) The free instrumental forms
      (a) The principal types are the *ricercar* and the fantasia MeyC, 556
         i) Although these types seemed to have been originally confined to lute and organ music, there was a continuous interchange between keyboard and lute music and ensemble music
            MeyC, 557
      (b) The *ricercar* and fantasia grew out of vocal forms that were musically the most highly developed; they were structurally modeled on the motet MeyC, 557
         i) Like the motet, the *ricercar* and fantasia set various clauses and sentences of the text to themes based on fragments of the plainsong MeyC, 557
            a - Thus they consisted of a series of sections that were mostly fugal or semi-homophonic developments of a thematic idea MeyC, 557
               1 - Although the sections generally overlapped, they always ended in a cadence
      (c) But there were differences in the ways in which the *ricercar* and the motet treated their imitation AtlR, 495
         i) In a motet, each point of imitation is based on a new motive and generally presented with the entry of each voice part
            AtlR, 495
            a - This is usually followed by non-imitative writing which leads to a cadence

    ii) In a *ricercar*, points of imitation are worked over far more insistently
      a - Thus, the *ricercar* became a completely imitative composition and as a result became the first instrumental genre to be based on systematic imitation AtlR, 494
    iii) A collection of imitative *ricercar* entitled *Musica nova* was published in 1540 AtlR, 494
      a - This is not Willaert's *Musica nova* of 1559
      b - A facsimile of *Musica nova* MusN
      c - A transcription of *Musica nova* MusNA
      d - With this collection, the imitative *ricercar* became the standard for the genre AtlR, 495
  (d) During this period, the fantasia differed from the *ricercar* only in the greater freedom of the melodic material which was nearly always freely invented MeyC, 558
  (e) There are three-part *ricercari* by willaert and Rore which are found in partbooks ReeMR, 549
    i) There is evidence that the music is for instrumental ensemble
      a - The keyboard is never mentioned in the titles of Willaert's compositions

2. English instrumental ensemble music
 a) Introduction HarEL, 263
  (1) The sixteenth century was primarily a formative period for idiomatic music for instruments HarEL, 264
  (2) The repertory of English ensemble music is primarily secular in provenance
    (a) Instruments other than the organ were not used in churches with choral foundations until the early seventeenth century
  (3) Ensemble music was used in the theater, civic occasions, education, and domestic circles
    (a) It was particularly important in official and domestic life at court
      i) Henry VIII established instrumental ensembles, particularly during the 1540s
      ii) These ensembles were dominated by foreign musicians
      iii) But, most of the identified composers of the surviving ensemble music were native and held posts in the Chapel Royal
  (4) At times it is impossible to discern three different kinds of music from one another, *e.i.* solo music, music especially written for instrumental ensemble, and music conceived for voices whose abstract musical qualities made their performance without a text plausible HarEL, 264
    (a) This is true particularly in predominantly contrapuntal music
      i) The same composition may be found in several sources whose repertory suggests performance by ensemble, lute, voices, or keyboard
 b) The Sources of ensemble music
  (1) Most of the ensemble music is found in manuscripts rather than printed sources HarEL, 265
    (a) Some of the sources of instrumental music post-date the composi-

tion of the repertory by several decades   HarEL, 272
- (b) The instrumental music was often copied alongside the vocal music such as Latin motets, English anthems, songs, *chansons*, and madrigals   HarEL, 272
  - i) The vocal music was not copied necessarily with the verbal texts
- (c) British Library, *MS Royal Appendix 58*   HarEL, 299
  - i) This manuscript is from the reign of Henry VIII   HarEL, 300
  - ii) It contains a small group of six dances as well as keyboard and lute music   HarEL, 316
    - a - The dances are presented in keyboard score
    - b - But, they are dances for polyphonic ensemble HarEL, 299
    - c - "The two pavans (one in triple time) and two galliards are indicative of the infiltration of new foreign dances into England..."   HarEL, 300
    - d - *The kyngs maske* and *The crocke* may have connections with masking and dramatic entertainment   HarEL, 300
      - 1 - It is also possible that the latter may have originated as a pair of French *branles*
    - e - A transcription of the six dances   ThoSD
- (2) The printed sources   HarEL, 278
  - (a) The earliest printed partbooks were the *XX songes* of 1530
    - i) They are titled, *XX Songes ix of iiii partes and xi of thre partes*   HarEP, 348
      - a - This is a printed copy of London: British Museum *MS. K.1.e.1.*   HanJ, 119
    - ii) This source originally comprised four small partbooks   HanJ, 95
      - a - The bass partbook and some fragments of the triplex and medius partbooks have survived   HarEL, 160
    - iii) There are three untexted pieces
      - a - They are at the end of seventeen three- and four-voice partsongs   HarEL, 160
      - b - One untexted piece is a shortened version of Cornysh's "fa la sol"   HarEL, 278
      - c - The other two are both based on *ut-re-mi-fa-sol-la* by Fayrfax and Cooper   HarEL, 278
    - iv) This was the first attempt at printing mensural polyphony in England   JosJ, 189
  - (b) After the *XX songes* of 1530 only a few ensemble works can be identified until ca. 1560-1570   HarEL, 279
    - i) They are mostly dances found in keyboard arrangements

3. French instrumental ensemble music
   a) In 1530, Attaingnant published a set of four partbooks, *Six Gaillardes et Six Pavanes avec trez chansons musicales a quatre parties*   PerMR, 784, fn. 21
      (1) They contain a dozen dances for instrumental consort as well as some *chansons* to be sung or played   PerMR, 784
         (a) The dances are balanced equally between *pavennes* and *gaillards*

                    (2)   A transcription of *Six Gaillardes et Six Pavanes*...   ThoN
          b) This was followed by *Neuf basses danses, deux branles, vingt et cinq Pavannes avec quinze Gaillardes en musique a quatre parties* (Paris 1530)
                                                                                            PerMR, 784, fn. 22
                    (1)   In this source a significant number of *pavannes* and *gaillardes* are rounded out by a pair of *branles* (brawls) and a series of *basses danses*
                                                                                            PerMR, 784
                          (a) There is also "a Latin translation of the brief tract on playing the lute, which opened the *Tres breve et familiere introduction* of 1529 and gave it its title, now ascribed to Oronce Finé"
                                    i) A facsimile of *Epithoma musice instrumentalis...* by Oronce Finé   HeaPC
                                    ii) A transcription of *Tres breve et familiere introduction...*   HeaPC
                    (2)   A transcription of *Neuf basses danses, deux branles, vingt et cinq Pavannes...*   ThoN

  4. Italian instrumental music
       a) It was revolutionized through the musical form, *canzon* (or *canzone*)
                                                                                            MeyC, 565
                    (1)   It grew essentially out of the French *chanson*
                    (2)   The instrumental *canzona* was known as *canzona da sonare*   RanH, 136
                    (3)   Italian composers took over this brilliant new form and adapted it to their own traditions
                          (a) Gardano published *Canzoni francese a due voci...buone da cantare et sonare* at Venice in 1539
                                    i) A facsimile of *Canzoni francese a due voci...*   GarCF
                          (b) Other collections followed
                    (4)   In time, as an instrumental form, the *canzon* borrowed characteristics from both the *ricercari* and the numerous dance movements in use at the time
                          (a) From the *ricercari*, the *canzon* took over the sectional arrangement of the motet   MeyC, 566
                          (b) From the dance movements, especially those in triple time, it took over many rhythmic and metrical features   MeyC, 566

Index of Persons

Aaron, Pietro, 123-125, 127, 128, 138, 144-146, 150-152, 155, 166, 178, 181, 196, 452
Agricola, Martin, 129-130, 155, 279, 478
Alamanni, 401
Albrecht, duke of Prussia, 285
Allwood, Richard, 471
Antico, Andrea, 385
Apiarius, Matthias, 447, 450
Ap Rhys, Philip, 467-468, 469, 470
Arcadelt, Jaques, 161, 162, 164, 200, 205, 246, 369, 403, 405-406, 407, 418, 420, 434
Aretino, Pietro, 395
Ariosto, Ludovico, 407
Aristotle, 181
Aristoxenus, 128, 452
Ashwell, Thomas, 323
Aston, Hugh, 309, 320, 324-326
Attaingnant, Pierre, 186, 249, 368, 370, 375, 387-390, 491, 493, 495

Bach, J. S. 259
Bacheler, Daniel, 498
Bapst, Valentin, 284
Barberiis, Melchior de, 496
Beausseron, 163
Bembo, Pietro, 398, 405
Bercham, Jachet de, 419, 420
Beringen, Marcelin, 290
Beringen, Godefroy, 290
Bermudo, Juan, 188, 457, 486-487
Bèze, Théodore, de, 287, 290
Blaurer, Ambrosius, 291

Blum, Michael, 284
Bourgeois, Louis, 287, 290, 291
Boyce, William, 361
Brandolini, Raffaele, 177
Brandt, Jobst vom, 448, 450
Brebate, A. de, 385
Breitengaser, Wilhelm, 450
Brewster, 498
Bridges, Thomas, 420
Bruck, Arnoldus de (Arnold von), 278, 279, 450, 451
Brumel, Antoine, 490
Brumel, Jacques, 481
Buchner, Hans or Johann (Hans von Constance), 474-476, 477, 478, 479
Bulman, 498
Burck, Joachim, 446

Calvin, John, 256, 286-287, 288, 289, 290
Cambio, Perissone, 433, 438
Caracciolo, Antonio, 435
Castellino, Alvise (Il Varoter), 424
Castiglione, Giovanni Antonio da. 126
Causton, Thomas, 358, 359
Cavazzoni, Girolamo, 456, 457, 483-485
Cavazzoni, Marco Antonio, 125, 126, 185, 455, 456, 457, 482-483
Celtes, Konrad, 446
Ceretto, Scipione, 499
Certon, Pierre, 205, 234, 375-376, 495
Chappuys, Claude, 369
Charles V, 435
Chemin, Nicolas du, 391

Cicero, 179
Cimello, Tomaso (Thomas), 198, 430, 434, 436, 437
Clemens (Clemens non Papa), Jacobus, 169, 209-210, 226, 242-244, 381
Collarde, 498
Colonia, Johannes, 428, 434
Compère, Loyset, 478, 490
Cooper, 504
Cordoba, Gonzalo Hernandéz de, 487
Corteccia, Francesco, 220, 224, 232, 407, 410-411, 414, 415, 420, 421, 431, 432, 433
Coverdale, Myles, 296, 362
Cranmer, Thomas, 300, 301, 302, 303, 305
Crécquillon, Thomas, 208, 229, 238-239, 379, 450
Cromwell, Thomas, 296
Crowley, Robert, 305
Cutting, Francis, 498

Dallam, Thomas, 473
Danckerts, Ghiselin, 166
Dante, Aligheri, 398
Day, John, 359
Decius, Nikolaus, 259
Del Lago, Giovanni, 126, 127-128, 145, 146, 178, 180-181
Del la Rue, Pierre, 367
Dietrich, Sixtus, 214, 231, 278, 281, 451, 477
Donato, Baldassare, 438
Dorico, Valerio, 403, 417, 424, 434
Ducis, Benedictus, 215, 231, 278

Edward VI (King of England), 302, 304, 463, 472
Egenolff, Christian, 447, 450
Elizabeth, Queen, 304

Farrant, Richard, 471
Fayrfax, robert, 504
Festa, Costanzo, 213, 226-227, 230, 231, 245, 397, 400, 402, 406, 415, 417, 418, 419, 420, 421, 434
Festa, Sebastiano, 402, 407, 417, 424
Févin, Antoine de, 490, 501
Finck, Heinrich, 478

Finé, Oronce, 505
Flaminio, Giovanni Antonio, 123
Fogliano, Lodovico, 126, 147-150, 179, 419
Fontana, Vincenzo, 430, 434
Formschneider, Hieronymus, 447, 450
Forster, Georg, 447, 448, 449, 450
Francis I, 288, 373, 374
Froschauer, Christoph, 291, 292
Fuchswild, Johann, 477

Gafurius, Franchinus, 150, 166
Ganassi, Sivestro, 499
Gardane, Antoine, (Gardano, Antonio) 378, 390-391, 403, 416, 417, 421, 424, 429, 430, 432, 433, 437, 438, 453
Gaytan, Juan, 487
Gero, Jhan, 165, 434
Ghibel, 165
Gintzler, Simon, 496
Glarean, Heinrich, 130-133, 138-140, 147, 180, 183
Gombert, Nicolas, 200, 207, 226, 239-242, 380, 450, 500, 501
Grammateus, Henricus, 152
Grazzini (Il Lasca), 410
Greffinger, Wolfgang, 446, 477
Greiter, Matthias, 288-289
Guilliaud, 143
Guyot, Jean (Castileti), 381

Heath, John, 471
Henry II, (king of France) 288
Henry VIII (king of England), 295, 301, 309, 463, 464, 504
Heyden, Sebald, 134
Hofhaimer, Paul, 446, 456, 474, 477, 478
Holborne, anthony, 498
Horace, 446, 452
Horn, Johannes (Jan Roh), 292, 293
Huss, John, 261, 268

Isaac, Heinrich, 278, 448, 451, 477, 478

Jacquet of Mantua, 220, 223, 224, 227, 232, 250-251
Johnson, Robert, 498
Janequin, Clément, 202, 234, 368, 369, 372, 373-374, 417, 495

Index of Persons

Jhan, Maistre, (Giovanni Nasco), 223, 420
Johnson, Robert, 358, 360, 441
Josquin des Prez, 161, 477, 478, 490, 500, 501

Kleber, Leonard, 458, 459, 460, 474, 476, 478-479, 480
Klug, Josef, 266, 267, 270, 274, 276, 284
Kotter, Johannes, 458, 459, 460, 474, 476-477, 479
Kriesstein, Melchior, 285, 391
Kugelmann, Johann, 285

Lafage, Pierre de, 490
Lampadius, Auctor, 134, 185
Landi, Antonio, 415
Lanfranco, Giovanni Maria, 133, 152, 167, 172-173, 182
Lassus, Orlandus, 221
Laufenberg, Heinrich von, 266
Layolle, François de, 203, 222, 235-237, 377, 400, 407, 420, 421, 422, 501
Le Cocq (Gallus), 381
Legge, Giovanni da, 125
Le Heurteur, Guillaume, 235, 377-378
Lemlin, Lorenz, 450
Lhéritier, Jean, 162, 163
Listenius, Nicolaus, 135, 137, 144, 154, 155, 177
Lorenzo the Magnificent, 410
Louis XII (king of France), 367
Ludford, Nicholas, 307, 310, 318, 322, 326-329, 366
Lufft, Hans, 274
Luther, Martin, 214, 251, 256, 257, 260, 262, 263, 264, 267, 268, 269, 270, 271, 272, 274-278, 281, 282, 283, 285

Machiavelli, Niccolò, 394, 395, 401, 404
Maio, Giovan Thomaso di, 198, 428-429
Manchicourt, Pierre de, 244-245, 380
Marot, Clément, 286, 288, 289, 290, 368, 369, 373, 374
Maurus, Rhabanus, 264
Merbecke, John, 300, 301, 305, 306, 317, 342
Michelangelo, 405, 410
Milán, Luis de, 192, 193, 443, 500

Milano, Francesco Canova da, 496, 497
Moderne, Jacques, 368, 385-387, 422
Morales, Cristóbal, 216-219, 228, 230, 233, 246, 252-253, 421, 501
Morely, Thomas, 308
Moulu, Pierre, 477, 490
Mudarra, alonso de, 443, 501
Muentzer, Thomas, 259
Mulliner, Thomas, 470
Munday, William, 309, 371

Nachtgall, Ottmar, 478
Narváez, Luis de, 193, 443, 500
Navarre, Marguerite de, 374
Newman, (Master Newman), 498
Nola, Giovane Domenico da, 198, 425, 437 427, 428, 429-430, 436, 437-438

Obrecht, Jacob, 456, 478, 490
Ockeghem, Johannes, 490
Oecolampadius, Johannes, 291
Okeland, Robert, 358
Othmayer, Casper, 450, 451
Ott, Johann (Hans), 447, 448, 450

Paolucci, Giuseppe, 193
Pasoti, 424
Passereau, Pierre, 372, 377
Petrarch, Francesco, 133, 393, 398, 401, 404, 410
Petrucci, Ottaviano dei, 417, 424
Phinot, Dominique, 223
Pilkington, Francis, 498
Pisano, Bernardo, 397, 399-400
Preston, Thomas, 463, 468-469, 470

Ramis, Bartolomé, 152, 166
Rauscher, Andreas, 274
Redford, John, 463, 465, 466-467, 470, 471
Regnault, Pierre. See Sandrin
Rener, Adam, 214
Resinarius (Harzer), Balthazar, 214, 278, 281
Rhau, Georg, 129, 130, 276, 278, 280, 281, 283, 447
Richafort, Jean, 206, 226, 237-238, 378-379, 450, 500
Robinson, Thomas, 498

Ronsard, Pierre de, 373
Rore, Cipriano de, 220, 224, 227, 248-249, 407, 411-413, 453, 454, 503
Rosseter, Philip, 498
Rossetti, Biagio, 170-172, 182
Rotta, Antonio, 496
Rousée, Jean, 477
Ruggo, 501
Rupsch, Conrad, 258
Ruscelli, 133
Ruzante (Angelo Beolco), 415, 423, 435

Saint-Gelais, Mellin de, 369
Saint-Gelais, Octovien de, 374
Salinas, Francisco, 153
Sandrin, 376, 495
Sannazaro, 405
Sanseverino, Ferrante, 415
Scaffen, Heinrich, 223
Schlick, Arnolt, 150, 474
Schmeltzl, Wolfgang, 447, 451
Schöffer, Peter, 447, 450
Schumann, Valentin, 284
Scotto, Girolamo, 404, 417, 420, 429, 432, 434, 437, 438
Scotto, Ottaviano, 385, 403, 418, 419, 420
Sedulius, Coelius, 264
Senfl, Ludwig, 214, 215, 225, 228, 251, 278-279, 280, 281, 446, 448, 449-450, 451, 454, 477, 478, 479
Sepúlveda, 501
Seraphim, Fra, 127
Sermisy, Claudin de, 202, 204, 219, 225, 229, 234, 368, 374-375, 376, 378, 417, 445, 490, 491, 495
Shelby, William, 471
Sheppard, John, 317, 320, 321, 342-343, 350-351, 353, 354, 356-357, 358, 360, 364, 441, 471
Sicher, 474, 476, 477-478, 479
Silvestrino, Francesco, 433
Spataro, Giovanni, 126, 127, 128, 145, 146, 452
Steigleder, Joh. Ulrich, 187
Sternhold, Thomas, 302
Stoltzer, Thomas, 278, 285, 451

Strozzi, Lorenzo, 410
Striggio, Alessandro, 416
Strozzi, giovambattista, 415
Sultzbach, 435
Susato, Tielman, 379, 380, 391-393

Tallis, Thomas, 307, 315-317, 341-342, 347-350, 352-353, 355-356, 357, 358, 360, 361, 362, 363, 441, 471
Taverner, John, 310-315, 318-320, 321, 322, 330-340, 345-347, 351-352, 353, 358, 359, 360, 471
Tinctoris, Johannes, 160
Tompkins, Thomas, 470
Tritonius, Petrus, (Peter Treibenreif), 183, 446
Tye, Christopher, 307, 312, 315, 320, 321, 340-341, 343, 358, 361, 471

Valderrábano, Enrique Enriquez de, 444, 501
Vanneo, Stephano, 155, 167
Verdelot, Philippe, 249-250, 394, 395, 396, 399, 402, 406, 417, 418, 419, 421, 450
Virdung, Sebastian, 130

Walther, Johann, 258, 260, 264, 265, 266, 267, 269, 270, 271, 275-278, 282
Weck, Hans, 460, 477
Weisse Michael, 292, 293
Whytbroke, William, 358
Whyte, Robert, 471
Wilder, Philip Van, 498
Willaert, Adrian, 133, 165, 169, 200, 211-212, 222-224, 231, 247-248, 381-382, 405, 406, 407, 408-410, 411, 413, 418, 419, 424, 431-433, 434, 435, 438, 451-454, 495, 501, 503
Winkworth, Catherine, 259

Zili, Dominik, 291
Zirler, Stephan, 450
Zuylen van Nyevelt, Willem van, 294
Zwick, Jean (Reformer), 291, 292
Zwick, Johannes (Poet), 291
Zwingli, Ulrich, 256, 285, 286

Index of Works

Agnus Dei, Redford, 466
Antiphonale (Plainsong), 297
Antiphon, *see* Processional; Ritual; Votive
A Plaine and Easie Introduction, Morely, 308
A Preface for All Good Hymnals, Luther, 274
Ars ludendi, Buchner, 475, 476
Ars transferendi, Buchner, 475
Arte prattica di contrappunto, Paolucci, 194
Assumpta est Maria, 481
Ave nobilissima creatura, Josquin, 161, 162
Ayn new kunstlich Buech, Grammateus, 152

Beatus Laurentius, Preston, 469
Benedicam Domino, Johnson, 441
Book of Common Prayer, The, (1549), 303, 306, 357, 361; __(1552), 306
Book of *Psaumes*, Certon, 288
Booke of common praier noted, Merbecke, 301, 305-306
Breve introduttione di musica misurata, Del Lago, 128, 180, 181
Breviary (Lessons, antiphons, responds, etc.), 297
Büchlein von den Proportionibus, Agricola, 130
Canzoni francese a due voci...buone da Cantare et sonare, Gardane, 505
Cathedral Music, Boyce, 361
Certaine Notes, Day, 359

Certaine Notes (*continued*)
  In trouble and adversity, Causton, 359
  O give thanks unti the Lord, Causton 359
Chanson
  Paris School
    Allez souspirs, Sermisy, 374
    Contentez vous, amy, de la pensée, Certon, 376
    En reveillant, Regnault, Sandrin, 376
    Frere Thibault, sejourné gros et gras, Certon, 375
    Il est bel et bon, Passereau, 372
    Je n'ay point plus d'affection , Sermisy, 371
    La Chasse, Janequin, 374
    Languir me fais sans l'avoir offensé, Certon, 376
    Las povre coeur, Janequin, 374
    Le Chant des Oiseaux, Janequin, 374
    Les cris de Paris, Janequin, 372
    Pour ung plaisir, Sermisy, 375
    Résveillies vous, Janequin, 417
    Reveillez vous, Sandrin, 376
    Sy mon travail vous peult donner plaisir, Regnault, Sandrin, 376
    Tant que vivrai, Sermisy, 375
    Vivre ne puis content sans ma maistresse, Certon, 376
  __ in the theater
    Content desir, Sermisy 384
    Doulce memoire, Sandrin, 384
    Il estroit une fillette, Janequin, 384
    Laissez moy planter le may, Bou-

Chanson (continued)
    in the theater *(continued)*
      teiller, 384
    Languir me fais, Sermisy, 384
    My levay par ung matin, Janequin, 385
    Puysqu'en amours, Sermisy, 384
  Provencial School
    Amour partes, Le Heurteur, 377
    Amu chercher vostre fortune, Gardane, 378
    Amy, souffrez que je vous aime, Le Heurteur, 378
    Au joly son du sansonnet, Passereau, 377
    Content desir, Gardane, 378. See also *Chanson* __ in the theater
    Helas! Amour, Le Heurteur, 378
    La fille qui n'a point, Layolle, 377
    Donna si raro, Layolle, 377
    Jouyssance vous donneray, Gardane, 378
    Ma dame ung jour, Le Heurteur, 378
    N'avons veu mal assenée, Gardane, 378
    O doulx regard, Gardane, 378
    Pour avoir paix avecques mon desir, Layolle, 377
    Troys jeunes bourgeoises, Le Heurteur, 378
    Vostre cueur je supply, Gardane, 378
  Netherlandish School
    Au joly boys je rencontrary, Clemens, 381
    Baises moy tant, tant, Willaert, 382
    Dame D'honneur vives en sperace, Crécquillon?, 380
    De mon triste deplaisir, Richafort, 379
    Falte d'argens, Josquin, 484; Cavazzoni, 484
    J'ay veu le cerf, Manchicourt, 380
    Je prens en grey la dure mort, Clemens, 381
    Jouissance vous donneray, Gombert, 380
    Le bergier et la bergier, Le Cocq (Gallus), 381
    Plusieurs regretz, Josquin, 482; Cavazzoni, 482
    Qui ne l'aymeroit, Gombert, 380
    Tru, tru, trut avant il fault boire, Richafort, 379
    Ung gay bergier prioit bergiere, Crécquillon, 379
    Vous êtes trop jeune, Gombert, 380
  Published sources of the
    Canzoni francese a due voci di Ant. Gardane et di altri autori, Gardane, 390
    Canzoni francese a due voci d'Antonio Gardane insieme auquel de altri autori, libro primo, Gardane, 391
    Chansons Nouvelles, Attaingnant, 387
    Chansons nouvelle en musique à quatre parties, Attaingnant, 387
    Dixseptiesme livre contenant xix chansons legères très musicales nouvelles à quatre parties, Attaingnant, 390
    La couronne et fleur des chansons à troy, Antico-Brebate, 385
    Le difficile des chanson: Premier livre contenant xxii chansons nouvelles à quatre parties en quatre livres, Moderne, 387
    Le difficile des chanson: Second livre contenant xxvi chansons nouvelles à quatre parties en quatre livres, Moderne, 387
    Le neufiesme livre des chansons à quatre parties, Susato, 380
    Le parangon des chansons. Premier (-Dixieseme) livre, Moderne, 368, 377, 385-387
    Live premier(-trentesixiesme) de chansons, Attaingnant, 389-390
    Motetti novi e chanzoni franciose a quatro sopra doi, Antico, 385
    Premier Livre de chansons à quatre parties, Chemin, 391
    Premier livre-Le treziesme livre, Susato, 391-393
    Primo libro de la canzoni franzese, Antico-Scotto, 385
    Quarante et duex chansons musicales à troys parties, Attaingnant, 388
    Secund livre contenant xxxi chansons musicales, Attaingnant, 375, 389

Index of Works   513

Chanson (continued)
  Published sources of the (continued)
    Second Livre de chansons à quatre parties, Chemin, 391
    Selectissimae...cantiones, Kriesstein, 391
    Trente chansons musicales à auatre parties nouvellement et tres correctement imprimés (1529), Attaingnant, 388
    Trente chansons musicales (1534), Attaingnant, 389
    Trente et huyt chansons musicales, Attaingnant, 388
    Trente et quatre chansons musicales à quatre parties, Attaingnant, 388
    Trente et sept chansons musicales, Attaingnant, 388
    Trente et six chansons musicales, Attaingnant, 388
    Trente et trois chansons nouvelles, Attaingnant, 388
    Trente troysiesme livre contenant xx chansons nouvelles à quatre en deux, Attaingnant, 390
    Trente et une chansons musicales à quatre parties, (1529), Attaingnant, 388
    Trente et une chansons musicales (1534), Attaingnant, 389
    Trente et ungyesme livre contenant xxx chansons nouvelles à quarte [parties] en deux volumes. De la facture et composition de maîstre Clément Jannequin... Attaingnant, 390
    Vingt et cinque chansons musicales reduictes en la tablature des Orgues Espinettes manicordions et telz semblables instrumentz musicaulx..., Attaingnant, 186, 491
    Vingt et six chansons musicales reduictes en la tablature des Orgues espinettes manicordions et telz semblables instrumentz musicaulx... 1531, Attaingnant, 491
    Vingt et huit chansons nouvelles, Attaingnant, 388
    Vingt et neuf chansons musicales à quatre parties, Attaingnant, 388
    Vingt et quatre chansons musicales à quatre parties composées par Clément Jennequin, Attaingnant, 388
    Vingt et sept chansons musicales (1531), Attaingnant 388
    Vingt et sept chansons musicales à quatre parties desquelles les plus convenables à la fleuste d'allemant... (1533) Attaingnant, 374, 389
    Vingt et six chansons musicales, Attaingnant, 186, 389
    Vingt deuxiesme livre, Attaingnant, 390
Christe qui lux, Redford, 466
Christ rising again, Sheppard, 364
Commedia di Callimaco e di Lucrezia, 395
Compendiolo di molti dubbi, segreti et sentenze intorno al canto fermo, et figurato, Aaron, 125-126
Compendium musices tam figurati quam plani cantus, Lampadius, 135, 185
Con lagrime e sospir, Willaert, 496
Contrapunctus: seu figurata musica..., Guaynard; Layolle?, 202, 203, 235
Credidi propter quod locutus est, Willaert, 223

Das gluet zu Speier, senfl, 449
De arte canendi, Heyden, 134
Décalogue (Ten Commandments), Calvin, 289
Declaración de instrumentos musicales, Bermudo, 188-189, 457, 486
De compositione cantus compendium, Lampadius, 135
De inventione, Cicero, 179
De laudibus musicae et poesos, Brandolini, 177
Deliver us good Lord, Tye, 361
De musica et poetica opusculum, Brandolini, 177
De musica libri VII, Salinus, 153
Deudsche Messe, Luther, 258, 261, 285
Deus in adjutorium, Senfl, 225
Diffusa est gratia, Preston, 469
Dixhuit basses dances...avec dixneuf branles... Attaingnant, 493, *495*

Dixhuit basses dances garnies de Recoupes et Tordions..., 495
Dixneuf chansons musicales...reduicts en la tabulature des Orgues espinettes Manicordions..., Attaingnant, 186, 462, 491
Dodecachordon, Glarean, 131-133, 138-140, 180, 183
Dolcemente s'adirà, Gero, 165
Dorian Service, Tallis, 363
Eecce nunc benedicite, Corteccia, 224
Ein kurtz deudsche Musica, Agricola, 129, 130
El Maestro. See *Libro de Música de Vihuela de Mano:...*
Epistole composte in lingua volgare, Del Lago, 127-128, 181
Eterne rerum, Redford, 466

Fantasia in re, Kleber, 479
Fantasie per sonar a due laute, Barberiis, 496
Farce de deulx, Marot, 384
Felix namque, Ap Rhys, 468; Preston, 468
Finale in re seeu preambalon, Kleber, 478
Formula missae et communionis pro Ecclesia Wittembergensi, Luther, 257
Fremuit spiritu Jesu, Clemens, 169
Frottole intabulate da sonar organi, Antico, 480-481
Fundamentum, sive ratio vera, quae docet quemvis cantum planum... Buchner, 475-476

Gaudetete in Domino semper, Corteccia, 224
Gesellschaftslied, 447-448
  Frische teutsche Liedein, Forster, 447. See also Lieder, Collections of secular German
  Liederbuch, Ott, 448
Glogauer Liederbuch, 184
Gloria Patri et Filio et Spiritui Sancto (Lesser Doxology), 225
Glorificamus, Redford, 467

Heare the voyce and prayer, Tallis, 362
Hesperiae cum laeta, 454. See also Motet, Venus Motet
Hofweisen, 447, 449
  Olm Ehr und Gunst, Forster?, 447
Hymnal, The (music for the hymns), 297
Hymnals
  Monophonic
    Achliederbuch, Jobst Gutknecht, 272-274
    Enchiridion, Lufft, 274
    Erfurt(er) Enchiridia(en), Jum Schwarzen Horn (Maler) and Zum Färbefass (Loersfeld), 260, 261, 264, 265, 267, 271, 272, 273, 274
    Geistliche Lieder auffs new gebessert zu Wittemberg, Klug, 264, 266, 267, 270, 271, 272, 274-276, 284
    Nüw gsangbüchle von vil schönen Psalmen und geistlichen liedern, (Constance Songbook of 1540) Zwick, 291-292
  Polyphonic
    Concentus novi trium vocum, Kugelmann, 285
    Cycle of, Festa, 231; Dietrich, 231; Ducis, 231
    Ein New Gesengbüchlen, Weisse, 292-293
    Ein Sangbüchlein aller Sontags Evangelien, Agricola, 279
    Enchiridion geistlicher gesenge und Psalmen für die leisen, Blum, 284
    Geystliche Gesangk Buchleyn (Walther Chorgesangbuch), Walther, 260, 261, 264, 265, 267, 268, 269, 270, 271, 272, 273, 276-278
    Geystliche Lieder: mit einer newen vorrhede D. Mart. Luth., Bapst, 266
    Geystliche Lieder...[und] Psalmen.. Bapst, 284
    Himni vesperorum totius anni secundum Romanam curiam diligentissime recogniti...cum quatuor ey quinque vocibus, Scotto (Jacquet), 232
    Himnnario secondo l'uso della chiesa romana et fiorentina, Corteccia, 232
    Hymnarium, Corteccia, 232
    Hymni per totum annum: 3, 4, 5, 6 vocibus, Festa, 231
    Hymnorum musica, Willaert, 231

Index of Works 515

*Newe deudsche geistliche Gesenge...
für die gemeinen Schulen*, Rhau, 278-279
Sacorum hymnorum liber primus, Rhau, 230
Hymns
  German
    All ehr und lob soll Gottes sein, 259
    Aallein Gott in der Höhe sei Ehre, 259
    Christe, du Lamm Gottes (Agnus Dei), 261
    Christum wir sollen loben schon, Luther, 264
    Da Jakob nu das Kleid ansah, Senfl. 278
    Es ist das Heil uns kommen her, 273, 274
    Gelobet seist du, Jesu Christ, Luther, 269, 283
    Gott der Vater wohn uns bei, Luther, 269
    Gott sey gelobet und gebenedeiet, Luther, 260, 270
    Herr Gott, dich loben wir, 264
    Ich will den Herrn Iben allezeit, 258
    Jesaja dem Propheten das geschah (German Sanctus), 260, 271
    Jesus Christus unser Heiland, Luther, 260, 261, 268
    Komm Gott Schöpfer, heileger Geist, Luther, 264
    Mit Fried und Freud ich fahr dahin, Agricola, 279, 280
    Nun bitten wir den Heiligen Geist, 259
    Nun freut euch, lieben Christen g'-mein (gmein), 272, 273; Ducis, 279
    Nun komm, der Heiden Heiland, Luther, 263, 264
  Latin
    Aeterne rerum Conditor, Redford, 467
    Ave maris stella, Sheppard, 356
    A solis ortus cardine, 264; Sheppard, 356; Redford, 466
    Aures ad nostras...preces, Festa, 231
    Christe redemptor omnium, Festa, 231; Sheppard, 357
    Conditor alme siderum, Bermudo, 487
    Deus tuorum militum, Tallis 355
    Eterne rex altissime, Redford, 466
    Iam Christus astra ascenderat, Tallis, 355
    In Dominicis Adventus et Quadragesimae, 271
    Jesus Christus, Nostra Salus, Huss, 261, 268
    Jesu salvator saeculi, Tallis, 355; Sheppard, 356
    Media vita in morte, Layolle, 236
    Pange lingua, Bermudo, 487
    Quod chorus vatum, Tallis, 355
    Sacris solemniis, Sheppard, 356
    Salvator mundi Domine, Tallis, 355; Sheppard, 356
    Sermone blando angelus, Tallis, 355
    Te Deum laudamus, 264
    Te lucis ante terminum, Tallis, 356
    Veni creator Spiritus, Rhabanus Maurus, 264; Bermudo, 487
    Veni redemptor gentium, 263; Redford, 467
    Vexilla regis prodeunt, Bermudo, 487
  Latin (non-liturgical)
    Dies est laetitae, 266
    In dulci jubilo, 266
    Puer natus in Bethlehem, 266
    Resonet in laudibus, 266

I cried unto the Lord, Sheppard, 360
If you love me, Tallis, 363
I give you a new commandment, Sheppard, 364
Il commodo, Landi, 415
Il marescalco, Aretino, 395
Il Petrarca, Ruscelli, 133
Il re di Spagna, 459
Il terzo libro di motetti a cinque voci, Gardano, 248, 454
Il Thoscanello de la musica, Aaron, 124-125, 150-152, 167, 178, 181, 196
In dulci iubilo, Sicher, 477; Kleber, 479
In nomine, 332
In pictura annae principis Estensis, Falletti, 454
Instruction pour le jeu l'orgue, 492
Intabolatura de lauto..., Bianchini, 497
Intabolatura de lauto, Primo libro, Gintz-

ler, 496; Rotta, 496
Intavolatura cioè Recercari, Canzoni, Hinni, Magnificati, Cavazzoni, 483
Intavolaturo di liuto, Milano, 497
Intavolatura d'organo cioè Misse Hinni Magnifficati...libro secondo, Cavazzoni, 484-*485*
Io che di viver, Arcadelt, 162, 164
Isagoge in musicen, Glarean, 131
I sacri et santi salmi di David profeta..., Rore, 224, 227; Jacquet, 224, 228
I salmi appertinenti alli vesperi per tutte le feste dell'anno..., Willaert, 222-223
I will exalt thee, Tye, 361
I will give thanks unto the Lord, Sheppard, 360
I will magnify thee, Taverner, 359

La Clizia, Machiavelli, 394, 395, 404
La Mandragola, Machiavelli, 394, 395, 404. See also *Commedia di Callimaco e di Lucrezia*
La pastorale, 415
Lamentationes Hieremiae Prophetae..., Montanus and Neuber, 229-230
La verginella, Ghibel, 165
La vaccaria, 415
Leisen
 Christ ist erstanden, 267, *283*
 Nun bitten wir den Heiligen Geist, Luther, 267
Letanie with Suffrages, Cranmer, 300-301, 304, 305
Lettione Seconda, Ganassi, 498, *499*
Libellus de rudimentis musicae, Rossetti, 170-172, 182
Liber decem missarum, Moderne, 1532 edition, 203, 204; 1540 edition, 204
Liber de natura et proprietate tonorum, Tinctoris, 160
Liber selectarum cantionum, 225
Libri tres de institutione harmonica, Aaron, 123, 166-167
Libro de Música de Vihuela de Mano: intitulado El Maestro, Milán, 192, 193, 443, 500
Libro de Música de Vihuela de Mano: intitulado Silva de Sirenas, Valderrábano, 444, 501

Lieder
 Non-liturgical songs
  Aus fremden Landen komm ich her, 268
  Christ lag in Todesbanden, Luther, 267
  Der tag ist so freudenreich, 266
  Ein Kind geborn zu Bethlehem, 266
  In Gottes Namen fahren wir, 275
  Joseph, lieber Joseph mein, 266
  Nun singet und seid froh, 266
  Singet frisch und wohlgemut, 266
  Von Himmel hoch, da komm ich her, Luther, 268
 Collections of secular German
  Frische teutsche Liedein, Forster, 447, 449, 450
  Fünff und sechzig teütscher Lieder, vormals imm Truck nie ussgangen, Schöffer & Apiarius, 450
  Gassenhawerlin und Reutterliedlin, Egenolff, 450
  Guter, seltzamer, und Künstreicher teutscher Gesang..., Schmeltzl, 451
  Mehrstimmiges deutsches *Liederbuch,* Ott, 450
  121 neue Lieder, Ott, 450
  Reutterische und Jegerische Liedlein, Othmayr, 451
Lord, let thy servant now depeart in peace, Tye, 361
Los seys libros del Delphin de múica, Narváez, Aaron, 193, 443, 500
Lucem tuam, Redford, 466, 467
Lucidario in musica di alcune opinione antiche e moderne, Aaron, 125, 146, 155
Lumen ad revelationem, 253

Madrigals
 Ancor che col partire, Rore, 413
 Aspro core, Willaert, 409
 Come lieta si mostra, Festa, 415
 Da bei rami scendea dolce, Arcadelt, 406
 Da la belle contrade, Rore, 412
 'Dormend' un giorno, Verdelot, 399
 Il bianco e dolce cigno, Arcadelt, 406
 Ingredere, Corteccia, 415
 Io dico e dissi e dirò, Corteccia, 411

Madrigals (continued)
   Madonna qual certezza, Verdelot, 399
   Madonna non so dir, Verdelot, 399
   Mentre che 'l cor', Willaert, 409
   Perch 'io veggio et mi spiace, Corteccia, 411
   Più che mai vaga, Festa, 415
   Quando nascesti amor?, Willaert, 409
   Quando ritrova, C. Festa, 400
   Quanto più m'arde, Willaert, 408
   Sacro e santo Imeneo, Corteccia, 415
   Una donna, Pisano, 400
   Vientene almo riposo, Corteccia, 414
   Voi ve n'andat' al cielo, Arcadelt, 406
Madrigal, The
   Published sources of
      Arcadelt il quinto libro di Madrigali di Archadelt a quatro voci..., Gardane, 421
      Cantus il primo libro di madrigali di Archedelt a quatro voci..., Gardane, 420
      Cantus libro primo de Madrigali a quattro voci di Francesco Corteccia..., G. Scotto, 420
      Cantus primo libro di Madrigali d'Archadelt a tre voci..., Gardane, 421
      Cinquanta Canzoni a quatro voci..., Moderne, 422
      Corteccia libro primo de Madrigali a cinque e a sei voci..., Gardane, 416, 422
      Corteccia libro secondo de Madrigali a quattro voci..., Gardane, 422
      Dei madrigali di Verdelotto et de altri eccellentissimi auttori a cinque voci, libro secondo, O. Scotto, 419
      Deli madrigali a tre voci, O. Scotto, 419
      Il primo libro de madrigali cromatici a cinque voci, Gardane, 412
      Il primo libro de madrigali di Verdelotto, G. Scotto, 417
      Il primo libro de madrigali di Verdelotto. Novamente stampato, et con somma diligentia corretto. O. Scotto, 418
      Il quarto libro di Madrigali d'Archadelt a quatro voci..., Gardane, 421
      It secondo libro de madrigali d'Archadelt, O. Scotto, 420
      Il secundo libro de madrigali di Verdelot, novamente stampati... (1534 edition), O. Scotto, 418
      Il secundo libro de madrigali di Verdelot insie con alcuni bellissimi madrigali di Adriano, et Constantio Festa... (1537 edition), O. Scotto, 418
      Il terzo libro de i madrigali novissimi de Archadelt, Gardane, 416
      Il terzo libro de i madrigali novissimi d'Archadelt a quattro voci, Scotto, 417
      Il terzo libro de madrigali di Verdelotto insieme con alcuni altribellissimi madrigali di Constantino Festa..., O Scotto, 419
      Il Vero Libro di Madrigali a tre voci di Constantio Festa, Gardane, 421
      Il vero secondo libro di madrigali d'Archadelt, Gardane, 416
      Primo libr di madrigali a quatro voci, G. Scotto, 420
      Madrigali a cinque Libro primo, O. Scotto, 419
      Madrigali de diversi musici libro primo, 396
      Madrigali novi de diversi excellentissimi musici libro prima de la serena, Dorico (1530 edition), 417; (1533 edition), 396, 403; (1534 edition), 418
      Musica di meser Bernardo Pisano sopra le canzone del Petrarcha, 397, 417
      Musica nova, Willaert, 404, 410
      Scotto. Di Girolamo Scotto I madrigali a tre voci, G. Scotto, 420
      Venticinque Canzoni a cinque voci..., Moderne, 422
Magnificat. *See also* Music __ for Vespers
   Benedicta, Ludford, 318
   Et exulavitt, Rore, 227
   __ *octavi toni*, Richafort, 226
   __ *octo tonorum*, Senfl, 228
   __ *on the first Tone*, Taverner, 318
   __ *on the second Tone*, Taverner, 319

Magnificat (*continued*)
   __on the sixth Tone, Taverner, 319
   __on the 8th tone, Morales, 228
   __quinti toni, Richafort, 226
   __sexti toni, Richafort, 226; Festa, 227
Magnificat sur les huit tons avec Te Deum laudamus et deux Preludes, le tout mys en la tabulature des Orgues espinettes et Manicordions... Attaingnant, 489
Maria Zart, Buchner, 476
Mascherate, 436-438. See also *Villanella*
  Madonna noi sapimo ben giocare, Cambio, 438
  Medici noi siamo o belle donne, Cambio, 438
  O anime devot'in caritate, Cambio, 438
  Tri ciechi siamo povr'inamorati, Cambio, 438
  Veniteve a pigliare la candelora, Cambio, 438
Mascherata, The
  Published sources of
    Canzone villanesche alla napolitana a quatro voci di Perissone novamente poste in luce..., Gardane, 438. See also *Villanella*, The __Published sources of
    Canzone villanesche alla napolitana di M. Adriano Wigliaret a quattro voci..., Scotto, 438. See also *Villanella*, The __Published sources of
    Canzone villanesche al modo napolitano a tre voci di Thomaso Cimello da Napoli con una bataglia villanescha a tre del medesimo autore npvamente poste in luce. Libro primo 1545, Gardane, 430
    Canzoni villanesche de Don Joan Dominico del Giovane de Nola, a tre voci novamente ristampate. Libro primo 1545, Scotto, 429
    Di Baldissera Donato il primo libro di canzon villanesche alla napolitana a quatro voci..., Gardane, 438
Mass
  Lady, Ludford, 328-329
  Requiem
    Missa Circumdederunt me, Richafort, 206, 207

Missa pro defunctis, Sermisy, 204; Clemens, 209; Morales, 217
Missa pro defunctis cum quatuor vocibus, nunc primum in lucem aedita, Certon, 205
__-Section
  Agnus Dei, Taverner, 340
  Alleluia Salve virgo, Taverner, 339
  Alleluia Veni electa mea, Taverner, 339-340
  Benedictus, Tallis, 357, 360; Preston, 469
  Benedictus sit pate, Ap Rhys, 467
  Christe eleison, Taverner, 338
  Confessio, Preston, 469
  Credo in unum Deum, Ap Rhys, 468
  Deus creator onium, Ap Rhys, 467
  Kyrie eleison angelicum sollemne, Buchner, 475
  Kyrie Leroy, Taverner, 338
  O Lamb of God, Heath, 358
Meistergesang, 442-443
Melopoiae sive harmoniae tetracenticae..., Tritonius (Peter Treibenreif), 183
Miserere, Redford, 466
Missa. See also Music __for the Mass
  __*Adieu mes amours*, Layolle, 203
  __*Adiuva me*, Certon, 205
  __*A la fontaine du prez*, Clemens, 210
  __*Apostolorum*, Cavazzoni, 485
  __*Aspice Domine*, Morales, 217
  __*Ave Maria*, Morales, 217; Ashwell, 323, 324
  __*Ave maris stella*, Morales, 217
  __*Ave Regina Coelorum*, Arcadelt, 205
  __*Benedicta*, Ludford, 326
  __*Benedicta es coelorum Regina*, Willaert? or Hesdin?, 212; Morales, 218
  __*Carminum*, Festa, 214
  __*Ces fascheux sotz*, Layolle, 204
  __*Christus resurgens*, Willaert, 212
  __*Christi virgo*, Ludford, 327
  __*Corona spinea*, Taverner, 332-*333*
  __*cum quatuor vocibus, ad imitationem cantionis Voulant honneur*, Sermisy, 205
  __*cum quatuor vocibus, ad imitationem moduli Ab initio*, Sermisy, 205
  __*cum quatuor vocibus paribus, ad imi-*

Missa (continued)
- tationem moduli *Tota pulchra es,* Sermisy, 205
- cum quinque vocibus, ad imitationem moduli *Quare fremuerunt gentes,* Sermisy, 205
- da pacem, Gombert, 207
- de Beata Virgine, Arcadelt, 161, 206; Morales, 216
- Decidle al cavallero, Morales, 216
- de Domina nostra, Festa, 214
- de feria, Beausseron, 163
- de la Dominica, Brumel?, 481
- Domine Deus omnipotens, Crécquillon, 209
- Domine quis habitavit, Sermisy, 204
- dominicales I, II, Sefl, 215
- Dulcis amica, Certon, 235
- Ecce quam bonum, Clemens, 209
- Et in terra pax, Festa, 214
- Euge bone, Tye, 340-341
- Forseulement, Gombert, 208
- Gaude Barbara, Willaert, 211; Morales, 218
- Gloria tibi Trinitas, Taverner, 331-332, 359
- Inclina cor meum [Deus], Ludford, 328
- in Die Sanctae Trinitatis, Ap Rhys, 467
- Jesu Christe, Ashwell, 323
- Je suis déshéritée, Gombert, 208
- Kein in der Welt so schön, Crécquillon, 208
- La Bataille de Marignan, Janequin, 202
- Languir my fault, Clemens, 210
- Lapidaverunt [Stephanum], Ludford, 327
- Laudate Deum, Willaert, 212
- L'aveuglé diu, Janequin, 202
- Leroy, Ludford, 328
- L'homme armé, Morales, 218
- Mater Christi, Taverner, 333, 334
- Meane [Sine nomine], Taverner, 335-336, 358
- Media vita, Gombert, 208
- Menta tota, Willaert, 212
- Mille regretz, Morales, 217
- Mittit as virgmem, Willaert, 212
- Miséricorde, Clemens, 210
- Mort m'a privé, Crécquillon, 209
- Nisi Dominus, Senfl, 215
- Noe, Noe, Arcadelt, 205
- O Dei genetrix, Richafort, 207
- Or combien, Clemens, 210
- O Michael, Taverner, 330-331
- O salutaris hostia, Layolle, 203
- Osculetur me, Willaert, 212
- Per arma justitiae, Merbecke, 323, 342
- Per signum crucis, Senfl, 215
- Peur natus [est nobis], Tallis, 342
- Playn Song, Taverner, 337-338; Tallis, 342
- Plurium motettorum, Sermisy, 204
- Quaeramus cum Pastoribus, Willaert, 211; Morales, 218
- Quam pulchra es, Gombert, 208
- Quem dicunt homines, Morales, 217
- Regnum mundi, Certon, 205; Ludford, 328
- Salve intemerata virgo, Tallis, 341
- Sancte Cuthberte, Ashwell, 324
- Sancte Wilhelmi [Samll Devotion], Taverner, 333, 334, 358
- Se dire je l'osoie, Crécquillon, 209
- se congie pris, Festa, 213
- Si bona suscepimus, Morales, 217
- Spes salutis, Clemens, 210
- sum quatuor vocibus ad imitationem Cantilenae Miséricorde, Clemens, 210
- Super fa re ut fa sol fa, Morales, 219
- Super ut re mi fa, sol, la, Morales, 219
- Sus le pont d'Avignon, Certon, 205
- Te Deum, Aston, 325
- tempore paschali, Gombert, 207
- tous regretz, Gombert, 208
- Tristezas me matan, Morales, 216
- Tu es vas electionis, Morales, 218
- Veni sponsa Christi, Richafort, 207
- Virtute magna, Clemens, 210
- Vitete manus meas, Aston, 325-326
- Videte miraculum, Ludford, 327
- Vulnerasti cor meum, Morales, 218
- Western Wynde, 322; Taverner, 336-

Missa (continued)
    337; Tye, 341; Sheppard, 342-343
Miserere, Ap Rhys, 468
Motectorum...liber primus quinque vocum,
    Gardano, 248
Motectorum quinque vocum liber secundus, Scotto, 241
Motet, The. *See also* Music __ for Diverse
    liturgical and non liturgical purposes
  Absterge Domine, Tallis, 360
  Angelus Domini, Clemens, 244
  Aspice, Domine, de sede sancta tua,
    Sermisy, 234; Jacquet?, 251
  Ave Maria, Layolle, 236
  Ave Regina coelorum, Mater Regis,
    Willaert, 248
  Ave rosa sine spinis, Jacquet, 252
  Ave sanctissima Maria, Verdelot, 250
  Ave Virgo, Crécquillon, 239
  Ave Virgo, Cecilia, Manchicourt, 244
  Ave Virgo sanctissima, Layolle, 236
  Beata Dei genitrix, Layolle, 237
  Beatus homo, Rore, 249
  Benedicta es coelorum Regina, Willaert,
    247
  Carole, magnus erat, Crécquillon, 239
  Christus resurgens, Richafort, 238
  Clare sanctorum senate apostolorum,
    Sermisy, 234
  Congregati sunt inimici nostri, Janequin, 234; Crécquillon, 239; Verdelot,
    250
  Diversi diversa orant, Gombert, 241
  Domine Deus conteris bella, Crécquillon, 238
  Domine Deus omnipotens, Sermisy, 235
  Emendemus in melius, Morales, 252
  Erravi sicut ovis, Clemens, 242
  Fremuit spiritu Jesu, Clemens, 242
  Gabriel archangelus, Verdelot, 250
  Gloria, laus et honor, Richafort, 238
  Hoc est praeceptum, Morales, 253
  Illuxit nunc sacra dies, Rore, 248
  Infelix ego, Rore, 249
  In te Domine speravi, Le Heurteur, 235
  In te, Domine, speravi, Verdelot, 250
  Inviolata, integra, Willaert, 248
  Jerusalem surge, Clemens, 244
  Jubilate Deo omnis, Morales, 233
  Lamentabatur Jacob, Morales, 253
  Libera me de morte eterna, Layolle, 236
  Mane nobiscum, Clemens, 243
  Mater Christi, Taverner, 360
  Mene gaude plurimum, Taverner, 360
  Misereatur mei, Richafort, 237
  Musica Dei donum, Clemens, 454
  Noe, Noe, Christum ascendentem, Le
    Heurteur, 235
  O quam moesta dies, Clemens, 242
  O sacrum convivium, Arcadelt, 246
  Parasti in dulcedine tua, Crécquillon,
    239
  Pater noster, Willaert, 247
  Pater peccavi, Manchicourt, 244; Morales, 252
  Peccantem me, Manchicourt, 244
  Praeparate corda vestra, Sermisy, 234
  Quem dicunt homines, Richafort, 238;
    Gombert, 240
  Quid non ebrietas designat, Willaert,
    169, 451
  Quis te victorem dica, Crécquillon, 239
  Regem archangelorum, Festa, 246
  Regem Regum, Festa, 245
  Repleatur os meum, Jacquet, 251
  Salutatio prima, Senfl, 251
  Salve, crux sancta, Willaert, 247
  Salve Virgo salutaris, Layolle, 235
  Salvum me fac, Jacquet, 251
  Sancte Antoni, Morales, 253
  Sed melius est, Crécquillon, 238
  Spem in alium, Jacquet, 251
  Stabat Mater dolorosa, Layolle, 236
  Stephanus autem, Layolle, 236
  Sufficiebat, Richafort, 237
  Super flumina, Gombert, 240
  Super ripam Jordanis, Clemens, 243
  Veni, Sancte Spiritus, Willaert, 248
  Venus Motet, Rore, 454
  Verbum bonum et suave, Willaert, 247
  Victimae paschali laudes, Willaert, 248
  Voce mea ad dominum, Sheppard, 360
  Vox in Rama, Clemens, 243, 244
Motetta cum quinque cicibus liber primus,
    Scotto, 242
Motetta...quinque vocum, Gardano, 248
Motetti C, Petrucci, 184
Motetti del fiore: Quartus liber motteto-

Index of Works 521

rum ad quinque et six voces, Moderne, 253
Mulliner Book, The, 439, 441, 467
Music
  __for diverse liturgical and non liturgical purposes
    Bicinia gallica, latina, germanica, 282
    Symphoniae jucundae atque adeo breves, Rhau, 281
    Tricinia...latina germanica et gallica, 281
  __for the Mass
    Officia de Nativitae, Rhau, 280
    Officia Paschalia, de Resurrectione et Ascensione Domini, Rhau, 280
    Opus decem missarum, Rhau, 280
    Selectae harmoniae de Passione Domini, Rhau, 280
  __for Vespers
    Novum et insigne opus musicum triginta sex antiphonarium, Dietrich, 281
    Novum opus musicum tres tomos sacrorum hymnorum continens, Dietrich, 281
    Postremum Vespertini officii opus, Rhau, 281
    Responsoriorum...libri duo, Resinarius, 281
    Sacrorum hymnorum liber primus, Rhau, 281
    Vesperarum precum officia, Rhau, 280
Musica, ab authre denuo recognita..., Listenius, 135-136, 137, 154, 177
Musicae..., Heyden, 134
Musicae, id est artis canendi libri duo, Heyden, 134
Musica choralis deudsch, Agricola, 129, 155
Musica figuralis deudsch, Agricola, 130
Musica getutscht, Virdung, 493
Musica instrumentalis deudsch, Agricola, 129-130
Musica nova, 503
Musica nova, Willaert, 453
Musica practica, Gafurius, 166
Musica quatuor vocum vulgo metecta liber primus, Scotto, 241
Musica theorica, Fogliano, 126-127, 147-150, 179
Musica vulgo motecta quinque vocum liber primus, Scotto, 241
My friends the things that do, 441

Neuf basses dances, deux branles, vingt et cinque Pavannes avec quinze Gaillardes en musique a quatre parties, 505
Nunc dimittis, 253, 361

O gloriosa Domina, 481
O happy dames, Mulliner Book, 360; Sheppard, 441
O Lord with all my heart (Benedicam Domino), Johnson, 360
O lux on the faburden, Redford, 466
O most holy and mighty Lord, Taverner, 360
Opus sacrarum cntionum, Crécquillon, 239
Order for Communion, 302
Orgeltabulatur, Sicher, 478; Kleber, *479*
Orlando furioso, Ariosto, 407, 411
O vecchia, tu che guardi, Colonia, 434

Passion
  St, Matthew, Alberti, Gasparo, 219; Sermisy, 220; Corteccia, 220
  St. John, Alberti, Gasparo, 219; Rore, 220; Corteccia, 220
Politica, Aristotle, 181
Practica musicae, Gafurius, 150, 166
Praeambulum in re, Kleber, 478
Praeambulum 6 vocum Lud. Senfl, Senfl, 479
Praeambulum in sol b moll, Kleber, 478
Precatus est Moyses, Redford, 467
Prélude sur chacun ton, 489
Primer of Henry VIII, 304
Processional, 343-344
  __Antiphons
    Salve regina...Ad te clamamus, Tye, 343
  __Hymns
    Gloria laus et honor, Tye, 343
    Salve festa dies, Sheppard, 343

Processional (*continued*)
Hymns (*continued*)
__Psalms with antiphons
In exitu Israel, Sheppard, 343
Laudate pueri, sheppard, 343
Proprium Missae in Dei Paschae, Preston, 469
Prose, 353
Inviolata, Sheppard, 353
Sospitati dedit aegros, Taverner, 353
Prose della volgar lingua, Bembo, 398
Psalms. *See also* Music __Music for Vespers
English
O God be merciful unto us (*Deus misere atur*), Tye, 357
German
Ach Gott von hymel sich dar en, see Ach Gott vom Himmel sieh darein
Ach Gott vom Himmel sieh darein, 272, 273; Agricola, 280
Aus tieffer not schrey ich zu dyr, 271, 273; Bruck, 279
De profundis clamavi ad te (Psalm 130), 271
Ein feste Burg, Luther, 271, 272; Agricola, 280
Es spricht der unweysen mund wol, 273
Ich will den Herrn lben allezeit, 258
Salvum me fac, Domine (Psalm 12), 272
Wohl dem, der in Gottes Furcht steht, 271
Latin
Beati omnes qui timent Dominum (Psalm 128), 271
Deus noster refugium et virtus, (Psalm 46), 271
Psalter, The (Psalms and their ferial antiphons), 297
Psalters
Dutch
Souterliedekens, 293-294
English
Goostly psalmes and spirituall songes drawen out of the holy Scripture, for the comforte and consolacyon of soch as love to rejoyse in God and his worde, 296-297
Psalms in English Metre, 295, 302
Psalter of David newly translated into Englysh metre, Crowley, 305
French
Monophonic Psalters
Aulcuns pseaulmes et cantiques mys en chant, Calvin, 286, 288-289
La forme des prières et chants ecclésiastiques, Calvin, 289
La Manyere de faire prières aux églises françoyses..., 289
Polyphonic Psalters
Le premier livre des Pseaulmes de David, contenant XXIV Psaulmes, composé par Loys Bourgeois en diversité de musique..., Bourgeois, 287, 291
Premier livre de psalmes mis en musique, Certon, 288
Pseaumes cinquante de David roy et et profète, traduictz en vers françois par Clément et mis musique par Loys Bourgeoys à quatre parties à voix de contrepoinct égal consonante au verbe, Bourgeois, 287, 290

Quatorze gaillardes, neuf pavennes, sept branles et deux basses dances le tout reduict de musique en la tabulature du jeu d'Orgues..., Attaingnant, 186, 461

Recanetum de musica aurea, Vanneo, 144, 167
Recerchari, Motetti, Canzoni, Libro I, Cavazzoni, 185, 482-483
Recordare, Buchner, 476
Reges Tharsis, Preston, 469
Regola Rubertina, Ganassi, 498, *499*
Remember not, O Lord God, our old iniquities (*Ne reminiscaris*), Tallis, 362
Repleatur os meum, Lhéritier, 163
Respond, The, 344-351
Audivi media nocte, Tallis, 347
Audivi vocem de caelo, Taverner, 346
[Candidi] facti sunt Nazarei, Tallis, 350
Dum transisset Sabbatum, Taverner, 345-346; Tallis, 350; __I, II, Shep-

Respond (*continued*)
    pard, 350
Gaude, gaude, gaude Maria, Sheppard, 350
Hodie nobis caelorum, Taverner, 347; Tallis, 348
[Homo] quidam fecit coenam, Tallis, 349
[Honor] virtus et potestas, Tallis, 349
In manus tuas I, II, III, Sheppard, 351
In pace in idipsum, Taverner, 347; Sheppard, 351
In pace si dedro, Tallis, 348
[Loquebantur] variis linguis, Tallis, 349
Non conturbetur cor vestrum I, Sheppard, 350, *II*, Sheppard, 351
[Videte] miraculum, Tallis, 349
Ricercar Tabulatura, Steigleder, 187
Rimario novo di tutte le concordanze del Petrarca raccolte di maniera, che quante volte sono nel detto autore, tante per tavo la ordinatissima ritrovare si potranno..., Lanfranco, 133
Ritual antiphon, 353-354
    Libera nos sava nos I, II, Sheppard, 354
    Media vita, Sheppard, 354
Rorbertsbridge fragment, 462
Romance, 441, 445
Rudimenta musicae in gratiam studiosae juventutis diligenter comportata, Listenius, 135, 137, 154
Rudimenta musices, Agricola, 129
Rudiments de musique, Guilliaud, 143

Sacrae Cantiones seu Moteti ut vocant, non minus instrumentis quam vocibus aptae, Rore, 249
Sancta Maria, Buchner, 476
Scintille di musica, Lanfranco, 133-134, 152-153, 167, 172-173, 182
Selectae Harmoniae quatuor vocum de passione Domini, Rhau, 266
Septem psalmi penitentiales, Layolle, 222
Sequence
  German
    Komm, Heiliger Geist, Herre Gott, Luther, 265
    Mitten wir im Leben sind, Luther, 265
  Latin

    Grates nunc omnes reddamus, 269, 283
    Media vita in morte sumus, 265
    Veni, Sancte Spiritus, 265
    Victimae paschali laudes, 267, 283
Six Gaillards et six Pavanes avec Treze chansons musicales a quatre parties, 495, 504
Small Catechism, Luther
    Christ, unser Herr, zum Jordan kam (Baptism), 275
    Dies sind die heiligen Gebot (Ten Commandments), 275
    Jesus Christus, unser Heiland (Communion), 275
    Mensch wiltu leben seliglich, 275
    Vater unser im Himmelreich (Lord's Prayer), 275
    Wir glauben all' an einen Gott (Creed), 260, 269, 275
Song of Simeon, Calvin, 289
Spania in re, Kleber, 460; Buchner, 460
Spanieler, Kotter, 460
Spaniol, Buchner, 460
Spaniol Kochersperg, , 460
Spanyöler Tancz, Weck, 460
Spataro Correspondence, 123, 126, 128
Spiegel der Orgelmacher und Organisten, Schlick, Arnolt, 150
Strambotto, 426
Submit yourselves, Sheppard, 364
Sub tuum presidium, Lhéritier, 162

Tablature pour le jeu d'orgues espinettes et manicordions sur le plain chant de Cunctipotens et Kyrie fons..., Attaingnant, 186, 489
Te Deum laudamus, 309, 465, 472; Aston, 320, Taverner, 321; Tye, 321; Sheppard, 321; Redford, 466
The bella, the bella, Taverner, 441
The bitter swete that straynes my yeldid hart, Sheppard, 441
The crocke, 504
The kyngs maske, 504
Tonale (Psalm-tones), 279
Trattato della natura et cognitione di tutti gli tuoni di canto figurato, Aaron, 125, 138, 144-146

Trattato sopra una differentia musicale,
   Dabckerts, 166
*Tres breve et familiere introduction pour
   entendre &? apprendre par soy mesmes
   a jouer toutes chansons reduictes en la
   tabulature du lutz*, 445-446, 495, 505
*Tres libros de música en cifras para Vi-
   huela*, Mudarra, 443, 501
*Treze motetz musicaulx avec ung Prelude
   le tout reduice...*, Attaingnant, 186, 462,
   490
*XX Songes ix of iiii partes and xi of thre
   partes*, 441, 504

Verse, The, 351-353
   Alleluya [ora pro nobis], Tallis, 352
   Ecce mater, Taverner, 351
   Euge caeli porta, Tallis, 352
   Jesu spes poenitenitbus, Taverner, 351
   Tam peccatum, Taverner, 352
   Traditur militibus, Taverner, 352
Villancico, 443, 444-445
Villanelle, 424-431
   A quando a quando haveva una vicina,
      Willaert, 434
   Canzone di Ruzante, 432
   Chi cerca de vedere donne belle, Colo-
      nia, 428
   Fontana che dai acqua a dui valluni,
      Nola, 434
   Io dich' è sturno, Nola, 428
   La Canzone di Ruzante: Zoia zentil,
      432
   Madonn'io non lo so, Nola, 427
   Na volta me gabasti o lusinghera, Nola,
      434
   O bene mio famme uno favore, Willaert,
      434
   O bene mio fam'no, Willaert, 431
   O dolce vita mia, Willaert, 165, 425;
      Nola, 425, 427
   Oime dolente ca ne nivino, Nola, 434
   O vita mia s'io v'amo anzi v'adoro,
      Fontana, 434
   Par Deo cha te conosco, Cimello, 434
Villanella, The
   __on the stage
      Commedia alla villanesca, Ruzante,
         435

Farsette, Caracciolo, 435
Farse caviole, 435
Gli ingannati, 435
Published sources of
   *Canzone villanesche al modo napoli-
      tano a tre voci di Thomaso Cimello
      da Napoli con una bataglia villanes-
      cha a tre del medesimo autore nova-
      mente poste in luce. Libro primo
      1545*, Gardane, 430
   *Canzone vilanesche di Giovan Thoma-
      so di Maio musico napolitano libro
      primo a tre voci*, Gardane, 429
   Canzone villanesca alla napolitana,
      425, 426, 427, 428, 430
   Canzone villanesche alla napolitana,
      424, 431
   *Canzone villanesche alla napolitana a
      quatro voci di Perissone novamente
      poste in luce*. Gardane, 433, 438
   *Canzone villanesche alla napolitana
      di M. Adriano Wigliaret a quatro
      voci... con la Canzona di Ruzante*,
      (1544, 1548, and 1563 editions),
      Scotto 432, 438
   *Canzone villanesche alla napolitana
      di M. Adriano Vvigliaret a quatro
      voci la Canzona di Ruzante...* Gar-
      dane, 432, 433
   *Canzone villanesche alla napolitana...
      libro primo*, Colonia, 434
   *Canzone villanesche di Vicenzo Fon-
      tana a tre voci alla napolitana no-
      vamente poste in luce. Libro primo.
      Villote di V. Fontana a 3*, Gardane,
      430
   *Canzoni villanesche de Don Joan Do-
      minico del Giovane de Nola, a tre
      voci novamente ristampate. Libro
      primo 1545*, Scotto, 429
   *Canzoni villanesche de Don Joan Do-
      minico del Giovane de Nola, a tre
      voci novamente ristampate. Libro
      secundo 1545*, Scotto, 430
   *Canzoni villanesche de Don Joan Do-
      minico del Giovane de Nola. Libro
      primo et secondo...* Scotto (1541
      edition), 429
   Canzonj vilanesche napolitane nove

Villanella, The __ on the stage *(continued)*
  scelte et di varij autori 1547, Sultzbach, 435
  Elletione de canzone alla napolitana a tre voci di Rinaldo Burno con altre scielte da diversi musici. Novamente poste in luce. Libro primo 1546, Scotto, 435
  Madrigali a quatro voci di Geronimo Scotto con alcuni alla misura di breve, Scotto, 434
  Madrigali a tre et arie napolitane, Dorico, 434
Villotte, 422-424
  __ alla mantovana, 422
  __ alla paduana, 422
  __ alla veneziana, 422
  L'ultimo di de maggio, S. Festa, 424
Villotta, The, 424
  Published sources of
    Fior de motetti e canzone novi, Pasoti and Dorico?, 424
    Il primo libro delle villotte, Gardane, 424
    Libro primo de la Croce, Pasoti and Dorico, 424
Von ordenung gottis diensts ynn der gemeyne, Luther, 257, 260
Votive antiphon, 308-317, 344
  Ave cujus conceptio, Ludford, 310
  Ave caput Christi, Tye, 315
  Ave Dei Patris filia, Taverner, 310-311; Tallis, 316; Merbecke, 317
  Ave Maria, Taverner, 313
  Ave Maria ancilla Trinitatis, Aston, 310; Ludford, 310
  Ave Maria [divae matris Annae], Aston, 309
  Ave rosa sine spinis, Tallis, 316
  Christe Jesu pastor bone, Taverner, 310, 313
  Domine Jesu Christe, Ludford, 307, 310;
  Gaudete coelicolae omnes, Sheppard, Merbecke, 317
  Fac nobis, Taverner, 314
  Gaude plurimum, Taverner, 310, 311-312, 317
  Gaude virgo christipera, Sheppard, 317
  Gaude virgo mater Christi, Aston, 309
  Igitur O Jesu, Sheppard, 317
  Illustrissima omnium, Sheppard, 317
  Mater Christe, Taverner, 310, 312-313
  O Baptista vates Christi, Aston, 310
  O splendor gloriae, Taverner, 310, 312
  Peccavimus cum partribus, Tye, 315
  Prudens Virgo, Taverner, 314
  Salve intemerata, Tallis, 315
  Salve Regina, Ludford, 310
  Salve regina pudica mater, Ludford, 310
  Sancte Deus, Taverner, 313; Tallis, 317
  Singularis privilegii, Sheppard, 317
  Sub tuum praesidium, Taverner, 314
  Sub tuum protectionem, Tye, 315
  Te matrem Dei laudamus, Aston, 309
  Virgo pura, Taverner, 314
Wohl auf, Forster, 449
Wol kumpt der May, Senfl, 449

Subject Index

Act of Supremacy, 295
An Act for the Uniformity of Service, 303, 304, 463, 472
Anglican church music
  Form and style, 360
  Composers, 361-364
Antiphon
  Ritual, 353-354
    Composers of, 354
  Processional, 343
  Votive, 308-317, 344
    Composers of, 309-317
    General style of, 308-309
Art song, 446-451
  Court song (*Hofweisen*), 447
  German Lied, 449-450
    Sources of, 450-451
  Gesellschaftlied, (Tenor song), 447-448
  Metrical ode, 446
  Song motets, 448-450

Bohemian-Moravian Brethern, 292
  __Songbooks, 292-293

Calvinist church music, 285-288
  __in Southern Switzerland, 285, 286-287
  Psalters
    Monophonic, 288-290
    Polyphonic, 290-291
      by Bourgeois, 287, 290-291
  __in Strasbourg, 286
Canticles, *see* Office music
Canzona (keyboard), 456-457

Canzona d'organo, 457
Canzona francese, 456
Carmen, 456
Canzone, Italian
  Definition of the, 393
  __in the theater, 394-395
  Music of the, 393-394
  Poetry of the, 393
Chanson
  Franco-Flemish (Netherlandish)
    General style of, 367
    Netherlandish style, 373
      Composers of, 378-382
  French
    General style, 367-368
      of poetry, 368-369
      of music, 369-370
  Parisian
    Composers of, 373-376
    General style of, 370-371
      Lyrical style, 371
      Program style, 371-372
      Narrative style, 372
  Provincial
    Composers of, 377-378
    General style of, 372-373
  Performance of the, 382-383
  __in the theater, 383-385
  Printed sources of the, 385-393
Chantries Act of 1547, 302
Choralmotette, 279
Chromaticism: "Chain Reactions", 168-169
Chromaticism: *Musica ficta*, 154

Horizontal precepts: *(fa supra la)*, 155-157
Horizontal precepts: Diminished fifths, 157-158
Vertical precepts: Intervals (*mi contra fa*), 158-160
Vertical precepts: Cross-relations (false relations), 160-165
   Satzfehler and other groups, 161-165
Vertical precepts: Contrapuntal progressions, 165-167
   Imperfect-to-perfect rule, 166-167
   Third above a cadence note, 167
   Sharps for leading tones, 167
Vertical precepts: Canon and imitation, 167
Clefs (Sixteenth century), 193
   Clef combinations, 193-195
     Chiavette, (High C*hiavette*),193, 194, 195
     Chiavi naturali, (Natural clefs), 193, 194, 195
     Chivi trasportati, (Low Chiavette), 193, 194
Contrafacta, 358-359
Coro spezzato (*coro battente*), 222

Dance music (keyboard), 459-462
   Alta danza, 459, 460
   Basse danse, 459
   Pass'e mezzo, 461
   Pavane, 461
   Piva, 459
   Quaternaria, 459
   Saltarello, 459, 461
   Sources of, 459-462. See also Manuscripts
   Style of, 460
Dictionary
   __of Musical terms, 128
   Rhyming, 133

Ensemble music, 501-505
   English, 503-504
     Sources of, 503-504
       Manuscripts, 503-504
       Printed, 504
     Free instrumental forms, 502-503
       Fantasia, 502
       Ricercar, 502-503
   French, 504-505
     Sources of, 504-505
   Italian, 505

Fantasia (keyboard), 457-458

Gamut, the, 127, 142-147
   Musica recta [*musica vera*], 142-144
     Solmization, 142
     Hexachords, 142-144
   Musica ficta, [the extension of the hand] 144-147
     Hexachords, 144-145
     Seventeen-step gamut, 145-146
     Twenty-one-step gamut, 146

Huguenots, 287
Hymnals (Protestant)
   Monophonic, 272
   Polyphonic, 276
Hymns (English). *See also* Mass __ German; Office music
   Polyphonic, 354-357
   Composers of, 354-357
   Processional, 343

Intablations (keyboard), 462
Intermedio, 394-395
Intervalic Systems
   Comma, the, 145
   Consonances, 147-148
   Dissonances, 147-148
Interval ratios
   Conflict between mathematics and ear, 179
Intonation
   Just intonation, 148-150
   Tuning systems, keyboard, 149-150
   Syntonic diatonic (Ptolemy), 148-149
Temperament
   Mean-tone, 150-152
   Equal, 152-153

Letter to Fra Seraphin, 181
Lincoln Cathedral Injunction of 1548, 304
Lute music, 493-498
   the instrument, 493
   in England, 497-498

Lute music (*continued*)
  in England (continued)
    Composers of, 498
    Sources of, 498
  in France, 493-495
    Musical forms, 493-494
      Basse danse, 493
      Branle, 494
      Pavenne, 494
    Performance of, 494
    Published sources of, 495
  in Italy, 495-497
    Composers of, 496-497
    Musical forms, 495
      Dances, 496
      Intabulations, 495
      Ricercari, 496
Lutheran church music, 283. *See also* Calvinist church music
  at Leipzig, 283
    Hymnals, 284
  at Augsburg, 285
    Published sources, 285
Lutheranism, 295

Madrigal
  Definition of, 395-396
  Early madrigal (1520s), 396-403
    Composers of, 399-403
      __in Florence, 396-397
      __in Rome, 397
    Music of the, 398
    Poetry of the, 397-398
    Sources of the, 401-403
  Early madrigal (1530s), 403-407
    Composers of the, 405-406
    Music of the, 404-405
    Music printing of the, 403-404
      Single impression, 403
    Poetry of the, 404
    Sources of the, 406-407
    __for ceremonial occasions, 415
    __for the theater, 414
    Intermedio, the, 414
  Late madrigal (1540s), 407-413
    Composers of the, 408-413
    Music of the, 407-408
    Poetry of the, 407
    Performance of the, 413-414
    __in the theater, 416
  Published sources of the, 416-422
    __for the theater, 416-417

Manuscripts
  Basle:
    __Basel University Library, *F. 1. 8.*, 479
    __Basle University Library, *MS. F. IX. 22*, 459, 476, *479*
    __Basle University Library, *MS. F. IX. 58*, 459, 476, 479
  Berkeley:
    __University of California Music Library, 419
  Berlin:
    __*40026 (Z26)*, 460, 478, 480
  Biblioteca apostolica vaticana, *MS Vat. lat. 5318*, 126
  Bologna:
    __Bibliotèca del Conservatorio (*Liceo Musicale*), 391
    __Civico Museo Bibliografico Musicale, 419
    __Civico Museo Bibliografico Musicale, *MS. Q 21*, 402,
  Brussels:
    __Bibliothèque du Conservatoire Royal de Musique, *Ms. 27731*, 407
  Cambridge:
    __Gonville and Caius College, *MS. 667*, 327, 329
    __King's College, *Rowe Music Library, MS. 316*, 311, 312, 359
    __Peterhouse, *MSS. 40, 41, 31, 32*, 311, 313, 314, 325, 334, 335, 336
    __Peterhouse, *MSS. 471-4* ('Peterhouse'), 317, 325, 328
    __St. John's college, *MS. K. 31*, 311, 325
    __University Library, *MS. Dd. 13.27*, 311, 325
  Castell' Arquato:
    1-CARc, 461
  Chicago:
    __Newberry Library Case, *MS-VM 1578. M91*, 402
  Clemsford:

Subject Index

__Essex Record Office, *MS. D/DP. Z. b/1*, 311, 312, 316, 336, 360
Eichstätt:
__Staatliche Bibliothek, 391
Florence:
__Biblioteca del Conservatorio, 391
__Biblioteca del Conservatorio di musica Luigi Cherubini, *MS. Basevi 2440*, 401
__Biblioteca del Conservatorio di musica Luigi Cherubini, *MS. Basevi 2495* (Strozzi partbooks), 406
__Biblioteca Marucelliana, 385
__Biblioteca Nazionale Centrale, *MS. Magl XIX. 99, 100, 101bis, 102*, 407
__Biblioteca Nazionale Centrale, *MS. Magl XIX. 122-125*, 406
__Biblioteca Nazionale Centrale, *MS. Magl XIX. 164-167*, 402, 423
Klagenfurt:
__Kärntner Landesarchiv, MS. 4/3, 480
London:
__British Library, *K. 8. b. 7(5)*, 236
__British Library, MS. Add. 30513 (*Mulliner Book*), 439, 441, 467, 470
__British Library, *MS. Royal Appendix 58*, 498
__British Library, *MS. Stowe 389*, 498
__British Museum, 392, 393
__British Museum, *MS. Harley 1709*, 311
__British Museum, MS. K.1.e.1., 441, 442
__British Museum, *MSS. Add. 15166*, 359
__British Museum, *Add. 15233*, 470
__British Museum, *MSS. Add. 17802-5* ('Gyffard'), 315, 337, 338, 339, 340, 341, 343, 347, 353
__British Museum, *MSS. Add. 18936-9*, 311
__British Museum, *MSS. Add. 22597*, 360
__British Museum, *MS. Add. 29246*, 311, 332, 333, 336
__British Museum, *Add. 29996*, 467, 468, 470
__British Museum, *Add. 30480-84*, 359
__British Museum, *MS. Add. 31390*, 346
__British Museum, *MS. Add. 34049*, 312
__British Museum, *MS. Add. 34191*, 311.
__British Museum, *MSS. Add. 41156-8*, 312
__British Museum, *MS. Royal Music Library 24 d. 2*, 312, 314, 315
__British Museum, *Roy App. 56*, 469
__British Museum, Roy App. 74-76 ('Lumley'), 357
__Lambeth Palace, *MS. 1*, 327, 329
__Public Record Office, S.P.I (Henry VIII), *vol. 246*, 439, 441
__Royal College of Music, *MS. 2035*, 311, 312, 332, 333, 336, 340
__Royal Music Library, *24 d. 2*, 332, 351, 352
__Westminster Abbey Library, 441
Lüneburg:
__Ratsbücherei und Stadtarchiv, 386
Munich:
__Bayerische Staatsbibliothek, 386, 388-389, 390, 391
__Bayerische Staatsbibliothek. *Cim. 52* (Rore codex), 249
New York:
__New York Public Library, Drexel *MSS. 4180-5*, 441
Oxford:
__The Bodleian Library, *MSS. Music School, e. 1-5*, 311, 312, 317, 337
__The Bodleian Library, *MS. Music School, e. 376-381*, Forrest-Heyther), 325, 331, 332, 333
__The Bodleian Library, *MS. Music School, e. 420-22 (Wanley)*, 313, 335, 336, 357-358, 362, 363
__The Bodleian Library, *MS. Music School, e. 423*, 311, 312
__The Bodleian Library, *MSS. Arch. f. e. 19-24 (Forrest-Heather)*, 324, 325, 326, 341, 342, 343
__Christ Church, *MS. 45*, 315

Manuscripts (continued)
　__Christ Church, *MS. 979-83*, 311, 312, 313, 315, 316, 332, 346, 349, 351
　__Christ Church, *MSS. 984-988*, 343
　__Christ Church Mus.389
New Haven:
　__Yale University, John Herrick Jackson Music Library, *Misc. MS. 179*, 402
Paris:
　__Bibliothèque Mazarine, 389
　__Bibliothèque Nationale, 385, 388, 391
　__Bibliothèque Nationale, *Rés. Vm^d 30.* 419
　__Bibliothèque Nationale, *MS. it. 1110*, 126
　__Bibliothèque Municipale, 385
Pistoia:
　__Archivio Capitolare, *B.7.7.*, 432
St.Gall:
　__Staatsbibl. *MS. 530*, 478, 479
Sutton Coldfield, Oscott College:
　__Old Library, *MS. Case B No. 4^{24}*, 402
Tenbury:
　__St. Michael's College, *MSS. 354-358*, 311, 312
　__St. Michael's College, *MSS. 341-344*, 312, 332, 333
　__St. Michaels College, *MSS. 354-358*, 312, 336
　__St. Michaels College, *MS. 1464*, 316, 332, 336, 342
　__St. Michaels College, *MSS. 1469-1471*, 312, 316, 332
　__St. Michaels College, *MS. 1486*, 312, 316, 317
Venice:
　__Biblioteca Marciana *MSS. It. Cl. IV, 1795-8*, 423
　__*1-Vm MS. Ital. 1227*, 461
Wien:
　__Österreichische Nationalbibliothek, 392
Wolfenbüttel:
　__Herzog-August-Bibliothek, 432, 433, 434

Worcester:
　__Worcestershire Record Office, *The Wilmott MS.*, 312, 316, 317
Zurich:
　__Stadtbibl. *Cod. 284*, 479
Mascherata, Neapolitan, 436-438
　Arrangements of the, 438
　Composers of the, 437-438
　Music of the, 437
　Poetry of the, 436
Mass
　English Pre-Reformation, 298-300
　　Extra-liturgical devotions, 300
　　Great Service, 300
　　Short Service, 298-300
　English Reformation
　　Composers, 323-343
　　General style of the, 321-323
　　Lady-Mass, 328-329
　German, 258-261. *See also* Lutheran church music
　　General style of texts and music, 261
　　Monophonic hymns
　　　Texts, 261
　　　Music, 262
　　Polyphonic hymns, 262-263
　　　Texts, 262
　　　Music, 263
　　Hymnals
　　　Monophonic, 272-276
　　　Polyphonic, 276-280
　　Sources of vernacular hymns, 263-272
　　　Centuries old German religious songs, 266
　　　Centuries old songs with rewritten texts (*contrafacta*), 267
　　　Chants from the Catholic Church, 264-265
　　　Latin hymn, the, 263
　　　Latin Passion, the, 265
　　　Non-liturgical music, 266
　　　The revised service, 258-261
　　　Songs written for Lutherans, 268-272
　　　Freely composed hymns, 272
　　　Psalm *Lieder*, 271-272
　　　Texts by Luther, 268-270
　　　Texts and music by Luther, 270-

Subject Index

Mass (continued)
    271
  Latin Catholic, 199-206
    General style of, 199-200
      __Mass Ordinary music, 199
        Cantus firmus Mass, 201
        Cyclic Mass, 200
        Freely composed Mass, 201
        Paraphrase Mass, 201
        Parody Mass (imitative), 200
        Plainsong Mass, 201
        Soggetto Mass, 201
      __Mass Propers music
        French, 202, 203
        Style of, 199
    Music for the Ordinary and Proper, 200
      Central European Mass, 214
        Composer of, 215
        Style of, 214
      Flemish Mass
        Composers of, 206
        Style of, 206
      French Mass
        Composers of, 202
        Style of, 201-202
      Roman Catholic Mass
        Composer of, 213
        Style of, 212
      Spanish Mass
        Composer of, 216
        Style of, 216
      Venetian Mass
        Composer of, 211
        Style of, 211
  Latin Protestant, (Luther), 257
    The retained parts of the Service, 257
    The retained traditional plainsong and polyphonic settings, 258
    The sequence, 258
    Sources of music taken from the Catholic Church, 280-282
    Diverse liturgical and non-liturgical purposes, 281-282
    Masses and Proper cycles, music for, 280
Meistergesang, 442-443
Modal theory, 138-140

Modes, 129, 132, 138
  Regular position, 139-140
  Irregular position, 139-140
Motet,
  Central European, 251
    Composers of, 251
    Style of, 251
  Ceremonial, 451-454
  English, 307
    Prayer-motets, 307, 344
  Flemish, 237
    Composers of, 237
    Some printed sources of, 241-242
  Florentine, 249
    Composers of, 249
    Style of, 249
  French, 233
    Composers of, 234
    Style of, 233
  General style of, 233
  __in the Mass, 200
  Imitative, 200
  Mantuan, 250
    Composers of, 250
  Roman Catholic. 245
    Composers of, 245
    Style of, 245
  Spanish, 252
    Composers, 252
    Style of, 252
  Venetian, 246
    Composers of, 247
Musica, 137
  __*Mensurabilis,* 154
  __*figuralis,* 154
  __*plana,* 154
  __*Poetica,* (Composition), 137, 154, 177, 178
  Art of composition
    Aesthetics, 180, 181
    Beat and accent, 181
    Expressive music (style), 180
    Mode determined by text, 180
    Music and poetry, 177, 180, 181
      Melody and text, 182
      Rules for text and music, 182
    Rhythm, 181
  Conflict between counterpoint and supremacy of text, 182-183

Musica (continued)
  __*Practica*, 137, 154
    Musica attiva, 137, 154
      __(Performance didactics), 177
  __*Theorica*, 137, 154
    Musica speculativa, 137
    Musica contemplativa, 137
    Musica arithmetica, 137
      __(Science), 177
    Music, Science of, 147
Musica ficta, 127, 144-147. *See also*
  Chromaticism; Gamut
Modulation, Secret, 135, 242
Mutation, 132

'Narrative' formula, 400
Note nere, 197-198, 396, 428
  A misura di breve, 197
  Chromaticho, 197
  Misura alla breve, 197

Office music (Catholic), 221
  __for Compline, 298
  __for Instruments, 283
  __for Lauds, 298
  __for Matins, 298
  Organ, use of, 283
  Polyphony for the Office, 199, 221
    Hymns, 230
      Composers of, 231-233
        Florentine, 232
        Mantuan, 232
        Roman Catholic, 231
        Venetian, 231
      Style of, 230
    Lamentations, 228
      Composers of, 229-230
        Flemish, 229
        French, 229
        Roman Catholic, 230
        Spanish, 230
      Style of, 229
    Magnificat, the, 225
      Composers of, 225-228
        Central European, 228
        English, 318-320
        Flemish, 226
        French, 225
        Mantuan, 227

        Roman Catholic, 226
        Spanish, 228
        Venetian, 227
      style of, 225, 318
    Psalms, 221
      Composers of the, 222-225
    Te Deum laudamus, 320-321
      Composers of the, 320-321
      Style of the, 320
    Prose, 353
      Composers of, 353
    Respond, 344-351
      Composers of, 344-351
      Style and performance of the, 344
    Verse, 351-353
    Vespers, music for, 297
Office music, (Protestant)
  Broadsheets, 272
  Catechism hymns, 275
  __for Vespers, 280-281
Organ music (Liturgical), 462-463
  __in England, 462-474
    Composers of, 465-469
    Daily Offices, 464
    General style of, 463
    Manuscripts of, 469-471. *See also*
      Manuscripts
    Organ Mass, 465
    the Organ, 472-473
      Chair organ, 472
      Great organ, 472
        __Pitch of, 473
        Specifications of, 473
    Performance of, 471-472
  __in France, 488-493
    General style of, 488
    the Organ, 491-493
      Beaune organ, 492
      Flemish organ, 492
      Specifications of, 492
      Italian style organ, 492
      Specifications of, 492
    Registration of, 491
    Sources of, 489-491
  __in Germany, 474-480
    Composers of, 474-479
    General style of, 474
    Manuscripts of, 479-480. *See also*
      Manuscripts

Organ Music (Liturgical) (continued)
　__In Germany (continued)
　　Notation of, 474
　　the Organ, 480
　　　Sweelinck organ, 480
　　　Lüneburg organ, 480
　__in Italy, 480-486
　　Composers of, 482-485
　　General style of, 482
　　Manuscripts of, 481-482. See also
　　　Manuscripts
　　the Organ, 485-486
　__in Spain, 486-488
　　Composers of, 486-487
　　the Organ, 487-488
　　　Barcelona organ
　　　　Nuestra Señora del Pino, the, 487
　　　Toledo organ
　　　　Organo del Emperador, 487
Ornamentation, 173-176
　English, 176
　Mordanten, 174
　　Tremolo, 174
　Groppo, 174
　Passaggi, 174, 176
　　Diminutions, 175-176

"Paulomines", 457
Partbooks, 184
Passion, the
　Composers of, 219
　　Flemish, 220
　　Florentine, 220
　　French, 219
　　Mantuan, 220
　Style of, 219
Performance practices
　__of English music
　　Choral practice, 365
　　__in the Cathedral, 364
　　__in the parish church, 365
　__of Latin music, 253
　__in Paris
　__in religious plays, 255
　__in Rome, 253
　__in Venice, 254
　__of Lutheran church music
　　Kantorei, the, 282
　　Lieder, the, 282-283

Pitch, 169-170, 366
Poetici, 178
Prelude (keyboard), 458-459
　Style of the, 458
Psalmody (style)
　Antiphonal, 222
　Responsoial, 222
　Direct, 222
Psalms, the, 221
　Antiphonal settings of, 223
　　Salmi a versi con le sue Risposte, 223
　　Salmi a versi senza Risposte, 223
　　Salmi spezzati, 223. See also *coro spezzato*
　Composers of, 222
　　Central European, 225
　　Florentine, 224
　　French, 222
　　Mantuan, 224
　　Venetian, 222
　Processional, 343
　Texts of, 221
　Psalm motets, 221
　Settings of, 221
Psalter (Dutch), 293-294
Psalter, The, (Book of Psalms and ferial antiphons), 297

Ricercar, (keyboard), 455-456
　Homophonic, 456
　Polyphonic, 456
Royal Injunction, the, 296

Sarum Use, 297
Score Arrangement, 184
　Keyboard scores, 185-187
　Manuscript scores, 185
　Notation of, 185
　Tabula, 185
Secular English vocal music, 438-442
　Court songs, 439
　General style of, 439-440
　　Texts and Music of, 440
　　　The carol, 440
　　　Political and topical poems, 440
　　　Love lyrics, 440
　Manuscripts of,. See also Manuscripts
　Published sources, 441-442

Signatures, conflicting ('Partial signatures'), 196
Solo song, 443-445
  French, 445-446
    Sources of, 445
  Spanish
    Music of, 444-445
      Romance, 445
      Villancicos, 444
    Sources of, 443-444
'Squares', 328
Suppression of 1540-1541, 296

Tablatures
  Griffschrift, (finger notation), 187
  Keyboard, 185, 187-189
    German, New, 188
    German, Old, 188
    Spanish (Neapolitan), 188-189
  Lute, 189-191
    Neapolitan (Spanish), 190
  Vihuela de mano, 192-193
  Viol, 191-192
  Tonschrift, (pitch notation), 187
Tactus, 134
Text Underlay
  Writings on, 170-173
Tiento (keyboard), 457
Tonality, 140-141
Trivium, 178
  Grammar, 178
  Rhetoric, 178, 179

Vihuela music, 499-501
  in Spain, 499-501
  Diferencia (variation), 500
  Sources of, 500-501
Villanella, 424-435
  Definition of, 424-425
  Early (canzone villanesca), 425-431
    Composers of the, 428-430
    Music of the, 426
    Musical form of the, 428
    Performance of the, 430
    Poetry of the, 426
    Style of the, 427-428
  Four-voice, 431-433
    Composers of the, 431-434
  Published sources of the, 434-435
Villotta, 422-424
  Lilolela, 422
  Manuscripts containing, 423
  Music of the, 423
  Nio, 423
  Poetry of the, 422
  Published sources of, 423-424
Viol, 498-499
  Tutors, 498
    Handling the instrument, 499
    Tablature for the, 499

ABOUT THE AUTHOR

BLANCHE GANGWERE has worked as a high school music teacher, a church organist, and choir director. She is also the author of *Music History from the Late Roman through the Gothic Periods, 313–1425* (Greenwood Press, 1986) and *Music History During the Renaissance Period, 1425–1520: A Documented Chronology* (Greenwood Press, 1991).

780.9031 G197m

Gangwere, Blanche.

Music history during the
 Renaissance period,